D1380764

Cisco Networking Academy Program: Second-Year Companion Guide
Second Edition

Cisco Systems, Inc.
Cisco Networking Academy Program

Cisco Press

Cisco Press
201 West 103rd Street
Indianapolis, IN 46290 USA

Cisco Networking Academy Program:
Second-Year Companion Guide
Second Edition

Cisco Systems, Inc.

Cisco Networking Academy Program

Copyright © 2002 Cisco Systems, Inc.

All rights reserved. No part of this book may be reproduced or transmitted in any form or by any means, electronic or mechanical, including photocopying, recording, or by any information storage and retrieval system, without written permission from the publisher, except for the inclusion of brief quotations in a review.

International Standard Book Number: 1-58713-029-7

Library of Congress Catalog Card Number: 2001087344

04   03   02   01   5   4   3   2

Second Printing   July 2001

Interpretation of the printing code: The rightmost double-digit number is the year of the book's printing; the rightmost single-digit, the number of the book's printing. For example, the printing code 01-2 shows that the second printing of the book occurred in 2001.

Trademark Acknowledgments

All terms mentioned in this book that are known to be trademarks or service marks have been appropriately capitalized. Cisco Press or Cisco Systems, Inc., cannot attest to the accuracy of this information. Use of a term in this book should not be regarded as affecting the validity of any trademark or service mark.

Warning and Disclaimer

This book is designed to provide information on networking fundamentals. Every effort has been made to make this book as complete and as accurate as possible, but no warranty or fitness is implied.

The information is provided on an as-is basis. Cisco Press and Cisco Systems, Inc., shall have neither liability nor responsibility to any person or entity with respect to any loss or damages arising from the information contained in this book or from the use of the discs or programs that may accompany it.

Feedback Information

At Cisco Press, our goal is to create in-depth technical books of the highest quality and value. Each book is crafted with care and precision, undergoing rigorous development that involves the unique expertise of members from the professional technical community.

Readers' feedback is a natural continuation of this process. If you have any comments regarding how we could improve the quality of this book, or otherwise alter it to better suit your needs, you can contact us at feedback@ciscopress.com. Please make sure to include the book title and ISBN in your message.

We greatly appreciate your assistance.

Publisher	*John Wait*
Executive Editor	*Carl Lindholm*
Product Manager	*Shannon Gross*
Cisco Systems Management	*Michael Hakkert*
	Tom Geitner
	William Warren
Managing Editor	*Patrick Kanouse*
Senior Project Editor	*Sheri Replin*
Technical Reviewers	*Wayne Lewis*
	Wayne Jarvimaki
	Cheryl Schmidt
	Richard Reynolds
	Tanna Kincaid
	Truett Clearman
	Charles Schultz
	Lynn Bloomer
	Elaine Horn
	Harry Lawhorn
	Mark McGregor
	Barb Nolley
Cover Designer	*Louisa Klucznik*
Compositor	*Steve Gifford*
Indexer	*Tim Wright*

Overview

Table of Contents

Preface

Since 1997, the Cisco Networking Academy Program has instituted an e-learning system approach that integrates the multimedia delivery of a networking curriculum with testing, performance-based skills assessment, evaluation, and reporting through a Web interface. The Cisco Networking Academy curriculum goes beyond traditional computer-based instruction by helping students develop practical networking knowledge and skills in a hands-on environment. In a lab setting that closely corresponds to a real networking environment, students work with the architecture and infrastructure pieces of networking technology. As a result, students learn the principles and practices of networking technology.

The Cisco Networking Academy Program provides in-depth and meaningful networking content, which is being used by Regional and Local Academies to teach students around the world by utilizing the curriculum to integrate networking instruction into the classroom. The focus of the Networking Academy program is on the integration of a Web-based network curriculum into the learning environment. This element is addressed through intensive staff development for instructors and innovative classroom materials and approaches to instruction, which are provided by Cisco. The participating educators are provided with resources, the means of remote access to online support, and the knowledge base for the effective classroom integration of the Cisco Networking Academy curriculum into the classroom learning environment. As a result, the Networking Academy program provides the means for the dynamic exchange of information by providing a suite of services that redefine the way instructional resources are disseminated, resulting in a many-to-many interactive and collaborative network of teachers and students functioning to meet diverse educational needs.

The Networking Academy curriculum is especially exciting to educators and students because the courseware is interactive. Because of the growing use of interactive technologies, the curriculum is an exciting new way to convey instruction with new interactive technologies that allow instructors and trainers to mix a number of media, including audio, video, text, numerical data, and graphics. Consequently, students can select different media from the computer screen and tweak their instructional content to meet their instructional needs, and educators have the option of either designing their own environment for assessment or selecting from the applicable assessments.

Finally, by developing a curriculum that recognizes the changing classroom and workforce demographics, the globalization of the economy, changing workforce knowledge and skill requirements, and the role of technology in education, the Cisco Networking Academy Program supports national educational goals for K–12 education. As support for the Networking Academy program, Cisco Press has published this book, *Cisco Networking Academy Program: Second-Year Companion Guide*, Second Edition, as a companion guide for the curriculum used in the Cisco Networking Academy Program.

Introduction

Cisco Networking Academy Program: Second-Year Companion Guide, Second Edition, is designed to act as a supplement to your classroom and laboratory experience with the Cisco Networking Academy Program, whose curriculum is designed to empower you to enter employment or further education and training in the computer networking field.

This book is designed to further train you beyond the online training materials that you have already used in this program, along with the topics pertaining to the Cisco Certified Network Associate (CCNA) exam. This book closely follows the style and format that Cisco has incorporated into the curriculum. In addition, this book follows the two-semester curriculum model that has already been developed for the Cisco Networking Academy Program. Finally, this book is complemented by a CD-ROM, which contains cross-referenced movies presented in an interactive multimedia format as learning reference materials.

This book introduces and extends your knowledge and practical experience with the design, configuration, and maintenance of switches, local-area networks (LANs), and virtual local-area networks (VLANs). The concepts covered in this book enable you to develop practical experience in skills related to configuring LANs, wide-area networks (WANs), Novell networks, Internetwork Packet Exchange (IPX) routing, Interior Gateway Routing Protocol (IGRP) protocols, and network troubleshooting. In addition, this book extends your knowledge and practical experience with WANs, Integrated Services Data Network (ISDN), Point-to-Point Protocol (PPP), and Frame Relay design, configuration, and maintenance. Finally, the topics discussed in this book enable you to develop practical experience in skills related to configuring WANs, ISDN, PPP, and Frame Relay protocols and network troubleshooting.

The Washington Project

Chapter 4 introduces the Washington Project. This project is designed to help you learn by allowing you to apply the knowledge that you have gained to a real-life example. The Washington Project is introduced in the first course of the curriculum. However, the actual project work is not done until Semesters 3 and 4 of the curriculum, which are covered in this book. As concepts are introduced in this book, you learn to apply them. Each chapter contains content, concepts, and topics that help you build the knowledge you need to complete the Washington Project.

A district in Phoenix, Arizona, is the field model for the Washington Project. You will be given architectural drawings (electronically) of the various schools in the district, along with the actual wiring drawings (also in electronic format). Your teacher will give you the completed design considerations, specifications, and technical requirements document as resources. You will be required to keep an engineering journal during the project, and you will be required to submit a final design document and make an oral presentation of your project design near the end of Course 4. Cisco Press also published *Cisco Networking Academy Program: Engineering Journal and Workbook*, Volume II, Second Edition, which is a supplement that provides additional information to help you succeed with the Washington Project.

The Goal of This Book

The goal of this book is to educate you about Cisco-supported networking technologies and to help you understand how to design and build networks and to configure Cisco routers. It is designed for use in conjunction with the Cisco Networking Academy curriculum or as a stand-alone reference.

The Book's Audience

The book is written for anyone who wants to learn about networking technologies. The main target audience for this book is students in high schools, community colleges, and four-year institutions. Specifically, in an educational environment, this book could be used both in the classroom as a textbook companion and in computer labs as a lab manual.

The secondary target audience is corporate training faculty and staff members. In order for corporations and academic institutions to take advantage of the capabilities of networking, a large number of individuals have to be trained in the design and development of networks.

A third target audience is general users. The book's user-friendly and nontechnical approach should be appealing to readers who prefer to stay away from technical manuals.

This Book's Features

Many of this book's features help facilitate a full understanding of the networking and routing covered in this book:

- **Chapter objectives**—At the beginning of each chapter is a list of objectives to be mastered by the end of the chapter. In addition, the list provides a reference to the concepts covered in the chapter, which can be used as an advanced organizer.
- **Figures, examples, and tables**—This book contains figures, examples, and tables that help explain theories, concepts, commands, and setup

sequences; they reinforce concepts and help you visualize the content covered in each chapter. In addition, examples and tables provide such things as command summaries with descriptions, examples of screen outputs, and practical and theoretical information.

- **Washington Project notes**—Beginning in Chapter 4, each chapter includes Washington Project notes. These notes relate to the concepts introduced in the chapter and provide information that will help you apply the knowledge that you have gained to the Washington Project.

- **Engineering Journal notes**—Starting in Chapter 4, each chapter includes engineering journal notes. These notes relate to the concepts introduced in the chapter and provide supplemental information above and beyond what you learn in the course that will help you apply what you're learning to real-world situations.

- **Chapter summaries**—At the end of each chapter is a summary of the concepts covered in the chapter; it provides a synopsis of the chapter and serves as a study aid.

- **Washington School District Project task**—Starting in Chapter 4, each chapter includes a School District project task. This task reinforces the concepts introduced in the chapter by allowing you to apply the knowledge that you have gained to the Washington Project.

- **Check Your Understanding**—The end of each chapter presents review questions that serve as an end-of-chapter assessment. In addition, the questions reinforce the concepts introduced in the chapter and help you test your understanding before you move on to new concepts.

- **Key terms**—In many chapters, after the review questions are key terms that provide a summary of the new terms that are covered in the chapter. These terms serve as a study aid. In addition, the key terms reinforce the concepts introduced in the chapter and help your understanding of the chapter material before you move on to new concepts. You can find the key terms highlighted in *blue* throughout the chapter where they are used in practice.

SKILL BUILDER

Throughout the book, you see references to the lab activities found in the *Cisco Networking Academy Program: Lab Companion*, Volume II, Second Edition. These labs allow you to make a connection between theory and practice.

e-LAB ACTIVITIES

In each chapter, e-Lab activities emphasize not only the conceptual material, but also the important practice that facilitates the learning of networking concepts. The e-Lab activities allow you to make a connection between theory and practice and, as a result, master the skills of the exercises presented. In addition, the e-Lab activities present you with the experience of troubleshooting problem scenarios.

MOVIES

Throughout this book, you see references to movies, which are located on the companion CD-ROM. These movies emphasize the conceptual material and help you to make a connection between theory and practice.

About the CD-ROM

This book is complemented by a CD-ROM, which contains e-Lab activities, practice questions, and movies presented in an interactive multimedia format as learning materials. The learning reference materials are cross-referenced and are aligned to the content in this book. These materials effectively support self-directed learning by allowing you to engage in your learning and skill building. Additionally, these learning reference materials provide the following:

- An easy-to-use graphical user interface
- Accuracy and conciseness feedback
- Frequent interaction with content
- Support for guided and exploratory navigation
- Guidance and external control over navigation
- Learner direction and support
- Flexibility to all learners, no matter what level of expertise they have

Finally, these learning reference materials emphasize not only the conceptual material, but also the important practice that facilitates the learning of networking concepts. These materials help you to make a connection between theory and practice.

Conventions Used in This Book

In this book, the following conventions are used:

- Important or new terms are *italicized*.
- Key terms, defined at the end of most chapters and in the Glossary, appear in *blue*.

- All code examples appear in monospace type, and parts of code use the following conventions:
  - Commands and keywords are in monospaced **bold** type.
  - Arguments, which are placeholders for values the user inputs, appear in monospaced *italics*.
  - Square brackets ([ ]) indicate optional keywords or arguments.
  - Braces ({ }) indicate required choices.
  - Vertical bars (|) are used to separate required choices.

This Book's Organization

This book is divided into 19 chapters, 4 appendixes, and a Glossary.

Chapter 1 presents a review of the Open System Interconnection (OSI) reference model and an overview of network planning and design considerations related to routing.

Chapter 2 discusses problems in LANs and possible solutions that can improve LAN performance. In addition, this chapter covers the advantages and disadvantages of using bridges, switches, and routers for LAN segmentation and the effects of switching, bridging, and routing on network throughput. Finally, this chapter presents Ethernet, Fast Ethernet, and VLANs and the benefits of these technologies.

Chapter 3 provides an overview of VLANs and switched internetworking, compares traditional shared LAN configurations with switched LAN configurations, and discusses the benefits of using a switched VLAN architecture.

Chapter 4 presents an overview of the LAN design process. In addition, the chapter discusses LAN design goals, network design issues, network design methodology, and the development of LAN topologies.

Chapter 5 discusses how routers can be used to connect two or more networks and how they are used to pass data packets between networks based on network protocol information. This chapter presents how routers operate and what kinds of protocols they use. Finally, this chapter covers routing and IP routing protocols and discusses Cisco's proprietary protocol IGRP.

Chapter 6 presents standard and extended access control lists (ACLs), which you use to control network traffic, and describes how ACLs are used as part of a security solution. In addition, this chapter includes tips, considerations, recommendations, and general guidelines for how to use ACLs, and includes the commands and configurations needed to create ACLs. Finally, this chapter provides examples of standard and extended ACLs and how to apply ACLs to router interfaces.

Chapter 7 covers Novell's IPX protocols, operation, and configuration. In addition, this chapter explains how Cisco routers are used in NetWare networks and discusses how to verify IPX operation and connectivity between routers, along with troubleshooting in IPX operations.

Chapter 8 covers network documentation, network security, network maintenance, server administration, and server maintenance.

Chapter 9 presents the various protocols and technologies used in WAN environments. This chapter describes the basics of WANs, including common WAN technologies, types of wide-area services, encapsulation formats, and link options. Finally, this chapter discusses point-to-point links, circuit switching, packet switching, virtual circuits, dialup services, and WAN devices.

Chapter 10 provides an overview of the methodologies used to design WANs. It includes a description of WAN communication and the process and considerations for designing a WAN. It all covers the process for gathering user requirements for WAN design, as well as the benefits of using a hierarchical design model.

Chapter 11 discusses the basic components, processes, and operations that define PPP communication. Additionally, this chapter describes how to configure and verify the configuration of PPP along with PPP authentication.

Chapter 12 presents the services, standards, components, operation, and configuration of ISDN communication.

Chapter 13 discusses Frame Relay services, standards, components, and operation. In addition, this chapter covers the configuration tasks for Frame Relay service, along with the commands for monitoring and maintaining a Frame Relay connection.

Chapter 14 provides information regarding managing a network using techniques such as documenting, monitoring, and troubleshooting.

Chapter 15 provides a review of the topics you need to know in order to succesfully pass the Network+ Certification Exam.

Chapter 16 presents a review of the topics covered in the CCNA Certification Exam, which assists in your preparation for the exam.

Chapter 17 provides an overview of emerging remote-access technologies. Additionally, it discusses the pros and cons of accessing the Internet via cable modems, wireless connections, and digital subscriber lines (xDSL).

Chapter 18 establishes virtual private networking as a clear case for security as an enabler, and a basic mechanism to do something new and different: using public networks for private communications.

Chapter 19 helps you work with your network design customer in the development of effective security strategies, and to help you select the right tools and products to implement the strategies.

Appendix A contains cross-referenced information about each of the e-Lab activities contained on the CD-ROM.

Appendix B provides the answers to the "Check Your Understanding" questions that you find at the end of each chapter.

Appendix C describes and defines the commands related to configuring and using Cisco routers that are used throughout this book. It is arranged alphabetically so that you can easily find information on a given command, and each command is also cross-referenced to the chapters where it is used so you can easily find more information.

Appendix D contains cross-referenced information about each of the movies contained on the CD-ROM.

The Glossary defines the terms and abbreviations related to networking used in this book.

Objectives

After reading this chapter, you will be able to

- Describe the overall function of the OSI reference model and the problems it solves
- Describe the characteristics of the physical layer of the OSI reference model
- Describe the characteristics of the data link layer of the OSI reference model
- Describe the characteristics of the network layer of the OSI reference model
- Describe the characteristics of the transport layer of the OSI reference model
- Describe the function of routing in networks
- Understand the different classes of routing protocols

Chapter 1

Review: The OSI Reference Model and Routing

Introduction

Networks are complex environments involving multiple media, multiple protocols, and interconnections to networks outside an organization's central office. Well-designed and carefully installed networks can reduce the problems associated with growth as a networking environment evolves.

Designing, building, and maintaining a *network* can be a challenging task. Even a small network that consists of only 50 routing nodes can pose complex problems that lead to unpredictable results. Large networks that feature thousands of nodes can pose even more complex problems. Despite improvements in equipment performance and media capabilities, designing and building a network is difficult.

This chapter provides a review of the Open System Interconnection (OSI) reference model and an overview of network planning and design considerations related to routing. Using the OSI reference model as a guide for network design can facilitate changes. Using the OSI reference model as a hierarchical structure for network design allows you to design networks in layers. The OSI reference model is at the heart of building and designing networks, with every layer performing a specific task to promote data communications. In this semester, Layer 1 through Layer 4 are the focus. These four layers define the following:

- The type and speed of LAN and WAN media
- How the data is sent across the media
- The type of addressing schemes
- How the data will be sent across the network and how flow control will be accomplished
- The type of routing protocol

The Layered Network Model: The OSI Reference Model

Network models use layers to simplify the networking functions. The separation of networking functions is called *layering*. To understand the importance of layering, let's consider the OSI reference model, a layered model for understanding and implementing computer communications. By using layers, the OSI reference model simplifies the tasks required for two computers to communicate with each other. Each layer focuses on specific functions, thereby allowing the networking designer to choose the right networking devices and functions for the layer. In the OSI reference model, each of the seven numbered layers indicate distinct functions.

The reasons for this division of network functions include the following:

- Layers divide the aspects of network operation into less complex elements.
- Layers define standard interfaces for plug-and-play compatibility.
- Layers enable engineers to specialize design and development efforts on modular functions.
- Layers promote symmetry in the different network modular functions so that they work together.
- Layers prevent changes in one area from affecting other areas, so each area can evolve more quickly.
- Layers divide the complexity of networking into separate, easy-to-learn operations.

MOVIE 1.1

The OSI Model Conceptual Framework

Protocols enabling communication.

As shown in Figure 1-1, each layer of the OSI reference model serves a specific function:

- *Application layer (Layer 7)*—This layer provides network services to user applications. For example, a word processing application is serviced by file transfer services at this layer.
- *Presentation layer (Layer 6)*—This layer provides data representation and code formatting, along with the negotiation of data transfer syntax. It ensures that the data that arrives from the network can be used by the application, and it ensures that information sent by the application can be transmitted on the network.

- *Session layer (Layer 5)*—This layer establishes, maintains, and manages sessions between applications.

- *Transport layer (Layer 4)*—This layer segments and reassembles data into a data stream. The transport layer has the potential to guarantee a connection and offer reliable transport.

- *Network layer (Layer 3)*—This layer determines the best way to move data from one place to another. The router operates at this layer. This layer uses logical addressing schemes that can be managed by an administrator. This layer uses the Internet Protocol (IP) addressing scheme, along with AppleTalk, DECnet, VINES, and IPX addressing schemes.

- *Data link layer (Layer 2)*—This layer provides physical transmission across the medium. It handles error notification, network topology, and flow control. This layer uses *Media Access Control (MAC)* addresses, which also are referred to as physical or hardware addresses.

- *Physical layer (Layer 1)*—This layer provides the electrical, mechanical, procedural, and functional means for activating and maintaining the physical link between systems. This layer uses such physical media as twisted-pair, coaxial, and fiber-optic cable.

SKILL BUILDER

OSI Model Review

This lab serves as a refresher to reinforce your understanding of the seven layers of the OSI model as they relate to the TCP/IP model.

FIGURE 1-1
The OSI reference model defines layer functions that can be used by any network products vendor to help guide the design and development of network products.

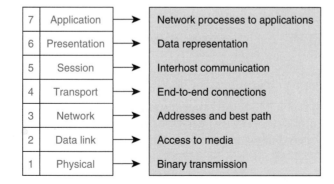

Peer-to-Peer Communication

The OSI reference model describes how information makes its way from application programs on different computers through a network medium. As the information to be sent descends through the layers of a given system, it looks less and less like a human language and more and more like the ones and zeros that a computer understands.

Each layer uses its own layer protocol to communicate with its peer layer in the other system. Each layer's protocol exchanges information, called *protocol data units (PDUs)*, between peer layers.

Figure 1-2 shows an example of OSI-type communication. Host A has information to send to Host B. The application program in Host A communicates with Host A's application layer, which communicates with Host A's presentation layer, which communicates with Host A's session layer, and so on, until Host A's physical layer is reached. The physical layer puts information on (and takes information off) the physical network medium. After the information traverses the physical network medium and is picked up by Host B, it ascends through Host B's layers in reverse order (first the physical layer, then the data link layer, and so on) until it finally reaches Host B's application layer.

FIGURE 1-2
In host-to-host peer-layer protocol communication, the layer below the current layer provides services to the current layer.

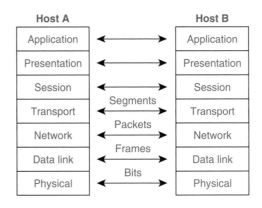

Although each Host A layer communicates with its adjacent layers, each layer in a host has a primary task it must perform. The primary task of each layer is to communicate with its peer layer in Host B. That is, the task of Layer 1 in Host A is to communicate with Layer 1 in Host B; Layer 2 in Host A communicates with Layer 2 in Host B; and so on.

The OSI reference model's layering prohibits direct communication between peer layers in different hosts. Each layer in Host A must therefore rely on services provided by adjacent Host A layers to help achieve communication with its Host B peer. Assume that Layer 4 in Host A must communicate with Layer

4 in Host B. To do this, Layer 4 in Host A must use the services of Layer 3 in Host A. Layer 4 is said to be the *service user*, and Layer 3 is the *service provider*. Layer 3 services are provided to Layer 4 at a *service access point (SAP)*, which is a location at which Layer 4 can request Layer 3 services.

Thus, as shown in Figure 1-2, the TCP segments become part of the network-layer *packets* (also called *datagrams*) exchanged between IP peers. In turn, the IP packets must become part of the datalink frames exchanged between directly connected devices. Ultimately, these frames must become bits as the data is finally transmitted by the physical-layer protocol using hardware.

Data Encapsulation

How does Layer 4 in Host B know what Layer 4 in Host A wants? Layer 4's specific requests are stored as control information, which is passed between peer layers in a *header* block that is attached to the actual application information. Each layer depends on the service function of the OSI reference model layer below it. To provide this service, the lower layer uses encapsulation to put the PDU from the upper layer into its data field; then, it can add whatever headers and trailers the layer will use to perform its function.

The concept of a header and data is relative, depending on the layer currently analyzing the information unit. For example, to Layer 3, an information unit consists of a Layer 3 header and the data that follows. Layer 3's data, however, can potentially contain headers from Layers 4, 5, 6, and 7. Further, Layer 3's header is simply data to Layer 2. This concept is illustrated in Figure 1-3. Finally, not all layers need to append headers. Some layers simply perform a transformation on the actual data they receive to make the data readable to their adjacent layers.

FIGURE 1-3
The network layer has the task of moving data through the network by encapsulating the data within a header.

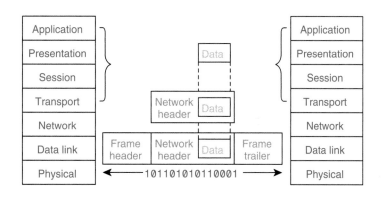

For example, the network layer provides a service to the transport layer, and the transport layer presents data to the network. The network layer then encapsulates the data within a header. This header contains the information required to complete the transfer, such as the source and destination logical addresses. The data link layer, in turn, provides a service to the network layer, encapsulating the network layer information in a frame. The frame header contains information required to complete the datalink functions. For example, the frame header contains physical addresses. The physical layer also provides a service to the data link layer by encoding the datalink frame into a pattern of ones and zeros for transmission on the medium (often copper wire or optical fiber).

For example, let's assume that Host A wants to send the following e-mail to Host B:

```
The small gray cat ran up the wall to try to catch the red bird.
```

Five conversion steps occur during data encapsulation, which enables the transmission of the e-mail to the appropriate destination:

Step 1   As a user sends an e-mail message, its alphanumeric characters are converted to data, starting at Layer 7 down through Layer 5, and are sent over the network.

Step 2   By using segments at Layer 4, the transport function packages data for the network transport and ensures that the message hosts at both ends of the e-mail system can reliably communicate.

Step 3   The data is placed into a packet (or datagram) at Layer 3 that contains a network header with source and destination logical addresses. Then, the network devices send the packets across the network along a chosen path.

Step 4   Each network device must put the packet into a frame at Layer 2. The frame allows the connection to the next directly connected network device on the link. Each device in the chosen network path requires framing to connect to the next device.

Step 5   The frame must be converted into a pattern of ones and zeros for transmission on the medium (often copper wire or optical fiber) at Layer 1. A clocking function enables the devices to distinguish these bits as they traverse the medium. The medium on the physical network can vary along the path used. For example, the e-mail message can originate on a LAN, cross a campus backbone, and go out a WAN link until it reaches its destination on another remote LAN.

The Physical Layer

Ethernet and IEEE 802.3 currently maintain the greatest share of any local-area network (LAN) protocol used. Today, the term *Ethernet* is often used to refer to all carrier sense multiple access collision detect (CSMA/CD) LANs that generally conform to Ethernet specifications, including IEEE 802.3.

When it was developed, Ethernet was designed to fill the middle ground between long-distance, low-speed networks and specialized, computer room networks carrying data at high speeds for very limited distances. Ethernet is good for applications where a local communication medium must carry sporadic, occasionally heavy traffic at high-peak data rates.

The term *Ethernet* refers to the family of LAN implementations that includes three principal categories:

- **Ethernet and IEEE 802.3**—LAN specifications that operate at 10 Mbps over coaxial and twisted-pair cable.
- **100-Mbps Ethernet**—Also known as *Fast Ethernet*, it specifies a LAN operating at 100 Mbps over twisted-pair cable.
- **1000-Mbps Ethernet**—Also known as *Gigabit Ethernet*, it specifies a LAN operating at 1000 Mbps (1 Gbps) over fiber-optic and twisted-pair cables.

Ethernet has survived as an essential media technology because of its tremendous flexibility and because it is simple to implement and understand. Although other technologies have been promoted as likely replacements, network managers have turned to Ethernet and its derivatives as effective solutions for a range of campus implementation requirements. To resolve Ethernet's limitations, creative users (and standards organizations) have created bigger and bigger Ethernet pipes. Critics might dismiss Ethernet as a technology that cannot grow, but its underlying transmission scheme continues to be one of the principal means of transporting data for contemporary campus applications.

Ethernet/802.3 Physical Connections

The Ethernet and IEEE 802.3 wiring standards define a bus topology LAN that operates at 10 Mbps.

Figure 1-4 illustrates the three defined wiring standards:

- **10Base2**—Known as *thin Ethernet* or *ThinNet*, 10Base2 allows network segments up to 185 meters on coaxial cable.
- **10Base5**—Known as *thick Ethernet*, 10Base5 allows network segments up to 500 meters on coaxial cable.
- **10BaseT**—10BaseT carries Ethernet frames on inexpensive twisted-pair wiring with individual cable runs of up to 100 meters.

Ethernet and IEEE 802.3 wiring standards specify a bus topology network with a connecting cable between the end stations and the actual network medium. In the case of Ethernet, that cable is called a *transceiver cable*. The transceiver cable connects to a transceiver device attached to the physical network medium. The IEEE 802.3 configuration is much the same, except that the connecting cable is referred to as an *attachment unit interface (AUI)*, and the transceiver is called a *media attachment unit (MAU)*. In both cases, the connecting cable attaches to an interface board (or interface circuitry) within the end station.

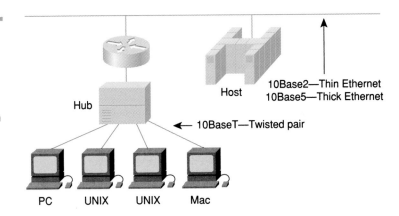

FIGURE 1-4
The 10Base2, 10Base5, and 10BaseT standards provide access for several stations on the same LAN segment.

Stations are attached to the segment by a cable that runs from an AUI in the station to a MAU that is directly attached to the Ethernet coaxial cable. 10BaseT Ethernet also uses a bus topology, but it is a logical bus because it is implemented in the circuitry of the hub or switch. Physically, 10BaseT Ethernet uses a star or extended-star topology, with all network nodes connected to the central hub or LAN switch.

The Data Link Layer

Access to the networking media occurs at the data link layer of the OSI reference model. The data link layer, where the MAC address is located, is adjacent to the physical layer. No two MAC addresses are ever alike. Thus, on a network, the *network interface card (NIC)* is where a device connects to the medium, and each NIC has a unique MAC address.

Before each NIC leaves the factory, the hardware manufacturer assigns it a MAC address. This address is programmed into a chip on the NIC. Because the MAC address is located on the NIC, if a computer's NIC is replaced, the physical address of the station changes to that of the new NIC's MAC address.

MAC addresses are written using a base 16 (hexadecimal) number. There are two formats for MAC addresses: 0000.0c12.3456 and 00-00-0c-12-34-56.

Imagine that you operate a motel. Room 207 has a lock called Lock A. Key A will open the door to Room 207. Room 410 has a lock called Lock F. Key F will open the door to Room 410.

You decide to swap the locks on Rooms 207 and 410. After you switch the two locks, Key A opens the door of Room 410, and Key F opens the door to Room 207.

In this analogy, the locks are like NICs. When the NICs are swapped, the matching keys also must be changed. In this analogy, the keys are like the MAC addresses.

On an Ethernet network, when one device wants to send data to another device, it can open a communication pathway to the other device by using its MAC address. When data is sent out on a network by a source, it carries the MAC address of its intended destination. As this data travels along the network media, the NIC in each device on the network checks to see if its MAC address matches the physical destination address carried by the frame. If no match is made, the NIC ignores the frame, and the frame continues along the network to the next station.

However, when a match is made, the NIC makes a copy of the frame, which it places in the computer where it resides at the data link layer. Even though this copy has been made by the NIC and placed on the computer, the original frame continues along the network where other NICs will be able to look at it to determine whether a match can be made.

The Ethernet/802.3 Interface

The Ethernet and 802.3 data links provide data transport across the physical link joining two devices. For example, as Figure 1-5 shows, the three devices can be directly attached to each other over the Ethernet LAN. The Apple Macintosh on the left and the Intel-based PC in the middle show MAC addresses used by the data link layer. The router on the right also uses MAC addresses for each of its LAN-side interfaces.

FIGURE 1-5
To indicate the 802.3 interface on a router, you use the *Cisco Internetwork Operating System (IOS)* interface type abbreviation E, followed by an interface number (for example, 0).

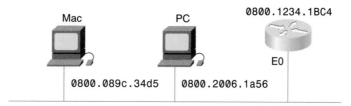

The Network Layer

Several protocols operate at the OSI reference model network layer:

- IP provides connectionless, *best-effort delivery* of routed datagrams (packets). It is not concerned with the content of the datagrams; instead, it looks for a way to move the datagrams to their destinations.
- *Internet Control Message Protocol (ICMP)* provides control and messaging capabilities.
- *Address Resolution Protocol (ARP)* determines the data link layer addresses for known IP addresses.
- *Reverse ARP (RARP)* determines network addresses when data link layer addresses are known.

IP Addressing and Subnets

In a TCP/IP environment, end stations communicate with servers, hosts, or other end stations. This occurs because each node using the TCP/IP protocol suite has a unique 32-bit logical address, known as the *IP address*. In addition, within a TCP/IP environment, each network is seen as a single unique address. That address must be reached before an individual host within that network can be contacted.

MOVIE 1.2

Determining Network Address

The IP destination retrieves an internal subnet mask.

Networks can be segmented into a series of smaller networks called *subnetworks*, as shown in Figure 1-6. Thus, an IP address is broken up into the network number, the subnetwork number, and the host number. Subnets use unique 32-bit subnet addresses that are created by borrowing bits from the host field. Subnet addresses are visible to other devices on the same network, but they are not visible to outside networks because detailed information about subnetting schemes is normally not shared with neighbor routers.

Subnets allow network address space to be used more efficiently. There is no change to how the outside world sees the network, but within the organization, there is additional structure. In Figure 1-7, network 172.16.0.0 is subdivided into four subnets: 172.16.1.0, 172.16.2.0, 172.16.3.0, and 172.16.4.0.

FIGURE 1-6
Each network has an address and each host is identified by a unique address on that network.

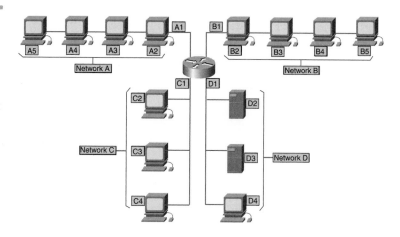

FIGURE 1-7
Routers determine the destination network by using the subnet address, limiting the amount of traffic on the other network segments.

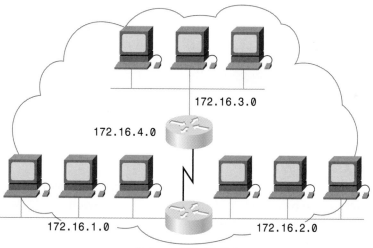

Path Determination

Path determination is the path traffic should take through the network cloud. As shown in Figure 1-8, routers evaluate the best known path for traffic. Path determination occurs at Layer 3, the network layer. Routing services use network topology information when evaluating network paths. This information can be configured by the network administrator or collected through dynamic processes running in the network.

The network layer connects to networks and provides best-effort end-to-end packet delivery services to its user, the transport layer. The network layer sends packets from the source network to the destination network based on the IP routing table. After the router determines which path to use, it can proceed with switching the packet. Switching involves taking the packet the router accepted on one interface and forwarding it to another interface or port that reflects the best path to the packet's destination.

MOVIE 1.3

Router Function

Path determination.

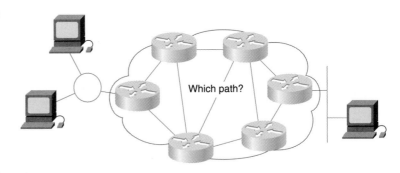

FIGURE 1-8
The path determination function enables a router to evaluate the available paths to a destination and to establish the preferred handling of a packet.

Which path?

Path Communication

For path communication to be truly practical, a network must consistently represent the paths available between routers. Each line between the routers in Figure 1-9 has a number that represents the subnetwork address that can be used by a routing process. These addresses must convey information that can be used by a routing process.

The network address contains both a path and a host part. The path portion identifies a path part used by the router within the network cloud; the host part identifies a specific port or device on the network. The router uses the network address to identify the source or destination network of a packet within a network. Figure 1-10 shows three network numbers coming from the router and three hosts sharing the network number 1. For some network layer protocols, a network administrator establishes this relationship by assigning network addresses ahead of time according to a network-addressing plan. For other network layer protocols, assigning addresses is partially or completely dynamic.

FIGURE 1-9
An address must have information about the path of media connections that are used by the routing process to pass packets from a source toward a destination.

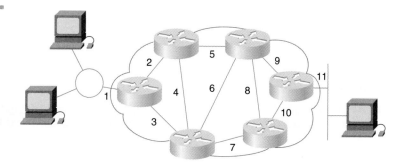

FIGURE 1-10
Most network-protocol addressing schemes use some form of a host or node address.

Network	Host
1	1 2 3
2	1
3	1

The consistency of Layer 3 addresses across the entire network also improves the use of bandwidth by preventing unnecessary broadcasts. Broadcasts cause unnecessary traffic and waste capacity on any devices or links that do not need to receive the broadcasts. By using consistent end-to-end addressing to represent the path of media connections, the network layer can find a path to the destination without unnecessary use of devices or links on the network.

ICMP

ICMP messages are carried in IP datagrams and are used to send error and control messages. ICMP uses the following types of defined messages; others exist, but are not included in the following list:

- Destination unreachable
- Time exceeded
- Parameter problem
- Source quench
- Redirect

- Echo
- Echo reply
- Timestamp
- Timestamp reply
- Information request
- Information reply
- Address request
- Address reply

Figure 1-11 shows a router receiving a packet that it is unable to deliver to its ultimate destination; because of this, the router sends an ICMP host unreachable message to the source. The message might be undeliverable because there is no known route to the destination. On the other hand, Figure 1-12 shows an echo reply that is a successful reply to a **ping** command.

e-LAB ACTIVITY 1.1

ping

In this activity, you demonstrate the use of the **ping** command to verify workstation connectivity.

MOVIE 1.5

Router Can't Deliver

ICMP destination unreachable message.

MOVIE 1.6

Reachability

TCP/IP host sends ICMP echo request.

ARP

To communicate on an Ethernet network, the source station must know the destination station's IP and MAC addresses. When the source has determined the IP address for the destination, the source's Internet protocol looks into its ARP table to locate the MAC address for the destination. If the Internet protocol locates a mapping of destination IP address to destination MAC address in its table, it binds the IP address with the MAC address and uses them to encapsulate the data. The data packet is then sent out over the networking media to be picked up by the destination.

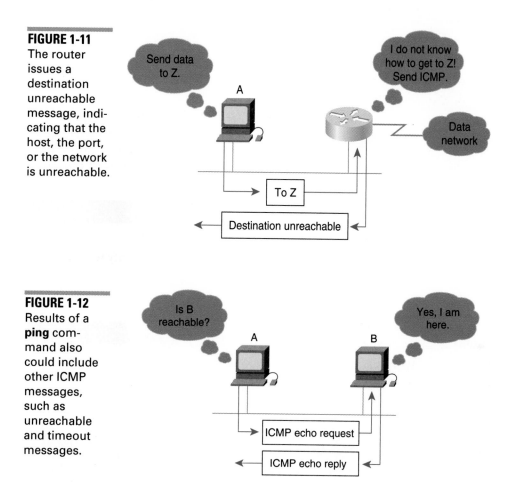

FIGURE 1-11
The router issues a destination unreachable message, indicating that the host, the port, or the network is unreachable.

FIGURE 1-12
Results of a **ping** command also could include other ICMP messages, such as unreachable and timeout messages.

When a network device wishes to send data, it checks its ARP table for the destination address. If the address is not found in the table, the sender broadcasts an ARP request in an attempt to discover the MAC address of the destination. Every device on the network receives this broadcast.

The term *local ARP* is used when both the requesting host and the destination host share the same medium, or wire (see Figure 1-13).

MOVIE 1.7

Address Resolution

Finding the MAC address.

FIGURE 1-13
Local ARP
resolves an
address by
looking at the
subnet mask.

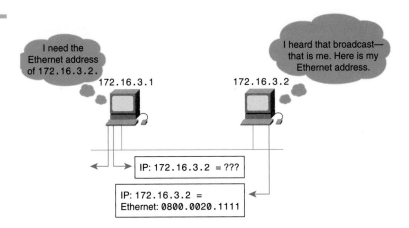

Routing

The network layer must relate to and interface with various lower layers.
Routers must be capable of seamlessly handling packets encapsulated into dif-
ferent lower-level frames without changing the packets' Layer 3 addressing.
Figure 1-14 shows an example of this with LAN-to-LAN routing. In this
example, packet traffic from Host 4 on Ethernet Network 1 needs a path to
Host 5 on Network 2.

When the router checks its routing table entries, it discovers that the best path
to Network 2 uses outgoing Port To0, the interface to a Token Ring LAN.
Although the lower-layer framing must change as the router switches packet
traffic from Ethernet on Network 1 to Token Ring on Network 2, the Layer 3
addressing for the source and destination remains the same. In Figure 1-14, the
destination address remains Network 2, Host 5, despite the different lower-
layer encapsulations.

Router Operations

Routers generally relay a packet from one data link to another. To relay a
packet, a router uses two basic functions: a path determination function and a
switching function. Figure 1-15 illustrates how routers use addressing for routing and switching functions.

FIGURE 1-14 The LAN hosts depend on the router and its consistent network addressing to find the best path.

Destination network	Direction and router port
1.0	← 1.1
2.0	→ 2.1
3.0	→ 3.1

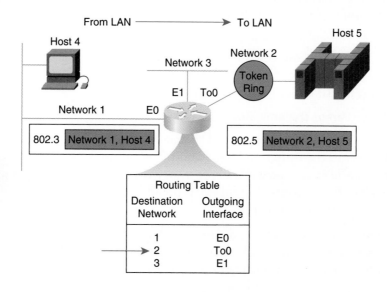

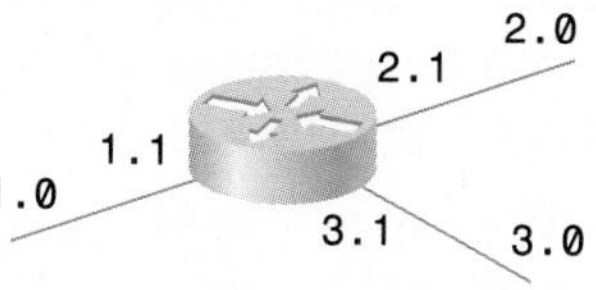

FIGURE 1-15 A router passes the packet to the next network along the path and uses the network portion of the address to make path selections.

The switching function allows a router to accept a packet on one interface and forward it on a second interface. The path determination function enables the router to select the most appropriate interface for forwarding a packet. The node portion of the address refers to a specific port on the router that leads to an adjacent router in that direction.

When a host application needs to send a packet to a destination on a different network, a datalink frame is received on one of a router's interfaces. The network layer process examines the header to determine the destination network and then references the routing table that associates networks to outgoing interfaces. The original frame is stripped off and discarded. The packet is again encapsulated in the datalink frame for the selected interface and stored in a *queue* for delivery to the next *hop* in the path.

This process occurs each time the packet switches through another router. At the router connected to the network containing the destination host, the packet is again encapsulated in the destination LAN's datalink frame type and delivered to the destination host.

Static Versus Dynamic Routes

Static routing is administered manually. A network administrator enters the route into the router's configuration. The administrator must manually update this static route entry whenever a network topology change requires an update. Static routing reduces overhead because routing updates are not sent (in the case of RIP, every 30 seconds).

Dynamic routing works differently. After the network administrator enters configuration commands to start dynamic routing, route knowledge is updated automatically by a routing process whenever new information is received from the network. Changes in dynamic knowledge are exchanged between routers as part of the update process.

Static routing has several useful applications. It allows a network administrator to specify what is advertised about restricted partitions. For security reasons, the administrator can hide parts of a network. Dynamic routing tends to reveal everything known about a network.

Additionally, when a network is accessible by only one path, a static route to the network can be sufficient. This type of partition is called a *stub network*. Configuring static routing to a stub network avoids the overhead of dynamic routing because routing updates are not sent.

A Default Route Example

Figure 1-16 shows a use for a *default route*—a routing table entry that is used to direct packets for which the next hop is not explicitly listed in the routing table. In this example, Company X routers possess specific knowledge of the topology of the Company X network, but not of other networks. Maintaining knowledge of every other network accessible by way of the Internet cloud is unnecessary and unreasonable, if not impossible.

Instead of maintaining specific network knowledge, each router in Company X is informed by the default route that it can reach any unknown destination by directing the packet to the Internet.

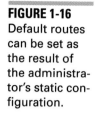

FIGURE 1-16
Default routes
can be set as
the result of
the administra-
tor's static con-
figuration.

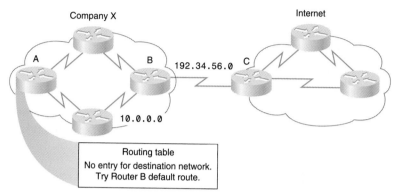

Routed Versus Routing Protocols

Confusion often exists between the similar terms *routed protocol* and *routing protocol*. The following definitions differentiate the terms:

- **Routed protocol**—Any network protocol that provides enough information in its network layer address to allow a packet to be forwarded from host to host based on the addressing scheme. Routed protocols define the format and use of the fields within a packet. Packets generally are conveyed from end system to end system. IP is an example of a routed protocol.

- **Routing protocol**—A protocol that supports a routed protocol by providing mechanisms for sharing routing information. Routing protocol messages move between the routers. A routing protocol allows the routers to communicate with other routers to update and maintain tables. TCP/IP examples of routing protocols are *Routing Information Protocol (RIP)*, *Interior Gateway Routing Protocol (IGRP)*, *Enhanced Interior Gateway Routing Protocol (Enhanced IGRP)*, and *Open Shortest Path First (OSPF)* protocol.

Routing Protocols

The success of dynamic routing depends on two basic router functions:

- Maintenance of a routing table
- Timely distribution of knowledge in the form of routing updates to other routers

Dynamic routing relies on a routing protocol to share knowledge. A routing protocol defines the set of rules used by a router when it communicates with neighboring routers. For example, a routing protocol describes

- How updates are sent
- What knowledge is contained in these updates

- When to send this knowledge
- How to locate recipients of the updates

Exterior routing protocols are used to communicate between autonomous systems. Interior routing protocols are used within a single autonomous system.

IP Routing Protocols

At the network layer (Layer 3) of the OSI reference model, a router can use IP routing protocols to accomplish routing through the implementation of a specific routing protocol. Examples of IP routing protocols include

- **RIP**—A distance-vector routing protocol
- **IGRP**—Cisco's distance-vector routing protocol
- **OSPF**—A link-state routing protocol
- **EIGRP**—A balanced-hybrid routing protocol

Classes of Routing Protocols

Most interior routing protocols can be classified as one of three basic types: distance vector, link state, or balanced-hybrid routing. The *distance-vector routing protocol* determines the direction (vector) and distance to any link in the network. The *link-state routing protocol* (also called the *shortest path first [SPF] protocol*) approach re-creates the exact topology of the entire network (or at least the partition in which the router is situated). The *balanced-hybrid protocol* combines aspects of the link-state and distance-vector protocols.

Convergence

Routing protocols, which are used to determine the best route for traffic from a particular source to a particular destination, are fundamental to dynamic routing. Whenever the topology of the network changes because of growth, reconfiguration, or failure, the network knowledge base also must change. The knowledge needs to reflect an accurate, consistent view of the new topology. This accurate, consistent view is called *convergence*.

When all routers in a network are operating with the same knowledge, the network is said to have converged. Fast convergence is a desirable network feature because it reduces the period of time that routers have outdated knowledge for making routing decisions that could be incorrect, wasteful, or both.

Distance-Vector Routing

Distance-vector routing protocols pass periodic copies of a routing table from router to router. Each router receives a routing table from its direct neighbor. (See Figure 1-17.) For example, Router B receives information from Router A. Router B adds a distance-vector number (such as a number of hops), increases the distance vector, and then passes the routing table to its other neighbor,

Router C. This same step-by-step process occurs in all directions between direct-neighbor routers.

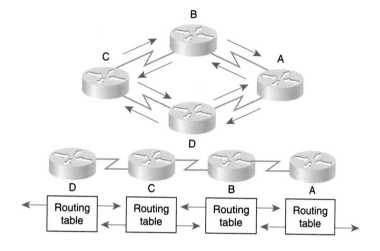

FIGURE 1-17
Regular
updates
between
routers
communicate
topology
changes.

In this way, the protocol accumulates network distances so it can maintain a database of network topology information. Distance-vector protocols do not allow a router to know the exact topology of a network.

Link-State Routing

The second basic protocol used for routing is the link-state protocol. Link-state routing protocols maintain a complex database of topology information. Whereas the distance-vector protocol has nonspecific information about distant networks and no knowledge of distant routers, a link-state routing protocol maintains full knowledge of distant routers and how they interconnect.

MOVIE 1.8
Link-State Protocols
A complex database of topology information.

Link-state routing uses *link-state advertisements (LSAs)*, a topological database, the SPF protocol, the resulting SPF tree, and finally, a routing table of paths and ports to each network. Engineers have implemented this link-state concept in OSPF routing.

MOVIE 1.9

OSPF Routers

Link-state advertisements.

Distance-Vector Routing Versus Link-State Routing

You can compare distance-vector routing to link-state routing in several key areas:

- Distance-vector routing gets all topological data from the routing table information of its neighbors. Link-state routing obtains a complete view of the network topology by accumulating information from LSAs from both neighboring and distant routers.
- Distance-vector routing determines the best path by adding to the metric value it receives as tables move from router to router. For link-state routing, each router works separately to calculate its own shortest path to destinations.
- With most distance-vector routing protocols, updates for topology changes come in periodic table updates. These tables pass from router to router, often resulting in slower convergence. With link-state routing protocols, updates usually are triggered by topology changes. Relatively small LSAs passed to all other routers usually result in faster time to converge on any network topology change.

MOVIE 1.10

Distance-Vector Protocols

Routing updates.

IP Routing Configuration Tasks

The selection of IP as a routed protocol involves the setting of global parameters. Global parameters include selecting a routing protocol, such as RIP or IGRP, and assigning IP network numbers without specifying subnet values.

IP Address Configuration

You use the **ip address** command to establish the logical network address of the interface. You use the **term ip netmask-format** command to specify the format of network masks for the current session. Format options are bit count, dotted-decimal (the default), and hexadecimal.

Dynamic Routing Configuration

Dynamic routing occurs when routers send periodic routing update messages to each other. Each time such a message is received and it contains new information, the router recalculates the new best route and sends new update information to other routers.

The following router commands start routing processes:

Command	Description
router *protocol*	Defines an IP routing protocol, which can be either RIP, IGRP, OSPF, or EIGRP.
network	The **network** subcommand is a mandatory configuration command for each routing process.

The following **network** command is required because it allows the routing process to determine which interfaces will participate in the sending and receiving of routing updates:

network Command	Description
network *network-number*	Specifies a directly connected network.

RIP

Key characteristics of RIP include the following:

- It is a distance-vector routing protocol.
- Hop count is used as the metric for path selection.
- The maximum allowable hop count is 15.
- Routing updates are broadcast every 30 seconds by default.

The **router rip** command selects RIP as the routing protocol. The **network** command assigns an IP-based network address range, which is directly connected to the router. The routing process associates interfaces with the proper addresses and begins packet processing on the specified networks (see Figure 1-18).

- **router rip**—Selects RIP as the routing protocol.
- **network 1.0.0.0**—Specifies a directly connected network.
- **network 2.0.0.0**—Specifies a directly connected network.

The Cisco A router interfaces connected to networks 1.0.0.0 and 2.0.0.0 will send and receive RIP updates.

FIGURE 1-18
Routing updates allow the router to learn the network topology.

1.4.0.0

Token Ring

2.6.0.0

T0

2.7.0.0
S1

E

2.5.0.0

S2

3.3.0.0   1.1.0.0

S0   A

2.2.0.0

2.1.0.0

C

B

D

1.2.0.0   2.3.0.0

Token Ring

Cisco A
router protocol rip
network 1.0.0.0
network 2.0.0.0

2.4.0.0

SKILL BUILDER

Router Lab Setup Review

This lab serves as a refresher for how the Cisco lab routers are set up and connected for the Semester 2 topology. This is a review of the Semester 2 network topology.

SKILL BUILDER

Router Subnets Review

This important lab demonstrates your understanding of how the Cisco lab is set up and how subnetting applies to multiple routers.

e-LAB ACTIVITY 1.2

ip address

In this activity, you demonstrate how to use the **ip address** command to connect to another router via the serial port.

e-LAB ACTIVITY 1.3

router rip

In this activity, you demonstrate how to use the **router rip** command to select RIP as the routing protocol.

The Transport Layer

As the transport layer sends its data segments, it can ensure the integrity of the data. One method of doing this is called *flow control*. Flow control avoids the problem of a source host overflowing the buffers in the destination host. Overflows can present serious problems because they can result in the loss of data.

Transport-layer services also allow users to request reliable data transport between hosts and destinations. To obtain such reliable transport of data, a connection-oriented relationship is used between the communicating end systems. Reliable transport can accomplish the following:

- Segment upper-layer applications
- Establish a connection
- Transfer data
- Provide reliability with windowing
- Use acknowledgment techniques

Segmenting Upper-Layer Applications

One reason for using a layered network model is so that several applications can share the same transport connection. Transport functionality is accomplished segment by segment. This means that different applications can send data segments on a first-come, first-served basis. Such segments can be intended for the same destination or for many different destinations.

Establishing a Connection

To establish a connection, one machine places a call that must be accepted by the other. Protocol software modules in the two operating systems communicate by sending messages across the network to verify that the transfer is authorized and that both sides are ready. After all synchronization has occurred, a connection is established, and the transfer of data begins. During transfer, the two machines continue to communicate with their protocol software to verify that data is received correctly.

Figure 1-19 depicts a typical connection between sending and receiving systems. When you first meet someone, you often greet the person by shaking his or her hand. The act of shaking hands is understood by both parties as a signal for a friendly greeting. We speak of connections on the network in the same way. The first handshake, or greeting, requests synchronization. The second and third handshakes acknowledge the initial synchronization request, as well as synchronize the connection parameters in the opposite direction. The final handshake segment is an acknowledgment used to inform the destination that both sides agree that a connection has been established. After the connection is established, data transfer begins.

MOVIE 1.11

Connection-Oriented Services

Three phases: connection establishment, data transfer, and connection termination.

FIGURE 1-19
For data transfer to begin, both the sending and receiving application programs must inform their respective operating systems that a connection will be initiated.

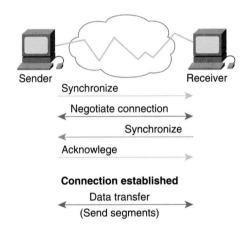

Data Transfer

When data transfer is in progress, congestion can arise for two different reasons. First, a high-speed computer might be able to generate traffic faster than a network can transfer it. Second, if many computers simultaneously need to send datagrams to a single destination, that destination can experience congestion, even though no single source caused the problem.

When datagrams arrive too quickly for a host or gateway to process, they are temporarily stored in memory. If the traffic continues, the host or gateway eventually exhausts its memory and must discard additional datagrams that arrive. Therefore, as shown in Figure 1-20, an indicator acts like a stoplight and signals the sender to stop sending data. When the receiver can handle additional data, the receiver sends a "ready" transport indicator, which is like a "go" signal. When it receives this indicator, the sender can resume segment transmission.

MOVIE 1.12

Three-Way Handshake

Sequence of messages exchanged to ensure transmission synchronization.

FIGURE 1-20
Instead of
allowing data
to be lost, the
transport func-
tion can issue a
"not ready"
indicator to the
sender.

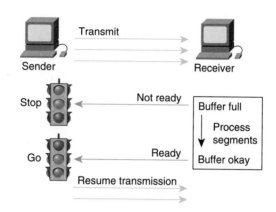

Reliability with Windowing

In the most basic form of reliable connection-oriented data transfer, data packets must be delivered to the recipient in the same order in which they were
transmitted. The protocol fails if any data packets are lost, damaged, duplicated, or received in a different order. The basic solution is to have a recipient
acknowledge the receipt of every data segment.

If the sender has to wait for an acknowledgment after sending each segment,
throughput is low. Because time is available after the sender finishes transmitting the data packet and before the sender finishes processing any received
acknowledgment, the interval is used for transmitting more data. The number
of data packets the sender is allowed to have outstanding without yet receiving
an acknowledgment is known as the *window*.

MOVIE 1.13

TCP Host Sends Packet

Window size.

Windowing is a method to control the amount of information transferred end-to-end. Some protocols measure information in terms of the number of packets; TCP/IP measures information in terms of the number of bytes.

MOVIE 1.14
Windowing
Window size, acknowledgment.

Acknowledgment Techniques

Reliable delivery guarantees that a stream of data sent from one machine will be delivered through a data link to another machine without duplication or data loss. Positive acknowledgment with retransmission is one technique that guarantees reliable delivery of data streams. Positive acknowledgment requires a recipient to communicate with the source, sending back an acknowledgment message when it receives data. The sender keeps a record of each data packet it sends and waits for an acknowledgment before sending the next data packet. The sender also starts a timer when it sends a segment, and it retransmits a segment if the timer expires before an acknowledgment arrives.

MOVIE 1.15
PAR
Positive acknowledgment and retransmission.

Figure 1-21 shows the sender transmitting Data Packets 1, 2, and 3. The receiver acknowledges receipt of the packets by requesting Packet 4. Upon receiving the acknowledgment, the sender sends Packets 4, 5, and 6. If Packet 5 does not arrive at the destination, the receiver acknowledges with a request to resend Segment 5. The sender resends Packet 5 and must receive an acknowledgment to continue with the transmission of Packet 7.

SKILL BUILDER
IOS Update/TFTP
This important lab demonstrates your understanding of how the Cisco lab is set up and how subnetting applies to multiple routers. You develop an addressing scheme based on a Class B network address and then subnet it to accommodate your current physical network with room for growth.

SKILL BUILDER

Router Memory Upgrade

In this lab, you determine what version and IOS your router is currently running and become familiar with the requirements to update to a newer version.

FIGURE 1-21
Positive acknowledgment requires a recipient to communicate with the source, sending back an acknowledgment message when it receives data.

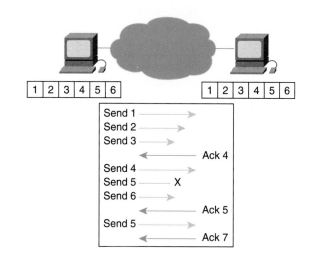

Summary

- By using layers, the OSI reference model simplifies the task required for two computers to communicate.

- Each layer's protocol exchanges information, called PDUs, between peer layers.

- Each layer depends on the service function of the OSI reference model layer below it. The lower layer uses encapsulation to put the PDU from the upper layer into its data field; then, it can add whatever headers and trailers the layer will use to perform its function.

- The term *Ethernet* is often used to refer to all CSMA/CD LANs that generally conform to Ethernet specifications, including IEEE 802.3.

- The Ethernet and 802.3 data links provide data transport across the physical link that joins two devices.

- IP provides connectionless, best-effort delivery routing of datagrams. It is not concerned with the content of the datagrams, but it looks for a way to move the datagrams to their destination.

- ICMP messages are carried in IP datagrams and are used to send error and control messages.

- ARP is used to map a known IP address to a MAC sublayer address to allow communication on a multiaccess medium, such as Ethernet.

- The switching function allows a router to accept a packet on one interface and forward it on a second interface.

- Routed protocols are network protocols that provide enough information in the network layer address to allow a packet to be forwarded from host to host based on the addressing scheme.

- Routing protocol supports routed protocols by providing mechanisms for sharing routing information. Routing protocol messages move between the routers.

- Most routing protocols can be classified into one of two basic protocols: distance-vector or link-state.

- Routers must be capable of seamlessly handling packets encapsulated into different lower-level frames without changing the packets' Layer 3 addressing.

- Examples of IP routing protocols include RIP, IGRP, OSPF, and EIGRP.

- Transport-layer services allow users to request reliable data transport between hosts and destinations.

Check Your Understanding

Complete all the review questions to test your understanding of the topics and concepts covered in this chapter. Answers are listed in Appendix B, "Check Your Understanding Answer Key."

1. Which OSI reference model layer best describes 10BaseT standards?

   A. The data link layer

   B. The network layer

   C. The physical layer

   D. The transport layer

2. Which of the following best describes the function of the transport layer of the OSI reference model?

   A. It sends data by using flow control.

   B. It provides the best path for delivery.

   C. It determines network addresses.

   D. It allows for network segmentation.

3. Which of the following functions does a router use to relay data packets between networks?

   A. Application and media

   B. Path determination and switching

   C. Broadcast and collision detect

   D. None of the above

4. Which of the following are two basic types of dynamic routing?

   A. Static and default

   B. TCP and UDP exchange

   C. Distance vector and link state

   D. None of the above

5. When all the routers in a network are operating with the same knowledge, the network is said to have done which of the following?

   A. Converged

   B. Formalized

   C. Reconfigured

   D. None of the above

6. Describe the purpose of data encapsulation.

7. Describe the main function of the transport layer of the OSI reference model.

8. Describe the purpose of ICMP.

9. Describe windowing in a TCP/IP implementation.

10. Describe the main function of the network layer of the OSI reference model.

11. What commands are used to associate a network with a RIP routing process?

   A. **router rip**
   area *area-id*

   B. **router rip**
   network *network-number*

   C. **router rip**
   neighbour *IP-address*

   D. **router rip**
   show IP route *summary*

12. Which of the following best decribes the TCP/IP protocol stack?

   A. Maps closely to the OSI reference model in the upper layers.

   B. Supports all standard physical and data-link protocols.

   C. Transfers information in a sequence of datagrams.

   D. Reassembles datagrams into complete messages at the receiving location.

13. Which best describes the structure of an encapsulated data packet?

   A. Segment header, network header, data, frame trailer

   B. Segment header, network header, data, segment trailer

   C. Frame header, network header, data, frame trailer

   D. Frame header, segment header, data, segment trailer

14. What technique is used with windowing to guarantee that a stream of data sent from one machine will be delivered through a data link to another machine without duplication or data loss?

A. Acknowledgment and retransmission

B. Encapsulation and broadcasting

C. Recovery and flow control

D. Synchronization and acknowledgment

15. What is one advantage of dynamic routing?

A. Takes little network overhead and reduces network traffic

B. Reduces unauthorized break-ins because security is tight

C. Adjusts automatically to topology or traffic changes

D. Requires little bandwidth to operate efficiently

16. Which best describes the function of the transport layer?

A. Uses the TCP protocol to segment and reassemble data into a data stream.

B. Establishes, maintains, and manages sessions between applications.

C. Provides network services to user applications.

D. Uses a MAC address to provide physical transmission across media and handles error notification, network topology, and flow control.

17. In the IP RIP routing protocol, how often are routing updates sent?

A. Every 30 seconds

B. Every 60 seconds

C. Every 90 seconds

D. Only when the admin directs the router to do so

18. Which of the following statements is true?

A. MAC addressing is a hierarchical addressing system, which has unique MAC addresses assigned.

B. IP addresses are used by bridges to enable the traveling of data across the network.

C. The address that is at the data link layer and hard-coded into the network interface card is the MAC address.

D. If a device is moved from one network to a different network, the MAC address of the device changes.

19. The advantage of using a layered model of networking is

A. Simplifying the network

B. For the purpose of standardization

C. Dividing the complexity of internetworking into discrete, more easily learned operation subsets

D. All of the above

20. A router routing a packet of data performs which of the following functions?

A. Simply adds another header to the packet frame, consisting of the final resolved destination machine's IP address.

B. Consults its routing tables to determine which of its ports it will need to send the data out on in order for it to reach its destination network

C. Broadcasts the data frame to all the ports except the port that the data arrived at

D. Performs all the above functions

Key Terms

application layer   Layer 7 of the OSI reference model. This layer provides network services to user applications. For example, a word processing application is serviced by file transfer services at this layer.

ARP (Address Resolution Protocol)   An Internet protocol used to map an IP address to a MAC address. Defined in RFC 826.

AUI (attachment unit interface)   An IEEE 802.3 interface between a MAU and a network interface card. The term *AUI* also can refer to the rear panel port to which an AUI cable might attach, such as those found on a Cisco LightStream Ethernet access card. Also called a *transceiver cable*.

balanced-hybrid protocol   A protocol that combines aspects of the link-state and distance-vector protocols.

best-effort delivery   This delivery occurs when a network system does not use a sophisticated acknowledgment system to guarantee reliable delivery of information.

Cisco Internetwork Operating System (IOS) software   Cisco system software that provides common functionality, scalability, and security for all products under the CiscoFusion architecture. The Cisco IOS software allows centralized, integrated, and automated installation and management of internetworks, while ensuring support for a wide variety of protocols, media, services, and platforms.

convergence   The speed and capability of a group of internetworking devices running a specific routing protocol to agree on the topology of an internetwork after a change in that topology.

data link layer   Layer 2 of the *OSI reference model*. This layer provides reliable transit of data across a physical link. The data link layer is concerned with physical addressing, network topology, line discipline, error notification, ordered delivery of frames, and flow control. The IEEE divided this layer into two sublayers: the MAC sublayer and the LLC sublayer. Sometimes, this layer is called simply the *link layer*. This layer roughly corresponds to the data link control layer of the SNA model.

datagram   A logical grouping of information sent as a network layer unit over a transmission medium without prior establishment of a virtual circuit. IP datagrams are the primary information units in the Internet. The terms *cell*, *frame*, *message*, *packet*, and *segment* also are used to describe logical information groupings at various layers of the OSI reference model and in various technology circles.

default route   A routing table entry that is used to direct frames for which a next hop is not explicitly listed in the routing table.

distance-vector routing protocol   A routing protocol that iterates on the number of hops in a route to find a shortest-path spanning tree. Distance-vector routing protocols call for each router to send its entire routing table in each update, but only to its neighbors. Distance-vector routing protocols can be prone to routing loops, but are computationally simpler than link-state routing protocols. Also called *Bellman-Ford routing algorithm*.

dynamic routing   Routing that adjusts automatically to network topology or traffic changes. Also called *adaptive routing*.

Enhanced IGRP (Enhanced Interior Gateway Routing Protocol)   An advanced version of IGRP developed by Cisco. Provides superior convergence properties and operating efficiency, and combines the advantages of link-state protocols with those of distance-vector protocols. Also called *EIGRP*.

flow control   A technique for ensuring that a transmitting entity does not overwhelm a receiving entity with data. When the buffers on the receiving device are full, a message is sent to the sending device to suspend the transmission until the data in the buffers has been processed. In IBM networks, this technique is called *pacing*.

header   Control information placed before data when encapsulating that data for network transmission.

hop   The passage of a data packet between two network nodes (for example, between two routers).

ICMP (Internet Control Message Protocol)   A network layer Internet protocol that reports errors and provides other information relevant to IP packet processing. Documented in RFC 792.

IGRP (Interior Gateway Routing Protocol)   A protocol developed by Cisco to address the problems associated with routing in large, heterogeneous networks.

IP address   A 32-bit address assigned to hosts by using TCP/IP. An IP address belongs to one of five classes (A, B, C, D, or E) and is written as four octets separated by periods (that is, dotted-decimal format). Each address consists of a network number, an optional subnetwork number, and a host number. The network and subnetwork numbers together are used for routing, and the host number is used to address an individual host within the network or subnetwork. A subnet mask is used to extract network and subnetwork information from the IP address. Also called an *Internet address*.

layering   The separation of networking functions used by the OSI reference model, which simplifies the tasks required for two computers to communicate with each other.

link-state routing protocol   A routing protocol in which each router broadcasts or multicasts information regarding the cost of reaching each of its neighbors to all nodes in the internetwork. Link-state protocols create a consistent view of the network and are therefore not prone to routing loops, but they achieve this at the cost of relatively greater computational difficulty and more widespread traffic (compared with distance-vector routing protocols).

LSA (link-state advertisement)   A broadcast packet used by link-state protocols that contains information about neighbors and path costs. LSAs are used by the receiving routers to maintain their routing tables. Sometimes called *link-state packets (LSPs)*.

MAC (Media Access Control)   The part of the data link layer that includes the 6-byte (48-bit) address of the source and destination, and the method of getting permission to transmit.

MAU (media attachment unit)   A device used in Ethernet and IEEE 802.3 networks that provides the interface between the AUI port of a station and the common medium of the Ethernet. The MAU, which can be built into a station or can be a separate device, performs physical-layer functions including the conversion of digital data from the Ethernet interface, collision detection, and injection of bits onto the network. Sometimes referred to as a *media access unit* (also abbreviated MAU) or as a *transceiver.*

network   A collection of computers, printers, routers, switches, and other devices that are able to communicate with each other over some transmission medium.

network layer   Layer 3 of the *OSI reference model*. This layer provides connectivity and path selection between two end systems. The network layer is the layer at which routing occurs. Corresponds roughly with the path control layer of the SNA model.

NIC (network interface card)   A board that provides network communication capabilities to and from a computer system. Also called an *adapter.*

OSPF (Open Shortest Path First) protocol   A link-state, hierarchical routing protocol proposed as a successor to RIP in the Internet community. OSPF features include least-cost routing, multipath routing, and load balancing.

packet   A logical grouping of information that includes a header containing control information and (usually) user data. Packets are most often used to refer to network layer units of data. The terms *datagram*, *frame*, *message*, and *segment* also are used to describe logical information groupings at various layers of the OSI reference model and in various technology circles.

path determination   The decision of which path traffic should take through the network cloud. Path determination occurs at the network layer of the OSI reference model.

PDU (protocol data unit)   The OSI term for a packet.

physical layer   Layer 1 of the OSI reference model. This layer defines the electrical, mechanical, procedural, and functional specifications for activating, maintaining, and deactivating the physical link between end systems. Corresponds with the physical control layer in the SNA model.

presentation layer   Layer 6 of the OSI reference model. This layer provides data representation and code formatting, along with the negotiation of data transfer syntax. It ensures that the data that arrives from the network can be used by the application, and it ensures that information sent by the application can be transmitted on the network.

queue   1. Generally, an ordered list of elements waiting to be processed. 2. In routing, a backlog of packets waiting to be forwarded over a router interface.

RARP (Reverse Address Resolution Protocol)   A protocol in the TCP/IP stack that provides a method for finding IP addresses based on MAC addresses.

RIP (Routing Information Protocol)   A protocol supplied with UNIX BSD systems. The most common Interior Gateway Protocol (IGP) in the Internet. RIP uses hop count as a routing metric.

routed protocol   A protocol that can be routed by a router. A router must be able to interpret the logical internetwork as specified by that routed protocol. Examples of routed protocols include AppleTalk, DECnet, and IP.

routing protocol   A protocol that accomplishes routing through the implementation of a specific routing protocol. Examples of routing protocols include IGRP, OSPF, and RIP.

session layer   Layer 5 of the OSI reference model. This layer establishes, maintains, and manages sessions between applications.

SPF (shortest path first) protocol   A routing protocol that iterates on length of path to determine a shortest-path spanning tree. Commonly used in link-state routing protocols. Sometimes called *Dijkstra's algorithm*.

static routing   Routing that is explicitly configured and entered into the routing table. Static routes take precedence over routes chosen by dynamic routing protocols.

stub network   A network that has only a single connection to a router.

subnet mask   A mask used to extract network and subnetwork information from the IP address.

subnetwork   A network that is segmented into a series of smaller networks.

transport layer   Layer 4 of the OSI reference model. This layer segments and reassembles data into a data stream. The transport layer has the potential to guarantee a connection and offer reliable transport.

window   The number of octets that the sender is willing to accept.

Objectives

After reading this chapter, you will be able to

- Describe the various LAN communication problems, such as
  - Collisions
  - CSMA/CD
  - Demands of multimedia applications on the network
  - Normal latency
  - Distances and repeaters
  - Excessive broadcasts
- Describe full-duplex transmitting and the Fast Ethernet standard as two methods to improve LAN performance
- Describe the effects of LAN segmentation with bridges, routers, and switches
- Describe switching
- Describe the operation and benefits of LAN switching
- Describe the Spanning-Tree Protocol
- Describe the benefits of VLANs

Chapter 2

LAN Switching

Introduction

Today, network designers are moving away from using bridges and hubs and are primarily using switches and routers to build networks. Chapter 1, "Review: The OSI Reference Model and Routing," provides a review of the OSI reference model and an overview of network planning and design considerations related to routing.

This chapter discusses problems in a local-area network (LAN) and possible solutions that can improve LAN performance. You will learn about LAN congestion and its effect on network performance and the advantages of LAN segmentation in a network. In addition, you will learn about the advantages and disadvantages of using bridges, switches, and routers for LAN segmentation and the effects of switching, bridging, and routing on network throughput. Finally, you will learn about Ethernet, Fast Ethernet, and VLANs, and the benefits of these technologies.

Network Demands

Today's LANs are becoming increasingly congested and overburdened. In addition to an ever-growing population of network users, several other factors have combined to expand the capabilities of traditional LANs:

- **Faster CPUs**—In the mid-1980s, the most common desktop workstation was a PC. At the time, most PCs could complete 1 million instructions per second (MIPS). Today, workstations with 50 to 75 MIPS of processing power are common, and input/output (I/O) speeds have increased accordingly. As a result, two workstations on the same LAN can easily saturate the network.

- **Faster operating systems**—The multitasking environment present in current desktop operating systems (Windows, UNIX, and Mac) allows for simultaneous network transactions. This increased capability has lead to stronger demand for network resources.

- **Network-intensive applications**—The use of *client/server applications* is increasing. Client/server applications allow administrators to centralize information, thus making it easy to maintain and protect. Client/server applications free users from the burden of maintaining information and the cost of providing enough hard disk space to store it. Given the cost benefit of client/server applications, such applications are likely to become even more widely used in the future.

The Ethernet/802.3 Interface

The most common LAN architecture is *Ethernet*. Ethernet is used to transport data between devices on a network, such as computers, printers, and file servers. As shown in Figure 2-1, all the devices are connected to the same delivery medium. Ethernet media use a data frame *broadcast* method of transmitting and receiving data to all *nodes* on the shared media.

The performance of a shared-medium Ethernet/802.3 LAN can be negatively affected by several factors:

- The data frame broadcast delivery nature of Ethernet/802.3 LANs
- *Carrier sense multiple access collision detect (CSMA/CD)* access methods allowing only one station to transmit at a time
- Multimedia applications with higher bandwidth demands such as video and the Internet
- Normal latency as the frames travel across the Layer 1 medium and through Layer 1, 2, and 3 networking devices and the latency added by the extension of Ethernet/802.3 LANs by adding repeaters
- Extending the distances of the Ethernet/802.3 LANs by using Layer 1 repeaters

MOVIE 2.1

Ethernet and 802.3 LANs

Broadcast networks.

FIGURE 2-1
Ethernet is known as a shared-medium technology used to transport data between devices on a network.

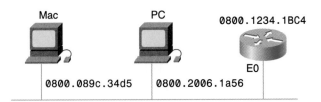

Ethernet using CSMA/CD and a shared medium can support data transmission rates of over 100 Mbps. CSMA/CD is an access method that allows only one station to transmit at a time. The goal of Ethernet is to provide a best-effort delivery service and allow all devices on the shared medium to transmit on an equal basis. As shown in Figure 2-2, one of the inherent problems with CSMA/CD technology is *collisions*.

MOVIE 2.2	
CSMA/CD LANs	
Ethernet and 802.3.	

MOVIE 2.3	
Collisions	
Backoff protocols that determine when to retransmit.	

FIGURE 2-2
CSMA/CD is an access method that allows only one station to transmit at a time, thus reducing collisions

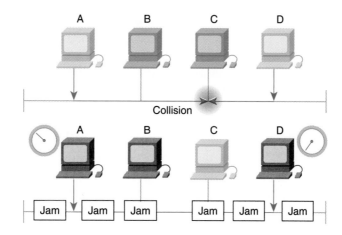

Half-Duplex Ethernet Design

Ethernet is a *half-duplex* technology. Each Ethernet host checks the network to see whether data is being transmitted before it transmits additional data. If the network is already in use, the transmission is delayed. Despite transmission deferral, two or more Ethernet hosts can transmit at the same time, which results in a collision. When a collision occurs, the hosts that first detects the collision will send a jam signal. Upon hearing the jam signal, each host will wait a random period of time before attempting to transmit. This process uses up all the available bandwidth, resulting in a total loss of transmission until the random period of time expires.

Ethernet LANs become saturated because users run network-intensive software, such as client/server applications, which cause hosts to transmit more often and for longer periods of time. The physical connector (for example, NIC) used by devices on an Ethernet LAN provides several circuits so that communications between devices can occur.

Congestion and Bandwidth

Technological advancements are producing faster and more intelligent desktop computers and workstations. The combination of more powerful computers/workstations and network-intensive applications has created a need for network capacity, or *bandwidth,* that is much greater than the 10 Mbps that is available on shared Ethernet/802.3 LANs.

Today's networks are experiencing an increase in the transmission of large graphics files, images, full-motion video, and multimedia applications, as well as an increase in the number of users on a network. All these factors place an even greater strain on bandwidth.

As more people utilize a network to share large files, access file servers, and connect to the Internet, network *congestion* occurs. This can result in slower response times, longer file transfers, and network users becoming less productive due to network delays. To relieve network congestion, more bandwidth is needed or the available bandwidth must be used more efficiently. The methods used to implement these solutions are discussed later in the chapter.

Latency

Latency, sometimes called *propagation delay,* is the time a frame, or packet, of data takes to travel from the source station or node to its final destination on the network. Because Ethernet LANs use CSMA/CD to provide best-effort delivery, there must be a certain amount of latency in the system to detect collisions and negotiate transmission rights on the network.

Latency does not depend solely on distance and number of devices. For example, if three switches separate two workstations, the workstations experience less latency than if two routers separated them. This is because routers conduct more complex and time-consuming decision making. The intermediate devices, the switches, greatly enhance network performance.

Ethernet Transmission Times

Transmission time is the time it takes a frame or packet (the data being placed into a packet or frame) to move from the *data link layer* to the *physical layer* (onto the physical cabling of the network). Table 2-1 represents the transmission time for four different packet sizes.

TABLE 2-1   Ethernet Transmission Times

Packet Size in Bytes	Transmission Time in Microseconds
64	51.2
512	410
1000	800
1518	1214

Each 10-Mbps Ethernet bit has a 100-ns window for transmission (bit time). Bit time is calculated by dividing the speed (10 Mbps) into 1 (reciprocal function). A *byte* is equal to 8 *bits*. Therefore, 1 byte takes a minimum of 800 ns to transmit. A 64-byte frame takes 51,200 ns, or 51.2 microseconds, to transmit (64 bytes at 800 ns equals 51,200 ns, and 51,200 ns/1000 equals 51.2 microseconds). Transmission time of a 1000-byte packet from Workstation 1 to the server or to Workstation 2 requires 800 microseconds due to the latency of the devices in the network.

Extending Shared-Media LANs by Using Repeaters

The distance that a LAN can cover is limited due to *attenuation*. Attenuation means that the signal weakens (that is, attenuates) as it travels through the network. Attenuation is caused by the resistance in the cable, or medium. An Ethernet *repeater* is a physical-layer device on the network that boosts or regenerates the signal on an Ethernet LAN. When you use an Ethernet repeater to extend the distance of a LAN, a single network can cover a greater distance and more users can share that same network, as shown in Figure 2-3. However, using repeaters and multiport repeaters also compounds the issue of broadcasts and collision effect on the overall performance of the shared-media LAN.

MOVIE 2.4

Repeater Advantages

Repeater cleans, amplifies, and resends.

MOVIE 2.5

Repeater Disadvantages

Can't filter traffic.

FIGURE 2-3
An Ethernet
repeater allows
for only one
transmission at
a time, con-
nects all nodes
to a single
communica-
tion channel,
and transmits
the same data
to all the
repeater's
ports.

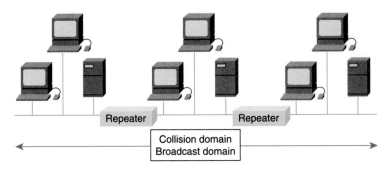

A multiport repeater is also known as a *hub*. In a shared-medium LAN that uses hubs, the broadcast and collision problems are compounded, and the total bandwidth of the LAN is 10 Mbps.

Improving LAN Performance

The performance of a shared-medium LAN can be improved by using one or more of the following solutions:

- Full-duplex Ethernet
- LAN segmentation

Full-Duplex Ethernet

Full-duplex Ethernet allows the transmission of a packet and the reception of a different packet at the same time. This simultaneous transmission and reception requires the use of two pairs of wires in the cable and a switched connection between each node. This connection is considered point-to-point and is collision free. Because both nodes can transmit and receive at the same time, there are no negotiations for bandwidth. Full-duplex Ethernet can use an existing shared medium as long as the medium meets minimum Ethernet standards:

Standard	Distance
10BaseT/100BaseTX	100 meters
100BaseFX	2 kilometers

To transmit and receive simultaneously, a dedicated *port* is required for each node. Full-duplex connections can use 10BaseT, 100BaseTX, or 100BaseFX media to create point-to-point connections. The *network interface cards (NICs)* on both ends need to have full-duplex capabilities.

MOVIE 2.6
Bridge Examines MAC Addresses
Store-and-forward devices.

The full-duplex Ethernet switch takes advantage of the two pairs of wires in the cable. This is done by creating a direct connection between the transmit (TX) at one end of the circuit and the receive (RX) at the other end. With these two stations connected this way, a collision-free domain is created because the transmission and receipt of data occurs on separate non-competitive circuits.

Ethernet usually can only use 50% to 60% of the 10 Mbps available bandwidth because of collisions and latency. Full-duplex Ethernet offers 100% of the bandwidth in both directions. This produces a potential 20-Mbps throughput—10-Mbps TX and 10-Mbps RX.

LAN Segmentation

A network can be divided into smaller units called *segments*. Each segment uses the CSMA/CD access method and maintains traffic between users on the segment. Figure 2-4 shows an example of a segmented Ethernet network. The entire network has 15 computers (6 file severs and 9 PCs). By using segments in a network, fewer users/devices are sharing the same 10 Mbps when communicating to one another within the segment. Each segment is its own *collision domain*, as shown in Figure 2-5.

By dividing the network into three segments, a network manager can decrease network congestion within each segment. When transmitting data within a segment, the five devices within each segment are sharing the 10-Mbps bandwidth per segment. In a segmented Ethernet LAN, data passed between segments is transmitted on the *backbone* of the network using a *bridge*, *router*, or *switch*.

FIGURE 2-4
Without seg-
menting the
network, all 15
devices would
need to share
the same 10-
Mbps band-
width and
would reside in
the same colli-
sion domain.

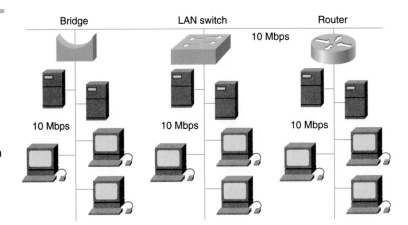

FIGURE 2-5
The backbone
network is its
own collision
domain and
uses CSMA/CD
to provide
best-effort
delivery ser-
vice between
segments.

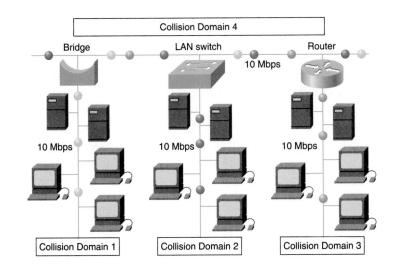

Segmentation with Bridges

Ethernet LANs that use a bridge to segment the LAN provide more bandwidth
per user because there are fewer users on each segment. In contrast, LANs that
do not use bridges for segmentation provide less bandwidth per user because
there are more users on a nonsegmented LAN.

Bridges "learn" a network's segmentation by building address tables (see Figure 2-6) that contain the address of each network device and which segment to
use to reach that device. Bridges are Layer 2 devices that forward data frames

according to the frames' Media Access Control (MAC) addresses. In addition, bridges are transparent to the other devices on the network.

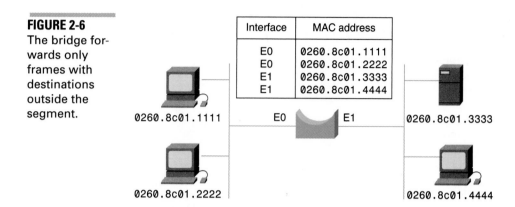

FIGURE 2-6
The bridge forwards only frames with destinations outside the segment.

Interface	MAC address
E0	0260.8c01.1111
E0	0260.8c01.2222
E1	0260.8c01.3333
E1	0260.8c01.4444

0260.8c01.1111   E0   E1   0260.8c01.3333

0260.8c01.2222   0260.8c01.4444

Bridges increase the latency in a network by 10% to 30%. This latency is due to the decision making required of the bridge or bridges in transmitting data. A bridge is considered a store-and-forward device because it must examine the destination address field and calculate the CRC in the frame check sequence field before forwarding the frame to all ports. If the destination port is busy, the bridge can temporarily store the frame until the port is available. The time it takes to perform these tasks slows the network transmissions, causing increased latency.

Segmentation with Routers

Routers are more advanced than typical bridges. A bridge is passive on the network and operates at the data link layer. A router operates at the *network layer* and bases all its decisions about forwarding between segments on the network-layer protocol address. Routers create the highest level of segmentation, as shown in Figure 2-7, by forwarding data to the hub, to which workstations are connected. A router makes forwarding decisions to segments by examining the destination address on the data packet and looking in its *routing table* for forwarding instructions.

A router must examine a packet to determine the best path for forwarding that packet to its destination. This process takes time. Protocols that require an *acknowledgment* from the receiver to the sender for every packet as it is delivered (known as *acknowledgment-oriented protocols*) have a 30% to 40% loss of throughput. Protocols that require minimal acknowledgments (*sliding-window* protocols) suffer a 20% to 30% loss of throughput. This is due to the fact that there is less data traffic between the sender and receiver (that is, fewer acknowledgments).

FIGURE 2-7
Routers deter-
mine to which
hub and seg-
ment the data
packet should
be forwarded.

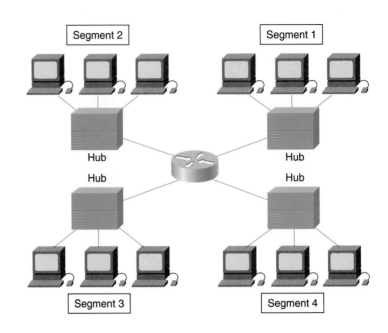

Segmentation with LAN Switches

LAN *switching* eases bandwidth shortages and network bottlenecks, such as those between several PCs and a remote file server. As shown in Figure 2-8, a switch can segment a LAN into microsegments, which are single-host segments. This creates collision-free domains from one larger collision domain. Although the LAN switch eliminates collision domains, all hosts connected to the switch are still in the same broadcast domain. Therefore, all nodes connected through the LAN switch can see a broadcast from just one node. A LAN switch is a very high-speed multiport bridge with one port for each node or segment of the LAN. Like bridges, switches make frame forwarding decisions by building a table of the MAC addresses of the hosts attached to each port.

MOVIE 2.7

LAN Switching

Dedicated collision-free communication between devices.

Switched Ethernet is based on Ethernet. Each node is directly connected to one of its ports or a segment that is connected to one of the switch's ports. This creates a 10-Mbps bandwidth connection between each node and each segment on the switch. A computer connected directly to an Ethernet switch is its own collision domain and accesses the full 10 Mbps.

A LAN that uses a Switched Ethernet *topology* creates a network that behaves as though it has only two nodes: the sending node and the receiving node. These two nodes share the 10-Mbps bandwidth between them, which means that nearly all the bandwidth is available for the transmission of data. Because a Switched Ethernet LAN uses bandwidth so efficiently, it can provide more throughput than Ethernet LANs connected by bridges or hubs. In a Switched Ethernet implementation, the available bandwidth can reach close to 100%.

FIGURE 2-8
A LAN switch is a very high-speed multi-port bridge with one port for each node or segment of the LAN.

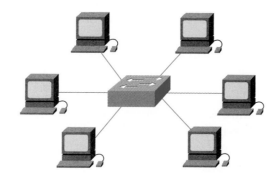

Ethernet switching increases the bandwidth available on a network by creating dedicated network segments (that is, point-to-point connections) and connecting those segments in a virtual network within the switch. This virtual network circuit exists only when two nodes need to communicate. This is why it is called a *virtual circuit*; it exists only when needed and is established within the switch. One drawback of switches is that they cost more than hubs. However, many businesses implement switch technology slowly by connecting hubs to switches until such a time that the hubs can be replaced.

Switching and Bridging Overview

Switching is a technology that decreases congestion in Ethernet, Token Ring, and Fiber Distributed Data Interface (FDDI) LANs by reducing traffic and increasing bandwidth. LAN switches often replace shared hubs and are designed to work with existing cable infrastructures so that they can be installed without disrupting existing network traffic.

Today in data communications, all switching equipment perform two basic operations:

- **Switching data frames**—This happens when a frame arrives on an input media and is transmitted to an output media.

■ **Maintaining switching operations**—In this operation, switches build and maintain switching tables.

The term *bridging* refers to a technology in which a device known as a bridge connects two or more LAN segments. A bridge transmits datagrams from one segment to their destinations on other segments. When a bridge is powered on and begins to operate, it examines the MAC address of the incoming datagrams and builds a table of known destinations. If the bridge knows that the destination of a datagram is on the same segment as the source of the datagram, it drops the datagram because there is no need to transmit it. If the bridge knows that the destination is on another segment, it transmits the datagram on that segment only. If the bridge does not know the destination segment, the bridge transmits the datagram on all segments except the source segment (a technique known as *flooding*). The primary benefit of bridging is that it limits traffic to certain network segments.

Both bridges and switches connect LAN segments, use a table of MAC addresses to determine the segment on which a datagram needs to be transmitted, and reduce traffic. Switches are more functional in today's network than bridges because they operate at much higher speeds than bridges and can support new functionality, such as *virtual LANs (VLANs)*. Bridges typically switch using software; switches typically switch using hardware.

LAN Switch Latency

Each switch used on an Ethernet 10-Mbps LAN adds latency to the network. However, the type of switching used can help overcome the built-in latency of some switches.

A switch between a workstation and a server adds 21 microseconds to the transmission process. A 1000-byte packet has a transmission time of 800 microseconds. A packet sent from a workstation to a server has a total transmission time of 821 microseconds (800 + 21 = 821). Because of the switching employed, known as *cut-through*, the MAC address of the destination device is read and the switch begins transmitting the packet before the packet completely arrives in the switch. This more than makes up for the inherent latency in the switch.

Layer 2 and Layer 3 Switching

There are two methods of switching data frames: Layer 2 and Layer 3 switching. Switching is the process of taking an incoming frame from one interface and delivering it out through another interface. Routers use Layer 3 switching to route a packet; switches (Layer 2 switches) use Layer 2 switching to forward frames.

The difference between Layer 2 and Layer 3 switching is the type of information inside the frame that is used to determine the correct output interface. With Layer 2 switching, frames are switched based on MAC address information. With Layer 3 switching, frames are switched based on network-layer information.

Layer 2 switching does not look inside a packet for network-layer information as does Layer 3 switching. Layer 2 switching looks at a destination MAC address within a frame. It sends the information to the appropriate interface if it knows the destination address location. Layer 2 switching builds and maintains a switching table that keeps track of which MAC addresses belong to each port or interface.

If the Layer 2 switch does not know where to send the frame, it broadcasts the frame out all its ports to the network to learn the correct destination. When the frame's reply is returned, the switch learns the location of the new address and adds the information to the switching table.

The manufacturer of the data communications equipment determines the Layer 2 addresses. They are unique addresses that are derived in two parts: the manufacturing (MFG) code and the unique identifier. The Institute of Electrical and Electronic Engineers (IEEE) assigns the MFG code to each vendor. The vendor assigns a unique identifier. Except in Systems Network Architecture (SNA) networks, users have little or no control over Layer 2 addressing because Layer 2 addresses are fixed with a device, whereas Layer 3 addresses can be changed. In addition, Layer 2 addresses assume a flat address space with universally unique addresses.

Layer 3 switching operates at the network layer. It examines packet information and forwards packets based on their network-layer destination addresses. Layer 3 switching also supports router functionality.

For the most part, the network administrator determines the Layer 3 addresses. Protocols such as IP, IPX, and AppleTalk use Layer 3 addressing. By creating Layer 3 addresses, a network administrator creates local areas that act as single addressing units (similar to streets, cities, states, and countries) and assigns a number to each local entity. If users move to another building, their end stations obtain new Layer 3 addresses, but their Layer 2 addresses remain the same.

Because routers operate at Layer 3 of the OSI reference model, they can adhere to and create a hierarchical addressing structure. Therefore, a routed network can tie a logical addressing structure to a physical infrastructure, for example, through TCP/IP subnets or IPX networks for each segment. Traffic flow in a switched (that is, flat) network is therefore inherently different from traffic flow in a routed (that is, hierarchical) network. Hierarchical networks offer more flexible traffic flow than flat networks because they can use the network hierarchy to determine optimal paths and contain broadcast domains.

Implications of Layer 2 and Layer 3 Switching

The increasing power of desktop processors and the requirements of client/ server and multimedia applications have created an increased need for greater bandwidth in traditional shared-media environments. These requirements are prompting network designers to replace hubs in wiring closets with switches.

Layer 2 switches use *microsegmentation* to satisfy the demands for more bandwidth and increased performance, but network designers are now faced with increasing demands for intersubnet communication. For example, every time a user accesses servers and other resources that are located on different subnets, the traffic must go through a Layer 3 device. Potentially, there is a tremendous bottleneck, which can threaten network performance. To avoid this bottleneck, network designers can add Layer 3 capabilities throughout the network, which alleviates the burden on centralized routers. Therefore, a switch improves bandwidth by separating collision domains and selectively forwarding traffic to the appropriate segments of a network.

How a LAN Switch Learns Addresses

An Ethernet switch can learn the address of each device on the network by reading the source address of each packet transmitted and noting the port where the frame entered the switch. The switch then adds this information to its forwarding database. Addresses are learned dynamically. This means that as new addresses are read, they are learned and stored in *content-addressable memory (CAM)*. When a source is read that is not found in CAM, it is learned and stored for future use.

Each time an address is stored, it is time stamped. This allows for addresses to be stored for a set period of time. Each time an address is referenced or found in CAM, it receives a new time stamp. Addresses that are not referenced during a set period of time are removed from the list. By removing aged or old addresses, CAM maintains an accurate and functional forwarding database.

The Benefits of Switching

Switches have many benefits. A LAN switch allows many users to communicate in parallel through the use of virtual circuits and dedicated network segments in a collision-free environment. This maximizes the bandwidth available on the shared medium. Also, moving to a switched LAN environment is very cost-effective because you can reuse existing hardware and cabling. Finally, the power of the switch combined with the software to configure LANs give network administrators great flexibility in managing the network.

Symmetric and Asymmetric Switching

Symmetric switching is one way to characterize a LAN switch according to the bandwidth allocated to each port on the switch. As shown in Figure 2-9, a symmetric switch provides switched connections between ports with the same bandwidth, such as all 10-Mbps ports or all 100-Mbps ports.

MOVIE 2.8

Symmetric Switching

Switch connections between ports of equal bandwidth.

SKILL BUILDER

Switch Characteristics

In this lab, you examine an Ethernet switch to gather information about its physical characteristics and begin to appreciate the function of switches in a network.

FIGURE 2-9
Even distribution of network traffic across the entire network optimizes a symmetric switch.

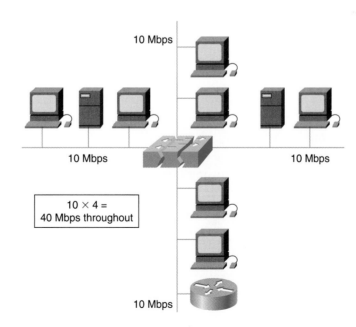

10 Mbps

10 Mbps

10 Mbps

10 Mbps

10 × 4 = 40 Mbps throughout

10 Mbps

As shown in Figure 2-10, an asymmetric LAN switch provides switched connections between ports of unlike bandwidth, such as a combination of 10-Mbps and 100-Mbps ports.

Asymmetric switching makes the most of client/server network traffic flows where multiple clients are communicating with a server at the same time, requiring more bandwidth dedicated to the switch port that the server is connected to in order to prevent a bottleneck at that port.

MOVIE 2.9

Asymmetric Switching

Switch connections between ports with different bandwidth.

FIGURE 2-10
Asymmetric
provides
switched
connections
between
10-Mbps
ports and
100-Mbps
ports.

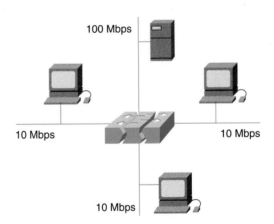

As you will learn in the next section, memory buffering in an asymmetric switch is required to allow traffic from the 100-Mbps port to be sent to a 10-Mbps port without causing too much congestion at the 10-Mbps port.

Memory Buffering

An Ethernet switch may use a buffering technique to store and forward packets to the correct port or ports. Buffering may also be used when the destination port is busy. The area of memory where the switch stores the destination and transmission data is called the *memory buffer*. This memory buffer can use two methods for forwarding packets, port-based memory buffering and shared memory buffering.

In port-based memory buffering, packets are stored in *queues* that are linked to specific incoming ports. A packet is transmitted to the outgoing port only when all the packets ahead of it in the queue have been successfully transmitted. It is possible for a single packet to delay the transmission of all the packets in memory because of a busy destination port. This delay occurs even if the other packets can be transmitted to open destination ports.

Shared memory buffering deposits all packets into a common memory buffer that is shared by all the ports on the switch. The amount of memory allocated to a port is determined by how much is required by each port. This is called *dynamic allocation of buffer memory*. The packets in the buffer are then linked dynamically to the transmit port; the packet is linked to the memory allocation of that transmit port. This allows the packet to be received on one port and transmitted on another port, without moving it into a different queue.

The switch maintains a map of the ports that a packet needs to be transmitted to. The switch clears out this map of destination ports only after the packet has been successfully transmitted. Because the memory buffer is shared, the packet is restricted by the size of the entire memory buffer, not just the allocation to one port. This means that larger packets can be transmitted with fewer dropped packets. This is important to 10/100 switching, where a 100-Mbps port can forward a packet to a 10-Mbps port.

Two Switching Methods

Two switching modes can be used to forward a frame through a switch:

- **Store-and-forward**—The entire frame is received before any forwarding takes place. The destination and/or the source addresses are read and filters are applied before the frame is forwarded. Latency occurs while the frame is being received; the latency is greater with larger frames because the entire frame takes longer to read. Error detection is high because of the time available to the switch to check for errors while waiting for the entire frame to be received.

MOVIE 2.10
Store-and-Forward Switching
Copies frame on board, checks frame's length and CRC.

- **Cut-through**—The switch reads the destination address before receiving the entire frame. The frame is then forwarded before the entire frame arrives. This mode decreases the latency of the transmission and has poor error detection. Fast-forward and fragment-free are two forms of cut-through switching:

— **Fast-forward switching**—Fast-forward switching offers the lowest level of latency by immediately forwarding a packet after receiving the destination address. Because fast-forward switching does not check for errors, there may be times when frames are relayed with errors. Although this occurs infrequently and the destination network adapter discards the faulty frame upon receipt. In networks with high collision rates, this can negatively affect available bandwidth. Use the fragment-free option to reduce the number of collision frames forwarded with errors. In fast-forward mode, latency is measured from the first bit received to the first bit transmitted, or first in, first out (FIFO).

— **Fragment-free switching**—Fragment-free switching filters out collision fragments, which are the majority of packet errors, before forwarding begins. In a properly functioning network, collision fragments must be smaller than 64 bytes. Anything greater than 64 bytes is a valid packet and is usually received without error. Fragment-free switching waits until the received packet has been determined not to be a collision fragment before forwarding the packet. In fragment-free mode, latency is measured as FIFO.

The latency of each switching mode depends on how the switch forwards the frames. The faster the switching mode, the smaller the latency in the switch. To accomplish faster frame forwarding, the switch takes less time to check for errors. The tradeoff is less error checking, which can lead to a higher number of retransmissions.

MOVIE 2.11

Cut-Through Switching

Switch reads the destination address before receiving the entire frame.

VLANs

An Ethernet switch physically segments a LAN into individual collision domains. However, each segment is still part of one broadcast domain. The total number of segments on a switch equals one broadcast domain. This means that all nodes on all segments can see a broadcast from a node one segment.

A VLAN is a logical grouping of network devices or users that are not restricted to a physical switch segment. The devices or users in a VLAN can be grouped by function, department, application, and so on, regardless of their physical segment location. A VLAN creates a single broadcast domain that is not restricted to a physical segment and is treated like a subnet.

SKILL BUILDER

Switch Management Console

This lab helps you develop a basic understanding of Ethernet switch management and helps prepare you for more-advanced switching lessons, such as VLANs.

SKILL BUILDER

Switch Port Options

In this lab, you work with the Management Console interface menus to configure a switch to operate in Fragment-Free switching mode. You also configure a port to enable full duplex and port fast operation.

Spanning-Tree Protocol

The main function of the *Spanning-Tree Protocol* is to allow duplicate switched/bridged paths without incurring the latency effects of loops in the network.

Bridges and switches make their forwarding decisions for *unicast* frames based on the destination MAC address in the frame. If the MAC address is unknown, the device floods the frame out all ports in an attempt to reach the desired destination. It also does this for all broadcast frames.

The Spanning-Tree Algorithm, implemented by the Spanning-Tree Protocol, prevents loops by calculating a stable spanning-tree network topology. When creating fault-tolerant networks, a loop-free path must exist between all Ethernet nodes in the network. The Spanning-Tree Algorithm is used to calculate a loop-free path. Spanning-tree frames, called *bridge protocol data units (BPDUs)*, are sent and received by all switches in the network at regular intervals and are used to determine the spanning-tree topology.

A switch uses Spanning-Tree Protocol on all Ethernet- and *Fast Ethernet* – based VLANs. Spanning-Tree Protocol detects and breaks loops by placing some connections in a standby mode, which are activated in the event of an active connection failure. A separate instance of Spanning-Tree Protocol runs within each configured VLAN, ensuring Ethernet topologies that conform to industry standards throughout the network.

Understanding Spanning-Tree Protocol States

The Spanning-Tree Protocol states are as follows:

- **Blocking**—No frames forwarded, BPDUs heard
- **Listening**—No frames forwarded, listening for frames
- **Learning**—No frames forwarded, learning addresses
- **Forwarding**—Frames forwarded, learning addresses
- **Disabled**—No frames forwarded, no BPDUs heard

The state for each VLAN is initially set by the configuration and later modified by the Spanning-Tree Protocol process. You can determine the status, cost, and priority of ports and VLANs by using the **show spantree** command. After the port-to-VLAN state is set, Spanning-Tree Protocol determines whether the port forwards or blocks frames. Ports can be configured to immediately enter Spanning-Tree Protocol forwarding mode when a connection is made instead of following the usual sequence of blocking, learning, and then forwarding. The capability to quickly switch states from blocking to forwarding rather than going through the transitional port states is useful in situations where immediate access to a server is required.

SKILL BUILDER

Switch Configuration Browser

This lab provides you with an opportunity to configure a switch for IP and Hypertext Transfer Protocol (HTTP) access. By assigning an IP address to the switch, you can ping it and telnet to it.

Summary

- The combination of more powerful computers/workstations and network-intensive applications has created a need for bandwidth that is much greater than the 10 Mbps available on shared Ethernet/802.3 LANs.
- As more people utilize a network to share large files, access file servers, and connect to the Internet, network congestion occurs.

- A network can be divided in smaller units, called *segments*. Each segment is considered its own collision domain.

- In a segmented Ethernet LAN, data passed between segments is transmitted across the network by a bridge, switch, or router.

- A LAN that uses a switched Ethernet topology creates a network that behaves like it only has two nodes—the sending node and the receiving node.

- A switch segments a LAN into microsegments, creating collision-free domains from one larger collision domain.

- Switches achieve high-speed transfer by reading the destination Layer 2 MAC address of the packet, much the way a bridge does.

- Ethernet switching increases the bandwidth available on a network by creating dedicated network segments (point-to-point connections) and connecting those segments in a virtual network within the switch.

- An asymmetric LAN switch provides switched connections between ports of unlike bandwidth, such as a combination of 10-Mbps and 100-Mbps ports.

- Symmetric switching is where all ports have the same bandwidth.

- Two switching modes can be used to forward frames through a switch: store-and-forward and cut-through.

- A VLAN is a grouping of network devices or users that is not restricted to a physical switch segment.

- The main function of the Spanning-Tree Protocol is to allow duplicate switched/bridged paths without suffering the latency effects of loops in the network.

Check Your Understanding

Complete all the review questions to test your understanding of the topics and concepts covered in this chapter. Answers are listed in Appendix B, "Check Your Understanding Answer Key."

1. Which of the following broadcast methods does an Ethernet medium use to transmit and receive data to all nodes on the network?

   A. A packet

   B. A data frame

   C. A segment

   D. A byte at a time

2. What is the minimum time it takes Ethernet to transmit 1 byte?

   A. 100 ns

   B. 800 ns

   C. 51,200 ns

   D. 800 microseconds

3. Characteristics of microsegmentation include which of the following?

   A. Dedicated paths between sender and receiver hosts

   B. Multiple traffic paths within the switch

   C. All traffic visible on network segment at once

   D. A and B

4. LAN switches are considered to be which of the following?

   A. Multiport repeaters operating at Layer 1

   B. Multiport hubs operating at Layer 2

   C. Multiport routers operating at Layer 3

   D. Multiport bridges operating at Layer 2

5. Asymmetric switching is optimized for which of the following?

   A. Client/server network traffic where the "fast" switch port is connected to the server

   B. An even distribution of network traffic

   C. Switches without memory buffering

   D. A and B

6. In _____ switching, the switch checks the destination address and immediately begins forwarding the frame, and in _____ switching, the switch receives the complete frame before forwarding it.

   A. Store-and-forward; symmetric

   B. Cut-through; store-and-forward

   C. Store-and-forward; cut-through

   D. Memory buffering; cut-through

7. The Spanning-Tree Protocol allows which of the following?

   A. Routers to communicate link states

   B. Switches to communicate hop counts

   C. Bridges to communicate Layer 3 information

   D. Redundant network paths without suffering the effects of loops in the network

8. Distinguish between cut-through and store-and-forward switching.

9. Describe full- and half-duplex Ethernet operation.

10. Describe the advantages of LAN segmentation that uses switches.

11. How would each segment be considered in a network segmented by switches?

    A. Network

    B. Campus network

    C. Collision domain

    D. WAN

12. In a full duplex Ethernet switch,

   A. Collisions are virtually eliminated.

   B. Two cable pairs and a switched connection between each node are used.

   C. Connections between nodes are considered point-to-point.

   D. All of the above.

13. Congestion causes which of the following effects?

   A. Lower reliability and low traffic

   B. High rate of collisions

   C. Network unpredictability and high error rates

   D. Lower response times, longer file transfers, and network delays

14. Host A transmits to another host, Host B. The communication is such that Host A stops sending information content packets and then Host B begins sending packets. Similarly, Host B stops when Host A starts transmitting again. Classify the transmission type as

   A. Full-duplex

   B. Half-duplex

   C. Simplex

   D. None of the above

15. Which of the following statements concerning packet forwarding in a LAN is not true?

   A. Store-and-forward packet-switching technique is the one in which frames are completely processed before being forwarded out to the appropriate port.

   B. Store-and-forward packet switching technique is slower than cut-through packet switching.

   C. Cut-through packet switching is also known as on-the-fly packet switching.

   D. Buffering is required in cut-through packet switching if the network connection or link is slow.

16. Which of the following is true for a LAN switch?

    A. Repairs network fragments known as microsegments.

    B. They are very high-speed multiport bridges.

    C. Higher latency is made up for by lower bandwidth.

    D. Requires new network interface cards on attached hosts.

17. How many collision domains would be created by a 16-port LAN switch?

    A. One

    B. Two

    C. Fourteen

    D. Sixteen

18. By creating a virtual circuit with LAN switching, what will result on that segment?

    A. Increased collisions

    B. Decreased available bandwidth

    C. Increased broadcasts

    D. Increased available bandwidth

19. How do switches learn the addresses of devices that are attached to their ports?

    A. Switches get the tables from a router.

    B. Switches read the source address of a packet entering through a port.

    C. Switches exchange address tables with other switches.

    D. Switches are not capable of building address tables.

20. What is the purpose of symmetric switching?

    A. To provide switch connections on ports with the same bandwidths.

    B. To make sure the network tables are symmetrical.

    C. To provide switched connections on ports with different bandwidths.

    D. Switches only provide asymmetrical switching.

Key Terms

acknowledgment   A notification sent from one network device to another to acknowledge that some event (for example, receipt of a message) has occurred. Sometimes abbreviated ACK.

attenuation   Loss of communication signal energy.

backbone   The structural core of the network, which connects all the components of the network so that communication can occur.

bandwidth   The difference between the highest and lowest frequencies available for network signals. Also, the rated throughput capacity of a given network medium or protocol.

bit   A binary digit used in the binary numbering system. Can be zero or one.

bridge   A device that connects and passes packets between two network segments that use the same communications protocol. Bridges operate at the data link layer (Layer 2) of the OSI reference model. In general, a bridge filters, forwards, or floods an incoming frame based on the MAC address of that frame.

bridge protocol data unit (BPDU)   A Spanning-Tree Protocol hello packet that is sent out at configurable intervals to exchange information among bridges in the network.

bridging   A technology in which a bridge connects two or more LAN segments.

broadcast   A data packet that is sent to all nodes on a network. Broadcasts are identified by a broadcast address.

byte   A series of consecutive binary digits that are operated on as a unit (for example, an 8-bit byte).

carrier sense multiple access collision detect (CSMA/CD)   A media-access mechanism wherein devices ready to transmit data first check the channel for a carrier. If no carrier is sensed for a specific period of time, a device can transmit. If two devices transmit at once, a collision occurs and is detected by all colliding devices. This collision subsequently delays retransmissions from those devices for some random length of time. Ethernet and IEEE 802.3 use CSMA/CD access.

content-addressable memory (CAM)   Memory that maintains an accurate and functional forwarding database.

client/server application   An application that is stored centrally on a server and accessed by workstations, thus making it easy to maintain and protect.

collision   In Ethernet, the result of two nodes transmitting simultaneously. The frames from each device collide and are damaged when they meet on the physical medium.

collision domain   In Ethernet, the network area within which frames that have collided are propagated. Repeaters and hubs propagate collisions; LAN switches, bridges, and routers do not.

congestion   Traffic in excess of network capacity.

cut-through   A packet-switching approach that streams data through a switch so that the leading edge of a packet exits the switch at the output port before the packet finishes entering the input port. A device using cut-through packet switching reads, processes, and forwards packets as soon as the destination address is looked up and the outgoing port is determined. Also known as *on-the-fly packet switching*.

data link layer   Layer 2 of the *OSI reference model*. This layer provides reliable transit of data across a physical link. The data link layer is concerned with physical addressing, network topology, line discipline, error notification, ordered delivery of frames, and flow control. The IEEE has divided this layer into two sublayers: the MAC sublayer and the LLC sublayer. Sometimes simply called link layer. Roughly corresponds to the data link control layer of the SNA model.

Ethernet   A shared medium that can support data transmission rates of up to 10 Mbps and uses CSMA/CD.

Fast Ethernet   Any of a number of 100-Mbps Ethernet specifications. Fast Ethernet offers a speed increase ten times that of the 10BaseT Ethernet specification, while preserving such qualities as frame format, MAC mechanisms, and MTU. Such similarities allow the use of existing 10BaseT applications and network management tools on Fast Ethernet networks. Based on an extension to the IEEE 802.3 specifi-cation.

fast-forward switching   Switching that offers the lowest level of latency by immediately forwarding a packet after receiving the destination address.

flooding   When a bridge transmits the datagram on all segments except the source segment.

fragment-free switching   A switching technique that filters out collision fragments, which are the majority of packet errors, before forwarding begins.

full-duplex Ethernet   A capability for simultaneous data transmission between a sending station and a receiving station.

half-duplex Ethernet   A capability for data transmission in only one direction at a time between a sending station and a receiving station.

hub   Generally, a device that serves as the center of a star-topology network. Also called a *multiport repeater*.

interface   1. A connection between two systems or devices. 2. In routing terminology, a network connection.

latency   The delay between the time a device requests access to a network and the time it is granted permission to transmit.

memory buffer   The area of memory where the switch stores the destination and transmission data.

microsegmentation   The division of a network into smaller segments, usually with the intention of increasing aggregate bandwidth to network devices.

network layer   Layer 3 of the OSI reference model. This layer provides connectivity and path selection between two end systems. The network layer is the layer at which routing occurs. Corresponds roughly with the path control layer of the SNA model.

network interface card (NIC)   A board that provides network communication capabilities to and from a computer system. Also called an *adapter*.

node   An endpoint of a network connection or a junction common to two or more lines in a network. Nodes can be processors, controllers, or workstations. Nodes, which vary in routing and other functional capabilities, can be interconnected by links, and serve as control points in the network. *Node* is sometimes used generically to refer to any entity that can access a network, and is frequently used interchangeably with device.

physical layer   Layer 1 of the OSI reference model. This layer defines the electrical, mechanical, procedural, and functional specifications for activating, maintaining, and deactivating the physical link between end systems. Corresponds with the physical control layer in the SNA model.

port   An interface on an internetworking device (such as a router). A female plug on a patch panel that accepts the same size plug as an RJ-45 jack. Patch cords are used in these ports to cross connect computers wired to the patch panel. It is this cross-connection that allows the LAN to function.

propagation delay   The time required for data to travel over a network from its source to its ultimate destination. Also called *latency*.

queue   1. Generally, an ordered list of elements waiting to be processed. 2. In routing, a backlog of packets waiting to be forwarded over a router interface.

repeater   A device that regenerates and propagates electrical signals between two network segments.

router   A network-layer device that uses one or more metrics to determine the optimal path along which network traffic should be forwarded. Routers forward packets from one network to another based on network layer information. Occasionally called a *gateway* (although this definition of gateway is becoming increasingly outdated).

routing table   A table stored in a router or some other internetworking device that keeps track of routes to particular network destinations and, in some cases, metrics associated with those routes.

segment   A section of a network that is bounded by bridges, routers, or switches.

sliding window   A window whose size is negotiated dynamically during the TCP session.

Spanning-Tree Protocol   A bridge protocol that utilizes the Spanning-Tree Algorithm, enabling a learning bridge to dynamically work around loops in a network topology by creating a spanning tree. Bridges exchange BPDU messages with other bridges to detect loops and then remove the loops by shutting down selected bridge interfaces. Refers to both the IEEE 802.1 Spanning-Tree Protocol standard and the earlier Digital Equipment Corporation Spanning-Tree Protocol on which it is based. The IEEE version supports bridge domains and allows the bridge to construct a loop-free topology across an extended LAN. The IEEE version is generally preferred over the Digital version.

store-and-forward   A packet-switching technique in which frames are completely processed before being forwarded out the appropriate port. This processing includes calculating the CRC and checking the destination address. In addition, frames must be temporarily stored until network resources (such as an unused link) are available to forward the message.

switch   A network device that filters, forwards, and floods frames based on the destination address of each frame. The switch operates at the data link layer of the OSI reference model.

switching   The process of taking an incoming frame from one interface and delivering it out through another interface.

topology   A physical arrangement of network nodes and media within an enterprise networking structure.

unicast   A message sent to a single network destination.

virtual circuit   A logical circuit created to ensure reliable communication between two network devices. A virtual circuit is defined by a VPI/VCI pair and can be either permanent (a PVC) or switched (an SVC). Virtual circuits are used in Frame Relay and X.25. In ATM, a virtual circuit is called a *virtual channel*. Sometimes abbreviated VC.

virtual LAN (VLAN)   A group of devices on a LAN that are configured (using management software) so that they can communicate as if they were attached to the same wire, when in fact they are located on a number of different LAN segments. Because VLANs are based on logical instead of physical connections, they are extremely flexible.

Objectives

After reading this chapter, you will be able to

- Explain what VLANs are
- Name reasons to create VLANs and describe the benefits of VLANs
- Describe the role that switches play in the creation of VLANs
- Describe VLAN frame filtering, frame identification, and frame tagging
- Describe how switches can be used with hubs
- Name and describe the three methods of VLAN implementation

Chapter 3

VLANs

Introduction

Chapter 2, "LAN Switching," discusses problems inherent in a LAN and possible solutions to improve LAN performance. You learned about the advantages and disadvantages of using bridges, *switches*, and *routers* for LAN segmentation and the effects of switching, bridging, and routing on network throughput. Finally, you briefly learned about the benefits of Fast Ethernet and *virtual local-area networks (VLANs)*.

This chapter provides an introduction to VLANs and switched internetworking, compares traditional shared LAN configurations with switched LAN configurations, and discusses the benefits of using a switched VLAN architecture.

VLAN Overview

A VLAN is a logical grouping of devices or users, as shown in Figure 3-1. These devices or users can be grouped by function, department, application, and so on, regardless of their physical *segment* location. VLAN configuration is done at the switch via software.

Existing Shared LAN Configurations

A typical LAN is configured according to the physical infrastructure it is connecting. Users are grouped based on their location in relation to the *hub* they are plugged in to and how the cable is run to the wiring closet. The router interconnecting each shared hub typically provides segmentation and can act as a *broadcast* firewall, whereas the segments created by switches do not. Traditional LAN segmentation does not group users according to their workgroup association or need for bandwidth. Therefore, they share the same segment and contend for the same bandwidth, although the bandwidth requirements might vary greatly by to workgroup or department.

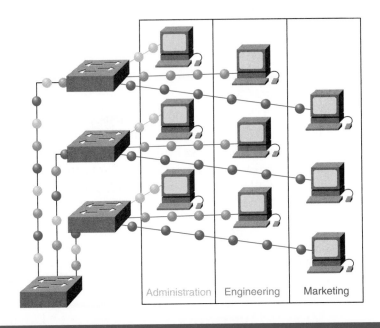

FIGURE 3-1
A VLAN is a group of network devices or users that is not restricted to a physical switch segment.

Administration | Engineering | Marketing

MOVIE 3.1

Broadcast Transmission

Source node to network.

Segmenting with Switching Architectures

LANs are increasingly being divided into workgroups connected via common backbones to form VLAN topologies. VLANs logically segment the physical LAN infrastructure into different subnets (or *broadcast domains*, for Ethernet) so that broadcast frames are switched only between *ports* within the same VLAN.

Initial VLAN implementations offered a port-mapping capability that established a broadcast domain between a default group of devices. Current network requirements demand VLAN functionality that covers the entire network. This approach to VLANs allows you to group geographically separate users in networkwide virtual topologies. VLAN configurations group users by logical association rather than physical location.

The majority of the networks currently installed provides very limited logical segmentation. Users are commonly grouped based on connections to the shared hub and the router ports between the hubs. This topology provides segmentation only between the hubs, which are typically located on separate floors, and not between users connected to the same hub. This imposes physical constraints on the network and limits how users can be grouped. A few shared-hub architectures have some grouping capability, but they restrict how you configure logically defined workgroups.

VLANs and Physical Boundaries

In a LAN that utilizes LAN switching devices, VLAN technology is a cost-effective and efficient way of grouping network users into virtual workgroups regardless of their physical location on the network. Figure 3-2 shows the difference between LAN and VLAN segmentation. Some of the main differences are as follows:

- VLANs work at Layer 2 and Layer 3 of the OSI reference model.
- Communication between VLANs is provided by Layer 3 routing.
- VLANs provide a method of controlling network broadcasts.
- The network administrator assigns users to a VLAN.
- VLANs can increase network security by defining which network nodes can communicate with each other.

FIGURE 3-2
Within a switched network, VLANs provide segmentation and organizational flexibility.

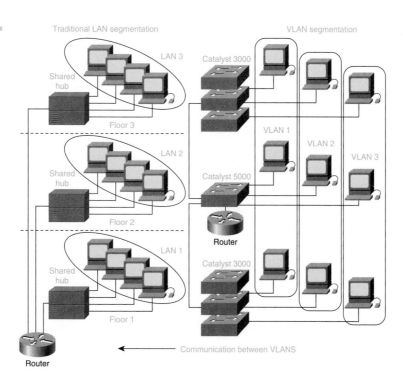

Using VLAN technology, you can group switch ports and their connected users into logically defined workgroups, such as the following:

- Coworkers in the same department
- A cross-functional product team
- Diverse user groups sharing the same network application or software

You can group these ports and users into workgroups on a single switch or on connected switches. By grouping ports and users together across multiple switches, VLANs can span single-building infrastructures, interconnected buildings, or even wide-area networks (WANs), as shown in Figure 3-3.

FIGURE 3-3
VLANs remove the physical constraints of workgroup communications.

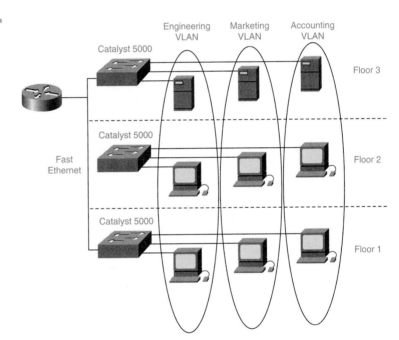

Transporting VLANs Across Backbones

Important to any VLAN architecture is the ability to transport VLAN information between interconnected switches and routers that reside on the corporate backbone. These transport capabilities consist of the following:

- Removing the physical boundaries between users
- Increasing the configuration flexibility of a VLAN solution when users move
- Providing mechanisms for interoperability between backbone system components.

The backbone commonly acts as the collection point for large volumes of traffic. It also carries end-user VLAN information and identification between switches, routers, and directly attached servers. Within the backbone, high-bandwidth, high-capacity links are typically chosen to carry the traffic throughout the enterprise.

Routers in VLANs

The traditional role of the router is to provide *firewalls*, broadcast management, and route processing and distribution. While switches take on some of these tasks, routers still remain vital in VLAN architectures because they provide connected routes between different VLANs. They also connect to other parts of the network that are either logically segmented with the more traditional subnet approach or require access to remote sites across wide-area links. Layer 3 communication, either embedded in the switch or provided externally, is an integral part of any high-performance switching architecture.

You can cost-effectively integrate external routers into the switching architecture by using one or more high-speed backbone connections. These are typically Fast Ethernet or ATM connections, and they provide benefits by

- Increasing the throughput between switches and routers
- Consolidating the overall number of physical router ports required for communication between VLANs

VLAN architecture not only provides logical segmentation, but with careful planning, it can greatly enhance the efficiency of a network.

Switched Networking Configuration

The problems associated with shared LANs and the emergence of switches are causing traditional LAN configurations to be replaced with switched VLAN networking configurations. Switched VLAN configurations vary from traditional LAN configurations in the following ways:

- Switches remove the physical constraints imposed by a shared-hub architecture because they logically group users and ports across the enterprise. Switches replace hubs in the wiring closet. Switches are easily installed with little or no cabling changes, and can completely replace a shared hub with per-port service to each user.
- Switches can be used to create VLANs in order to provide the segmentation services traditionally provided by routers in LAN configurations.

Switches are one of the core components of VLAN communications. As shown in Figure 3-4, they perform critical VLAN functions by acting as the entry point for end-station devices into the switched fabric and for communication across the enterprise.

Each switch has the intelligence to make filtering and forwarding decisions by *frame*, based on VLAN metrics defined by network managers. The switch can also communicate this information to other switches and routers within the network.

The most common approaches for logically grouping users into distinct VLANs are frame filtering and frame identification. Both of these techniques look at the frame when it is either received or forwarded by the switch. Based on the set of rules defined by the administrator, these techniques determine where the frame is to be sent, filtered, or broadcast. These control mechanisms can be centrally administered (with network management software) and are easily implemented throughout the network.

FIGURE 3-4
You can use switches to group users, ports, or logical addresses into common communities of interest.

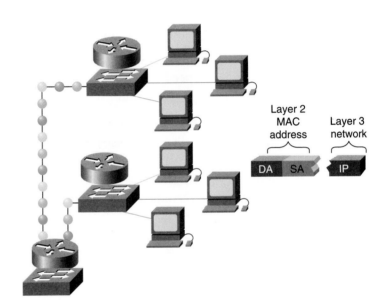

Frame filtering examines particular information about each frame. A filtering table is developed for each switch; this provides a high level of administrative control because it can examine many attributes of each frame. Depending on the sophistication of the *LAN switch*, you can group users based on a station's *Media Access Control (MAC) addresses* or network-layer *protocol* type. The switch compares the frames it filters with table entries, and it takes the appropriate action based on the entries.

In their early days, VLANs were filter-based and they grouped users based on a filtering table. This model did not scale well because each frame had to be referenced to a filtering table.

Frame tagging uniquely assigns a VLAN ID to each frame. The VLAN IDs are assigned to each VLAN in the switch configuration by the switch administrator. This technique was chosen by the *Institute of Electrical and Electronic Engineers (IEEE)* standards group because of its *scalability*. Frame tagging is gaining recognition as the standard trunking mechanism; in comparison to frame filtering, it can provide a more scalable solution to VLAN deployment that can be implemented campus-wide. IEEE 802.1q states that frame tagging is the way to implement VLANs.

VLAN frame tagging is an approach that has been specifically developed for switched communications. Frame tagging places a unique identifier in the header of each frame as it is forwarded throughout the network backbone. The identifier is understood and examined by each switch prior to any broadcasts or transmissions to other switches, routers, or end-station devices. When the frame exits the network backbone, the switch removes the identifier before the frame is transmitted to the target end station. Layer 2 frame identification requires little processing or administrative overhead.

VLAN Implementations

A VLAN makes up a switched network that is logically segmented by functions, project teams, or applications, without regard to the physical location of users. Each switch port can be assigned to a VLAN. Ports assigned to the same VLAN share broadcasts. Ports that do not belong to that VLAN do not share these broadcasts. This improves the overall performance of the network. The following sections discuss three VLAN implementation methods that can be used to assign a switch port to a VLAN. They are

- Port-centric VLANs
- Static
- Dynamic

Port-Centric VLANs

In *port-centric VLANs*, all the nodes connected to ports in the same VLAN are assigned the same VLAN ID. Figure 3-5 shows VLAN membership by router port, which make an administrator's job easier and the network more efficient because

- Users are assigned by port.
- VLANs are easily administered.
- It provides increased security between VLANs.
- Packets do not "leak" into other domains.

SKILL BUILDER

Creating VLANs

In this lab, you work with Ethernet virtual local-area networks (VLANs). VLANs can separate groups of users based on function rather than physical location.

SKILL BUILDER

Switch Management VLANs

In this lab, you work with virtual local-area networks (VLANs). You console into the switch and view the menu options available to manage VLANs and check the current VLAN configuration.

FIGURE 3-5
In port-centric VLANs, membership is easily controlled across the network. Also, all nodes attached to the same port must be in the same VLAN.

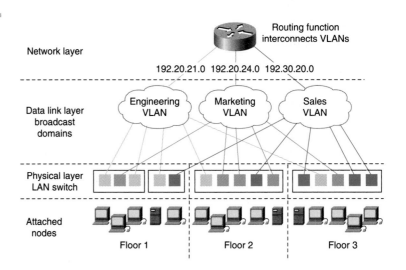

Static VLANs

Static VLANs are ports on a switch that you statically assign to a VLAN. These ports maintain their assigned VLAN configurations until you change them. Although static VLANs require the administrator to make changes, they are secure, easy to configure, and straightforward to monitor. Static VLANs work well in networks in which moves are controlled and managed.

Dynamic VLANs

Dynamic VLANs are ports on a switch that can automatically determine their VLAN assignments. Dynamic VLAN functions are based on MAC addresses, logical addressing, or protocol type of the data packets. When a station is initially connected to an unassigned switch port, the appropriate switch checks the MAC address entry in the VLAN management database and dynamically configures the port with the corresponding VLAN configuration. The major benefits of this approach are less administration within the wiring closet when a user is added or moved and centralized notification when an unrecognized user is added to the network. Typically, more administration is required up front to set up the database within the VLAN management software and to maintain an accurate database of all network users.

Benefits of VLANs

VLANs provide the following benefits:

- They reduce administration costs related to solving problems associated with moves, additions, and changes.
- They provide controlled broadcast activity.
- They provide workgroup and network security.
- They save money by using existing hubs.

Adding, Moving, or Changing User Locations

Companies are continuously reorganizing. On average, 20% to 40% of the workforce physically moves every year. These moves, additions, and changes are one of a network manager's biggest headaches and one of the largest expenses related to managing the network. Many moves require recabling, and almost all moves require new station addressing and hub and router reconfigurations.

VLANs provide an effective mechanism for controlling these changes and reducing much of the cost associated with hub and router reconfigurations. Users in a VLAN can share the same network address space (that is, the IP subnet), regardless of their location. When users in a VLAN are moved from one location to another, as long as they remain within the same VLAN and are connected to a switch port, their network addresses do not change. A location change can be as simple as plugging a user in to a port on a VLAN-capable switch and configuring the port on the switch to that VLAN, as shown in Figure 3-6.

VLANs are a significant improvement over the typical LAN-based techniques used in wiring closets because they require less rewiring, configuration, and debugging. Router configuration is left intact; a simple move for a user from one location to another does not create any configuration modifications in the router if the user stays in the same VLAN.

Controlling Broadcast Activity

Broadcast traffic occurs in every network. Broadcast frequency depends on the types of applications, the types of servers, the amount of logical segmentation, and how these network resources are used. Although applications have been fine-tuned over the past few years to reduce the number of broadcasts they send out, new multimedia applications are being developed that are broadcast and *multicast* intensive.

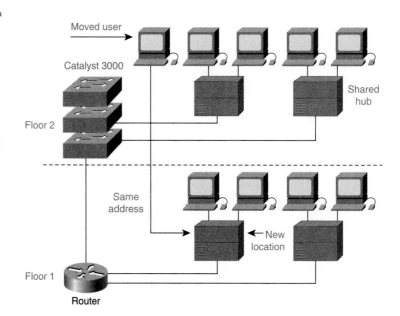

FIGURE 3-6
VLAN-capable switches simplify the rewiring, configuration, moving of users, and debugging that are required to get a user back online.

You need to take preventive measures to ensure against broadcast-related problems. One of the most effective measures is to properly segment the network with protective firewalls that, as much as possible, prevent problems on one segment from damaging other parts of the network. Thus, although one segment may have excessive broadcast conditions, the rest of the network is protected with a firewall commonly provided by a router. Firewall segmentation provides reliability and minimizes the overhead of broadcast traffic, allowing for greater throughput of application traffic.

When no routers are placed between the switches, broadcasts (Layer 2 transmissions) are sent to every switched port. This is commonly referred to as a *flat network*, where there is one broadcast domain across the entire network. The advantage of a flat network is that it can provide both low-latency and high-throughput performance and it is easy to administer. The disadvantage is that it increases vulnerability to broadcast traffic across all switches, ports, backbone links, and users.

VLANs are an effective mechanism for extending firewalls from the routers to the switch fabric and protecting the network against potentially dangerous broadcast problems. Additionally, VLANs maintain all the performance benefits of switching.

You create firewalls by assigning switch ports or users to specific VLAN groups both within single switches and across multiple connected switches. Broadcast traffic within one VLAN is not transmitted outside the VLAN, as shown in Figure 3-7. Conversely, adjacent ports do not receive any of the broadcast traffic generated from other VLANs. This type of configuration substantially reduces the overall broadcast traffic, frees bandwidth for real user traffic, and lowers the overall vulnerability of the network to *broadcast storms*.

FIGURE 3-7
Restricting both the number of switch ports within a VLAN and the users residing on these ports can easily control the size of a broadcast domain.

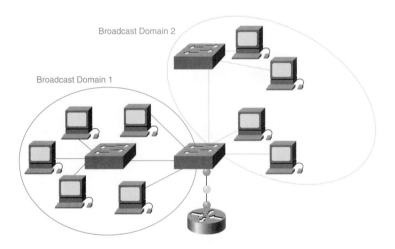

Broadcast Domain 2

Broadcast Domain 1

The smaller the VLAN group, the smaller the number of users affected by broadcast traffic activity within the VLAN group. You can also assign VLANs based on the application type and the number of applications broadcasts. You can place users sharing a broadcast-intensive application in the same VLAN group and distribute the application across the campus.

Providing Better Network Security

The use of LANs has increased at a very high rate over the past several years. As a result, LANs often have confidential, mission-critical data moving across them. Confidential data requires security through access restriction. One problem of shared LANs is that they are relatively easy to penetrate. By plugging in to a live port, an intrusive user has access to all traffic within the segment. The larger the group, the greater the potential access.

One cost-effective and easy administrative technique to increase security is to segment the network into multiple broadcast groups, as shown in Figure 3-8, which allows the network manager to

- Restrict the number of users in a VLAN group
- Disallow another user from joining without first receiving approval from the VLAN network management application
- Configure all unused ports to a default low-service VLAN

FIGURE 3-8
VLANs provide security fire-walls, restrict individual user access, and flag any unwanted intrusion to a network manager.

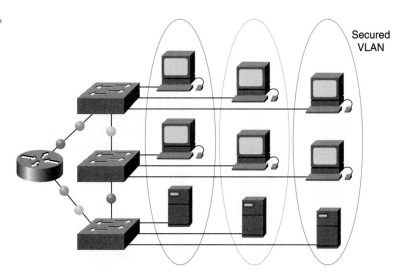

Secured VLAN

Implementing this type of segmentation is relatively straightforward. Switch ports are grouped together based on the type of applications and access privileges. Restricted applications and resources are commonly placed in a secured VLAN group. On the secured VLAN, the router restricts access into the group as configured on both the switches and the routers. Restrictions can be placed based on station addresses, application types, or protocol types.

You can add more security enhancements by using *access control lists*, which will be covered in Chapter 6, "ACLs." These are especially useful when communicating between VLANs. On the secured VLAN, the router restricts access to the VLAN as configured on both switches and routers. You can place restrictions on station addresses, application types, protocol types, or even by time of day.

Saving Money by Using Existing Hubs

Over the past several years, network administrators have installed a significant number of hubs. Many of these devices are being replaced with newer switching technologies. Because network applications require more dedicated bandwidth and performance directly to the desktop, these hubs still perform useful functions in many existing installations. Network managers save money by connecting existing hubs to switches.

Each hub segment connected to a switch port can be assigned to only one VLAN, as shown in Figure 3-9. Stations that share a hub segment are all assigned to the same VLAN group. If an individual station needs to be reassigned to another VLAN, the station must be relocated to the corresponding hub. The interconnected switch fabric handles the communication between the switching ports and automatically determines the appropriate receiving segments. The more the shared hub can be broken into smaller groups, the greater the *microsegmentation* and the greater the VLAN flexibility for assigning individual users to VLAN groups.

By connecting hubs to switches, you can configure hubs as part of the VLAN architecture. You can also share traffic and network resources directly attached to switching ports with VLAN designations.

SKILL BUILDER

Switch Firm Ware Update/TFTP

In this lab, you learn to display information about current Switch Firmware, learn about switch memory and update options, and how to use a TFTP Server to update a switch to a new version of the Firmware software.

SKILL BUILDER

Multi-Switch VLANs

In this lab, you work with Ethernet virtual local-area networks (VLANs). VLANs can separate groups of users based on function rather than physical location. Normally, all the ports on a switch are in the same default VLAN 1.

FIGURE 3-9
The connections between hubs and switches provide opportunities for VLAN segmentation.

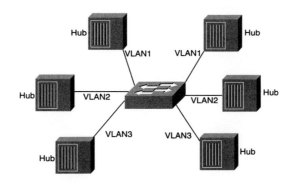

Summary

- An Ethernet switch is designed to physically segment a LAN into individual *collision domains*.

- A typical LAN is configured according to the physical infrastructure it connects.

- In a LAN that uses LAN switching devices, VLAN technology is a cost-effective and efficient way of grouping network users into virtual workgroups, regardless of their physical location on the network.

- VLANs work at Layer 2 and Layer 3 of the OSI reference model.

- Important to any VLAN architecture is the ability to transport VLAN information between interconnected switches and routers that reside on the corporate backbone.

- The problems associated with shared LANs and switches are causing traditional LAN configurations to be replaced with switched VLAN networking configurations.

- The most common approaches for logically grouping users into distinct VLANs are frame filtering and frame identification (frame tagging).

- There are three main types of VLANs: port-centric VLANs, static VLANs, and dynamic VLANs.

- VLANs provide the following benefits:
  - They reduce administration costs related to solving problems associated with moves, additions, and changes.
  - They provide controlled broadcast activity.
  - They provide workgroup and network security.
  - They save money by using existing hubs.

Check Your Understanding

Complete all the review questions to test your understanding of the topics and concepts covered in this chapter. Answers are listed in Appendix B, "Check Your Understanding Answer Key."

1. Describe the benefits of VLANs.

2. What is the effect of VLANs on LAN broadcasts?

3. What are the three main VLAN implementations?

4. What is the purpose of VLAN frame tagging?

5. The phrase *microsegmentation with scalability* means which of the following?

    A. The ability to increase networks without creating collisions domains

    B. The ability to put a huge number of hosts on one switch

    C. The ability to broadcast to more nodes at once

    D. All of the above

6. Switches, as the core element of VLANs, provide the intelligence to do which of the following?

    A. They group users, ports, or logical addresses into a VLAN.

    B. They make filtering and forwarding decisions.

    C. They communicate with other switches and routers.

    D. All of the above.

7. Each _____ segment connected to a _____ port can be assigned to only one VLAN.

    A. Switch; hub

    B. Hub; router

    C. Hub; switch

    D. LAN; hub

8. Which of the following is *not* an advantage of using static VLANS?

   A. They are secure.

   B. They are easy to configure.

   C. They are easy to monitor.

   D. They automatically configure ports when new stations are added.

9. Which of the following is *not* a criterion on which VLANs can be based?

   A. Port ID

   B. Protocol

   C. MAC address

   D. All of the above are criteria on which VLANs can be based

10. Which of the following is a beneficial effect of adding a VLAN?

    A. Switches do not need to be configured.

    B. Broadcasts can be controlled.

    C. Confidential data can be protected.

    D. Physical boundaries that prevent user groupings can be removed.

11. Which of the following statements pertaining to virtual LANs is false?

    A. The most common approaches for logically grouping users into distinct VLANs are frame filtering and frame identification.

    B. VLAN benefits include tighter network securtiy with establishment of secure user groups.

    C. Bridges form one of the core components of VLAN communications.

    D. VLANs help in distributing traffic load.

12. What Layer 3 function on a switch allows you to easily manipulate devices that reside in different IP subnets?

    A. Transparent bridging

    B. Segmentation

    C. Reduction of collision domains

    D. VLANs

13. What device is needed for a packet to be passed from one VLAN to another?

  A. Bridge

  B. Router

  C. Switch

  D. Hub

14. Which layer of the OSI model does frame tagging occur?

  A. Layer 1

  B. Layer 2

  C. Layer 3

  D. Layer 4

15. _____ allows switches to share address tables while _____ assigns a user-defined VLAN ID to each frame.

  A. Frame tagging; frame forwarding

  B. Frame identification; frame removal

  C. Frame filtering; frame tagging

  D. Frame tagging; frame filtering

16. Which of the following is *not* a beneficial effect of adding a VLAN?

  A. Switches do need configuring.

  B. Nodes within a VLAN which are physically moved do not change network addresses.

  C. Confidential data can be protected.

  D. Physical boundaries which prevent user groupings can be removed.

17. True or False: VLANs are more flexible in handling moves and additions of ports than routers.

  A. True

  B. False

18. Which of the following is *not* a benefit of VLANs?

  A. Multicast control

  B. Broadcast control

  C. Reduce router interfaces required

  D. None of the above

19. Why create VLANs?

  A. Moves, adds, and changes are made simpler.

  B. There is less administrative overhead.

  C. The router can switch faster.

  D. Both A and B.

Key Terms

access control list (ACL)   A list kept by a Cisco router to control access to or from the router for a number of services (for example, to prevent packets with a certain IP address from leaving a particular interface on the router).

broadcast   A data packet that is sent to all nodes on a network. Broadcasts are identified by a broadcast address.

broadcast domain   The set of all devices that will receive broadcast frames originating from any device within the set. Broadcast domains are typically bounded by routers because routers do not forward broadcast frames.

broadcast storm   An undesirable network event in which many broadcasts are sent simultaneously across all network segments. A broadcast storm uses substantial network bandwidth and, typically, causes network time-outs.

collision domain   In Ethernet, the network area within which frames that have collided are propagated. Repeaters and hubs propagate collisions; LAN switches, bridges, and routers do not.

dynamic VLAN   A VLAN that is based on the MAC addresses, the logical addresses, or the protocol type of the data packets.

firewall   A router or an access server, or several routers or access servers, designated as a buffer between any connected public networks and a private network. A firewall router uses access control lists and other methods to ensure the security of the private network.

flat network   A network in which there are no routers placed between the switches, broadcasts and Layer 2 transmissions are sent to every switched port, and there is one broadcast domain across the entire network.

frame   A logical grouping of information sent as a data link–layer unit over a transmission medium. Often refers to the header and trailer, used for synchronization and error control, that surround the user data contained in the unit. The terms *datagram*, *message*, *packet*, and *segment* are also used to describe logical information groupings at various layers of the OSI reference model and in various technology circles.

hub   A hardware or software device that contains multiple independent but connected modules of network and internetwork equipment. Hubs can be active (where they repeat signals sent through them) or passive (where they do not repeat, but merely split, signals sent through them).

Institute of Electrical and Electronic Engineers (IEEE)   A professional organization whose activities include the development of communications and network standards. IEEE LAN standards are the predominant LAN standards today.

LAN switch   A high-speed switch that forwards packets between data-link segments. Most LAN switches forward traffic based on MAC addresses. LAN switches are often categorized according to the method they use to forward traffic: cut-through packet switching or store-and-forward packet switching. An example of a LAN switch is the Cisco Catalyst 5000.

Media Access Control (MAC) address   A standardized data link layer address that is required for every port or device that connects to a LAN. Other devices in the network use these addresses to locate specific ports in the network and to create and update routing tables and data structures. A MAC address is 6 bytes long. MAC addresses are controlled by the IEEE and are also known as hardware addresses, MAC-layer addresses, and physical addresses.

microsegmentation   The division of a network into smaller segments, usually with the intention of increasing aggregate bandwidth to network devices.

multicast   Single packets copied by a network and sent out to a set of network addresses. These addresses are specified in the destination address field.

port   An interface on an internetworking device (such as a router).

port-centric VLAN   A VLAN in which all the nodes in the same VLAN are attached to the same switch port.

protocol   A formal description of a set of rules and conventions that govern how devices on a network exchange information.

router   A network-layer device that uses one or more metrics to determine the optimal path along which network traffic should be forwarded. Routers forward packets from one network to another based on network-layer information. Occasionally called a *gateway* (although this definition of gateway is becoming increasingly outdated).

scalability   The ability of a network to grow without any major changes to the overall design.

segment   A section of a network that is bounded by bridges, routers, or switches.

static VLAN   A VLAN in which the ports on a switch are statically assigned.

switch   A network device that filters, forwards, and floods frames based on the destination address of each frame. The switch operates at the data link layer of the OSI reference model.

VLAN (virtual LAN)   A group of devices on a LAN that are configured (using management software) so that they can communicate as if they were attached to the same wire, when, in fact, they are located on a number of different LAN segments. Because VLANs are based on logical instead of physical connections, they are extremely flexible.

Objectives

After reading this chapter, you will be able to

- Explain LAN design goals
- Identify LAN design issues
- Explain network design methodology
- Describe how to gather and analyze network equipment
- Identify Layer 1 (media and topology) design issues
- Identify Layer 2 (LAN switching) design issues
- Identify Layer 3 (routing) design issues
- Describe the physical and logical network implementation documentation

LAN Design

Introduction

Chapter 3, "VLANs," provided an introduction to virtual LANs (VLANs) and switched internetworking, compared traditional shared *local-area network (LAN)* configurations with switched LAN configurations, and discussed the benefits of using a switched VLAN architecture. Despite improvements in equipment performance and *media* capabilities, network design is becoming more difficult. The trend is toward increasingly complex environments involving multimedia (or multiple media types) and interconnection to networks outside any single organization's controlled LAN. Keeping all the many factors in mind is important because carefully designing networks can reduce the hardships associated with growth as a networking environment evolves.

One of the most critical steps to ensure a fast and stable network is the design of the network. If a network is not designed properly, many unforeseen problems can arise, and network growth can be jeopardized. This design process is truly an in-depth process. This chapter provides an overview of the LAN design process. In addition, LAN design goals, network design issues, network design methodology, and the development of LAN topologies are covered in this chapter.

Washington Project: Designing the Network
In this chapter, you will begin the process of designing the LAN at your specific site within the Washington School District WAN. As concepts and requirements are introduced, you will be able to apply them in your network design. You will need to make sure to address the following requirements: • The LAN is meant to serve different "workgroups" of staff members and students. This logical division will require the use of VLANs and will be a major design decision. For example, VLANs should be used to secure the administrators' machines from the students' machines.   • Access to the Internet from any site in the school district, via the District WAN, is also an integral part of this implementation.   • A series of servers is needed to facilitate online automations of all the district's administrative functions and many of the curricular functions.   <div align="right">*continues*</div>

Washington Project: Designing the Network (Continued)
• Because this network implementation must be functional for a minimum of 7–10 years, all design considerations should include at least 100x (times) growth in the LAN throughput, 2x (times) growth in WAN throughput, and 10x (times) growth in the Internet connection throughput.
• A minimum of 1.0 Mbps to any host computer in the network and 100 Mbps to any server host in the network is required.
• Only two routed protocols may be implemented in the network: TCP/IP and Novell IPX.

LAN Design Goals

Designing a network can be a challenging task and involves more than just connecting computers together. A network requires many features in order to be scalable and manageable. To design reliable, scalable networks, network designers must realize that each of the major components of a network has distinct design requirements. Even a network that consists of only 50 routing nodes can pose complex problems that lead to unpredictable results. Attempting to design and build networks that contain thousands of nodes can pose even more complex problems.

The first step in designing a LAN is to establish and document the goals of the design. These goals are particular to each organization or situation. However, the following requirements tend to show up in most network designs:

■ **Functionality**—The network must work. That is, it must allow users to meet their job requirements. The network must provide user-to-user and user-to-application connectivity with reasonable speed and reliability.

■ **Scalability**—The network must be able to grow. That is, the initial design should grow without any major changes to the overall design.

■ **Adaptability**—The network must be designed with an eye toward future technologies, and it should include no element that would limit implementation of new technologies as they become available.

■ **Manageability**—The network should be designed to facilitate network monitoring and management to ensure ongoing stability of operation.

These requirements are specific to certain types of networks and more general in other types of networks. This chapter discusses how to address these requirements.

Network Design Components

With the emergence of high-speed technologies such as *Asynchronous Transfer Mode (ATM)* and more complex LAN architectures that use LAN switching and VLANs over the past several years, many organizations have been upgrading existing LANs or planning, designing, and implementing new LANs.

To design LANs for high-speed technologies and multimedia-based applications, network designers should address the following critical components of the overall LAN design:

- The function and placement of servers
- Collision detection
- Segmentation
- Bandwidth versus broadcast domains

These components are discussed in the following sections.

Function and Placement of Servers

One of the keys to designing a successful network is to understand the function and placement of servers needed for the network. Servers provide file sharing, printing, communication, and application services, such as word processing. Servers typically do not functions as workstations; rather, they run specialized operating systems, such as NetWare, Windows NT, UNIX, and Linux. Today, each server usually is dedicated to one function, such as e-mail or file sharing.

Servers can be categorized into two distinct classes: *enterprise servers* and *workgroup servers*. An enterprise server supports all the users on the network by offering services, such as e-mail or Domain Name System (DNS), as shown in Figure 4-1. E-mail or DNS is a service that everyone in an organization (such as the Washington School District) would need because it is a centralized function. On the other hand, a workgroup server supports a specific set of users, offering services such as word processing and file sharing, which are services only a few groups of people would need.

Enterprise servers should be placed in the *main distribution facility (MDF)*. This way, traffic to the enterprise servers has to travel only to the MDF and does not need to be transmitted across other networks. Ideally, workgroup servers should be placed in the *intermediate distribution facilities (IDFs)* closest to the users accessing the applications on these servers. You merely need to directly connect servers to the MDF or IDF. By placing, workgroup servers close to the users, traffic only has to travel the network infrastructure to that IDF, and does not affect other users on that network segment. Within the MDF and IDFs, the Layer 2 LAN switches should have 100 Mbps or more allocated for these servers.

FIGURE 4-1
The differences between enterprise servers and workgroup servers involve the services needed.

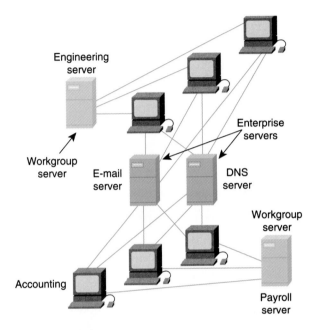

Washington Project: Server Placement and Function

You should categorize all file servers for the Washington School District as enterprise or workgroup types and then place servers in the network topology according to the anticipated traffic patterns of users and according to the following functions:

- **DNS and E-Mail Services**—Each district hub location should contain a DNS server to support the individual schools serviced out of that location. Each school should also contain a host for DNS and e-mail services (that is, a local post office) that will maintain a complete directory of the staff members and students for that location.

- **The Administrative Server**—Each school location should have an administration server for the student tracking, attendance, grading, and other administrative functions. This server should run TCP/IP as its protocol suite and should be made available only to teachers and staff members.

- **The Library Server**—The school district is implementing an automated library information and retrieval system for an online curricular research library. This server should run TCP/IP as its OSI Layer 3 and Layer 4 protocol and should be made available to anyone at the school site.

Washington Project: Server Placement and Function (Continued)
• **Application Server**—All computer applications, such as word processing and spreadsheet software, should be housed in a central server at each school location.
• **Other Servers**—Any other servers implemented at the school sites should be considered departmental (workgroup) servers and should be placed according to user group access needs. An example would be a server running an instructional application for a specific school site.

Intranets

One common configuration of a LAN is an *intranet*. Intranet Web servers differ from public Web servers in that, without the needed permissions and passwords, the public does not have access to an organization's intranet. Intranets are designed to be accessed by users who have access privileges to an organization's internal LAN. Within an intranet, Web servers are installed in the network, and browser technology is used as the common front end to access information, such as financial data or graphical, text-based data stored on those servers.

The addition of an intranet to a network can cause an increase in needed network bandwidth. Because bandwidth has to be added to the network backbone, network administrators should also consider acquiring robust desktops to get faster access into intranets. New desktop computers and servers should be outfitted with 10/100/1000-Mbps Ethernet network interface cards (NICs) to provide the most configuration flexibility, thus enabling network administrators to dedicate bandwidth to individual end stations as needed.

Collision Detection

You should decide carefully on the selection and placement of networking devices to be used in the LAN in order to decrease the collision detection and media contention on a network.

An Ethernet node gets access to the wire by contending with other Ethernet nodes for the right to do so. When your network grows to include more nodes on the shared segment or wire, and these nodes have more and more messages to transmit, the chance that a node will contend successfully for its share of the wire gets much worse, and the network bogs down. The fact that contention media access does not scale or allow for growth is Ethernet's main disadvantage.

As shown in Figure 4-2, as traffic increases on the shared media, the rate of collisions also increases. Although collisions are normal events in Ethernet, an excessive number of collisions further (sometimes dramatically) reduces available bandwidth. In most cases, the actual available bandwidth is reduced to a fraction (about 35% to 40%) of the full 10 Mbps. This reduction in bandwidth can be remedied by segmenting the network by using bridges, switches, or routers.

FIGURE 4-2
In a shared bus topology, collisions reduce the effective available bandwidth.

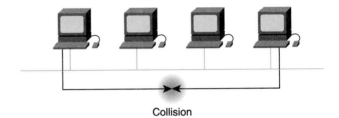

Collision

Segmentation

Segmentation is the process of splitting a single collision domain into two or more collision domains, as shown in Figure 4-3. Layer 2 (the data link layer) bridges or switches can be used to segment a logical bus topology and create separate collision domains, which results in more bandwidth being available to individual stations. Notice in Figure 4-3 that the entire bus topology still represents a single *broadcast domain* because, although bridges and switches do not forward collisions, they forward broadcast packets.

All broadcasts from any host in the same broadcast domain are visible to all other hosts in the same broadcast domain. Broadcasts must be visible to all hosts in the broadcast domain in order to establish connectivity. The scalability of the bandwidth domain depends on the total amount of traffic, and the scalability for a broadcast domain depends on the total broadcast of the traffic. It is important to remember that bridges and switches forward broadcast (FF-FF-FF-FF-FF-FF) traffic, and that routers normally do not.

FIGURE 4-3
Routers and switches are used for segmentation.

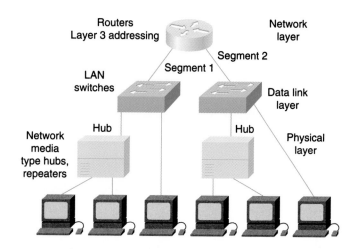

Routers
Layer 3 addressing

Network layer

Segment 2

Segment 1

LAN switches

Data link layer

Hub

Hub

Network media type hubs, repeaters

Physical layer

Bandwidth Versus Broadcast Domains

A bandwidth domain is everything associated with one port on a bridge or switch. In the case of an Ethernet switch, a bandwidth domain is also known as a collision domain. As shown in Figure 4-4, a switch can create one bandwidth domain per port. All workstations within one bandwidth domain compete for the same LAN bandwidth resource. All the traffic from any host in the bandwidth domain is visible to all the other hosts. In the case of an Ethernet collision domain, two stations can transmit at the same time, causing a collision.

FIGURE 4-4
A collision domain has shared bandwidth, and a broadcast domain is visible across a subnet.

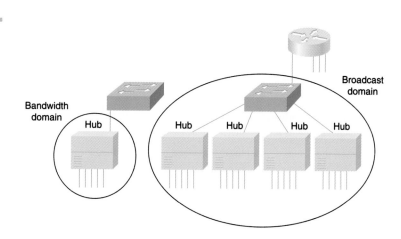

Broadcast domain

Bandwidth domain

Hub

Hub

Hub

Hub

Hub

Network Design Methodology

For a LAN to be effective and serve the needs of its users, it should be designed and implemented according to a planned series of systematic steps, which include the following:

1. Gathering the users' requirements and expectations

2. Analyzing requirements

3. Designing the Layer 1, 2, and 3 LAN structure (that is, topology)

4. Documenting the logical and physical network implementation

These steps are described in the following sections.

Gathering Requirements

The first step in designing a network should be to gather data about the organizational structure. This information includes the organization's history and current status, projected growth, operating policies and management procedures, office systems and procedures, and the viewpoints of the people who will be using the LAN. You need to answer the following questions: Who are the people who will be using the network? What is their level of skill, and what are their attitudes toward computers and computer applications?

Answering these and similar questions will help determine how much training will be required and how many people will be needed to support the LAN.

Washington Project: Understanding the Customer

First and foremost, you must understand the customer. In the case of the Washington School District, you need to talk to major users of the network; find out their geographic location, their current applications, their plans for the future; and determine who the major players will be in helping you design the network. After you have gathered data on the district's organizational structure, you need to

- Determine where information flows in the district

- Find out where shared data resides and who uses it

- Determine whether data outside the district—for example, data on the Internet—is accessed

- Define the issues or problems that need to be addressed

Ideally, the information gathering process helps clarify and identify the problems. You also need to determine whether there are documented policies in place. Has some data been declared mission critical? Have some operations been declared mission critical? (*Mission-critical* data and operation are those that are considered key to businesses, and access to them is critical to the business running on a daily basis.) What protocols are allowed on the network? Are only certain desktop hosts supported?

Next, you should determine who in the organization has authority over addressing, naming, topology design, and configuration. Some companies have a central Management Information Systems (MIS) department that controls everything. Some companies have very small MIS departments and, therefore, must delegate authority to departments. Focus on identifying the resources and constraints of the organization. Organization resources that can affect the implementation of a new LAN system fall into two general categories: computer hardware/software and human resources. An organization's existing computer hardware and software must be documented, and projected hardware and software needs identified. How are these resources currently linked and shared? What financial resources does the organization have available? Documenting these types of things helps you estimate costs and develop a budget for the LAN. You should make sure you understand performance issues of any existing network.

Analyzing Requirements

The next step in designing a network is to analyze the requirements of the network and its users that were gathered in the last step. Network user needs constantly change. For example, as more voice- and video-based network applications become available, the pressure to increase network bandwidth will become intense.

Another component of the analysis phase is assessing the user requirements. A LAN that is incapable of supplying prompt and accurate information to its users is of little use. Therefore, you must take steps to ensure that the information requirements of the organization and its workers are met.

Washington Project: Availability
Find out what *availability* means to your customer. In the case of the Washington School District, you need to conduct a detailed analysis of current and projected needs in order to help meet this need. Analysis of network requirements includes analyzing the district's business and technical goals.   You need to answer the following questions: • What applications will be implemented?   • What new networks will be accessed?   • What are the success criteria?   • What level of reliability must the WAN and LANs have?   • How can you tell if the new design is successful?

Availability and Network Traffic

Availability measures the usefulness of the network. Many things affect availability, including the following:

- Throughput
- Response time
- Access to resources

Every customer has a different definition of *availability*. For example, there may be a need to transport voice and video over the network. However, these services require more bandwidth than is available on the network or backbone. You can increase availability by adding more resources, but resources drive up cost. Network design seeks to provide the greatest availability for the least cost.

Washington Project: Determining Network Traffic Load

You need to determine the network traffic load for the Washington School District before developing a network structure and acquiring hardware.

Additionally, when analyzing the district's technical requirements, you should estimate the traffic load caused by applications in packet size (for example, you need to estimate the size of files in bytes per second that need to be transmitted over the network).

Certain types of network use can generate large volumes of traffic and, therefore, can cause congestion, including congestion of the following:

- Internet access
- Computers loading software from a remote site
- Anything that transmits images or video
- Central database access
- Department file servers

You should estimate worst-case traffic load on the network during the busiest times for users and during regularly scheduled network services, such as file server backups.

Designing the Network Topology

After determining the overall requirements for the network, the next step is to decide on an overall LAN topology that will satisfy the user requirements. In this curriculum, we concentrate on *star topology* and extended star topology. As you have seen, the star/extended star topology, which is illustrated in Figure 4-5, uses Ethernet 802.3 carrier sense multiple access collision detect (CSMA/CD) technology. The reason that this curriculum focuses on a CSMA/CD star topology is that it is by far the dominant configuration in the industry.

FIGURE 4-5
The star and extended star topologies are the most widely used models in networking and are extremely stable.

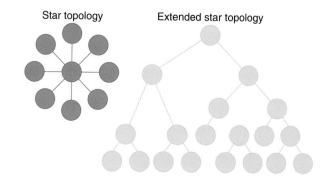

Star topology   Extended star topology

The major pieces of a LAN topology design can be broken into three unique categories of the OSI reference model—the network layer, the data link layer, and the physical layer—shown previously in Figure 4-3. These components are discussed in the following sections.

Designing the Layer 1 Topology

In this section, we examine Layer 1 star and extended star topologies.

Washington Project: Speed and Expansion
For the Washington School District network, you need to build the Layer 1 components of the district network with speed and expansion capabilities. As you know, the physical layer controls the way data is transmitted between the source and a destination node. Therefore, the type of media and topology you select helps you determine how much data can travel across the network and how quickly.

Cabling

The physical cabling is one of the most important components to consider when designing a network. Design issues include the type of cabling to be used (typically copper or fiber) and the overall structure of the cabling. Layer 1 cabling media include types such as *Category 5 unshielded twisted-pair (UTP)* and *fiber-optic cable*, along with the *EIA/TIA 568* standard for layout and connection of wiring schemes.

In addition to distance limitations, you should carefully evaluate the strengths and weaknesses of various topologies because a network is only as effective as its underlying cable. Most network problems are caused by Layer 1 issues. If you are planning any significant changes for a network, you should do a complete cable audit to identify areas that require upgrades and rewiring.

Whether you are designing a new network or recabling an existing one, fiber-optic cable is preferable for use in the backbone and risers, with Category 5

UTP cable in the horizontal runs. The cable upgrade should take priority over any other needed changes, and enterprises should ensure—without exception—that these systems conform to well-defined industry standards, such as the EIA/TIA 568 specifications.

The EIA/TIA 568 standard specifies that every device connected to the network should be linked to a central location with horizontal cabling, as shown in Figure 4-6. This is true if all the hosts that need to access the network are within the 100-meter distance limitation for Category 5 UTP Ethernet, as specified by EIA/TIA 568B standards. Table 4-1 lists cable types and their characteristics.

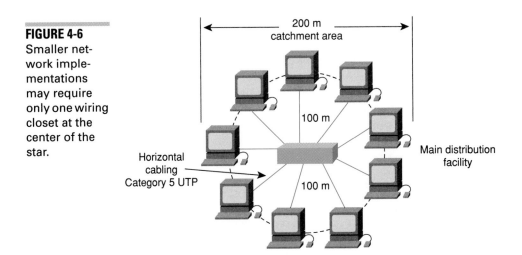

FIGURE 4-6
Smaller network implementations may require only one wiring closet at the center of the star.

TABLE 4-1   Cable Type Characteristics and IEEE 802.3 Values

Characteristic	10BaseT	10BaseFL	100BaseTX	100BaseFX
Data rate	10 Mbps	10 Mbps	100 Mbps	100 Mbps
Signaling method	Baseband	Baseband	Baseband	Baseband
Medium type	Category 5 UTP	Fiber-optic	Category 5 UTP	Multi-mode fiber (two strands)
Maximum length	100 meters	2000 meters	100 meters	400 meters

Star Topology

In a simple star topology, as shown in Figure 4-7, with only one wiring closet, the MDF includes one or more *horizontal cross-connect (HCC)* patch panels. HCC patch cables are used to connect the Layer 1 horizontal cabling with the Layer 2 LAN equipment ports. The LAN switch is connected to an Ethernet port on the Layer 3 router by using a standard Category 5 Ethernet patch cable. At this point, the end host has a complete physical connection to the router port.

Washington Project: Catchment Areas
You should review the TCS overview to determine what the user expects for the number of horizontal cable runs to each room that the MDF or IDF will be servicing in its *catchment area*.

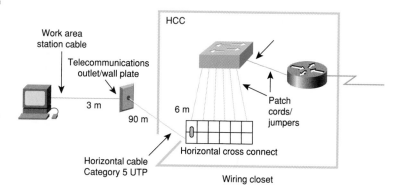

FIGURE 4-7
The number of horizontal cable runs and the size (that is, the number of ports) of the HCC patch panels should be determined by the user's requirements.

Extended Star Topology

When hosts in larger networks are outside the 100-meter limitation for Category 5 UTP Ethernet, it is not unusual to have more than one wiring closet. By creating multiple wiring closets, multiple catchment areas are created. The secondary wiring closets are referred to as IDFs (see Figure 4-8). TIA/EIA 568-A standards specify that IDFs should be connected to the MDF by using *vertical cabling*, also called *backbone cabling*.

As shown in Figure 4-9, a *vertical cross-connect (VCC)* is used to interconnect the various IDFs to the central MDF. Because the vertical cable lengths typically are longer than the 100-meter limit for Category 5 UTP cable, as shown in Figure 4-10, fiber-optic cabling normally is used.

Washington Project: Connection Speeds
In the Washington School District network, the vertical cabling should carry all data traffic between the IDFs and MDFs. Therefore, the speed of this connection should be designed to be the fast link in the network. All traffic across the district network backbone will traverse this link, so this link should be at least 100 Mbps.

FIGURE 4-8
Extended star
topology in a
multibuilding
campus.

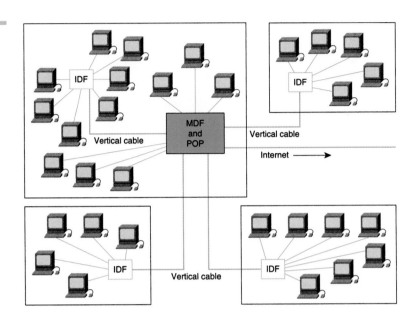

FIGURE 4-9
The major
difference
between the
MDF and the
IDFs is the
implementa-
tion of another
patch panel in
the IDF, which
can be the
VCC.

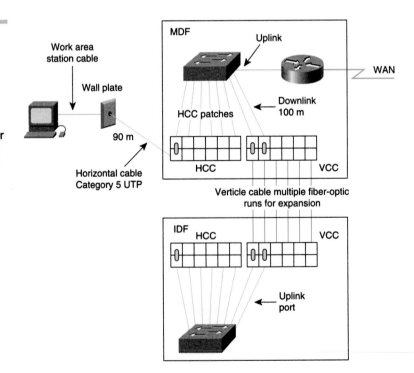

FIGURE 4-10
All vertical cabling is connected to the MDF to create a single LAN segment.

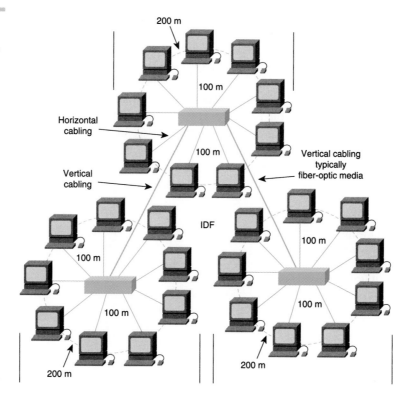

Fast Ethernet—MDF-to-IDF Vertical Cabling

Fast Ethernet is Ethernet that has been upgraded to 100 Mbps. This type uses the standard Ethernet broadcast-oriented logical bus topology of *10BaseT*, along with the familiar CSMA/CD method for Media Access Control (MAC). The Fast Ethernet standard is actually several different standards based on copper-pair wire (*100BaseTX*) and on fiber-optic cable (*100BaseFX*), and it is used to connect the MDF to the IDF, as shown in Figure 4-11.

Layer 1 Documentation

As shown in Figure 4-12, the logical diagram is the network topology model without all the detail of the exact installation path of the cabling. The logical diagram is a snapshot view of the LAN implementations and is useful in troubleshooting problems and implementing expansion in the future. It is the basic road map of the LAN. Elements of the logical diagram include

- The exact locations of the MDF and IDF wiring closets.
- The type and quantity of cabling used to interconnect the IDFs with the MDF, along with how many spare cables are available for increasing the

bandwidth between the wiring closets. For example, if the vertical cabling between IDF 1 and the MDF is running at 80% utilization, you can use two additional pairs to double the capacity.

■ Detailed documentation, as shown in the cut sheet in Figure 4-13, of all cable runs, the identification numbers, and which port on the HCC or VCC the run is terminated on. For example, say Room 203 has lost connectivity to the network. By examining the cutsheet, you can see that Room 203 is running off cable run 203-1, which is terminated on HCC 1 port 13. You can now test that run by using a cable tester to determine whether the problem is a Layer 1 failure. If it is, you can simply use one of the other two runs to get the connectivity back and then troubleshoot run 203-1.

FIGURE 4-11
Fast Ethernet connects the MDF to the IDF by utilizing bandwidth at 100 Mbps using CSMA/ CD technology.

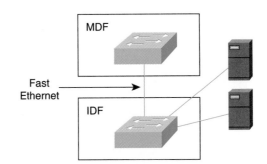

FIGURE 4-12
The logical diagram is a snapshot of the overall view of the LAN implementation and is useful in troubleshooting problems and implementing expansion in the future.

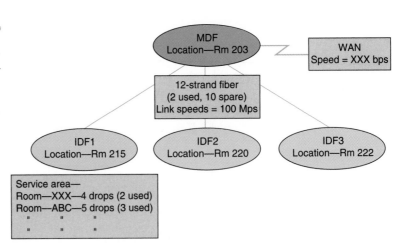

FIGURE 4-13
The cutsheet becomes a valuable tool in troubleshooting any Layer 1 network problems.

IDF1
Location—Rm 215

Connection	Cable ID	Cross Connection Paired # / Port #	Type of Cable	Status
IDF1 to Rm 203	203-1	HCC1/Port 13	Category 5 UTP	Used
IDF1 to Rm 203	203-2	HCC1/Port 14	Category 5 UTP	Not used
IDF1 to Rm 203	203-3	HCC2/Port 3	Category 5 UTP	Not used
IDF1 to MDF	IDF1-1	VCC1/Port 1	Multimode fiber	Used
IDF1 to MDF	IDF1-2	VCC1/Port 2	Multimode fiber	Used

Washington Project: LAN Wiring Scheme Requirements

As you're planning the wiring for the Washington School District network, you need to take into account certain LAN requirements related to user access, segmentation, infrastructure, cabling, MDFs, and IDFs. Therefore, you should address the requirements described here when designing the network.

Requirement 1

Two LAN segments need to be implemented in each school and the district office. One LAN needs to be designated for student/curriculum usage and the other needs to be designated for administration usage.

Requirement 2

The LAN infrastructure needs to be based on Ethernet LAN switching, which will allow for a migration to faster speeds (that is, more bandwidth) to the individual computers and between MDFs and IDFs without revamping the physical wiring scheme to accommodate future applications. The transport speeds need be Ethernet 10BaseT, 100BaseTX, and 100BaseFx.

Requirement 3

Horizontal cabling needs to be Category 5 UTP and needs to have the capacity to accommodate 100 Mbps. Vertical (backbone) cabling needs to be Category 5 UTP or fiber-optic multimode cable. The cabling infrastructure needs to comply with EIA/TIA 568-A and EIA/TIA 569 standards.

Requirement 4

In each location, an MDF room needs to be established as the central point to which all LAN cabling will be terminated. This will also be the point of presence (POP) for the WAN connection. The IDF should service its geographical area, and the IDF should be connected directly to the MDF in a star or extended star topology.

Designing the Layer 2 LAN Topology

As you learned in Chapter 2, "LAN Switching," and Chapter 3, "VLANs," the purpose of Layer 2 devices in the network is to provide flow control, error detection, error correction, and to reduce congestion in the network. The two most common Layer 2 devices (other than the NIC, which every host on the network must have) are bridges and LAN switches. Devices at this layer determine the size of the collision domains. This section concentrates on the implementation of LAN switching at Layer 2.

Washington Project: Layer 2 Design Goals
The following are Layer 2 LAN topology design goals for the sites of the Washington School District network:
• You should install LAN switching devices that use microsegmentation in order to reduce the collision domain size.
• You should create VLANs and unique broadcast domains based on user workgroups.

Collisions and collision domain size are two factors that negatively effect the performance of a network. By using LAN switching, you can microsegment the network, thus eliminating collisions and reducing the size of collision domains. As shown in Figure 4-14, another important characteristic of a LAN switch is how it can allocate bandwidth on a per-port basis, thus allowing more bandwidth to vertical cabling, uplinks, and servers. This type of switching is referred to as *asymmetric switching*, and it provides switched connections between ports of unlike bandwidth, such as a combination of 10-Mbps and 100-Mbps ports.

FIGURE 4-14
An example of asymmetric switching.

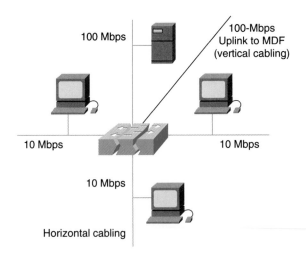

100 Mbps

100-Mbps Uplink to MDF (vertical cabling)

10 Mbps

10 Mbps

10 Mbps

Horizontal cabling

As you have learned, microsegmentation means using bridges and switches to boost performance for a workgroup or a backbone. Typically, boosting performance in this manner involves Ethernet switching. As shown in Figure 4-15, switches can be used with hubs to provide the appropriate level of performance for different users and servers.

FIGURE 4-15
You can avoid congestion on a LAN by using microsegmentation to eliminate collision domains.

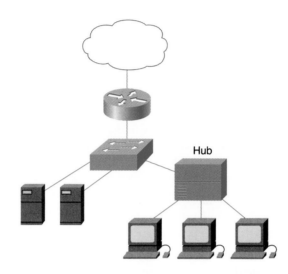

Hub

By installing LAN switching at the MDF and IDFs and vertical cable between the MDF and the IDFs, the vertical cable is carrying all the data traffic between the MDF and the IDFs; therefore, the capacity of this run must be larger than that of the runs between the IDFs and workstations.

Horizontal cable runs using Category 5 UTP must be no longer than 90 meters, which allows links at 10 Mbps or 100 Mbps. In a normal environment, 10 Mbps is adequate for the horizontal cable drop. Because asymmetric LAN switches allow for mixing 10-Mbps and 100-Mbps ports on a single switch, the next task is to determine the number of 10-Mbps and 100-Mbps ports needed in the MDF and every IDF. This can be determined by going back to the user requirements for the number of horizontal cable drops per room and the number of drops total in any catchment area, along with the number of vertical cable runs.

For example, say user requirements dictate that 4 horizontal cable runs be installed to each room. The IDF that services a catchment area covers 18 rooms; therefore, 4 drops × 18 rooms = 72 LAN switch ports.

Washington Project: LAN Topology Requirements

As you're planning the LAN topology for your school site, you need to keep in mind certain requirements for rooms that need access to the network and the room's wiring POP.

Requirement 1

Each room requiring connection to the network needs to be able to support 24 workstations and be supplied with four Category 5 UTP runs for data, with one run terminated at the teacher's workstation. These cable runs should be terminated in the closest MDF or IDF. All Category 5 UTP cable runs need to be tested end-to-end for 100-Mbps bandwidth capacity.

Requirement 2

A single location in each room needs to be designated as the wiring POP for that room. It needs to consist of a lockable cabinet containing all cable terminations and electronic components (that is, data hubs or switches). From this location, data services need to be distributed within the room via decorative wire molding. Network 1 needs to be allocated for general curriculum use, and Network 2 needs to be allocated for administrative use.

Layer 2 Switch Collision Domains

To determine the size of a collision domain, you must determine how many hosts are physically connected to any single port on the switch. This also affects how much network bandwidth is available to any host.

In an ideal situation, there is only one host connected on a LAN switch port. This would make the size of the collision domain 2 (the source host and destination host). Because of this small collision domain, there should be almost no collisions when any two hosts are communicating with each other.

Another way to implement LAN switching is to install shared LAN hubs on the switch ports and connect multiple hosts to a single switch port, as shown in Figure 4-16. All hosts connected to the shared LAN hub share the same collision domain and bandwidth, as shown in Figure 4-17.

Note that some older switches, such as the Catalyst 1700, don't truly support sharing the same collision domain and bandwidth because they don't maintain multiple MAC addresses mapped to each port. In that case, there are many broadcasts and ARP requests.

Using a Layer 2 Switch with Hubs

Shared-media hubs are generally used in a LAN switch environment to create more connection points at the end of the horizontal cable runs. Make sure that design specifications are adhered to, that bandwidth requirements are met, and that collision domains are kept to a minimum, as shown in Figure 4-18.

FIGURE 4-16
When you're using hubs, the size of the collision domain increases and bandwidth is shared.

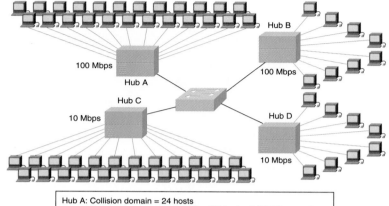

Hub A: Collision domain = 24 hosts
Bandwidth average = 100 Mbps/24 host = 4.167 Mbps per host

Hub B: Collision domain = 8 hosts
Bandwidth average = 100 Mbps/8 host = 12.5 Mbps per host

Hub C: Collision domain = 24 hosts
Bandwidth average = 10 Mbps/24 host = .4167 Mbps per host

Hub D: Collision domain = 8 hosts
Bandwidth average = 10 Mbps/8 host = 1.25 Mbps per host

FIGURE 4-17
In a pure LAN switched environment, the size of the collision domain is 2 hosts, and in a LAN that uses hubs, the collision domain is much larger.

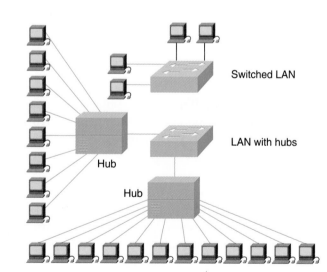

FIGURE 4-18
You can use hubs to supply more connection points for a host.

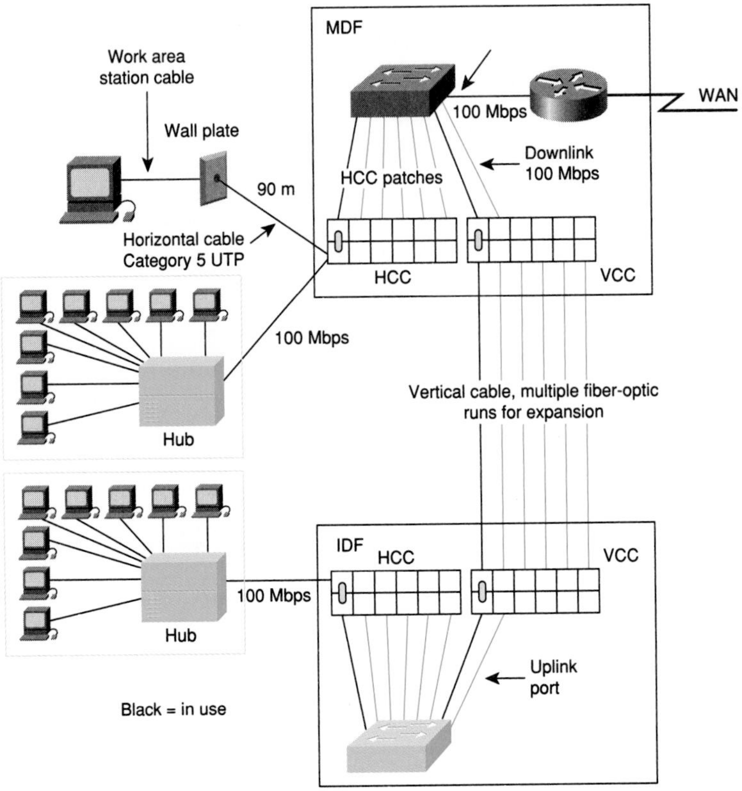

Layer 2 Migration to Higher Bandwidth

As the network grows, the need for more bandwidth increases. In the vertical cabling between MDF and IDFs, unused fiber optics can be connected from the VCC to 100-Mbps ports on the switch. The network in Figure 4-19 doubles the capacity of the vertical cabling in the network in Figure 4-18 by bringing up another link.

In the horizontal cabling, you can increase the bandwidth by a factor of 10 by repatching from the HCC to a 100-Mbps port on the switch and changing from a 10-Mbps hub to 100-Mbps hub. When sizing the Layer 2 LAN switch, it is important to make sure there are enough 100-Mbps ports to allow for this migration to higher bandwidth. It is important to document the speed at which each active cable drop is running.

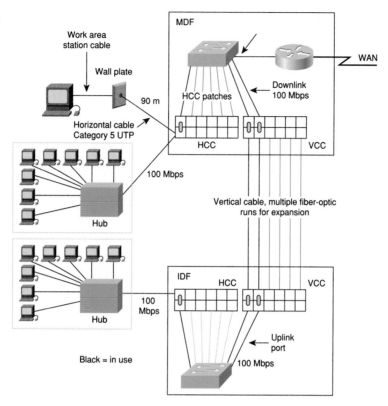

FIGURE 4-19
Migration to higher bandwidth is as simple as patching to a higher-speed port or adding more higher-speed ports.

Designing the Layer 3 LAN Topology

Layer 3 (the network layer) devices, such as routers, can be used to create unique LAN segments and allow communication between segments based on Layer 3 addressing, such as IP addressing. Implementation of Layer 3 devices, such as routers, allows for segmentation of the LAN into unique physical and logical networks. Routers also allow for connectivity to *wide-area networks (WANs)*, such as the Internet.

Layer 3 Router Implementation

As shown in Figure 4-20, Layer 3 routing determines traffic flow between unique physical network segments based on Layer 3 addressing, such as IP network and subnet. The router is one of the most powerful devices in the network topology.

Washington Project: Layer 3 Design Goals
The following are Layer 3 LAN topology design goals for your site:
• Build a path between LAN segments that will filter the flow of data packets.
• Isolate ARP protocol broadcast.

continues

Washington Project: Layer 3 Design Goals (Continued)
• Isolate collisions between segments.
• Filter Layer 4 services between segments.

FIGURE 4-20
Layer 3 routing addresses issues such as the need for physically separate subnets.

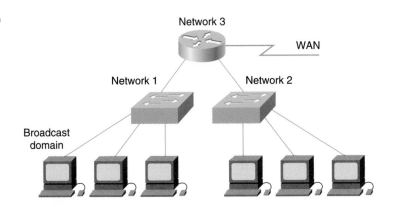

As you have learned, a router forwards data packets based on destination addresses. A router does not forward LAN-based broadcasts such as ARP requests. Therefore, the router interface is considered the entry and exit point of a broadcast domain and stops broadcasts from reaching other LAN segments.

VLAN Implementation

One important issue in a network is the total number of broadcasts, such as ARP requests. By using VLANs, you can limit broadcast traffic to within a VLAN and thus create smaller broadcast domains, as shown in Figure 4-22. VLANs can also be used to provide security by creating the VLAN groups according to function, as shown in Figure 4-21.

In Figure 4-22, a physical port association is used to implement VLAN assignment. Ports P0, P1, and P4 have been assigned to VLAN 1. VLAN 2 has ports P2, P3, and P5. Communication between VLAN 1 and VLAN 2 can occur only through the router. This limits the size of the broadcast domains and uses the router to determine whether VLAN 1 can talk to VLAN 2. This means you can create a security scheme based on VLAN assignment.

Using Routers to Create Scalable Networks

Routers provide scalability because they can serve as firewalls for broadcasts, as shown in Figure 4-20. In addition, because Layer 3 addresses typically have structure, routers can provide greater scalability by dividing networks and subnets, as shown in Figure 4-23, therefore, adding structure to Layer 3 addresses. The ways in which greater scalability in networks can occur are shown in Table 4-2. When the networks are divided into subnets, the final step is to develop and document the IP addressing scheme to be used in the network.

FIGURE 4-21
VLANs provide broadcast containment and security.

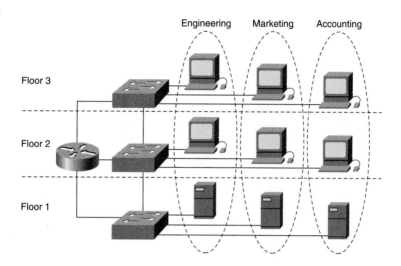

FIGURE 4-22
Routers provide communication between VLANs.

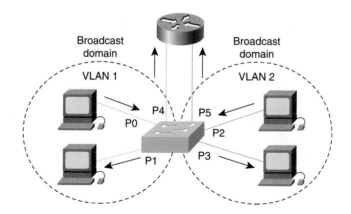

Routing technology filters data-link broadcasts and multicasts. By adding router ports with additional subnet or *network addresses*, you can segment the internetwork as required. Network protocol addressing and routing provide built-in scaling. When deciding whether to use routers or switches, remember to ask, "What problem am I trying to solve?" If your problem is protocol related rather than contention oriented, then routers are appropriate. Routers solve problems with excessive broadcasts, protocols that do not scale well, security issues, and network-layer addressing. Routers, however, are more expensive and harder to configure than switches.

FIGURE 4-23
A router pro-
vides structure
to a network by
dividing net-
works and
subnets.

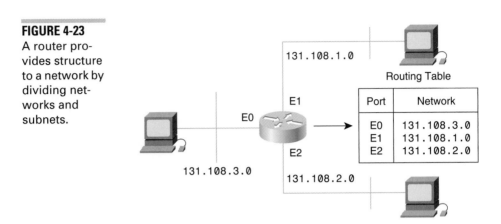

TABLE 4-2   **Logical Addressing, Mapped to the Physical Network**

Logical Address	Physical Network Devices
x.x.x.1–x.x.x.10	Router, LAN, and WAN ports
x.x.x.11–x.x.x.20	LAN switches
x.x.x.21–x.x.x.30	Enterprise servers
x.x.x.31–x.x.x.80	Workgroup servers
x.x.x.81–x.x.x.254	Hosts

Washington Project: Addressing

The district office should develop a complete TCP/IP addressing and naming convention scheme for all hosts, servers, and network interconnection devices. The implementation of unauthorized addresses should be prohibited. All computers located on the administrative networks should have static addresses. Curriculum computers should obtain addresses by utilizing Dynamic Host Configuration Protocol (DHCP). DHCP provides a mechanism for allocating IP addresses dynamically so that addresses can be reused when hosts no longer need them. While the district office should design, implement, and enforce the overall addressing scheme for the network, DHCP should be administered by the local sites within the confines of the address blocks they were assigned.

Using Routers to Impose Logical Structure

As shown in Figure 4-23, routers can be used to provide IP subnets to add structure to addresses. With bridges and switches, all unknown addresses must be flooded out of every port. With routers, hosts using protocols with net-work-layer addressing can solve the problem of finding other hosts without *flooding.* If the destination address is local, the sending host can *encapsulate* the packet in a data-link *header* and send a *unicast* frame directly to the station. The router does not see the frame and, of course, does not need to flood the frame. The sending host might have to use ARP, which would cause a broadcast, but the broadcast is only a local broadcast and is not forwarded by the router. If the destination is not local, the sending station transmits the packet to the router. The router sends the frame to the destination or to the next hop, based on its routing table. Given this routing functionality, it is clear that large, scalable LANs need to incorporate some routers.

Using a Layer 3 Router for Segmentation

Figure 4-24 is an example of an implementation that has multiple physical networks. All data traffic from Network 1 destined for Network 2 has to go through the router. In this implementation, there are two broadcast domains. The two networks have unique Layer 3 IP addressing network/subnetwork addressing schemes.

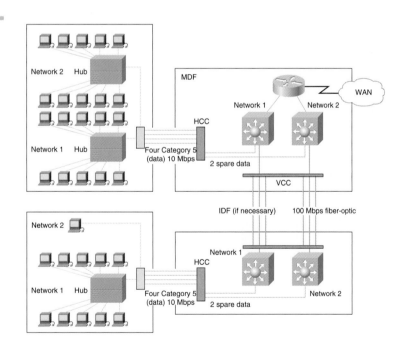

FIGURE 4-24
In this implementation, the router serves as the central point in the LAN for traffic destination, and robust security is implemented.

In a structured Layer 1 wiring scheme, multiple physical networks are easy to create simply by patching the horizontal cabling and vertical cabling into the appropriate Layer 2 switch using patch cables. As we will see in future chapters, this implementation provides for robust security implementation. In addition, the router is the central point in the LAN for traffic destination.

Documenting the Logical and Physical Network Implementation

After you have developed the IP addressing scheme for the customer, you should document it by site and by network within the site, as shown previously in Table 4-2. A standard convention should be set for addressing important hosts on the network. This addressing scheme should be kept consistent throughout the entire network, as shown in Figure 4-25. By creating addressing maps, you can get a snapshot of the network, as shown in Figure 4-26. Creating physical maps of the network, as shown in Figure 4-27, helps you troubleshoot the network.

SKILL BUILDER

Switched LAN Design

This lab helps you prepare for the threaded Case Study. In this lab, you are given some basic requirements for a small LAN that spans multiple buildings. Your focus is on the physical topology and data link layer components.

FIGURE 4-25
Networks with good documentation are easy to troubleshoot when problems occur.

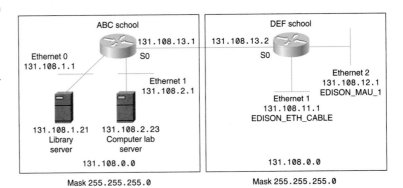

FIGURE 4-26
Networks with good documentation such as this reduce network problem load.

IP Network 131.108.0.0
Subnet Mask = 255.255.255.0

XYZ school district	
ABC school	**DEF school**
131.108.1.0 through 131.108.10.0 Subnet mask = 255.255.255.0 Router name = ABC Router Ethernet 0 = 131.108.1.0 Ethernet 1 = 131.108.2.0 Ethernet 2 = 131.108.3.0	131.108.11.0 through 131.108.21.0 Subnet mask = 255.255.255.0 Router name = DEF Router Ethernet 0 = 131.108.11.0 Ethernet 1 = 131.108.12.0

FIGURE 4-27
Physical maps indicate where MDFs and IDFs are located and where a host is connected to the network.

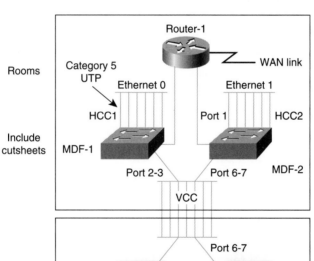

Summary

- One of the most critical factors in ensuring a fast and stable network is the design of the network. If a network is not designed properly, many unforeseen problems may arise, and network growth can be jeopardized.
- LAN design goals include functionality, scalability, adaptability, and manageability.
- Network design issues include function and placement of servers, collision detection, segmentation, and bandwidth versus broadcast domains.
- The design process includes the following:
  - Gathering the users requirements and expectations
  - Determining data traffic patterns now and in the future based on growth and server placements
  - Defining all the Layer 1, 2, and 3 devices, along with the LAN and WAN topology
  - Documenting the physical and logical network implementation

Washington School District Project Task: LAN Design

In this chapter, you learned concepts that help you begin the design process for the Washington School District network. As part of the LAN design process, you need to complete the following tasks:

1. Gather all information required to design a LAN for your group's assigned site in the Washington School District, starting with the TCS Overview but doing additional research as needed.

2. Design the LAN for your school based on the requirements gathered in Step 1, in the context of developing an overall IP addressing scheme for the school district. First, each group will separately develop an IP addressing scheme for the entire school district. This can be done a variety of ways, and diversity is encouraged so the class thinks through the pros and cons of different IP addressing schemes. Some ideas to consider are Class A, B, and C networks with proper subnetting; Network Address Translation (NAT); and private network numbers. Each group will present their IP addressing scheme and the class will agree on the best implementation. The class will elect this one group as the Network Operations Center (NOC) contact who will control the distribution of all IP addresses. After the NOC distributes IP address blocks to school sites, the

individual school site groups can assign static and dynamic IP addresses within their individual LANs.

3. Develop and document an overall LAN design based on the user and district requirements. To properly design your site's LAN, complete these tasks:

■ A user requirements document (your interpretation and proposal of what is meant by the TCS Overview, the District and site needs, and your instructor's assignments)

■ An overall design document, which includes a logical LAN design (logical topology) of the school and a complete physical design (physical topology) that includes:

— Details of all MDFs/IDFs in the rooms, including a to-scale diagram

— The number of HCCs, VCCs, and LAN switch ports required to meet the existing and projected growth needs

■ LAN Electronics List: what devices (hubs, switches, routers, servers, others) are needed

■ Specifications on the type and quantity of cable media for all horizontal and vertical runs

■ Specifications on security, VLANs, and the separation of staff and student networks

■ The overall district IP addressing scheme and how it is applied at the local school site

■ An analysis of the pros and cons of the proposed LAN design

4. Apply the CCNA Certification Exam Learning Objectives to your specific design. This will require a paragraph on how the learning objectives relate to your design. Learning objectives can be grouped together for the purpose of explanation. In this way, you will be studying for the CCNA Certification Exam as you work through the case study.

CCNA Certification Exam Learning Objectives

OSI Model

■ Identify and describe the functions of each of the seven layers of the OSI reference model.***

■ Describe the different classes of IP addresses [and subnetting].***

■ Define and explain the 5 conversion steps of data encapsulation.***

NOTE

*** are explicit CCNA Exam objectives; unmarked are knowledge assumed by the exam.

Addressing

- Define and describe the function of a MAC address.
- Describe data link addresses and network addresses, and identify the key differences between them.***
- Identify the functions of the TCP/IP transport-layer protocols.***
- Identify the functions of the TCP/IP network-layer protocols.***
- Describe the different classes of IP addresses [and subnetting].***

Ethernet

- Describe the network congestion problem in Ethernet networks.***
- Describe full- and half-duplex Ethernet operation.***
- Describe the features and benefits of Fast Ethernet.***
- Describe the guidelines and distance limitations of Fast Ethernet.***

Segmentation

- Describe LAN segmentation using bridges.***
- Describe LAN segmentation using routers.***
- Describe LAN segmentation using switches.***
- Describe the benefits of network segmentation with bridges.***
- Describe the benefits of network segmentation with routers.***
- Describe the benefits of network segmentation with switches.***

LAN Switching

- Name and describe two switching methods.***
- Distinguish between cut-through and store-and-forward LAN switching.***
- Describe the benefits of virtual LANs.***

Flow Control

- Define flow control and describe the three basic methods used in networking.***

Check Your Understanding

Complete all the review questions to test your understanding of the topics and concepts covered in this chapter. Answers are listed in Appendix B, "Check Your Understanding Answer Key."

1. What are the four main goals of any network design?

2. What is the purpose of Layer 2 devices in a network design?

3. What is the purpose of Layer 3 devices in a network design?

4. What are the two major categories of servers that you should consider in a network design, and what are their purposes?

5. What are the main aspects of a network that should be documented and why?

6. Which of the following is likely to cause congestion?

   A. Internet access

   B. Central database access

   C. Video and image transmission

   D. All of the above

7. Which of the following is *not* a cause of excessive broadcasts?

   A. Too many client packets looking for services

   B. Too many server packets announcing services

   C. Too many routing table updates

   D. Too many network segments

8. A primary data link layer design goal is the selection of _____ devices, such as bridges or LAN switches, used to connect _____ media to form LAN segments.

   A. Layer 3; Layer 2

   B. Layer 1; Layer 2

   C. Layer 2; Layer 1

   D. Layer 2; Layer 3

9. Which of the following specifications for 10BaseT is wrong?

   A. Data rate = 10 Mbps

   B. Max length = 400 meters

   C. Signaling method = baseband

   D. Media = Category 5 UTP

10. Which of the following are benefits of implementing Layer 3 devices in your LAN:

    A. Allows segmentation of the LAN into unique physical and logical networks

    B. Filters data-link broadcasts and multicasts and allows for WAN connectivity

    C. Provides logical structure to the network

    D. All of the above

11. Match the following terms with their definitions:

    1. Functionality

    2. Scalability

    3. Adaptability

    4. Manageability

    5. Networks should facilitate monitoring

    6. Network must be able to grow without major changes to overall design

    7. Network must be able to incorporate new technologies

    8. Network must provide user-to-user application conectivity with reasonable speed and reliability.

    A. 1 and 8; 2 and 6; 3 and 7; 4 and 5

    B. 1 and 8; 2 and 7; 3 and 6; 4 and 5

    C. 1 and 8; 2 and 7; 3 and 5; 4 and 6

    D. 1 and 5; 2 and 6; 3 and 7; 4 and 8

12. What type of switching occurs when connecting to devices of unlike bandwidth? (Choose two.)

    A. Prometric

    B. Symmetric

    C. Asymmetric

    D. Full-duplex

13. What similar effect(s) will both the router and switch have on a LAN segment?

    A. Reduction of broadcasts

    B. Reduction of collision domains

    C. Increased bandwidth

    D. Both B and C

14. What device provides logical segmentation of a LAN?

    A. Router

    B. Bridge

    C. Switch

    D. Hub

15. In what two ways does a router segment a LAN?

    A. Reduces the broadcast domain

    B. Creates more logical segments

    C. Reduces bandwidth

    D. Both A and B

16. Which of the following is *not* a benefit of implementing Layer 3 devices in your LAN?

    A. Allows segmentation of the LAN into unique physical and logical networks

    B. Allows for WAN connectivity

    C. Provides logical structure to the network

    D. Increases the size of the LAN

17. Which of the following is an example of an enterprise server?

    A. CAD server at a large company

    B. DNS server for a school district

    C. Administrative records (grades and transcripts) server at a school

    D. Payroll and accounting server

18. Microsegmentation with switches will

  A. Create additional broadcast domains

  B. Decrease network segments

  C. Create additional collision domains

  D. Both A and C

19. If an increasing number of broadcasts are causing network congestion, which of the following could be a solution?

  A. A bridge

  B. A router

  C. A switch configured with VLANs

  D. Both B and C

20. An introduction of a switch will create which of the following?

  A. An additional broadcast domain

  B. An additional collision domain

  C. An additional network segment

  D. All of the above

Key Terms

10BaseT   A 10-Mbps baseband Ethernet specification using two pairs of twisted-pair cabling (Category 3, 4, or 5): one pair for transmitting data and the other for receiving data. 10BaseT, which is part of the IEEE 802.3 specification, has a distance limit of approximately 100 meters per segment.

100BaseFX   A 100-Mbps baseband Fast Ethernet specification using two strands of multimode fiber-optic cable per link. To guarantee proper signal timing, a 100BaseFX link cannot exceed 400 meters in length. Based on the IEEE 802.3 standard.

100BaseTX   A 100-Mbps baseband Fast Ethernet specification using two pairs of either UTP or STP wiring. The first pair of wires is used to receive data; the second is used to transmit. To guarantee proper signal timing, a 100BaseTX segment cannot exceed 100 meters in length. Based on the IEEE 802.3 standard.

asymmetric switching   A type of switching that provides switched connections between ports of unlike bandwidth, such as a combination of 10-Mbps and 100-Mbps ports.

ATM (Asynchronous Transfer Mode)   An international standard for cell relay in which multiple service types (such as voice, video, or data) are conveyed in fixed-length (53-byte) cells. Fixed-length cells allow cell processing to occur in hardware, thereby reducing transit delays. ATM is designed to take advantage of high-speed transmission media, such as E3, SONET, and T3.

backbone cabling   Cabling that provides interconnections between wiring closets, between wiring closets and the POP, and between buildings that are part of the same LAN.

broadcast domain   The set of all devices that will receive broadcast frames originating from any device within the set. Broadcast domains are typically bounded by routers because routers do not forward broadcast frames.

catchment area   A zone that falls within an area that can be served by an internetworking device such as a hub.

Category 5 cabling   One of five grades of UTP cabling described in the EIA/TIA 568B standard. Category 5 cabling can transmit data at speeds up to 100 Mbps.

contention   An access method in which network devices compete for permission to access the physical medium.

EIA/TIA 568   A standard that describes the characteristics and applications for various grades of UTP cabling.

encapsulate   To wrap data in a particular protocol header. For example, Ethernet data is wrapped in a specific Ethernet header before network transit. Also, when bridging dissimilar networks, the entire frame from one network simply is placed in the header used by the data link layer protocol of the other network.

enterprise server   A server that supports all the users on a network by offering services such as e-mail or Domain Name System (DNS).

Ethernet   A baseband LAN specification invented by Xerox Corporation and developed jointly by Xerox, Intel, and Digital Equipment Corporation. Ethernet networks use CSMA/CD and run over a variety of cable types at 10 Mbps. Ethernet is similar to the IEEE 802.3 series of standards.

Fast Ethernet   Any of a number of 100-Mbps Ethernet specifications. Fast Ethernet offers a speed increase ten times that of the 10BaseT Ethernet specification, while preserving such qualities as frame format, MAC mechanisms, and MTU. Such similarities allow the use of existing 10BaseT applications and network management tools on Fast Ethernet networks. Based on an extension to the IEEE 802.3 specification.

fiber-optic cable   A physical medium capable of conducting modulated light transmission. Compared with other transmission media, fiber-optic cable is more expensive but is not susceptible to electromagnetic interference, and it is capable of higher data rates. Sometimes called *optical fiber.*

flooding   A traffic-passing technique used by switches and bridges in which traffic received on an interface is sent out all the interfaces of that device except the interface on which the information was originally received.

HCC (horizontal cross-connect)   A wiring closet where the horizontal cabling connects to a patch panel that is connected by backbone cabling to the MDF.

header   Control information placed before data when encapsulating that data for network transmission.

IDF (intermediate distribution facility)   A secondary communications room for a building using a star networking topology. The IDF is dependent on the MDF.

intranet   An internal network that is to be accessed by users who have access to an organization's internal LAN.

LAN (local-area network)   A high-speed, low-error data network covering a relatively small geographic area (up to a few thousand meters). LANs connect workstations, peripherals, terminals, and other devices in a single building or other geographically limited area. LAN standards specify cabling and signaling at the physical and data link layers of the OSI model. Ethernet, FDDI, and Token Ring are widely used LAN technologies.

MDF (main distribution facility)   The primary communications room for a building. The central point of a star networking topology where patch panels, hub, and router are located.

media   Plural of *medium.* The various physical environments through which transmission signals pass. Common network media include twisted-pair, coaxial, fiber-optic cable, and the atmosphere (through which microwave, laser, and infrared transmission occurs). Sometimes called *physical media.*

network address   A network-layer address referring to a logical, rather than a physical, network device. Also called a *protocol address.*

protocol   A formal description of a set of rules and conventions that govern how devices on a network exchange information.

routing table   A table stored in a router or some other internetworking device that keeps track of routes to particular network destinations and, in some cases, metrics associated with those routes.

segmentation   The process of splitting a single collision domain into two or more collision domains in order to reduce collisions and network congestion.

star topology   A LAN topology in which endpoints on a network are connected to a common central switch by point-to-point links. A ring topology that is organized as a star implements a unidirectional closed-loop star, instead of point-to-point links.

unicast   A message sent to a single network destination.

UTP (unshielded twisted-pair)   A four-pair wire medium used in a variety of networks. UTP does not require the fixed spacing between connections that is necessary with coaxial-type connections. There are five types of UTP cabling commonly used: Category 1 cabling, Category 2 cabling, Category 3 cabling, Category 4 cabling, and Category 5 cabling.

VCC (vertical cross-connect)   A connection that is used to interconnect the various IDFs to the central MDF.

vertical cabling   *See* backbone cabling.

WAN (wide-area network)   A data communications network that serves users across a broad geographic area and often uses transmission devices provided by common carriers. Frame Relay, SMDS, and X.25 are examples of WAN technologies.

workgroup server   A server that supports a specific set of users and offers services, such as word processing and file sharing, which are services that only a few groups of people would need.

After reading this chapter, you will be able to

- Describe the routing functions of the network layer and how these functions relate to path determination in a router
- Describe routed and routing protocols
- Describe interior and exterior protocols
- Describe routing protocol characteristics and configuration
- Describe IGRP features, operation, and configuration tasks

Chapter 5

Routing Protocols: IGRP

Introduction

In Chapter 4, "LAN Design," you learned about LAN design goals and methodology. In addition, you learned about design considerations related to Layers 1, 2, and 3 of the Open System Interconnection (OSI) reference model. Reliability, connectivity, ease of use, ease of modification, and ease of implementation are other issues that need to be considered in building networks:

- To be reliable, a network must provide a means for error detection as well as the capability to correct the error.

- To provide connectivity, a network must be able to incorporate a variety of hardware and software products in such a way that they can function together.

- To be easy to use, a network must perform in such a way that users need to have no concern for or knowledge of the network's structure or implementation.

- To be easy to modify, a network must allow itself to evolve and adapt as needs change or expand, or as new technologies emerge.

- Finally, to be easy to implement, a network must follow industry-wide networking standards, and it must allow for a variety of configurations that meet network users' needs.

In this chapter, you learn how the use of routers can help you address these issues. In addition, this chapter discusses how routers can be used to connect two or more networks and how they are used to pass data packets between networks based on network protocol information. You also learn that a router can have more than one Internet Protocol (IP) address because it is attached to more than one network. As you learned in *Cisco Systems Networking Academy: First-Year Companion Guide*, Second Edition, an important function of routers is to examine incoming data packets and make path selections based on information stored in their routing tables. In this chapter, you learn more about how routers operate and what kinds of protocols they use. Finally, this chapter describes routing and IP routing protocols and discusses Cisco's proprietary implementation of *Interior Gateway Routing Protocol (IGRP)*.

Washington Project: Routing Protocols and Implementing IGRP
The concepts covered in this chapter will help you understand routing protocols. Routing protocols, such as IGRP, route routed (routable) protocols, such as IP and IPX, through a network. This chapter will help you apply IGRP to the network design you have been creating for the Washington School District project. In addition, you will learn how to implement IGRP and all the IGRP-required configurations needed for the network implementations.

MOVIE 5.1
Router Function
Sending data packets.

Network-Layer Basics

As you have learned, the network layer interfaces to networks and provides the best effort end-to-end packet delivery services to its user, the transport layer. The network layer sends packets from the source network to the destination network. To send packets from the source to the destination, path determination needs to occur at the network layer. This function is usually the responsibility of the router.

Network-Layer Path Determination

The *path determination* function enables a router to evaluate the available paths to a destination and to establish the best path for routing a packet. *Routing* refers to the process of choosing the best path over which to send packets and how to cross multiple physical networks. This is the basis of all Internet communication. Most routing protocols simply use the shortest and best path, but they use different methods to find the shortest and best path. The sections that follow explain some of the ways routing protocols find the shortest and best paths.

MOVIE 5.2
Path Switching
The network layer finds a path to the destination.

Packet routing in a network is similar to traveling by car. Routers, through the use of protocols, make path decisions based on routing tables, and people driving cars determine their paths examining maps, analyzing road conditions, and reading road signs.

Routing Tables

In IP networks, the router forwards packets from the source network to the destination network based on the IP routing table. After the router determines which path to use, it can proceed with switching the packet. This means it accepts the packet on one interface and forwards it to another interface that is the next *hop* on the best path to the packet's destination. This is why routing protocols are so important because each router that handles the packet must know what to do with the packet.

Routing tables store information about possible destinations and how to reach each of the destinations. Routing tables need to store only the network portion of IP addresses for routing. This keeps the tables small and efficient.

MOVIE 5.3

IP Routing Table

Destination network address and next-hop pairs.

Entries in the routing tables contain an IP address of the next hop along the route to the destination. Each entry specifies only one hop and points to a router that is directly connected, which means that it can be reached across a single network.

Routing protocols fill routing tables with a variety of information. For example, a router uses the destination/next-hop routing table when it receives an incoming packet. The router uses its routing table to check the destination address and attempts to associate the address with a next hop. A destination/next-hop routing table tells a router that a particular destination can be best reached by sending the packet to a particular router that represents the next hop on the way to the final destination.

Routers must communicate with each other in order to build tables through the use of routing protocols and through the transmission of a variety of messages. The routing update message is one such message. Routing updates generally consist of all or a portion of a routing table. By analyzing routing updates from all routers, a router can build a detailed picture of network topology. When routers understand the network topology, they can determine the best routes to network destinations.

Representing Distance with Metrics

It is important that a routing table be up-to-date because its primary purpose is to provide the best information for the router. Each routing protocol interprets the *best path* in its own way. The protocol generates a value, called the *metric*, for each path through the network. Typically, the smaller the metric, the better the path. Routing tables can also contain information about the desirability of a path. Routers compare metrics to determine the best routes. Metrics differ depending on the design of the routing protocol being used. Several common metrics are described later in this chapter.

A variety of metrics can be used to define the best path. Some routing protocols, such as Routing Information Protocol (RIP), use only one metric, and some routing protocols, such as IGRP, use a combination of metrics. The metrics most commonly used by routers are shown in Table 5-1.

TABLE 5-1   Commonly Used Metrics

Metric Type	Description
Hop count	The number of routers a packet must go through to reach a destination. The lower the hop count, the better the path. Path length is used to indicate the sum of the hops to a destination.
Bandwidth	The data capacity of a link.
Delay	The length of time required to move a packet from end to end on the network.
Load	The amount of utilization of a link.
Reliability	The error rate of each network link.
Ticks	The delay on a data link using IBM PC clock ticks (approximately 55 milliseconds).
Cost	The arbitrary value, usually based on bandwidth, dollar expense, or other measurement, that is assigned by a network administrator.

The Network-Layer Communication Path

After examining a packet's destination protocol address, the router determines that it either knows or does not know how to forward the packet to the next hop. If the router does not know how to forward the packet and there is no default route, it typically drops the packet. If the router knows how to forward the packet, it changes the destination physical address (MAC address) to that of the next hop and transmits the packet.

The next hop may not be directly connected to the ultimate destination host. If it is not directly connected to the ultimate destination, the next hop is usually another router, which executes the same routing decision process as the previous router. This process is illustrated in Figure 5-1.

FIGURE 5-1
As a packet moves through the network, its physical address changes, but its protocol address remains constant.

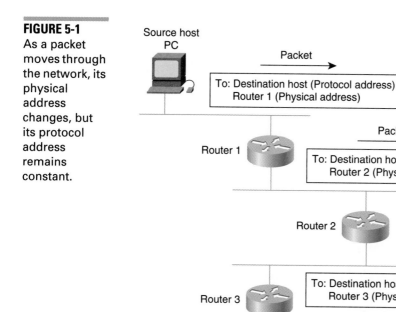

Addressing: The Network and the Host

The network address consists of a network portion and a host portion; the network portion is used by the router within the network cloud. To see whether the destination is on the same physical network, the network portion of the destination IP address is extracted and compared with the source's network address.

When a packet traverses a network, the source and destination IP addresses are never changed. A physical address is determined by the IP routing protocol and software and is known as the *next-hop address*.

The network portion of the IP address is used to make path selections. A router is responsible for passing the packet to the next network along the path.

The switching function allows a router to accept a packet on one interface and forward it on a second interface. The path determination function enables the router to select the most appropriate interface for forwarding a packet.

Routed Versus Routing Protocols

Confusion about the terms *routed protocol* and *routing protocol* is common. *Routed protocols* are protocols that are moved over a network. Examples of such protocols are Transmission Control Protocol/Internet Protocol (TCP/IP) and Internetwork Packet Exchange (IPX). *Routing protocols* route routed protocols through a network. Examples of these protocols include IGRP, Enhanced IGRP, Open Shortest Path First (OSPF), Exterior Gateway Protocol (EGP), *Border Gateway Protocol (BGP)*, OSI routing, Advanced Peer-to-Peer Networking (APPN), Intermediate System-to-Intermediate System (IS-IS), and RIP. Put simply, computers (or *end systems*) use routed protocols, such as IP, to "talk to each other," whereas routers (or *intermediate systems*) use routing protocols to "talk to each other" about networks and paths.

Multiprotocol Routing

Routers are capable of *multiprotocol routing*, which means they support multiple independent routing protocols, such as IGRP and RIP. This capability allows a router to deliver packets from several routed protocols, such as TCP/IP and IPX, over the same data links.

SKILL BUILDER

Routed and Routing Protocols

This lab reinforces your knowledge and understanding of routed and routing protocols, the primary protocols that enable a router to function. You review examples of each type of protocol and use various IOS commands at the router to discover which routed and routing protocols are currently running or are active on the router.

e-LAB ACTIVITY 5.1

Routed and Routing Protocols

In this activity, you work through several tasks to discover which routed and routing protocols are currently running or active on a the router.

Washington Project: Multiprotocol Routing
Based on user requirements, the Washington School District network needs to handle multiprotocol routing. The district requires that both TCP/IP and IPX routing protocols be handled over the network.

IP Routing Protocols

Routing is the process of determining where to send data packets destined for addresses outside the local network. Routers gather and maintain routing information to enable the transmission and receipt of such data packets. Routing information takes the form of entries in a routing table, with one entry for each identified route. Routing protocols allow a router to create and maintain routing tables dynamically and to adjust to network changes as they occur.

MOVIE 5.4
Route Processor
Using routing protocols to determine optimum paths.

Routing protocols can be differentiated from one another based on several key characteristics:

- First, the particular goals of the protocol designer affect the operation of the resulting routing protocol.
- Second, there are various types of routing protocols. Each protocol has a different effect on network and router resources.
- Third, as discussed earlier in this chapter, routing protocols use a variety of metrics to identify the best routes.

Routing protocols are broadly divided into two classes: interior protocols and exterior protocols. *Interior protocols* are used for routing information within networks that are under a common network administration. All IP interior protocols must be specified with a list of associated networks before routing activities can begin. A routing process listens to updates from other routers on these networks and broadcasts its own routing information on those same networks. The interior protocols Cisco supports include RIP and IGRP.

Exterior protocols are used to exchange routing information between networks that do not share a common administration. Exterior routing protocols include EGP and BGP. Exterior routing protocols require the following information before routing can begin:

- A list of neighbor (also called peers) routers with which to exchange routing information
- A list of networks to advertise as directly reachable

The following sections discuss routing protocol characteristics in more detail.

Washington Project: IGRP Design Goals

Throughout the rest of the chapter, you learn the concepts and configuration techniques to help address the following design goals for IGRP implementation in the Washington School District network:

- The network should use stable routing, and no routing loops should occur.
- The network should quickly respond to changes in the network topology.
- The network should have low overhead, and IGRP itself should not use more bandwidth than is actually needed for its task.
- The network design should take into account error rates and level of traffic on different paths.

The Optimal Route

Optimal route refers to the ability of the routing protocol to select the best route. The best route depends on the metrics and metric weightings used to make the calculation. For example, one routing protocol might use the number of hops and the delay, but might weigh the delay more heavily in the calculation.

Simplicity and Efficiency

Routing protocols are also designed to be as simple and efficient as possible. Efficiency is particularly important when the software implementing the routing protocol must run on a device with limited physical resources.

Robustness

Routing protocols must be robust. In other words, they should perform correctly in the face of unusual or unforeseen circumstances, such as hardware failures, high load conditions, and incorrect implementations. Because routers are located at network junction points, they can cause considerable problems when they fail. The best routing protocols are often those that have withstood the test of time and proven stable under a variety of network conditions.

Rapid Convergence

Routing protocols must converge rapidly. *Convergence* is the speed and ability of a group of networking devices running a specific routing protocol to agree on the topology of a network after a change in that topology. When a network event, such as a change in a network's topology, causes routes to either go down or become available, routers distribute routing update messages. Routing update messages are sent to routers, thereby causing the recalculation of optimal routes and eventually causing all routers to agree on these routes. Routing protocols that converge slowly can cause routing loops or network outages.

Figure 5-2 shows a routing loop. In this case, a packet arrives at Router 1 at Time T1. Router 1 has already been updated and knows that the best route to the destination calls for Router 2 to be the next stop. Router 1 therefore forwards the packet to Router 2. Router 2 has not yet been updated and believes that the best next hop is Router 1. Therefore, Router 2 forwards the packet back to Router 1. The packet will continue to bounce back and forth between the two routers until Router 2 receives its routing update or until the packet has been switched the maximum number of times allowed. Different routing protocols have different maximums; the network administrator usually can define lower maximums. For example, IGRP has a maximum hop count of 255, it defaults to 100, and it is usually set to 50 or less.

FIGURE 5-2
Routing loops occur until the routing update has occurred or until the packet has been switched the maximum number of times allowed.

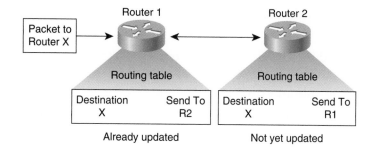

Flexibility

Routing protocols should also be flexible. In other words, they should quickly and accurately adapt to a variety of network circumstances. For example, assume that a network segment has gone down. Many routing protocols quickly select the next-best path for all routes that normally use a given segment. Routing protocols can be programmed to adapt to changes in network bandwidth, router queue size, network delay, and other variables.

Static Routing

Static routing protocols are hardly protocols at all. Before routing begins, the network administrator establishes static routing table mappings. These mappings do not change unless the network administrator changes them. Protocols that use static routes are simple to design and work well in environments where network traffic is predictable and network design is simple.

Because static routing systems cannot react to network changes, they are generally considered unsuitable for today's large, constantly changing networks. These networks require dynamic routing protocols.

Dynamic Routing

Dynamic routing protocols adjust to changing network circumstances. They do this by analyzing incoming routing update messages. If a message indicates that a network change has occurred, the routing software recalculates routes and sends out new routing update messages. These messages permeate the network, prompting routers to recalculate their routing tables accordingly.

Dynamic routing protocols can be supplemented with static routes where appropriate. For example, a *gateway of last resort* (that is, a router to which all unroutable packets are sent) may be designated. This router acts as a central storing place for all unroutable packets, ensuring that all messages are at least handled in some way.

Routing Approaches

As you learned, most routing protocols can be classified into three basic approaches:

- The distance-vector routing approach determines the direction (vector) and distance to any link in the network. Examples of distance-vector routing protocols are IGRP and RIP.

- The link-state (also called shortest path first) approach re-creates the exact topology of the entire network (or at least the partition in which the router is situated). Examples of link-state routing protocols are OSPF, IS-IS, and NetWare Link Services Protocol (NLSP).

- The hybrid approach combines aspects of the link-state and distance-vector approaches. An example of a hybrid routing approach is Enhanced IGRP.

IP Routing Configuration

Each routing protocol must be configured separately. With any routing protocol, you must follow two basic steps:

1. Create the routing process with one of the router commands.

2. Configure the protocol specifics.

As you learned earlier, the interior protocols such as IGRP and RIP must have a list of networks specified before routing activities can begin. In addition, you learned that the routing process listens to updates from other routers on these networks and broadcasts its own routing information on those same networks. IGRP has the additional requirement of an autonomous system (AS) number.

Washington Project: AS Numbers
AS number consistency is a design issue. You need to have the same number throughout the Washington School District network. The AS is assigned a 16-bit number by the Internet Assigned Numbers Authority.

With any of the IP routing protocols, you need to create the routing process, associate networks with the routing process, and customize the routing protocol for your particular network. Choosing a routing protocol is a complex task. When choosing a routing protocol, you should consider the following:

- Network size and complexity
- Network traffic levels
- Security needs
- Reliability needs
- Network delay characteristics
- Organizational policies
- Organizational acceptance of change

Understanding IGRP Operation

IGRP is a Cisco proprietary protocol that was developed to supercede RIP. IGRP is a distance-vector interior routing protocol. Distance-vector routing protocols call for each router to send all or a portion of its routing table in a routing update message at regular intervals to each of its neighboring routers. As routing information spreads throughout the network, routers can calculate distances to all nodes within the network.

IGRP uses a combination of metrics. Network delay, bandwidth, reliability, and load are all factored into the routing decision. Network administrators can determine the settings for each of these metrics. IGRP uses either the settings determined by the administrator or the default settings of bandwidth and delay to automatically calculate best routes.

MOVIE 5.5
IGRP
Multipath routing.

IGRP provides a wide range for its metrics. For example, reliability and load can have any value between 1 and 255; bandwidth can have values reflecting speeds from 1200 bps to 10 Gbps; and delay can have any value from 1 to 2^{24}. Wide metric ranges allow an adequate metric setting in networks with widely varying performance characteristics. As a result, network administrators can influence route selection in an intuitive fashion. This is accomplished by weighting each of the four metrics—that is, telling the router how much to value a particular metric. The default values related to the weightings for IGRP give the most importance to bandwidth, which makes IGRP superior to RIP. In contrast, RIP does not weigh metrics because it only uses one—hop count.

Interior, System, and Exterior IGRP Routes

Cisco's primary goal in creating IGRP was to provide a robust protocol for routing within an *autonomous system (AS)*. An AS is a collection of networks under common administration sharing a common routing strategy, as shown in Figure 5-3.

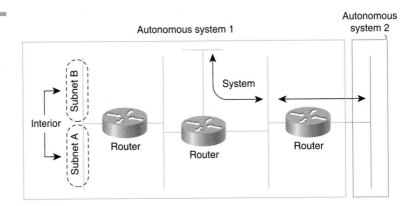

FIGURE 5-3
Autonomous systems are subdivided by areas.

IGRP uses a combination of user-configurable metrics, including network delay, bandwidth, reliability, and load. IGRP advertises three types of routes: interior, system, and exterior (as shown in Figure 5-3). *Interior routes* are routes between subnets in the network attached to a router interface. If the network attached to a router is not subnetted, IGRP does not advertise interior routes. Additionally, subnet information is not included in IGRP updates, which poses a problem for discontiguous IP subnets or Variable Length Subnet Masking (VLSM)-based networks.

System routes are routes to other major networks within the AS. The router derives system routes from directly connected network interfaces and system route information provided by other routers that use IGRP. System routes do not include subnetting information.

Exterior routes are routes to networks outside the AS that are considered when identifying a gateway of last resort. The router chooses a gateway of last resort from the list of exterior routes that IGRP provides. The router uses the gateway of last resort if it does not have a better route for a packet and the destination is not a connected network. If the AS has more than one connection to an external network, different routers can choose different exterior routers as the gateway of last resort.

Creating the IGRP Routing Process

To configure IGRP, you need to create the IGRP routing process. The router commands needed to implement IGRP on a router are explained in this section. This section also describes the processes the routers go through to ensure that the neighbor routers are aware of the status of all networks in the AS. These status reports include the frequency with which routing table updates are sent and the effects of the updates on bandwidth utilization.

SKILL BUILDER

Migrating RIP to IGRP

In this lab, you work with two dynamic interior routing protocols: Router Information Protocol (RIP) and Interior Gateway Routing Protocol (IGRP).

e-LAB ACTIVITY 5.2

Migrating RIP to IGRP

In this activity, you work through several tasks for migrating from RIP to IGRP.

Engineering Journal: Configuring IGRP

To create the IGRP routing process, you need to perform the tasks described here, starting in global configuration mode.

Enable an IGRP routing process by using the command **router igrp**, which places you in router configuration mode. The full syntax of this command is as follows:

router igrp *autonomous-system*

The argument *autonomous-system* identifies the routes to other IGRP routers and is used to tag the routing information passed along. When an IGRP routing process is configured, an AS number must be specified. This number may or may not be assigned. The AS number is used to tag updates

continues

belonging to one of up to four IGRP routing processes. You use the **no router igrp** command to shut down the routing process on the AS specified by the *autonomous-system* argument:

no router igrp *autonomous-system*

You associate networks with an IGRP routing process by using the command **network**. The full syntax of this command is as follows:

network *network-number*

The argument *network-number* is a network number in dotted-decimal IP notation. Note that this number must not contain subnet information. You can specify multiple **network** commands.

You use the **no network** command with the network number to remove a network from the list:

no network *network-number*

In the following example, a router is configured for IGRP and assigned to AS 109. In the last two lines, two network commands assign the two networks to a list of networks to receive IGRP updates:

```
Router(config)# router igrp 109
network 131.108.0.0
network 192.31.7.0
```

IGRP sends updates to the interfaces in the specified networks. If an interface's network is not specified, it is not advertised in any IGRP updates.

e-LAB ACTIVITY 5.3

router igrp

In this activity, you demonstrate how to use the **router igrp** command to select RIP as the routing protocol.

Enhancing IGRP Stability

IGRP provides a number of features that are designed to enhance its stability, including the following:

- Holddowns
- Split horizons
- Poison reverse updates

These features are described in the following sections.

Holddowns

When a router learns that a network is further away than was previously known or when it learns that the network is down, the route to that network is placed into *holddown*. During the holddown period, the route is advertised, but incoming advertisements about that network from any router other than the one that originally advertised the network's new metric are ignored. This mechanism is often used to help avoid routing loops in the network, but has the effect of increasing the topology convergence time.

Holddowns are used to prevent regular update messages from reinstating a route that may have gone bad. When a router goes down, neighboring routers detect this via the lack of regularly scheduled update messages. These routers then calculate new routes and send routing update messages to inform their neighbors of the route change. This activity begins a wave of triggered updates that filter through the network. These triggered updates do not instantly arrive at every network device. It is therefore possible for Device A, which has not yet been informed of a network failure, to send a regular update message (indicating that a route that has just gone down is still good) to Device B, which has just been notified of the network failure. In this case, Device B would now contain (and potentially advertise) incorrect routing information.

Holddowns tell routers to hold down any changes that might affect routes for some period of time. The holddown period is usually calculated to be just greater than the period of time necessary to update the entire network with a routing change. This can prevent routing loops caused by slow convergence.

Split Horizons

A *split horizon* occurs when a router tries to send information about a route back in the direction from which it came. For example, consider Figure 5-4. Router 1 initially advertises that it has a route to Network A. As a result, there is no reason for Router 2 to include this route back to Router 1 because Router 1 is closer to Network A. The split-horizon rule says that Router 2 should strike this route from any updates it sends to Router 1.

FIGURE 5-4
Because Router 1 is closer to Network A, Router 2 should strike updates to Router 1 about its route to Network 2.

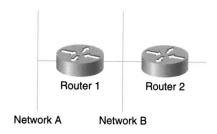

Router 1   Router 2

Network A   Network B

The split-horizon rule helps prevent routing loops. For example, consider the case where Router 1's interface to Network A goes down. Without split horizons, Router 2 continues to inform Router 1 that it can get to Network A (through Router 1). If Router 1 does not have sufficient intelligence, it might actually pick up Router 2's route as an alternative to its failed direct connection, causing a routing loop. Although holddowns should prevent this, split horizons are implemented in IGRP because they provide extra protocol stability.

Poison Reverse Updates

Whereas split horizons should prevent routing loops between adjacent routers, *poison reverse updates* are intended to defeat larger routing loops. Increases in routing metrics generally indicate routing loops. Poison reverse updates are then sent to remove the route and place it in holddown. A router poisons the route by sending an update with a metric of infinity to a router that originally advertised a route to a network. Poisoning the route can help speed convergence.

Engineering Journal:
The timers basic and
no metric holddown Commands

The following are descriptions of the timers basic and no metric holddown commands used to help you control routing updates.

The timers basic Command

The **timers basic** command lets you control how often IGRP sends updates. The default is once every 90 seconds. In order to allow for dropped packets, IGRP can't time out expired routes until several minutes have elapsed. When IGRP removes a route, it can't adopt a new one for several more minutes because of holddown.

The first thing to do is to speed up the time constants. Use 15 seconds instead of 90 for the basic time constant. This allows routes to expire after 45 seconds. All the other times decrease proportionally.

Actually, the expiration time turns out not to be as important as you might expect. Normally, routes don't just expire. They are killed because a keepalive fails on some interface. Keepalives normally occur every 10 seconds, so it takes 30 seconds to detect an interface down that way. You should use a keepalive of 4 on T1 lines where you care about speed of routing adjustment. This lets you detect a failure in 12 seconds.

The no metric holddown Command

The other critical parameter to change in order to accept a new route is **no metric holddown**. This disables holddowns, meaning that after a route has been removed, a new one is accepted immediately. There are good theoretical reasons for using holddowns. For example, there could be cases where, without holddowns, an old route can never get out of the system.

e-LAB ACTIVITY 5.4

timers basic

In this activity, you demonstrate how to use the **timers basic** command to control how often IGRP sends updates.

IGRP Metric Information

IGRP uses several types of metric information. For each path through an AS, IGRP records the segment with the lowest bandwidth, the accumulated delay, the smallest *maximum transmission unit (MTU)*, and the reliability and load.

Variables are used to weight each metric, and by default, bandwidth is given the most importance when calculating the best path. For a network of one medium (such as a network that uses all Ethernet), this metric reduces to a hop count. For a network of mixed media (for example, Ethernet and serial lines running from 9600 baud to T1 rates), the route with the lowest metric reflects the most desirable path to a destination.

IGRP Updates

A router running IGRP sends an IGRP update broadcast every 90 seconds. It declares a route inaccessible if it does not receive an update from the first router in the route within three update periods (270 seconds). After seven update periods (630 seconds), the router removes the route from the routing table. IGRP uses flash update and poison reverse to speed up the convergence of the routing protocol.

MOVIE 5.6

IGRP Update

Timer controls frequency of router update messages.

A *flash update* is the sending of an update sooner than the standard periodic update interval for notifying other routers of a metric change. Poison reverse updates are intended to defeat larger routing loops that are caused by increases in routing metrics. The poison reverse updates are sent to remove a route and place it in holddown, which keeps new routing information from being used for a certain period of time.

Maximum Hop Count

IGRP has a maximum hop count of 255, which is normally set lower than the default 100. Because IGRP uses triggered (flash) updates, counting to 100 may not take too long. However, you should set the maximum hop count to something smaller, unless you have an enormous network. It should be a number at least as large as the maximum number of routers a route might ever have to go through in the network. If you exchange IGRP routing with an external network, the hop count must include your network plus that external network. When you compute hop count, take into account what the configuration would look like if a few lines went down.

Here's a sample router statement that uses all the features explained in this section; you should use your own network number in place of 128.6.0.0:

```
Router(config)# router igrp 46
Router(config-router)# timers basic 15 45 0 60
Router(config-router)# network 128.6.0.0
Router(config-router)# no metric holddown
Router(config-router)# metric maximum-hop 50
```

With this statement, routing generally adapts to change within 45 seconds, assuming that the keepalive interval, which is the period of time between messages sent by a network device, has been set to 4.

SKILL BUILDER

Configuring IGRP

In this lab, you work with the Cisco Interior Gateway Routing Protocol (IGRP). Routing protocols are used by routers to communicate between themselves in order to exchange information about the networks they can reach and the desirability of the routes available.

SKILL BUILDER

Multi-Path

In a previous lab, you saw how to set up the RIP routing protocol on Cisco routers. In this lab, you configure the routers to use IGRP and see how IGRP uses metrics to select the best path.

SKILL BUILDER

NeoTrace and traceroute

In this lab, you use the shareware utility NeoTrace to determine the path that data travels through an Internetwork. In Semester 2, you completed a lab using the Cisco IOS traceroute command. NeoTrace uses graphics to depict the results of the **traceroute** command.

e-LAB ACTIVITY 5.5

Configuring IGRP

In this activity, you work through several tasks to configure IGRP.

Summary

- Network-layer routing functions include network addressing and best path selection for traffic.

- Routing tables store information on possible destinations and how to reach each of the destinations.

- Routed protocols are protocols that are routed over a network, and routing protocols are protocols that maintain routing tables between routers.

- Routing protocols can be either static or dynamic.

- Interior protocols are used for routing networks that are under a common network administration, and exterior protocols are used to exchange routing information between networks that do not share a common administration.

- IGRP is a distance-vector interior gateway protocol and uses a combination of user-configurable metrics including network delay, bandwidth, reliability, and load.

- The stability of IGRP is improved by using holddowns, split horizons, and poison reverse updates.

- To configure IGRP, you must follow two basic steps to create the IGRP routing process: Create the routing process with one of the router commands and configure the protocol specifics.

Washington School District Project Task: Routing Protocols and Configuring IGRP

In this chapter, you learned concepts and configuration processes that help you implement IGRP as the routing protocol in the Washington School District network. As part of the IGRP configuration and implementation, you need to complete the following tasks:

1. Identify and gather the information required to implement IGRP at the schools' networks and across the district network. Add the information you gather to the existing user requirements and LAN design.

NOTE

It is best to complete these activities in conjunction with an IGRP lab.

2. Identify and document the networks that will be advertised by the routers in the school district and add that information to the requirements and LAN design. Study and report on the effects of a dynamic routing protocol such as IGRP on the overall performance and maintenance of the entire school district network.

3. Identify and document the IGRP AS number for the school district.

4. Document the router command sequence needed to implement IGRP on the school's router and document the changes in the router configuration.

5. Describe the process that the routers go through to ensure that the neighbor routers are aware of the status of all networks in the AS. This will include the frequency with which routing table updates are sent and the effects of the updates on bandwidth utilization.

6. Identify the best settings for maximum hops, hold-down timer, update timer, and so on. Also, document appropriate bandwidth settings for serial interfaces.

7. Continue LAN design tasks: site wiring designs, LAN logical designs, typical MDF and IDF designs and electronics tables, and a site-specific LAN electronics list

8. Apply the CCNA Certification Exam Learning Objectives to your specific design. This will require a paragraph on how the learning objectives relate to your design. Learning objectives can be grouped together for the purpose of explanation. In this way, you will be studying for their CCNA Certification Exam as you work through the case study.

CCNA Certification Exam Learning Objectives

OSI Model

> **NOTE**
>
> *** are explicit CCNA objectives; unmarked are knowledge assumed by the exam.

- Describe the three major portions of an IP address.
- Describe the functions of the TCP/IP network-layer protocols and how they are used for path determination.

Routing Protocols

- Add the IGRP routing protocol to your configuration.
- Describe the function of a router in delivering data packets between different networks
- Describe the function and limitations of static route entries in a Router.

- Describe the functions and advantages of dynamic routing protocols.
- Describe the difference between routed and routing protocols.
- Describe the function of a routing table in the router.
- Describe what a routing metrics is and what the various components mean.
- Describe the difference between distance-vector and link-state routing protocols.
- Describe what convergence is in a network.
- Describe what an autonomous network is and what general type of protocol is used to communicate between autonomous networks.

Check Your Understanding

Complete all the review questions to test your understanding of the topics and concepts covered in this chapter. Answers are listed in Appendix B, "Check Your Understanding Answer Key."

1. At what layer of the OSI model does path determination take place and what is that layer's function?

2. How does a router determine on which interface to forward a data packet?

3. What does the term *multiprotocol routing* mean?

4. What two basic router factors does a dynamic routing protocol depend on?

5. What does the term *convergence* mean in network implementation?

6. After a router determines which path to use for a packet, it can then proceed with which of the following?

    A. A broadcast

    B. Storing the packet in a routing table

    C. Choosing a routing protocol

    D. Switching the packet

7. The success of dynamic routing depends on which of the following?

    A. Manually entering routes

    B. Maintaining a routing table

    C. Periodic routing updates

    D. B and C

8. _____ routing protocols determine the direction and distance to any link in the internetwork; _____ routing protocols are also called shortest path first.

    A. Distance-vector; link-state

    B. Distance-vector; hybrid

    C. Link-state; distance-vector

    D. Dynamic; static

9. Which of the following is *not* what a variable IGRP uses to determine a composite metric?

    A. Bandwidth.

    B. Delay.

    C. Load.

    D. IGRP uses all of these.

10. To select IGRP as a routing protocol, which command do you use?

    A. show igrp

    B. router network igrp

    C. enable igrp

    D. router igrp

11. IGRP is a _____ based protocol.

    A. Time

    B. Cost

    C. Distance-vector

    D. Link-state

12. What is one advantage of dynamic routing?

    A. Takes little network overhead and reduces network traffic

    B. Reduces unauthorized break-ins because security is tight

    C. Adjusts automatically to topology or traffic changes

    D. Requires little bandwidth to operate efficiently

13. IGRP does *not* use which of the following as part of the metric?

    A. Bandwith

    B. Delay

    C. Load

    D. Hop count

14. Which one of the following configuration commands should be configured to broadcast the network 10.1.1.0/24 using IGRP?

    A. RouterA#network 10.1.1.0

    B. RouterA(config-router)#network 10.1.1.0

    C. RouterA(config)#network 10.0.0.0

    D. RouterA(config-router)#network 10.0.0.0

15. To enable IGRP routing, you must type **router igrp**.

    A. True

    B. False

16. What is a valid metric for IGRP?

    A. Reliability

    B. Hop count

    C. MTU

    D. Both A and C

17. For routers to communicate IGRP without redistribution, they must be in the same _____.

    A. Autonomous system

    B. Interior gateway

    C. Exterior gateway

    D. Domain

18. Which of the following are true of administrative distance?

    A. Measures the distance to a destination network

    B. Only applies to IGRP and EIGRP

    C. Measures the "reliability" of an IP routing protocol

    D. The higher the value, the more important the routing information

19. What is the default route on an IP network? (Choose one.)

    A. This is the route that will be chosen first by IP for delivery of a datagram.

    B. The address of the nearest downstream neighbor in a Token Ring network.

    C. At the router, it is a route manually defined as the path to take when no route to the destination is known.

    D. Any dynamic route listing in a routing table.

20. Which of the following are true about this configuration line?

```
Router_A(config)#ip route 172.17.10.0 ... 255.255.255.0.172.16.10.1.255
```

A. If Router_A receives a packet with a destination IP subnet address of 172.17.10.0, the packet will be placed on the 172.16.10.0 wire.

B. If Router_A receives a packet with a destination IP subnet address of 172.17.10.0, the packet will be sent to 172.16.10.1 (if there is no dynamic entry in the routing table).

C. 255 is the administrative distance (AD).

D. Both B and C.

Key Terms

AS (autonomous system)   A collection of networks under common administration sharing a common routing strategy. Also referred to as a *routing domain*. The AS is assigned a 16-bit number by the Internet Assigned Numbers Authority.

bandwidth   The difference between the highest and lowest frequencies available for network signals. Also, the rated throughput capacity of a given network medium or protocol.

BGP (Border Gateway Protocol)   An interdomain routing protocol that replaces Exterior Gateway Protocol (EGP). BGP exchanges reachability information with other BGP systems and is defined by RFC 1163.

convergence   The speed and ability of a group of internetworking devices running a specific routing protocol to agree on the topology of an internetwork after a change in that topology.

cost   An arbitrary value, typically based on hop count, media bandwidth, or other measures, that is assigned by a network administrator and used to compare various paths through an internetwork environment. Cost values are used by routing protocols to determine the most favorable path to a particular destination: the lower the cost, the better the path.

delay   The time between the initiation of a transaction by a sender and the first response received by the sender. Also, the time required to move a packet from source to destination over a given path.

dynamic routing   Routing that adjusts automatically to network topology or traffic changes.

exterior protocol   A protocol that is used to exchange routing information between networks that do not share a common administration.

flash update   The process of the sending of an update sooner than the standard periodic update interval for notifying other routers of a metric change.

gateway of last resort   A router to which all unroutable packets are sent.

holddown   An IGRP feature that rejects new routes for the same destination for some period of time.

hop   The passage of a data packet between two network nodes (for example, between two routers).

hop count   A routing metric used to measure the distance between a source and a destination. RIP uses hop count as its sole metric.

interior protocol   A protocol that is used for routing networks that are under a common network administration.

IGRP (Interior Gateway Routing Protocol)   A protocol developed by Cisco to address the problems associated with routing in large, heterogeneous networks.

load   The amount of activity on a network resource, such as a router or link.

metric   A standard of measurement (for example, path length) that is used by routing protocols to determine the optimal path to a destination.

MTU (maximum transmission unit)   Maximum packet size, in bytes, that a particular interface can handle.

multiprotocol routing   Routing in which a router delivers packets from several routed protocols, such as TCP/IP and IPX, over the same data links.

next-hop address   The IP address that is computed by the IP routing protocol and software.

path determination   The decision of which path traffic should take through the network cloud. Path determination occurs at the network layer of the OSI reference model.

poison reverse update   An IGRP feature intended to defeat larger routing loops. Poison reverse updates explicitly indicate that a network or subnet is unreachable, rather than imply that a network is unreachable by not including it in updates.

reliability   The ratio of expected to received keepalives from a link. If the ratio is high, the line is reliable. Used as a routing metric.

routed protocol   A protocol that can be routed by a router. A router must be able to interpret the logical internetwork as specified by that routed protocol. Examples of routed protocols include AppleTalk, DECnet, and IP.

routing protocol   A protocol that accomplishes routing through the implementation of a specific routing protocol. Examples of routing protocols include IGRP, OSPF, and RIP.

split horizon   An IGRP feature designed to prevent routers from picking up erroneous routes. Split horizon prevents loops between adjacent routers and keeps down the size of update messages.

static routing   Routing that is explicitly configured and entered into the routing table. Static routes take precedence over routes chosen by dynamic routing protocols.

tick   The delay on a data link using IBM PC clock ticks (approximately 55 milliseconds). One tick is $\frac{1}{18}$ second.

Objectives

After reading this chapter, you will be able to

- Define and describe the purpose and operation of ACLs
- Explain the processes involved in testing packets with ACLs
- Describe ACL configuration commands, global statements, and interface commands
- Define and explain the function and operation of wildcard masks bits and the wildcards **any** and **host**
- Describe standard ACLs
- Describe extended ACLs
- Describe named ACLs
- Monitor and verify selected ACL operations on the router

Chapter 6

ACLs

Introduction

Network administrators must figure out how to deny unwanted access to the network while allowing appropriate access. Although security tools, such as passwords, callback equipment, and physical security devices are helpful, they often lack the flexibility of basic traffic filtering and the specific controls most administrators prefer. For example, a network administrator might want to allow users access to the Internet but might not want external users telnetting into the LAN.

Routers provide basic traffic filtering capabilities, such as blocking Internet traffic, with *access control lists (ACLs)*. An ACL is a sequential collection of **permit** or **deny** statements that apply to addresses or upper-layer protocols. In this chapter, you learn about using standard and extended ACLs as a means to control network traffic and how ACLs are used as part of a security solution.

In addition, this chapter includes tips, considerations, recommendations, and general guidelines on how to use ACLs, and includes the commands and configurations needed to create ACLs. Finally, this chapter provides examples of standard and extended ACLs and how to apply ACLs to router interfaces.

Washington School District Project: ACLs
In this chapter, you learn the concepts and configuration commands that will help you use and implement ACLs in the Washington School District network. In addition, as ACL concepts and commands are introduced, you will be able to apply ACLs to your school site design and implementation.

ACL Overview

ACLs are lists of instructions you apply to a router's interface. These lists tell the router what kinds of packets to accept and what kinds of packets to deny. Acceptance and denial can be based on certain specifications, such as source address, destination address, and port number.

ACLs enable you to manage traffic and scan specific packets by applying the ACL to a router interface. Any traffic going through the interface is tested against certain conditions that are part of the ACL.

ACLs can be created for all routed network protocols, such as Internet Protocol (IP) and Internetwork Packet Exchange (IPX), to filter packets as the packets pass through a router. ACLs can be configured at the router to control access to a network or subnet. For example, in the Washington School District, ACLs could be used to prevent student traffic from entering the administrative network.

ACLs filter network traffic by controlling whether routed packets are forwarded or blocked at the router's interfaces. The router examines each packet to determine whether to forward or drop it, based on the conditions specified in the ACL. ACL conditions could be the source address of the traffic, the destination address of the traffic, the upper-layer protocol, or other information.

ACLs must be defined on a per-protocol basis. In other words, you must define an ACL for every protocol enabled on an interface if you want to control traffic flow for that interface. (Note that some protocols refer to ACLs as *filters*.) For example, if your router interface were configured for IP, AppleTalk, and IPX, you would need to define at least three ACLs. As shown in Figure 6-1, ACLs can be used as a tool for network control by adding the flexibility to filter the packets that flow in or out of router interfaces.

FIGURE 6-1
Using ACLs, you can deny traffic based on packet tests, such as addressing or traffic type.

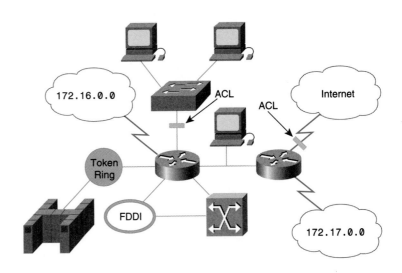

Washington Project: Security Requirements
The LAN design for all schools in the Washington School District requires that each school have two networks: one for curriculum and the other for administration. Each unique LAN segment should be connected to a separate Ethernet port on the router to service that LAN. Such routers exist; search www.cisco.com for more information. As part of the security solution, you need to devise an ACL for the local site access router that will deny users access from the curriculum LAN segment into the administrative LAN segment, yet continue to give the administrative LAN complete access to the curriculum LAN segment.
One exception to this ACL is that the router is to pass any *Domain Name System (DNS)* or e-mail traffic to the DNS/e-mail server, which is located on the administration LAN segment. This is traffic originating on the LAN that is accessed by the students. Therefore, if a student is surfing the Web and needs the DNS server to resolve host names, this ACL will allow for host name resolution. In addition, this ACL will allow students to send and receive e-mail.

Reasons to Create ACLs

There are many reasons to create ACLs. For example, ACLs can be used to

- Limit network traffic and increase network performance. For example, ACLs can designate certain packets to be processed by a router before other traffic, on the basis of a protocol. This is referred to as *queuing*, which ensures that routers will not process packets that are not needed. As a result, queuing limits network traffic and reduces network congestion.

- Provide traffic flow control. For example, ACLs can restrict or reduce the contents of routing updates. These restrictions are used to limit information about specific networks from propagating through the network.

- Provide a basic level of security for network access. For example, ACLs can allow one host to access a part of your network and prevent another host from accessing the same area. In Figure 6-2, Host A is allowed to access the Human Resources network, and Host B is prevented from accessing the Human Resources network. If you do not configure ACLs on your router, all packets passing through the router could be allowed onto all parts of the network.

- Decide which types of traffic are forwarded or blocked at the router interfaces. For example, you can permit e-mail traffic to be routed, but at the same time block all telnet traffic.

> ## Washington Project: Using ACLs
>
> When you use ACLs on the local site access routers, all traffic from the curriculum LANs should be prohibited on the administration LAN. You can make exceptions to this requirement by allowing applications, such as e-mail and directory services, to pass freely because they pose minimal risk.
>
> E-mail and DNS need to be available throughout the district, and these types of services should not allow any unauthorized access to the administration network. All the ACLs you create need to be controlled at the district office, and you need to review exceptions to the ACLs prior to implementation.

FIGURE 6-2
You can use ACLs to prevent traffic from being routed to a network.

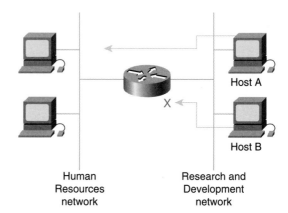

Human Resources network

Host A

Host B

Research and Development network

Creating an ACL in the Correct Order

The order in which you place ACL statements is important. When the router is deciding whether to forward or block a packet, the Cisco Internetwork Operating System (IOS) software tests the packet against each condition statement in the order in which the statements were created. After a match is found, no more condition statements are checked.

If you create a condition statement that permits all traffic, no statements added later will ever be checked. If you need additional statements in a standard or extended ACL, you must delete and re-create it with the new condition statements. This is why it's a good idea to edit a router configuration on a PC using a text editor and then send it to the router using Trivial File Transfer Protocol (TFTP).

NOTE

Each additional condition statement that you enter is added to the end of the ACL statements. Also, you cannot delete individual statements in numbered ACLs after they have been created. You can only delete an entire ACL.

Using ACLs

You can create an ACL for each protocol you want to filter for each router interface. For some protocols, you create one ACL to filter inbound traffic, and one ACL to filter outbound traffic.

After an ACL statement checks a packet for a match, the packet can be denied or permitted to use an interface in the access group. Cisco IOS ACLs check the packet and upper-layer headers, as shown in Figure 6-3.

FIGURE 6-3
ACLs check the
packet and
upper-layer
headers.

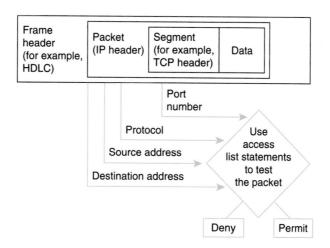

How ACLs Work

An ACL is a group of statements that define how packets

- Enter inbound interfaces
- Relay through the router
- Exit outbound interfaces of the router

As shown in Figure 6-4, the beginning of the communication process is the same, whether ACLs are used or not. As a packet enters an interface, the router checks to see whether the packet is routable or bridgeable. Now, the router checks whether the inbound interface has an ACL. If one exists, the packet is now tested against the conditions in the list. If the packet is allowed it will then be checked against routing table entries to determine the destination interface ACLs do not filter packets that originate in the router itself, but on packets from other sources.

Next, the router checks whether the destination interface has an ACL. If it does not, the packet can be sent to the destination interface directly; for example, if it will use E0, which has no ACLs, the packet uses E0 directly.

FIGURE 6-4
ACLs do not filter packets that originate in the router itself, but on packets from other sources.

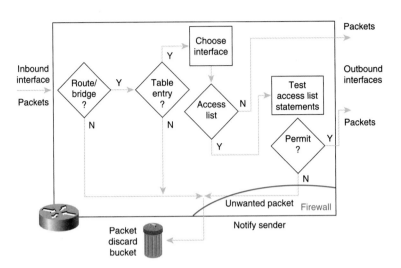

ACL statements operate in sequential, logical order. If a condition match is true, the packet is permitted or denied and the rest of the ACL statements are not checked. If the packet does not match any of the written ACL statements, the packet will match the final implicit **deny any** statement. This means that even though you will not see the **deny** any as the last line of an ACL, it is there.

In Figure 6-5, for instance, by matching the first test, a packet is denied access to the destination. It is discarded and dropped into the *bit bucket*, and it is not exposed to any ACL tests that follow. If the packet does not match the conditions of the first test, it drops to the next statement in the ACL.

ACLs allow you to control what clients can access on your network. Conditions in an ACL file can

- Screen out certain hosts to either allow or deny access to part of your network
- Grant or deny users permission to access only certain types of files, such as FTP or HTTP

Washington Project: User Permission
You need to develop a user ID and password policy for all computers in the District. This policy should be published and strictly enforced. Finally, you need make sure that all computers in the district network will have full access to the Internet.

FIGURE 6-5
ACLs evaluate incoming packets and notify the sender if a packet is unwanted.

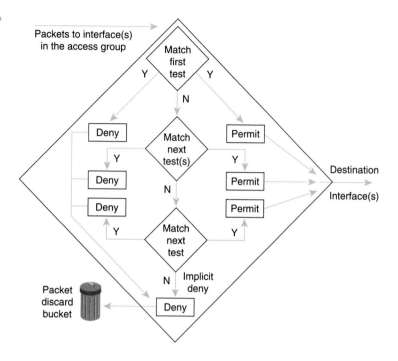

NOTE

For logical completeness, an ACL must have conditions that test true for all packets using the ACL. A final implied statement covers all packets for which conditions did not test true. This final test condition matches all other packets and results in a deny. Instead of proceeding in or out an interface, all remaining packets are dropped. So, if you want to avoid this, the last statement of your ACL should be a **permit any**. Note that the implicit **deny any** is not listed in your configuration file. Because this statement is not listed, some network administrators prefer to explicitly enter the **deny** statement, so that it appears in configuration information, which is good for record keeping.

ACL Configuration Tasks

In practice, ACL commands can be lengthy character strings. Key tasks covered in this section for creating ACLs include the following:

- You create ACLs by using the global configuration mode.
- Specifying an ACL number from 1 to 99 instructs the router to accept standard ACL statements. Specifying an ACL number from 100 to 199 instructs the router to accept extended ACL statements.
- You must carefully select and logically order the ACL. Permitted IP protocols must be specified; all other protocols should be denied.
- You should select which IP protocols to check; any other protocols are not checked. Later in the procedure, you can also specify an optional destination port for more precision.

You can understand the general ACL configuration commands by grouping the commands into two general steps:

Step 1   Define the ACL by using the following command:

```
Router(config)# access-list access-list-number
    {permit | deny} {test-conditions}
```

A global statement identifies the ACL. Specifically, the 1–99 range is reserved for standard IP. This number refers to the type of ACL. In Cisco IOS Release 11.2 or newer, ACLs can also use an ACL name, such as education_ group, rather than a number.

The **permit** or **deny** term in the global ACL statement indicates how packets that meet the test conditions are handled by Cisco IOS software. **permit** usually means the packet will be allowed to use one or more interfaces that you will specify later.

The final term or terms specifies the test conditions used by the ACL statement.

Step 2   Next, you need to apply ACLs to an interface by using the **access-group** command, as in this example:

```
Router(config-if)# {protocol} access-group access-list-number
```

All the ACL statements identified by access-list-number are associated with one or more interfaces. Any packets that pass the ACL test conditions can be permitted to use any interface in the access group of interfaces.

> **NOTE**
>
> The **access-list** command is used when an ACL is being created, and the **access-group** command is used when the same ACL is being applied to an interface.

Grouping ACLs to Interfaces

Although each protocol has its own set of specific tasks and rules that are required to provide traffic filtering, in general most protocols require the two basic steps described in the preceding section, "ACL Configuration Tasks." The first step is to create an ACL definition, and the second step is to apply the ACL to an interface.

ACLs are assigned to one or more interfaces and can filter inbound traffic or outbound traffic, depending on the configuration. Outbound ACLs are generally more efficient than inbound, and are therefore preferred. A router with an inbound ACL must check every packet to see whether it matches the ACL condition before switching the packet to an outbound interface.

Assigning a Unique Number to Each ACL

When configuring ACLs on a router, you must identify each ACL uniquely by assigning a number to the protocol's ACL. When you use a number to identify an ACL, the number must be within the specific range of numbers that is valid for the protocol.

You can specify ACLs by numbers for the protocols listed in Table 6-1. Table 6-1 also lists the range of ACL numbers that is valid for each protocol.

TABLE 6-1   Protocols with ACLs Specified by Numbers

Protocol	Range
IP	1–99
Extended IP	100–199
AppleTalk	600–699
IPX	800–899
Extended IPX	900–999
IPX Service Advertising Protocol	1000–1099

After you create a numbered ACL, you must assign it to an interface for it to be used. If you want to alter an ACL containing numbered ACL statements, you need to delete all the statements in the numbered ACL by using the command **no access-list** *list-number.*

Engineering Journal:
Numbered ACL Configuration Example

The following example defines ACLs 1 and 2:

```
interface ethernet 0
 ip address 1.1.1.1 255.0.0.0
 ip access-group 1 in
 ip access-group 2 out
!
access-list 1 permit 5.6.0.0 0.0.255.255
access-list 1 deny 7.9.0.0 0.0.255.255
!
access-list 2 permit 1.2.3.4
access-list 2 deny 1.2.0.0 0.0.255.255
```

Suppose the interface receives 10 packets from 5.6.7.7 and 14 packets from 1.2.23.21. The first log will look like this:

```
list 1 permit 5.6.7.7 1 packet
list 2 deny 1.2.23.21 1 packet
```

Using Wildcard Mask Bits

A *wildcard mask* is a 32-bit number that is divided into four octets, with each octet containing 8 bits. A wildcard mask bit 0 means "check the corresponding bit value" and a wildcard mask bit 1 means "do not check (ignore) that corresponding bit value" (see Figure 6-6).

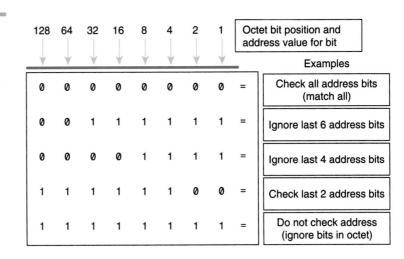

FIGURE 6-6
By carefully setting wild-card masks, you can select one or several IP addresses for permit or deny tests.

A wildcard mask is paired with an IP address. Address bits use the numbers one and zero to identify how to treat the corresponding IP address bits.

ACLs use wildcard masking to identify a single address or multiple addresses for permit or deny tests. The term *wildcard masking* is a nickname for the ACL mask-bit matching process and comes from of an analogy of a wildcard that matches any other card in a poker game.

Although both are 32-bit quantities, wildcard masks and IP subnet masks operate differently. Recall that the zeros and ones in a subnet mask determine the network, subnet, and host portions of the corresponding IP address. The zeros and ones in a wildcard, as just noted, determine whether the corresponding bits in the IP address should be checked or ignored for ACL purposes.

As you have learned, the zero and one bits in an ACL wildcard mask cause the ACL to either check or ignore the corresponding bit in the IP address. In Figure 6-7, this wildcard masking process is applied.

Say you want to test an IP address for subnets that will be permitted or denied. Assume that the IP address is a Class B address (that is, the first two octets are the network number) with 8 bits of subnetting (the third octet is for subnets). You want to use IP wildcard mask bits to permit all packets from any host in the 172.30.16.0 to 172.30.31.0 subnets. Figure 6-7 shows an example of how to use the wildcard mask to do this.

To begin, the wildcard mask checks the first two octets (172.30), using corresponding zero bits in the wildcard mask.

NOTE

Wildcard masking for ACLs operates differently from IP subnet masking. A zero in a bit position of the ACL mask indicates that the corresponding bit in the address must be checked; a one in a bit position of the ACL mask indicates that the corresponding bit in the address can be ignored. Thus, wildcard bit masks often look like inverted subnet masks (for example, 0.0.255.255 versus 255.255.0.0).

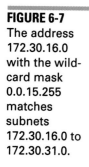

FIGURE 6-7
The address 172.30.16.0 with the wild-card mask 0.0.15.255 matches subnets 172.30.16.0 to 172.30.31.0.

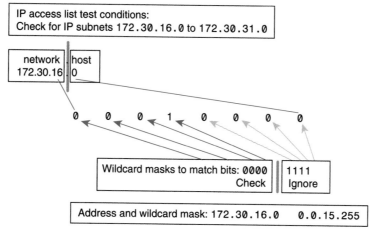

Because there is no interest in individual host addresses (a host ID does not have .00 at the end of the address), the wildcard mask ignores the final octet, using corresponding one bits in the wildcard mask.

In the third octet, the wildcard mask is 15 (00001111), and the IP address is 16 (00010000). The first four zeros in the wildcard mask tell the router to match the first four bits of the IP address (0001). Because the last four bits are ignored, all numbers in the range of 16 (00010000) to 31 (00011111) will match because they begin in the pattern 0001.

For the final (least-significant) four bits in this octet, the wildcard mask ignores the value because in these positions, the address value can be binary zero or binary one, and the corresponding wildcard bits are ones.

In this example, the address 172.30.16.0 with the wildcard mask 0.0.15.255 matches subnets 172.30.16.0 to 172.30.31.0. The wildcard mask does not match any other subnets.

Using the Wildcard any

Working with decimal representations of binary wildcard mask bits can be tedious. For the most common uses of wildcard masking, you can use abbreviations. These abbreviations reduce the amount of typing you need to do when configuring address test conditions. For example, say you want to specify that any destination address will be permitted in an ACL test. To indicate any IP address, you would enter 0.0.0.0, as shown in Figure 6-8; then, to indicate that the ACL should ignore (that is, allow without checking) any value, the corresponding wildcard mask bits for this address would be all ones (that is, 255.255.255.255). You can use the abbreviation any to communicate this same test condition to Cisco IOS ACL software. Instead of typing 0.0.0.0 255.255.255.255, you can use the word any by itself as the keyword.

For example, instead of using this:

```
Router(config)# access-list 1 permit 0.0.0.0  255.255.255.255
```

you can use this:

```
Router(config)# access-list 1 permit any
```

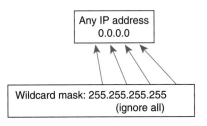

FIGURE 6-8
You can use the wildcard **any** instead of a long wildcard mask string when you want to match any address.

Using the Wildcard host

A second common condition where Cisco IOS permits an abbreviation in the ACL wildcard mask is when you want to match all the bits of an entire IP host address. For example, say you want to specify that a specific IP host address will be permitted in an ACL test. To indicate a host IP address, you would enter the full address (for example, 172.30.16.29, as shown in Figure 6-9); then, to indicate that the ACL should check all the bits in the address, the corresponding wildcard mask bits for this address would be all zeros (that is, 0.0.0.0). You can use the abbreviation **host** to communicate this same test condition to Cisco IOS ACL software. In the example, instead of typing 172.30.16.29 0.0.0.0, you can use the word **host** in front of the address.

For example, instead of using this:

```
Router(config)# access-list 1 permit 172.30.16.29  0.0.0.0
```

you can use this:

```
Router(config)# access-list 1 permit host 172.30.16.29
```

FIGURE 6-9
An example of using the wild-card **host** in an ACL test condition is the string **host 172.30.16.29.**

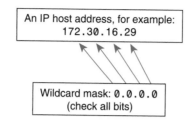

An IP host address, for example:
172.30.16.29

Wildcard mask: 0.0.0.0
(check all bits)

Standard ACLs

You use *standard ACLs* when you want to block all traffic from a network or a specific host, allow all traffic from a specific network, or deny protocol suites. Standard ACLs check the source address of packets that could be routed. The result permits or denies output for an entire protocol suite (for example, TCP/IP), based on the network, subnet, and host addresses. For example, in Figure 6-10, packets coming in E0 are checked for source address and protocol. If they are permitted, the packets are output through S0, which is grouped to the ACL. If they are not permitted, they are dropped.

FIGURE 6-10
Packets coming from E0 are checked for source address and protocol.

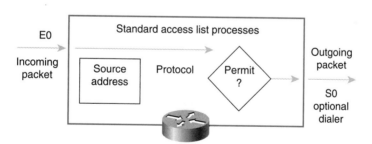

Standard ACL Examples

As you have learned, you use the standard version of the **access-list** global configuration command to define a standard ACL with a number. This command is used in global configuration command mode.

The full syntax of the command is

```
Router(config)# access-list access-list-number {permit | deny}
    source [source-wildcard] [log]
```

You use the **no** form of this command to remove a standard ACL. This is the syntax:

```
Router(config)# no access-list access-list-number
```

The following is a description of the parameters used in this syntax:

Parameter	Description
access-list-number	Number of an ACL. This is a decimal number from 1 to 99 (for a standard IP ACL).
deny	Denies access if the conditions are matched.
permit	Permits access if the conditions are matched.
source	Number of the network or host from which the packet is being sent. There are two ways to specify the *source*: • Use a 32-bit quantity in four-part, dotted-decimal format. • Use the keyword **any** as an abbreviation for a *source* and *source-wildcard* of 0.0.0.0 255.255.255.255.
source-wildcard	(Optional) Wildcard bits to be applied to the source. There are two ways to specify the *source-wildcard*: • Use a 32-bit quantity in four-part, dotted-decimal format. Place ones in the bit positions you want to ignore. • Use the keyword **any** as an abbreviation for a *source* and *source-wildcard* of 0.0.0.0 255.255.255.255. (Optional) Causes an informational logging message about the packet that matches the entry to be sent to the console. (The level of messages logged to the console is controlled by the **logging console** command.)

Parameter	Description
log	The message includes the ACL number, whether the packet was permitted or denied, the source address, and the number of packets. The message is generated for the first packet that matches, and then at five-minute intervals, including the number of packets permitted or denied in the prior five-minute interval.

You use the **show access-lists** EXEC command to display the contents of all ACLs. In addition, you use the **show access-lists** EXEC command followed by the name or number of one ACL.

The following example of a standard ACL allows access for hosts on the three specified networks:

```
access-list 1 permit 192.5.34.0  0.0.0.255
access-list 1 permit 128.88.0.0  0.0.255.255
access-list 1 permit 36.0.0.0  0.255.255.255
! (Note: all other access implicitly denied)
```

In the example, the wildcard bits apply to the host portions of the network addresses. Any host with a source address that does not match the ACL statements will be rejected.

To specify a large number of individual addresses more easily, you can omit the wildcard if it is all zeros. Thus, the following two configuration commands have the same effect:

```
access-list 2 permit 36.48.0.3
access-list 2 permit 36.48.0.3  0.0.0.0
```

The **ip access-group** command applies an existing ACL to an interface. Remember that only one ACL per port per protocol per direction is allowed. The format of the command is

```
Router(config-if)#ip access-group access-list-number {in | out}
```

Where the parameters have the following meanings:

Parameter	Description
access-list-number	Indicates the number of the ACL to be linked to this interface.
in | **out**	Selects whether the ACL is applied to the incoming or outgoing interface. If **in** or **out** is not specified, **out** is the default.

The standard ACL configuration examples in the following sections refer to the network shown in Figure 6-11. The first example permits traffic from source network 172.16.0.0. The second example denies traffic from a specific

NOTE

To remove an ACL, first enter the **no ip access-group** command, including list number, for each interface where the list had been used, and then enter the **no access-list** command (with list number).

host with the address 172.16.4.13 and permits all other traffic. The third example denies traffic from a specific subnet with the address 172.16.4.0 and permits all other traffic.

e-LAB ACTIVITY 6.1

access-list

In this activity, you demonstrate how to use the **access-list** command to define a standard IP ACL.

e-LAB ACTIVITY 6.2

show access-lists

In this activity, you demonstrate how to use the **show access-lists** command to display the contents of all current ACLs.

Standard ACL Example 1: Permitting Traffic from a Source Network

In this example, the ACL allows only traffic from source network 172.16.0.0 to be forwarded. Non-172.16.0.0 network traffic is blocked. Example 6-1 shows how the ACL allows only traffic from source network 172.16.0.0 to be forwarded and non-172.16.0.0 to be blocked.

FIGURE 6-11
This network is an example of two subnets connected by a router.

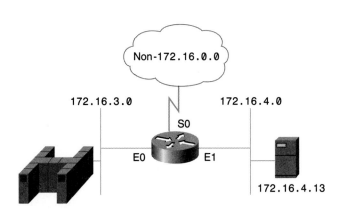

Example 6-1   *Permitting Traffic from Source Network 172.16.0.0*

```
access-list 1 permit 172.16.0.0  0.0.255.255
(implicit deny any - not visible in the list)
(access-list 1 deny 0.0.0.0  255.255.255.255)
```

Example 6-1 *Permitting Traffic from Source Network 172.16.0.0 (Continued)*

```
interface ethernet 0
ip access-group 1 out
interface ethernet 1
ip access-group 1 out
```

The following are the fields in the output shown in Example 6-1:

Field	Description
1	ACL number; indicates that this is a simple list.
permit	Traffic that matches selected parameters will be forwarded.
172.16.0.0	IP address that will be used with the wildcard mask to identify the source network.
0.0.255.255	Wildcard mask; zeros indicate positions that must match and ones indicate "don't care" positions.

Also, in Example 1, the command **ip access-group 1 out** applies the ACL to an outgoing interface.

Standard ACL Example 2: Denying a Specific Host

Example 6-2 shows how an ACL is designed to block traffic from a specific address, 172.16.4.13, and to allow all other traffic to be forwarded on interface Ethernet 0. The first **access-list** command uses the **deny** parameter to deny traffic from the identified host. The address mask 0.0.0.0 in this line requires the test to match all bits.

Example 6-2 *Denying a Specific Host*

```
access-list 1 deny 172.16.4.13  0.0.0.0
access-list 1 permit 0.0.0.0  255.255.255.255
(implicit deny any)
(access-list 1 deny 0.0.0.0  255.255.255.255)

interface ethernet 0
ip access-group 1 out
```

The following are the fields in the output shown in Example 6-2:

Field	Description
1	ACL number; indicates that this is a simple list.
deny	Traffic that matches selected parameters will not be forwarded.
host	Shorthand for the wildcard mask 0.0.0.0.

continues

Field	Description
permit	Traffic that matches selected parameters will be forwarded.
0.0.0.0	IP address of the source host; all zeros indicate a placeholder.
255.255.255.255	Wildcard mask; zeros indicate positions that must match, ones indicate "don't care" positions. All ones in the mask indicate that all 32 bits will not be checked in the source address.

In the second **access-list** command, the 0.0.0.0 255.255.255.255 IP address/ wildcard mask combination identifies traffic from any source. This combination can also be written using the keyword **any**. All zeros in the address indicate a placeholder, and all ones in the wildcard mask indicate that all 32 bits will not be checked in the source address.

Any packet that does not match the first line of the ACL will match the second one and be forwarded.

Standard ACL Example 3: Denying a Specific Subnet

Example 6-3 shows how an ACL is designed to block traffic from a specific subnet, 172.16.4.0, and to allow all other traffic to be forwarded. Note the wildcard mask, 0.0.0.255: The zeros in the first three octets indicate that those bits will be tested for matches while the last octet of all ones indicates a don't care condition for matching the last octet of the IP address (the host portion. Note also that the **any** abbreviation has been used for the IP address of the source.

Example 6-3   *Denying a Specific Subnet*

```
access-list 1 deny 172.16.4.0  0.0.0.255
access-list 1 permit any
(implicit deny any)
access-list 1 deny any

interface ethernet 0
ip access-group 1 out
```

The following are the fields in the output shown in Example 6-3:

Field	Description
1	This ACL is designed to block traffic from a specific subnet, 172.16.4.0, and to allow all other traffic to be forwarded.
deny	Traffic that matches selected parameters will not be forwarded.
172.16.4.0	IP address of the source subnet.

Field	Description
0.0.0.255	Wildcard mask; zeros indicate positions that must match, ones indicate don't care positions. The mask with zeros in the first three octets indicates that those positions must match; the 255 in the last octet indicates a don't care condition.
permit	Traffic that matches selected parameters will be forwarded.
any	Abbreviation for the IP address of the source; all zeros indicate a placeholder and the wildcard mask 255.255.255.255. All ones in the mask indicates that all 32 bits will not be checked in the source address.

SKILL BUILDER

Standard ACLs

In this lab, you work with standard access control lists (ACLs) to regulate the traffic that is allowed to pass through a router based on the source, either a specific host (typically a workstation or server) or an entire network (any host or server on that network).

e-LAB ACTIVITY 6.3

Standard ACLs

In this activity, you work through several tasks to configure standard ACLs.

Extended ACLs

Extended ACLs are used most often to test conditions because they provide a greater range of control than standard ACLs. You would use an extended ACL when you want to allow Web traffic but deny File Transfer Protocol (FTP) or telnet from non-company networks. Extended ACLs check for both source and destination packet addresses. They also can check for specific protocols, port numbers, and other parameters. This gives you more flexibility to describe what checking the ACL will do. Packets can be permitted or denied output based on where the packet originated and based on its destination. For example, in Figure 6-10, the extended ACL can allow e-mail traffic from E0 to specific S0 destinations, while denying remote logins or file transfers.

In Figure 6-10, let's assume that Interface E0 has been applied to an extended ACL, created from precise, logical statements. Before a packet can proceed to that interface, it is tested by the ACL associated with that interface.

Based on the extended ACL tests, the packet can be permitted or denied. For inbound lists, this means that permitted packets will continue to be processed. For outbound lists, this means that permitted packets will be sent directly to E0. If test results deny permission, the packet will be discarded. The router's ACL provides firewall control to deny use of the E0 interface. When packets are discarded, some protocols return a packet to the sender, stating that the destination was unreachable.

For a single ACL, you can define multiple statements. Each of these statements should reference the same identifying name or number to tie the statements to the same ACL. You can have as many condition statements as you want, limited only by the available memory. Of course, the more statements you have, the more difficult it will be to comprehend and manage your ACL. Therefore, documenting ACLs prevents confusion.

The standard ACL (numbered 1 to 99) might not provide the traffic-filtering control you need. Standard ACLs filter traffic based on a source address and mask. Standard ACLs also permit or deny the entire Internet Protocol (IP) suite. You might need a more precise way to control traffic and access.

For more precise traffic-filtering control, you use extended ACLs. Extended ACL statements check for source address and for destination address. In addition, at the end of the extended ACL statement, you gain additional precision from a field that specifies the optional TCP or User Datagram Protocol (UDP) protocol port number. These can be the well-known port numbers for TCP/IP. A few of the most common port numbers are shown in Table 6-2.

TABLE 6-2   Common Port Numbers

Common Port Number (Decimal)	IP Protocol
20	FTP data
21	FTP program
23	Telnet
25	Simple Mail Transport Protocol (SMTP)
69	TFTP
53	DNS

You can specify the logical operation that the extended ACL will perform on specific protocols. Extended ACLs use a number in the range 100 to 199.

Extended ACL Examples

The complete form of the **access-list** command is

```
Router(config-if)# access-list access-list-number {permit | deny}
    protocol source [source-mask destination destination-mask
    [operator operand] [established] [log]
```

Where the parameters have the following meanings:

Parameter	Description
access-list-number	Identifies the list using a number in the range 100 to 199.
permit | **deny**	Indicates whether this entry allows or blocks the specified address.
protocol	The protocol, such as IP, TCP, UDP, ICMP, GRE, or IGRP.
source and **destination**	Identifies source and destination addresses.
source-mask and *destination-mask*	Wildcard mask; zeros indicate positions that must match, ones indicate don't care positions.
operator *operand*	lt, gt, eq, neq (less than, greater than, equal, not equal), and a port number.
established	Allows TCP traffic to pass if the packet uses an established connection (for example, has ACK bits set).

The **ip access-group** command applies an extended ACL to an interface. Remember that only one ACL per interface, per direction, per protocol is allowed. The format of the command is

```
Router(config-if)#ip access-group access-list access-list-number {in | out}
```

Where the parameters have the following meanings:

Parameter	Description
access-list-number	Indicates the number of the ACL to be linked to this interface.
in | **out**	Selects whether the ACL is applied to the incoming or outgoing packet on the interface. If **in** or **out** is not specified, **out** is the default.

e-LAB ACTIVITY 6.4

access-list

In this activity, you demonstrate how to use the **access-list** command to define an extended IP ACL.

e-LAB ACTIVITY 6.5

ACL

Using access list parameters to block traffic.

Destination and source addresses or specific protocols using extended ACLs need to be identified with numbers in the range 100 to 199. Upper-level TCP or UDP port numbers in addition to the other tests in extended ACLs need to be identified with a number in the range 100 to 199. Some of the well-known reserved port numbers are shown in Table 6-3.

TABLE 6-3   Reserved Well-Known Port Numbers

Decimal	Keyword	Description	TCP/UDP
0		Reserved	
1–4		Unassigned	
20	FTP-DATA	FTP (data)	TCP
21	FTP	FTP	TCP
23	TELNET	Terminal connection	TCP
25	SMTP	SMTP	TCP
42	NAMESERVER	Host name server	UDP
53	DOMAIN	DNS	TCP/ UDP
69	TFTP	TFTP	UDP
70		Gopher	TCP/IP
80		WWW	TCP

TABLE 6-3   Reserved Well-Known Port Numbers (Continued)

Decimal	Keyword	Description	TCP/UDP
133–159		Unassigned	
160–223		Reserved	
161		FNP	UDP
224–241		Unassigned	
242–255		Unassigned	

The extended ACL configuration examples in the following sections refer to the network shown in Figure 6-11. The first example denies FTP for E0. The second example denies only Telnet out of E0 and permits all other traffic.

Extended ACL Example 1: Denying FTP for E0

Example 6-4 shows an extended ACL that blocks FTP traffic.

Example 6-4   *Denying FTP for E0*

```
access-list 101 deny tcp 172.16.4.0
   0.0.0.255 172.16.3.0  0.0.0.255  eq 21
access-list 101 permit ip 172.16.4.0
   0.0.0.255 0.0.0.0 255.255.255.255
(implicit deny any)
(access-list 101 deny ip 0.0.0.0
   255.255.255.255  0.0.0.0  255.255.255.255)

interface ethernet 0
ip access-group 101
```

The following are the fields in the output shown in Example 6-4:

Field	Description
101	ACL number; indicates extended ACL.
deny	Traffic that matches selected parameters will be blocked.
tcp	Transport-layer protocol.
172.16.4.0 and 0.0.0.255	Source address and mask; the first three octets must match, but the last octet does not matter.
172.16.3.0 and 0.0.0.255	Destination address and mask; the first three octets must match, but the last octet does not matter.

continues

Field	Description
eq021	Specifies the well-known port number for FTP.
eq 20	Specifies the well-known port number for FTP data.

The **interface E0 access-group 101** command applies ACL 101 to outgoing interface E0. Note that blocking port 21 prevents FTP commands from being transmitted, thus preventing FTP file transfers. Blocking port 20 prevents the traffic itself from being transmitted but does not block FTP commands. FTP servers can easily be configured to work on different ports. You should understand that well-known port numbers are just that: well-known. There are no guarantees that services will be on those ports, although they usually are.

Example 6-5 shows an ACL that denies telnet traffic (eq 23) from 172.16.4.0 being sent out interface E0. All traffic from any other source to any destination is permitted, as indicated by the keyword **any**. Interface E0 is configured with the **access-group 101 out** command; that is, ACL 101 is applied to outgoing interface E0.

Example 6-5   *Allowing Only Mail of Interface E0; Denying All Other Traffic*

```
access-list 101 deny tcp 172.16.4.0  0.0.0.255 any eq 23
access-list 101 permit ip any any
(implicit deny any)
(access-list 101 deny ip 0.0.0.0  255.255.255.255
    0.0.0.0  255.255.255.255)

interface ethernet 0
ip access-group 101 out
```

The following are the fields in the output shown in Example 6-5:

Field	Description
101	ACL number; indicates extended ACL.
deny	Traffic that matches selected parameters will be discarded.
tcp	Transport-layer protocol.
172.16.4.0 and 0.0.0.255	Source address and mask; the first three octets must match, but the last octet does not matter.
0.0.0.0 and 255.255.255.255	Destination address and mask; no octet values matter.
eq 23	Specifies well-known port number for SMTP.

Field	Description
access-group 101	Command links ACL 101 to outgoing port interface E0.

Using Named ACLs

Named ACLs allow standard and extended IP ACLs to be identified with an alphanumeric string (name) instead of the current numeric (1 to 199) representation. Named ACLs can be used to delete individual entries from a specific ACL. This enables you to modify your ACLs without deleting and then reconfiguring them. Use named ACLs when

- You want to intuitively identify ACLs using an alphanumeric name.
- You have more than 99 standard and 100 extended ACLs to be configured in a router for a given protocol.

Consider the following before implementing named ACLs:

- Named ACLs are not compatible with Cisco IOS releases prior to Release 11.2.
- You cannot use the same name for multiple ACLs. In addition, ACLs of different types cannot have the same name. For example, it is illegal to specify a standard ACL named George and an extended ACL with the same name.

To name the ACL, use the following command:

```
Router(config)# ip access-list {standard | extended} name
```

In ACL configuration mode, specify one or more conditions allowed or denied. This determines whether the packet is passed or dropped:

```
Router(config {std- | ext-}nacl)# deny {source [source-wildcard] | any}
```

or

```
Router(config {std- | ext-}nacl)# permit {source [source-wildcard] | any}
```

The following configuration creates a standard ACL named Internetfilter and an extended ACL named marketing_group:

```
interface ethernet0/5
ip address 2.0.5.1 255.255.255.0
ip access-group Internetfilter out
ip access-group marketing_group in
...
ip access-list standard Internetfilter
permit 1.2.3.4
```

continues

```
deny any
ip access-list extended marketing_group
permit tcp any 171.69.0.0 0.255.255.255 eq telnet

deny tcp any any
deny udp any 171.69.0.0  0.255.255.255 lt 1024

deny ip any log
```

e-LAB ACTIVITY 6.6

ip access-list

In this activity, you demonstrate how to use the ip   **access-list** command to name a ACL.

The deny Command

You use the **deny** ACL configuration command to set conditions for a named ACL. The full syntax for this command is

```
deny {source [source-wildcard] | any} [log]
```

You use the **no** form of this command to remove a deny condition, using the following syntax:

```
no deny {source [source-wildcard] | any}
```

The following example sets a deny condition for a standard ACL named Internetfilter:

```
ip access-list standard Internetfilter
 deny 192.5.34.0  0.0.0.255
 permit 128.88.0.0  0.0.255.255
 permit 36.0.0.0  0.255.255.255
 ! (Note: all other access implicitly denied)
```

e-LAB ACTIVITY 6.7

deny

In this activity, you demonstrate how to use the **deny** command to set conditions for a named ACL.

The permit Command

You use the permit access-list configuration command to set conditions for a named standard ACL. The full syntax of this command is

```
permit {source [source-wildcard] | any} [log]
```

You use the no form of this command to remove a condition from an ACL, using the following syntax

```
no permit {source [source-wildcard] | any}
```

You use this command in access list configuration mode, following the **ip access-list** command, to define the conditions under which a packet passes the ACL.

The following example is for a standard ACL named Internetfilter:

```
ip access-list standard Internetfilter
 deny 192.5.34.0  0.0.0.255
 permit 128.88.0.0  0.0.255.255
 permit 36.0.0.0  0.255.255.255
! (Note: all other access implicitly denied)
```

In this example, **permit** and **deny** statements have no number, and **no** removes the specific test from the named ACL:

```
Router(config {std- | ext-}nacl)# {permit | deny} {ip ACL test conditions}
{permit | deny} {ip ACL test conditions}
no {permit | deny} {ip ACL test conditions}
```

This example activates the IP named ACL on an interface:

```
Router(config-if)# ip access-group {name | 1-199 {in | out} }
```

The following is a configuration output example:

```
ip access-list extended come_on
permit tcp any 171.69.0.0 0.255.255.255 eq telnet

deny tcp any any
deny udp any 171.69.0.0 0.255.255.255 lt 1024

deny ip any any
interface ethernet0/5
ip address 2.0.5.1 255.255.255.0
ip access-group over_out out
ip access-group come_on in
ip access-list standard over_and
permit 1.2.3.4

deny any
```

Using ACLs with Protocols

ACLs can control most protocols on a Cisco router. You enter a number in the protocol number range as the first argument of the global ACL statement. The router identifies which ACL software to use based on this numbered entry. Many ACLs are possible for a protocol. You select a different number from the protocol number range for each new ACL; however, you can specify only one ACL per protocol per interface. For some protocols, you can group up to two ACLs to an interface: one inbound ACL and one outbound ACL. With other protocols, you group only one ACL, which checks both inbound and outbound packets. If the ACL is inbound, when the router receives a packet, the

Cisco IOS software checks the ACL's condition statements for a match. If the packet is permitted, the software continues to process the packet. If the packet is denied, the software discards the packet by placing it in the bit bucket. If the ACL is outbound, after receiving and routing a packet to the outbound interface, the software checks the ACL's condition statements for a match. If the packet is permitted, the software transmits the packet. If the packet is denied, the software discards the packet by sending it to the bit bucket.

> ## Engineering Journal:
> ## Naming or Numbering an IP Protocol
>
> The name or number of an IP protocol can be one of the keywords **eigrp**, **gre**, **icmp**, **igmp**, **igrp**, **ip**, **ipinip**, **nos**, **ospf**, **tcp**, or **udp**, or an integer in the range **0** to **255**, representing an IP protocol number. To match any Internet protocol (including ICMP, TCP, and UDP), use the keyword **ip**. The protocols and their corresponding numbers are listed in RFC 1700, along with port numbers.

Placing ACLs

NOTE

For most protocols, if you define an inbound ACL for traffic filtering, you should include precise ACL condition statements to permit routing updates. If you do not, you might lose communication from the interface when routing updates are blocked by the **deny all** traffic statement at the end of the ACL. This can be avoided by adding a **permit any** statement to the end of any ACL you create.

As you learned earlier, ACLs are used to control traffic by filtering packets and eliminating unwanted traffic at a destination. Depending on where you place an ACL statement, you can reduce unnecessary traffic. Traffic that will be denied at a remote destination should not use network resources along the route to that destination.

Suppose an enterprise's policy aims to deny telnet or FTP traffic on Router A to the switched Ethernet LAN on Router D's E1 port, as shown in Figure 6-12. At the same time, other traffic must be permitted. Several approaches can accomplish this policy. The recommended approach uses an extended ACL. It specifies both source and destination addresses. Place this extended ACL in Router A. Then, packets do not cross Router A's Ethernet, do not cross the serial interfaces of Routers B and C, and do not enter Router D. Traffic with different source and destination addresses can still be permitted.

The rule is to put the extended ACLs as close as possible to the source of the traffic denied. Standard ACLs do not specify destination addresses, so you have to put the standard ACL as near the destination as possible. For example, as shown in Figure 6-12, you should place either a standard or an extended ACL on E0 of Router D to prevent traffic from Router A.

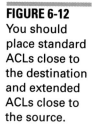

FIGURE 6-12
You should place standard ACLs close to the destination and extended ACLs close to the source.

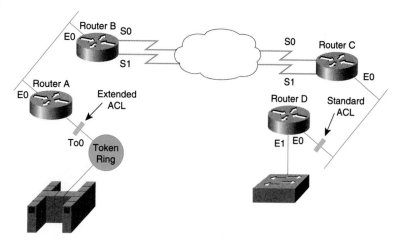

Using ACLs with Firewalls

ACLs should be used in *firewall* routers, which are often positioned between the internal network and an external network, such as the Internet. The firewall router provides a point of isolation so that the rest of the internal network structure is not affected. You can also use ACLs on a router positioned between two parts of the network to control traffic entering or exiting a specific part of the internal network.

To provide the security benefits of ACLs, you should at a minimum configure ACLs on *border routers*, which are routers situated on the boundaries of the network. This provides basic security from the outside network, or from a less controlled area of the network, into a more private area of the network.

On these border routers, ACLs can be created for each network protocol configured on the router interfaces. You can configure ACLs so that inbound traffic, outbound traffic, or both are filtered on an interface.

Washington Project: Firewall Implementation
The Internet connectivity you need to implement in the Washington School District requires a double firewall implementation with all the applications that are exposed to the Internet residing on a public backbone network. You need to ensure that all connections initiated from the Internet into each school's private network will be refused.

Setting Up a Firewall Architecture

A firewall architecture is a structure that exists between you and the outside world to protect you from intruders. In most circumstances, intruders come from the global Internet and the thousands of remote networks it interconnects.

Typically, a network firewall consists of several different machines, as shown in Figure 6-13.

FIGURE 6-13
A typical fire-
wall architec-
ture protects a
network from
intruders from
the Internet.

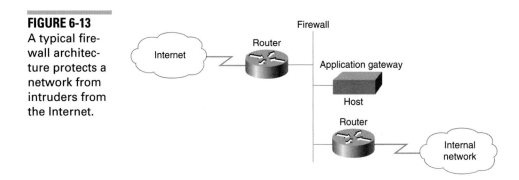

In this architecture, the router that is connected to the Internet (that is, the exterior router) forces all incoming traffic to go to the application gateway. The router that is connected to the internal network (that is, the interior router) accepts packets only from the application gateway.

In effect, the gateway controls the delivery of network-based services both into and from the internal network. For example, only certain users might be allowed to communicate with the Internet, or only certain applications might be permitted to establish connections between an interior and exterior host.

If the only application that is permitted is mail, then only mail packets should be allowed through the router. This protects the application gateway and avoids overwhelming it with packets that it would otherwise discard.

Engineering Journal:
Using a Firewall Router

This section uses the scenario illustrated in Figure 6-13 to describe the use of ACLs to restrict traffic to and from a firewall router.

Having a designated router act as a firewall is good because it clearly identifies the router's purpose as the external gateway and avoids encumbering other routers with this task. In the event that the internal network needs to isolate itself, the firewall router provides the point of isolation so that the rest of the internal network structure is not affected.

In the firewall router configuration that follows, subnet 13 of the Class B network is the firewall subnet, and subnet 14 provides the connection to the worldwide Internet via a service provider:

```
interface ethernet 0
ip address B.B.13.1 255.255.255.0
interface serial 0
ip address B.B.14.1 255.255.255.0
```

```
router igrp
network B.B.0.0
```

This simple configuration provides no security and allows all traffic from the outside world onto all parts of the network. To provide security on the firewall router, you need to use ACLs and access groups.

An ACL defines the actual traffic that will be permitted or denied, and an access group applies an ACL definition to an interface. ACLs can be used to deny connections that are known to be security risks and then permit all other connections, or to permit connections that are considered acceptable and deny all the rest. For firewall implementation, the latter is the more secure method.

The best place to define an ACL is on a host, using a text editor. You can create a file that contains the **access-list** commands and then upload the file onto the router. Before uploading the access control definition, any previous definition of this ACL is removed by using the following command:

```
no access-list 101
```

The **access-list** command can now be used to permit any packets returning to machines from already established connections. With the **established** keyword, a match occurs if the TCP datagram has the acknowledgment (ACK) or reset (RST) bits set:

```
access-list 101 permit tcp 0.0.0.0 255.255.255.255
    0.0.0.0 255.255.255.255 established
```

After the ACL has been loaded onto the router and stored into nonvolatile random-access memory (NVRAM), you assign it to the appropriate interface. In this example, traffic coming from the outside world via serial 0 is filtered before it is placed on subnet 13 (ethernet 0). Therefore, the **access-group** command, which assigns an ACL to filter incoming connections, must be assigned to ethernet 0 as follows:

```
interface ethernet 0
ip access-group 101
```

To control outgoing access to the Internet from the network, you define an ACL and apply it to the outgoing packets on serial 0 of the firewall router. To do this, returning packets from hosts using Telnet or FTP must be allowed to access the firewall subnetwork B.B.13.0.

If you have several internal networks connected to the firewall router and the router is using output filters, traffic between internal networks will see a reduction in performance created by the ACL filters. If input filters are used only on the interface going from the router to the outside world, internal networks will not see any reduction in performance.

Verifying ACLs

The **show ip interface** command displays IP interface information and indicates whether any ACLs are set. The **show access-lists** command displays the contents of all ACLs. By entering the ACL name or number as an option for this command, you can see a specific list, as shown in Example 6-6.

Example 6-6 *Show IP Interface*

```
Router> show

Ethernet0 is up, line protocol is up
    Internet address is 192.54.22.2, subnet mask is 255.255.255.0
    Broadcast address is 255.255.255.255
    Address determined by nonvolatile memory
    MTU is 1500 bytes
Helper address is 192.52.71.4
Secondary address 131.192.115.2, subnet mask 255.255.255.0
Outgoing ACL 10 is set
Inbound ACL is not set
Proxy ARP is enabled
Security level is default
Split horizon is enabled
ICMP redirects are always sent
ICMP unreachables are never sent
ICMP mask replies are never sent
IP fast switching is enabled
Gateway Discovery is disabled
IP accounting is disabled
TCP/IP header compression is disabled
Probe proxy name replies are disabled
    Router>
```

SKILL BUILDER

Extended ACLs

In this lab, you work with extended ACLs to regulate the traffic that is allowed to pass through the router based on the source and type of traffic. ACLs are an important tool to control which packets and what type of packets should be allowed to pass through a router from one network to another.

SKILL BUILDER

Extended ACLs Internet

This lab simulates a real-world example. You work with multiple extended access control lists (ACLs) to simulate regulating the traffic that is allowed to pass through multiple routers to various servers and the Internet.

e-LAB ACTIVITY 6.8

show ip interface

In this activity, you demonstrate how to use the **show ip interface** command to display IP interface information.

e-LAB ACTIVITY 6.9

Extended ACLs

In this activity, you work through several tasks to configure extended ACLs.

Summary

■ ACLs perform several functions within a Cisco router, including implementing security/access procedures.

■ ACLs are used to control and manage traffic.

■ For some protocols, you can apply up to two ACLs to an interface: one inbound ACL and one outbound ACL.

■ With ACLs, after a packet is checked for a match with the ACL statement, it can be denied or permitted the use of an associated interface.

■ Wildcard mask bits use the number one and the number zero to identify how to treat the corresponding IP address bits.

■ The two main types of ACLs are standard ACLs and extended ACLs.

■ ACLs can be configured for all routed network protocols to filter those protocols' packets as the packets pass through a router.

■ ACLs are typically used in firewall routers, which are often positioned between the internal network and an external network such as the Internet.

Washington School District Project Task: Using ACLs

In this chapter, you have learned concepts and configuration processes that will help you implement ACLs. In the previous chapters, you learned the concepts of how data traffic flows across a LAN; in this chapter, you studied the methods for controlling the flow of these data packets based on Layer 2 and 3 addressing and Layer 4 services. The TCS Overview dictates that each school will have two networks: one for curriculum and the other for administration. Each unique LAN segment is connected to a separate Ethernet port on the router. You should devise an ACL for the router that will deny anyone from the curriculum LAN access into the administrative LAN segment, yet continue to give the administrative LAN complete access into the curriculum LAN segment. One exception to this ACL is the router is to pass any DNS or e-mail packets to the DNS/E-mail server, which is located on the Administration LAN segment. In response to the network design and security requirements, you need to complete the following tasks:

1. Document why you would need ACLs and create a logical diagram describing the overall effect of these ACLs on the entire district network.

2. Document what type of ACL will be placed on the high-end, powerful, district core router(s), and where they will be placed and why.

3. Document the router command sequence required to implement each ACL on each of the local school site access router's interfaces, and document the resulting changes to the router configuration.

4. Document the effect of each ACL as it relates to traffic flow across individual school LANs and the overall district network.

5. Continue LAN design tasks: site wiring designs, LAN logical designs, typical MDF and IDF designs and electronics tables, and a site-specific LAN electronics list.

6. Apply the CCNA Certification Exam Learning Objectives to your specific design. This requires a paragraph on how the learning objectives relate to your design. Learning objectives can be grouped together for the purpose of explanation. In this way, you will be studying for the CCNA Certification Exam as you work through the case study.

CCNA Certification Exam Learning Objectives

General

NOTE

*** are explicit CCNA exam objectives; unmarked are knowledge assumed by the exam.

- Describe what an access control list is.
- Describe the function of access control lists on routers.
- Describe the reasons access control lists are used.
- Describe how segmentation with routers and access control lists are related.
- Configure standard and extended access lists to filter IP traffic.***
- Monitor and verify selected access list operations on the router.***

OSI Model

- Define what layers of the OSI model standard access control lists function at and what fields in the data packet header it is concerned with.
- Define what layers of the OSI model extended access control lists function at and what fields in the data packet header it is concerned with.

Check Your Understanding

Complete all the review questions to test your understanding of the topics and concepts covered in this chapter. Answers are listed in Appendix B, "Check Your Understanding Answer Key."

1. What is the purpose of ACLs?

2. What condition do standard ACLs use for IP data packets?

3. How do extended ACLs differ from standard ACLs?

4. How do ACLs compare each data packet to the conditions in the list?

5. How are standard and extended ACLs differentiated in the router?

6. Which of the following commands would you use to find out whether there are any ACLs set on an interface?

   A. show running-config

   B. show ip protocols

   C. show ip interface

   D. show ip network

7. What do you call the additional 32 bits of information in the **access-list** statement?

   A. Wildcard bits

   B. Access bits

   C. Zero bits

   D. One bits

8. Using **Router(config)# access-list 156.1.0.0 0.0.255.255** is equivalent to saying which of the following?

   A. "Deny my network only."

   B. "Permit a specific host."

   C. "Permit my network only."

   D. "Deny a specific host."

9. When you issue a permit entry into an ACL that is accompanied by an implicit deny all, all traffic except that listed in the permit statement will be denied.

   A. True

   B. False

10. The **show access-lists** command is used to do which of the following?

    A. Monitor whether ACLs are set

    B. Monitor ACL statements

    C. Monitor ACL debugging

    D. Monitor groupings

11. If you want to permit traffic based on its addressing or protocol type, you would use which of the following commands?

    A. Router #access-list access-list number {permit | deny} {test conditions}

    B. Router (config)#access-list access-list number {permit | deny} {test conditions}

    C. Router (config-if)#access-list access-list number {permit | deny} {test conditions}

    D. None of the above

12. Which one of the following would access list most likely be used for?

    A. Decrease the amount of content in routing updates

    B. Log in to an ATM switch

    C. Identify packets for priority mailing

    D. None of the above

13. There are two types of access lists: _____, which check the source address of the packet and will usually permit or deny an entire protocol suite, and _____, which allows more complex address and protocol specifications.

    A. Extended; standard

    B. Standard; extended

    C. Extended; simple

    D. None of the above

14. Standard IP access lists permit or deny routing of a packet based on the IP address it originates from and the protocol suite it is destined for.

   A. True

   B. False

15. When configuring dial-on-demand routing, one uses _____ to filter _____ flow. This packet flow usually comes from a _____ connection. Controlling this flow helps protect the network's expanding resources without _____ legitimate traffic.

   A. Dialer maps; segments; MAN; fast-switching

   B. Access groups; frames; LAN; discarding

   C. Access lists; packets; WAN; impeding

   D. None of the above

16. One might use the _____ command to find out whether there were any access lists set on an interface.

   A. show running-config

   B. show ip protocols

   C. show ip interface

   D. None of the above

17. Correlate the commands that are used for monitoring the access list to their respective functions. Mark the wrong correlation.

   A. show access-lists: Displays access list parameters.

   B. show access-lists: Displays a specific list's content.

   C. show access-lists: Displays interface information.

   D. show ip interface: Displays whether access lists are set.

18. Access lists impart network security based on which of the following factors?

   A. The data content of the packets.

   B. The destination subnet/host/network for the packets.

   C. The source subnet/host/network of the packets.

   D. The type of the network they are routed through.

19. What type of networking device would be needed to implement access lists to increase network security?

A. Hub

B. Router

C. Bridge

D. Switch

20. What does the following access list allow?

`access-list 1 permit 204.211.19.162 0.0.0.0`

A. "Deny my network only."

B. "Permit a specific host."

C. "Permit only my network."

D. None of the above

Key Terms

ACL (access control list)   A list kept by a Cisco router to control access to or from the router for a number of services (for example, to prevent packets with a certain IP address from leaving a particular interface on the router).

bit bucket   The destination of discarded bits as determined by the router.

border router   A router situated at the edges, or end, of the network boundary, which provides a basic security from the outside network, or from a less controlled area of the network, into a more private area of the network.

DNS (Domain Name System)   A system used in the Internet for translating names of network nodes into addresses.

extended ACL (extended access control list)   An ACL that checks for source address and destination address.

firewall   A router or an access server, or several routers or access servers, designated as a buffer between any connected public networks and a private network. A firewall router uses access control lists and other methods to ensure the security of the private network.

queuing   A process in which ACLs can designate certain packets to be processed by a router before other traffic, on the basis of a protocol.

standard ACL (standard access control list)   An ACL that filters based on a source address and mask. Standard ACLs permit or deny the entire TCP/IP protocol suite.

wildcard mask   A 32-bit quantity used in conjunction with an IP address to determine which bits in an IP address should be ignored when comparing that address with another IP address. A wildcard mask is specified when setting up an ACL.

Objectives

After reading this chapter, you will be able to

- Explain how Cisco routers are used in NetWare networks

- Describe the Novell NetWare protocol suite

- Describe Novell IPX addressing

- Describe Novell encapsulation

- Explain how Novell uses RIP for routing

- Describe Service Advertising Protocol

- Configure both the router Ethernet and serial interfaces with IPX addresses

- Describe how to discover IPX addresses on remote routers

- Describe how to verify IPX operation and connectivity between routers

- Explain troubleshooting in IPX operations

Chapter 7

Novell IPX

Introduction

Novell *NetWare* is a *network operating system (NOS)* that connects PCs and other *clients* to NetWare *servers*. NetWare servers provide a variety of network services to their clients, including file sharing, printer sharing, directory services, and Internet access. Many NetWare servers function as application platforms for shared databases and as Internet and intranet servers. With more than 5 million networks and more than 50 million clients, Novell has the largest share of the NOS market.

In addition to Transmission Control Protocol/Internet Protocol (TCP/IP), Novell's *Internetwork Packet Exchange (IPX)* is another protocol that is commonly implemented in the networking industry. Until Novell's NetWare 5.0 release in 1998, all NetWare networks used IPX. As with AppleTalk, Novell migrated NetWare to IP. Therefore, IPX networks are networks that must still be supported due to their installed base. In this chapter, you will learn about Novell's IPX protocols, operation, and configuration.

Washington Project: IPX Implementation
In this chapter, you will learn how to implement Novell IPX in the Washington School District network. The school district needs a workgroup server in each computer lab at the school sites. The computer labs are located on the curriculum LAN segments of their respective sites. Both IP and IPX services need to be advertised across the school district network to other curriculum LAN segments.

Cisco Routers in NetWare Networks

Cisco and Novell have collaborated for many years to develop and improve NetWare-based networking. Although many of the NetWare protocols were initially designed for use on small, homogeneous LANs, Cisco has added features to optimize NetWare protocols performance in large and diverse networking environments. Cisco supports many unique enhancements to the basic NetWare protocol suite. These enhancements are part of the *Cisco Internetwork Operating System (IOS) software*.

MOVIE 7.1

Large Novell Installations

Hundreds of file, print, and gateway services available.

The Novell NetWare Protocol Suite

NOTE

A datagram is one unit of *encapsulated* data that traverses a network and requires no acknowledgment. IP and User Datagram Protocol (UDP) use datagrams. The word *datagram* is often used as an adjective to describe protocols and networks that break data into discrete units and require no acknowledgment.

Novell, Inc., developed and introduced NetWare in the early 1980s. NetWare uses a *client/server* architecture. Clients (sometimes called *workstations*) request services, such as file and printer access, from servers. Unlike Windows NT networks, NetWare servers are dedicated servers and cannot be used as clients. Figure 7-1 shows the NetWare protocol suite, the media access protocols that NetWare and Cisco support, and the relationship between the NetWare protocols and the Open System Interconnection (OSI) reference model.

FIGURE 7-1
The NetWare protocol stack supports all common media access protocols.

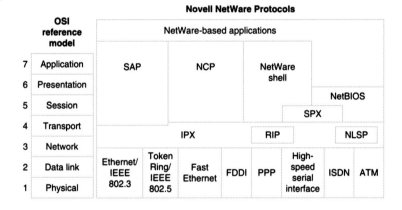

NOTE

SPX is a common NetWare transport layer (Layer 4) protocol. A reliable, connection-oriented protocol (similar to TCP), SPX adds to the datagram service provided by IPX.

Novell NetWare is a proprietary suite of protocols and includes the following:

- A connectionless protocol that does not require an acknowledgment for each port
- A Layer 3 protocol that defines the network and node addresses
- Novell Routing Information Protocol (RIP)—which is different from IP RIP—to facilitate the exchange of routing information
- *Service Advertising Protocol (SAP)* to advertise network services
- NetWare Core Protocol (NCP) to provide client-to-server connections and applications
- *Sequenced Packet Exchange (SPX)* service for Layer 4 connection-oriented services

IPX Overview

IPX is the NetWare Layer 3 protocol used to route packets through interconnected networks. IPX is connectionless (similar to IP in TCP/IP networks) and operates within the same network.

MOVIE 7.2
Novell NetWare
Based on client/server architecture.

IPX is similar to TCP/IP and operates within the same network implementation as TCP/IP, provided that you have a multiprotocol router. Some of the characteristics of IPX are

- It is used in a client/server environment.
- It uses the *network.node* IPX addressing structure.
- Its logical address contains an interface MAC address.
- IPX interface configuration supports multiple data-link encapsulations.
- Novell RIP uses the distance-vector metrics of ticks and hops.
- *SAP* and *Get Nearest Server (GNS)* broadcasts connect clients and servers.

IPX uses distance-vector routing (such as RIP) or link-state routing (such as *NetWare Link Services Protocol [NLSP]*). IPX RIP sends routing updates every 60 seconds. RIP uses ticks (network delay) and hop count as its *routing metrics*, and if the hop count is greater than 15, the packet will be discarded.

Novell IPX Addressing

Novell IPX addressing uses a two-part address—the network number and the node number—as shown in Figure 7-2. The node number is usually the *Media Access Control (MAC) address* for a network interface in the end node. Novell IPX supports multiple logical networks on an individual interface; each network requires a single encapsulation type. The IPX network number, which is assigned by the network administrator, can be up to eight *base 16 (hexadecimal)* digits in length.

Figure 7-3 shows two IPX networks, 4a1d and 3f. The IPX node number is 12 hexadecimal digits in length. This number is usually the MAC address, obtained from a network interface that has a MAC address. The use of the MAC address in the logical IPX address eliminates the need for Address Resolution Protocol (ARP). Serial interfaces use the MAC address of the Ethernet interface for their IPX node address. Figure 7-3 shows the IPX node

> **NOTE**
>
> To make best-path decisions, IPX uses a tick as the metric, which is the delay expected when using a particular length. One tick is $1/18$ second. If two paths have an equal tick count, IPX RIP uses the hop count. Although they are similar, Novell's version of RIP is not compatible with RIP implementations used in other networking protocol suites, such as TCP/IP.

0000.0c56.de33 on the 4a1d network. Another node address is 0000.0c56.de34 on the 3f network.

FIGURE 7-2
A Novell IPX address has 80 bits: 32 bits for the network number and 48 bits for the node number.

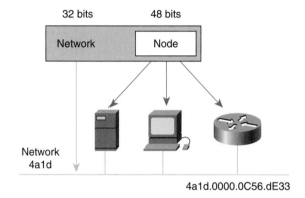

Regardless of whether you're using a LAN or a WAN interface, you assign the same IPX network numbers to the routers that are in use by the IPX devices. The best and recommended way to obtain a Novell network address is to ask the network administrator for one. The network administrator must specify the correct IPX network address on the Cisco router for the same network where you want IPX enabled. On the Cisco router, you must use the same IPX network address as the address that already exists on that network, which is typically specified by the NetWare administrator. If you cannot obtain an IPX address from the network administrator, you can get the IPX address directly from a neighbor router. To do this, you Telnet to the neighbor router and use the **show protocols** or **show ipx interface** command.

FIGURE 7-2
A Novell IPX address has 80 bits: 32 bits for the network number and 48 bits for the node number.

FIGURE 7-3
Each device in an IPX network has a unique address.

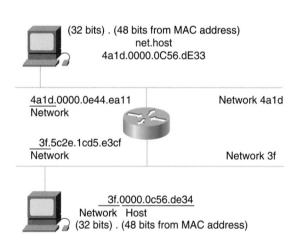

e-LAB ACTIVITY 7.1

show protocols

In this activity, you demonstrate how to use the **show protocols** command to display the configured protocols.

Engineering Journal:
The show ipx interface Command

To display the status of the IPX interfaces configured in the router and the parameters configured on each interface, use the **show ipx interface** in privileged EXEC command mode.

The full syntax of the command is

```
show ipx interface [interface unit]
```

The argument *interface* is the interface and can be one of the following types: asynchronous, dialer, Ethernet (IEEE 802.3), FDDI, loopback, null, serial, Token Ring, or tunnel. The argument *unit* is the number of the interface. For example, `ethernet 0` specifies the first Ethernet interface.

The following is sample output from the **show ipx interface** command:

```
Router# show ipx interface ethernet 1
Ethernet1 is up, line protocol is up
   IPX address is C03.0000.0c05.6030, NOVELL-ETHER [up] line-up,
      RIPPQ: 0, SAPPQ : 0
   Delay of this Novell network, in ticks is 1
   IPXWAN processing not enabled on this interface.
   IPX SAP update interval is 1 minute(s)
```

The following are the fields shown in this output:

Field	Description
Ethernet1 is..., line protocol is...	The type of interface and whether it is currently active and inserted into the network (up) or inactive and not inserted (down).
IPX address is...	The network and node address of the local router interface, followed by the type of encapsulation configured on the interface and the interface's status.
NOVELL-ETHER	The type of encapsulation being used on the interface, if any.
[up] line-up	Indicates whether IPX routing is enabled or disabled on the interface. Line-up indicates that IPX routing has been enabled with the **ipx routing** command. Line-down indicates that it is not enabled. The word in square brackets provides more detail about the status of IPX routing when it is in the process of being enabled or disabled.
RIPPQ:	The number of packets in the RIP queue.

continues

Field	Description
SAPPQ:	The number of packets in the SAP queue.
Secondary address is...	The address of a secondary network configured on this interface, if any, followed by the type of encapsulation configured on the interface and the interface's status. This line is displayed only if you have configured a secondary address with the **ipx network** command.
Delay of this Novell network, in ticks...	The value of the ticks field (configured with the **ipx delay** command).
IPXWAN processing...	Indicates whether IPXWAN processing has been enabled on this interface with the **ipx ipxwan** command.
IPX SAP update interval	Indicates the frequency of outgoing SAP updates (configured with the **ipx sap-interval** command).

Washington Project: IPX Addressing Issues

When planning IPX addressing, you do not need to worry about numbering hosts as you would for TCP/IP. This is because the host address for a workstation is usually the MAC address of that station's network interface card. However, you need to develop a scheme for the IPX network numbers in the Washington School District WAN. Remember that a router can't have two interfaces that belong to the same logical (IP, IPX, and so on) network or subnet; therefore, you cannot use the same network number throughout the district WAN.

When you develop your IPX network numbering scheme, keep in mind that IPX network numbers can be up to 32 bits (or 8 hexadecimal digits), but they usually contain leading zeros to "pad out" the address. For example, the number 21 can be used as a valid IPX network number because leading zeros can be added to expand 21 into 32 bits (written as 8 hexadecimal digits): 00000021.

Some network administrators convert the IP network address to hexadecimal and use the result as the IPX network number. For example, the subnet 169.199.69.128 /27 would become A9C74580. But there's no rule that says you have do this. You can use the leading zeros feature to create very simple IPX network numbers (such as 10, 20, 30, and so on).

You will see later in this chapter that, because of Layer 2 issues, a router interface may need to exist on two logical networks—that is, have two network numbers simultaneously. After you have read about Novell frame encapsulation types, you should check the TCS Overview carefully to see if your addressing scheme needs to account for this.

Novell Encapsulations

NetWare supports multiple encapsulations (that is, *frame* types), all of which are supported by Cisco routers, for the Ethernet family of protocols.

Xerox, Intel, and Digital (known collectively as DIX) first released a standard for Ethernet in 1980, called *Ethernet Version I*. Two years later, DIX replaced this standard with *Ethernet Version II*, which is the standard encapsulation type for TCP/IP. The Institute of Electrical and Electronic Engineers (IEEE) 802.3 committee began work on an improved Ethernet frame in 1982. The 802.3 committee was responsible for work on this project, but Novell could not wait for the committee to officially release the new frame specification. In 1983, Novell released its frame specifications based on the partial results of the 802.3 committee. Novell called this frame type 802.3 (Ethernet 802.3); this specification is sometimes called *Ethernet raw* because the IEEE hadn't finished "cooking" it. Two years later, the IEEE finally released the final 802.3 specification, which included the logical link control (LLC) header. The LLC contains fields that identify service access points, and these fields make the IEEE's specification (now called 802.2) incompatible with Novell's 802.3. Because the IEEE 802.2 frame includes service access points, the Cisco IOS software refers to 802.2 as *Ethernet SAP* (Novell calls it *Ethernet_802.2*). Compatibility issues between 802.2 and 802.3 prompted the development of a fourth major frame type: *Ethernet SNAP*. The most important thing to remember about these four frame types is that they are not compatible with each other. If a Novell server uses 802.3 framing, and a Cisco router is configured to encapsulate using 802.2, then these two nodes cannot talk to each other.

The Cisco IOS software and Novell terms for these encapsulations are

- Ethernet 802.3 is also called raw Ethernet and is the default for NetWare versions 2 through 3.11.
- Ethernet 802.2 or SAP (also called Novell Ethernet_802.2 or 802.3) is the standard IEEE frame format, including an 802.2 LLC header. With the release of NetWare 3.12 and 4.x, this encapsulation became Novell's new standard frame format and is also used for OSI routing.
- Ethernet II or ARPA (also called Novell Ethernet_II or Ethernet Version II) uses the standard Ethernet Version II header and is used with TCP/IP.
- Ethernet SNAP or snap (also called Novell Ethernet_SNAP or snap) extends the IEEE 802.2 header by adding a Subnetwork Access Protocol (SNAP) header, which provides an "encapsulation type" code similar to that defined in the Ethernet Version II specification and used with TCP/IP and AppleTalk.

Cisco Encapsulation Names

Cisco hardware and Cisco IOS software support all the different Ethernet/802.3 encapsulations used by NetWare. Cisco equipment can tell the difference between these various packet types, regardless of how they are encapsulated. Multiple encapsulations are supported on a single LAN interface, allowing older and newer NetWare nodes to coexist on the same LAN segment as long as you configure multiple logical networks. Multiple IPX-encapsulation support reduces equipment expense, minimizes configuration complexity, and eases migration from one IPX encapsulation method to another.

NOTE

Multiple IPX encapsulations can be specified on an interface, but only if multiple IPX network numbers have also been assigned. Although several IPX encapsulation types can share the same interface, Novell clients and servers with different IPX encapsulation types cannot communicate directly with each other.

NOTE

Make sure to use the Cisco name for the appropriate IPX encapsulation and that the IPX encapsulation types of the clients, servers, and routers all match. Also note that the default Ethernet IPX encapsulation type on Cisco routers does not match the default Ethernet IPX encapsulation type on Novell servers after NetWare 3.11.

When you configure an IPX network, you might need to specify an encapsulation type on the Novell servers and clients or on the Cisco router. Table 7-1 helps you specify the appropriate IPX encapsulation type by matching the Novell term to the equivalent Cisco IOS term for the same frame types.

TABLE 7-1   Cisco Encapsulation Names

Encapsulation Type	Novell IPX Name	Cisco IOS Name
Ethernet	Ethernet_802.3 Ethernet_802.2 Ethernet_II Ethernet_SNAP	novell-ether sap arpa snap
Token Ring	Token-Ring Token-Ring_SNAP	sap snap
FDDI	FDDI_SNAP FDDI_802.2 FDDI_RAW	snap sap novell-fddi

<table>
<tr><th colspan="1">Washington Project: IPX Addressing and Encapsulation Types</th></tr>
<tr><td>When configuring routers for the Washington School District, you should note what Novell servers are connected to a router's interface. If those servers are running NetWare 3.12 or 4.x, you must configure that interface to use Ethernet SAP as a frame type. If two NetWare servers connect to the same router port and use different frame types, you have to configure the router interface for multiple framing types. Thus, you must create multiple logical networks (that is, the interface will have two IPX addresses that have the same host number but different network numbers).</td></tr>
</table>

IPX Packet Format

The IPX packet is the basic unit of Novell NetWare networking. The following descriptions summarize the IPX packet fields:

Field	Description	
Checksum	Provides integrity checking	2
Packet Length	Length of packet (in bytes)	2
Transport Control	Number of routers a packet can traverse before it is discarded	1
Packet Type	Defines the Novell Service which created the packet (SPX, NCP, NLSP, RIP, SAP, or NetBios)	1

NOTE

NetWare 3.11 is old technology, and some network administrators have migrated to 3.12 or 4.x. As a result, if you have a new server that is using IPX, and you have a Cisco router, you should specify sap as the frame type. This is necessary because if your server speaks Ethernet 802.2 and your workstation speaks only Ethernet_802.3, they can't talk to each other. The Cisco router will default to 802.3. Newer servers do not use the default, so an encapsulation configuration is usually necessary.

Field	Description	
Destination Network	The network address of the destination network; part of the overall IPX destination address	4
Destination Node	The MAC address of the destination node; part of the overall IPX destination address	6
Destination Socket	Similar to TCP/UDP port numbers, this is the address of the process running in the destination node.	2
Source Network	The network address of the source address; part of the overall IPX source address	4
Source Node	The MAC address of the source node; part of the overall IPX source address	6
Source Socket	Similar to TCP/UDP port numbers, this is the address of the process running in the source node.	2
Data	Upper Layer Data	Variable

Novell Routing Using RIP

Connecting existing Novell LANs together and supporting large numbers of NetWare clients and servers presents special challenges in areas such as network management and scalability. Cisco IOS software provides several key features designed to make very large Novell networks possible.

Cisco IOS software supports the standard Novell RIP, which provides a basic solution for networking Novell LANs together. However, the frequent update messages, the slow convergence when the network topology changes, and the greater than 15 hop count limitation of Novell RIP make it a poor choice for larger networks or networks connected via WAN links.

Novell RIP uses two metrics to make routing decisions: ticks (a time measure) and hop count (a count of each router transversed). Novell RIP checks its two distance-vector metrics by first comparing the ticks for alternate paths. Utilizing ticks as a metric provides a better measurement of the speed of the link. If two or more paths have the same tick value, Novell RIP compares the hop count. If two or more paths have the same hop count, the router load shares. *Load sharing* is the use of two or more paths to route packets to the same destination evenly among multiple routers to balance the work and improve network performance.

A router's Novell RIP routing table is different from its IP routing table because the router maintains a routing table for every IPX protocol that is enabled. Therefore, each IPX-enabled router periodically passes copies of its Novell RIP routing table to its direct neighbor. The neighbor IPX routers add distance vectors as required before passing copies of their Novell RIP tables to their own neighbors.

A "best information" split-horizon protocol prevents the neighbor from broadcasting Novell RIP tables about IPX information back to the networks from which it received that information. Novell RIP also uses an information aging mechanism to handle conditions where an IPX-enabled router goes down without any exact message to its neighbors. Periodic updates reset the aging timer. Routing table updates are sent at 60-second intervals. This update frequency can cause excessive overhead traffic on some networks.

MOVIE 7.3

Simple Split Horizon

Prevents routing loops.

e-LAB ACTIVITY 7.2

ipx routing

In this activity, you demonstrate how to use the **ipx routing** command to enable IPX routing.

Engineering Journal:
The ipx routing Command

To enable IPX routing, use the **ipx routing** in global configuration mode. The full syntax of the command is

    ipx routing [*node*]

To disable IPX routing, use the **no** form of this command:

    no ipx routing [*node*]

The argument *node* indicates the node number of the router. This is a 48-bit value represented by a dotted triplet of four-digit hexadecimal numbers (xxxx.xxxx.xxxx).

If you omit *node*, the router uses the hardware MAC address currently assigned to it as its node address. This is the MAC address of the first Ethernet, Token Ring, or FDDI interface card. If no satisfactory interfaces are present in the router (such as only serial interfaces), you must specify *node*.

The **ipx routing** command enables the IPX RIP and SAP services on the router. If you omit the argument node and if the MAC address later changes, the IPX node address automatically changes to the new address. However, connectivity might be lost between the time that the MAC address changes and the time that the IPX clients and servers learn the router's new address. The following example enables IPX routing:

```
Router(config)# ipx routing
```

Engineering Journal:
The ipx maximum-paths Command

To set the maximum number of equal-cost paths the router uses when forwarding packets, use the **ipx maximum-paths** in global configuration mode. The full syntax of this command is

```
ipx maximum-paths paths
```

To restore the default value of 1, use the no form of this command:

```
no ipx maximum-paths paths
```

The argument *paths* indicates the maximum number of equal-cost paths the router will use and can be a value from 1 to 512. The default value is 1.

The **ipx maximum-paths** command is designed to increase throughput by allowing the router to choose among several equal-cost, parallel paths. (Note that when paths have differing costs, the router chooses lower-cost routes before higher-cost routes.) IPX load shares on a packet-by-packet basis in round-robin fashion, regardless of whether you are using fast switching or process switching. That is, the first packet is sent along the first path, the second packet along the second path, and so on. When the final path is reached, the next packet is sent to the first path, the next to the second path, and so on.

Limiting the number of equal-cost paths can save memory on routers with limited memory or very large configurations. Additionally, in networks with a large number of multiple paths and end systems with the limited ability to cache out-of-sequence packets, performance might suffer when traffic is split between many paths. In the following example, the router uses up to three parallel paths:

```
Router(config)# ipx maximum-paths 3
```

Engineering Journal:
Cisco's Enhanced IGRP

One of Cisco's greatest strengths for connecting NetWare LANs is the enhanced version of Cisco's Interior Gateway Routing Protocol (IGRP). *Enhanced IGRP* provides support for NetWare and AppleTalk networks, in addition to TCP/IP. Enhanced IGRP is a distance-vector routing protocol, but features the fast convergence on changes in the network topology of a link-state routing protocol. Enhanced IGRP issues routing updates only when the network topology changes, transmits only the changed information, and limits the distribution of the update information to those routers affected by the change. As a result, Enhanced IGRP provides low routing overhead, low router CPU utilization, and moderate memory requirements.

Unlike link-state protocols, Enhanced IGRP does not require networks to be designed with an explicit address hierarchy, which gives network administrators greater flexibility in connecting and extending existing networks. Enhanced IGRP also makes use of multiple metrics (delay, bandwidth, reliability, and load) to build a more accurate view of the overall network topology and make more efficient use of network bandwidth. Enhanced IGRP can reduce backbone traffic on large NetWare networks by as much as 40% to 50%. Many large public and private NetWare networks have been implemented using Enhanced IGRP on the network backbone because of its excellent scalability and performance.

To create an IPX Enhanced IGRP routing process, perform the following tasks:

Task	Command
Enable an IPX Enhanced IGRP routing process in global configuration mode.	**ipx router eigrp** *autonomous-system-number*
Enable Enhanced IGRP on a network in IPX router configuration mode.	**network** {*network-number* | *all*}

The following example enables RIP on Networks 1 and 2, and Enhanced IGRP on Network 1:

```
Router# ipx routing
!
interface ethernet 0
 ipx network 1
!
interface ethernet 1
 ipx network 2
!
ipx router eigrp 100
 network 1
```

The following example enables RIP on Network 2, and Enhanced IGRP on Network 1:

```
Router# ipx routing
!
interface ethernet 0
 ipx network 1
!
interface ethernet 1
 ipx network 2
!
ipx router eigrp 100
 ipx network 1
!
ipx router rip
 no ipx network 1
```

Service Advertising Protocol

NetWare's SAP allows network resources, including file and print servers, to advertise their network addresses and the services they provide. Each service is identified by a number, called a SAP identifier. SAP updates are sent every 60 seconds.

Intermediate network devices, like routers, listen to the SAP updates and build a table of all known services and associated network addresses. When a Novell client requests a particular network service and a NetWare server is located on the segment, it responds to the client request. The Cisco router does not respond to the GNS request. If there are no NetWare servers on the local network, the Cisco router responds with a server address from its own SAP table. The client can then contact the service directly.

All the servers on NetWare networks can advertise their services and addresses. All versions of NetWare support SAP broadcasts to announce and locate registered network services. Adding, finding, and removing services on the network is dynamic because of SAP advertisements.

Each SAP service is an object type identified by a number. The following are examples:

Number	SAP Service
4	NetWare file server
7	Print server
24	Remote bridge server (router)

Workstations do not keep SAP tables—only routers and servers keep SAP tables. All servers and routers keep a complete list of the services available throughout the network in SAP tables. Like RIP, SAP also uses an aging mechanism to identify and remove SAP table entries that become invalid.

MOVIE 7.4

SAP

Network resources advertise services.

By default, service advertisements occur at 60-second intervals. However, although service advertisements might work well on a LAN, broadcasting services can require too much bandwidth to be acceptable on large networks, or in networks linked on WAN serial connections.

Routers do not forward SAP broadcasts. Instead, each router builds its own SAP table and forwards the SAP table to other routers. By default, this occurs every 60 seconds, but the router can use access control lists to control the SAPs accepted or forwarded.

Cisco IOS software also allows network administrators to display SAP table entries by name rather than by SAP identifier. By presenting network configuration information in a more readable format, this feature makes maintaining networks and diagnosing network problems easier.

Engineering Journal: Configurable RIP and SAP Update Timers and Packet Sizes

NetWare clients and servers rely on RIP and SAP update messages, both of which occur every 60 seconds by default, to transmit routing information and to provide current information on available network services. Once each minute, RIP and SAP update timers trigger broadcast packets to inform the network of changes in the internal tables of a particular device. These update packets can wreak havoc on network performance, however, particularly in the case of large, continually changing networks with relatively slow backbones.

Cisco IOS software supports configurable RIP and SAP update timers on a per-interface basis. By appropriately configuring the RIP and SAP update timers, network administrators can control the amount of traffic introduced to the network by RIP and SAP, thereby saving precious bandwidth.

Cisco IOS software also allows the size of the RIP and SAP packets to be increased (up to the MTU of the underlying network). By increasing the size of the RIP and SAP packets, the overall number of update packets can be reduced, making more efficient use of available bandwidth.

Get Nearest Server Protocol

NetWare clients automatically discover available network services because Novell servers and routers announce the services by using SAP broadcasts. One type of SAP advertisement is GNS, which enables a client to quickly locate the nearest server for login.

The NetWare client/server interaction begins when the client powers up and runs its client startup programs. These programs use the client's network adapter on the LAN and initiate the connection sequence for the NetWare command shell to use. The connection sequence is a broadcast that comes from a client using SAP. The nearest NetWare file server responds with another SAP; the protocol type is GNS. From that point on, the client can log in to the target server, make a connection, set the packet size, and proceed to use server resources.

If a NetWare server is located on the segment, it responds to the client request. The Cisco router does not respond to the GNS request. If there are no

NetWare servers on the local network, the Cisco router responds with a server address from its own SAP table.

Cisco IOS software allows NetWare clients to be located on LAN segments where there are no servers. When a NetWare client wants to locate a NetWare server, it issues a NetWare GNS request. Cisco routers listen to NetWare traffic, identify eligible servers, and forward the GNS requests specifically to them. By filtering GNS packets, you can explicitly exclude selected servers, providing greater security and flexibility in network design.

In responding to GNS requests, Cisco IOS software can also distribute clients evenly among the available servers. For example, assume that Clients A and B both issue GNS requests, as shown in Figure 7-4. The Cisco router sends a GNS response to Client A, telling it to communicate with Server 1, and a GNS response to Client B, telling it to communicate with Server 2.

FIGURE 7-4
A GNS request is a broadcast from a client needing a server.

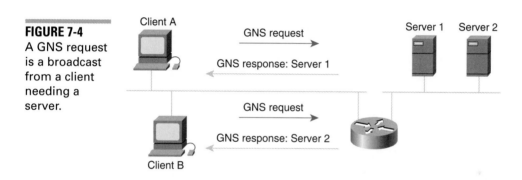

By supporting serverless LAN segments and distributing clients evenly among available servers, Cisco IOS software provides network-based load sharing, improves application availability, and minimizes the need to configure and manage large numbers of local servers, assuming that the servers are identical.

Novell IPX Configuration Tasks

Configuring the router for IPX routing involves both global and interface tasks.

Global IPX configuration tasks include the following:

- Start the IPX routing process.
- Enable load sharing if appropriate for your network.

Interface IPX configuration tasks include the following:

- Assign unique network numbers to each interface. Multiple network numbers can be assigned to an interface, allowing support of different encapsulation types.
- Set the optional IPX encapsulation type if it is different from the default.

These IPX configuration tasks are described in more detail in the following sections.

Novell IPX Global Configuration

The **ipx routing** command enables Novell IPX routing. If no node address is specified, the Cisco router uses the MAC address of the interface. If a Cisco router has only serial interfaces, an address must be specified. In addition, the **ipx maximum-paths** command enables load sharing. As previously stated, this is the maximum number of parallel paths to the destination; the default is 1 and the maximum is 512.

Assigning IPX Network Numbers to Interfaces

When assigning IPX network numbers to interfaces that support multiple IPX networks, you can also configure primary and secondary IPX networks.

The first logical network you configure on an interface is considered the *primary network*. Any additional networks are considered *secondary networks*. Again, each IPX network on an interface must use a distinct encapsulation, and it should match that of the clients and servers using the same network number. Assigning the second network number is necessary if an additional encapsulation type is linked to an individual network.

To assign network numbers to interfaces that support multiple IPX networks, you normally use subinterfaces. A *subinterface* is a mechanism that allows a single physical interface to support multiple logical interfaces or networks. That is, several logical interfaces or networks can be associated with a single hardware interface. Each subinterface must use a distinct encapsulation, and the encapsulation must match that of the clients and servers using the same network number.

Washington Project: Configuring Subinterfaces
If a router's interface needs to exist on two different IPX networks to accommodate two different frame types or two different IP subnets, or if you run out of host space, then you need to configure subinterfaces.

The example shown in Figure 7-5 illustrates both the global configuration of Novell IPX and the assignment of network numbers to interfaces. The following describes the commands used in the example:

Command	Description
ipx routing	Selects IPX for routing, and starts IPX RIP.
ipx maximum-paths 2	Allows load sharing over parallel metric paths to the destination. The number of parallel paths used is limited to two.

Command	Description
interface ethernet 0.1	Indicates the first subinterface on interface E0.
encapsulation novell-ether	Specifies that Novell's unique frame format is used on this network segment. Cisco's keyword is **novell-ether**; Novell's terminology is **Ethernet_802.3**.
ipx network 9e	The network number assigned to subinterface E0.1.
interface ethernet 0.2	Indicates the second subinterface on interface E0.
ipx network 6c	The network number assigned to subinterface E0.2.
encapsulation sap	Specifies that Ethernet 802.2 frame format is used on this network segment. Cisco's keyword is **sap**.

FIGURE 7-5
A Novell IPX configuration example of assigning network numbers to interfaces.

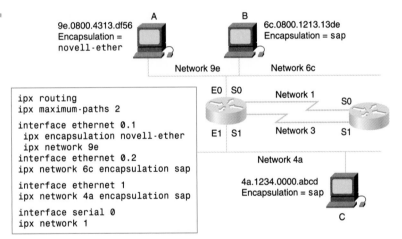

```
ipx routing
ipx maximum-paths 2

interface ethernet 0.1
 ipx encapsulation novell-ether
 ipx network 9e
interface ethernet 0.2
ipx network 6c encapsulation sap

interface ethernet 1
ipx network 4a encapsulation sap

interface serial 0
ipx network 1
```

Verifying IPX Operation

When IPX routing is configured, you can monitor and troubleshoot IPX by using the commands listed in Table 7-2.

e-LAB ACTIVITY 7.3

ipx routing

In this activity, you work through several tasks to configure IPX.

TABLE 7-2   **IPX Monitoring and Troubleshooting Commands**

Command	Displays
Monitoring Commands	
show ipx interface	IPX status and parameters.
show ipx route	Routing table contents.
show ipx servers	IPX server list.
show ipx traffic	Number and type of packets
Troubleshooting Commands	
debug ipx routing activity	Information about RIP update packets.
debug ipx sap	Information about SAP update packets.
ping	Information about a particular node that is capable of responding to network requests.

SKILL BUILDER

IPX Routing

In previous labs, you worked with the TCP/IP routed protocol or the Internet Protocol (IP). In this lab, you work with Novell's Internetwork Packet Exchange (IPX) routed protocol. OSI Layer 3 protocols, such as IP and IPX, contain information in their packets to indicate what network the packet came from and what network it is going to.

Monitoring and Managing an IPX Network

Cisco IOS software includes a variety of tools for configuring, monitoring, and managing the network. These tools make NetWare networks easier to set up and can be essential when unforeseen network conditions are encountered.

Engineering Journal:
Simple Network Management Protocol

Cisco IOS software supports the NetWare Management Information Base (MIB), which is available from Novell, for Simple Network Management Protocol (SNMP), which allows a network administrator to

- Manually delete a neighbor and all its routes from the routing table
- Display all IPX-related interface settings, including the IPX address of the interface, the state of the line hardware, whether IPX protocol processing is enabled or disabled, and the delay to various destinations

- Display the contents of name, neighbor, and routing tables
- Display statistics about IPX protocol traffic, such as
  - —Total number of IPX packets received
  - —Number and type of packet errors
  - —Total number of broadcast packets received, sent, and forwarded
  - —Number of echo packets sent and received
- Log important IPX protocol operations, including RIP, SAP, echo, and routing activities

Monitoring the Status of an IPX Interface

The **show ipx interface** command shows the status of IPX interface and IPX parameters configured on each interface.

In Example 7-1, the first highlighted line shows the IPX address, the type of encapsulation, and the status of the interface. The second highlighted area shows that the SAP filters are not set. The last highlighted line shows that fast switching is enabled.

Example 7-1   *show ipx interface Command Sample Output*

```
Router# show ipx interface ethernet 0
Ethernet0 is up, line protocol is up
  IPX address is 3010.aa00.0400.0284 NOVELL_ETHER [up] line-up RIPPQ: 0, SAPPQ: 0
  Delay of this Novel network, in ticks, is 1
  IPXWAN processing not enabled on this interface
  IPX SAP update interval is 1 minute(s)
  IPX type 20 propagation packet forwarding is disabled
  Outgoing access list is not set
  IPX Helper access list is not set
  SAP Input filter list is not set
  SAP Output filter list is not set
  SAP Router filter list is not set
  SAP GNS output filter list is not set
  Input filter list is not set
  Output filter list is not set
  Router filter list is not set
  Netbios Input host access list is not set
  Netbios Input bytes access list is not set
  Netbios Output host access list is not set
  Netbios Output bytes access list is not set
  Update time is 60 seconds
  IPX accounting is disabled
  IPX fast switching is configured (enabled)
  IPX SSE switching is disabled
  RIP packets received 1, RIP packets sent 10006
  SAP packets received 1, SAP packets sent 6
```

You can manually set the tick metric to configure the tick delay on an interface. You use the command **ipx delay** *number*, where *number* is the ticks to associate with an interface. This command manually overrides the following defaults on the Cisco router:

- For LAN interfaces, 1 tick
- For WAN interfaces, 6 ticks

e-LAB ACTIVITY 7.4

show ipx interface ethernet 0

Use **show ip interface** to display the status of the IPX interfaces configured in the Cisco IOS software and the parameters configured on each interface.

Monitoring IPX Routing Tables

The **show ipx route** command displays the contents of the IPX routing table.

In Example 7-2, the first highlighted line provides routing information for a remote network:

- The R represents the information learned from a RIP update.
- The network is number 3030.
- The network is located six ticks or one hop away. (This information is used to determine best routes. If there is a tie between ticks, hops are used to break the tie.)
- The next hop in the path is router 3021.0000.0c03.13d3.
- The information was updated 23 seconds ago.
- The next-hop router is reachable out interface Serial1.
- There is an equal-metric route to a different next-hop router, reachable through interface Serial 0 (for load sharing).

The second line of highlighting provides information about a direct connection:

- The network number is 3010.
- The encapsulation type is NOVELL-ETHER.
- The C represents the information learned from a directly connected primary network.

Example 7-2   *show ipx route Command Sample Output*

```
Router# show ipx route
Codes: C - Connected primary network, c - Connected secondary network,
  R - RIP, E - EIGRP, S - Static, W - IPXWAN connected
5 total IPX routes

Up to 2 parallel paths allowed. Novell routing protocol variant in use

R Net 3030 [6/1] via 3021.0000.0c03.13d3, 23 sec, Serial1
  via 3020.0000.0c03.13d3, 23 sec, Serial0
```

Example 7-2 *show ipx route* Command Sample Output *(Continued)*

```
C Net 3020 (X25), Serial0
C Net 3021 (HDLC), Serial1
C Net 3010 (NOVELL-ETHER), Ethernet0
C Net 3000 (NOVELL-ETHER), Ethernet1
```

The following describes the fields shown in Example 7-2:

Field	Description
Codes	Codes defining how the route was learned: C—Directly connected primary network. c—Directly connected secondary network. R—Route learned from a RIP update. E—Route learned from an Enhanced IGRP update. S—Statically defined route, defined via the **ipx route** command. W—Directly connected route, determined via IPXWAN.
5 Total IPX routes	The number of routes in the IPX routing table.
Parallel paths allowed	The maximum number of parallel paths for which the router has been configured with the **ipx maximum-paths** command.
Novell routing protocol variant in use	Indicates whether the router is using the IPX-compliant routing protocols (default).
Net 1	The network to which the route goes.
[6/1]	*Delay/Metric. Delay* is the number of IBM clock ticks reported to the destination network. *Metric* is the number of hops reported to the same network. *Delay* is used as the primary routing metric, and *Metric* (hop count) is used as a tie breaker.
via network.node	The address of a router that is the next hop to the remote network.
Age	The amount of time, in hours, minutes, and seconds, that has elapsed since information about this network was last received.
Uses	The number of times this network has been looked up in the routing table. This field is incremented when a packet is process-switched, even if the packet is eventually filtered and not sent. Therefore, this field represents a fair estimate of the number of times a route gets used.

continues

Field	Description
Ethernet0	The interface through which packets to the remote network will be sent.
(NOVELL-ETHER) (HDLC) (SAP)(SNAP)	The encapsulation (frame) type.

e-LAB ACTIVITY 7.5

show ipx route

In this activity, you demonstrate how to use the **show ipx route** command to display the content of the IPX routing table.

Monitoring the Novell IPX Servers

The **show ipx servers** command lists the IPX servers discovered through SAP advertisements. The output of the **show ipx servers** command shows the following information:

- The service learned about the server from a SAP update
- The server name, network location, device address, and source socket number
- The ticks and hops for the route (taken from the routing table)
- The number of hops (taken from the SAP protocol)
- The interface through which to reach the server

To list the IPX servers discovered through SAP advertisements, use the **show ipx servers** command in user EXEC mode. The full syntax of this command is:

```
show ipx servers [sorted [name | net | type]]
```

The following describes the keywords used in the command:

Keyword	Description
sorted	(Optional) Sorts the display of IPX servers according to the keyword that follows.
name	(Optional) Displays the IPX servers alphabetically by server name.
net	(Optional) Displays the IPX servers numerically by network number.
type	(Optional) Displays the IPX servers numerically by SAP service type. This is the default.

Example 7-3 is sample output from the **show ipx servers** command.

Example 7-3 *show ipx servers Command Sample Output*

```
Router> show ipx servers
Codes: P - Periodic, I - Incremental, H - Holddown, S - Static
1 Total IPX Servers
Table ordering is based on routing and server info
Type  Name     Net Address                 Port     Route Hops  Itf
P     4 MAXINE  AD33000.0000.1b04.0288:0451 332800/ 1     2     Et3
```

The following describes the fields shown in Example 7-3:

Field	Description
Codes	Codes defining how the server was learned: • P—The server information was learned via the normal periodic SAP updates. • I—The server information was learned by using the incremental SAP capability in IPX Enhanced IGRP. • H—The server is believed to have gone down, and the router will no longer advertise this server's services. • S—The server is defined statically, via the ipx sap command.
Total IPX Servers and server info	The number of servers in the list.
Table order is based on routing and server info	Entries listed are based on the routing information associated with this SAP. Server information is used as a tie breaker.
Type	The SAP service number.
Name	The server name.
Net	The network number of the server.
Address	The node address of the server.
Port	The socket number.
Route	The metric/hop count for the route to the network.
Hops	The SAP-advertised number of hops from the router to the server's network.
Itf	The interface through which this server was first discovered.

e-LAB ACTIVITY 7.6

show ipx servers

In this activity, you demonstrate how to use the **show ipx servers** command to display the IPX server list.

Monitoring IPX Traffic

You use the **show ipx traffic** command to get information about the number and type of IPX packets received and transmitted by the router.

Notice in Example 7-4 that a large percentage of the total number of packets received and sent were RIP advertisements because this sample was taken from a lab network with essentially no user traffic on it. This output shows how much overhead traffic IPX generates.

Example 7-4   *show ipx traffic Command Sample Output*

```
Router# show ipx traffic
Rcvd:   32124925 total, 1691992 format errors, 0 checksum errors,
            67 bad hop count,
        18563 packets pitched, 452467 local destination, 0 multicast
Bcast:  452397 received, 1237193 sent
Sent:   2164776 generated, 31655567 forwarded
        0 encapsulation failed, 2053 no route
SAP:    3684 SAP requests, 10382 SAP replies
        259288 SAP advertisements received, 942564 sent
        0 SAP flash updates sent, 0 SAP poison sent
        0 SAP format errors
RIP:    0 RIP format errors
Echo:   Rcvd 0 requests, 0 replies
        Sent 0 requests, 0 replies
        4252 unknown, 0 SAPs throttled, freed NDB len 0
Watchdog:
        0 packets received, 0 replies spoofed
Queue lengths:
        IPX input: 1, SAP 0, RIP 0, GNS 0
        Total length for SAP throttling purposes: 1/(no preset limit)
IGRP:   Total received 0, sent 0
        Updates received 0, sent 0
        Queries received 0, sent 0
        Replies received 0, sent 0
        SAPs received 0, sent 0
```

e-LAB ACTIVITY 7.7

show ipx traffic

In this activity, you demonstrate how to use the **show ipx traffic** command to display the number and type of packets.

The following describes the fields that might possibly be shown in Example 7-4:

Field	Description
Rcvd:	A description of the packets the router has received.
644 total	The total number of packets the router has received.
1705 format errors	The number of bad packets discarded (for example, packets using a frame type not configured on an interface).
0 checksum errors	The number of packets containing a checksum error.
0 bad hop count	The number of packets discarded because their hop count exceeded 16 (that is, the packets timed out).
0 packets pitched	The number of times the router has discarded packets. This can happen when a type 20 propagation or all-networks broadcast fails the **ipx type-20-input-checks** command; when a type 20 propagation packet handling detects a loop, detects an excessive hop count, or is malformed; when RIP or SAP packets are received for the wrong network; when the router receives its own broadcast; or when the router receives local packets from the wrong source network.
644 local destination	The number of packets sent to the local broadcast address or specifically to the router.
0 multicast	The number of packets received that were addressed to multiple destinations.
Bcast:	A description of the broadcast packets the router has received and sent.
589 received	The number of broadcast packets received.
324 sent	The number of broadcast packets sent. It includes broadcast packets the router is either forwarding or has generated.
Sent:	A description of the packets that the router generated and then sent, and the ones the router has received and then routed to other destinations.
380 generated	The number of packets the router transmitted that it generated itself.
0 forwarded	The number of packets the router transmitted that it forwarded from other sources.
0 encapsulation failed	The number of packets the router was unable to encapsulate.

continues

Field	Description
4 no route	The number of times the router could not locate in the routing table a route to the destination.
SAP:	A description of the SAP packets the router has sent and received.
1 SAP requests	The number of SAP requests the router has received.
1 SAP replies	The number of SAP replies the router has sent in response to SAP requests.
61 SAP advertisements received	The number of SAP advertisements the router has received from another router.
120 sent	The number of SAP advertisements the router has generated and then sent.
0 SAP flash updates sent	The number of SAP advertisements the router has generated and then sent as a result of a change in its routing table.
0 SAP poison sent	The number of times the router has generated an update indicating that a service is no longer reachable.
0 SAP format errors	The number of SAP advertisements that were incorrectly formatted.
RIP:	A description of the RIP packets the router has sent and received.
0 RIP format errors	The number of RIP packets that were incorrectly formatted.
Echo:	A description of the **ping** replies and requests the router has sent and received.
Rcvd 55 request 0 replies	The number of **ping** requests and replies received by the router.
Sent 0 requests, 55 replies	The number of **ping** requests and replies sent by the router.
0 unknown	The number of unrecognized packets sent to the router.
0 SAPs throttled	The number of SAP packets discarded because they exceeded buffer capacity.

Field	Description
freed NDB length	The number of network descriptor blocks (NDBs) that have been removed from the network but still need to be removed from the router's routing table.
Watchdog:	A description of the watchdog packets the router has handled.
0 packets received	The number of watchdog packets the router has received from IPX servers on the local network.
0 replies spoofed	The number of times the router has responded to a watchdog packet on behalf of the remote client.
Queue lengths	A description of outgoing packets currently in buffers that are waiting to be processed.
IPX input	The number of incoming packets waiting to be processed.
SAP	The number of incoming SAP packets waiting to be processed.
RIP	The number of incoming RIP packets waiting to be processed.
GNS	The number of incoming GNS packets waiting to be processed.
Total length for SAP throttling purposes	The maximum number of incoming RIP and SAP packets allowed in the buffer. Any SAP request packets received beyond this number are discarded.
unknown counter	The number of packets the router was unable to forward, for example, because no route was available.

Troubleshooting IPX Routing

Cisco IOS software supports a **debug** command and a **ping** command, allowing network administrators to view and track almost any aspect of network traffic. Cisco's **debug** support can be essential to network administrators in monitoring, managing, and troubleshooting Novell networks.

The **debug ipx routing activity** command displays information about IPX routing update packets that are transmitted or received.

A router sends an update every 60 seconds. Each update packet can contain up to 50 entries. If there are more than 50 entries in the routing table, the update includes more than 1 packet.

In Example 7-5, the router is sending updates but not receiving them. Updates received from other routers would also appear in this listing.

Example 7-5   *debug ipx routing activity Command Sample Output*

```
Router# debug ipx routing activity
IPX routing debugging is on
Router#
IPXRIP: positing full update to 3010.ffff.ffff.ffff via Ethernet0 (broadcast)
IPXRIP: positing full update to 3000.ffff.ffff.ffff via Ethernet1 (broadcast)
IPXRIP: positing full update to 3020.ffff.ffff.ffff via Serial0 (broadcast)
IPXRIP: positing full update to 3021.ffff.ffff.ffff via Serial1 (broadcast)
IPXRIP: sending update to 3020.ffff.ffff.ffff via Serial0
IPXRIP: arc=3020.0000.0c03.14d8m dst=3020.ffff.ffff.ffff, packet sent
   network 3021, hops 1, delay 6
   network 3010, hops 1, delay 6
   network 3000, hops 1, delay 6
IPXRIP: sending update to 3021.ffff.ffff.ffff via Serial1
IPXRIP: arc=3021.0000.0c03.14d8m dst=3021.ffff.ffff.ffff, packet sent
   network 3020, hops 1, delay 6
   network 3010, hops 1, delay 6
   network 3000, hops 1, delay 6
IPXRIP: sending update to 3010.ffff.ffff.ffff via Ethernet0
IPXRIP: arc=3010.aa00.0400.0284, dst=3010.ffff.ffff.ffff, packet sent
   network 3030, hops 2, delay 7
   network 3020, hops 1, delay 1
   network 3021, hops 1, delay 1
   network 3000, hops 1, delay 1
IPXRIP: sending update to 3000.ffff.ffff.ffff via Ethernet1
```

The **debug ipx routing activity** command should be used with caution, as with any **debug** command. It uses a great deal of router resources and could cause the router to "crash" and bring the network down.

e-LAB ACTIVITY 7.8

debug ipx routing activity

In this activity, you demonstrate how to use the **debug ipx routing activity** command to display information about IPX routing update packets that are transmitted or received.

Troubleshooting IPX SAP

The **debug ipx sap [events | activity]** command displays information about IPX SAP packets that are transmitted or received. One of the two choices ([events | activity]) at the end of the command is required. The events option provides less detail in the command output, while activity provides more detail.

Like RIP updates, these SAP updates are sent every 60 seconds and may contain multiple packets. As shown in Example 7-6, each SAP packet appears as multiple lines in the output, including a packet summary message and a service detail message.

Example 7-6 *debug ipx sap Command Sample Output*

```
Router# debug ipx sap events
IPX SAP debugging is on
Router#
NovellSAP: at 0023F778
I SAP Response type 0x2 len 160 arc:160.0000.0c00.070d
dest:160.ffff.ffff.ffff(452)
    type 0x4, "HELLO2", 199.0002.0004.0006(451), 2 hops
    type 0x4, "HELLO1", 199.0002.0004.0008(451), 2 hops
    Novell SAP: sending update to 160
    NovellSAP: at 169080
    O SAP Update type 0x2 len 96 ssoc; 0x452 dest: 160.ffff.ffff.ffff(452)
    Novell: type 0x4 "Magnolia", 42.0000.0000.0000(451), 2 hops
```

SAP responses may be one of the following:

- **0x1**—General query
- **0x2**—General response
- **0x3**—GNS request
- **0x4**—GNS response

In each line of the SAP response of the sample output, the address and distance of the responding or target router is listed.

The IPX ping Command

Cisco IOS software provides an IPX version of the **ping** command to aid in network troubleshooting. The **ping** command enables network administrators to verify that a particular node is capable of responding to network requests. This feature helps determine whether a physical path exists through a station that is causing network problems. IPX **ping** is a Novell standard and can be used with Novell clients and servers and network devices.

The Privileged IPX ping Command

To check host reachability and network connectivity, use the **ping** in privileged EXEC command mode. The full syntax of the command is

```
ping [ipx] [network.node]
```

The following is a description of the parameters used in this command:

Parameter	Description
ipx	(Optional) Specifies the IPX protocol.
network.node	(Optional) The address of the system to **ping**.

The privileged **ping** command provides a complete **ping** facility for users who have system privileges.

The privileged **ping** command works only on Cisco routers running IOS Release 8.2 or later. Novell IPX devices do not respond to this command.

You cannot **ping** a router from itself. To abort a **ping** session, type the escape sequence. By default, this is Ctrl-^-X or Ctrl-^-6-X. You enter this by simultaneously pressing the Ctrl, Shift, and 6 keys, letting go, and then pressing the X key.

e-LAB ACTIVITY 7.9

debug ipx sap

Use the **debug ipx sap** command to display information about IPX SAP packets that are transmitted or received.

Table 7-3 describes the test characters displayed in **ping** responses.

TABLE 7-3   ping Response Test Characters

ping Test Character	Meaning
!	Each exclamation point indicates the receipt of a reply from the target address.
.	Each period indicates that the network server timed out while waiting for a reply from the target address.
U	A destination unreachable error protocol data unit (PDU) was received.
C	A congestion experienced packet was received.
I	A user interrupted the test.
?	An unknown packet type.
&	Packet lifetime exceeded.

The sample display in Example 7-7 shows input to and output from the privileged **ping** command.

Example 7-7   *Privileged ping Command Output*

```
Router# ping
Protocol [ip]: ipx
Target Novell Address: 211.0000.0c01.f4cf
Repeat Count [5]:
Datagram Size [100]:
Timeout in seconds [2]:
```

Example 7-7   *Privileged **ping** Command Output (Continued)*

```
Verbose [n]:
Type escape sequence to abort.
Sending 5 100-byte Novell echoes to 211.0000.0c01.f4cf, timeout is 2 seconds.
!!!!!
Success rate is 100%, round trip min/avg/max  = 1/2/4 ms.
```

e-LAB ACTIVITY 7.10

Privileged IPX ping

In this activity, you demonstrate how to use the privileged IPX **ping** command to check host reachability and network connectivity.

The User IPX ping Command

To check host reachability and network connectivity, use the user-level ping command in EXEC command mode. As opposed to the privileged ping command, the user-level **ping** command provides a basic **ping** facility for users who do not have system privileges. This command is equivalent to a simplified form of the privileged **ping** command. It sends five 100-byte IPX Cisco echoes.

The full syntax of the command is

> **ping** [**ipx**] {*host* | *address*}

The following is a description of the parameters used in the syntax:

Parameter	Description
ipx	(Optional) Specifies the IPX protocol.
host	The host name of the system to **ping**.
address	The address of the system to **ping**.

The user-level **ping** command works only on Cisco routers running IOS Release 8.2 or later. Novell IPX devices do not respond to this command.

You cannot **ping** a router from itself. If the system cannot map an address for a host name, it returns an **%Unrecognized host or address** error message.

Example 7-8 shows input to and output from the user-level **ping** command:

Example 7-8   *User-Level **ping** Command Output*

```
Router> ping ipx 211.0000.0c01.f4cf
Type escape sequence to abort.
Sending 5, 100-byte Novell Echoes to 211.0000.0c01.f4cf, timeout is 2 seconds:
...
Success rate is 0 percent (0/5)
```

e-LAB ACTIVITY 7.11

User IPX ping

In this activity, you demonstrate how to use the user IPX **ping** command to check host reachability and network connectivity.

Summary

- Novell IPX is a proprietary suite of protocols and includes the following:
  - A datagram, connectionless protocol that does not require an acknowledgment for each packet.
  - A Layer 3 protocol that defines the network and internode addresses.
- Novell NetWare uses RIP to facilitate the exchange of routing information and SAP to advertise network services. NetWare uses NCP to provide client-to-server connections and applications, and SPX for Layer 4 connection-oriented services.
- IPX is the NetWare Layer 3 protocol and specifies a connectionless datagram, similarly to an IP packet in TCP/IP networks.
- The default encapsulation types on Cisco router interfaces and their keywords are Ethernet (novell-ether), Token Ring (sap), and FDDI (snap).
- Novell RIP is a distance-vector routing protocol and uses two metrics to make routing decisions: ticks and hop count.
- NetWare's SAP allows network resources to advertise their network addresses and the services they provide.
- GNS enables a client to locate the nearest server for login.
- The router configuration for IPX routing involves both global and interface tasks.

Washington School District Project Task: Configuring Novell IPX

In this chapter, you learned concepts and configuration processes that will help you implement IPX in the Washington School District network. You will investigate how Novell IPX protocol behaves on your assigned school's network. The school district has approved the implementation of a workgroup server in each of the computer labs at the school sites. The computer labs are located on the curriculum LAN segments of their respective sites. The condition for implementation is that only NetWare file server services will be advertised across the school district network to other curriculum LAN segments. As part of the IPX configuration and implementation, you need to complete the following tasks:

1. Document the effects of Novell IPX traffic on your school's LAN and the district WAN including projected increase in traffic loads and traffic patterns.

2. Submit a proposal for the overall district IPX network number addressing scheme and be prepared to present this to the class. An addressing scheme will be selected by the class based on the proposals.

3. Document the changes in the router configuration to conform with the users requirements, including changes in the ACLs, list the appropriate commands needed to implement these changes, and document the resulting changes in the router configuration.

4. Continue LAN design tasks: site wiring designs, LAN logical designs, typical MDF and IDF designs and electronics tables, and a site-specific LAN electronics list.

5. Apply the CCNA Certification Exam Learning Objectives to your specific design. This will require a paragraph on how the learning objectives relate to your design. Learning objectives can be grouped together for the purpose of explanation. In this way, you will be studying for the CCNA Certification Exam as you work through the case study.

> **NOTE**
>
> These tasks should be completed in conjunction with the IPX lab activities. Consult with your instructor to assist you with these tasks.

CCNA Certification Exam Learning Objectives

General

- Describe connectionless data packet delivery over a network.

Novell IPX Protocol

- Describe the format for IPX addressing and how unique networks are identified.
- Describe the function of the Service Advertisement Protocol (SAP) within IPX.
- Describe the three major types of SAP advertisements.
- Describe the concept of client/server in a Novell network.

> **NOTE**
>
> *** are explicit CCNA Exam objectives; unmarked are knowledge assumed by the exam.

- Describe the function and process of Get Nearest Server (GNS) in a Novell network.
- Monitor Novell IPX operation on the router.* * *
- List the required IPX address and encapsulation type.* * *
- Enable the Novell IPX protocol and configure interfaces.* * *
- Configure IPX access lists and SAP filters to control basic Novell traffic.* * *

Routing

- Describe the concept of multi-protocol routing.
- Describe what function of the router will control the flow of SAP advertisements across the network.

Check Your Understanding

Complete all the review questions to test your understanding of the topics and concepts covered in this chapter. Answers are listed in Appendix B, "Check Your Understanding Answer Key."

1. In an IPX network, what is used for the host address?

2. What command do you use to set the maximum number of equal-cost paths the router uses when forwarding packets?

3. What command mode must the router be in before you can issue the **ipx routing** command?

4. What command do you issue to verify IPX address assignment on a router?

5. What command displays information about IPX SAP packets that are transmitted or received?

6. A Novell IPX address has 80 bits: 32 for the _____ and 48 for the _____.

    A. Network number; IP address

    B. Node number; MAC address

    C. Network number; node number

    D. MAC address; node number

7. When you configure an IPX network, you might need to specify an encapsulation type on which of the following?

    A. Just the Novell servers

    B. Just the Cisco routers

    C. Sometimes A and B

    D. Always A and B

8. Novell NetWare uses _____ to facilitate the exchange of routing information and _____ to advertise network services.

    A. NCP; RIP

    B. RIP; SAP

    C. SPX; NCP

    D. SAP; RIP

9. The syntax for configuring Novell IPX globally is which of the following?

   A. ipx routing *[node]*

   B. router ipx

   C. ipx route *[node]*

   D. router rip

10. Fill in the commands: _____ displays IPX status and parameters; _____ displays the contents of the IPX routing table; and _____ lists servers discovered through SAP advertisements.

   A. show ipx traffic; show ipx route; show ipx routing activity

   B. show ipx interface; show ipx route; show ipx servers

   C. show ipx interface; show ipx; show ipx servers

   D. show ipx; show ipx route; show ipx

11. In this sequence of commands

```
Router (config-if)# interface Ethernet 0.2
Router (config-subif)# ipx encapsulation novel-ether
Router (config-subif)# ipx network 9c
```

   the 0.2 is _____, and the 9c is _____.

   A. Router subinterface; router interface

   B. Attached network; router interface

   C. Router subinterface; attached network

   D. Encapsulation; router interface

12. How do you get the status of IPX interface and IPX parameters configured on each interface?

   A. show ipx status

   B. show ipx protocol

   C. show ipx interface

   D. show router ipx

13. The IPX node number can be up to how many digits in length?

   A. 8 hexadecimal

   B. 10 hexadecimal

   C. 6 hexadecimal

   D. 12 hexadecimal

14. The IPX network number can be up to how many digits in length?

   A. 8 hexadecimal

   B. 10 hexadecimal

   C. 6 hexadecimal

   D. 12 hexadecimal

15. Which of the following statements is true?

   A. The use of the IPX node number in the protocol eliminates the need for address resolution.

   B. The IPX node number can be up to 8 hexadecimal digits in lenth.

   C. The IPX node number is assigned by the network administrator.

   D. The IPX network number is obtained from the network interface.

16. Which of the following commands enable load sharing?

   A. interface serial0

   B. ipx maximum-paths

   C. ipx routing

   D. ipx network 6c

17. The encapsulation that needs to be specified in the router in order to configure an IPX with the FDDI 802.2 is

   A. snap

   B. Novell-FDDI

   C. Arpa

   D. sap

18. The default encapsulation types on Cisco router interfaces and their keywords are

   A. Ethernet: *arpa*

   B. Token Ring: *snap*

   C. Ethernet: *novell-ether*

   D. FDDI: *Novell-FDDI*

19. What is the command **ipx network network-no** specifically used for?

A. Selects IPX for routing and starts IPX RIP

B. Allows load sharing over parallel metric paths to the destination

C. Network number assigned to a specific subinterface

D. Specifies the frame encapsulation that is used on this network segment

20. What function does the command **show ipx traffic** specifically perform?

A. Displays number and types of packets

B. Information about RIP update packets

C. IPX status and parameters

D. Routing table contents

Key Terms

base 16 hexadecimal   A number representation using the digits 0 through 9, with their usual meaning, plus the letters A through F, to represent hexadecimal digits with values 10 to 15. The rightmost digit counts ones, the next counts multiples of 16, the next is $16^2=256$, and so on.

Cisco IOS (Internetwork Operating System) software   Cisco system software that provides common functionality, scalability, and security for all products under the CiscoFusion architecture. The Cisco IOS software allows centralized, integrated, and automated installation and management of internetworks, while ensuring support for a wide variety of protocols, media, services, and platforms.

client   A node or software program (front-end device) that requests services from a server.

client/server   The architecture of the relationship between a workstation and a server in a network.

Enhanced IGRP (Enhanced Interior Gateway Routing Protocol)   An advanced version of IGRP developed by Cisco. Provides superior convergence properties and operating efficiency, and combines the advantages of link-state protocols with those of distance-vector protocols.

encapsulate   To wrap data in a particular protocol header. For example, Ethernet data is wrapped in a specific Ethernet header before network transit. Also, when bridging dissimilar networks, the entire frame from one network is simply placed in the header used by the data link–layer protocol of the other network.

frame   A logical grouping of information sent as a data link–layer unit over a transmission medium. Often refers to the header and trailer, used for synchronization and error control, that surround the user data contained in the unit.

GNS (Get Nearest Server)   A request packet sent by a client on an IPX network to locate the nearest active server of a particular type. An IPX network client issues a GNS request to solicit either a direct response from a connected server or a response from a router that tells it where on the internetwork the service can be located. GNS is part of IPX SAP.

IPX (Internetwork Packet Exchange)   A NetWare network-layer (Layer 3) protocol used for transferring data from servers to workstations. IPX is similar to IP and XNS.

load sharing   The use of two or more paths to route packets to the same destination evenly among multiple routers to balance the work and improve network performance.

MAC (Media Access Control) address   A standardized data link–layer address that is required for every port or device that connects to a LAN. Other devices in the network use these addresses to locate specific ports in the network and to create and update routing tables and data structures. MAC addresses are each 6 bytes long, and they are controlled by the IEEE. Also known as a hardware address, a MAC-layer address, or a physical address.

NetWare   A popular distributed NOS developed by Novell. Provides transparent remote file access and numerous other distributed network services.

NLSP (NetWare Link Services Protocol)   A link-state routing protocol based on IS-IS. The Cisco implementation of NLSP also includes MIB variables and tools to redistribute routing and SAP information between NLSP and other IPX routing protocols.

NOS (network operating system)   The operating system used to run a network such Novell NetWare and Windows NT.

routing metric   A method by which a routing protocol determines that one route is better than another. This information is stored in routing tables. Metrics include bandwidth, communication cost, delay, hop count, load, MTU, path cost, and reliability. Sometimes referred to simply as a metric.

SAP (Service Advertising Protocol)   An IPX protocol that provides a means of informing network clients, via routers and servers, of available network resources and services.

server   A node or software program that provides services to clients.

SPX (Sequenced Packet Exchange)   A reliable, connection-oriented protocol that supplements the datagram service provided by network-layer protocols. Novell derived this commonly used NetWare transport protocol from the SPP of the XNS protocol suite.

subinterface   One of a number of virtual interfaces on a single physical interface.

Objectives

After completing this chapter, you will be able to perform tasks related to the following:

- Network documentation
- Network security
- Environmental factors
- Network performance
- Server administration
- Network troubleshooting

Network Management, Part I

Introduction

Network management involves many different areas, including network documentation, network security, network maintenance, server administration, and server maintenance. This is not an all-inclusive list, but it is more than enough to be covered at this time.

Each one of the listed topics is just as important as the rest, and none of them should be overlooked. The problem is that many administrators feel that when the network is up and running, the job is over. This statement couldn't be further from the truth. When a network setup is done, that is when the real job of a network administrator starts.

Network Documentation

The first and most critical component for a good network is documentation. Documentation is the most talked about and least performed task in a network. Documentation represents the network administrator's memory. First of all, it consists of your engineering journal, but it does not stop there. Documentation also includes these components:

- Diagrams that indicate the path of the physical wiring layout
- The type of cable
- The length of each cable
- The type of termination for the cable
- The physical location of each wall plate or patch panel
- A labeling scheme for easy identification of each wire

MDF and IDF Layouts

This document contains a physical and logical layout of the main distribution facility and all of the intermediate distribution facilities in the network. It includes the physical layout of rack mounts, auxiliary equipment, and servers in the distribution facility. It also includes patch panel labels to identify cable terminations, as well as identification and configuration details of all equipment located in the distribution facility.

Server and Workstation Configuration Details

Server and workstation configuration details are to be filled out about each host attached to the network. Information on these sheets is standardized and contains such things as the make and model of the computer, its serial number, floppy drives, hard drives, DVD/CD-ROM drive, sound and network cards, the amount of RAM, and any other physical details of the computer (see Figure 8-1 and Figure 8-2). This information also includes configuration details about the computer, including the IRQ, DMA, and base memory address configuration details of the peripheral cards.

FIGURE 8-1
The Computer Hardware Configuration worksheet.

Computer Hardware Configuration Worksheet
One sheet per computer

File Server or Workstation:	
Physical Location:	
Make and Model:	
Serial #:	
Company Inv. #:	

Removable Media Drives:

Manufacturer	Drive Letter	Capacity	Internal/External	Internal drive bay #

Fixed Media Drives:

Manufacturer	Drive Letter	Capacity	Internal/External	Internal drive bay #

Memory current/maximum:	Current:		Maximum:	

Peripheral Cards:

Manufacturer:	Model:	Type:	IRQ	DMA	Base Memory Addr.

Network Interface Cards:

Manufacturer:	Node Addr.	Model:	Lan Driver:	IRQ	DMA	Base Memory Addr.

Comments:	

FIGURE 8-2
The Printer Configuration worksheet.

Printer Configuration Worksheet						
One sheet per printer						
Physical Location:						
Make and Model:						
Serial #:						
Company Inv. #:						
Printer ID #:						
Memory current/maximum:	Current:			Maximum:		
Paper Bins	Bin #1 paper type		Bin #2 paper type		Bin #3 paper type	
Printer Configuration:						
Serial	Port	Baud Rate	Stop bits	Parity	Xon/Xoff	Interrupt
Parallel	Port	Polling				Interrupt
Network	IP addr.	Polling	MAC addr.			
Print Queues:						
Print Operators:						
Comments:						

Lastly, this document contains the physical location, user, and network identification (IP address, MAC address, subnet, and topology) information about the computer. Be sure to also include purchase date and warranty information in this document.

Software Listings

A listing of standard and special software used on each machine in the network is necessary as well, to document the standard configuration installation details of each software package. This list includes the operating system and application software (see Figure 8-3).

Maintenance Records

It is also valuable to keep a list of all repairs that have been done to all equipment included in the network (see Figure 8-4). This will help an administrator predict possible future problems with existing hardware and software.

FIGURE 8-3
The Computer Software Configuration worksheet.

Computer Software Configuration Worksheet					
One sheet per computer					
Computer Inv. #:					
Operating System(s)					
Manufacturer	Version	Service updates	Network capable	Security	
Application software					
Manufacturer	Version	Service updates	Network capable	Install directory	Data directory

FIGURE 8-4
The Computer Repair worksheet.

Computer Repair Worksheet				
One sheet per computer				
Computer Inv#:			**Date:**	
Type of problem:	**Hardware:**		**Software:**	
Problem Description:				
Warranty Coverage:	**Yes:**	**No:**	**Location of Repair:**	
Repair description:				
Department Charged:				
Authorized By:				
Repair Completed By:				
Comments:				

Security Measures

This document not only includes "soft" security, such as user rights, password definition, and firewall support, but it also addresses physical security. Physical or hard security includes things as simple as identifying how the MDF and IDFs are locked, who has access to these rooms and why, how the hosts are protected (security cables and alarms), and who has physical access to the system (see Figures 8-5 and 8-6).

FIGURE 8-5
The Network
Security Room
form.

Network Security Room Form One per room					
Physical location:				**Date:**	
Physical security:	Door lock	Windows	False Ceiling	Fire suppression	Locking cabinets

Servers Tape Backup:					
Server Name:	Type	Media	Off-site Loc.	Tape set name	Start day-of-week
Server #1					
Server #2 .					
Server #3					

Authorized Access:	Name	Department	Function

Comments:	

User Policies

User policies are documents that can be the most important and beneficial to the network administrator. They contain information on how the users can interact with the network. These policies include what is and what is not permissible on the network. This documentation should also include the consequences of violating user policies. Other aspects of user policies include what the minimum user ID and password length should be and rules for the content of passwords. User policies need to be created with the management of the company to make sure that these policies are acceptable and will be enforced. As a network administrator, you want to create the most secure and functional network possible for your company, while still ensuring that network policies don't conflict with company policies or limit the users access to necessary resources.

FIGURE 8-6
The Network
Security User
form.

Network Security User Form One per user				
Physical location:			**Date:**	
User name:			**User ID:**	
Department:			Dept. manager:	
Password length:			Home Dir:	
Date ID expires:			Local access:	
Access hours:			Print access:	
Remote access:			Admin. Access:	
Inclusive groups:	Group name	Group rights	Local/Global	Restrictions
Network Duties/Privileges:				
Comments:				

The Network Security User form.

The information recorded in the documents mentioned creates the network documentation set for your system. This documentation set helps ensure that maintenance and upgrades to the network work in a more orderly fashion. This documentation also gives the administrator a starting place to return to if an upgrade goes wrong or if recovery from a network failure is necessary. One last point about network documentation is that it continuously needs to be updated with the latest upgrades and configuration changes to the network. If this doesn't happen, the documentation will not have a great deal of relevance to your current network implementation.

Network Security

Network security involves two major components. The first is keeping your network safe from unauthorized access, and the second is ensuring your ability to recover data from catastrophic events.

The first part of security refers back to the network documentation section of the chapter. It involves making the network as secure as possible against unauthorized access. This is done by establishing security policies, such as minimum password length, maximum password age, unique passwords (not allowing the same password repeated), and allowing the user to log on to the network only at particular times of the day or days of the week. These parameters can be directly controlled by the network administrator and will be enforced by the network operating system.

Security also involves making sure that users are aware of the company's network policies and then that they follow those policies. Examples of such policies might be not letting users use family or pet names for passwords. Another example is making sure that users are logged out of the network or have a password-protected screen saver activated any time they leave their computer. These are the types of rules that can be followed only if the users understand and follow the established network policies.

Data Recovery

Data recovery, the second part of network security, involves protecting data from loss. Multiple methods exist for this, and usually more than one method is used at the same time to protect the data. As shown in Figure 8-7, three popular data protection methods are tape backup of data, fault-tolerant disk configurations, and the use of uninterruptible power supplies (UPS) to prevent equipment shutdowns during electrical power outages. We will talk about these three methods in detail in the following paragraphs.

FIGURE 8-7
UPS, tape backup
unit, and disk
array.

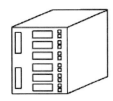

Tape backup is the process of duplicating all stored data to magnetic tape. Tape is used because of its cost and capacity: Tape cartridges are much less expensive and contain much greater storage capacity than comparable removable hard disks. The drawback of tape for general usage, however, is that it stores data sequentially, the same way that music is recorded on a tape cassette. This means that, just as trying to find a single song on a cassette is difficult to do efficiently, the same is true of trying to find a specific file on a data tape. But because the data for a backup is recorded sequentially and is recovered the same way, this isn't a problem for this usage.

It is important to do a tape backup as completely and quickly as possible because it can be quite a drain on system resources (network bandwidth and server processor power). To allow the complete backup to occur most efficiently, different types of backups have been developed. Most of the backup types work with a flag or switch called the *archive bit*. The archive bit is stored with a file and is turned on whenever that file is created or modified. This flag tells the backup process whether the file needs to be backed up. If a file is stored to tape during the backup process, the flag normally is turned off, saying that the current file is backed up to tape.

Most companies recommend that tapes and backups be stored in some type of fire safe or take the tapes off the premises in case of fire or water damage.

Backup Operations

The five types of back up operations are as follows:

1. **Full backup**—All files on the disk are stored to tape, and the archive bit for all files is set to off.

2. **Incremental backup**—This type backs up all the files that have been created or modified since the last full backup. It is important to remember two things about an incremental backup: first, like differential backup, it works only in conjunction with a full backup; second, that any file created or modified since the last full backup has its archive bit turned back on so that it will be saved to tape during the next incremental backup. The backup then copies only those files with archive bits set on. Once backed-up, the archive bits of these files are turned off (0).

3. **Differential backup**—This type backs up all the files that have been created or modified since the last full backup. This sounds the same as an incremental backup, but the difference is that even though the file is saved to tape, the archive bit is not reset. This means that each time a differential backup is done, all the files modified or created since the last full backup will be stored again.

4. **Copy backup**—This backup type backs up user-selected files to tape. This backup also does not reset the archive bit to off.

5. **Daily backup**—This type backs up only the files that are modified on the day of the backup. This backup also does not reset the archive bit to off.

The first three backup procedures are the most widely used. Here is a sample way of doing first an incremental backup and then a differential backup.

To do an incremental backup, first do a full backup on Monday; this would reset all the archive bits on the files. On Tuesday, an incremental backup would be performed to a separate tape. This stores all the files modified on Tuesday to tape and resets their archive bit. This process is repeated for all the other business days of the week, each with a separate tape. This gives a complete backup of all files modified during that week. On the following Monday, the entire process starts over again. The advantage of this type of backup scheme is that it requires the least amount of time per day to do the backup, so it has the least impact on the network resources. The disadvantage is that if you need to restore the backup, it requires that you first restore the full backup tape and then all the incremental backup tapes in order, which takes a great deal of time. In addition, if one of the tapes is bad, you lose that information.

To do a differential backup, first do a full backup on Monday to reset all the archive bits on the files. On Tuesday a differential backup would be performed to a separate tape. This stores all the files modified on Tuesday to tape, but it doesn't reset their archive bit. This process is repeated for all the other business days of the week, each with the same tape. This process also gives a complete backup of the network data. Its advantages are that it requires only two tapes to make and restore the backup, if necessary. The disadvantages of this method are that each day, the files that were backed up on previous days are stored again, which takes a lot more of the network resources per day. Also, if the deferential backup tape is damaged and the restore was preformed on Friday, four days' worth of data are lost and must be re-entered.

Just as a note, a full backup that is done each day requires only one tape to restore the data, but it is impractical to run a full backup each day because of the amount of dedicated time that it requires. Neither the copy backup nor the daily backup resets the archive bit, and both are used for backup of selected files.

Another important consideration when doing system backup is the data that is on the user workstations. Is the data stored on a workstation being backed up—and if so, how? The data that is stored on the workstations is just as—and sometimes more—important than the data stored on the network servers. The particular method of backup for workstations depends on the situation. The following paragraphs discuss different scenarios for workstation backup.

The first method is used for a workstation that creates and works on a large amount of data that is used by only that workstation. In this case, an individual tape drive might work best because it allows for very large amounts of data to be backed up and does not impact the network throughput. The downside of the method is that it puts the responsibility for the backup in the hands of the user.

A second way to do workstation backup is to copy all data files to a removable storage device such as a floppy or ZIP disk drive. This saves the expense, time, and complication of doing a tape backup, but it still leaves the responsibility in the hands of the user.

Finally, the last method is to create directories on the servers for all users to store their data. This solution removes the user's responsibility of doing the backup. Instead, the backup is done when the servers are backed up, eliminating the need for special devices on the workstation to do the backup. The drawbacks of this solution are that the policies of where data is to be stored must be clearly defined. The users must understand where they are storing the data to make sure that it is done correctly. Also, if a network communication problem occurs, the data may not be available to the users until the problem is corrected.

As you have seen, with any solution, there are potential problems. Each situation will have a "best case" solution for that particular time and place. The only wrong solution is to ignore the need to back up all data on the system.

Redundancy Techniques

The next method of protecting data is through fault-tolerant storage devices. This is categorized by Redundant Array of Inexpensive Disks (RAID) levels 0 to 5. All the basic RAID types will be shown, but we will look specifically at the three levels of most importance. The types are as follows:

- **RAID 0**—Stripes data across multiple disks, with no parity, so there is no redundancy.

- **RAID 1**—Uses disk mirroring (disk duplexing) to write data to two identical partitions on separate hard disks, thus creating an automatic backup. Disk duplexing uses two hard-disk controller cards as well as two hard disks to prevent the controller card from being the single point of failure for the system, as in disk mirroring.

- **RAID 2**—Writes data across multiple hard disks, with error checking. This system is not used anymore because it requires expensive disk modifications to work.

- **RAID 3**—Stripes data 1 byte at a time and has a dedicated parity drive. This is a good but expensive redundancy choice. Because of the expense, this solution is not used very often.

- **RAID 4**—Stripes data one sector at a time and has a dedicated parity drive. This is an expensive redundancy choice that is very slow writing data to the disk. Because of the expense and the slowness of writing, this solution is not used very often.

- **RAID 5**—Stripes data and parity across multiple disks (at least three for RAID 5). By mixing the parity across all the disks, a separate parity disk is not required, and yet full data redundancy is achieved. Data writes to the disk are still slow, but the cost isn't so high. One other important fact about

RAID 5 is that on a Windows NT system, the boot and system partitions cannot be located on a RAID 5 disk array.

Other RAID levels exist, but they are beyond what is needed here. In fact, not all network operating systems support the RAID levels mentions. The three RAID levels that are supported by most operating systems are RAID 0, RAID 1, and RAID 5. The key points to remember are that RAID 0 is used for speed and provides *no* data redundancy (backup). RAID 1 provides full data redundancy but requires twice as much storage space because all data must be written to two separate disks; this method still involves a single point of failure in the controller card. This problem is taken care of by the other variation of RAID 1, which uses disk duplexing, in which the disk controller is duplicated also.

RAID 5 requires a minimum of three disks (four in a Windows NT system because the system and boot partitions cannot be on the RAID set), and the partition size must be the same on each disk. RAID 5 is popular because it provides very fast data reads from disk, which gives better throughput to the network. One last important point about RAID 5 and Windows NT is that, to have full redundancy, this must be done. You need at least five disks—the first two will be set up as RAID 1 (disk mirroring) for the system and boot partitions, and the last three data disks will be set up with RAID 5. This provides full redundancy with the speed advantage that RAID 5 supplies.

The last term that you will see when working with hard disk storage is volumes. A *volume* refers to a physical unit of storage. A good analogy would be to think of an encyclopedia set. Each book in the set normally is called a volume. Some books hold more that one volume (for example, the XYZ volume). Finally, think of the whole set of encyclopedias as a single unit. This concept is true of the disk volume set also, with one volume name that includes space from multiple disks that are referenced as a single unit. This information is important because volume sets are used quite often in network systems. One last thing about volume sets is that they provide *no* data redundancy; they are just a way to refer to large storage areas as a single unit.

Environmental Factors

Another part of good network management is dealing with the environmental factors that can affect a network. Controlling these factors will create a more stable and reliable network.

When installing new equipment, always follow the owner's manual setup procedures. This will resolve many problems that might come up by "doing it yourself." Make sure that all of the equipment's power switches are *off* before hooking it up. This also holds true if you buy a new peripheral card (an accessory that goes with your computer); make sure that the computer power is *off* before you install it and that you ground (discharge) yourself before touching the inside of the computer. The best way to ground yourself is to use a grounding strap. Without proper grounding, it is possible to build up an electric charge as great as 20,000 volts. This charge can be created by just walking on a synthetic rug with leather shoes or by sliding around to get comfortable in a plastic chair.

Another cause of static is lack of humidity in the air, so it is important to make sure that the rooms that hold equipment have proper temperature and humidity control. Static charges are also sneaky; you may not even know that there is a charge built up until it is discharged, causing damage. A static voltage discharge can burn out many of the ICs (electrical components) in network and computer equipment. To eliminate this problem, you might want to purchase antistatic or ground mats along with grounding straps.

Keep dust and dirt out of the keyboards, disk drives, and equipment air vents. Keeping the environment in which equipment is used clean and free of contaminants does this. Tar and nicotine are very sticky contaminants that are a part of cigarette smoke—smoking around computer equipment is a sure way to eventually damage the equipment. Never set coffee, soft drinks or any contained liquid on or above a piece of network or computer equipment. If the liquid spills and gets inside the machine, it will almost certainly cause the machine to burn out (and sometimes actually burn up).

Don't let the equipment overheat; computers and other network equipment have built-in fans to cool them. Make sure not to block any of the equipment's cooling vents, either. Make sure that your work area leaves the computers vents open. Also make sure that you place the computer on a solid support area (don't set it on a snack tray). Vibration and sudden shocks can loosen components inside the computer.

Power Conditioning

Protect your equipment from irregularities in your building's electrical wiring. The easiest way to protect your network and computer equipment is to put it on separate circuits in your building. This will solve some but not all power-related problems. Other devices that can be used to control electrical irregularities are listed here:

- **Isolating transformer**—Controls voltage spikes and high-frequency noise.
- **Regulators**—Maintains a constant output voltage, despite changes in the power line's voltage over a long period of time. It handles such problems as brownouts and voltage surges.
- **Line conditioner**—Is a regulator with an isolating transformer built in.

- **Uninterruptible power supply**—Basically, is a battery charger that charges a battery that, in turn, powers the computer. This device will allow the computer to run even if there is a power failure.

EMI and RFI

Other sources of problems with network communications can actually be the equipment itself. Computer components, such as power supplies and monitors, as well as fluorescent lights, large electric motors, and electrical wiring, can cause electromagnetic interference (EMI) and radio frequency interference (RFI) that can be picked up by other equipment and improperly shielded cables. Components of a device might be failing, but those components make it look like another part is causing the problem. These types of problems can be very difficult to diagnose and, as is shown later in the chapter, are usually discovered by the use of diagnostic software and hardware.

Software Viruses

All of the previous topics that can affect the performance of a network have dealt with the physical aspect of the network. The last factor that we will talk about that can affect the performance of your network is software—specifically, a type of software with the sole purpose of disrupting the operation of a network. The following paragraphs describe the different types of infectious software.

A *worm* is a program that propagates itself across computers, usually by creating copies of itself in each computer's memory. A worm might duplicate itself in one computer so often that it causes the computer to crash. Sometimes written in separate "segments," a worm is introduced unknowingly into a host or network system either for "fun" or with intent to damage or destroy information. The term comes from a science-fiction novel and has generally been superseded by the term *virus*.

A *virus* is a program that "infects" computer files (usually other executable programs) by inserting copies of itself in those files. This is usually done in such a manner that the copies will be executed when the file is loaded into memory, allowing them to infect still other files, and so on. Viruses often have damaging side effects, sometimes intentionally, sometimes not. The latest variation is to send these viruses over the Internet as e-mail attachments.

A *Trojan horse* is a destructive program disguised as a game, a utility, or an application. When run, a Trojan horse does something devious to the computer system while appearing to do something useful.

We all try to avoid having things happen to our computers, whether it is physical damage or software damage. The following tips can prevent an infection by a virus to your network or computers:

- Be careful about getting software, without knowing specifically where it comes from. Many times, software that is distributed through illegal channels is a prime carrier of viruses. This is because no system has been established for checking the software.

- Be wary of other people using your computer with their disks. Any kind of file can carry a virus. It doesn't have to be a program file; it could just as well be a data file that has a virus infecting it.

- Use a current virus-checker on all computers. Many companies sell or provide virus checkers.

There are many other ways of detecting and preventing viruses that cannot be covered here. If you are worried about viruses, you can obtain other articles and reports through the Internet.

Network Performance

Along with network security and redundancy, another important consideration in network management is network performance. Network performance is a measurement of a network's quickness and reliability. A good comparison to a network is an automobile. You want your car to lock (security) and to have a spare tire (redundancy), but this is only part of the car. The other part is how fast it can accelerate from 0 to 60 (quickness), and when you step on the brakes, whether they work (reliability).

These aspects of performance need to be checked to see if performance is being maintained. To continue our analogy, if your car is not performing well, you can take it in for a tuneup. The difference between networks and cars is that most car models have standard performance levels; most networks do not. Every combination of computer and network hardware, software, and cabling will have a different network performance. This leads us to the conclusion that to know when the network is performing poorly, we must have a measurement to compare the performance against. This measurement is called a *baseline*. A baseline is established after the network has been installed and configured properly.

To establish a baseline, a network monitor package or tool, such as the Fluke LANMeter or Windows NT network monitor program, can be used. These tools record several types of network performance data, including network utilization percentage, collision counts, frame errors, and broadcast traffic. By establishing a baseline measurement when the network system is at optimum normal performance levels, the network administrator will have a comparison value to use to determine the health of the network.

As the network grows and changes, the baseline measurement needs to be periodically updated, just like any other documentation. As a system is upgraded, it is important to remember that as hardware is upgraded, so should the software drivers that control that hardware. If an upgrade or new program is installed, the service or repair packs supplied by the software company need to be reinstalled. In the case of the new hardware installation, the old software driver may not take advantage of the new hardware features or may not be compatible at all. This could create a serious performance problem. The reason for the reinstallation of the service packs is to prevent files that are part of the new programs installation process or that are older than the file that is in the service pack from causing problems.

When making changes to the network, such as moving a piece of equipment from one location to another (as shown in Figure 8-8), it is important to verify the proper operation of that piece of equipment in its new location before updating your baseline measurement. This is especially important when making changes to reduce network traffic on a particular network segment. Even though the device was working properly on the old segment, it may not be working for the new segment, and this will have an effect on network performance. Always verify the operation of a device thoroughly after an equipment move; this includes network functionality and all critical applications.

FIGURE 8-8
PC moved from one segment to another.

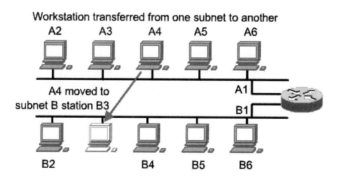

Workstation transferred from one subnet to another

Server Administration

Network administrators need to be aware of two types of networks: peer-to-peer and client/server networks.

Figure 8-9 shows a peer-to-peer network, which is also known as a workgroup network. It is designed for small numbers of workstations; Microsoft recommends no more that ten users in a peer-to-peer network.

FIGURE 8-9
A peer-to-peer
network.

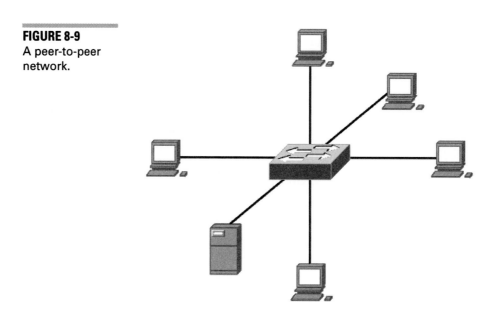

Advantages of a peer-to-peer network are that it is cheaper to create and operate than a client/server network, it allows users to control their own resources, it does not require a dedicated server, and no additional software is required besides a suitable operation system.

Among the disadvantages, no central point of management is provided, and each user must create IDs for each user that shares resources on a machine. Each time a user changes a password, all passwords on shared resources must be changed individually. If a shared workstation is turned off or otherwise unavailable, those resources are not available. The last disadvantage was mentioned before—if there are more than ten users or if the network will grow to more than ten users in the next year, a peer-to-peer network is not a good choice.

Examples of peer-to-peer operating systems are Windows for Workgroups, Windows 95, Windows 98, and LANtastic.

Client/Server Network

The other type of network is a client/server network, as shown in Figure 8-10. Network operating systems are the heart of the client/server network. These systems control the resources and management of the local-area network.

Among the advantages of client/server networks is a centralized point of user, security, and resource management. Dedicated servers also can be used to more effectively provide specific resources to clients. In addition, these networks provide access to all allowed resources with one network ID and password.

One disadvantages of a client/server network is that there is now a single point of failure in the network. If the server "goes down," all server resources are unavailable to the clients. In fact, the clients may not even operate without the server. Network operation and maintenance now require specially trained personnel to maintain the network. This, along with special network software and hardware, add greatly to the cost of operation. Even with the disadvantages, though, a client/server network is really the only choice for businesses with more than ten users. Examples of client/server operating systems are UNIX, Novell NetWare, and Windows NT.

FIGURE 8-10
A client/server network.

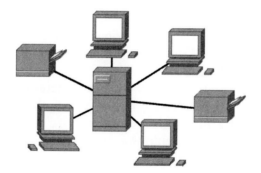

The UNIX operating system comes in many variations, as implemented by different companies. Companies that provide UNIX include Sun Microsystems, IBM, Hewlett-Packard, and Santa Cruz Operation (SCO). Free versions of UNIX also exist, including FreeBSD and Linux, the latter of which has great popularity at the present time.

UNIX is a multiuser operating system that supports multiprocessing, multitasking, and multithreaded applications. The operating system is kernel-based, which isolates the hardware layer of the computer from improperly operating applications and primarily uses the Network File System (NFS, Sun Microsystems's implementation). The NFS file system provides for both file and directory security access on the server. UNIX also provides for centralized user and resource control through the operating system. Because of the multiple versions of UNIX in production, it is difficult to contrast all the variations and releases of this software. The previous description gives the common features available in all UNIX "flavors." Clients that work best with UNIX are usually specific to the developer of the operating system.

In discussing NetWare and Windows NT, we must also talk about the different versions that have evolved over the years. First, we will cover Novell NetWare. The versions of NetWare that will be covered are version 3.12, version 4.11, and version 5.0. These versions primarily differ in their handling of directory services.

NetWare version 3.12 uses an object called the *bindery* to manage multiple users and resources. The drawback is that bindery services create a server-centric network, which is focused on the individual server as the point of control. This creates a problem with a multiple-server network. Each server still must have an individual ID for each user, even though the passwords could be synchronized so that changing one would change the password on all servers; this defeats the purpose of centralized management. To be fair, this is a time issue—version 3.12 was in existence before the great explosion of multiserver networks. This is one of the major improvements in NetWare version 4.11.

NetWare versions 4.11 and 5.0 use an object called *Novell Directory Services* (NDS) to manage users and resources. The advantage over version 3.12 is that NDS creates a network-centric network, which is focused on the entire network as the point of control. This focus consolidates management to a single point, and servers are treated just as objects within the context of the network. This allows a single ID and password to authorize users for all resources across the network, and it provides for easier network organization and management.

All versions of NetWare use a combination of two file services, the first being a file allocation table (FAT), which is the file system used for DOS. The second is the directory entry table (DET) which is a proprietary Novell file system that provides for both file and directory security on the server. Clients that work well with NetWare are numerous; they include all versions of Windows, DOS, Macintosh, and OS-2. NetWare's strong points are user and file resource management.

Windows NT is the last operating system to be discussed. There are two versions of Windows NT to cover. Windows NT version 4.0 server and workstation were developed with the Windows 95 user interface. This provides a consistent "look and feel" interface across all Windows products. Windows NT handles user and resource management through the use of domains (see Figure 8-11). A domain is a logical grouping of users and resources under the control of one server, called the primary domain controller (PDC). Domains also support the use of secondary servers called *backup domain controllers*

(BDCs). BDCs balance the workload of the PDC and provide for redundancy of user and resource objects.

A third type of server, called a *stand-alone server*, is allowable in a domain. This server is primarily set up to support one particular application and to dedicate its resources to that application. Another variation of a domain is called a *multidomain model*. In this model, separate domains are connected by trusting/trusted relationships, which allows users to cross domain boundaries to use resources.

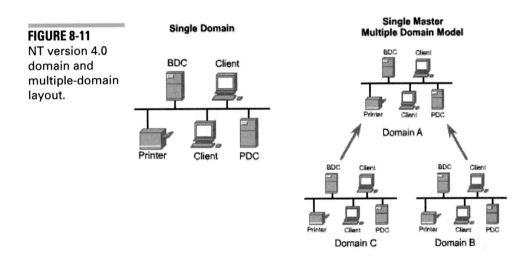

FIGURE 8-11
NT version 4.0 domain and multiple-domain layout.

The Windows 2000 Server management structure will change from domains to an Active Directory structure. Active Directory is based on a network-centric model, like NDS, rather that a domain-centered model.

Windows NT is just like UNIX, a multiuser operating system that supports multiprocessing, multitasking, and multithreaded applications. The operating system, just like UNIX, is kernel-based, which isolates the hardware layer of the computer from improperly operating applications, and uses both the FAT16 file system and NT's own proprietary system, New Technology File System (NTFS). With FAT16, Windows NT provides just directory (or also known as folder)–level security; no individual file security is provided. NTFS provides both file- and directory-level security and permissions.

The reason that Windows NT supports both of these operating systems is that it has the capability to coexist with another operating system on the same machine. This doesn't mean that both systems can run at the same time, but the computer can run Windows NT or the other operating system. For the other operating system to have file access, the file system must be FAT16. Just as a point of interest, Windows 95 and 98 support FAT32; Windows NT doesn't. So, FAT16 would be the choice for running Windows NT and Windows 95 on the same computer. Windows NT works best with its own client, Windows NT Workstation, but it also works well with Windows for Workgroups, Windows 95 and 98, and Macintosh clients.

No matter which network operating system is used, the main function of the NOS is to control the network. This is accomplished by establishing network user rights, login accounts (user IDs), passwords, and groups, along with system profiles and policies. These terms will be identified more completely in the following sections.

Network Control

A login account identifies the network user to the network system. This account, along with the user's password, identifies and gives access to the network system's resources. This account ID also holds the user responsible for actions on the network. This should be stated in the security documents identified earlier in the chapter. Just because the network user has an account does not mean that the network resources are completely available to this user. User rights determine the user's resource availability.

User rights are set by an administrator to permit or deny access to particular resource on a network. For example, even though a user is connected to the network and a network printer is also connected the network, the user may not be able to print to that printer. If the user is not assigned the right or permission to use the printer, access to that resource will be denied. If the user *is* assigned the right or permission, then the printer will be available. This is true of printers, data and program files, and any other "resources" on the network. There is one administrative problem with assigning rights to users: If there are a lot of users on a network system, assigning and modifying rights for each individual user can take most of the administrator's time. This problem is resolved by the use of groups.

Groups are a logical grouping of users on the network. The rights and permissions are given to the group instead of to an individual user. Then if a user needs these rights, he or she is assigned to the groups and, by this action, is given the rights assigned to the group. This is also true if the rights to a resource need to be changed; a change to the group will reflect that change to all of the group's members. This doesn't mean that rights can't be assigned to individual users, but the more efficient way in large networks is to work with groups.

The terms *policy* and *profiles* have to do not with system resources, but with how the user interacts with the workstation. Profiles allow a user to customize a user interface on a computer and then be able to use that profile at any computer that user connects to the network. This is called a *roaming profile*. Another type of profile will bring up the same user interface for everyone without allowing changes to be made. This is called a *mandatory profile* and is used in situations in which many people have to use the same physical computer. If users are on the same computers all the time and do not need to go to other computers, they may have a local profile. A local profile is stored not on the network like the first two profiles, but on the local computer.

Policies deal with the control of the resources on the local computer. A policy that prevents a user from storing data on the workstation's local hard or floppy drive can improve security by preventing data from being taken out of the building. Policies can also prevent users from accidentally making changes to their system configuration information. Things such as video card settings, hard disk configuration, and network card settings are aspects of the workstation that the majority of users have no need to change; if these are changed, this can cause a lot of extra unnecessary work for help desk and network personnel.

All the aspects that we have just discussed can be summarized this way: Network rights, login accounts, passwords, and groups, along with profiles and policies, provide a way for the system administrator to control access and restrictions to network services and to control the local user workstation. Being a network administrator is also a set of rights and privileges granted on the network. Not all users have the right to change other users' rights and privileges; these rights are reserved for certain groups that have been given administrator rights. By being part of a group that has administrator rights, you also are an administrator.

Network Troubleshooting

Network troubleshooting is a systematic process applied to solve a problem on a network. A good way to get started would be to use the Dartmouth Design Matrix that was used in the network design phase of the course. This is a very good tool for establishing a systematic analysis technique for troubleshooting. Another technique for troubleshooting is the scientific method. The first list gives the actual scientific method, and the second list shows the scientific method specifically pointed at troubleshooting.

Scientific Method:

> **Step 1**   Observe some aspect of the universe.
>
> **Step 2**   Invent a theory that is consistent with what you have observed.

Step 3   Use the theory to make predictions.

Step 4   Test those predictions by experiments or further observations.

Step 5   Modify the theory in the light of your results.

Step 6   Go back to Step 3.

Scientific Method for Troubleshooting:

Step 1   Identify the network/user problem.

Step 2   Gather data about the network/user problem.

Step 3   Analyze data to come up with a possible solution to the problem.

Step 4   Implement a solution to the network to attempt correction to the system.

Step 5   If the problem isn't resolved, undo previous changes and modify the data.

Step 6   Go back to Step 3.

Analyze Network Troubleshooting

Here is an example of this method of troubleshooting. A user on your network calls the help desk to report that his computer can no longer get to the Internet. The help desk fills out the error report form and forwards it to you, the network support department.

You call and talk to the user, who tells you that he has done nothing differently than he has always done to get to the Internet. You check the hardware logs for the network and find out that the user's computer was upgraded last night. Your first solution is that the computer's network drivers must be incorrectly configured. You go to the machine and check the network configuration information on the computer. It seems to be correct, so you **ping** the server on that subnet. It doesn't connect.

The next solution is to check to see if the workstation cable is plugged in. You check both ends of the cable and then try **ping**ing the server again. It doesn't connect again.

Next you **ping** 127.0.0.1, the loopback address for the computer. The **ping** is successful, so that eliminates a possible problem between the computer, driver configuration, and the NIC card.

You decide then that there might be a problem with the server for this network segment. There is another networked computer at the next desk, so you **ping** the server's address and get a successful result. This eliminates the server, the backbone, and the server's connection to the backbone as the problem.

You then go to the IDF and switch the port for the workstation, go back to the workstation, and try to **ping** the server again. The solution still does not work. This narrows your search to the horizontal cabling or the workstation patch cable. You go back to the IDF, put the cable back in the original switch port, get a new workstation patch cable, and return to the workstation.

You replace the workstation cable and try to **ping** the server again. This time it is successful, so you have fixed the problem.

The last step is to document the problem solution on the error report form and return it to the help desk so that it can be logged as completed.

As you can see, this example was a step-by-step process of eliminating the possible causes of the network problem. Each possible problem was addressed in turn and was individually eliminated. If you make multiple changes at once, the process can be confused, and the solution cannot be precisely identified. As the solutions were implemented and found not to resolve the problem, the data was re-evaluated and new problem solutions were formulated. This process continued until the actual problem was found and resolved. The problem was then documented for future use.

No matter what type of problems will be encountered on a network system, the process for resolving them will be the same. This is the process that was outlined previously in the chapter.

Summary

Now that you have completed this chapter, you should have a firm understanding of the following:

- Network documentation, such as the following:
  - Cut sheet diagrams
  - MDF and IDF layouts
  - Server and workstation configuration details
  - Software listings
  - Maintenance records
  - Security measures
  - User policies

■ Network security processes, such as these:

— Network access techniques: security policies and network policies

— Server data recovery techniques:

Tape backup

Full backup

Incremental backup

Differential backup

Copy backup

Daily backup

■ Workstation data-recovery techniques:

— Tape backup

— Disk copy

— Server directory

■ Redundancy techniques:

— RAID 0

— RAID 1

— RAID 2

— RAID 3

— RAID 4

— RAID 5

■ Environmental factors:

— Static

— Dust and dirt

— Heat

— Power conditioning

— EMI and RFI

— Software viruses:

Worms

Viruses

Trojan horses

■ Network performance:

— Network baseline

— Documentation updates

— Change verification

- Server administration:
    — Peer-to-peer networks
    — Client/server networks
    — Network control
- Network troubleshooting techniques, such as these:
    — Scientific method
    — Analyze network
    — Troubleshooting

Washington School District Project Task: Finishing the TCS

In this chapter, you learned some basic principles of network management that would help you administer the LAN that you have designed. As the semester ends, you need to complete the following tasks to make sure that the LAN part of your Web-based TCS solution is finished:

- LAN user requirements document
- Site LAN wiring plan (physical topology)
- Site LAN logical topology (including IP addressing scheme)
- Wiring closet diagrams
- LAN electronics spreadsheet
- LAN media spreadsheet
- IGRP implementation
- ACL implementation
- IPX implementation
- LAN pros and cons

Check Your Understanding

Complete all the review questions to test your understanding of the topics and concepts covered in this chapter. Answers are listed in Appendix B, "Check Your Understanding Answer Key."

1. Which type of backup only saves the files that were modified on the same day as the backup operation?

    A. Full backup

    B. Daily backup

    C. Copy backup

    D. Differential backup

2. Raid 1 features what type of disk redundancy?

    A. Disk striping

    B. Disk backup

    C. Disk duplexing

    D. No redundancy

3. A network baseline is the comparison value to measure a network's

    A. Security

    B. Design

    C. Structure

    D. Performance

4. A peer-to-peer network establishes what type f relationship between end stations?

    A. Client-to-client

    B. Client-to-server

    C. Server-to-server

    D. Server-to-Internet

5. Which type of file system does Windows NT use for security purposes?

    A. Fat 16

    B. Fat 32

    C. NTFS

    D. NFS

6. A document that shows the physical layout of a building's network wiring is called a

    A. Cut sheet

    B. Layout diagram

    C. Floorplan

    D. Access list

7. What is the minimum number of drives required for RAID 5?

    A. 1

    B. 2

    C. 3

    D. 4

8. In a client sever network the ability of a user to access certain files while not being able to access other files are the user

    A. Accesses

    B. Rights

    C. Abilities

    D. Securities

9. What is the IP address of the internal loopback?

    A. 10.10.10.1

    B. 255.255.255.0

    C. 127.0.0.1

    D. 192.0.0.1

10. One way to prevent static-electricity damage is to

    A. Turn off the electricity when working on the computer.

    B. Wear rubber gloves to insulate the equipment

    C. Use only plastic tools

    D. Use a grounding strap

Objectives

After reading this chapter, you will be able to

- Describe the purpose and function of WANs
- Describe the various WAN devices
- Describe WAN operation
- Understand WAN encapsulation formats
- Understand WAN link options

Chapter 9

WANs

Introduction

This chapter introduces the various protocols and technologies used in *wide-area network (WAN)* environments. You will learn about the basics of WANs, including common WAN technologies, types of wide-area services, encapsulation formats, and link options. In this chapter, you also will learn about point-to-point links, circuit switching, packet switching, virtual circuits, dialup services, and WAN devices.

Washington Project: WAN Implementation
The Washington School District WAN should connect all school and administrative offices with the district office for the purpose of delivering data. The information presented in this chapter will help you understand and design a district WAN that connects all the schools and administrative offices.

WAN Technology Overview

A WAN is a data communications network that operates beyond a LAN's geographic scope. One way that a WAN is different from a LAN is that, with a WAN, you must subscribe to an outside WAN service provider, such as a *regional Bell operating company (RBOC)* to use WAN *carrier network* services. A WAN uses data links, such as Integrated Services Digital Network (ISDN) and Frame Relay, that are provided by carrier services to access bandwidth over wide-area geographies. A WAN connects the locations of an organization to each other, to locations of other organizations, to external services (such as databases), and to remote users. WANs generally carry a variety of traffic types, such as voice, data, and video.

WAN technologies function at the three lowest layers of the OSI reference model: the physical layer, the data link layer, and the network layer. Figure 9-1 illustrates the relationship between the common WAN technologies and the OSI reference model.

WAN Services

Telephone and data services are the most commonly used WAN services. Telephone and data services are connected from the building *point of presence (POP)* to the WAN provider's *central office (CO)*. The CO is the local telephone company office to which all local loops in a given area connect and in which circuit switching of subscriber lines occurs.

MOVIE 9.1
WAN Technology
Identify WAN components.

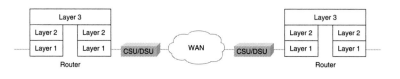

FIGURE 9-1
WAN technologies operate at the three lowest levels of the OSI reference model.

MOVIE 9.2
Data
Goes through layers, is given a header at each layer, and is passed on to next layer.

An overview of the WAN cloud (shown in Figure 9-2) organizes WAN provider services into three main types:

- **Call setup**—Sets up and clears calls between telephone users. Also called *signaling*, call setup uses a separate telephone channel not used for other traffic. The most commonly used call setup is *Signaling System 7 (SS7)*, which uses telephone control messages and signals between the transfer points along the way to the called destination.

- *Time-division multiplexing (TDM)*—Information from many sources has bandwidth allocation on a single medium. Circuit switching uses signaling to determine the call route, which is a dedicated path between the sender and the receiver. By multiplexing traffic into fixed time slots, TDM avoids congested facilities and variable delays. Basic telephone service and ISDN use TDM circuits.

■ **Frame Relay**—Information contained in frames shares bandwidth with other WAN Frame Relay subscribers. Frame Relay is statistical multiplexed service, unlike TDM, which uses Layer 2 identifiers and permanent virtual circuits. In addition, Frame Relay packet switching uses Layer 3 routing with sender and receiver addressing contained in the packet.

FIGURE 9-2
There are three types of WAN service providers.

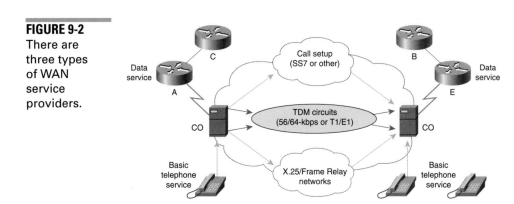

WAN Service Providers

Advances in technology over the past decade have made a number of additional WAN solutions available to network designers. When you're selecting an appropriate WAN solution, you should discuss the costs and benefits of each with your service providers.

When your organization subscribes to an outside WAN service provider for network resources, the provider gives connection requirements to the subscriber, such as the type of equipment to be used to receive services. As shown in Figure 9-3, the following are the most commonly used terms associated with the main parts of WAN services:

■ *Customer premises equipment (CPE)*—Devices physically located on the subscriber's premises. Includes both devices owned by the subscriber and devices leased to the subscriber by the service provider.

■ *Demarcation (or demarc)*—The point at which the CPE ends and the local loop portion of the service begins. Often occurs at the POP of a building.

■ *Local loop (or "last-mile")*—Cabling (usually copper wiring) that extends from the demarc into the WAN service provider's central office.

■ *CO switch*—A switching facility that provides the nearest point of presence for the provider's WAN service.

■ *Toll network*—The collective switches and facilities (called *trunks*) inside the WAN provider's cloud. The caller's traffic may cross a trunk to a primary center, then to a sectional center, and then to a regional- or international-carrier center as the call travels the long distance to its destination.

MOVIE 9.3

Sending Packets Through Network

Paths selected dynamically.

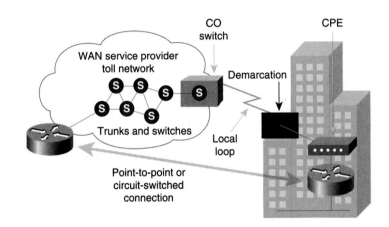

FIGURE 9-3
An organization makes connections to destinations as point-to-point calls.

A key interface in the customer site occurs between the *data terminal equipment (DTE)* and the *data circuit-terminating equipment (DCE)*. Typically, the DTE is the router, and the DCE is the device used to convert the user data from the DTE into a form acceptable to the WAN service's facility. As shown in Figure 9-4, the DCE is the attached *modem*, *channel service unit/data service unit (CSU/DSU)*, or *terminal adapter/network termination 1 (TA/NT1)*.

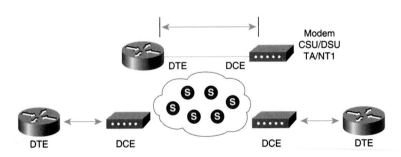

FIGURE 9-4
Data communication over WANs interconnects DTEs so that they can share resources over a wide area.

The WAN path between the DTEs is called the link, circuit, channel, or line. The DCE primarily provides an interface for the DTE into the communication link in the WAN cloud. The DTE/DCE interface acts as a boundary where responsibility for the traffic passes between the WAN subscriber and the WAN provider.

The DTE/DCE interface uses various protocols (such as HSSI and V.35) that establish the codes that the devices use to communicate with each other. This communication determines how call setup operates and how user traffic crosses the WAN.

WAN Virtual Circuits

A *virtual circuit* is a logical circuit, as opposed to a point-to-point circuit, created to ensure reliable communication between two network devices. Two types of virtual circuits exist: *switched virtual circuits (SVCs)* and *permanent virtual circuits (PVCs)*.

SVCs are virtual circuits that are dynamically established on demand and terminated when transmission is complete. Communication over an SVC consists of three phases: circuit establishment, data transfer, and circuit termination. The establishment phase involves creating the virtual circuit between the source and destination devices. Data transfer involves transmitting data between the devices over the virtual circuit, and the circuit-termination phase involves tearing down the virtual circuit between the source and destination devices. SVCs are used in situations where data transmission between devices is sporadic. SVCs increase bandwidth used due to the circuit establishment and termination phases, but decrease the cost associated with constant virtual-circuit availability.

A PVC is a permanently established virtual circuit that consists of one mode: data transfer. PVCs are used in situations where data transfer between devices is constant. PVCs decrease the bandwidth use associated with the establishment and termination of virtual circuits, but increase costs due to constant virtual-circuit availability.

Washington Project: WAN Technology Design
The WAN technology required for the Washington District WAN's link to the Internet is a Frame Relay PVC running at T1 speed.

WAN Signaling Standards and Capacity

WAN links can be ordered from the WAN provider at various speeds that are stated in bits per second (bps) capacity. This bps capacity determines how fast data can be moved across the WAN link. WAN bandwidth is often provisioned in the United States by using the North American Digital Hierarchy, shown in Table 9-1.

TABLE 9-1   **WAN Link Types and Bandwidth**

Line Type	Signal Standard	Bit Rate Capacity
56	DSO	56 kbps
64	DSO	64 kbps
T1	DS1	1.544 Mbps
E1	ZM	2.048 Mbps
E3	M3	34.064 Mbps
J1	Y1	2.048 Mbps
T3	DS3	44.736 Mbps
OC-1	SONET	51.84 Mbps
OC-3	SONET	155.54 Mbps
OC-9	SONET	466.56 Mbps
OC-12	SONET	622.08 Mbps
OC-18	SONET	933.12 Mbps
OC-24	SONET	1244.16 Mbps
OC-36	SONET	1866.24 Mbps
OC-48	SONET	2488.32 Mbps

WAN Devices

WANs use numerous types of devices, including the following:

- Routers, which offer many services, including LAN and WAN interface ports.
- WAN switches, which connect to WAN bandwidth for voice, data, and video communication.
- Modems, which interface voice-grade services. Modems include CSUs/DSUs and TA/NT1 devices that interface ISDN services.
- Communication servers, which concentrate dial-in and dial-out user communication.

Figure 9-5 shows the icons used for these WAN devices.

FIGURE 9-5
The main WAN
devices are
routers, WAN
switches,
modems, and
communica-
tion servers.

 Router

 WAN switch

 Modem CSU/DSU TA/NT1

 Communication server

Routers

Routers are devices that implement the network service. They provide interfaces for a wide range of links and subnetworks at a wide range of speeds. Routers are active and intelligent network devices and thus can participate in managing the network. Routers manage networks by providing dynamic control over resources and supporting the tasks and goals for networks. These goals are connectivity, reliable performance, management control, and flexibility.

WAN Switches

A WAN switch is a multiport networking device that typically switches such traffic as Frame Relay, *X.25*, and Switched Multimegabit Data Service (SMDS). WAN switches typically operate at the data link layer of the OSI reference model. Figure 9-6 illustrates two routers at remote ends of a WAN that are connected by WAN switches. In this example, the switches filter, forward, and flood frames based on the destination address of each frame.

Washington Project: Deployment of Switches
As part of the Washington School District network design and implementation, you need to determine what type of switches to obtain, how many of them to obtain, and where to place them in the network. Possible locations include the MDFs and IDFs in the school locations and at the main district office. Additionally, you need to determine what types of switches are needed, such as LAN or WAN switches, and whether they need to be Layer 2 or Layer 3 switches. Finally, you need to determine the segmentation and security required to establish the types, number, and placement of switches in the network.

Modems

A modem is a device that interprets digital and analog signals by modulating and demodulating the signal, enabling data to be transmitted over voice-grade telephone lines. At the source, digital signals are converted to a form suitable for transmission over analog communication facilities. At the destination, these analog signals are returned to their digital form. Figure 9-7 illustrates a simple modem-to-modem connection through a WAN.

FIGURE 9-6
WAN switches can connect two routers at remote ends of a WAN.

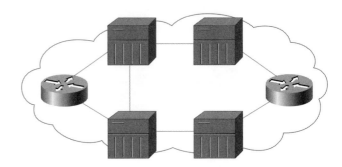

FIGURE 9-7
A WAN can handle analog and digital signals through a modem connection.

CSUs/DSUs

A CSU/DSU is a digital-interface device—or sometimes two separate digital devices—that adapts the physical interface on a DTE device (such as a terminal) to the interface of a DCE device (such as a switch) in a switched-carrier network. Figure 9-8 illustrates the placement of the CSU/DSU in a WAN implementation. Sometimes, CSUs/DSUs are integrated in the router box.

FIGURE 9-8
In a WAN, the CSU/DSU is placed between the switch and the terminal.

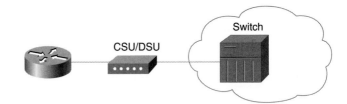

Washington Project: Deployment of CSUs/DSUs
As part of the Washington School District network design and implementation, you need to determine what kind of CSU/DSUs to obtain, how many of them to obtain, and where to place them in the network. Possible locations include the MDFs in the school locations and at the main district office, where the WAN links will be terminated. Keep in mind that CSUs/DSUs need to be located close to routers.

ISDN Terminal Adapters

An ISDN Terminal Adapter (TA) is a device used to connect ISDN Basic Rate Interface (BRI) connections to other interfaces. A TA is essentially an ISDN modem. Figure 9-9 illustrates the placement of a TA in an ISDN environment.

FIGURE 9-9
In a WAN, the TA connects the ISDN to other interfaces, such as the switches.

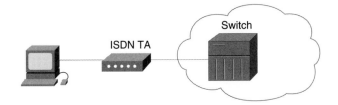

WANs and the OSI Reference Model

WANs use the OSI reference model layered approach to encapsulation, just as LANs do, but they are mainly focused on the physical and data link layers. WAN standards typically describe both physical-layer delivery methods and data link layer requirements, including addressing, flow control and encapsulation. WAN standards are defined and managed by a number of recognized authorities, including the following agencies:

- International Telecommunication Union-Telecommunication Standardization Sector (ITU-T), formerly the Consultative Committee for International Telegraph and Telephone (CCITT)
- International Organization for Standardization (ISO)
- *Internet Engineering Task Force (IETF)*
- *Electronic Industries Association (EIA)*
- *Telecommunications Industries Association (TIA)*

The WAN Physical Layer

WAN physical-layer protocols describe how to provide electrical, mechanical, operational, and functional connections for WAN services. Most WANs require an interconnection that is provided by a communications service provider (such as an RBOC), an alternative carrier (such as an Internet service provider), or a *post, telephone, and telegraph (PTT)* agency.

The WAN physical layer also describes the interface between the DTE and the DCE. Typically, the DCE is the service provider, and the DTE is the attached device, as shown in Figure 9-10.

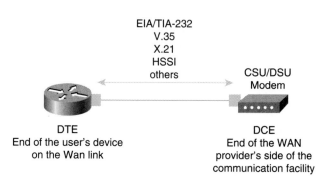

FIGURE 9-10
The service provider circuit typically terminates at a DTE (for example, a router), and a DCE (for example, at the customer site).

Several physical-layer standards define the rules governing the interface between the DTE and the DCE:

- **EIA/TIA-232** —A common physical-layer interface standard developed by EIA and TIA that supports unbalanced circuits at signal speeds of up to 64 kbps. It closely resembles the V.24 specification, and was formerly known as RS-232. This standard has been in place for many years.

- **EIA/TIA-449**—A popular physical-layer interface developed by EIA and TIA. It is essentially a faster (up to 2 Mbps) version of EIA/TIA-232, capable of longer cable runs.

- **EIA/TIA-612/613**—A standard describing High Speed Serial Interface (HSSI), which provides access to services at T3 (45 Mbps), E3 (34 Mbps), and Synchronous Optical Network (SONET) STS-1 (51.84 Mbps) rates. The actual rate of the interface depends on the external DSU and the type of service to which it is connected.

- **V.24**—An ITU-T standard for a physical-layer interface between DTE and DCE.

- **V.35**—An ITU-T standard describing a synchronous, physical-layer protocol used for communications between a network access device and a packet network. V.35 is most commonly used in the United States and in Europe.

- **X.21**—An ITU-T standard for serial communications over synchronous digital lines. The X.21 protocol is used primarily in Europe and Japan.

- **G.703**—An ITU-T electrical and mechanical specification for connections between telephone company equipment and DTE using British Naval connectors (BNCs) and operating at E1 data rates.

- **EIA-530**—Two electrical implementations of EIA/TIA-449: RS-422 (for balanced transmission) and RS-423 (for unbalanced transmission).

The WAN Data Link Layer

The WAN data link layer defines how data is encapsulated for transmission to remote sites. WAN data-link protocols describe how frames are carried between systems on a single data path.

Figure 9-11 shows the common data-link encapsulations associated with WAN lines, which are

- *Frame Relay*—By using simplified encapsulation with no error correction mechanisms over high-quality digital facilities, Frame Relay can transmit data very rapidly compared to the other WAN protocols.

- **Point-to-Point Protocol (PPP)**—Described by RFC 1661, PPP was developed by the IETF. PPP contains a protocol field to identify the network-layer protocol.

- **ISDN**—A set of digital services that transmits voice and data over existing phone lines.

- *Link Access Procedure, Balanced (LAPB)*—For packet-switched networks, LAPB is used to encapsulate packets at Layer 2 of the X.25 stack. It can also be used over a *point-to-point link* if the link is unreliable or there is an inherent delay associated with the link, such as in a satellite link. LAPB provides *reliability* and flow control on a point-to-point basis.

- **Cisco/IETF**—Used to encapsulate Frame Relay traffic. The Cisco option is proprietary and can be used only between Cisco routers.

- **High-Level Data Link Control (HDLC)**—An ISO standard, HDLC might not be compatible between different vendors because of the way each vendor has chosen to implement it. HDLC supports both point-to-point and multipoint configurations.

FIGURE 9-11
The choice of encapsulation protocol depends on the WAN technology and the communicating equipment.

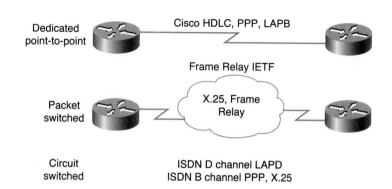

WAN Frame Encapsulation Formats

The two most common point-to-point WAN encapsulations are HDLC and PPP. All the serial line encapsulations share a common frame format, which has the following fields, as shown in Figure 9-12:

- **Flag**—Indicates the beginning and end of the frame and is set to the *hexadecimal (base 16)* pattern 7E.
- **Address**—A 1- or 2-byte field to address the end station in multidrop environments.
- **Control**—Indicates whether the frame is an information, a supervisory, or an unnumbered type frame. It also contains specific function codes.
- **Data**—The encapsulated data.
- **FCS**—The frame check sequence (FCS).
- **Flag**—The trailing 7E flag identifier.

FIGURE 9-12
Point-to-point encapsulations generally are used on dedicated WAN lines.

PPP

Flag	Address	Control	Protocol	Data	FCS	Flag

HDLC

Flag	Address	Control	Proprietary	Data	FCS	Flag

Each WAN connection type uses a Layer 2 protocol to encapsulate traffic while it is crossing the WAN link. To ensure that the correct encapsulation protocol is used, you need to configure the Layer 2 encapsulation type to use for each serial interface on a router. The choice of encapsulation protocol depends on the WAN technology and the communicating equipment. Encapsulation protocols that can be used with the WAN connection types covered in this chapter are PPP and HDLC.

PPP Encapsulation

PPP is a standard serial-line encapsulation method (described in RFC 1332 and RFC 1661). This protocol can, among other things, check for link quality during connection establishment. In addition, there is support for authentication through Password Authentication Protocol (PAP) and Challenge Handshake Authentication Protocol (CHAP). PPP is covered in depth in Chapter 11, "PPP."

Engineering Journal:
PPP Link Negotiation

PPP ensures interoperability between networking vendors by using several additional protocols, including the following:

- LCP for negotiating basic line interoperability
- A family of network control protocols for negotiating individual Layer 3 protocols and their options (such as IP Control Protocol [IPCP] for IP and options such as compression)

When the PPP link is negotiated, a link control protocol is negotiated to establish the link and then additional network control protocols are negotiated.

You can use the command **show interfaces** to check the status of the LCP and the network control protocol and to test the interoperability of the network layers. There are also excellent **debug ppp** commands for troubleshooting.

To configure the serial line to use PPP, use the **encapsulation ppp** command, as follows:

```
Router(config)# interface serial 0
Router(config-if)# encapsulation ppp
```

HDLC Encapsulation

HDLC is a data link layer protocol derived from the *Synchronous Data Link Control (SDLC)* encapsulation protocol. HDLC is Cisco's default encapsulation for serial lines. This implementation is very streamlined; there is no windowing or flow control, and only point-to-point connections are allowed. The address field is always set to all ones. Furthermore, a 2-byte proprietary type code is inserted after the control field, which means that HDLC framing is not interoperable with other vendors' equipment.

If both ends of a dedicated-line connection are routers or access servers running *Cisco Internetwork Operating System (IOS) software*, HDLC encapsulation typically is used. Because HDLC encapsulation methods can vary, you should use PPP with devices that are not running Cisco IOS software.

Washington Project: PPP Encapsulation

Although both PPP and HDLC are appropriate frame types for point-to-point connections, you should use PPP on point-to-point links in the Washington School District network. PPP offers the following advantages:

- Interoperability between networking vendors
- LCP for negotiating basic line interoperability
- A family of network control protocols for negotiating individual Layer 3 protocols

WAN Link Options

In general, as shown in Figure 9-13, two types of WAN link options are available: dedicated lines and switched connections. Switched connections, in turn, can be either circuit switched or packet switched. The following sections describe these types of link options.

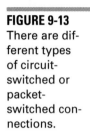

FIGURE 9-13
There are different types of circuit-switched or packet-switched connections.

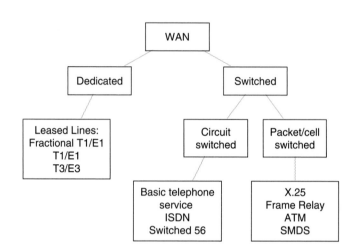

Dedicated Lines

Dedicated lines, also called *leased lines*, provide full-time service. Dedicated lines typically are used to carry data, voice, and occasionally video. In data network design, dedicated lines generally provide core or backbone connectivity between major sites or campuses, as well as LAN-to-LAN connectivity.

Dedicated lines generally are considered reasonable design options for WANs. With dedicated lines, you need a router port and a circuit for each remote site. When dedicated line connections are made, a router port is required for each connection, along with a CSU/DSU and the actual circuit from the service provider. The cost of dedicated-line solutions can become significant when they are used to connect many sites.

Dedicated, full-time connectivity is provided by point-to-point serial links. Connections are made using the router's synchronous serial ports with typical bandwidth use of up to 2 Mbps (E1) available through the use of a CSU/DSU. Different encapsulation methods at the data link layer provide flexibility and reliability for user traffic. Dedicated lines of this type are ideal for high-volume environments with a steady-rate traffic pattern. Use of available bandwidth is a concern because you have to pay for the line to be available even when the connection is idle.

Washington Project: Dedicated Lines
The Washington School District should use dedicated lines (T1) for its WAN core. You need to determine how many links this will involve and what kinds of equipment must be purchased (such as CSUs/DSUs).

Dedicated lines also are referred to as point-to-point links because their established path is permanent and fixed for each remote network reached through the carrier facilities. A point-to-point link provides a single, pre-established WAN communications path from the customer premises through a carrier network, such as a telephone company, to a remote network. The service provider reserves point-to-point links for the private use of the customer. Figure 9-14 illustrates a typical point-to-point link through a WAN. Point-to-point is used for direct physical links or for virtual links consisting of multiple physical links.

FIGURE 9-14
A typical point-to-point link operates through a WAN to a router, and to end systems on both ends of the link.

Packet-Switched Connections

Packet switching is a WAN switching method in which network devices share a permanent virtual circuit (PVC), which is like a point-to-point link that transports packets from a source to a destination across a carrier network, as shown in Figure 9-15. Frame Relay, SMDS, and X.25 are all examples of packet-switched WAN technologies.

Switched networks can carry variable-size frames (packets) or fixed-size cells. The most common packet-switched network type is Frame Relay.

Frame Relay

Frame Relay was designed to be used over high-speed, high-quality digital facilities. As a result, Frame Relay does not offer much error checking or reliability, but expects upper-layer protocols to attend to these issues.

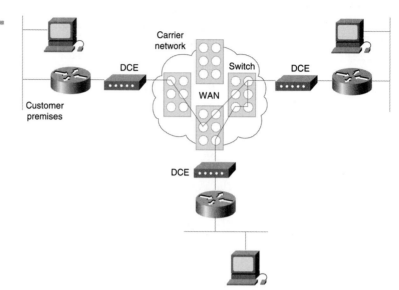

FIGURE 9-15
Packet switching transfers packets across a carrier network.

Frame Relay is a packet-switching data communications technology that can connect multiple network devices on a multipoint WAN, as shown in Figure 9-16. The design of Frame Relay WANs can affect certain aspects (such as split horizon) of higher-layer protocols such as IP, IPX, and Apple-Talk. Frame Relay is called a *non-broadcast multi-access technology* because it has no broadcast channel. Broadcasts are transmitted through Frame Relay by sending packets to all network destinations.

FIGURE 9-16
Frame Relay is a packet-switched data network technology designed to be simpler and faster than older technologies (such as X.25) that connect multiple network devices.

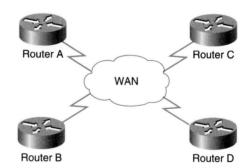

Frame Relay defines the connection between a customer DTE and a carrier DCE. The DTE is typically a router, and the DCE is a Frame Relay switch. (In this case, DTE and DCE refer to the data link layer, not the physical layer.) Frame Relay access is typically at 56 kbps, 64 kbps, or 1.544 Mbps.

Frame Relay is a cost-effective alternative to point-to-point WAN designs. Each site can be connected to every other by a virtual circuit. Each router needs only one physical interface to the carrier. Frame Relay is implemented mostly as a carrier-provided service but can also be used for private networks.

Frame Relay service is offered through a PVC. A PVC is an unreliable data link. A *data-link connection identifier (DLCI)* identifies a PVC. The DLCI number is a local identifier between the DTE and the DCE that identifies the logical circuit between the source and destination devices. The Service Level Agreement (SLA) specifies the *committed information rate (CIR)* provided by the carrier, which is the rate, in bits per second, at which the Frame Relay switch agrees to transfer data. (These topics are covered in depth in Chapter 13, "Frame Relay.")

MOVIE 9.4

DLCIs Become Unique Network Addresses for DTE Devices

Frame Relay network changes to reflect origin of source.

As you'll learn further in Chapter 13, two common topologies can be used in a Frame Relay solution:

- *Fully meshed topology*—Every Frame Relay network device has a PVC to every other device on the multipoint WAN. Any update sent by one device is seen by every other. If this design is used, the entire Frame Relay WAN can be treated as one data link.

- *Partially meshed topology*—This is also often called a star topology or hub-and-spokes topology. In a partially meshed topology, not every device on the Frame Relay cloud has a PVC to every other device.

Circuit-Switched Connections

Circuit switching is a WAN switching method in which a dedicated physical circuit is established, maintained, and terminated through a carrier network for each communication session. Used extensively in telephone company networks, circuit switching operates much like a normal telephone call. ISDN is an example of a circuit-switched WAN technology.

Circuit-switched connections from one site to another are brought up when needed and generally require low bandwidth. Basic telephone service connections are generally limited to 28.8 kbps without compression, and ISDN connections are limited to 64 or 128 kbps. Circuit-switched connections are used primarily to connect remote users and mobile users to corporate LANs. They are also used as backup lines for higher-speed circuits, such as Frame Relay and dedicated lines.

DDR

Dial-on-demand routing (DDR) is a technique in which a router can dynamically initiate and close circuit-switched sessions when transmitting end stations need them. When the router receives traffic destined for a remote network, a circuit is established, and the traffic is transmitted normally. The router maintains an idle timer that is reset only when interesting traffic is received. (*Interesting traffic* refers to traffic the router needs to route.) If the router receives no interesting traffic before the idle timer expires, however, the circuit is terminated. Likewise, if uninteresting traffic is received and no circuit exists, the router drops the traffic. When the router receives interesting traffic, it initiates a new circuit.

MOVIE 9.5

Dial Backup

Activates backup serial line to be used when traffic is too heavy or when primary line fails.

DDR enables you to make a standard telephone connection or an ISDN connection only when required by the volume of network traffic. DDR may be less expensive than a dedicated-line or multipoint solutions. DDR means that the connection is brought up only when a specific type of traffic initiates the call or when you need a backup link. These circuit-switched calls, indicated by the broken lines in Figure 9-17, are placed using ISDN networks. DDR is a substitute for dedicated lines when full-time circuit availability is not required. In addition, DDR can be used to replace point-to-point links and switched multi-access WAN services.

DDR can be used to provide backup load sharing and interface backup. For example, you might have several serial lines, but you want the second serial line to be used only when the first line is very busy so that load sharing can occur. When your WAN lines are used for critical applications, you might want a DDR line configured in case the primary lines go down. In this case, the secondary line enables itself so traffic can still get across.

FIGURE 9-17
Using ISDN,
connections
are made when
traffic requires
them.

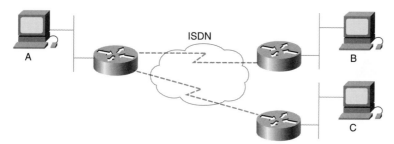

Compared to LAN or campus-based networking, the traffic that uses DDR is typically low volume and periodic. DDR initiates a WAN call to a remote site only when there is traffic to transmit.

When you configure for DDR, you must enter configuration commands that indicate what protocol packets make-up interesting traffic to initiate the call. To do this, you enter access control list statements to identify the source and destination addresses, and you choose specific protocol selection criteria for initiating the call. Then you must establish the interfaces where the DDR call initiates. This step designates a dialer group. The dialer group associates the results of the access control list specification of interesting packets to the router's interfaces for dialing a WAN call.

ISDN

Telephone companies developed ISDN with the intention of creating a totally digital network. ISDN devices include the following:

- **Terminal Equipment 1 (TE1)**—Designates a device that is compatible with the ISDN network. A TE1 connects to an NT of either Type 1 or Type 2.
- **Terminal Equipment 2 (TE2)**—Designates a device that is not compatible with ISDN and requires a TA.
- **TA**—Converts standard electrical signals into the form used by ISDN so that non-ISDN devices can connect to the ISDN network.
- **NT Type 1 (NT1)**—Connects four-wire ISDN subscriber wiring to the conventional two-wire local loop facility.
- **NT Type 2 (NT2)**—Directs traffic to and from different subscriber devices and the NT1. The NT2 is an intelligent device that performs switching and concentrating.

As shown in Figure 9-18, ISDN interface reference points include the following:

- The S/T interface defines the interface between a TE1 and an NT. The S/T also is used to define the TA-to-NT interface.

■ The R interface defines the interface between a TE2 and the TA.

■ The U interface defines the two-wire interface between the NT and the ISDN cloud.

FIGURE 9-18
ISDN is an end-to-end digital network technology used for voice, data, fax, and video.

TE1 — Four wires — NT — Two wires to central office — Service provider

TE1

S/T interface   U interface

TE2   TA

R interface

There are two ISDN services: Basic Rate Interface (BRI) and Primary Rate Interface (PRI). ISDN BRI operates mostly over the copper twisted-pair telephone wiring in place today. ISDN BRI delivers a total bandwidth of a 144 kbps line into three separate channels. Two of the channels, called *B (bearer) channels*, operate at 64 kbps and are used to carry voice or data traffic. The third channel, the *D (delta) channel*, is a 16-kbps signaling channel used to carry instructions that tell the telephone network how to handle each of the B channels. ISDN BRI often is referred to as *2B+D*. ISDN is covered in depth in Chapter 12, "ISDN."

ISDN provides great flexibility to the network designer because of its capability to use each of the B channels for separate voice or data applications. For example, one ISDN 64-kbps B channel can download a long document from the corporate network while the other B channel browses a Web page. When you're designing a WAN, you should be careful to select equipment that has the right feature to take advantage of ISDN's flexibility.

MOVIE 9.6

ISDN BRI Service
B channel and D channel.

Summary

- A WAN is used to interconnect LANs that are separated by a large geographic distance.
- A WAN provides a data path between routers and the LANs that each router supports.
- Many types of WAN services are available to the WAN subscriber, which must know how to interface to the WAN provider's service.
- WAN devices include WAN switches, modems, and ISDN TAs.
- A WAN mainly operates at the OSI physical and data link layers.
- WAN encapsulation formats include PPP and HDLC encapsulation.
- WAN link options include dedicated lines such as point-to-point links, packet-switched connections such as Frame Relay, and circuit-switched connections such as DDR and ISDN.

Washington School District Project Task: WANs

In this chapter, you have learned about the WAN technologies that enable you to interconnect all the individual Washington School District sites into the WAN topology.

You need to complete the following tasks:

1. Select WAN services for the district WAN-to-site, WAN core-to-WAN core, and WAN-to-Internet connections.

2. Determine the costs and the range of WAN services.

3. Begin documenting the WAN design.

4. Apply the CCNA Certification Exam Learning Objectives to your specific design. This requires a paragraph on how the learning objectives relate to your design. Learning objectives can be grouped together for the purpose of explanation. In this way, you will be studying for the CCNA Certification Exam as you work through the case study.

CCNA Certification Exam Learning Objectives

WANs

- Differentiate between the following WAN services: Frame Relay, ISDN/LAPD, HDLC, and PPP.

Check Your Understanding

Complete all the review questions to test your understanding of the topics and concepts covered in this chapter. Answers are listed in Appendix B, "Check Your Understanding Answer Key."

1. How many data paths are used by WAN data-link protocols to carry frames between systems?

   A. Two

   B. One

   C. Four

   D. Undetermined

2. At what layer of the OSI reference model would you find the DCE or DTE equipment?

   A. The network layer

   B. The data link layer

   C. The physical layer

   D. The transport layer

3. A CSU/DSU generally is used as what type of equipment?

   A. Router

   B. DTE

   C. Switch

   D. DCE

4. Which of the following encapsulation types is associated with synchronous serial lines?

   A. PPP

   B. HDLC

   C. Frame Relay

   D. All of the above

5. What encapsulation type would you select for a link if speed were the most important factor?

   A. Frame Relay

   B. PPP

   C. HDLC

   D. SLIP

6. Devices that are located at a service subscriber's site are referred to as what?

   A. Customer owned equipment

   B. Subscriber devices

   C. Customer premises equipment

   D. Subscriber premises equipment

7. The WAN path between DTEs is known as what?

   A. The link

   B. The circuit

   C. The channel

   D. All of the above

8. Which WAN services can be used with a router?

   A. Frame Relay

   B. ISDN

   C. PPP

   D. All of the above

9. Which of the following is an example of a packet-switched protocol?

   A. ISDN

   B. Frame Relay

   C. PPP

   D. HDLC

10. Which protocol does PPP use for establishing and maintaining point-to-point connections?

A. HDLC

B. LCP

C. LAPD

D. Cisco IETF

11. What type of link is typically used by WANs?

A. Serial

B. Parallel

C. Full-duplex

D. High-speed

12. Which encapsulation type is the default encapsulation for serial interfaces on a Cisco router?

A. PPP

B. HDLC

C. Frame Relay

D. X.25

13. Which type of service uses time-division multiplexing (TDM)?

A. Frame Relay

B. ISDN

C. X.25

D. SS7

14. What type of ISDN adapter is used to connect ISDN Basic Rate Interface (BRI) connections to other interfaces?

A. Link adapter

B. Network adapter

C. Terminal adapter

D. Line adapter

15. How does Cisco's HDLC protocol handle windowing?

  A. The sender sets the window size.

  B. The recipient sets the window size.

  C. Windowing is not supported.

  D. Both sender and receiver agree on the size.

16. Which protocol would you select if you were looking for a protocol that supported multiple upper-layer protocols as well as being RFC-based?

  A. PPP

  B. HDLC

  C. SLIP

  D. Frame Relay

17. Which switched data link layer protocol uses High-Level Data Link Control (HDLC) encapsulation between connected devices to handle multiple virtual circuits?

  A. X.25

  B. Frame Relay

  C. PPP

  D. None of the above

18. Which of the following statements pertaining to ISDN is true?

  A. The ISDN BRI offers two B channels (of 16 kbps) and one D channel (of 64 kbps).

  B. The D channel, operating at 16 kbps, is meant to carry user data.

  C. The ISDN BRI offers 23 B channels (of 64 kbps) and one D channel (of 64 kbps).

  D. The total bit rate of the ISDN BRI is 1.533 Mbps.

19. If you are connected to the World Wide Web on one ISDN B channel, what can you do on the other channel?

  A. Send a fax

  B. Receive a phone call

  C. Download a file

  D. All of the above

Key Terms

ATM (Asynchronous Transfer Mode)   An international standard for cell relay in which multiple service types (such as voice, video, or data) are conveyed in fixed-length (53-byte) cells. Fixed-length cells allow cell processing to occur in hardware, thereby reducing transit delays. ATM is designed to take advantage of high-speed transmission media such as E3, SONET, and T3.

B channel (bearer channel)   In ISDN, a full-duplex, 64-kbps channel used to send user data.

carrier network   A service provider's network.

CIR (committed information rate)   The rate in bits per second at which the Frame Relay switch agrees to transfer data.

Cisco IOS (Internetwork Operating System) software   Cisco system software that provides common functionality, scalability, and security for all products under the CiscoFusion architecture. Cisco IOS software allows centralized, integrated, and automated installation and management of internetworks, while ensuring support for a wide variety of protocols, media, services, and platforms.

CO (central office)   The local telephone company office to which all local loops in a given area connect and in which circuit switching of subscriber lines occurs.

CPE (customer premises equipment)   Terminating equipment, such as terminals, telephones, and modems, supplied by the telephone company, installed at customer sites, and connected to the telephone company network.

CSU/DSU (channel service unit/data service unit)   A digital interface device that connects end-user equipment to the local digital telephone loop.

DCE (data circuit-terminating equipment)   The device used to convert the user data from the DTE into a form acceptable to the WAN service's facility.

D channel (delta channel)   A full-duplex, 16-kbps (BRI) or 64-kbps (PRI) ISDN channel.

DDR (dial-on-demand routing)   A technique with which a router can dynamically initiate and close circuit-switched sessions as transmitting end stations need them.

demarcation (demarc)   The point at which the CPE ends and the local loop portion of the service begins. Often occurs at the POP of a building.

DLCI (data-link connection identifier)   A value that specifies a PVC or an SVC in a Frame Relay network. In the basic Frame Relay specification, DLCIs are locally significant (that is, connected devices can use different values to specify the same connection). In the LMI extended specification, DLCIs are globally significant (that is, DLCIs specify individual end devices).

DTE (data terminal equipment)   A device at the user end of a user-to-network interface that serves as a data source, destination, or both. A DTE connects to a data network through a DCE device (for example, a modem) and typically uses clocking signals generated by the DCE. DTEs include such devices as computers, protocol translators, and multiplexers.

EIA (Electronic Industries Association)   A group that specifies electrical transmission standards. EIA and TIA have developed numerous well-known communications standards together, including EIA/TIA-232 and EIA/TIA-449.

Frame Relay   An industry-standard, switched data link–layer protocol that handles multiple virtual circuits using HDLC encapsulation between connected devices. Frame Relay is more efficient than X.25, the protocol for which it is generally considered a replacement.

fully meshed topology   A topology in which every Frame Relay network device has a PVC to every other device on the multipoint WAN.

hexadecimal (base 16)   A number representation using the digits 0 through 9, with their usual meaning, plus the letters A through F, to represent hexadecimal digits with values 10 to 15. The rightmost digit counts ones, the next counts multiples of 16, the next is $16^2=256$, and so on.

IETF (Internet Engineering Task Force)   A task force consisting of more than 80 working groups responsible for developing Internet standards. The IETF operates under the auspices of ISOC.

LAPB (Link Access Procedure, Balanced)   A data link layer protocol in the X.25 protocol stack. LAPB is a bit-oriented protocol derived from HDLC.

local loop   Cabling (usually copper wiring) that extends from the demarc into the WAN service provider's central office.

modem (modulator-demodulator)   A device that converts digital and analog signals. At the source, a modem converts digital signals to a form suitable for transmission over analog communication facilities. At the destination, the analog signals are returned to their digital form. Modems allow data to be transmitted over voice-grade telephone lines.

NT1 (network termination 1)   A type of device that interfaces with ISDN services.

partially meshed topology   A topology in which not every device on the Frame Relay cloud has a PVC to every other device.

point-to-point link   A link that provides a single, pre-established WAN communications path from the customer premises through a carrier network, such as a telephone company, to a remote network. Also called a dedicated line or a leased line.

POP (point of presence)   The point of interconnection between the communication facilities provided by the telephone company and the building's main distribution facility.

PTT (post, telephone, and telegraph)   A government agency that provides telephone services. PTTs exist in most areas outside North America and provide both local and long-distance telephone services.

PVC (permanent virtual circuit)   A virtual circuit that is permanently established. PVCs save bandwidth associated with circuit establishment and teardown in situations where certain virtual circuits must exist all the time.

RBOC (regional Bell operating company)   A local or regional telephone company that owns and operates telephone lines and switches in one of seven U.S. regions. The RBOCs were created by the divestiture of AT&T.

reliability   The ratio of expected to received keepalives from a link. If the ratio is high, the line is reliable. Used as a routing metric.

SDLC (Synchronous Data Link Control)   An SNA data link–layer communications protocol. SDLC is a bit-oriented, full-duplex serial protocol that has spawned numerous similar protocols, including HDLC and LAPB.

SS7 (Signaling System 7)   A standard common channel signaling system developed by Bellcore. It uses telephone control messages and signals between the transfer points along the way to the called destination.

star topology   A LAN topology in which endpoints on a network are connected to a common central switch by point-to-point links. A ring topology that is organized as a star implements a unidirectional closed-loop star instead of point-to-point links.

SVC (switched virtual circuit)   A virtual circuit that is dynamically established on demand and is torn down when transmission is complete. SVCs are used in situations in which data transmission is sporadic.

TA (terminal adapter)   A device used to connect ISDN BRI connections to existing interfaces such as EIA/TIA-232. Essentially, an ISDN modem.

TDM (time-division multiplexing)   A circuit-switching signal used to determine the call route, which is a dedicated path between the sender and the receiver.

TIA (Telecommunications Industries Association)   An organization that develops standards relating to telecommunications technologies. Together, TIA and EIA have formalized standards, such as EIA/TIA-232, for the electrical characteristics of data transmission.

toll network   The collective switches and facilities (called trunks) inside the WAN provider's cloud.

virtual circuit   A logical circuit created to ensure reliable communication between two network devices. A virtual circuit is defined by a VPI/VCI pair and can be either permanent (a PVC) or switched (an SVC). Virtual circuits are used in Frame Relay and X.25. In ATM, a virtual circuit is called a virtual channel. Sometimes abbreviated VC.

WAN (wide-area network)   A data communications network that serves users across a broad geographic area and often uses transmission devices provided by common carriers. Frame Relay, SMDS, and X.25 are examples of WAN technologies.

X.25   An ITU-T standard that defines how connections between DTEs and DCEs are maintained for remote terminal access and computer communications in public data networks. Frame Relay has superseded X.25 to some degree.

Objectives

After reading this chapter, you will be able to

- Describe WAN communication
- Describe the process and considerations for designing a WAN
- Describe the process for gathering user requirements for WAN design
- Describe the benefits of using a hierarchical design model, and identify and describe the three layers of the hierarchical model
- Describe the placement of ISDN and Frame Relay
- Describe how placement of enterprise servers and workgroup servers affects traffic patterns across the WAN
- Describe backbone service requirements
- Describe the benefits of switches and Layer 2 services
- Describe the benefits of routers and Layer 3 services
- Describe multiple- and single-protocol routing
- Identify and describe WAN reliability options

Chapter 10

WAN Design

Introduction

Today's network administrators must manage complex wide-area networks (WANs) in order to support the growing number of software applications that are built around Internet Protocol (IP) and the Web. These WANs place a great demand on network resources and require high-performance networking technologies. WANs are environments that incorporate multiple media, multiple protocols, and interconnection to other networks such as the Internet. Growth and manageability of these network environments are achieved by the often complex interaction of protocols and features.

Despite improvements in equipment performance and media capabilities, WAN design is becoming more difficult. Carefully designed WANs can reduce problems associated with growing networking environment. To design reliable, scalable WANs, network designers must keep in mind that each WAN has specific design requirements. This chapter provides an overview of the methodologies utilized to design WANs.

Washington Project: WAN Design
In this chapter, you learn about WAN design processes that will enable you to implement WAN services requirements into the Washington School District network design. The district WAN should connect all school and administrative offices with the district office for the purpose of delivering data.

WAN Communication

WAN communication occurs between geographically separated areas. When a local end station wants to communicate with a remote end station (that is, an end station located at a different site), information must be sent over one or more *WAN links*. Routers within WANs are connection points of a network. These routers determine the most appropriate path through the network for the required data streams.

As you have learned in Chapter 9, "WANs," WAN communication is often called a service because the network provider often charges users for the WAN services it provides. *Circuit-switching* and *packet-switching* technologies are two types of WAN services, each of which has advantages and disadvantages. For example, circuit-switched networks offer users dedicated bandwidth that cannot be infringed upon by other users. In contrast, packet switching is a method in which network devices share a single point-to-point link to transport packets from a source to a destination across a carrier network. Packet-switched networks have traditionally offered more flexibility and used network bandwidth more efficiently than circuit-switched networks.

Traditionally, relatively low throughput, high delay, and high error rates have characterized WAN communication. WAN connections are also characterized by the cost of renting media (that is, wire) from a service provider to connect two or more campuses together. Because the WAN infrastructure is often rented from a service provider, WAN network designs must optimize the cost of bandwidth and bandwidth efficiency. For example, all technologies and features used in WANs are developed to meet the following design requirements:

- Optimize WAN bandwidth
- Minimize cost
- Maximize the effective service to the end users

Recently, traditional shared-media networks are being overtaxed because of the following new network requirements:

- Network usage has increased as enterprises utilize client/server, multimedia, and other applications to enhance productivity.
- The rate of change in application requirements has accelerated and will continue to do so (for example, Internet "push" technologies).
- Applications increasingly require distinct network qualities of service due to services they provide end users.
- An unprecedented number of connections are being established among offices of all sizes, remote users, mobile users, international sites, customers/suppliers, and the Internet.
- The explosive growth of corporate intranets and extranets has created a greater demand for bandwidth.
- The increased use of enterprise servers continues to grow to serve the business needs of organizations.

Compared to current WANs, the new WAN infrastructures must be more complex, based on new technologies, and able to handle an ever-increasing (and rapidly changing) application mix with required and guaranteed service levels. In addition, with a 300% traffic increase expected in the next five years, enterprises will feel even greater pressure to contain WAN costs.

WAN connections generally handle important information and are optimized for price and performance. The routers connecting the campuses, for example, generally apply traffic optimization, multiple paths for redundancy, dial backup for disaster recovery, and quality of service (QoS) for critical applications. Table 10-1 summarizes the various WAN technologies that support such WAN requirements.

TABLE 10-1 Summary of WAN Technologies

WAN Technology	Typical Uses
Leased line	Leased lines can be used for Point-to-Point Protocol (PPP) networks and hub-and-spokes topologies, or backups of other types of links.
Integrated Services Digital Network (ISDN)	ISDN can be used for cost-effective remote access to corporate networks. It provides support for voice and video as well as a backup for another type of link.
Frame Relay	Frame Relay provides a cost-effective, high-speed, low-latency mesh topology between remote sites. It can be used in both private and carrier-provided networks.

LAN/WAN Integration

Distributed applications need increasingly more bandwidth, and the explosion of Internet use is driving many LAN architectures to the limit. Voice communications have increased significantly, with more reliance being placed on centralized voice mail systems for verbal communications. The network is the critical tool for information flow. Networks are being required to cost less, yet support the emerging applications and larger number of users with increased performance.

Until now, local- and wide-area communications have remained logically separate. In the LAN, bandwidth is free and connectivity is limited only by hardware and implementation costs. In the WAN, bandwidth is the overriding cost, and delay-sensitive traffic such as voice has remained separate from data.

Internet applications such as voice and real-time video require better, more predictable LAN and WAN performance. These multimedia applications are fast becoming an essential part of the business productivity toolkit. As companies begin to consider implementing new intranet-based, bandwidth-intensive multimedia applications, such as video training, videoconferencing, and voice over IP, the impact of these applications on the existing networking infrastructure will become a serious concern.

For example, if a company has relied on its corporate network for business-critical IP traffic and wants to integrate an online video-training application, the network must be able to provide guaranteed QoS. This QoS must deliver the multimedia traffic, but does not allow it to interfere with the business-critical traffic. Consequently, network designers need greater flexibility in solving multiple internetworking problems without creating multiple networks or writing off existing data communication investments.

The First Steps in Designing a WAN

Designing a WAN can be a challenging task. The discussions that follow outline several areas that you should carefully consider when planning a WAN implementation. The steps described here can lead to improved WAN cost and performance. Businesses can continually improve their WANs by incorporating these steps into the planning process.

Two primary goals drive WAN design and implementation:

- **Application availability**—Networks carry application information between computers. If the applications are not available to network users, the network is not doing its job.
- **Total cost of ownership**—Information Systems (IS) department budgets often run in the millions of dollars. As large businesses increasingly rely on electronic data for managing business activities, the associated costs of computing resources will continue to rise. A well-designed WAN can help to balance these objectives. When properly implemented, the WAN infrastructure can optimize application availability and allow the cost-effective use of existing network resources.

In general, WAN design needs to take into account three general factors:

- **Environmental variables**—Environmental variables include the location of hosts, servers, terminals, and other end nodes; the projected traffic for the environment; and the projected costs for delivering different service levels.
- **Performance constraints**—Performance constraints consist of network reliability, traffic throughput, and host/client computer speeds (for example, network interface cards and hard drive access speeds).
- **Networking variables**—Networking variables include the network topology, line capacities, and packet traffic. Characterizing network traffic is critical to successful WAN planning, but few planners perform this key step well, if at all.

Engineering Journal:
Traffic Characterization

In WAN design, nothing is more critical than characterizing the types of traffic that will be carried by the WAN.

Types of traffic include

- Voice/fax
- Transaction data (for example, SNA)
- Client/server data
- Messaging (for example, e-mail)
- File transfers
- Batch data
- Network management
- Videoconferencing

Analyzing and categorizing traffic is the basis for key design decisions. Traffic drives capacity, and capacity drives cost. Time-proven processes for measuring and estimating traffic exist for traditional networks, but not for WANs.

Traffic characteristics include

- Peak and average volume
- Connectivity and volume flows
- Connection orientation
- Latency tolerance, including length and variability
- Network availability tolerance
- Error rate tolerance
- Priority
- Protocol type
- Average packet length

Because many network planners do not have the planning and design techniques needed to deal with WAN traffic complexities and uncertainties, they typically guess the bandwidth capacity, which results in costly, over-engineered networks or poorly performing, under-engineered ones.

The overall goal of WAN design is to minimize cost based on these elements while delivering service that does not compromise established availability requirements. You face two primary concerns: availability and cost. These issues are essentially at odds. Any increase in availability must generally be reflected as an increase in cost. Therefore, you must carefully weigh the relative importance of resource availability and overall cost.

The first step in the design process is to understand the business requirements, which are covered in the following sections. WAN requirements must reflect the goals, characteristics, business processes, and policies of the business in which they operate.

Gathering Requirements

When designing a WAN, you need to start by gathering data about the business structure and processes. Next, you need to determine who the most important people will be in helping you design the network. You need to speak to major users and find out their geographic location, their current applications, and their projected needs. The final network design should reflect the user requirements.

In general, users primarily want application availability in their networks. The chief components of application availability are response time, throughput, and reliability:

- Response time is the time between entry of a command or keystroke and the host system's execution of the command or delivery of a response. Applications in which fast response time is considered critical include interactive online services, such as automated tellers and point-of-sale machines.

- Throughput-intensive applications generally involve file-transfer activities. However, throughput-intensive applications also usually have low response-time requirements. Indeed, they can often be scheduled at times when response-time-sensitive traffic is low (for example, after normal work hours).

- Although reliability is always important, some applications have genuine requirements that exceed typical needs. Organizations that conduct all business activities online or over the telephone require nearly 100% uptime. Financial services, securities exchanges, and emergency, police, and military operations are a few examples. These situations require a high level of hardware and redundancy. Determining the cost of downtime is essential in determining the importance of reliability to your network.

You can assess user requirements in a number of ways. The more involved your users are in the process, the more likely your evaluation will be accurate. In general, you can use the following methods to obtain this information:

- **User community profiles**—Outline what different user groups require. This is the first step in determining network requirements. Although many general users have the same requirements of e-mail, they may also have different needs, such as sharing local print servers in their area.

- **Interviews, focus groups, and surveys** build a baseline for implementing a network. Understand that some groups might require access to common servers. Others might want to allow external access to specific internal computing resources. Certain organizations might require IS support systems to be managed in a particular way, according to some external standard.

The least formal method of obtaining information is to conduct interviews with key user groups. Focus groups can also be used to gather information and generate discussion among different organizations with similar (or dissimilar) interests. Finally, formal surveys can be used to get a statistically valid reading of user sentiment regarding a particular service level.

- **Human factors tests**—The most expensive, time-consuming, and possibly revealing method of assessing user requirements is to conduct a test involving representative users in a lab environment. This is most applicable when you're evaluating response time requirements. For example, you might set up working systems and have users perform normal remote host activities from the lab network. By evaluating user reactions to variations in host responsiveness, you can create benchmark thresholds for acceptable performance.

After gathering data about the corporate structure, you need to determine where information flows in the company. Find out where shared data resides and who uses it. Determine whether data outside the company is accessed.

Make sure you understand the performance issues of any existing network. If time permits, analyze the performance of the existing network.

Washington Project: Understanding the Customer

First and foremost, you must understand your customers; in the case of the Washington School District, your customers include teachers, students, staff members, and administrators.
 	
You need to determine whether the district has documented policies in place. You need to answer questions like the following:
 	
  • Has district data been declared mission critical?
  • Have district operations been declared mission critical?
  • What protocols are allowed on the district network?
  • Are only certain desktop hosts supported in the district?
 	
Mission-critical data and operations are considered key to the business, and access to them is critical to the business running on a daily basis. You need to determine who in the district has authority over mission-critical data and operations, along with addressing, naming, topology design, and configuration. Some districts have a central Management Information System (MIS) department that controls everything. Some districts have very small MIS departments and, therefore, must pass on authority to departments and local school sites.

Analyzing Requirements

You need to analyze network requirements, including the customer's business and technical goals. What new applications will be implemented? Are any applications Internet based? What new networks will be accessed? What are the success criteria? (How will you know if the new design is successful?)

Availability measures the usefulness of the network. Many things affect availability, including throughput, response time, and access to resources. Every customer has a different definition of *availability*. You can increase availability by adding more resources. Resources drive up cost. Network design seeks to provide the greatest availability for the least cost.

Washington Project: Analyzing Availability
You need to find out what availability means to your customers in the Washington School District. These customers are teachers, students, administrators, and staff members. When analyzing your the district's technical requirements, estimate the traffic load caused by applications and by normal protocol behavior (for example, a new node joining the network). Estimate worst-case traffic load during the busiest times for users and during regularly scheduled network services, such as file server backups. This will help you understand what availability means to your customers.

The objective of analyzing requirements is to determine the average and peak data rates for each source over time. Try to characterize activity throughout a normal work day in terms of the type of traffic passed, level of traffic, response time of hosts, and the time to execute file transfers. You can also observe utilization on existing network equipment over the test period.

Engineering Journal:
Traffic Measurement

Depending on the traffic type, you should use one of the following four techniques to analyze and measure traffic:

- **Network management software**—For some types of traffic, you can use network management software to analyze traffic statistics.
- **Existing measurements**—You can place network analysis equipment on servers and analyze packet flows from router statistics for existing network segments.
- **The estimation process**—Where existing measurements cannot be attained (for example, the application does not yet exist), you can use an estimation process. You should work with the application developers and the network administrator to estimate transaction rates, lengths, and flows to derive traffic statistics.
- **Comparative sources**—You can find a known source that is likely to have similar characteristics and adjust the traffic statistics accordingly.

If the tested network's characteristics are close to those of the new network, you can estimate the new network's requirements based on the projected number of users, applications, and topology. This is a best-guess approach to traffic estimation given the lack of tools to measure detailed traffic behavior.

In addition to monitoring an existing network, you can measure activity and traffic generated by a known number of users attached to a representative test network and then use your results to predict activity and traffic for your anticipated population.

One problem with defining workloads on networks is that it is difficult to accurately pinpoint traffic load and network device performance as functions of the number of users, type of application, and geographic location. This is especially true without a real network in place.

Washington Project: Analyzing Network Traffic Load and Traffic Problems

Before you develop a district network structure and provision hardware, you need to determine the network traffic load that the district WAN needs to handle. You should determine all the sources of traffic and define what source characteristics must be ascertained. At this step, it is very important to define the sources in sufficient detail that source traffic can be measured or estimated.

Additionally, you need to evaluate applications that might cause traffic problems in the Washington School District WAN. The following applications can generate large volumes of traffic and therefore can cause network problems such as congestion:

- Internet access
- Computers loading software from a remote site
- Anything that transmits images or video
- Central database access
- Department file servers

The introduction of new sources or applications into the Washington School District WAN must be projected, along with likely growth rates. Obviously, this step requires considerable consultation with district end users and application developers. Finally, district network management data is an important source that you should not overlook because it could take up more than 15% of the total traffic volume.

Consider the following factors that influence the dynamics of the network:

- **The time-dependent nature of network access**—Peak periods can vary; measurements must reflect a range of observations that includes peak demand.

- **Differences associated with the type of traffic**—Routed and bridged traffic place different demands on network devices and protocols; some protocols are sensitive to dropped packets; some application types require more bandwidth.

- **The random nature of network traffic**—Exact arrival time and specific effects of traffic are unpredictable.

Each traffic source has its own metric, and each must be converted to bits per second. You should standardize traffic volumes to obtain per-user volumes. Finally, you should apply a factor to account for protocol overhead, packet fragmentation, traffic growth, and safety margin. By varying this factor, you can conduct what-if analyses. For example, you could run Microsoft Office from a server and then analyze the traffic volume generated from users sharing the application on the network. This volume will help you determine the bandwidth and server requirements to install Microsoft Office on the network.

Sensitivity Testing

From a practical point of view, sensitivity testing involves breaking stable links and observing what happens. When working with a test network, this is relatively easy. You can disturb the network by removing an active interface, and monitor how the change is handled by the network: how traffic is rerouted, the speed of convergence, whether any connectivity is lost, and whether problems arise in handling specific types of traffic. You can also change the level of traffic on a network to determine the effects on the network when traffic levels approach media saturation.

Identifying and Selecting Networking Capabilities

After you understand your networking requirements, you must identify and then select the specific capabilities that fit your computing environment. The following sections will help you with these tasks.

Identifying and Selecting a Networking Model

Hierarchical models for network design allow you to design networks in layers. To understand the importance of layering, consider the OSI reference model, a layered model for understanding computer communications. By using layers, the OSI reference model simplifies the tasks required for two computers to communicate. Hierarchical models for network design also use layers to simplify the task required for internetworking. Each layer can be focused on specific functions, thereby allowing the networking designer to choose the right systems and features for the layer.

Using a hierarchical design can facilitate changes. Modularity in network design allows you to create design elements that can be replicated as the network grows. Also, because networks will require upgrades, the cost and complexity of making the upgrade are constrained to a small subset of the overall network. In large flat or meshed network architectures, changes tend to affect a large number of systems. You can also facilitate the identification of failure-points in a network by structuring the network into small, easy-to-understand elements. Network managers can easily understand the transition points in the network, which helps identify failure points.

The Hierarchical Network Design Model

Network designs tend to follow one of two general design strategies: mesh or hierarchical. In a mesh structure, the network topology is flat; all routers perform essentially the same functions, and there is usually no clear definition of where specific functions are performed. Expansion of the network tends to proceed in a haphazard, arbitrary manner. In a hierarchical structure, the network is organized in layers, each of which has one or more specific functions. Benefits to using a hierarchical model include the following:

- **Scalability**—Networks that follow the hierarchical model can grow much larger without sacrificing control or manageability because functionality is localized and potential problems can be recognized more easily. An example of a very large-scale hierarchical network design is the Public Switched Telephone Network.

- **Ease of implementation**—A hierarchical design assigns clear functionality to each layer, thereby making network implementation easier.

- **Ease of troubleshooting**—Because the functions of the individual layers are well defined, the isolation of problems in the network is less complicated. Temporarily segmenting the network to reduce the scope of a problem also is easier.

- **Predictability**—The behavior of a network using functional layers is fairly predictable, which makes capacity planning for growth considerably easier; this design approach also facilitates modeling of network performance for analytical purposes.

- **Protocol support**—The mixing of current and future applications and protocols is much easier on networks that follow the principles of hierarchical design because the underlying infrastructure is already logically organized.

- **Manageability**—All the benefits listed here contribute to greater manageability of the network.

Using the Hierarchical Design Model

A hierarchical network design includes the following three layers:

- The core layer provides optimal transport between sites
- The distribution layer, which provides policy-based connectivity
- The access layer, which provides workgroup and user access to the network

Figure 10-1 shows a high-level view of the various aspects of a hierarchical network design.

FIGURE 10-1
A hierarchical network design presents three layers—core, distribution, and access—with each layer providing different functionality.

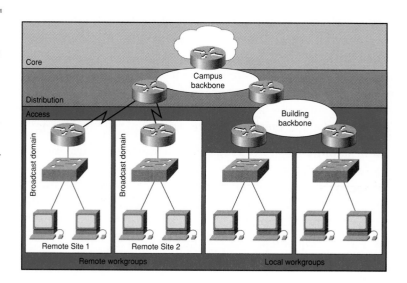

Three-Layer Model Components

A layer is identified as a point in the network where an OSI reference model Layer 3 (network layer) boundary occurs: The three layers are bound by Layer 3 devices or other devices that separate the network into broadcast domains. As shown in Figure 10-1, the three-layer model consists of core, distribution, and access layers, each of which has specific functions:

- *Core layer*—The core layer provides fast wide-area connections between geographically remote sites, tying a number of campus networks together in a corporate or enterprise WAN. Core links are usually point-to-point, and there are rarely any hosts in the core layer. Core services (for example, *T1/T3*, Frame Relay, SMDS) typically are leased from a telecom service provider.
- *Distribution layer*—The distribution layer gives network services to multiple LANs within a WAN environment. This layer is where the

WAN backbone network is found. This layer is implemented on large sites and is used to interconnect buildings.

- *Access layer*—The access layer is usually a LAN or a group of LANs, typically Ethernet or Token Ring, that provide users with frontline access to network services. The access layer is where almost all hosts are attached to the network, including servers of all kinds and user workstations. Chapter 4, "LAN Design," focuses on the design of the access layer.

A three-layer model can meet the needs of most *enterprise networks*. However, not all environments require a full three-layer hierarchy. In some cases, a two-layer design may be adequate, or even a single-layer flat network. In these cases, however, a hierarchical structure should be planned to allow these network designs to expand to three layers as the need arises. The following sections discuss in more detail the functions of the three layers. Then, we'll move on to discuss one- and two-layer hierarchies.

Core-Layer Functions

The core layer's function is to provide a fast path between remote sites, as shown in Figure 10-2. This layer of the network should not perform any packet manipulation, such as using access control lists and performing filtering, that would slow down the switching of packets. The core layer is usually implemented as a WAN. The WAN needs redundant paths so that the network can withstand individual *circuit* outages and continue to function. Load sharing and rapid convergence of routing protocols are also important design features. Efficient use of bandwidth in the core is always a concern.

FIGURE 10-2
The core layer optimizes transport between remote sites by creating redundant paths and providing load sharing, effective use of bandwidth, and rapid convergence.

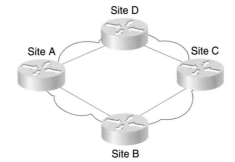

Site D

Site A

Site C

Site B

> ### Washington Project: The WAN Core
>
> The WAN core for the Washington School District network should be a high-speed switching backbone designed to switch packets as quickly as possible. School locations should connect into the WAN core based on proximity to the core from the school locations.

Distribution-Layer Functions

The distribution layer of the network is the demarcation point between the access and core layers and helps to define and differentiate the core. The purpose of this layer is to provide boundary definition, and it is the layer at which packet manipulation occurs. In the WAN environment, the distribution layer can include several functions, such as the following:

- Address or area aggregation
- Departmental or workgroup access to the core layer
- Broadcast/multicast domain definition
- Virtual LAN (VLAN) routing
- Any media transitions that need to occur
- Security

The distribution layer would include the campus backbone with all its connecting routers, as shown in Figure 10-3. Because policy is typically implemented at this level, we can say that the distribution layer provides policy-based connectivity. *Policy-based connectivity* means that the routers are programmed to allow only acceptable traffic on the campus backbone. Note that good network design practice would not put end stations (such as servers) on the backbone. Not putting end stations on the backbone frees up the backbone to act strictly as a transit path for traffic between workgroups or campus-wide servers.

FIGURE 10-3
The distribution layer controls access to services and network advertisements, and it defines path metrics.

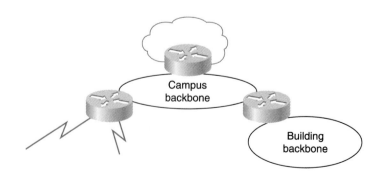

In non-campus environments, the distribution layer can be a point at which remote sites access the corporate network. The distribution layer can be summarized as the layer that provides policy-based connectivity.

Access-Layer Functions

The access layer is the point at which local end users are allowed into the network, as shown in Figure 10-4. This layer can also use access control lists or filters to further optimize the needs of a particular set of users. In the campus environment, access-layer functions can include the following:

- Shared bandwidth
- Switched bandwidth
- MAC-layer filtering
- Microsegmentation

FIGURE 10-4
The access layer connects workgroups to backbones.

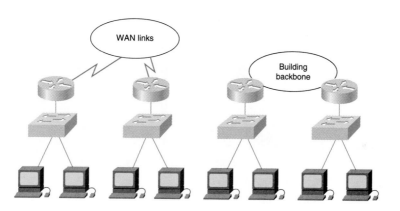

The access layer connects users into LANs, and LANs into WAN backbones or WAN links. This approach enables designers to distribute services of devices operating at this layer. The access layer allows logical segmentation of the network and grouping of users based on their function. Traditionally, this segmentation is based on organizational boundaries (such as Marketing, Administration, or Engineering). However, from a network management and control perspective, the main function of the access layer is to isolate broadcast traffic to the individual workgroup or LAN. (You studied this layer in great detail in Chapter 4.) In non-campus environments, the access layer can give remote sites access to the corporate network via some wide-area technology, such as Frame Relay, ISDN, or leased lines, which are covered in the following chapters.

One-Layer Design

Not all networks require a three-layer hierarchy. A key design decision becomes the placement of servers: They can be distributed across multiple LANs or concentrated in a central server farm location. Figure 10-5 shows a distributed server design. A one-layer design is typically implemented if there are only a few remote locations in the company, and access to applications is mainly done via the local LAN to the site file server. Each site is its own broadcast domain.

FIGURE 10-5
A one-layer design is sufficient in many smaller networks.

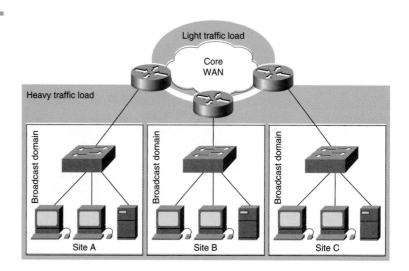

Two-Layer Design

In a two-layer design, a WAN link is used to interconnect separate sites, as shown in Figure 10-6. Inside the site, multiple LANs may be implemented, with each LAN segment being its own broadcast domain. The router at Site A becomes a concentration point from WAN links.

Washington Project: The Two-Layer Hierarchical Model
The Washington School District WAN should be based on a two-layer hierarchical model. Three regional hubs should be established—one each at the district office/data center, the service center, and Shaw Butte Elementary School—to form a fast WAN core network.

FIGURE 10-6
In a two-layer design, VLANs can be implemented to create separate logical networks.

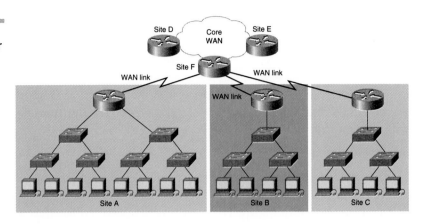

Hierarchical WAN Design Advantages

One of the advantages of a hierarchical WAN design is that it provides a method for controlling data traffic patterns by putting Layer 3 routing points throughout the network. Because routers have the ability to determine paths from the source host to destination hosts based on Layer 3 addressing, data traffic flows up the hierarchy only as far as it needs to find the destination host, as shown in Figure 10-7.

FIGURE 10-7
Routers are data path decision points.

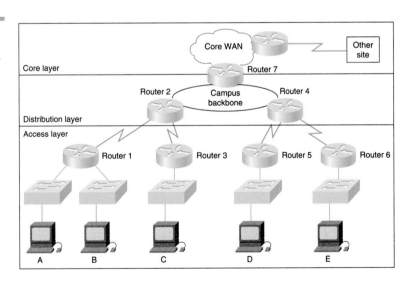

If Host A were to establish a connection to Host B, the traffic from this connection would travel to Router 1 and be forwarded back down to Host B. Notice in Figure 10-8 that this connection does not require that any traffic be placed on the link between Router 1 and Router 2, thus conserving the bandwidth on that link.

In a two-layer WAN hierarchy, which is shown in Figure 10-9, the traffic only travels up the hierarchy as far as needed to get to the destination, thus conserving bandwidth on other WAN links.

Server Placement

The placement of servers as it relates to who will be accessing them affects traffic patterns in the WAN. If you place an enterprise server in the access layer of Site 1, as shown in Figure 10-10, all traffic destined for that server is forced to go across links between Routers 1 and 2. This consumes major quantities of bandwidth from Site 1.

FIGURE 10-8
Data flows up the hierarchy based on source/ destination addressing.

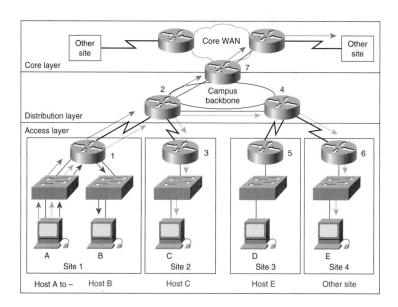

If you place the enterprise server at a higher layer in the hierarchy, as shown in Figure 10-11, the traffic on the link between Routers 1 and 2 is reduced and is available for users at Site 1 to access other services. In Figure 10-12, a workgroup server is placed at the access layer of the site where the largest concentration of users is located, and traffic crossing the WAN link to access this server is limited. Thus, more bandwidth is available to access resources outside the site.

FIGURE 10-9
The traffic patterns in a two-layer WAN hierarchy are governed by host source and destination addresses, and path determinations of the router.

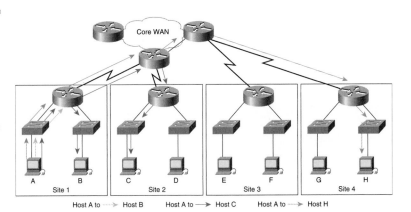

FIGURE 10-10
Unnecessary traffic consumes bandwidth; in this case, the server is poorly placed and causes the unnecessary traffic.

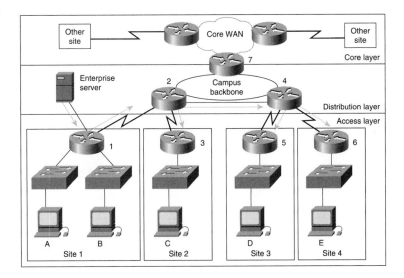

Frame Relay and ISDN WAN Links

It is not uncommon for remote sites to access the WAN core layer by using WAN technologies other than *dedicated links*. As shown in Figure 10-13, Frame Relay and ISDN are two such alternatives. If a remote site is small and has low demand for access to services in the corporate network, ISDN would be a logical choice for this implementation. Perhaps another remote site is too distant for a leased line to be affordable. Frame Relay is an appropriate choice because distance is not a factor in its pricing.

SKILL BUILDER

WAN Commands

This lab introduces wide-area networks (WANs) and the part routers play in them.

SKILL BUILDER

WAN Acronyms

The computer and networking field uses an incredible number of acronyms and abbreviations, sometimes called TLAs (Three Letter Acronyms). This exercise highlights some of the more common acronyms and terminology used.

Washington Project: The Frame Relay Link

You should provide access to the Internet or any other outside network connections through the Washington School District office by using a Frame Relay WAN link. For security purposes, no other connections should be permitted.

FIGURE 10-11
Moving servers to correct locations frees up bandwidth.

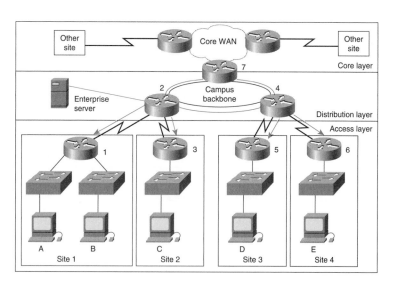

FIGURE 10-12
Placement of servers should be based on user needs.

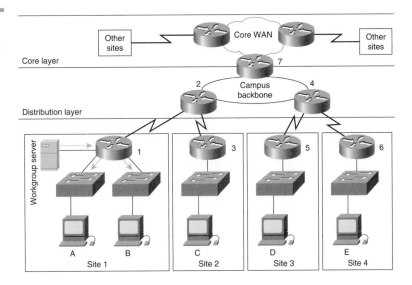

FIGURE 10-13
Different WAN technologies can be used to access the WAN core.

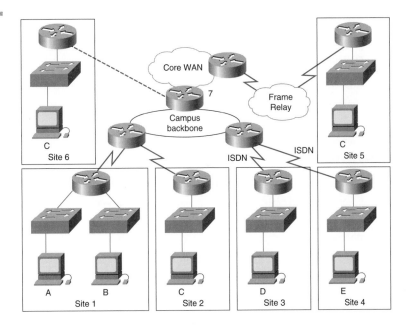

Washington School District Project Task: WAN Design

In this chapter, you learned about the WAN design process, so now you can focus on interconnecting all the individual Washington School District sites into a WAN topology that satisfies the users' requirements.

Complete the following tasks:

1. Create a WAN design that includes the following:

   ■ WAN link speeds and upgrade path

   ■ A model of traffic flow between schools showing a two- or three-layer WAN hierarchy

   ■ A list of additional equipment, such as CSUs/DSUs (channel service units/data service units) and router interfaces required to implement the districtwide WAN

   ■ A list of what kind of redundancy is needed to ensure WAN uptime

   (*Hint*: Consult the Washington School District Project technical requirements.)

2. Document all the router commands necessary for reconfiguration of routers in order to implement the WAN design.

3. Document how a WAN implementation affects routing updates between routers.

Summary

■ WAN design includes gathering and analyzing requirements, such as traffic load and response time.

■ The most scalable design for WAN implementation is a hierarchical model, with each layer performing a particular function.

■ The hierarchical design model consists of core-layer functions, distribution-layer functions, and access-layer functions.

■ Enterprise WANs can be made up of several different WAN technologies, such as Frame Relay and ISDN.

■ Placement of servers is critical for controlling traffic patterns across the WAN.

Check Your Understanding

Complete all the review questions to test your understanding of the topics and concepts covered in this chapter. Answers are listed in Appendix B, "Check Your Understanding Answer Key."

1. Which of the following are initial concerns in a WAN design?

   A. Determining whether data outside the company is accessed

   B. Determining who is involved in the design from the customer standpoint

   C. Determining where shared data resides and who uses it

   D. All of the above

2. When analyzing network load requirements, you should check worst-case traffic load during what time of the day?

   A. The busiest time

   B. The least busiest time

   C. During network backups

   D. After regular work hours

3. When designing the WAN, where should application servers be placed?

   A. On the enterprise backbone

   B. Close to the users

   C. Near the point of presence

   D. Any place the designer chooses

4. Which of the following is not a benefit of a hierarchical design model?

   A. Scalability

   B. Ease of implementation

   C. A flat topology

   D. Ease of troubleshooting

5. In most cases, when designing the core layer, your main concern should be which of the following?

   A. Efficient use of bandwidth

   B. Workgroup access

    C. Server placement

    D. Enterprise server placement

6. Which of the following would be placed on the network backbone?

    A. Server

    B. Routers

    C. Workstations

    D. Application servers

7. Which layer connects users into the LAN?

    A. Workgroup

    B. Core

    C. Access

    D. Distribution

8. Which layer connects a LAN into a WAN link?

    A. Distribution

    B. Workgroup

    C. Core

    D. Access

9. In a one-layer design, the placement of what device becomes extremely important?

    A. Server

    B. Router

    C. Workstation

    D. Switch

10. In a two-layer design, what device would you use to segment the LAN into individual broadcast domains?

    A. Switches

    B. Routers

    C. Hubs

    D. Repeaters

11. The campus backbone is typically based on what?

   A. FDDI

   B. Token Ring

   C. Ethernet

   D. Fast Ethernet

12. In a hierarchical design, what is a router function?

   A. Broadcast packets

   B. Perform bridging

   C. Perform switching

   D. Data path decision point

13. If a server is accessed by more than one workgroup, where should it be placed in a hierarchical design?

   A. In a workgroup

   B. At the distribution layer

   C. At the core layer

   D. At the access layer

14. The function of the core layer of the network is

   A. To provide access to services

   B. To serve as a distribution point

   C. To switch packets

   D. None of the above

15. The layer that provides policy-based connectivity is

   A. The access layer

   B. The core layer

   C. The distribution layer

   D. All of the above

Key Terms

access layer   The layer at which a LAN or a group of LANs, typically Ethernet or Token Ring, provides users with frontline access to network services.

circuit   A communications path between two or more points.

circuit switching   A switching system in which a dedicated physical circuit path must exist between the sender and the receiver for the duration of the "call." Used heavily in the telephone company network. Circuit switching can be contrasted with contention and token passing as a channel-access method, and with message switching and packet switching as a switching technique.

core layer   The layer that provides fast wide-area connections between geographically remote sites, tying a number of campus networks together in a corporate or enterprise WAN.

dedicated link   A communications link that is indefinitely reserved for transmissions rather than switched as transmission is required.

distribution layer   The layer in which the distribution of network services occurs to multiple LANs within a WAN environment. This layer is where the WAN backbone network is found, typically based on Fast Ethernet.

enterprise network   A corporation, agency, school, or other organization's network that ties together its data, communication, computing, and file servers.

Frame Relay   An industry-standard, switched data link–layer protocol that handles multiple virtual circuits using HDLC encapsulation between connected devices. Frame Relay is more efficient than X.25, the protocol for which it is generally considered a replacement.

leased line   A transmission line reserved by a communications carrier for the private use of a customer. A leased line is a type of dedicated line.

link   A network communications channel consisting of a circuit or transmission path and all related equipment between a sender and a receiver. Most often used to refer to a WAN connection. Sometimes referred to as a line or a transmission link.

packet switching   A networking method in which nodes share bandwidth with each other by sending packets.

T1   A digital WAN carrier facility that transmits DS-1-formatted data at 1.544 Mbps through the telephone-switching network, using AMI or B8ZS coding.

T3   A digital WAN carrier facility that transmits DS-3-formatted data at 44.736 Mbps through the telephone switching network.

WAN link   A WAN communications channel consisting of a circuit or transmission path and all related equipment between a sender and a receiver.

Objectives

After reading this chapter, you will be able to

- Identify and describe the basic components defining PPP communication
- Define and describe the use of LCP and NCP frames in PPP
- Understand the process for configuring and verifying PPP
- Describe and explain PPP authentication
- Define and describe the use of password authentication
- Define and describe the use of CHAP

Chapter 11

PPP

Introduction

You studied wide-area network (WAN) technologies in Chapter 9, "WANs." Now it is important to understand that WAN connections are controlled by protocols that perform the same basic functions as Layer 2 LAN protocols, such as Ethernet. In a LAN environment, in order to move data between any two nodes or routers, a data path must be established, and flow control procedures must be in place to ensure delivery of data. This is also true in the WAN environment and is accomplished by using WAN protocols, such as Point-to-Point Protocol (PPP).

In this chapter, you will learn about the basic components, processes, and operations that define *Point-to-Point Protocol (PPP)* communication. In addition, this chapter discusses the use of *Link Control Protocol (LCP)* and *Network Control Protocol (NCP)* frames in PPP. Finally, you will learn how to configure and verify the configuration of PPP. Along with PPP authentication, you will learn to use *Password Authentication Protocol (PAP)* and *Challenge Handshake Authentication Protocol (CHAP)*.

Washington Project: Applying PPP
You learned about WAN design and developed the Washington School District's WAN design to allow connectivity between all sites in the district. Without a Layer 2 protocol, the physical WAN links have no mechanism to transmit data and implement flow control. In this chapter, you apply PPP as the data link–layer protocol to be used in the district WAN implementation.

PPP Overview

In the late 1980s, *Serial Line Internet Protocol (SLIP)* was limiting the Internet's growth. PPP was created to solve remote Internet connectivity problems. Additionally, PPP was needed to be able to dynamically assign IP addresses and allow for use of multiple protocols. PPP provides router-to-router and host-to-network connections over both synchronous and asynchronous circuits (see Figure 11-1).

PPP is the most widely used and most popular WAN protocol because it offers all the following features:

- Control of data link setup
- Provides for dynamic assignment of IP addresses

- Network protocol multiplexing
- Link configuration and link quality testing
- Error detection
- Negotiation options for capabilities such as network-layer address and data compression negotiations.

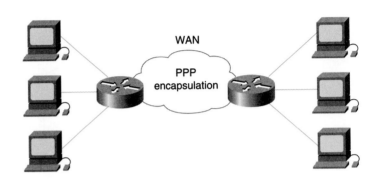

FIGURE 11-1
PPP provides reliable connections between routers.

PPP Components

PPP addresses the problems of Internet connectivity by employing three main components:

- A method for encapsulating datagrams over serial links. PPP uses High-Level Data Link Control (HDLC) as a basis for encapsulating datagrams over point-to-point links.
- A Link Control Protocol (LCP) for establishing, configuring, and testing the data-link connection.
- A family of Network Control Protocols (NCPs) for establishing and configuring different network-layer protocols. PPP is designed to allow the simultaneous use of multiple network-layer protocols. Today, PPP supports other protocols besides IP, including Internetwork Packet Exchange (IPX) and AppleTalk. As shown in Figure 11-2, PPP uses its NCP component to encapsulate multiple protocols.

MOVIE 11.1

PPP Components

Three components: HDLC Encapsulation, Link Control Protocol, Network Control Programs (NCPs).

FIGURE 11-2
PPP can carry packets from several protocol suites by using NCP.

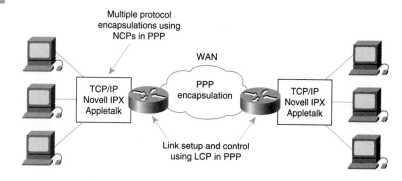

PPP Layer Functions

PPP uses a layered architecture, as shown in Figure 11-3. With its lower-level functions, PPP can use

- Synchronous physical media, such as those that connect Integrated Services Digital Network (ISDN) networks (which are covered in Chapter 12, "ISDN").

- Asynchronous physical media, such as those that use basic telephone service for modem dialup connections.

FIGURE 11-3
PPP is a data link layer protocol with network-layer services.

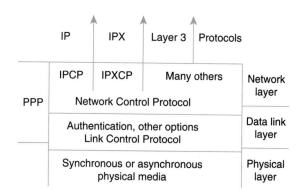

With its higher-level functions, PPP supports or encapsulates several network-layer protocols with NCPs. These higher-layer protocols include the following:

- **BCP**—Bridge Control Protocol
- **IPCP**—Internet Protocol Control Protocol
- **IPXCP**—Internetwork Packet Exchange Control Protocol

These are functional fields containing standardized codes to indicate the network-layer protocol type that PPP encapsulates.

PPP Frame Formats

As shown in Figure 11-4, the fields of a PPP frame are as follows:

- **Flag**—Indicates the beginning or end of a frame and consists of the binary sequence 01111110.

- **Address**—Consists of the standard broadcast address, which is the binary sequence 11111111. PPP does not assign individual station addresses.

- **Control**—1 byte that consists of the binary sequence 00000011, which calls for transmission of user data in an unsequenced frame. A connectionless link service similar to that of *Logical Link Control (LLC)* Type 1 is provided.

- **Protocol**—2 bytes that identify the protocol encapsulated in the data field of the frame.

- **Data**—0 or more bytes that contain the datagram for the protocol specified in the protocol field. The end of the data field is found by locating the closing flag sequence and allowing 2 bytes for the frame check sequence (FCS) field. The default maximum length of the data field is 1500 bytes.

- **FCS**—Normally 16 bits (2 bytes). Refers to the extra characters added to a frame for error control purposes.

FIGURE 11-4
PPP uses the frame structure of the International Organization for Standardization (ISO) HDLC procedures.

Field length, in bytes

1	1	1	2	Variable	2 or 4
Flag	Address	Control	Protocol	Data	FCS

PPP Session Establishment

PPP provides a method of establishing, configuring, maintaining, and terminating a point-to-point connection. To establish communications over a point-to-point link, PPP goes through four distinct phases:

1. **Link establishment and configuration negotiation**—An originating PPP node sends LCP frames to configure and establish the data link.

2. **Link-quality determination**—The link is tested to determine whether the link quality is sufficient to bring up network-layer protocols. Note that this is an optional phase.

3. **Network-layer protocol configuration negotiation**—The originating PPP node sends NCP frames to choose and configure network-layer protocols. The chosen network-layer protocols—such as TCP/IP, Novell IPX, and AppleTalk—are configured, and packets from each network-layer protocol can be sent.

4. **Link termination**—The link remains configured for communications until LCP or NCP frames close the link or until some external event occurs (for example, an inactivity timer expires or a user intervenes).

There are three classes of LCP frames:

- **Link establishment frames**—Used to establish and configure a link.
- **Link termination frames**—Used to terminate a link.
- **Link maintenance frames**—Used to manage and debug a link.

LCP frames are used to accomplish the work of each of the LCP phases: (1) link establishment; (2) link quality; (3) network-layer protocol; (4) link termination. These phases will be described in the following sections.

Phase 1: Link Establishment and Configuration Negotiation

In the link establishment and configuration negotiation phase, each PPP device sends LCP packets to configure and establish the data link. LCP packets contain a configuration option field that allows devices to negotiate the use of options, such as the maximum receive unit, compression of certain PPP fields, and the link authentication protocol. If a configuration option is not included in an LCP packet, the default value for that configuration option is assumed.

Before any network-layer datagrams (for example, IP) can be exchanged, LCP must first open the connection and negotiate the configuration parameters. This phase is complete when a configuration acknowledgment frame has been sent and received.

MOVIE 11.2

PPP Link Establishment

Establish communications.

MOVIE 11.3

PPP Configuration Acknowledgment

Negotiate parameters.

Phase 2: Link-Quality Determination

LCP allows an optional link-quality determination phase following the link establishment and configuration negotiation phase. In the link-quality determination phase, the link is tested to determine whether the link quality is good enough to bring up network-layer protocols.

In addition, after the link has been established and the authentication protocol decided on, the client or user workstation can be authenticated. Authentication, if used, takes place before the network-layer protocol configuration phase begins. LCP can delay transmission of network-layer protocol information until this phase is completed.

PPP supports two authentication protocols: PAP and CHAP. Both of these protocols are detailed in RFC 1334, "PPP Authentication Protocols." These protocols are covered later in the section "PPP Authentication."

> **MOVIE 11.4**
>
> **LCP: Link Quality Determination**
> Test links.

Phase 3: Network-Layer Protocol Configuration Negotiation

When LCP finishes the link-quality determination phase, network-layer protocols can be separately configured by the appropriate NCP and can be brought up and taken down at any time.

In this phase, the PPP devices send NCP packets to choose and configure one or more network-layer protocols (such as IP). When each of the chosen network-layer protocols has been configured, datagrams from each network-layer protocol can be sent over the link. If LCP closes the link, it informs the network-layer protocols so that they can take appropriate action. When PPP is configured, you can check its LCP and NCP states by using the **show interfaces** command.

> **MOVIE 11.5**
>
> **Network-Layer Protocols**
> Configuration by appropriate NCP.

e-LAB ACTIVITY 11.1

show interfaces

In this activity, you demonstrate how to use the **show interfaces** command to displays statistics for all interfaces configured on the router or access server.

Phase 4: Link Termination

LCP can terminate the link at any time. This is usually done at the request of a user but can happen because of a physical event, such as the loss of a carrier or a timeout.

MOVIE 11.6

LCP Link Termination

LCP can terminate the link at any time.

Washington Project: Enabling PPP Encapsulation

You can enable PPP on serial lines to encapsulate IP and other network-layer protocol datagrams. To do so, enable PPP encapsulation in interface configuration mode, using the **encapsulation ppp** command:

Step 1   Enter interface configuration mode for the desired interface.

Step 2   Configure the interface for PPP encapsulation:

Router(config-if)# `encapsulation ppp`

e-LAB ACTIVITY 11.2

encapsulation ppp

In this activity, you demonstrate how to use the **encapsulation ppp** command to set PPP as the encapsulation method used by a serial or ISDN interface.

PPP Authentication

The authentication phase of a PPP session is optional. After the link is established, and the authentication protocol chosen, the peer can be authenticated. If it is used, authentication takes place before the network-layer protocol configuration phase begins.

The authentication options require that the calling side of the link enter authentication information to help ensure that the user has the network administrator's permission to make the call. Peer routers exchange authentication messages.

When configuring PPP authentication, you can select PAP or CHAP. In general, CHAP is the preferred protocol. A brief description of each follows:

- **PAP**—As shown in Figure 11-5, PAP provides a simple method for a remote node to establish its identity, using a two-way handshake. After the PPP link establishment phase is complete, a username/password pair is repeatedly sent by the remote node across the link until authentication is acknowledged or the connection is terminated.

   PAP is not a strong authentication protocol. Passwords are sent across the link in clear text, and there is no protection from playback or repeated trial-and-error attacks. The remote node is in control of the frequency and timing of the login attempts.

FIGURE 11-5
PAP is activated only upon initial link establishment.

- **CHAP**—CHAP is used to periodically verify the identity of the remote node, using a three-way handshake, as shown in Figure 11-6. This is done upon initial link establishment and can be repeated any time after the link has been established. CHAP offers features such as periodic verification to improve security; this makes CHAP more effective than PAP. PAP verifies only once, which makes it vulnerable to hacks and modem playback. Further, PAP allows the caller to attempt authentication at will (without first receiving a challenge), which makes it vulnerable to brute-force attacks, whereas CHAP does not allow a caller to attempt authentication without a challenge.

   After the PPP link establishment phase is complete, the host sends a challenge message to the remote node. The remote node responds with a value. The host checks the response against its own value. If the values match, the authentication is acknowledged. Otherwise, the connection is terminated.

   CHAP provides protection against playback attacks through the use of a variable challenge value that is unique and unpredictable. The use of repeated challenges is intended to limit the time of exposure to any single attack. The local router (or a third-party authentication server, such as

Netscape Commerce Server) is in control of the frequency and timing of the challenges.

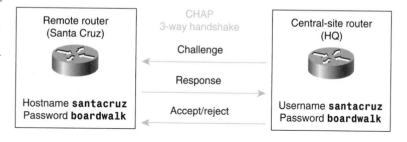

FIGURE 11-6
CHAP is used at the startup of a link, and periodically after that, to verify the identity of the remote node by using a three-way handshake.

Configuring PPP Authentication

To configure PPP authentication, do the following:

Step 1 On each router, define the username and password to expect from the remote router:

```
Router(config)#username name password secret
```

The arguments are described as follows:

name—This is the hostname of the remote router. Note that it is case sensitive.

secret—On Cisco routers, the *secret* password must be the same for both routers.

NOTE

When PPP is configured, you can check its LCP and NCP states by using the **show interfaces** command.

e-LAB ACTIVITY 11.3

username *name* **password** *password*

In this activity, you demonstrate how to use the **username** *name* **password** *password* command to specify the password to be used in CHAP caller identification and PAP.

Engineering Journal: Adding a Username

You should add a username entry for each remote system with which the local router communicates. You should also add a username entry for each remote system from which the router requires authentication. Finally, the remote device must also have a username entry for the local router.

To enable the local router to respond to remote CHAP challenges, one username name entry must be the same as the host name entry that has already been assigned to the device. With CHAP, you should use secret passwords that are known only to the authenticator and peer.

Step 2 Enter interface configuration mode for the desired interface.

Step 3 Configure the interface for PPP encapsulation:

```
Router(config-if)# encapsulation ppp
```

Step 4 Configure PPP authentication:

```
Router(config-if)# ppp authentication {chap | chap pap | pap chap | pap}
```

Step 5 If CHAP and PAP are enabled, the first method specified is requested during the link negotiation phase. If the peer suggests using the second method or simply refuses the first method, the second method is tried.

Step 6 In Cisco IOS Release 11.1 or later, if you choose PAP and are configuring the router that will send the PAP information (in other words, the router responding to a PAP request), you must enable PAP on the interface. PAP is disabled by default; to enable PAP, use the following command:

```
Router(config-if)# ppp pap sent-username username password password
```

e-LAB ACTIVITY 11.4

PPP Configuration

In this activity, you work through several tasks for configuring PPP.

Configuring CHAP Authentication

The following methods can be used to simplify CHAP configuration tasks on the router:

- **You can use the same hostname on multiple routers**—When you want remote users to think they are connecting to the same router when authenticating, configure the same hostname on each router:

```
Router(config-if)# ppp chap hostname hostname
```

- **You can use a password to authenticate to an unknown host**—This is to limit the number of username/password entries in the router. To use this, configure a password that will be sent to hosts that want to authenticate the router:

```
Router(config-if)# ppp chap password secret
```

This password is not used when the router authenticates a remote device.

e-LAB ACTIVITY 11.5

ppp chap hostname *hostname*

In this activity, you demonstrate how to use the **ppp chap hostname** *hostname* command to create a pool of dialup routers that appear to be the same host when authenticating with CHAP.

SKILL BUILDER

PPP Configuration

This lab focuses on PPP (Point-to-Point Protocol).

Summary

- PPP is the most widely used WAN protocol.
- PPP addresses the problems of Internet connectivity by providing an LCP and a family of NCPs to negotiate optional configuration parameters and facilities.
- A PPP session has four phases:
  — Link establishment
  — Link quality determination
  — Network-layer protocol configuration
  — Link termination
- You can select PAP or CHAP when configuring PPP authentication.
- PAP is not a strong authentication protocol.
- CHAP provides protection against playback attacks through the use of a variable challenge value that is unique and unpredictable.
- You configure the interface for PPP encapsulation by using the **encapsulation ppp** command.
- When PPP is configured, you can check its LCP and NCP states by using the **show interfaces** command.

Washington School District Project Task: PPP

In this chapter, you learned concepts and configuration processes that will help you configure PPP in the Washington School District network. As part of the configuration, you need to complete the following tasks:

1. Apply PPP to the existing WAN designs and describe the effects.

2. Document the router commands necessary to implement PPP on the router interfaces and how the router configuration changes.

3. Describe the benefits of PPP as a Layer 2 WAN protocol versus other options.

4. Apply the CCNA Certification Exam Learning Objectives to your specific design. This requires a paragraph on how the learning objectives relate to your design. Learning objectives can be grouped together for the purpose of explanation. In this way, you will be studying for the CCNA Certification Exam as you work through the case study.

NOTE

*** are explicit CCNA Exam objectives; unmarked are knowledge assumed by the exam.

CCNA Certification Exam Learning Objectives

OSI Model

- Describe the OSI model layer(s) at which the Point-to-Point Protocol (PPP) operates and its function at those layers.

Point-to-Point Protocol

- Describe what major types of WAN links are supported by PPP.
- Describe what the function of the Network Control Protocol (NCP) is within PPP.
- Describe what the function of the Link Control Protocol (LCP) is within PPP.
- Describe the functions of PAP and CHAP in a PPP implementation.
- Identify PPP operations to encapsulate WAN data on Cisco routers.***

Check Your Understanding

Complete all the review questions to test your understanding of the topics and concepts covered in this chapter. Answers are listed in Appendix B, "Check Your Understanding Answer Key."

1. PPP is generally considered to be the successor to what protocol?

2. PPP supports which physical interfaces?

3. Which of the following is the network-layer protocol supported by PPP?

   A. Novell IPX

   B. TCP/IP

   C. AppleTalk

   D. All of the above

4. NCPs are used by PPP to do which of the following?

   A. Establish links

   B. Encapsulate multiple protocols

   C. Convert packets into cells

   D. Establish connections

5. In a PPP frame, what field identifies whether you have encapsulated IPX or TCP/IP?

   A. Flag

   B. Control

   C. Protocol

   D. FCS

6. When you're running PPP, LCP is responsible for which of the following?

   A. Establishment, maintenance, and termination of the point-to-point connection

   B. Maintenance of several links

   C. Router updates

   D. Compression

7. How many phases are involved in PPP session establishment?

    A. Two

    B. Three

    C. Four

    D. One

8. What type of handshaking occurs when PAP is the selected PPP authentication protocol?

    A. One-way

    B. Two-way

    C. Three-way

    D. Four-way

9. What command on the router can you use to check the LCP and NCP states for PPP?

    A. router> **show interfaces**

    B. router(config)# **show interfaces**

    C. router# **show interfaces**

    D. router(config-if)# **show interfaces**

10. When would PPP most likely be used at a local workstation for Internet connectivity?

    A. When the workstation is directly connected to a LAN

    B. When the workstation is directly connected to a router

    C. When the workstation needs dialup access to the Internet

    D. It will never be used on a workstation

11. What protocol would you use to establish a remote connection over ISDN?

    A. PPP

    B. SLIP

    C. PAP

    D. CHAP

12. When PPP is load balancing across several links, what feature is being taken advantage of?

   A. PAP

   B. Stacker

   C. Compression

   D. Multilink

13. The first step in establishing connections over PPP links involves

   A. The originating PPP node sending a session startup message to the nearest PPP neighbor

   B. Routers along the path negotiating authentication facilities prior to PPP link activation

   C. PPP nodes advertising for dynamic address allocation or querying servers for address assignment

   D. The originating node sending Link Control Protocol (LCP) frames to configure the data link

14. PPP link establishment requires the LCP to open a connection,

   A. Negotiate configuration parameters, and send and receive a configuration acknowledgment frame

   B. Test the link, and determine whether the link quality is sufficient to bring up network protocols

   C. Poll PPP nodes, and determine whether a path to a Network Control Protocol (NCP) server exists

   D. And query the nearest adjacent upstream PPP neighbor to obtain routing metrics (such as hop count)

15. In PPP, if LCP terminates a link,

   A. The destination node attempts to establish a new link.

   B. NCP sends a link maintenance frame.

   C. The originating node reestablishes connection sessions.

   D. LCP informs the network-layer protocols.

Key Terms

CHAP (Challenge Handshake Authentication Protocol)   A security feature supported on lines using PPP encapsulation that prevents unauthorized access. CHAP does not itself prevent unauthorized access, but it identifies the remote end; the router or access server then determines whether that user is allowed access.

LCP (Link Control Protocol)   A protocol that provides a method of establishing, configuring, maintaining, and terminating the point-to-point connection.

LLC (logical link control)   The higher of the two data link–layer sublayers defined by the IEEE. The LLC sublayer handles error control, flow control, framing, and MAC-sublayer addressing. The most prevalent LLC protocol is IEEE 802.2, which includes both connectionless and connection-oriented variants.

NCP (Network Control Program)   A program that routes and controls the flow of data between a communications controller and other network resources.

PAP (Password Authentication Protocol)   An authentication protocol that allows PPP peers to authenticate one another. The remote router attempting to connect to the local router is required to send an authentication request. Unlike CHAP, PAP passes the password and host name or username in cleartext (that is, unencrypted). PAP does not itself prevent unauthorized access, but it identifies the remote end; the router or access server then determines whether that user is allowed access. PAP is supported only on PPP lines.

PPP (Point-to-Point Protocol)   A successor to SLIP, a protocol that provides router-to-router and host-to-network connections over synchronous and asynchronous circuits.

SLIP (Serial Line Internet Protocol)   A standard protocol for point-to-point serial connections using a variation of TCP/IP. The predecessor of PPP.

Objectives

After reading this chapter, you will be able to

- Describe ISDN and its components
- Describe ISDN standards
- Describe ISDN encapsulation
- Describe ISDN uses
- Describe BRI and PRI
- Describe ISDN configuration tasks
- Describe dial-on-demand routing

Chapter 12

ISDN

Introduction

Many types of WAN technologies can be implemented to solve connectivity issues for users who need network access from remote locations. In Chapter 11, "PPP," you learned about Point-to-Point Protocol (PPP). In this chapter, you will learn about the services, standards, components, operation, and configuration of *Integrated Services Digital Network (ISDN)* communication. ISDN is specifically designed to solve the low-bandwidth problems that small offices or dial-in users have with traditional telephone dial-in services. ISDN also provides backup links. Backup links are technologies used in case a main network connection is lost.

Telephone companies developed ISDN with the intention of creating a totally digital network. ISDN was developed to use the existing telephone wiring system, and it works very much like a telephone. When you make a data call with ISDN, the WAN link is brought up for the duration of the call and is taken down when the call is completed; it's very similar to how you call a friend on the phone and then hang up when you are done talking. Actually, the same structure is used to carry your phone call. The phone company digitizes the analog signal from your phone into 8-bit packets at the rate of a 8000 samples per second to produce a 64-kbps data stream. (In the U.S., 1 bit is robbed for in-band signaling to produce a 7 bit x 8000 or 56 kbps data stream.) Students need to know ISDN because it is a major technology used for users who dial-in from a remote location and for backup links.

Washington Project: ISDN Connectivity
In this chapter, you learn the concepts and configuration process needed to implement an ISDN connection in the Washington School District WAN. You need to provide an ISDN connection for a remote site that needs part-time connectivity to the district.

ISDN Overview

ISDN allows multiple digital signals to be transmitted over existing telephone wiring. This became possible when the telephone company switches were upgraded to handle digital signals. ISDN is generally viewed as an alternative to leased lines, which can be used for telecommuting and networking small and remote offices into LANs.

NOTE

The 8000 bits per second sample and frame rate is central to the telephone transport system and is accurately controlled by atomic clocks.

Telephone companies developed ISDN as part of an effort to standardize subscriber services. This included the *User-Network Interface (UNI)*, which is how the screen looks when the user dials into the network and network capabilities. Standardizing subscriber services makes it more possible to ensure international compatibility. The ISDN standards define the hardware and call setup schemes for end-to-end digital connectivity, which help achieve the goal of worldwide connectivity by ensuring that ISDN networks easily communicate with one another. Basically, the digitizing function is done at the user site rather than the telephone company.

ISDN's ability to bring digital connectivity to local sites has many benefits, including the following:

- ISDN provides access to digital video, circuit-switched data, and telephone network services by using the normal phone network that is circuit-switched.

- ISDN offers much faster call setup than modem connections because it uses out-of-band (*D, or delta, channel*) signaling. For example, some ISDN calls can be set up in less than one second.

- ISDN provides a faster data transfer rate than modems by using the *bearer channel (B channel of 64 kbps)*. When multiple B channels are used, ISDN offers users more bandwidth on WANs. For example, if you use two B channels, the bandwidth capability is 128 Kbps because each B channel handles 64 Kbps.

- ISDN can provide a clear data path over which to negotiate PPP links.

You should ensure in the design phase that the equipment selected has the feature set that takes advantage of ISDN's flexibility. In addition, you must keep in mind the following ISDN design issues:

- **Security issues**—Because network devices can now be connected over the Public Switched Telephone Network (PSTN), it is crucial to design and confirm a robust security model for protecting the network.

- **Cost-containment issues**—A primary goal of selecting ISDN for your network is to avoid the cost of full-time data services (such as leased lines or Frame Relay). Therefore, it is very important to evaluate your data traffic profiles and monitor ISDN usage patterns to ensure that your WAN costs are controlled.

ISDN Components

ISDN components include terminals, *terminal adapters (TAs)*, network-termination (NT) devices, line-termination equipment, and exchange-termination equipment. Table 12-1 provides a summary of the ISDN components. ISDN terminals come in two types, Type 1 or Type 2, as shown in

Figure 12-1. Specialized ISDN terminals are referred to as *Terminal Equipment type 1 (TE1)*. Non-ISDN terminals such as Data Terminal Equipment (DTE) that predate the ISDN standards are referred to as *Terminal Equipment type 2 (TE2)*. TE1s connect to the ISDN network through a four-wire, twisted-pair digital link. TE2s connect to the ISDN network through a TA. The ISDN TA can be either a standalone device or a board inside the TE2. If the TE2 is implemented as a stand-alone device, it connects to the TA via a standard physical-layer interface.

Beyond the TE1 and TE2/TA devices, the next connection point in the ISDN network is the *Network Termination type 1 (NT1)* or *Network Termination type 2 (NT2)* device. These network-termination devices connect the four-wire subscriber wiring to the conventional two-wire local loop. In North America, the NT1 is a *customer premises equipment (CPE)* device. In most parts of the world besides North America, the NT1 is part of the network provided by the carrier. The NT2 is a more complicated device, typically found in digital *Private Branch eXchanges (PBXs)*, that performs Layer 2 and Layer 3 protocol functions services. An NT1/2 device also exists; it is a single device that combines the functions of an NT1 and an NT2.

TABLE 12-1   ISDN Components

Component	Description
Terminal Equipment type 1 (TE1)	Designates a device that is compatible with the ISDN network. A TE1 connects to a Network Termination of either type 1 or type 2.
Terminal Equipment type 2 (TE2)	Designates a device that is not compatible with ISDN and requires a terminal adapter.
Terminal adapter (TA)	Converts standard electrical signals into the form used by ISDN so that non-ISDN devices can connect to the ISDN network.
Network Termination type 1 (NT1)	Connects four-wire ISDN subscriber wiring to the conventional two-wire local loop facility. Many devices have built-in NT1s.
Network Termination type 2 (NT2)	Directs traffic to and from different subscriber devices and the NT1. The NT2 is an intelligent device that performs switching and concentrating.

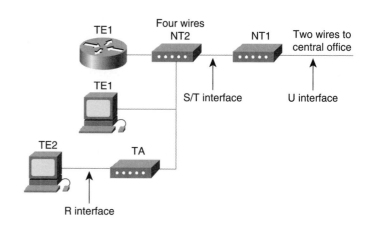

FIGURE 12-1
ISDN compo-
nents enable
connections
between two
devices.

ISDN Reference Points

Because CPEs cover a wide variety of capabilities and require a variety of services and interfaces, the standards refer to interconnects by reference points rather than specific hardware requirements. *Reference points* are a series of specifications that define the connection between specific devices, depending on their function in the end-to-end connection. It is important to know about these interface types because a CPE device, such as a router, may support different reference types; the reference points supported will determine what specific equipment is required for purchase.

Table 12-2 provides a summary of the reference points that affect the customer side of the ISDN connection (see Figure 12-2).

TABLE 12-2 ISDN Reference Points

Reference Point	Description
R	References the connection between a non–ISDN-compatible device and a TA.
S	References the points that connect into the NT2 or customer switching device. It is the interface that enables calls between the various parts of the CPE.
T	References the outbound connection from the NT2 to the ISDN network or NT1, and is electrically identical to the S interface.
U	References the connection between the NT1 and the ISDN network owned by the phone company. The U reference point is relevant only in North America, where the NT1 function is not provided by the service provider.

A sample ISDN configuration is shown in Figure 12-3, where three devices are attached to an ISDN switch at the *central office (CO)*. Two of these devices are ISDN compatible, so they can be attached through an S reference point to NT2 devices. The third device (a standard, non-ISDN telephone) attaches through the R reference point to a TA. Although they are not shown, similar user stations are attached to the far-right ISDN switch.

SKILL BUILDER

ISDN Terms and Devices

This exercise serves as a study guide to help reinforce your understanding of basic ISDN terms and devices to which they relate.

FIGURE 12-2
Reference points define logical interfaces between functional groupings, such as TAs and NT1s.

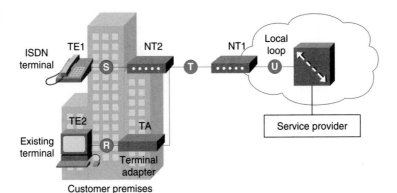

FIGURE 12-3
Several devices can access different types of networks through an ISDN switch.

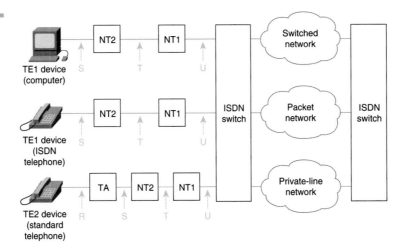

Washington Project: ISDN Equipment and Media
You need to identify what additional equipment and media will be necessary to implement an ISDN link in the Washington School District WAN design.

ISDN Switch Types

For proper ISDN operation, it is important that the correct switch type is configured on the ISDN device. The most common type in the United States is AT&T's 5ESS and Nortel's DMS-100. The most common type in Japan is NTT. U.K.'s most common types are Net3 and Net5. ISDN service providers use a variety of switch types for their ISDN services. Services offered by carriers vary considerably from nation to nation and region to region. Just like modems, each switch type operates slightly differently and has a specific set of call setup requirements. As a result, before you can connect a router to an ISDN service, you must be aware of the switch types used at the CO. You specify this information during router configuration so the router can place ISDN network-level calls and send data.

ISDN Service Profile Identifiers

In addition to learning about the switch type your service provider uses, you also need to know what *service profile identifiers (SPIDs)* are assigned to your connection. The ISDN carrier provides a SPID to identify the line configuration of the ISDN service. SPIDs are a series of characters (that can look like phone numbers) that identify you to the switch at the CO. After you're identified, the switch links the services you ordered to the connection.

ISDN Standards

Work on standards for ISDN began in the late 1960s. A comprehensive set of ISDN recommendations was published in 1984 and is continuously updated by the Consultative Committee for International Telegraph and Telephone (CCITT), now the International Telecommunication Union Telecommunication Standardization Sector (ITU-T). ITU-T groups and organizes the ISDN protocols as described in Table 12-3.

TABLE 12-3   ISDN Protocols

Protocols That Begin with This Letter...	Are Used for These Purposes
E	These protocols recommend telephone network standards for ISDN. For example, the E.164 protocol describes international addressing for ISDN.

TABLE 12-3   ISDN Protocols (Continued)

Protocols That Begin with This Letter...	Are Used for These Purposes
I	These protocols deal with concepts, terminology, and general methods. The I.100 series includes general ISDN concepts and the structure of other I-series recommendations; the I.200 series deals with service aspects of ISDN; the I.300 series describes network aspects; the I.400 series describes how the UNI (User-Network Interface) is provided.
Q	These protocols cover how switching and signaling should operate. The term *signaling* in this context means the process of call setup used. Q.921 describes the ISDN data-link processes of *Link Access Procedure on the D channel (LAPD)*, which functions like Layer 2 processes in the Open System Interconnection (OSI) reference model. *Q.931* specifies OSI reference model Layer 3 functions.

Q.921 recommends the data-link processes on the ISDN D Channel.

Q.931 governs the network-layer functionally between the terminal endpoint and the local ISDN switch. This protocol does not impose an end-to-end recommendation. The various ISDN providers and switch types can and do use various implementations of Q.931. Other switches were developed before the standards groups finalized this standard.

Because switch types are not standard, when configuring the router, you need to specify the ISDN switch you are connecting to. In addition, Cisco routers have **debug** commands to monitor Q.931 and Q.921 processes when an ISDN call is initiated or being terminated.

ISDN and the OSI Reference Model

ISDN utilizes a suite of ITU-T standards spanning the physical, data link, and network layers of the OSI reference model:

- **The physical layer**—The ISDN *Basic Rate Interface (BRI)* physical-layer specification is defined in ITU-T I.430. The ISDN *Primary Rate Interface (PRI)* physical-layer specification is defined in ITU-T I.431.
- **The data link layer**—The ISDN data link–layer specification is based on LAPD and is formally specified in ITU-T Q.920 and ITU-T Q.921.

■ **The network layer**—The ISDN network layer is defined in ITU-T Q.930 (also known as I.451). Together, these two standards specify user-to-user, circuit-switched, and packet-switched connections.

The ISDN Physical Layer

ISDN physical-layer (Layer 1) frame formats differ depending on whether the frame is outbound (from terminal to network—the TE frame format) or inbound (from network to terminal—the NT frame format). Both of the frames are 48 bits long, of which 36 bits represent data. Acutally, the frames are two 24-bit frames in succession consisting of two 8-bit B channels, a 2-bit D channel, and 6 bits of framing information $(2*(2*B+2D+6F) = 32B+4D+12F = 36BD+12F = 48BDF)$. Both physical-layer frame formats are shown in Figure 12-4. The bits of an ISDN physical-layer frame are used as follows:

■ **Framing bit**—Provides synchronization

■ **Load balancing bit**—Adjusts the average bit value

■ **Echo (E channel) of previous D channel bits**—Used for contention resolution when several terminals on a passive bus contend for a channel

■ **Activation bit**—Activates devices

■ **Spare bit**—Unassigned

■ **B1 channel 8 bits**

■ **B2 channel bits**

■ **8 added channel bit count bits**

■ **D channel bits**—Used for user data

FIGURE 12-4
ISDN physical-layer frame formats are 48 bits long, of which 36 bits represent data.

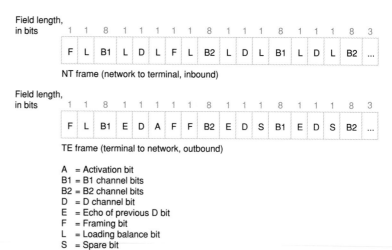

Multiple ISDN user devices can be physically attached to one circuit. In this configuration, collisions can result if two terminals transmit simultaneously. ISDN therefore provides features to determine link contention. These features are part of the ISDN D channel, which is described in more detail later in this chapter.

The ISDN Data Link Layer

Layer 2 of the ISDN signaling protocol is LAPD. LAPD is similar to High-Level Data Link Control (HDLC) and *Link Access Procedure, Balanced (LAPB)*. LAPD is used across the D channel to ensure that control and signaling information flows and is received properly (see Figure 12-5).

NOTE

Each of the ISDN BRI frames are sent at a rate of 8000 per second. There are 24 bits in each frame (2*8B+2D+6F = 24) for a bit rate of 8000*24 = 192 Kbps. The effective data rate is 8000*(2*8B+2D) = 8000*18 = 144 kbps.

FIGURE 12-5
The LAPD frame format is very similar to that of HDLC.

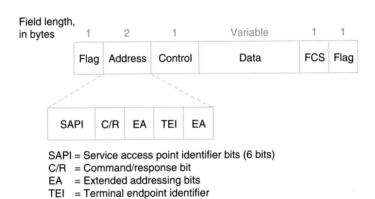

The LAPD *flag* and *control* fields are identical to those of HDLC. The LAPD *address* field can be either 1 or 2 bytes long. If the extended address bit of the first byte is set, the address is 1 byte; if it is not set, the address is 2 bytes. The first address field byte contains the *Service Access Point Identifier* (SAPI), which identifies the portal at which LAPD services are provided to Layer 3. The Command/Response (C/R) bit indicates whether the frame contains a command or a response. The *Terminal Endpoint Identifier* (TEI) field identifies either a single terminal or multiple terminals. All 1s in the TEI field indicate a broadcast.

The ISDN Network Layer

Two Layer 3 specifications are used for ISDN signaling: ITU-T I.450 (also known as ITU-T Q.930) and ITU-T I.451 (also known as ITU-T Q.931). Together, these protocols support user-to-user, circuit-switched, and packet-switched connections. A variety of call establishment, call termination, information, and miscellaneous messages are specified, including setup, connect, release, user information, cancel, status, and disconnect. Figure 12-6 shows the typical stages of an ISDN circuit-switched call.

FIGURE 12-6
ISDN circuit switching includes a variety of call stages.

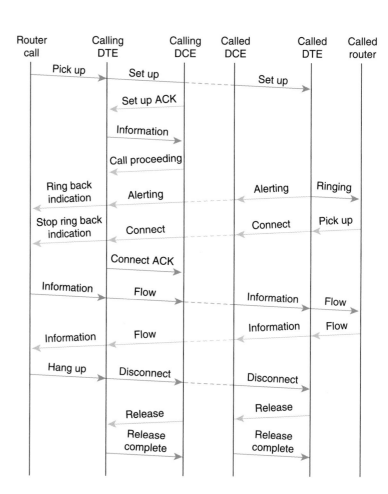

ISDN Encapsulation

When you're deploying remote access solutions, several encapsulation choices are available. The two most common encapsulations are PPP and HDLC. ISDN defaults to HDLC. However, PPP is much more robust than HDLC because it provides an excellent mechanism for authentication and negotiation of compatible link and protocol configuration. With PPP, you can enable Challenge Handshake Authentication Protocol (CHAP), a popular authentication protocol for call screening. One of the other encapsulations for end-to-end ISDN is LAPB.

ISDN interfaces allow only a single encapsulation type. After an ISDN call has been established, the router can use an ISDN cloud to carry any of the network-layer protocols required, such as IP to multiple destinations.

PPP

Most networking designs use PPP for encapsulation. PPP is a powerful and modular peer-to-peer mechanism used to establish data links, provide security, and encapsulate data traffic. PPP links can then be used by network protocols such as IP and IPX to establish network connectivity.

PPP is an open standard specified by RFC 1661. PPP was designed with several features that make it particularly useful in remote access applications. PPP uses Link Control Protocol (LCP) to initially establish the link and agree on configuration. There are built-in security features in the protocol; Password Authentication Protocol (PAP) and Challenge Handshake Authentication Protocol (CHAP) make robust security design easier. CHAP is a popular authentication protocol for call screening.

PPP consists of several components:

- **PPP framing**—RFC 1662 discusses the implementation of PPP in HDLC-like framing. There are differences in the way PPP is implemented on asynchronous and synchronous links.

  When one end of the link uses synchronous PPP (such as an ISDN router) and the other uses asynchronous PPP (such as an ISDN TA connected to a PC serial port), two techniques are available to provide framing compatibility. The preferable method is to enable synchronous-to-asynchronous PPP frame conversion in the ISDN TA.

- **LCP**—PPP LCP provides a method of establishing, configuring, maintaining, and terminating a point-to-point connection. Before any network-layer datagrams (for example, IP) can be exchanged, LCP must first open the connection and negotiate configuration parameters. This phase is complete when a configuration acknowledgment frame has been both sent and received.

- **PPP authentication**—PPP authentication is used to provide primary security on ISDN and other PPP encapsulated links. The PPP authentication protocols (PAP and CHAP) are defined in RFC 1334 (and you can find more information about them in Chapter 11, "PPP"). After LCP has established the PPP connection, you can implement an optional authentication protocol before proceeding to the negotiation and establishment of the Network

Control Programs. If authentication is needed, it must be negotiated as an option at the LCP establishment phase. Authentication can be bidirectional (each side authenticates the other—CHAP) or unidirectional (one side, typically the called side, authenticates the other—PAP).

PPP authentication is enabled with the **ppp authentication** interface command. PAP and CHAP can be used to authenticate the remote connection. CHAP is considered a superior authentication protocol because it uses a three-way handshake to avoid sending the password in cleartext on the PPP link.

ISDN Uses

ISDN has many uses in networking. This section discuss the following ISDN uses:

- Remote access
- Remote nodes
- *Small office/home office (SOHO)* connectivity, as shown in Figure 12-7

FIGURE 12-7
One use of ISDN is for SOHO dialup connectivity.

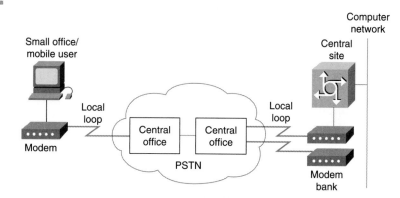

MOVIE 12.1

ISDN Applications

Integration of telecommuting services.

Remote Access

Remote access involves connecting users located at remote locations through dialup connections. The remote location can be a telecommuter's home, a mobile user's hotel room, or a small remote office. The dialup connection can be made via an analog connection using basic telephone service or via ISDN. Connectivity is affected by speed, cost, distance, and availability.

Remote access links generally represent the lowest-speed link in the enterprise. Any improvements in speed are desirable. The cost of remote access tends to be relatively low, especially for basic telephone service. ISDN service fees can vary widely, and they often depend on the geographic area, service availability, and billing method. There may be distance limitations, such as being out of a geographic range, with regard to dialup services, especially with ISDN.

Remote Nodes

With the remote nodes method, as shown in Figure 12-8, the users connect to the local LAN at the central site for the duration of the call. Aside from having a lower-speed connection, the user sees the same environment the local user sees. The connection to the LAN is typically through an access server. This device usually combines the functions of a modem and those of a router. When the remote user is logged in, he or she can access servers at the local LAN as if they were local.

FIGURE 12-8
With ISDN, a remote user can appear as a network node.

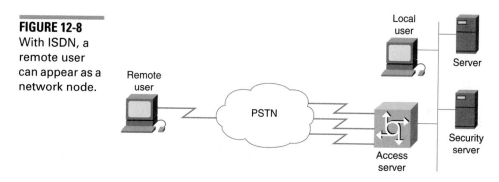

This method offers many advantages. It is the most secure and flexible, and it is the most scalable. Only one PC is required for the remote user, and many client software solutions are available. The only additional hardware required at the remote location is a modem. The main disadvantage of this method is the additional administrative overhead required to support the remote user. Because of its many advantages, this solution is used in the remainder of the design examples in this chapter.

The full-time telecommuter/teleworker is one who normally works out of the home. This user is usually a power user who needs access to the enterprise networks for large amounts of time. This connection should be reliable and available at all times. Such a requirement would generally point to ISDN as the connection method, as shown in Figure 12-9. With this solution, the ISDN connection can be used to service any phone needs, as well as to connect the workstation.

Washington Project: ISDN Requirement
A small remote site requires connectivity to the Washington School District WAN from time to time. You should use ISDN technology to make the small site a remote node on the WAN.

FIGURE 12-9
For an ISDN connection, components include an ISDN router and client software.

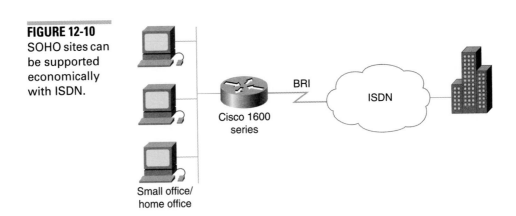

SOHO Connectivity

A small office or home office consisting of a few users requires a connection that provides faster, more reliable connectivity than an analog dialup connection. In the configuration shown in Figure 12-10, all the users at the remote location have equal access to services located at the corporate office through an ISDN router. This offers to the casual or full-time SOHO sites the capability to connect to the corporate site or the Internet at much higher speeds than are available over phone lines and modems.

FIGURE 12-10
SOHO sites can be supported economically with ISDN.

SOHO designs typically involve dialup only (SOHO-initiated connections) and can take advantage of emerging address translation technology to simplify design and support. Using these features, the SOHO site can support multiple devices, but appears as a single IP address.

Engineering Journal:
Dial Backup

You can use ISDN as a backup service for a leased-line connection between remote offices and the central office. If the primary connectivity goes down, an ISDN circuit-switched connection is established, and traffic is rerouted over ISDN. When the primary link is restored, traffic is redirected to the leased line, and the ISDN call is released.

ISDN dial backup can also be configured based on traffic thresholds or limits as a dedicated primary link. If traffic load exceeds a user-defined value on the primary link, the ISDN link is activated to increase bandwidth between the two sites, as shown in Figure 12-11.

FIGURE 12-11
ISDN can back up primary connectivity between sites.

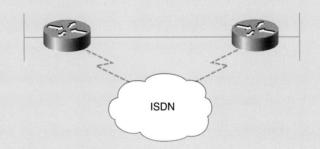

ISDN Services: BRI and PRI

There are two ISDN services: BRI and PRI. The ISDN BRI service offers two 8-bit B channels and one 2-bit D channel, often referred to as *2B+D*, as shown in Figure 12-12. ISDN BRI delivers a total bandwidth of a 144-kbps line into three separate channels (8000 frames per second * (2*8-bit channel+2-bit D channel) = 8000*18 = 144 kbps). BRI B channel service operates at 64 kbps (8000 frames per second* 8-bit B channel) and is meant to carry user data and voice traffic.

FIGURE 12-12
BRI, which is used for ISDN services, offers two B channels and one D channel.

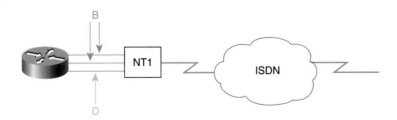

ISDN provides great flexibility to the network designer because of its ability to use each of the B channels for separate voice and/or data applications. For example, a long document can be downloaded from the corporate network over one ISDN 64-kbps B channel while the other B channel is being used to connect to browse a Web page.

The third channel, the D channel, is a 16-kbps (8000 frames per second*2-bit D channel) signaling channel used to carry instructions that tell the telephone network how to handle each of the B channels. BRI D channel service operates at 16 kbps and is meant to carry control and signaling information, although it can support user data transmission under certain circumstances. The D channel signaling protocol occurs at Layers 1 through 3 of the OSI reference model.

Terminals cannot transmit into the D channel unless they first detect a specific number of ones (indicating no signal) corresponding to a preestablished priority. If the TE detects a bit in the echo (E) channel that is different from its D bits, it must stop transmitting immediately. This simple technique ensures that only one terminal can transmit its D message at one time. This technique is similar and has the same effect as collision detection in Ethernet LANs. After successful D message transmission, the terminal has its priority reduced by requiring it to detect more continuous ones before transmitting. Terminals cannot raise their priority until all other devices on the same line have had an opportunity to send a D message. Telephone connections have higher priority than all other services, and signaling information has a higher priority than nonsignaling information.

ISDN PRI service offers 23 8-bit channels and 1 8-bit D channel, plus 1 framing bit in North America and Japan, yielding a total bit rate of 1.544 Mbps (8000 frames per second*(23*8-bit B channels+8-bit D channel+1 bit framing) = 8000*8*24.125 = 1.544 Mbps) (the PRI D channel runs at 64 kbps). ISDN PRI in Europe, Australia, and other parts of the world provides 30 8-bit B channels plus one 8-bit framing channel, for a total interface rate of 2.048 Mbps (8000 frames per second*(30*8-bit B channels+8-bit D channel+8-bit framing channel = 8000*8*32 = 2.048 Mbps).

In the T1/E1 and higher data rate frames, the B channels are strung together like boxcars in a freight train. Like boxcars in a switchyard, the B channels are rearranged and moved to other frames as they traverse the PSTN until they reach their destination. This path through the switch matrix establishes a synchronous link between the two endpoints. This allows continous voice communications without pauses, dropped data, or degradation. ISDN takes advantage of this digital transmission structure for the transfer of digital data.

Establishing BRI Connectivity

Based on application need and traffic engineering, BRI or PRI services are selected for ISDN connectivity from each site. Traffic engineering might require multiple BRI services or multiple PRIs at some sites. Once connected to the ISDN fabric by BRI or PRI interfaces, the design of ISDN end-to-end services must be implemented.

The BRI local loop is terminated at the customer premise at an NT1. The interface of the local loop at the NT1 is called the U reference point. On the customer premise side of the NT1 is the S/T reference point. Figure 12-13 shows a typical BRI installation.

FIGURE 12-13
The BRI local loop is connected to ISDN.

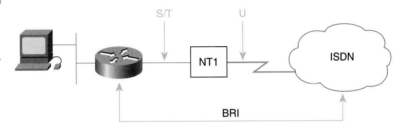

BRI Hardware

Two common types of ISDN CPE are available for BRI services: LAN routers and PC TAs. Some BRI devices offer integrated NT1s and integrated TAs for analog telephones.

ISDN LAN routers provide routing between ISDN BRI and the LAN by using dial-on-demand routing (DDR). DDR automatically establishes and releases circuit-switched calls, providing transparent connectivity to remote sites based on networking traffic. DDR also controls establishment and release of secondary B channels based on load thresholds. Multilink PPP is used to provide bandwidth aggregation when using multiple B channels. Some ISDN applications may require the SOHO user to take direct control over ISDN calls.

PC TAs connect to PC workstations either by the PC bus or externally through the communications ports (such as RS-232) and can be used similarly to analog (such as V.34) internal and external modems.

PC TAs can provide a single PC user with direct control over ISDN session initiation and release, similar to using an analog modem. Automated mechanisms must be provided to support the addition and removal of the secondary B channel. Cisco 200 Series PC cards can provide ISDN services to a PC.

ISDN Configuration Tasks

You must specify global and interface parameters to prepare the router for operation in an ISDN environment.

Global parameter tasks include the following:

- Select the switch that matches the ISDN provider's switch at the CO. This requirement is necessary because, despite standards, signaling specifics differ regionally and nationally.

- Set destination details. This involves indicating static routes from the router to other ISDN destinations and establishing the criteria for interesting packets in the router that initiate an ISDN call to the appropriate destination.

Interface parameter tasks include the following:

- Select interface specifications. Specify the interface type BRI and the number for this ISDN BRI port. The interface uses an IP address and subnet mask.

- Configure ISDN addressing with DDR dialer information and any ID supplied by the ISDN service provider. Indicate that the interface is part of the dialer group, using the interesting packets set globally. Additional commands place the ISDN call to the appropriate destination.

- Following interface configuration, you can define optional features, including time to wait for the ISDN carrier to respond to the call and seconds of idle time before the router times out and drops the call.

- Next, BRI configuration involves configuration of ISDN, switch type, and ISDN SPIDs. The following section provides examples and descriptions of ISDN configuration tasks.

Engineering Journal:
ISDN Commands

The **interface bri** *interface-number* command designates the interface used for ISDN on a router acting as a TE1. If the router does not have a native BRI (that is, it is a TE2 device), it must use an external ISDN terminal adapter. On a TE2 router, use the command **interface serial** *interface-number*.

Use the **encapsulation ppp** command if you want PPP encapsulation for your ISDN interface. This is the case if you want any of the rich LCP options that PPP offers (for example, CHAP authentication). You must use PPP PAP or CHAP if you will receive calls from more than one dialup source.

Configuring ISDN BRI

To configure BRI and enter interface configuration mode, use the **interface bri** command in global configuration mode. The full syntax of the command is

> **interface bri** *number*

The *number* argument describes the port, connector, or interface card number. The numbers are assigned at the factory at the time of installation or when added to a system, and can be displayed by using the **show interfaces** command.

---

e-LAB ACTIVITY 12.1

interface *interface-type interface-number*

In this activity, you demonstrate how to use the **interface** *interface-type interface-number* command to configure an interface type and enters interface configuration mode.

Example 12-1 configures BRI 0 to call and receive calls from two sites, use PPP encapsulation on outgoing calls, and use CHAP authentication on incoming calls.

Example 12-1   *Receiving Calls from Two Sites*

```
interface bri 0
encapsulation ppp
no keepalive
dialer map ip 131.108.36.10 name EB1 234
dialer map ip 131.108 36.9 name EB2 456
dialer-group 1
isdn spid1 0146334600
isdn spid2 0146334610
isdn T200 1000
ppp authentication chap
```

Defining a Switch Type

Before using ISDN BRI, you must define the **isdn switch-type** global command to specify the CO switch to which the router connects.

The Cisco IOS command output shown in Example 12-2 helps illustrate the supported BRI switch types (in North America, the most common types are 5ESS, DMS100, and NI-1).

Example 12-2   *Supported BRI Switch Types*

```
kdt-3640(config)# isdn switch-type ?
  basic-1tr6     1TR6 switch type for Germany
  basic-5ess     AT&T 5ESS switch type for the U.S.
  basic-dms100   Northern DMS-100 switch type
```

continues

> **NOTE**
>
> For Cisco IOS releases up to 11.2, the configured ISDN switch type is a global command (note that this also means you cannot use BRI and PRI cards in the same Cisco IOS chassis). In Cisco IOS 11.3T or later, multiple switch types in a single Cisco IOS chassis are supported.

Example 12-2   *Supported BRI Switch Types (Continued)*

```
basic-net3    NET3 switch type for the UK and Europe
basic-ni1     National ISDN-1 switch type
basic-nwnet3  NET3 switch type for Norway
basic-nznet3  NET3 switch type for New Zealand
basic-ts013   TS013 switch type for Australia
ntt           NTT switch type for Japan
vn2           VN2 switch type for France
vn3           VN3 and VN4 switch types for France
```

To configure a CO switch on the ISDN interface, use the **isdn switch-type** command in global configuration command mode. The full syntax of the command is

isdn switch-type *switch-type*

The argument *switch-type* indicates the service provider switch type. *switch-type* defaults to **none**, which disables the switch on the ISDN interface. To disable the switch on the ISDN interface, specify **isdn switch-type none**.

The following example configures the AT&T 5ESS switch type:

isdn switch-type basic-5ess

e-LAB ACTIVITY 12.2

isdn switch-type

In this activity, you demonstrate how to use the **isdn switch-type** command specifies the central office switch type on the ISDN interface.

Defining SPIDs

SPIDs allow multiple ISDN devices, such as voice and data devices, to share the local loop. In many cases, such as when you're configuring the router to connect to a DMS-100, you need to input the SPIDs.

Engineering Journal:
DMS-100 Switches

DMS-100 switches support only two SPIDs per BRI: one SPID for each B channel. If both B channels will be used for data only, you need to configure the router for both SPIDs (one for each B channel). You cannot run data and voice over the same B channel simultaneously. The absence or presence of a channel's SPID in the router's configuration dictates whether the second B channel can be used for data or voice.

Remember that ISDN is typically used for dialup connectivity. The SPIDs are processed during each call setup operation.

You use the **isdn spid2** command in interface configuration mode to define at the router the SPID number that has been assigned by the ISDN service provider for the B2 channel. The full syntax of the command is

```
isdn spid2 spid-number [ldn]
```

The optional *LDN* argument is for a local dial directory number. On most switches, the number must match the called party information coming in from the ISDN switch in order to use both B channels.

You use the **no isdn spid2** command to disable the specified SPID, thereby preventing access to the switch. If you include the LDN (local directory number) in the **no** form of this command, the access to the switch is permitted, but the other B channel might not be able to receive incoming calls. The full syntax of the command is

```
no isdn spid2 spid-number [ldn]
```

The *spid-number* argument indicates the number identifying the service to which you have subscribed. This value is assigned by the ISDN service provider and is usually a 10-digit telephone number with some extra digits. By default, no SPID number is defined.

e-LAB ACTIVITY 12.3

isdn spid

In this activity, you demonstrate how to use the **isdn spid** command to define at the router the service profile identifier (SPID) number that has been assigned by the ISDN service provider for the B1 channel.

Engineering Journal:
The *ldn* Argument

The *ldn* argument is optional and indicates the local directory number (LDN), as delivered by the service provider in the incoming setup message. This is a seven-digit number also assigned by the service provider.

This command is required for DMS-100 and National ISDN-1 (NI-1) switches only. You must define the LDN if you want to receive any incoming calls on the B1 channel. The ISDN switch checks for the LDN to determine whether both channels can be used to transmit and receive data. If the LDN is not present, only the B2 channel can be used for full-duplex communication. However, the other channel can still be used for making outgoing calls.

The following example defines, on the router, a SPID and an LDN for the B2 channel:

```
isdn spid2 415555121202 5551214
```

Each SPID points to line setup and configuration information. When a device attempts to connect to the ISDN network, it performs a D channel Layer 2 initialization process that causes a TEI

continues

to be assigned to the device. The device then attempts D channel Layer 3 initialization. If SPIDs are necessary but not configured or are configured incorrectly on the device, the Layer 3 initialization fails, and the ISDN services cannot be used.

No standard format for SPIDs exists. As a result, SPID numbers vary depending on the switch vendor and the carrier.

A typical Cisco IOS SPID configuration is as follows:

```
interface bri 0
isdn spid1 0835866201 8358662
isdn spid2 0835866401 8358664
```

These commands also specify the LDN, which is the seven-digit number assigned by the service provider and used for call routing. The LDN is not necessary for establishing ISDN-based connections, but it must be specified if you want to receive incoming calls on a B2 channel. The LDN is required only when two SPIDs are configured (for example, when you're connecting to a DMS or NI1 switch). Each SPID is associated with an LDN. Configuring the LDN causes incoming calls to the B2 channel to be answered properly. If the LDN is not configured, incoming calls to the B2 channel might fail.

BRI Configuration Example

This section is based on the output shown in Example 12-3, which shows a BRI configuration.

Example 12-3   *A Sample BRI Configuration*

```
! set up switch type, static route and dialer for ISDN on Cisco A
isdn switch-type basic-5ess
ip route 172.16.29.0.255.255.255.0 172.16.126.2
dialer-list 1 protocol ip permit
!
! configure BRI interface for PPP; set address and mask
interface bri 0
ip address 172.16.126.1 255.255.255.0
!
! refer to protocols in dialer-list to identify interesting packets
dialer-group 1
!
! select call start, stop, and other ISDN provider details
dialer wait-for-carrier time 15
dialer idle-timeout 300
isdn spid1 0145678912
! call setup details for router
dialer map ip 172.16.126.2 name cisco-b 445
```

The following is a description of the commands and parameters shown in Example 12-3:

Command/Parameter	Description
isdn switch-type	Selects the AT&T switch as the CO ISDN switch type for this router.

Command/Parameter	Description
dialer-list 1 protocol ip permit	Associates permitted IP traffic with the dialer group 1. The router will not start an ISDN call for any other packet traffic with dialer group 1.
interface bri 0	Selects an interface with TA and other ISDN functions on the router.
dialer-group 1	Associates the BRI 0 interface with dialing access group 1.
dialer wait-for-carrier-time	Specifies a 15-second maximum time for the provider to respond after the call initiates.
dialer idle-timeout	The number of seconds of idle time before the router drops the ISDN call. Note that a long duration is configured to delay termination.

The following is a description of the *dialer map* parameters shown in Example 12-3:

dialer map Parameter	Description
ip	Name of protocol.
172.16.126.2	Destination address.
name	An identification for the remote side router. Refers to the called router.
445	ISDN connection number used to reach this DDR destination.

Confirming BRI Operations

To confirm BRI operations, use the **show isdn status** command to inspect the status of your BRI interfaces. In Example 12-4, the TEIs have been successfully negotiated and ISDN Layer 3 (end-to-end) is ready to make or receive calls.

Example 12-4   *show isdn status Command Output*

```
kdt-1600#show isdn status
The current ISDN Switchtype = basic-ni1
ISDN BRI0 interface
    Layer 1 Status:
        ACTIVE
    Layer 2 Status:
        TEI = 109, State = MULTIPLE_FRAME_ESTABLISHED
        TEI = 110, State = MULTIPLE_FRAME_ESTABLISHED
    Spid Status:
```
continues

Example 12-5 *show isdn status Command Output (Continued)*

```
TEI 109, ces = 1, state = 8(established)
        spid1 configured, spid1 sent, spid1 valid
        Endpoint ID Info: epsf = 0, usid = 1, tid = 1
    TEI 110, ces = 2, state = 8(established)
        spid2 configured, spid2 sent, spid2 valid
        Endpoint ID Info: epsf = 0, usid = 3, tid = 1
Layer 3 Status:
    0 Active Layer 3 Call(s)
Activated dsl 0 CCBs = 0
Total Allocated ISDN CCBs = 0
```

e-LAB ACTIVITY 12.4

show isdn status

In this activity, you demonstrate how to use the **show isdn status** command to display the status of all ISDN interfaces or, optionally, a specific digital signal link (DSL) or a specific ISDN interface.

Dial-on-Demand Routing

When building networking applications, you must determine how ISDN connections will be initiated, established, and maintained. DDR creates connectivity between ISDN sites by establishing and releasing circuit-switched connections as needed by networking traffic. DDR can provide network routing and directory services in numerous ways to provide the illusion of full-time connectivity over circuit-switched connections.

To provide total control over initial DDR connections, you must carefully consider the following issues:

- Which sites can initiate connections based on traffic?

- Is dialout required to SOHO sites? Is dialout required for network or workstation management? Which sites can terminate connections based on idle links?

- How are directory services and routing tables supported across an idle connection?

- What applications need to be supported over DDR connections? For how many users do they need to be supported?

- What unexpected protocols might cause DDR connections? Can they be filtered?

Verifying DDR Operation

The following commands can be used to verify that DDR is operating:

Command	Description
ping/telnet	When you ping or Telnet a remote site or when interesting traffic triggers a link, the router sends a change in link status message to the console.
show dialer	Used to obtain general diagnostic information about an interface configured for DDR, such as the number of times the dialer string has been successfully reached, and the idle timer and the fast idle timer values for each B channel. Current call-specific information is also provided, such as the length of the call and the number and name of the device to which the interface is currently connected.
show isdn active	Use this command when using ISDN. It shows that a call is in progress and lists the numbered call.
show isdn status	Used to show the statistics of the ISDN connection.
show ip route	Displays the routes known to the router, including static and dynamically learned routes.

e-LAB ACTIVITY 12.5

ping

Use the **ping** command to confirm connectivity.

Troubleshooting DDR Operation

The following commands can be used to troubleshoot DDR operation:

Command	Description
debug isdn q921	Verifies that you have a connection to the ISDN switch.
debug dialer	Shows such information as what number the interface is dialing.
clear interface	Used to clear a call that is in progress. In a troubleshooting situation, it is sometimes useful to clear historical statistics to track the current number of successful calls relative to failures. Use this command with care. It sometimes requires that you clear both the local and remote routers.

You troubleshoot SPID problems by using the **debug isdn q921** command.
In Example 12-6, you can see that **isdn spid1** was rejected by the ISDN switch.

Example 12-6   *Troubleshooting SPID Problems*

```
kdt-1600# debug isdn q921
ISDN Q921 packets debugging is on
kdt-1600# clear interface bri 0
kdt-1600#
*Mar  1 00:09:03.728: ISDN BR0: TX -> SABMEp sapi = 0  tei = 113
*Mar  1 00:09:04.014: ISDN BR0: RX <- IDREM  ri = 0  ai = 127
*Mar  1 00:09:04.018: %ISDN-6-LAYER2DOWN:
        Layer 2 for Interface BRI0, TEI 113 changed to down
*Mar  1 00:09:04.022: %ISDN-6-LAYER2DOWN:
        Layer 2 for Interface BR0, TEI 113 changed to down
*Mar  1 00:09:04.046: ISDN BR0: TX -> IDREQ  ri = 44602  ai = 127
*Mar  1 00:09:04.049: ISDN BR0: RX <- IDCKRQ  ri = 0  ai = 113
*Mar  1 00:09:05.038: ISDN BR0: RX <- IDCKRQ  ri = 0  ai = 113
*Mar  1 00:09:06.030: ISDN BR0: TX -> IDREQ  ri = 37339  ai = 127
*Mar  1 00:09:06.149: ISDN BR0: RX <- IDREM  ri = 0  ai = 113
*Mar  1 00:09:06.156: ISDN BR0: RX <- IDASSN  ri = 37339  ai = 114
*Mar  1 00:09:06.164: ISDN BR0: TX -> SABMEp sapi = 0  tei = 114
*Mar  1 00:09:06.188: ISDN BR0: RX <- UAf sapi = 0  tei = 114
*Mar  1 00:09:06.188: %ISDN-6-LAYER2UP:
        Layer 2 for Interface BR0, TEI 114 changed to up
*Mar  1 00:09:06.200: ISDN BR0: TX ->
        INFOc sapi = 0  tei = 114  ns = 0  nr = 0  i =
             0x08007B3A06383932393833
*Mar  1 00:09:06.276: ISDN BR0: RX <-
        INFOc sapi = 0  tei = 114  ns = 0  nr = 1  i =
             0x08007B080382E43A
*Mar  1 00:09:06.283: ISDN BR0: TX -> RRr sapi = 0  tei = 114  nr = 1
*Mar  1 00:09:06.287: %ISDN-4-INVALID_SPID: Interface BR0,
     Spid1 was rejected
```

You check the status of the Cisco 700 ISDN line with the **show status** command, as shown in Example 12-7.

Example 12-7   *Checking the Status of the Cisco 700 ISDN Line*

```
kdt-776> show status
Status     01/04/1995 18:15:15
Line Status
  Line Activated
  Terminal Identifier Assigned    SPID Accepted
  Terminal Identifier Assigned    SPID Accepted
Port Status    Interface Connection Link
  Ch:  1     Waiting for Call
  Ch:  2     Waiting for Call
```

Summary

- ISDN provides an integrated voice/data capability that uses the public switched network.

- ISDN components include terminals, TAs, NT devices, and ISDN switches.

- ISDN reference points define logical interfaces between functional groupings, such as TAs and NT1s.

- ISDN is addressed by a suite of ITU-T standards, spanning the physical, data link, and network layers of the OSI reference model.

- The two most common encapsulation choices for ISDN are PPP and HDLC.

- ISDN has many uses, including remote access, remote nodes, and SOHO connectivity.

- There are two ISDN services: BRI and PRI.

- ISDN BRI delivers a total bandwidth of a 144 kbps line into three separate channels and a usable bandwidth of 128 kbps.

- BRI configuration involves the configuration of a BRI interface, an ISDN switch type, and ISDN SPIDs.

- DDR establishes and releases circuit switched connections as needed.

Washington School District Project Task: ISDN

In this chapter, a new site was brought into the network. This site is small and only requires connectivity from time to time. The decision has been made to connect it into the WAN core network using ISDN technology. As part of the ISDN configuration and implementation, you need to complete the following tasks:

1. Describe how ISDN will be inserted in the WAN implementation, how data will be sent across the ISDN link, and the benefits of ISDN for a small site.

2. Document the use of ISDN in the WAN design, including providing the following:

- A drawing of the implementation with all major reference points

- A description of overall bandwidth available to the site and how data communications will take place

- A description of all data communications equipment needed to accomplish the implementation

3. Document the router commands needed to implement ISDN on the router and document the resulting changes in the local site access router configurations.

4. Apply the CCNA Certification Exam Learning Objectives to your specific design. This requires a paragraph on how the learning objectives relate to your design. Learning objectives can be grouped together for the purpose of explanation. In this way, you will be studying for the CCNA Certification Exam as you work through the case study.

CCNA Certification Exam Learning Objectives

General

NOTE

*** are explict CCNA Exam objectives; unmarked are knowledge assumed by the exam.

- Describe the user requirement for implementing ISDN to a site.
- Describe at what layer of a hierarchical WAN model an ISDN link should be installed.

OSI Model

- Define what three layers of the OSI model ISDN standards are.

ISDN

- Describe the three data channels used in ISDN BRI and describe their functions.
- Describe what ISDN protocols that start with "Q" address.
- Describe what ISDN protocols that start with "I" address.
- Describe what ISDN protocols that start with "E" address.
- Describe the five major devices in an ISDN implementation.
- Describe the four major reference points in an ISDN implementation.
- Describe the function of Point-to-Point Protocol in an ISDN implementation.
- Describe why it is important to know the ISDN switch type when configuring an ISDN connection.
- Describe the funtion of SPID numbers and why it is important when configuring an ISDN connection.
- State a relevant use and context for ISDN networking. ***
- Identify ISDN protocols, function groups, reference points, and channels. ***
- Describe Cisco's implementation of ISDN BRI. ***

Check Your Understanding

Complete all the review questions to test your understanding of the topics and concepts covered in this chapter. Answers are listed in Appendix B, "Check Your Understanding Answer Key."

1. What is the top speed at which ISDN operates?

2. How many B channels does ISDN use?

3. How many D channels does ISDN use?

4. The ISDN service provider must provide the phone number and what type of identification number?

5. Which channel does ISDN use for call setup?

6. At the central site, what device can be used to provide the connection for dialup access?

   A. Switch

   B. Router

   C. Bridge

   D. Hub

7. For which of the following locations would ISDN service *not* be adequate?

   A. A large concentration of users at a site

   B. A small office

   C. A single-user site

   D. None of the above

8. Protocols that begin with E are used to specify what?

   A. Telephone network standards.

   B. Switching and signaling.

   C. ISDN concepts.

   D. It is not used with ISDN.

9. If you want to use CHAP for authentication when using ISDN, what protocol should you select?

A. HDLC

B. SLIP

C. PPP

D. PAP

10. On a router, which of the following commands do you use to set the ISDN switch type?

A. Router> **isdn switch-type**

B. Router# **isdn switch-type**

C. Router(config-if)# **isdn switch-type**

D. Router(config)# **isdn switch-type**

11. What service is generally viewed as an alternative to Frame Relay and T1 service?

A. ISDN

B. T3

C. ATM

D. FDDI

12. When a user logs in remotely to the network, what type of access will the user have?

A. No access to services

B. Only access for remote users

C. The same as if they were logging in locally

D. Access to all services

13. How does ISDN's data transfer rate compare to a modem?

A. It's the same.

B. It's faster.

C. It's slower.

D. ISDN does not have a set transfer rate.

14. Compared to regular phone service, how does ISDN compare when setting up a call?

   A. ISDN is slower.

   B. ISDN call setup is the same.

   C. ISDN is faster.

   D. ISDN does not set up calls.

15. A power user who telecommutes would most likely need what type of connection?

   A. T1

   B. T3

   C. Regular dial-up access

   D. ISDN

Key Terms

2B+D   In reference to the ISDN BRI service, two B channels and one D channel.

B channel (bearer channel)   In ISDN, a full-duplex, 64-kbps channel used to send user data.

BRI (Basic Rate Interface)   An ISDN interface composed of two B channels and one D channel for circuit-switched communication of voice, video, and data.

CO (central office)   The local telephone company office to which all local loops in a given area connect and in which circuit switching of subscriber lines occurs.

CPE (customer premises equipment)   Terminating equipment, such as terminals, telephones, and modems, supplied by the telephone company, installed at customer sites, and connected to the telephone company network.

D channel (delta channel)   A full-duplex, 16-kbps (BRI) or 64-kbps (PRI) ISDN channel.

ISDN (Integrated Services Digital Network)   A communication protocol, offered by telephone companies, that permits telephone networks to carry data, voice, and other source traffic.

LAPB (Link Access Procedure, Balanced)   A data link–layer protocol in the X.25 protocol stack. LAPB is a bit-oriented protocol derived from HDLC.

LAPD (Link Access Procedure on the D channel)   An ISDN data link–layer protocol for the D channel. LAPD was derived from LAPB and is designed primarily to satisfy the signaling requirements of ISDN basic access. Defined by ITU-T Recommendations Q.920 and Q.921.

NT1 (Network Termination type 1)   A device that connects four-wire ISDN subscriber wiring to the conventional two-wire local loop facility.

NT2 (Network Termination type 2)   A device that directs traffic to and from different subscriber devices and the NT1. The NT2 is an intelligent device that performs switching and concentrating.

PBX (Private Branch Exchange)   A digital or an analog telephone switchboard located on the subscriber premises and used to connect private and public telephone networks.

PRI (Primary Rate Interface)   An ISDN interface to primary rate access. Primary rate access consists of a single 64-kbps D channel plus 23 (T1) or 30 (E1) B channels for voice or data.

Q.931   A protocol that recommends a network layer between the terminal endpoint and the local ISDN switch. Q.931 does not impose an end-to-end recommendation. The various ISDN providers and switch types can and do use various implementations of Q.931.

reference point   A specification that defines the connection between specific devices, depending on their function in the end-to-end connection.

signaling   In the ISDN context, the process of call setup used, such as call establishment, call termination, information, and miscellaneous messages, including setup, connect, release, user information, cancel, status, and disconnect.

SOHO (small office/home office)   A small office or home office consisting of a few users requiring a connection that provides faster, more reliable connectivity than an analog dialup connection.

SPID (service profile identifier)   A number that some service providers use to define the services to which an ISDN device subscribes. The ISDN device uses the SPID when accessing the switch that initializes the connection to a service provider.

TA (terminal adapter)   A device used to connect ISDN BRI connections to existing interfaces, such as EIA/TIA-232. Essentially, an ISDN modem.

TE1 (Terminal Equipment type 1)   A device that is compatible with the ISDN network. A TE1 connects to a Network Termination of either type 1 or type 2.

TE2 (Terminal Equipment type 2)   A device that is not compatible with ISDN and requires a terminal adapter.

UNI (User-Network Interface)   A specification that defines an interoperability standard for the interface between products (a router or a switch) located in a private network and the switches located within the public carrier networks. Also used to describe similar connections in Frame Relay networks.

Objectives

After reading this chapter, you will be able to

- Describe the operation of Frame Relay
- Describe the functions of DLCIs in Frame Relay
- Describe Cisco's implementation of Frame Relay
- Describe the process for configuring and verifying Frame Relay
- Describe the Frame Relay subinterfaces
- Describe how Frame Relay uses subinterfaces to solve the problem of split horizon

Chapter 13

Frame Relay

Introduction

You learned about Point-to-Point Protocol (PPP) in Chapter 11, "PPP," and Integrated Services Digital Network (ISDN) in Chapter 12, "ISDN." You learned that PPP and ISDN are two types of WAN technologies that can be implemented to solve connectivity issues between geographically distant locations. In this chapter, you will learn about another type of WAN technology, *Frame Relay*, that can be implemented to solve connectivity issues for users who need access to geographically distant locations.

In this chapter, you will learn about Frame Relay services, standards, components, and operation. In addition, this chapter describes the configuration tasks for Frame Relay service, along with the commands for monitoring and maintaining a Frame Relay connection.

Washington Project: Implementing Frame Relay
In this chapter, you learn the concepts and configuration procedures that enable you to add Frame Relay to the Washington School District network design. In addition, you learn the steps to implement a Frame Relay link to the Internet per the specification in the TCS Overview. Implementing Frame Relay is the final step in your design and implementation of the district network.

Frame Relay Technology Overview

Frame Relay is a Consultative Committee for International Telegraph and Telephone (CCITT) and American National Standards Institute (ANSI) standard that defines a process for sending data over a *public data network (PDN)*. It is a high performance, efficient data-link technology used in networks throughout the world. Frame Relay is a way of sending information over a WAN by dividing data into packets. Each packet travels through a series of switches in a Frame Relay network to reach its destination. It operates at the physical and data link layers of the OSI reference model, but it relies on upper-layer protocols such as TCP for error correction.

Frame Relay was originally conceived as a protocol for use over ISDN interfaces. Today, Frame Relay is an industry-standard, switched data link layer protocol that handles multiple virtual circuits using High-Level Data Link Control

(HDLC) encapsulation between connected devices. Frame Relay uses virtual circuits to make connections through a connection-oriented service.

The network providing the Frame Relay interface can be either a carrier-provided public network or a network of privately owned equipment, serving a single enterprise. A Frame Relay network can consist of computers, servers, and so on, on the user end; Frame Relay access equipment such as routers or modems; and Frame Relay network devices such as switches, routers, CSU/DSUs, or multiplexers. As you have learned, user devices are often referred to as data terminal equipment (DTE), whereas network equipment that interfaces to DTE is often referred to as data circuit-terminating equipment (DCE), as shown in Figure 13-1.

FIGURE 13-1
Frame Relay defines the interconnection process between a router and the service provider's local access switching equipment.

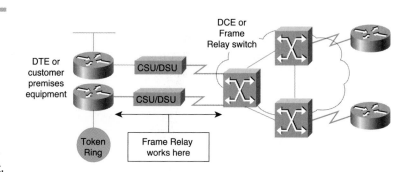

Frame Relay Terminology

Following are some terms that are used in this chapter to discuss Frame Relay:

- *Access rate*—The clock speed (port speed) of the connection (local loop) to the Frame Relay cloud. It is the rate at which data travels into or out of the network.

- *Data-link connection identifier (DLCI)*—As shown in Figure 13-2, a DLCI is a number that identifies the logical circuit between the source and destination device. The Frame Relay switch maps the DLCIs between each pair of routers to create a permanent virtual circuit (PVC).

- *Local Management Interface (LMI)*—A signaling standard between the customer premises equipment (CPE) device and the Frame Relay switch that is responsible for managing the connection and maintaining status between the devices. LMIs can include support for a keepalive mechanism, which verifies that data is flowing; a multicast mechanism, which can provide the network server with its local DLCI; multicast addressing, providing a few DLCIs to be used as multicast (multiple destination) addresses and the ability to give DLCIs global (whole Frame Relay network) significance rather than just local significance (DLCIs used only to the local switch); and a status mechanism, which provides an ongoing status on the DLCIs known to the switch. There are several LMI types, and routers need to be told which LMI type is being used. Three types of LMIs are supported: **cisco**, **ansi**, and **q933a**.

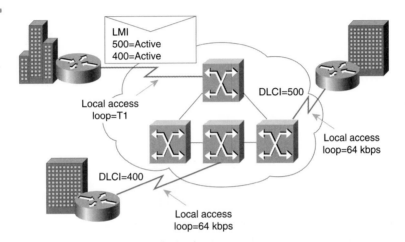

FIGURE 13-2
The DLCI value identifies the logical connection that is multiplexed into the physical channel.

- **Committed information rate (CIR)**—The CIR is the guaranteed rate, in bits per second, that the service provider commits to providing.

- **Committed burst**—The maximum number of bits that the switch agrees to transfer during a time interval. (It is noted as Bc.)

- **Excess burst**—The maximum number of uncommitted bits that the Frame Relay switch attempts to transfer beyond the CIR. Excess burst is dependent on the service offerings available by the vendor, but is typically limited to the port speed of the local access loop.

- *Forward explicit congestion notification (FECN)*—A bit set in a frame that notifies a DTE that congestion avoidance procedures should be initiated by the receiving device. When a Frame Relay switch recognizes congestion in the network, it sends a FECN packet to the destination device, indicating that congestion has occurred.

- *Backward explicit congestion notification (BECN)*—A bit set in a frame that notifies a DTE that congestion avoidance procedures should be initiated by the sending device. As shown in Figure 13-3, when a Frame Relay switch recognizes congestion in the network, it sends a BECN packet to the source router, instructing the router to reduce the rate at which it is sending packets. If the router receives any BECNs during the current time interval, it decreases the transmit rate by 25%.

- **Discard eligibility (DE) indicator**—A set bit that indicates the frame may be discarded in preference to other frames if conjestion occurs. When the router detects network congestion, the Frame Relay switch will drop packets with the DE bit set first. The DE bit is set on the oversubscribed traffic (that is, the traffic that was received after the CIR was met).

FIGURE 13-3
A Frame Relay switch sends BECN packets to reduce congestion.

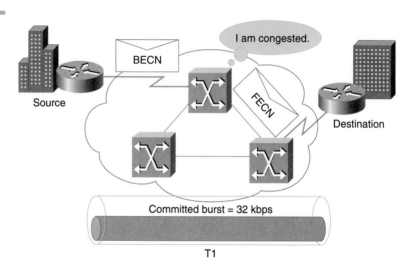

MOVIE 13.1

Congestion Handled by FECN

Frame Relay switch recognizes congestion in the network.

Frame Relay Operation

Frame Relay can be used as an interface to either a publicly available carrier-provided service or to a network of privately owned equipment. You deploy a public Frame Relay service by putting Frame Relay switching equipment in the central office of a telecommunications carrier. In this case, users get economic benefits from traffic-sensitive charging rates, and don't have to spend the time and effort to administer and maintain the network equipment and service.

No standards for interconnecting equipment inside a Frame Relay network currently exist. Therefore, the support of Frame Relay interfaces does not necessarily dictate that the Frame Relay protocol is used between the network devices. Thus, traditional circuit switching, packet switching, or a hybrid approach combining these technologies can be used, as shown in Figure 13-4.

FIGURE 13-4
You can use Frame Relay as an interface to a network by interconnecting equipment such as Frame Relay switches and routers.

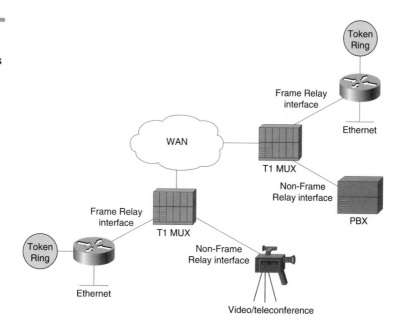

The lines that connect user devices to the network equipment can operate at a speed selected from a broad range of data rates. Speeds between 56 kbps and 1.544 Mbps are typical, although Frame Relay can support lower and higher speeds.

Frame Relay Multiplexing

As an interface between user and network equipment (see Figure 13-5), Frame Relay provides a means for multiplexing many logical data conversations, referred to as *virtual circuits*, through a shared physical *medium* by assigning DLCIs to each DTE/DCE pair of devices.

Frame Relay's multiplexing provides more flexible and efficient use of available bandwidth. Therefore, Frame Relay allows users to share bandwidth at a reduced cost. For example, say you have a WAN using Frame Relay, and the Frame Relay is equivalent to a group of roads. The phone company usually owns and maintains the roads. You can choose to rent out a road (or path) exclusively for your company (dedicated), or you can pay less to rent a path on shared roads. Of course, Frame Relay could also be run entirely over private networks; however, it's rarely used in this manner.

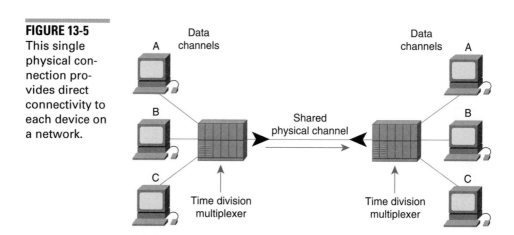

FIGURE 13-5
This single physical connection provides direct connectivity to each device on a network.

Frame Relay standards address *permanent virtual circuits (PVCs)* that are administratively configured and managed in a Frame Relay network. Frame Relay PVCs are identified by DLCIs, as shown in Figure 13-6. Frame Relay DLCIs have local significance. That is, the values themselves are not unique in the Frame Relay WAN. Two DTE devices connected by a virtual circuit might use a different DLCI value to refer to the same connection, as shown in Figure 13-6.

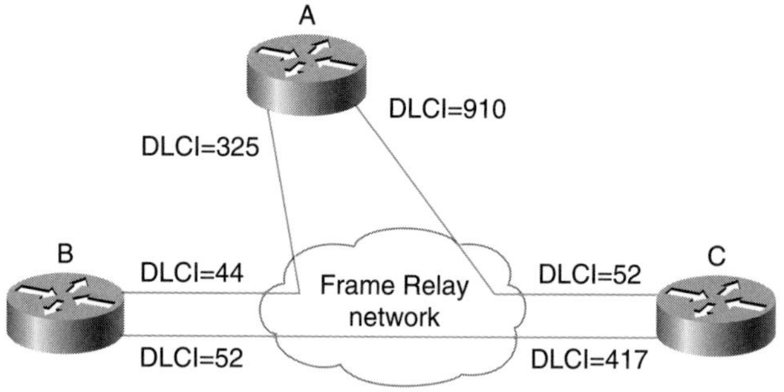

FIGURE 13-6
The end devices at two different ends of a connection can use different DLCI numbers to refer to the same connection.

When Frame Relay provides a means for multiplexing many logical data conversations, first the service provider's switching equipment constructs a table mapping DLCI values to outbound ports. When a frame is received, the switching device analyzes the connection identifier and delivers the frame to the associated outbound port. The complete path to the destination is established before the first frame is sent.

Frame Relay Frame Format

The Frame Relay frame format is shown in Figure 13-7. The flag fields indicate the beginning and end of the frame. Following the leading flag field are 2 bytes of address information. Ten bits of these 2 bytes make up the actual circuit ID (that is, the DLCI).

The following are the Frame Relay frame fields:

- **Flag**—Indicates the beginning and the end of the Frame Relay frame.
- **Address**—Indicates the length of the address field. Although Frame Relay addresses are currently all 2 bytes long, the address bits allow for the possible extension of address lengths in the future. The eighth bit of each byte of the address field is used to indicate the address. The address contains the following information:
  - **DLCI Value**—Indicates the DLCI value. Consists of the first 10 bits of the Address field.
  - **Congestion Control**—The last 3 bits in the address field, which control the Frame Relay congestion notification mechanisms. These are the FECN, BECN, and DE bits.
- **Data**—Variable-length field that contains encapsulated upper-layer data.
- **FCS**—Frame check sequence (FCS), used to ensure the integrity of transmitted data.

FIGURE 13-7
The Flag fields delimit the beginning and end of the frame.

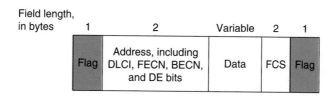

Frame Relay Addressing

In Figure 13-8, assume two PVCs, one between Atlanta and Los Angeles, and one between San Jose and Pittsburgh. Los Angeles uses DLCI 22 to refer to its PVC with Atlanta, whereas Atlanta refers to the same PVC as DLCI 82. Similarly, San Jose uses DLCI 12 to refer to its PVC with Pittsburgh and Pittsburgh uses DLCI 62. The network uses internal mechanisms to keep the two locally significant PVC identifiers distinct.

FIGURE 13-8
An example of the use of DLCIs in a Frame Relay network.

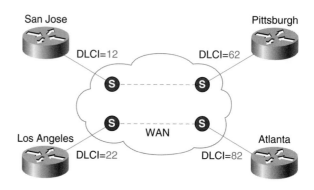

DLCI address space is limited to 10 bits. This creates a possiblility of 1024 DLCI addresses. The usable portion of these addresses are determined by the LMI type used. The Cisco LMI type supports a range of DLCI addresses from DLCI 16-992 for carrying user data. The remaining DLCI addresses are reserved for vendor implementation. This includes LMI messages and multicast addresses.

Cisco's Implementation of Frame Relay: LMI

There was a major development in Frame Relay's history in 1990 when Cisco Systems, StrataCom, Northern Telecom, and Digital Equipment Corporation formed a group to focus on Frame Relay technology development and accelerate the introduction of interoperable Frame Relay products. This group developed a specification conforming to the basic Frame Relay protocol, but extended it with features that provide additional capabilities for complex internetworking environments. These Frame Relay extensions are referred to as LMI (local management interface).Three LMI types can be invoked by the router: **ansi, cisco,** and **q933a**.

LMI Operation

The main functions of the LMI process are

- To determine the operational status of the various PVCs that the router knows about
- To transmit keepalive packets to ensure that the PVC stays up and does not shut down due to inactivity (see Figure 13-9)
- To tell the router what PVCs are available

FIGURE 13-9
LMI provides for management of connections.

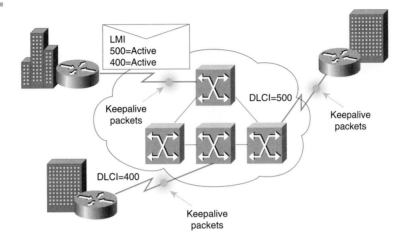

LMI Extensions

In addition to the basic Frame Relay protocol functions for transferring data, the Frame Relay specification includes LMI extensions that make supporting large, complex internetworks easier. Some LMI extensions are referred to as *common* and are expected to be implemented by everyone who adopts the specification. Other LMI functions are referred to as *optional*. A summary of the LMI extensions follows:

- **Virtual circuit status messages (common)**—Provide communication and synchronization between the network and the user device, periodically reporting the existence of new PVCs and the deletion of already existing PVCs, and generally providing information about PVC integrity. Virtual circuit status messages prevent the sending of data over PVCs that no longer exist.

- **Multicasting (optional)**—Allows a sender to transmit a single frame but have it delivered by the network to multiple recipients. Thus, multicasting supports the efficient conveyance of routing protocol messages and address resolution protocols that typically must be sent to many destinations simultaneously.

- **Global addressing (optional)**—Gives connection identifiers global rather than local significance, allowing them to be used to identify a specific interface to the Frame Relay network. Global addressing makes the Frame Relay network resemble a local-area network (LAN) in terms of addressing; address resolution protocols therefore perform over Frame Relay exactly as they do over a LAN.

■ **Simple flow control (optional)**—Provides for an XON/XOFF flow control mechanism that applies to the entire Frame Relay interface. It is intended for devices whose higher layers cannot use the congestion notification bits and that need some level of flow control.

MOVIE 13.2

Multicast Transmission

Data packets sent through network.

LMI Frame Format

The Frame Relay specification also includes the LMI procedures. LMI messages are sent in frames distinguished by an LMI-specific DLCI (defined in the consortium specification as DLCI = 1023). The LMI frame format is shown in Figure 13-10.

After the flag and LMI DLCI fields, the LMI frame contains 4 mandatory bytes. The first of the mandatory bytes (*unnumbered information indicator*) has the same format as the LAPB *unnumbered information* (UI) frame indicator, with the poll/final bit set to zero. The next byte is referred to as the *protocol discriminator*, which is set to a value that indicates LMI. The third mandatory byte (*call reference*) is always filled with zeros.

The final mandatory byte is the *message type* field. Two message types have been defined: *Status* messages and *status-enquiry* messages. *Status* messages respond to status-enquiry messages. Examples of these messages are (1) keepalives (messages sent through a connection to ensure that both sides will continue to regard the connection as active) and (2) a status message of an individual report on each DLCI defined for the link. These common LMI features are expected to be a part of every implementation that conforms to the Frame Relay specification.

FIGURE 13-10
In LMI frames, the basic protocol header is the same as in normal Frame Relay frames.

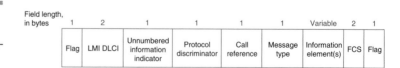

	Field length, in bytes	1	2	1	1	1	1	Variable	2	1
		Flag	LMI DLCI	Unnumbered information indicator	Protocol discriminator	Call reference	Message type	Information element(s)	FCS	Flag

Together, status and status-enquiry messages help verify the integrity of logical and physical links. This information is critical in a routing environment because routing protocols make decisions based on link integrity.

Next is an information element (IE) field of a variable number of *bytes*. Following the message type field is some number of IEs. Each IE consists of a 1-byte *IE identifier*, an *IE length* field, and 1 or more bytes containing actual data.

Global Addressing

In addition to the common LMI features, several optional LMI extensions are extremely useful in an internetworking environment. The first important optional LMI extension is *global addressing*. With this extension, the values inserted in the DLCI field of a frame are globally significant addresses of individual end-user devices (for example, routers). This is implemented as shown previously in Figure 13-8.

As noted earlier, the basic (nonextended) Frame Relay specification supports only values of the DLCI field that identify PVCs with local significance. In this case, there are no addresses that identify network interfaces or nodes attached to these interfaces. Because these addresses do not exist, they cannot be discovered by traditional address resolution and discovery techniques. This means that with normal Frame Relay addressing, static maps must be created to tell routers which DLCIs to use to find a remote device and its associated internetwork address.

In Figure 13-8, note that each interface has its own identifier. Suppose that Pittsburgh must send a frame to San Jose. The identifier for San Jose is 12, so Pittsburgh places the value 12 in the DLCI field and sends the frame into the Frame Relay network. Each router interface has a distinct value as its node identifier, so individual devices can be distinguished. This permits routing in complex environments. Global addressing provides significant benefits in a large, complex network. The Frame Relay network now appears to the routers on its periphery like any LAN.

Multicasting

Multicasting is another valuable optional LMI feature. Multicast groups are designated by a series of four reserved DLCI values (1019 to 1022). Frames sent by a device using one of these reserved DLCIs are replicated by the network and sent to all exit points in the designated set. The multicasting extension also defines LMI messages that notify user devices of the addition, deletion, and presence of multicast groups. In networks that take advantage of dynamic routing, routing information must be exchanged among many routers. Routing messages can be sent efficiently by using frames with a multicast DLCI. This allows messages to be sent to specific groups of routers.

Inverse ARP

The Inverse ARP mechanism allows the router to automatically build the Frame Relay map, as shown in Figure 13-11. The router learns the DLCIs that are in use from the switch during the initial LMI exchange. The router then sends an Inverse ARP request to each DLCI for each protocol configured on the interface if the protocol is supported. The return information from the Inverse ARP is then used to build the Frame Relay map.

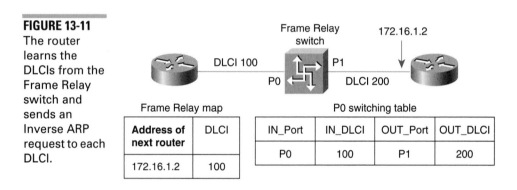

FIGURE 13-11
The router learns the DLCIs from the Frame Relay switch and sends an Inverse ARP request to each DLCI.

Frame Relay map

Address of next router	DLCI
172.16.1.2	100

P0 switching table

IN_Port	IN_DLCI	OUT_Port	OUT_DLCI
P0	100	P1	200

Frame Relay Mapping

The router next-hop address determined from the routing table must be resolved to a Frame Relay DLCI, as shown in Figure 13-12. The resolution is done through a data structure called a *Frame Relay map*. The routing table is then used to supply the next-hop protocol address or the DLCI for outgoing traffic. This data structure can be statically configured in the router, or the Inverse ARP feature can be used for automatic setup of the map.

Frame Relay Switching Tables

The Frame Relay switching table consists of four entries: two for incoming port and DLCI, and two for outgoing port and DLCI, as shown in Figure 13-13. The DLCI could, therefore, be remapped as it passes through each switch; the fact that the port reference can be changed is why the DLCI does not change even though the port reference might change.

FIGURE 13-12
Responses to
Inverse ARP
requests are
entered in an
address-to-
DLCI mapping
table on the
router or
access server.

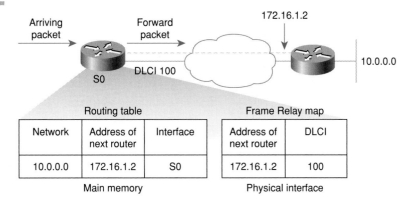

FIGURE 13-13
Routers use
Inverse ARP to
find the remote
IP address and
create a map-
ping of local
DLCIs and their
associated
remote IP
addresses.

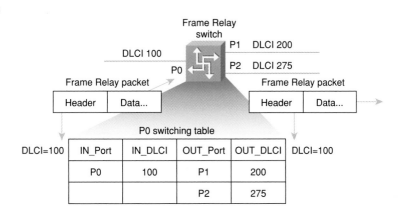

Engineering Journal:
Frame Relay Operation Summary

Now that you have learned the basic Frame Relay operations, you can use the following steps, which are illustrated in Figures 13-14 and 13-15 to implement Frame Relay:

Step 1   Order Frame Relay service from a service provider or create a private Frame Relay cloud.

Step 2   Connect each router, either directly or through a channel service unit/ digital service unit (CSU/DSU), to the Frame Relay switch.

Step 3   When the CPE router is enabled, it sends a Status Inquiry message to the Frame Relay switch. The message notifies the switch of the router's status, and asks the switch for the connection status of the other remote routers.

continues

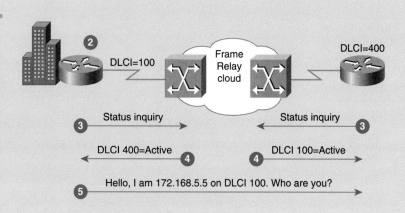

FIGURE 13-14
If Inverse ARP is not working or if the remote router does not support Inverse ARP, you need to configure the routes (that is, the DLCIs and IP addresses) of the remote routers.

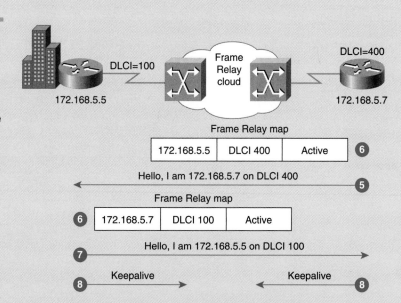

FIGURE 13-15
The router changes the status of each DLCI, based on the response from the Frame Relay switch.

Step 4   When the Frame Relay switch receives the request, it responds with a Status message that includes the DLCIs of the remote routers to which the local router can send data.

Step 5   For each active DLCI, each router sends an Inverse ARP request packet, introducing itself and asking for each remote router to identify itself by replying with its network-layer address.

Step 6   For every DLCI that the router learns about through an Inverse ARP message, a map entry is created in the router's Frame Relay map table. This includes the local

DLCI, the remote router's network-layer address, and the state of the connection. Note that the DLCI is the router's locally configured DLCI, not the DLCI that the remote router is using. Three possible connection states appear in the Frame Relay map table:

- **Active state**—Indicates that the connection is active and that routers can exchange data.
- **Inactive state**—Indicates that the local connection to Frame Relay switch is working, but the remote router's connection to Frame Relay switch is not working.
- **Deleted state**—Indicates that no LMI is being received from the Frame Relay switch or no service between the CPE router and Frame Relay switch is occurring.

Step 7 Every 60 seconds, the routers exchange Inverse ARP messages.

Step 8 By default, every 10 seconds or so (this is configurable), the CPE router sends a keepalive message to the Frame Relay switch. The purpose of the keepalive message is to verify that the Frame Relay switch is still active.

Frame Relay Subinterfaces

To enable the sending of complete routing updates in a Frame Relay network, you can configure the router with logically assigned interfaces called *subinterfaces*. Subinterfaces are logical subdivisions of a physical interface. In a subinterface configuration, each PVC can be configured as a point-to-point connection, which allows the subinterface to act as a dedicated line, as shown in Figure 13-16.

FIGURE 13-16
Routing updates can be sent out through subinterfaces as if they were from separate physical interfaces.

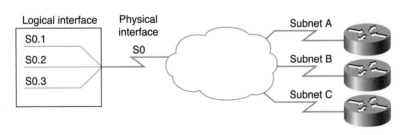

Early implementation of Frame Relay required that a router (that is, a DTE device) have a WAN serial interface for every PVC.

By logically dividing a single physical WAN serial interface into multiple virtual subinterfaces, the overall cost of implementing a Frame Relay network can be reduced. As shown in Figure 13-17, a single router interface can service many remote locations through individual unique suberinterfaces.

FIGURE 13-17
Each subinterface is considered a unique network and a unique DLCI number.

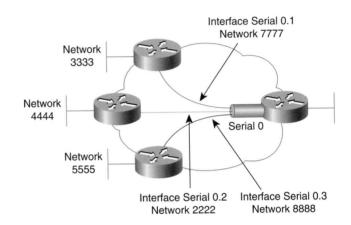

Split Horizon Routing Environments

Split horizon reduces routing loops by not allowing a routing update received on one physical interface to be sent back out to that same interface (see Figure 13-18). As a result, if a remote router sends an update to the headquarters router that is connecting multiple PVCs over a single physical interface, the headquarters router cannot advertise that route through the same physical interface to other remote routers (see Figure 13-19).

Resolving Reachability Issues with Subinterfaces

You can configure subinterfaces to support the following connection types:

- **Point-to-point**—A single subinterface is used to establish one PVC connection to another physical interface or subinterface on a remote router. In this case, the interfaces would be in the same subnet, and each interface would have a single DLCI. Each point-to-point connection is its own subnet. In this environment, broadcasts are not a problem because the routers are point-to-point and act like a leased line.

- **Multipoint**—A single subinterface is used to establish multiple PVC connections to multiple physical interfaces or subinterfaces on remote routers. In this case, all the participating interfaces would be in the same subnet, and each interface would have its own local DLCI. In this environment, because the subinterface is acting like a regular Frame Relay network, routing updates are subject to split horizon.

FIGURE 13-18
With split horizon, if a router learns a protocol's route on an interface, it does not send information about that route back on that interface.

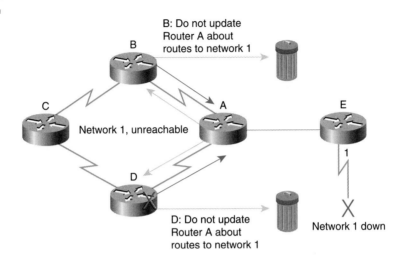

B: Do not update
Router A about
routes to network 1

Network 1, unreachable

D: Do not update
Router A about
routes to network 1

Network 1 down

FIGURE 13-19
With split horizon, routing updates received at a central router cannot be advertised out the same physical interface to other routers.

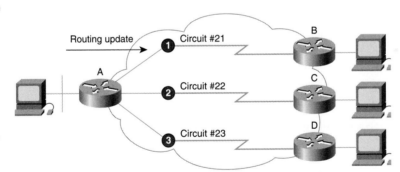

Routing update

Circuit #21

Circuit #22

Circuit #23

Basic Frame Relay Configuration

A basic Frame Relay configuration assumes that you want to configure Frame Relay on one or more physical interfaces (see Figure 13-20), and that LMI and Inverse ARP are supported by the remote router(s). In this type of environment, the LMI notifies the router about the available DLCIs. Inverse ARP is enabled by default, so it does not appear in configuration output. Use the following steps to configure basic Frame Relay:

Step 1   Select the interface and go into interface configuration mode:

```
router(config)# interface serial 0
```

Step 2   Configure a network-layer address, for example, an IP address:

```
router(config-if)# ip address 192.168.38.40 255.255.255.0
```

Step 3   Select the encapsulation type used to encapsulate data traffic end-to-end:

```
router(config-if)# encapsulation frame-relay [cisco | IETF]
```

where

cisco is the default, which you use if connecting to another Cisco router.

ietf is used for connecting to a non-Cisco router.

Step 4   If you're using Cisco IOS Release 11.1 or earlier, specify the LMI type used by the Frame Relay switch:

```
router(config-if)# frame-relay lmi-type {ansi | cisco | q933a}
```

where **cisco** is the default.

With IOS Release 11.2 or later, the LMI type is autosensed, so no configuration is needed.

Step 5   Configure the bandwidth for the link:

```
router(config-if)# bandwidth kilobits
```

This command affects routing operation by protocols such as IGRP, because it is used to define the metric of the link.

Step 6   If Inverse ARP was disabled on the router, reenable it (Inverse ARP is on by default):

```
router(config-if)# frame-relay inverse-arp [protocol] [dlci]
```

where

protocol is the supported protocols, including IP, IPX, AppleTalk, DECnet, VINES, and XNS.

dlci is the DLCI on the local interface that you want to exchange Inverse ARP messages.

FIGURE 13-20
When you have reliable connections to the local Frame Relay switch at both ends of the PVC, it is time to start planning the Frame Relay configuration.

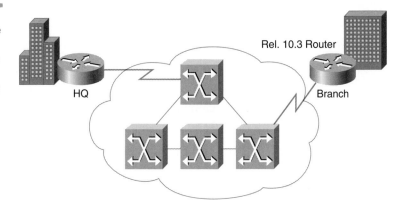

Engineering Journal: Configuring Security

Use the following steps to configure the router with some security measures, such as the router host name and the password used to prevent unauthorized access to the router:

Step 1   Configure the router with a host name, which is used in prompts and default configuration filenames. For PPP authentication, the host name entered with this command must match the username of the central site router:

Router(config)# **hostname 1600**

Step 2   Specify a password to prevent unauthorized access to the router:

1600(config)# **enable password** 1600user

Verifying Frame Relay Operation

After configuring Frame Relay, you can verify that the connections are active by using the following **show** commands:

Command	Description
show interfaces serial	Displays information about the multicast DLCI, the DLCIs used on the Frame Relay–configured serial interface, and the LMI DLCI used for the LMI.

continues

Command	Description
show frame-relay pvc	Displays the status of each configured connection as well as traffic statistics. This command is also useful for viewing the number of BECN and FECN packets received by the router.
show frame-relay map	Displays the network-layer address and associated DLCI for each remote destination that the local router is connected to.
show frame-relay lmi	Displays LMI traffic statistics. For example, it shows the number of status messages exchanged between the local router and the Frame Relay switch.

e-LAB ACTIVITY 13.1

show interfaces

In this activity, you demonstrate how to use **show interfaces serial** command to check the DLCI nformation on serial 0.

Confirming That the Line Is Up

Complete the following steps to confirm that the line is up:

Step 1 From the privileged EXEC command mode, enter the **show interfaces serial 0** command, as follows:

```
1600# show interfaces serial 0
Serial0 is up, line protocol is up
Hardware is QUICC Serial
MTU 1500 bytes, BW 1544 Kbit,
    DLY 20000 usec, rely 255/255, load 1/255
Encapsulation FRAME-RELAY,
    loopback not set, keepalive set (10 sec)
LMI enq sent 163, LMI stat recvd 136,
    LMI upd recvd 0, DTE LMI up
LMI enq recvd 39, LMI stat sent 0, LMI upd sent 0
LMI DLCI 1023 LMI type is CISCO frame relay DTE
Broadcast queue 0/64, broadcasts sent/dropped 27/0,
    interface broadcasts 28
Last input 00:00:01, output 00:00:05, output hang never
Last clearing of "show interface" counters never
Input queue: 0/75/0 (size/max/drops);
    Total output drops: 0
```

```
Queuing strategy: weighted fair
Output queue: 0/64/0 (size/threshold/drops)
Conversations 0/1 (active/max active)
Reserved Conversations 0/0 (allocated/max allocated)
5 minute input rate 0 bits/sec, 0 packets/sec
5 minute output rate 0 bits/sec, 0 packets/sec
1813 packets input, 109641 bytes, 0 no buffer
Received 1576 broadcasts, 0 runts, 0 giants
13 input errors, 0 CRC, 13 frame, 0 overrun,
    0 ignored, 0 abort
1848 packets output, 117260 bytes, 0 underruns
0 output errors, 0 collisions, 32 interface resets
0 output buffer failures, 0 output buffers swapped out
29 carrier transitions
DCD=up DSR=up DTR=up RTS=up CTS=up
```

e-LAB ACTIVITY 13.2

show interfaces

In this activity, you demonstrate how to use **show interfaces serial** command to check the DLCI nformation on serial 1.

Step 2 Confirm that the following messages (shown in bold in Step 1) appear in the command output:

— serial0 is up, line protocol is up—The Frame Relay connection is active.

— LMI enq sent 163, LMI stat recvd 136—The connection is sending and receiving data. The number shown in your output will probably be different.

— LMI type is CISCO—The LMI type is configured correctly for the router.

Step 3 If the message does not appear in the command output, take the following steps:

— Confirm with the Frame Relay service provider that the LMI setting is correct for your line.

— Confirm that keepalives are set and that the router is receiving LMI updates.

Step 4 To continue configuration, reenter global configuration mode.

Confirming the Frame Relay Maps

Complete the following steps to confirm the Frame Relay maps:

Step 1   From privileged EXEC mode, enter the **show frame-relay map** command. Confirm that the status defined, active message appears for each serial subinterface:

```
1600# show frame-relay map
Serial0.1 (up): point-to-point dlci, dlci 17(0x11,0x410),
    broadcast,
status defined, active
```

Step 2   If the message does not appear, follow these steps:

— Confirm that the central-site router is connected and configured.

— Check with the Frame Relay carrier to verify that the line is operating correctly.

Step 3   To continue configuration, reenter global configuration mode.

e-LAB ACTIVITY 13.3

show frame-relay map

In this activity, you demonstrate how to use the **show frame-relay map** command to display the current map entries and information about the connections.

Confirming Connectivity to the Central Site Router

Complete the following steps to confirm connectivity to the central site router:

Step 1   From privileged EXEC mode, enter the **ping** command, followed by the IP address of the central site router.

Step 2   Note the percentage in the Success rate... line (shown in bold in the example):

```
1600# ping 192.168.38.40
Type escape sequence to abort.
Sending 5, 100-byte ICMP Echos to 192.168.38.40,
    timeout is 2 seconds:
!!!!!
Success rate is 100 percent (5/5),
    round-trip min/avg/max = 32/32/32 ms
1600#
```

If the success rate is 10% or greater, this verification step is successful.

Step 3 To continue configuration, reenter global configuration mode.

e-LAB ACTIVITY 13.4

ping

In this activity, you demonstrate how to use the **ping** command to confirm connectivity.

Engineering Journal:
Configuring the Ethernet Interface

Use the following steps to configure the Ethernet interface (which connects the router to the local network) for IP and IPX routing and network addresses:

Step 1 Enter configuration mode for the Ethernet interface:

`1600(config)# interface ethernet 0`

Step 2 Configure this interface with an IP address and a subnet mask:

`1600(config-if)# ip address 172.16.25.1 255.255.255.0`

Step 3 Enable IPX routing on this interface:

`1600(config-if)# ipx network number`

Step 4 Enable the interface and the configuration changes that you have just made on the interface:

`1600(config-if)# no shutdown`

Step 5 Exit configuration mode for this interface:

`1600(config-if)# exit`

Configuring the Serial Interface for a Frame Relay Connection

Use the following steps to configure the serial interface for Frame Relay packet encapsulation:

Step 1 Enter configuration mode for the serial interface:

`1600(config)# interface serial 0`

Step 2 Set the encapsulation method on this interface to Frame Relay:

`1600(config-if)# encapsulation frame-relay`

Step 3 Enable the configuration changes on this interface:

`1600(config-if)# no shutdown`

e-LAB ACTIVITY 13.5

interface serial 0

In this activity, you demonstrate how to use the **interface serial 0** command to configure the serial interface for Frame Relay packet encapsulation.

Verifying Frame Relay Configuration

You can verify your configuration to this point by confirming that an active PVC is active on the Frame Relay line, as follows:

Step 1   Wait 60 seconds after entering the **encapsulation frame-relay** command.

Step 2   From privileged EXEC mode, enter the **show frame-relay pvc** command.

Step 3   Confirm that the PVC STATUS=ACTIVE message appears in the command output:

```
1600# show frame-relay pvc

PVC Statistics for interface Serial0 (Frame Relay DTE)

DLCI = 17, DLCI USAGE = LOCAL, PVC STATUS = ACTIVE, INTERFACE =
  Serial0.1

input pkts 45 output pkts 52 in bytes 7764

out bytes 9958 dropped pkts 0 in FECN pkts 0

in BECN pkts 0 out FECN pkts 0 out BECN pkts 0

in DE pkts 0 out DE pkts 0

pvc create time 00:30:59, last time pvc status changed 00:19:21
```

Step 4   Record the number shown in the DLCI = message. (In this example, the number is 17.) You use this number to finish configuring the Frame Relay interface.

Step 5   If there is no output after entering the command, use the **show interfaces serial 0** command to determine whether the serial interface is active. An example of this command is in the next section. The first line of the command output should be this:

```
Serial0 is up, line protocol is up
```

If the first line of the command output is Serial0 is up, line protocol is down, you should confirm that the LMI type for the Frame Relay switch is correct by checking for the LMI type is CISCO message in the same command output.

Step 6   To continue configuration, reenter global configuration mode.

e-LAB ACTIVITY 13.6

show frame-relay pvc

In this activity, you demonstrate how to use the **show frame-relay pvc** command to display statistics about PVCs for Frame Relay interfaces.

Engineering Journal:
Configuring Command-Line Access to the Router

Use the following steps to configure some parameters that control access to the router, including the type of terminal line used with the router, how long the router waits for a user entry before it times out, and the password used to start a terminal session with the router:

Step 1 Specify the console terminal line:

```
1600(config)#  line console 0
```

Step 2 Set the interval so that the EXEC command interpreter waits until user input is detected:

```
1600(config-line)#  exec-timeout 5
```

Step 3 Specify a virtual terminal for remote console access:

```
1600(config-line)#  line vty 0 4
```

Step 4 Specify a password:

```
1600(config-line)#  password lineaccess
```

Step 5 Enable password checking at terminal session login:

```
1600(config-line)#  login
```

Step 6 Exit configuration mode:

```
1600(config-line)#  end
```

Configuring Subinterfaces

To configure subinterfaces on a physical interface as shown in Figure 13-21, do the following:

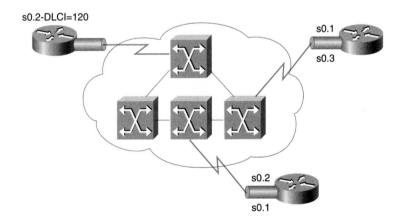

FIGURE 13-21 In point-to-point subinterface, each point-to-point connection requires its own subnet.

s0.2-DLCI=120

s0.1
s0.3

s0.2
s0.1

Step 1 Select the interface that you want to create subinterfaces on and get into interface configuration mode.

Step 2 Remove any network-layer address assigned to the physical interface. If the physical interface has an address, frames will not be received by the local subinterfaces.

Step 3 Configure Frame Relay encapsulation.

Step 4 Select the subinterface you want to configure:

```
router(config-if)# interface serial number.subinterface-number
        {multipoint | point-to-point}
```

where

number.subinterface-number is the subinterface number in the range 1 to 4294967293. The interface number that precedes the period must match the interface number to which this subinterface belongs.

multipoint is used if you want the router to forward broadcasts and routing updates that it receives. Select this if routing IP and you want all routers in same subnet (see Figure 13-22).

FIGURE 13-22
With a multipoint configuration, you need only a single network or subnet.

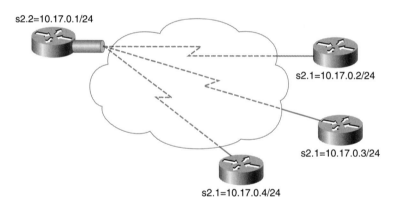

s2.2=10.17.0.1/24

s2.1=10.17.0.2/24

s2.1=10.17.0.3/24

s2.1=10.17.0.4/24

point-to-point is used if you do not want the router to forward broadcasts or routing updates and if you want each pair of point-to-point routers to have its own subnet (see Figure 13-23).

You are required to select either **multipoint** or **point-to-point**; there is no default.

Step 5 Configure a network-layer address on the subinterface. If the subinterface is point-to-point, and you are using IP, you can use the **ip unnumbered** command:

```
router(config-if)# ip unnumbered interface
```

If you use this command, it is recommended that the interface is the loopback interface. This is because the Frame Relay link will not work if this command is pointing to an interface that is not fully operational, and a loopback interface is not very likely to fail.

FIGURE 13-23
In a point-to-point subinterface configuration, subinterfaces act as leased line.

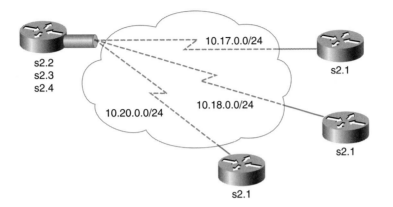

Step 6 If you configured the subinterface as multipoint or point-to-point, you must configure the local DLCI for the subinterface to distinguish it from the physical interface:

```
router(config-if)# frame-relay interface-dlci dlci-number
```

where

dlci-number defines the local DLCI number being linked to the subinterface. This is the only way to link an LMI-derived PVC to a subinterface because LMI does not know about subinterfaces.

This command is required for all point-to-point subinterfaces. It is also required for multipoint subinterfaces for which Inverse ARP is enabled. It is not required for multipoint subinterfaces configured with static route maps.

Do not use this command on physical interfaces.

Configuring Optional Commands

The following commands can be used when necessary for enhanced router operation:

```
router(config-if)# frame-relay map protocol protocol-address dlci
    [broadcast] [ietf | cisco | payload-compress packet-by-packet]
```

> **NOTE**
>
> If you defined a subinterface for point-to-point communication, you cannot reassign the same subinterface number to be used for multipoint communication without first rebooting the router. Instead you can avoid using that subinterface number and use a different subinterface number.

e-LAB ACTIVITY 13.7

interface serial

In this activity, you demonstrate how to use the **interface serial** command to select the interface and enters interface configuration mode.

The following is a description of this syntax:

Parameter	Description
protocol	Defines the supported protocol, bridging, or logical link control.
protocol-address	Defines the network-layer address of the destination router interface.
dlci	Defines the local DLCI used to connect to the remote protocol address.
broadcast	(Optional) Forwards broadcasts to this address when multicast is not enabled. Use this if you want the router to forward routing updates.
ietf	cisco	(Optional) Select the Frame Relay encapsulation type for use. Use **ietf** only if the remote router is a non-Cisco router. Otherwise, use **cisco**.
payload-compress packet-by-packet	(Optional) Packet-by-packet payload compression using the Stacker method.

Normally, Inverse ARP is used to request the next-hop protocol address for a specific connection. Responses to Inverse ARP are entered in an address-to-DLCI map (that is, Frame Relay map) table, as shown in Figure 13-24. The table is then used to route outgoing traffic. When Inverse ARP is not supported by the remote router, when configuring OSPF over Frame Relay, or when you want to control broadcast traffic while using routing, you must define the address-to-DLCI table statically. The static entries are referred to as *static maps*.

With Frame Relay, you can increase or decrease the keepalive interval. You can extend or reduce the interval at which the router interface sends keepalive messages to the Frame Relay switch. The default is 10 seconds, and the following is the syntax:

```
router(config-if)# keepalive number
```

where *number* is the value, in seconds, that is usually 2 to 3 seconds faster (that is, a shorter interval) than the setting of the Frame Relay switch to ensure proper synchronization.

FIGURE 13-24
Responses to the Inverse ARP request of the next-hop protocol address are entered in an address-to-DLCI map.

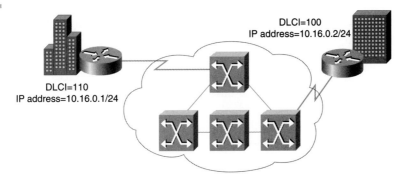

DLCI=100
IP address=10.16.0.2/24

DLCI=110
IP address=10.16.0.1/24

If an LMI type is not used in the network, or when you are doing back-to-back testing between routers, you need to specify the DLCI for each local interface by using the following command:

```
router(config-if)# frame-relay local-dlci number
```

where *number* is the DLCI on the local interface to be used.

e-LAB ACTIVITY 13.8

keepalive

In this activity, you demonstrate how to use the **keepalive** command to enable the LMI mechanism for serial lines using Frame Relay encapsulation.

e-LAB ACTIVITY 13.9

Frame Relay Config

In this activity, you work through several tasks to configure basic Frame Relay.

SKILL BUILDER

Frame Relay Configuration

This lab focuses on the Frame Relay Packet Switching Protocol for connecting devices on a wide-area network (WAN).

Summary

- Frame Relay WAN technology provides a flexible method of connecting LANs over Frame Relay WAN links.
- Frame Relay provides a packet-switching data communication capability that is used across the interface between user devices (such as routers, bridges, and host machines) and network equipment (such as switching nodes).
- Frame Relay uses virtual circuits to establish connections across the WAN.

The main purposes of the LMI process are to

- Determine the operational status of the various PVCs that the router knows about
- Transmit keepalive packets to ensure that the PVC stays up and does not shut down due to inactivity
- Tell the router what PVCs are available
- The Inverse ARP mechanism allows the router to automatically build the Frame Relay map
- The router next-hop address determined from the routing table must be resolved to a Frame Relay DLCI

Frame Relay can divide a single physical WAN interface into multiple subinterfaces.

- Split horizon reduces routing loops by not allowing a routing update received on one physical interface to be advertised through the same physical interface.

Washington School District Project Task: Frame Relay

In this chapter, you learned concepts and configuration processes that will help you implement a Frame Relay data link in the Washington School District network. You will design and implement the Frame Relay link to the Internet per the TCS Overview. This is the final step in the district network implementation. As part of the configuration and implementation, you need to complete the following tasks:

1. Describe how Frame Relay will be inserted in the WAN implementation, what speed will be required, and the benefits of Frame Relay.

2. Document the insertion of Frame Relay in the WAN implementation, including:

   ■ DLCI numbers

   ■ The value of the CIR

   ■ A description of all data communication equipment needed to accomplish implementation

3. Document the router commands needed to implement Frame Relay on the firewall router and how the router configuration changes.

4. Apply the CCNA Certification Exam Learning Objectives to your specific design. This requires a paragraph on how the learning objectives relate to your design. Learning objectives can be grouped together for the purpose of explanation. In this way, you study for the CCNA Certification Exam as you work through the case study.

CCNA Certification Exam Learning Objectives

NOTE

***are explicit CCNA Exam Objectives; unmarked are knowledge assumed by the exam.

General

■ Describe at what layer of the hierarchical WAN model an ISDN link should be installed.

OSI Model

■ Describe what layers of the OSI model Frame Relay standards address and their functions at these layers.

Frame Relay

■ Describe DLCIs and their functions in a Frame Relay implementation.

■ Describe LMIs and their function in a Frame Relay implementation.

■ Describe a permanent virtual circuit (PVC).

■ Describe connection-oriented network service and connectionless network service, and identify the key differences between them. ***

■ Describe committed information rate (CIR) and its function.

■ Describe forward explicit congestion notification (FECN) and its function.

■ Describe backward explicit congestion notification (BECN) and its function.

■ Describe discard eligibility (DE) and its function.

■ Recognize key Frame Relay terms and features. ***

■ List commands to configure Frame Relay LMIs, maps, and subinterfaces. ***

■ List commands to monitor Frame Relay operation in the router. ***

Check Your Understanding

Complete all the review questions to test your understanding of the topics and concepts covered in this chapter. Answers are listed in Appendix B, "Check Your Understanding Answer Key."

1. How does Frame Relay handle multiple conversations on the same physical connection?

   A. It duplexes the conversations.

   B. It multiplexes the circuits.

   C. It converts it to an ATM cell.

   D. Multiple conversations are not allowed.

2. Which of the following protocols are used by Frame Relay for error correction?

   A. Physical and data-link protocols

   B. Upper-layer protocols

   C. Lower-layer protocols

   D. Frame Relay does not do error correction

3. Which of the following does Frame Relay do to make its DLCIs global?

   A. It broadcasts them.

   B. It sends out unicasts.

   C. It sends out multicasts.

   D. DLCIs can't become global.

4. Which of the following is the data rate at which the Frame Relay switch agrees to transfer data?

   A. Committed information rate

   B. Data transfer rate

   C. Timing rate

   D. Baud rate

5. Which of the following assigns DLCI numbers?

   A. The end user

   B. The network root

C. A DLCI server

D. The service provider

6. DLCI information is included in which of the following fields of the Frame Relay header?

A. The Flag field

B. The Address field

C. The Data field

D. The Checksum field

7. Which of the following does Frame Relay use to keep PVCs active?

A. Point-to-point connections.

B. Windows sockets.

C. Keepalives.

D. They become inactive.

8. How does Frame Relay use Inverse ARP requests?

A. It maps IP addresses to MAC addresses.

B. It maps MAC addresses to IP addresses.

C. It maps MAC addresses to network addresses.

D. It uses the IP address-to-DLCI mapping table.

9. Which of the following does Frame Relay use to determine the next hop?

A. An ARP table

B. A RIP routing table

C. A Frame Relay map

D. A IGRP routing table

10. For which of the following does Frame Relay use split horizon?

A. To increase router updates.

B. To prevent routing loops.

C. To raise convergence times.

D. Frame Relay does not use split horizon.

11. Frame Relay operates at which of the following layers?

  A. Layer 2

  B. Layer 3

  C. Layer 4

  D. Layer 1

12. Which of the following statements is correct?

  A. The purpose of DTE equipment is to provide clocking and switching services in a network.

  B. Proposals for the standardization of the Frame Relay were initially presented to the CCITT.

  C. The older versions of Frame Relay are referred to collectively as the Local Management Interface (LMI).

  D. Switched virtual circuits are permanent connections used in situations requiring only sporadic data transfer between DTE devices across Frame Relay.

13. Which command is used (at the prompt) to enter the configuration mode for the serial interface for Frame Relay packet encapsulation?

  A. # Configure terminal

  B. # encapsulation frame-relay

  C. # frame-relay interface dlci *number*

  D. # interface serial0

14. If a **show interface serial 0** command is executed and if the message that appears is "Serial line is up, line protocol is up," the exact correct interpretation of the message is

  A. The connection is sending and receiving data.

  B. The LMI is configured correctly for the router.

  C. The Frame Relay connection is active.

  D. The central-site router is up and connected.

15. What does **show interfaces serial** do?

    A. Displays information about the multicast DLCI, the DLCIs used on the Frame-Relay configured serial interface, and the LMI DLCI used for the local-management interface.

    B. Displays the status of each configured connection and traffic statistics. This command is also useful for viewing the number of DECN and FECN packets received by the router.

    C. Displays the network-layer address and associated DLCI for each remote destination that the local router is connected to.

    D. Displays LMI traffic statistics. For example, it shows the number of status messages exchanged between the local router and the Frame Relay switch.

16. FECN and BECN are

    A. Error-checking mechanisms

    B. Congestion-notification mechanisms

    C. Flow-control mechanisms

    D. Keepalive mechanisms

17. Frame Relay virtual circuits

    A. Always require session establishment and tear down.

    B. Are only used when data transfer is sporadic.

    C. Provide permanent communication paths across Frame Relay networks.

    D. Provide a logical, bidirectional communication path between network devices.

18. Frame Relay implements a CRC to

    A. Perform flow control across virtual circuits

    B. Perform error-checking functions

    C. Manage address resolution functions

    D. Manage BECN and FECN operation

19. Which of the following is *not* one of the Frame Relay LMI extensions?

    A. Algorithmically generated MAC addresses

    B. Multicast groups

C. Global addressing

D. Virtual circuit status messages

Key Terms

BECN (backward explicit congestion notification)   A bit set by a Frame Relay network in frames traveling in the opposite direction of frames encountering a congested path. DTE devices receiving frames with the BECN bit set can request that higher-level protocols take flow control action as appropriate.

DLCI (data-link connection identifier)   A value that specifies a PVC or an SVC in a Frame Relay network. In the basic Frame Relay specification, DLCIs are locally significant (that is, connected devices can use different values to specify the same connection). In the LMI extended specification, DLCIs are globally significant (that is, DLCIs specify individual end devices).

FECN (forward explicit congestion notification)   A bit set by a Frame Relay network to inform DTE devices receiving the frame that congestion was experienced in the path from source to destination. DTE devices receiving frames with the FECN bit set can request that higher-level protocols take flow-control action as appropriate.

Frame Relay   An industry-standard, switched data link layer protocol that handles multiple virtual circuits using HDLC encapsulation between connected devices. Frame Relay is more efficient than X.25, the protocol for which it is generally considered a replacement.

LMI (Local Management Interface)   A set of enhancements to the basic Frame Relay specification. LMI includes support for a keepalive mechanism, which verifies that data is flowing; a multicast mechanism, which provides the network server with its local DLCI and the multicast DLCI; global addressing, which gives DLCIs global rather than local significance in Frame Relay networks; and a status mechanism, which provides an ongoing status report on the DLCIs known to the switch.

local access rate   The clock speed (port speed) of the connection (local loop) to the Frame Relay cloud. It is the rate at which data travels into or out of the network.

media   Plural of medium. The various physical environments through which transmission signals pass. Common network media include twisted-pair, coaxial, and fiber-optic cable, and the atmosphere (through which microwave, laser, and infrared transmission occurs). Sometimes called physical media.

PDN (public data network)   A network operated either by a government (as in Europe) or by a private concern to provide computer communications to the public, usually for a fee. PDNs enable small organizations to create a WAN without all the equipment costs of long-distance circuits.

PVC (permanent virtual circuit)   A virtual circuit that is permanently established. PVCs save bandwidth associated with circuit establishment and tear-down in situations where certain virtual circuits must exist all the time.

Objectives

After reading this chapter, you will be able to

- Describe the administrative side of network management
- Describe how to monitor a network
- Describe how to troubleshoot a network

Chapter 14

Network Management, Part II

Introduction

Now that you know how to design and build networks, you can perform tasks such as selecting, installing, and testing cable, along with determining where wiring closets will be located. However, network design and implementation are only part of what you need to know. You must also know how to maintain the network and keep it functioning at an acceptable level. This means that you must know how to troubleshoot problems when they arise. In addition, you must know when it is necessary to expand or change the network's configuration to meet the changing demands placed on it. In this chapter, you begin to learn about managing a network using techniques such as documenting, monitoring, and troubleshooting.

The Administrative Side of Network Management

The view of a network is important. A *network* is a collection of devices that interact with one another to provide communication. When a network administrator looks at a network, it should be looked at as a whole entity, not individual parts. In other words, each device in a network affects other devices and the network as a whole. As shown in Figure 14-1, nothing is isolated when it's connected to a network.

A good analogy for the network, in this instance, is an automobile. A car is a collection of parts that provide transportation. The engine provides power to move the car, but it doesn't work well if the fuel system goes bad or if the tires are flat. Brakes are also important components, but once again, without the hydraulic system, the brakes won't work and the car won't stop. Without all the components working together, the car does not perform its designated task: transportation.

The same is true with a network system. If the network server is set up to work with the IPX/SPX protocol and the hosts aren't, they won't be able to communicate. Also, if the system is working fine and the administrator changes the protocols on only one end, the system stops working. One device affects how other devices function. Another example is having a DNS server located at IP address 192.150.11.123. All your hosts are configured to find the DNS server at this IP address. If a network technician changes the IP address of the DNS server without changing the host identifiers, the hosts no longer have DNS services.

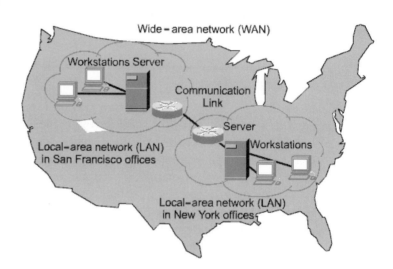

FIGURE 14-1
Basic network setup.

The important thing to remember when dealing with a network is to view it as a single unit instead of a group of individual connected devices. This also applies to the wide-area connections that are used when connecting to the Internet. Changes that are made to the routers at your location directly affect the efficiency and reliability of communication throughout the entire system.

Understanding and Establishing the Boundaries of the Network

In an enterprise network, it is important that the network staff members know their responsibilities. Is it the responsibility of the network staff to diagnose problems on a user's desktop, or is it simply to determine that a user's problem is not communication-related? Does the network staff's responsibility extend only as far as the horizontal cabling wall plate, or does that responsibility extend all the way to the NIC?

These definitions are important to a networking department because they affect the workload of each person and the cost of network services for the enterprise. The greater the responsibility of a network staff, the greater the resource cost. Imagine a restaurant owned and operated by a single individual. Only one person is responsible for all tasks, including cooking, serving, washing dishes, and paying the bills. The human-resource cost of the restaurant is relatively low, but possibilities for growth and expansion are limited until the owner hires cooks, waiters, bussers, and accountants. When responsibilities are divided, the restaurant can serve more people more efficiently. The trade-off, of course, is that resource costs have risen along with growth and expansion.

Just as the restaurant example showed, the job of network support can encompass all aspects of the network, or it can be limited to just certain components. These responsibilities need to be defined and enforced on a department-by-department basis. The key to understanding this relationship is that making the responsibility area too large can overburden the resources of the department, but making the area too small can make it difficult to effectively resolve the problems on the network.

Costs of a Network

Network administration encompasses many responsibilities, including cost analysis. This means determining not only the cost of network design and implementation, but also the cost of maintaining, upgrading, and monitoring the network. Determining the cost of network installation is not a particularly difficult task for most network administrators. Equipment lists and costs can be readily established; labor costs can be calculated using fixed rates. Unfortunately, the cost of building the network is just the beginning.

Some of the other cost factors that must be considered are the following:

- Network growth over time
- Technical and user training
- Repairs
- Software deployment

These cost factors are much more difficult to project than the cost of building the network. The network administrator must be able to look at historical and company growth trends to project the cost of growth in the network. A manager must look at new software and hardware to determine whether the company needs to implement them (and when), as well as to determine what staff training is needed to support these new technologies.

The cost of redundant equipment for mission-critical operations should also be added to the cost of maintaining the network. Think of running an Internet-based business that uses a single router to connect to the Internet. If that router fails, your company is out of business until you replace that router, which could cost the company thousands of dollars in lost sales. A wise network administrator might keep a spare router on the premises to minimize the time that the company is offline.

Error Report Documentation

As mentioned in the previous semester's materials, effective network management requires thorough documentation, so when problems arise, some form of error document should be generated (see Figure 14-2). This document is used to gather the basic information necessary to identify and assign a network problem, and it also provides a way of tracking the progress and eventual solution of the problem. Problem reports provide justification to senior management for hiring new staff, purchasing equipment, and providing additional training. This documentation also provides solutions to recurring problems that have already been resolved.

Computer Repair Worksheet One sheet per computer			
Computer Inv#:		**Date:**	
Type of problem:	Hardware:	Software:	
Problem Description:			
Warranty Coverage:	Yes:	No:	**Location of Repair:**
Repair description:			
Technician Name:			
Department Charged:			
Authorized By:			
Comments:			

FIGURE 14-2
Error report documentation.

All the material presented so far in this chapter deal with the nontechnical issues of network management. The rest of this chapter deals with the tools that are available to monitor and diagnose problems on a wide-area network (WAN).

Monitoring the Network

Although there are many reasons to monitor a network, the two primary reasons are to predict changes for future growth and to detect unexpected changes in network status. Unexpected changes might include things such as a router or switch failing, a hacker trying to gain illegal access to the network, or a communication link failure. Without the ability to monitor the network, an administrator can only react to problems as they occur instead of preemptively preventing these problems.

In the previous semester, network management topics were covered with primary focus on local-area networks. Monitoring a WAN involves many of the same basic management techniques as managing a local-area network (LAN). One of the major differences between WANs and LANs is the physical placement of equipment. The placement and use of monitoring tools becomes critical to the uninterrupted operation of the WAN.

Connection Monitoring

One of the most basic forms of connection monitoring takes place every day on a network. The process of users logging on to the network verifies that connections are working properly, or the networking department will soon be contacted. This is not the most efficient or preferable method of connection monitoring available, however. Simple programs can enable the administrator to enter a list of host IP addresses so that these addresses are periodically **ping**ed. If a connection problem exists, the program will alert the administrator by the **ping** output. This is an inefficient and primitive way to monitor the network, but it is better than nothing.

Another aspect of this type of monitoring is that it determines that there is a communication breakdown only somewhere between the monitoring station and the target device. The fault could be a bad router, switch, or network segment. The **ping** test indicates only that the connection is down; it does not indicate where the problem is.

Checking all the hosts on a WAN using this type of monitoring involves many resources. If the network has 3000 hosts on it, **ping**ing all the network devices and hosts can use a great deal of system resources. A better way is to **ping** just a few of the important hosts, servers, routers, and switches to verify their connectivity. These **ping** tests will not give true data unless workstations are always left on. Again, this method of monitoring should be used only if no other method is available.

Traffic Monitoring

Traffic monitoring is a more sophisticated method of network monitoring. It looks at the actual packet traffic on the network and generates reports based upon the network traffic. Programs, such as Microsoft Windows NT Network Monitor and Fluke's Network Analyzer, are examples of this type of software. These programs not only detect failing equipment, but they also determine whether a component is overloaded or poorly configured. The drawback to this type of program is that it normally works on a single segment at a time; if data needs to be gathered from other segments, the monitoring software must be moved to that segment. You can overcome this by using agents on the remote network segments (as shown in Figure 14-3). Equipment, such as switches and routers, can generate and transmit traffic statistics as part of their operating system. So, how is the data gathered and organized in one central location to be useful to the network administrator? The answer: the *Simple Network Management Protocol*.

FIGURE 14-3
SNMP layout.

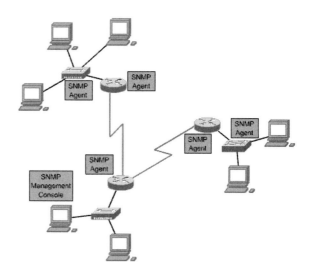

Simple Network Management Protocol

Simple Network Management Protocol (SNMP) is a protocol that allows management to transmit statistical data over the network to a central management console. SNMP is a component of the Network Management Architecture, which consists of four major components:

- **Management station**—The network manager's interface into the network system. It has the programs to manipulate data and control the network. The management station also maintains a Management Information Base (MIB) extracted from the devices under its management.

- **Management agent**—The component that is contained in the devices that are to be managed. Bridges, routers, hubs, and switches might contain SNMP agents to allow them to be controlled by the management station. The management agent responds to the management station in two ways. First, through polling, the management station requests data from the agent, and the agent responds with the requested data. Second, trapping is a data-gathering method designed to reduce traffic on the network and process on the devices being monitored. Instead of the management station polling the agents at specific intervals continuously, thresholds (top or bottom limits) are set on the managed device. If this threshold on the device is exceeded, the managed device sends an alert message to the management station. This eliminates the need to continuously poll all the managed devices on the network. Trapping is beneficial on networks with a large number of devices that need to be managed. It reduces the amount of SNMP traffic on the network to provide more bandwidth for data transfer.

■ **Management Information Base (MIB)**—Has a database structure and resides on each device that is managed. The database contains a series of objects, which are resource data gathered on the managed device. Some of the categories in the MIB include port interface data, TCP data, and ICMP data.

■ **Network management protocol**—Used is SNMP. SNMP is an application layer protocol designed to communicate data between the management console and the management agent. It has three key capabilities: the capability to GET the management console retrieving data from the agent, to PUT the management console setting object values on the agent, and to TRAP the agent notifying the management console of significant events.

The key word to remember in Simple Network Management Protocol is *simple*. When SNMP was developed, it was designed to be a short-term system that would later be replaced. But just like TCP/IP, it has become one of the major standards in Internet/intranet management configurations. Over the last few years, enhancements have been added to SNMP to expand its monitoring and management capabilities. One of the greatest enhancements to SNMP is called *Remote Monitoring (RMON)*. RMON extensions to SNMP give you the ability to look at the network as a whole instead of looking at individual devices.

Remote Monitoring

Probes gather remote data in Remote Monitoring (RMON). A probe has the same function as an SNMP agent. A probe has RMON capabilities; an agent does not. When working with RMON, as with SNMP, a central management console is the point of data collection. An RMON probe is located on each segment of the network monitored. These probes can be dedicated hosts, resident on a server, or can be included in a standard networking device, such as a router or a switch. These probes gather the specified data from each segment and relay it to the management console. Redundant management consoles provide two major benefits to network management processes. First is the capability to have more than one network administrator in different physical locations monitor and manage the same network (for example, one in New York and one in San Jose). Second is the all-important concept of redundancy. Having two or more management consoles means that if one console fails, the other console still can be used to monitor and control the network until the first console is repaired (see Figure 14-4).

The RMON extension to the SNMP protocol creates new categories of data. These categories add more branches to the MIB database. Each of the major categories is explained in the following list:

■ **The Ethernet Statistics Group**—Contains statistics gathered for each monitored subnetwork. These statistics include counters (incremental that start from zero) for bytes, packets, errors, and frame size. The other type of data reference is an index table. The table identifies each monitored Ethernet device, which allows counters to be kept for each individual Ethernet device. The Ethernet Statistics Group provides a view of the overall load and health of a subnetwork by measuring different types of errors, including CRC, collisions, and over- and undersized packets.

FIGURE 14-4
Network with dual management consoles.

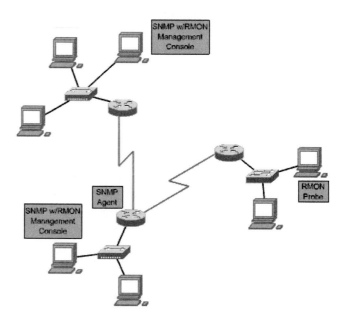

- **The History Control Group**—Contains a data table that records samples of the counters in the Ethernet Statistics Group over a specified period of time. The default time set up for sampling is every 30 minutes (1800 seconds), and the default table size is 50 entries, giving a total of 25 hours of continuous monitoring. As the history is created for the specified counter, a new entry is created in the table at each sample interval until the limit of 50 is reached. Then as each new entry is created, the oldest entry in the table is deleted. These samples provide a baseline of the network and can be used to compare against the original baseline to resolve problems or to update the baseline as the network changes.

- **The Alarm Group**—Uses user-specified limits called *thresholds*. If the data counters being monitored cross the thresholds, a message or alarm is sent to the specified people. This process, known as an *error trap*, can automate many functions of network monitoring. Instead of having a person constantly and directly monitoring the network or waiting for a user to identify a problem with the network, the network process itself can send messages to the network personnel because of a failure or, more importantly, an impending failure. This is an important component of preemptive troubleshooting.

■ **The Host Group**—Contains counters maintained about each host discovered on the subnetwork segment. Some of the counter categories maintained are packets, octets, errors, and broadcasts. Types of counters associated with each of the previously mentioned items could be, for example, total packets, packets received, and packets sent, along with many counters specific to the type of item.

■ **The Host TOPN Group**—Used to prepare reports about a group of hosts that top a statistical list based on a measured parameter. The best way to describe this group is by example. A report could be generated for the top ten hosts generating broadcasts for a day. Another report might be generated for the most packets transmitted during the day. This category provides an easy way to determine who and what type of data traffic most occupies the selected subnetwork.

■ **The Matrix Group**—Records the data communication between two hosts on a subnetwork. This data is stored in the form of a matrix (a multidimensional table). One of the reports that can be generated from this category is which host utilizes a server. Reorganizing the matrix order can create other reports. For example, one report might show all users of a particular server, while another report shows all the servers used by a particular host.

■ **The Filter Group**—Provides a way that a management console can instruct an RMON probe to gather selected packets from a specific interface on a particular subnetwork. This selection is based on the use of two filters, the data and the status filter. The data filter is designed to match or not match particular data patterns, which allows for the selection of that particular data. The status filter is based on the type of packet looked at, such as a CRC packet or a valid packet. These filters can be combined using logical "and" and "or" to create very complicated conditions. The filter group enables the network administrator to selectively look at different types of packets to provide better network analysis and troubleshooting.

■ **The Packet Capture Group**—Allows the administrator to specify a method to use to capture packets that have been selected by the Filter Group. By capturing specified packets, the network administrator can look at the exact detail for packets that meet the basic filter. The packet group also specifies the quantity of the individual packet captured and the total number of packets captured.

- **The Event Group**—Contains events generated by other groups in the MIB database. An example is a counter exceeding the threshold for that counter specified in the Alarm Group. This action would generate an event in the Event Group. Based on this event, an action could be generated, such as issuing a warning message to all the people listed in the Alarm Groups parameters or creating a logged entry in the event table. An event is generated for all comparison operations in the RMON MIB extensions.

- **The Token Ring Group**—Contains counters specific to Token Ring networks. Although most of the counters in the RMON extensions are not specific to any type of data-link protocol, the Statistics and History Groups are. They are particularly attuned to the Ethernet protocol. The Token Ring Group creates counters necessary to monitor and manage Token Ring networks using RMON.

Remember that RMON is an extension to the SNMP protocol. Specifically, this means that although RMON enhances the operation and monitoring capabilities of SNMP, SNMP is still required for RMON to operate on a network. As a last point, it is important to mention that there are later revisions of both SNMP and RMON, labeled as SNMPv2 and RMON2. This curriculum does not cover all the new capabilities of these versions.

Troubleshooting Networks

Problems happen! Even when the network is monitored, the equipment is reliable, and the users are careful, things will go wrong. The test of a good network administrator is the ability to analyze, troubleshoot, and correct problems under pressure of a network failure that causes company downtime. The suggestions in this section review troubleshooting techniques and offer other tools for troubleshooting a network. This is a review of previous and some additional techniques for troubleshooting a network. As stated previously, these techniques can be the best tools in curing network problems.

The first and most important thing in troubleshooting networks is to use your engineering journal and to take notes. Note-taking can define a clear path to diagnosing a problem. It can tell you what you have already tried and what effect that had on the problem. This can be extremely valuable to the troubleshooter so that previous attempts at resolving the problem won't be needlessly repeated. Taking notes is also valuable if the problem is handed off to another technician because it prevents that person from having to redo all that work. A copy of these notes should be included with the resolution of the problem when the trouble ticket on this job is completed. This provides a reference for similar problems that might happen.

Another essential element of preemptive troubleshooting is *labeling*. Label everything, including both ends of a horizontal cable run. This label should include not only the number of the cable but also where the other end is located and the usage of the cable, such as voice, data, or video. This type of label can be even more valuable than a wiring cut sheet when it comes to troubleshooting because it is located right where the unit is, not stuck in a drawer somewhere. Along with the wire labels, labeling each port on a hub, switch, or router as to location, purpose, and point of connection greatly improves the ease with which problems can be solved.

Finally, all other components attached to the network should also be labeled as to their location and purpose. With this type of labeling, all components can be located, and their purpose on the network can be easily defined. Proper labeling, used with the network documentation created when the network was built and updated, will give a complete picture of the network and its relationships. One other important reminder from the previous semester is that the documentation is useful only if it is current. All changes made to the network must be documented both on the devices or wire that is changed and in the paper documentation used to define the complete network.

The first step in network troubleshooting is to define the problem. This definition can be a consolidation of many different sources. One of the sources could be a trouble ticket or help desk report, which initially identifies a problem. Another source might be a phone conversation with the user where you discuss the problem to gather more information about it. Network monitoring tools can provide a more complete idea about the specific problem that needs to be resolved. Other users and your own observations will provide information. Evaluating all this information might give the troubleshooter a much clearer starting place to resolve the problem, rather than by working from any one source.

Troubleshooting Methods

The process of elimination and divide and conquer techniques are the most successful methods for network troubleshooting. The following scenarios explain these techniques.

The Process of Elimination Technique

Imagine that a user on your network calls the help desk to report that his computer can no longer connect to the Internet. The help desk fills out the error report form and forwards it to you, the network support department.

You call and talk to the user, who tells you that he has done nothing differently to get to the Internet. You check the hardware logs for the network and find out that the user's computer was upgraded last night. Your first hypothesis is that the computer's network drivers must be incorrectly configured. You go to the machine and check the network configuration information on the computer. It seems to be correct, so you **ping** the server on that subnet. It doesn't connect (see Figure 14-5).

FIGURE 14-5
Bad ping output.

```
C:\WINDOWS>ping 110.0.1.1

Pinging 110.0.1.1 with 32 bytes of data:

Request timed out.

Request timed out.

Request timed out.

Request timed out.

Ping statistics for 110.0.1.1:
        Packets: Sent = 4, Received = 0, Lost = 4 (100% loss),
Approximate round trip times in milli-seconds:
        Minimum = 0ms, Maximum = 0ms, Average = 0ms
```

The next solution is to check to see if the workstation cable is plugged in. You check both ends of the cable and try **ping**ing the server again.

Next, you **ping** 127.0.0.1, the loopback address for the computer (see Figure 14-6). The **ping** is successful, so that eliminates a possible problem between the computer, the driver configuration, and the NIC card.

You decide that there might be a problem with the server for this network segment. Another networked computer is at the next desk, so you **ping** the server's address, and the result is successful (see Figure 14-7). This eliminates the server, the backbone, and the server's connection to the backbone as the problem.

You then go to the IDF and switch the port for the workstation, go back to the workstation, and try to **ping** the server again. The solution still does not work (see Figure 14-8). This narrows your search down to the horizontal cabling or the workstation patch cable. You go back to the IDF, put the cable back in the original switch port, get a new workstation patch cable, and return to the workstation.

FIGURE 14-6
Loopback ping
output.

```
C:\WINDOWS>ping 127.0.0.1

Pinging 127.0.0.1 with 32 bytes of data:

Reply from 127.0.0.1: bytes=32 time=1ms TTL=128

Reply from 127.0.0.1: bytes=32 time<10ms TTL=128

Reply from 127.0.0.1: bytes=32 time<10ms TTL=128

Reply from 127.0.0.1: bytes=32 time<10ms TTL=128

Ping statistics for 127.0.0.1:

    Packets: Sent = 4, Received = 4, Lost = 0 (0% loss),

Approximate round trip times in milli-seconds:

    Minimum = 0ms, Maximum = 1ms, Average = 0ms
```

FIGURE 14-7
Next ping
output.

```
C:\WINDOWS>ping 110.0.1.1

Pinging 110.0.1.1 with 32 bytes of data:

Reply from 110.0.1.1: bytes=32 time=1ms TTL=128

Reply from 110.0.1.1: bytes=32 time<10ms TTL=128

Reply from 110.0.1.1: bytes=32 time<10ms TTL=128

Reply from 110.0.1.1: bytes=32 time<10ms TTL=128

Ping statistics for 110.0.1.1:

    Packets: Sent = 4, Received = 4, Lost = 0 (0% loss),

Approximate round trip times in milli-seconds:

    Minimum = 0ms, Maximum = 1ms, Average = 0ms
```

You replace the workstation cable and try to **ping** the server again (see Figure 14-9). This time, you are successful, so the problem is fixed.

The last step is to document the problem solution on the error report form and return it to the help desk so that it can be logged as completed.

FIGURE 14-8
Bad ping output.

```
C:\WINDOWS>ping 110.0.1.1

Pinging 110.0.1.1 with 32 bytes of data:

Request timed out.
Request timed out.
Request timed out.
Request timed out.

Ping statistics for 110.0.1.1:
        Packets: Sent = 4, Received = 0, Lost = 4 (100% loss),
Approximate round trip times in milli-seconds:
        Minimum = 0ms, Maximum = 0ms, Average = 0ms
```

FIGURE 14-9
Next ping
output.

```
C:\WINDOWS>ping 110.0.1.1

Pinging 110.0.1.1 with 32 bytes of data:

Reply from 110.0.1.1: bytes=32 time=1ms TTL=128
Reply from 110.0.1.1: bytes=32 time<10ms TTL=128
Reply from 110.0.1.1: bytes=32 time<10ms TTL=128
Reply from 110.0.1.1: bytes=32 time<10ms TTL=128

Ping statistics for 110.0.1.1:
        Packets: Sent = 4, Received = 4, Lost = 0 (0% loss),
Approximate round trip times in milli-seconds:
        Minimum = 0ms, Maximum = 1ms, Average = 0ms
```

The Divide and Conquer Technique

Here, you combine two networks that work fine when not connected (see Figure 14-10), but when they are joined, the entire combined network fails (see Figure 14-11).

The first step to correct this problem is to divide the network back into two separate networks and verify that the two still operate correctly when separated. If this is true, then you remove all the subnet connections for one of the connecting routers and reconnect it to the other working network. Verify that it is still working correctly.

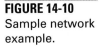

FIGURE 14-10
Sample network example.

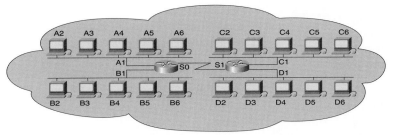

FIGURE 14-11
The network without the A and B subnetworks.

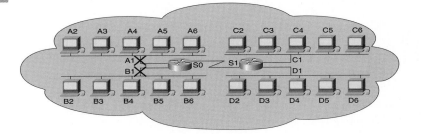

If the network is still functioning, add each of that router's subnetworks back into the router until the overall system fails (see Figure 14-12). Remove the last subnet that was added, and see if the whole network returns to its normal operation.

FIGURE 14-12
The network without the B subnetwork.

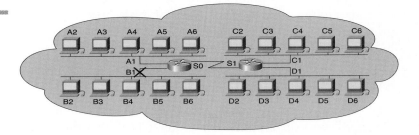

If the network is again functioning normally, remove the hosts from the network segment (see Figure 14-13), and replace them one at a time, again checking to see when the network fails (see Figure 14-14). When you find the offending device, remove it and verify that the network returns to normal.

FIGURE 14-13
The B network segment without the hosts.

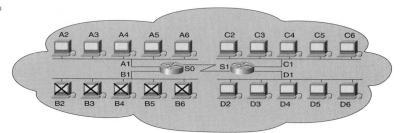

FIGURE 14-14
The B network segment without one host.

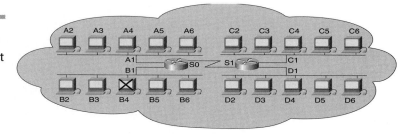

If the network still functions normally, you have isolated the faulty piece of equipment. It is now possible to troubleshoot this individual piece of equipment to find out why it was causing the entire network to crash. If nothing proves to be wrong with this device upon analysis, it might be that this device, in conjunction with another device on the opposite network, is causing the problem. To find the other end of the problem, you have to repeat the process used previously.

First, reconnect the host that caused the network to fail. Then, disconnect all the subnetworks from the other router. Check that the network has returned to operating status.

If the network is functioning again, add each of that router's subnetworks back into the router until the overall system fails. Remove the last subnet that was added before the failure and see if the whole network returns to its normal operation.

FIGURE 14-15
The network without the C and D subnetworks.

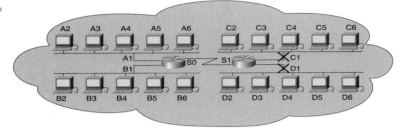

If the network again functions normally, remove the hosts from the network segment and replace them one at a time (see Figure 14-16), again checking to see when the network fails (see Figure 14-17). When you find the offending device, remove it and verify that the network returns to normal.

FIGURE 14-16
The C network segment without the hosts.

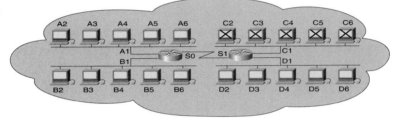

FIGURE 14-17
The C network segment without one host.

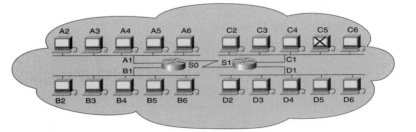

If the network still functions normally, you have isolated the other faulty piece of equipment. It is now possible to troubleshoot this individual piece of equipment to find out why it was causing the entire network to crash. If nothing proves to be wrong with this device upon analysis, compare the two hosts and find the reason for their conflict. By resolving this conflict, you will be able to reconnect both stations into the network and it will still function normally (see Figure 14-18).

FIGURE 14-18
The complete
functioning
network.

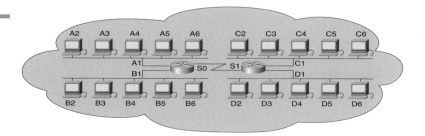

Software Tools

Along with the processes described previously, software tools are available for the network administrator to use to solve network connectivity problems. These tools can help in LAN troubleshooting, but they are especially helpful in a WAN troubleshooting situation.

We will look at the commands that are available to a network administrator in most client software packages. These commands include **ping**, **tracert** (traceroute), **telnet**, **netstat**, **ARP**, and **IPconfig** (WinIPcfg).

ping

ping sends ICMP echo packets to verify connections to a remote host. The output in Figure 14-19 displays whether the **ping** is successful. The output shows the number of packets responded to and the return time of the echo.

FIGURE 14-19
ping output.

```
C:\WINDOWS>ping    127.0.0.1

Pinging 127.0.0.1 with 32 bytes of data:

Reply from 127.0.0.1: bytes=32 time=1ms TTL=128
Reply from 127.0.0.1: bytes=32 time<10ms TTL=128
Reply from 127.0.0.1: bytes=32 time<10ms TTL=128
Reply from 127.0.0.1: bytes=32 time<10ms TTL=128

Ping statistics for 127.0.0.1:
        Packets: Sent = 4, Received = 4, Lost = 0 (0% loss),
Approximate round trip times in milli-seconds:
        Minimum = 0ms, Maximum = 1ms, Average = 0ms
```

```
C:\WINDOWS>ping    110.0.1.1

Pinging 110.0.1.1 with 32 bytes of data:

Request timed out.
Reply from 140.189.8.65: Destination host unreachable.
Request timed out.
Request timed out.

Ping statistics for 110.0.1.1:
        Packets: Sent = 4, Received = 1, Lost = 3 (75% loss),
Approximate round trip times in milli-seconds:
        Minimum = 0ms, Maximum = 0ms, Average = 0ms
```

```
ping [-t] [-a] [-n count] [-l length] [-f] [-i ttl] [-r count] destination
```

-t	**ping** until interrupted
-a	Resolves hostname and **ping** address
-n	Counts *x* number of pings
-l	Specifies length; send specified size echo packets
-f	Issues the "DO NOT FRAGMENT" command to gateways
-i	Here, **ttl** sets the TTL field
-r	Here, *count* records the route of the outgoing and returning packets
destination	Specifies the remote host to **ping**, by domain name or by IP address

tracert (traceroute)

tracert (**traceroute**) shows the route that a packet took to reach its destination. The output in Figure 14-20 shows the **trace** command.

FIGURE 14-20
tracert output.

```
C:\WINDOWS>tracert    192.31.7.130

Tracing route to CISCO.com [192.31.7.1301]
over a maximum of 30 hops:

    1    1 ms   <10 ms   <10 ms    198.150.221.254
    2    2 ms     1 ms     2 ms    198.150.15.252
    3    4 ms     2 ms     2 ms    198.150.12.1
    4   23 ms     4 ms     4 ms    UWMadison -sl-0-1.core.wiscnet.net [140.189.64.9]
    5    4 ms     5 ms     5 ms    UWMadisonISP-atml-0-3.core.wiscnet.net [140.189.8.65]
    6    8 ms    14 ms     8 ms    NChicagol-core0.nap.net [207.227.0.201]
    7    9 ms    10 ms    10 ms    4.0.5.233
    8   64 ms    64 ms    67 ms    p2-1.paloalto-nbr2.bbnplanet.net [4.24.7.18]
    9   67 ms    65 ms    69 ms    p0-0-0.paloalto-cr18.bbnplanet.net [4.0.3.86]
   10   66 ms    75 ms    75 ms    h1-0. cisco bbnplanet.net [4.1.142.238]
   11   66 ms    68 ms    70 ms    sty.cisco.com [192.31.7.39]
   12   67 ms    77 ms    76 ms    CISCO.COM [192.31.7.130]

Trace complete.
```

```
C:\WINDOWS>tracert 198.150.12.2

Tracing route to 198.150.12.2 over a maximum of 30 hops

    1    1 ms   <10 ms     1 ms    198.150.221.254
    2    1 ms     1 ms     2 ms    198.150.15.252
    3    *         *         *      Request timed out.
    4    *         *         *      Request timed out.
    5    *
C:\WINDOWS>
```

```
tracert [-d] [-h maximum_hops] [-j host-list] [-w timeout] target_name
```

-d	Specifies that IP addresses shouldn't be resolved to host names
-h	*max_hops*—Gives the maximum number of hops searched
-j	*host-list*—Specifies the loose source route
-w	Specifies the timeout to wait the number of milliseconds specified for each reply

telnet

This is a terminal emulation program that enables you to run interactive commands on the Telnet server. Until a connection is established, no data will pass; if the connection breaks, telnet will inform you. This is good for testing login configuration parameters to a remote host (see Figure 14-21).

FIGURE 14-21
telnet output.

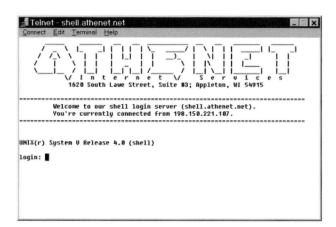

netstat

netstat displays protocol statistics and current TCP/IP network connections (see Figure 14-22).

FIGURE 14-22
netstat output.

```
C:\WINDOWS>netstat-a

Active Connections

    Prothocal Address          Foreign AddressState
    TCP matc-tag--:80          MATCNT:0          LISTENING
    TCP matc-tag--:135         MATCNT:0          LISTENING
    TCP matc-tag--:1025                  MATCNT:0              LISTENING
    TCP matc-tag--:1028                  MATCNT:0              LISTENING
    TCP matc-tag--:137         MATCNT:0          LISTENING
    TCP matc-tag--:138         MATCNT:0          LISTENING
    TCP matc-tag--:nbsession             MATCNT:0              LISTENING
    UDP matc-tag--:1028        *:*
    UDP matc-tag--:nbname      *:*
    UDP matc-tag--:nbdatagram            *:*
```

```
C:\WINDOWS>netstat-e
Interface Statistics

                              Received          Sent

    Bytes            4599931    364384056
    Unicast packets  348078     57374
    Non-unicast packets 109119 4774
    Discards         0          0
    Errors           0          0          0
    Unknown protocols           989407
```

`netstat [-a] [-e] [-n] [-s] [-p proto] [-r] [interval]`

-a	Displays all connections and listening ports. (Server-side connections are normally not shown.)
-e	Displays Ethernet statistics. This may be combined with the -s option.
-n	Displays addresses and port numbers in numerical form.
-p *proto*	Shows connections for the protocol specified by proto; proto may be **tcp** or **udp**. If used with the -s option to display per-protocol statistics, **proto** may be **tcp**, **udp**, or **ip**.
-r	Displays the contents of the routing table.
-s	Displays per-protocol statistics. By default, statistics are shown for TCP, UDP, and IP; the **-p** option may be used to specify a subset of the default.
interval	Redisplays selected statistics, pausing *interval* seconds between each display. Press CTRL+C to stop redisplaying statistics. If this is omitted, **netstat** will print the current configuration information once.

ARP

ARP gathers hardware addresses of local hosts and the default gateway. You can view the ARP cache and check for invalid or duplicate entries (see Figure 14-23).

FIGURE 14-23
ARP.

```
C:\WINDOWS>arp-a

Interface: 198.150.221.107 on Interface 0x2000002
  Internet Address    Physical Address    Type
  198.150.221.254     00-10-2f-0b-44-00   dynamic
```

```
arp -a [inet_addr] [-N [if_addr]]
arp -d inet_addr [if_addr]
arp -s inet_addr ether_addr [if_addr]
```

-a or -g	Displays the current contents of the ARP cache
-d	Deletes the entry specified by *inet_addr*
-s	Adds a static entry to the cache
-N	Displays the ARP entries for the specified physical address
inet_addr	Gives the IP address, in dotted decimal format
if_addr	Gives the IP address whose cache should be modified
ether_addr	Shows the MAC address in hex separated by hyphens

IPconfig (Windows NT)/WinIPcfg (Windows 95/98)

These Windows utilities display IP addressing information for the local network adapter(s) or a specified NIC (see Figure 14-24).

```
ipconfig [/all | /renew [adapter] | /release [adapter]]
```

/all	Shows all information about adapter(s)
/renew	Renews DHCP lease information for all local adapters if none is named
/release	Releases DHCP lease information disabling TCP/IP on this adapter

SKILL BUILDER

AUX Dial-Up

This lab focuses on the Frame Relay Packet Switching Protocol for connecting devices on a wide-area network (WAN).

FIGURE 14-24
WinIPcfg.

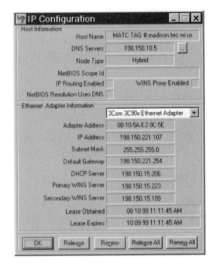

These are the tools that enable a network administrator to remotely monitor and control the network. It is important to implement the proper security when using SNMP and RMON so that the network is not violated.

Summary

Now that you have completed this chapter, you should understand the following:

- The administrative side of network management
- How to establish the boundaries of the network
- Costs of a network
- Error report documentation
- How to monitor the network
- Connection monitoring
- Traffic monitoring

■ Simple Network Management Protocol

■ Remote Monitoring (RMON)

■ Troubleshooting methods

■ Software tools for troubleshooting

Washington School District Project Task: Finishing the TCS

In this chapter, you learned about network management techniques that can help you run the individual school site LANs and the overall Washington School District WAN.

You now need to complete all TCS LAN and WAN tasks from Semesters 3 and 4. You should finish your Web-based portfolio solution to the TCS. You can use this as part of an "electronic resume" on a CD or a Web site to show your accomplishments. Be sure that you have completed the following tasks:

■ WAN requirements document

■ WAN physical topology

■ WAN logical topology, including IP addressing scheme

■ WAN electronics

■ WAN media

■ PPP implementation

■ ISDN implementation

■ Frame Relay implementation

■ Traffic flow and routing update analysis

■ WAN pros and cons

Check Your Understanding

1. Which protocol supports network management?

   A. SMTP

   B. NFS

   C. SNMP

   D. FTP

   E. IPX

2. To list your IP setting on a Windows NT computer, you would run the _____ command.

   A. ip

   B. ipconfig

   C. winipcfg

   D. show ip

   E. config

3. One troubleshooting method used in network troubleshooting is

   A. Loopback readout

   B. Divide and conquer

   C. Ping of death test

   D. Trace the fault

   E. Reset the server

4. If the server is set up using the Internet protocol, the clients must use which protocol to communicate with it?

   A. IPX

   B. UDP

   C. IP

   D. telnet

   E. HTTP

5. What is the most basic form of connection monitoring?

   A. WINIPCFG

   B. Tracert

   C. NetMonitor

   D. LanMeter

   E. Logging on

6. RMON is an extension of what protocol?

   A. SNMP

   B. UDP

   C. IPX

   D. PING

   E. SMTP

7. What does the *-n* protocol option stand for in the **ping** command?

   A. The network number of the ping area

   B. The no repeat option

   C. Count *x* number of pings

   D. Never stop until interrupted

   E. Nothing

8. How is the remote data gathered with RMON?

   A. Commands

   B. Tables

   C. Lists

   D. Probes

   E. User interaction

9. The cost of _____ equipment for mission critical operations needs to be added to the cost of maintaining the network.

   A. Redundant

   B. Expensive

   C. Mechanical

   D. Security

   E. Welding

Network+ Certification Exam Review

Introduction

This chapter provides a review of the topics that you need to know to successfully pass the Network+ certification exam. Each of the topics covered in this chapter correspond to the topics on the Network+ certification exam.

Basic Networking Topologies

In this section, you review the following topologies:

- Star
- Bus
- Mesh
- Ring

Star Topology

In a star topology, all devices are connected to a common central location, typically a hub or a switch (see Figure 15-1). When a node sends data to the central location, the central device retransmits the information and sends it to the destination. Because all cabling is connected to a central device, if one link fails, only that portion of the network will fail. The rest of the network will not be affected. However, if the central device fails, the entire network will also fail. A star topology can have a maximum of 1024 nodes on a LAN and is commonly used for 10BaseT (IEEE 802.3) and 100BaseTX (IEEE 802.3u) Ethernet.

Advantages of star topologies include reliability and ease of maintenance and installation. Monitoring and troubleshooting can be maintained at the central device, providing easier maintenance. Star topologies allow for greater reliability because each node is connected to the central device by a segment. If one segment breaks, only that node loses access to the network, so the rest of the network is not affected. Because each node is connected to the central device, star topologies also allow for an easy network layout, providing the network administrator easier installation over the other topologies. A disadvantage of this topology is cost. With each device being connected to the central location, more cabling is required than with other topologies. In addition, there is the cost of the central device.

FIGURE 15-1
Star topology.

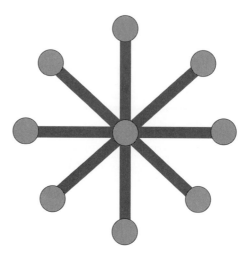

Bus Topology

A bus topology connects multiple devices onto one main cable and is sometimes referred to as a backbone, trunk, or segment (see Figure 15-2). Terminators must be connected at each end of the topology to absorb any reflected signals. If coaxial cable is used without terminators, reflected signals will echo across the network, causing the entire network to be unusable.

FIGURE 15-2
Bus topology.

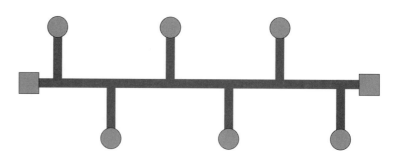

Advantages of a bus topology are cost and ease of installation. Because this topology uses a simple cable layout, it costs less and is easier to implement than the other topologies.

A disadvantage is that if a cable segment or the backbone breaks or fails, the network will fail. Another disadvantage is that only one node can transmit data onto the network at a time. If two or more nodes attempt to send data at the same time, a collision will occur; this will require a recovery procedure, thereby slowing down the network. After the collision has occurred, all the data must be re-sent. A process called *carrier sense multiple access collision detect* (CSMA/CD) prevents the occurrence of another collision. CSMA/CD is a process in which each node waits its turn to retransmit data.

Mesh Topology

Normally used for WANs, a mesh topology connects every device on the network and provides a path to and from each device (see Figure 15-3). An advantage is that because all the devices are connected to each other, the network has a higher fault tolerance and reliability. If a cable segment breaks along the network, the devices will find the quickest way to reroute the packet to its destination. Therefore, the data will most often always reach its destination.

FIGURE 15-3
Complete mesh
topology.

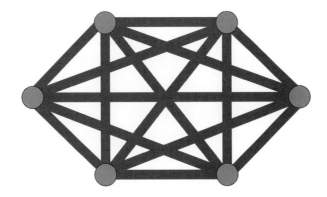

Disadvantages of this topology are cost and difficulty in management. Because there are numerous connections to and from each device, there is a large number of cabling requirements, causing a mesh topology to be somewhat expensive. If a segment breaks on the network, with the complex design of the mesh topology, finding the exact problem location can be very difficult. Therefore, maintaining the network can be very complex.

Ring Topology

In ring topologies, each device on the network is connected with two other devices (see Figure 15-4). There is no beginning or end of the cable. This particular topology forms a complete ring. The devices on this network use a transceiver to communicate with their neighbors. Transceivers also act like repeaters to regenerate each signal as it is passed through the device.

FIGURE 15-4
Ring topology.

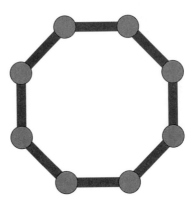

Advantages include better performance because each device receives a turn to transmit signals and has equal access to the network. An additional advantage is that the signal is regenerated by each device it passes through, thereby preventing the signal from degrading.

A disadvantage of using this topology is that if one device on the cable fails, the entire network will also fail. Locating the failure can sometimes be difficult. Another disadvantage is that if any changes are made to the network, including adding to or moving devices, the disruption will cause the network to fail.

Segments and Backbones

This section reviews the terms *segments* and *backbones*.

Segments

In networking, the term *segment* has several meanings. First, in a narrow sense, it can refer to a trunk (main line) of cabling, which connects devices to a concentration device (hubs, MAUs, or switches). Second, *segment* can also refer to a logical grouping of devices that communicate within a given subnet separated ("segmented") by bridges, switches, or routers. The term *segment* is sometimes synonymous with a collision or broadcast domain (see Figure 15-5).

Backbones

The term *backbone* also has several meanings within networking. First, a backbone is most often the main cable (or trunk) to which all nodes and devices connect. Second, backbones are the foundations of both LANs and WANs where servers, routers, and concentrating devices (such as switches and hubs) are connected by a high-bandwidth connection. Because of its desirable electrical characteristics, such as immunity to noise and grounding problems, optical fiber is now more commonly chosen for backbone cabling than coaxial cable and UTP.

FIGURE 15-5
Segmenting collision domains.

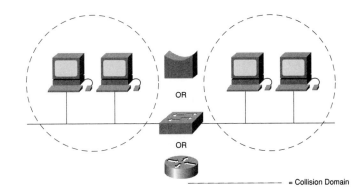

OR

OR

———————————— = Collision Domain

The Major Network Operating Systems

In this section, you review Microsoft Windows NT/2000, Novell NetWare, and UNIX.

Microsoft Windows NT/2000 Server

An extremely popular local-area network operating system is Microsoft Windows NT/2000 Server, which uses a graphical user interface (GUI) that looks very similar to that of the other Windows desktops. However, Windows NT/2000 is designed with different utilities to manage servers. Windows NT uses the User Manager for Domains to administer domain users and group administration programs, and it allows administrators to choose from two file systems: New Technology File System (NTFS) or File Allocation Table (FAT).

Novell NetWare

Novell NetWare, also an extremely popular local-area network operating system, is designed to support LANs such as Ethernet and Token Ring networks. To manage the resources available on the network, NetWare uses the NetWare Directory Services (NDS), in which both a physical and a logical file system are used to arrange files and dates. NetWare's primary file system is a combination of the File Allocation Table (FAT) and the Directory Entry Table (DET). Layer 3 protocols used in this OS are the Internetwork Package Exchange (IPX) protocol and the Internet Protocol (IP).

UNIX

Developed at the University of California, Berkeley, UNIX was designed for database management. UNIX is an important network operating system because its key features include multitasking, multiusers, and networking capabilities. UNIX has the capability to operate multiple processes while users are working with applications on the same machine. Multiple versions of UNIX exist, including Sun Microsystems' Solaris, IBM's AIX, Silicon Graphics' IRIX, Linux, and Hewlett-Packard's HP-UX. However, the operation of all versions is similar.

Windows NT Features

Windows NT has the capability to support and effectively function with a number of client software, including the following: MS-DOS, Windows 9x, Windows 3.11 for Workgroups, Windows NT Workstation 4.0, OS/2, LAN Manager, Macintosh, NetWare, Intel, Windows 2000 and UNIX clients. However, of these programs, Windows NT Workstation best serves Windows NT Server because of their common NTFS file system and system management architecture.

Windows 9x clients must have Client for Microsoft Networks installed to connect to an NT server, and must have Microsoft Client for NetWare Networks installed for proper connection to a NetWare server. However, there are two disadvantages when a Windows client connects to a Novell server: The TCP/IP protocol cannot be used to connect to a NetWare server, causing slower access, and Microsoft Client for NetWare Networks cannot understand the directory service and security system for NetWare v4.0 and v5.0. Novell Client 32 allows Windows 9x clients to connect to the NetWare server using either IPX/SPX or TCP/IP; it also gives full support for the NDS. The current version of Novell Client 32 is 3.3.

Novell NetWare Features

Novell NetWare works well with many operating systems, including DOS, Windows 3.11, Windows 9x, and Windows NT Workstation.

Prior to its 5.0 release, Novell NetWare was mainly a text-based network operating system, with a few functions administered from the server console and most administrative functions executed on a client workstation (which was logged onto the server). NetWare 3.x primarily used IPX/SPX as its protocol, while the newer versions NetWare 4.x and 5.x use TCP/IP or IPX/SPX as their protocols. Similar to the Windows platforms, NetWare also uses GUI for its applications.

UNIX Features

UNIX is a command-line–driven platform, which is accessed by terminal sessions from other operating systems or on the same machine. Windows 95 clients can access UNIX using terminal emulation programs. UNIX clients, such as Sparc (Solaris) workstations from Sun Microsystems, work best with their manufacturer's proprietary NOS.

A recent relative of UNIX is Linux, which was developed as an open source operating system. Developers who want to modify the platform can purchase or download a copy of the source code and modify it based on their own needs.

Windows NT Directory Services

In the not too distant past, users who wanted access to resources on a group of servers needed an account and password on each server. With Windows NT, the domain controller allows users to have only one account and password, and yet have access to all servers on the domain.

The domain controller manages user access to the network and stores the security account information into a common security database, called the *Security Access Manager (SAM)*. The SAM verifies passwords, enables users to store and secure information, and searches for information on the network. When a user has successfully logged into the database, the domain controller issues an access token to the user. Access tokens allow users to access any service without having to type in each password.

Novell NetWare Directory Services

Novell NetWare 3.*x* relies on a security database, called the *Bindery,* that uses only IPX/SPX. NetWare 4.*x* and 5.*x* rely on Novell Directory Services (NDS), which is a built-in directory service that uses TCP/IP or IPX/SPX. NDS is based on the Internet Directory Standard X.500, which uses a resource called the NDS tree to organize all user and resource information. The NDS tree allows users to log into the network and access any of the resources that are available.

UNIX Directory Services

The UNIX directory services use a file system called the *Network File System (NFS)*. This NFS grants users permission to certain parts of the file system and controls the security of the UNIX systems. Because the shared files are transparent, NFS users can view and edit files on other UNIX hosts.

UNIX systems running SAMBA communicate using Server Message Block (SMB). When UNIX connects to the Windows network with SMB, Microsoft clients and servers view UNIX system as if it were another Windows device. UNIX also uses DNS to resolve transport layer names into logical network addresses.

IP, IPX, and NetBEUI: Associating Them with Their Functions

In this section, you review IP, IPX, and NetBEUI, along with their associated functions.

Internet Protocol

Internet Protocol (IP) is a routable protocol that works at the network layer of the OSI model and the Internet layer of the TCP/IP model. IP provides packet delivery and addressing for source and destination. Connectionless IP and the connection-oriented TCP are the de facto protocol standards of the Internet.

Because IP is a connectionless service, it is unreliable and does not guarantee the delivery of data or the order in which it was sent. Working with IP at Layer 4, the connection-oriented protocol TCP provides reliable and orderly delivery of packets.

Internetwork Packet Exchange

Internetwork Packet Exchange (IPX) is a connectionless routable protocol that also works at the network layer of the OSI model. IPX is the network layer protocol used by Novell NetWare.

IPX is very efficient and scalable, has no performance issues, contains no addressing problems, and is capable of being used with Ethernet (1500-byte packet size) and Token Ring (4000-byte packet size) networks using the proper network interface card (NIC) drivers. However, IPX is largely being replaced by the IP protocol.

NetBIOS Extended User Interface

The NetBIOS Extended User Interface (NetBEUI), which is commonly used for smaller LANs, is a nonroutable protocol that operates at the network and transport layers of the OSI model. Because NetBEUI is a nonroutable protocol, it is quick and easy to configure. Configuration is minimal after NetBEUI is installed and bound to a network adapter. However, because it is nonroutable, it cannot participate in Internet communications and therefore is limited in its usefulness and scalability.

RAID Overview

A technology called *Redundant Array of Inexpensive Disks (RAID)* was created to minimize data loss when disk problems occur. Each RAID level is defined by differences in performance, reliability, and cost.

Mirroring

RAID 1, disk mirroring, is a common way to back up data. All information written to the first drive is also written to the mirror drive, making the two disk drives identical. A disk controller card connects to both the drives and writes the data in parallel to each of them. This single controller card creates a single point of failure for disk mirroring. An advantage is redundancy; however, disadvantages are cost and the amount of disk space required.

Duplexing

RAID 1, duplexing, provides fault tolerance for both data and the disk controller. Duplexing is disk mirroring with a separate controller for each drive. With its second controller, duplexing has improved fault tolerance over mirroring, and it is much faster than mirroring because the data can be written to both drives at the same time. The main disadvantage is the cost of the second controller card.

Striping

RAID 2, striping data, is a process in which the data is spread out onto a number of disks. A minimum of three hard disks is needed, with three or more different drives sharing the data. With more than one disk sharing the data, the process makes the input/output (I/O) faster. Parity is also an option with data striping. Striping with parity works on RAID 5, which provides redundancy by interweaving data onto several drives and has a distributed checksum for parity.

Volumes

Volumes is a method in which there are at least two volumes on the server, on either the same physical disk or multiple disks. Normally, two volumes are used: a system volume and a data volume. The system volume holds all the operating system files, which allow the network to run. The data volume holds all the varieties of user data. Because of volumes, more physical disks can be added without administrative work being done to reorganize the logical structure of the storage.

Tape Backups

One of the oldest and cheapest ways to store data is by using a magnetic tape. Three types of magnetic tapes can be used to store data: quarter-inch tape (QIC), digital audio tape (DAT), and digital linear tapes (DLT).

QIC, which is rarely used these days, is used mostly for smaller networks and was one of the first standards used for PC backups. The earliest QIC had the capability to hold up to 40 MB of data; the most recent QIC has a capacity of up to 2 GB.

DAT, which was originally used for audio and video, provides digital recording for tape backups. DAT uses a SCSI connection and is used in most medium-sized networks; it has a maximum capacity of 24 GB.

DLT, a form of tape backup that is becoming a more popular method, has the capacity of up to 80 GB. Although this method is expensive, it is very fast and reliable. Like DAT, DLT uses a SCSI connection.

The OSI Model

In this section, you review the OSI model and the protocols, services, functions that pertain to each layer.

Application Layer

The application layer (the seventh layer) of the OSI model provides network services, which are closest to the user. Programs such as Internet Explorer, Netscape Communicator, Eudora Pro, and other end-user application software are examples of services provided by the application layer to the user. This layer establishes communication with intended partners and synchronizes agreement on procedures for error recovery and control of data integrity.

The protocols that function at this layer are Server Message Block (SMB) and Network Control Program (NCP).

Services that provide network access include these:

- Telnet and File Transfer Protocol (FTP)
- Trivial File Transfer Protocol (TFTP)
- Network File System (NFS)
- Simple Network Management Protocol (SNMP)
- Simple Mail Transfer Protocol (SMTP)
- Hypertext Transfer Protocol (HTTP)

Devices that function up to this layer include hosts and gateways.

Presentation Layer

The presentation layer ensures that the information that the application layer of one system sends is readable by the application layer of another system. If necessary, the presentation layer translates among multiple data formats by using a common format.

The presentation layer also provides data encryption to ensure protection as data journeys through the network. When the encrypted data is received, it decrypts and formats the message before passing it along to the application layer.

Protocols include NCP. Data formats include ASCII, EBCDIC, encrypted, JPEG, GIF, MPEG, QuickTime, Flash, WAV, AVI, and MP3. Devices functioning up to this layer include hosts and gateways.

Session Layer

The session layer establishes, manages, and terminates sessions between two communicating hosts, and provides its services to the presentation layer. It also synchronizes dialogue between the two hosts and manages their data exchange. The session layer also offers provisions for efficient data transfer, class of service, security authorization, and exception reporting of session layer, presentation layer, and application layer problems.

Three types of dialogs used in the session layer are simplex, half-duplex, and full-duplex. A simplex dialog allows information to flow from one device to another without requiring a reply transmission.

A half-duplex dialog, which is also known as a two-way alternate (TWA) transmission, allows data to flow in two directions from one device to another; however, each device cannot send a transmission until the previous signal has been completely received. When one device sends a transmission and requires the destination device to respond, the destination device must wait until the initial transmission is complete before it can send its response.

A full-duplex dialog, which is also known as a two-way simultaneous (TWS) transmission, allows devices to send data to another device without having to wait until the wire is clear. When a device transmits a signal, the destination device does not have to wait until the signal is complete to send a reply to the source device. Full-duplex enables two-way traffic to occur simultaneously during one communication session. A telephone is an example of a full-duplex dialog.

Protocols include NFS, Structured Query Language (SQL), Remote Procedure Call (RPC), X-Window System, AppleTalk Session Protocol (ASP), and Digital Network Architecture Session Control Protocol (DNA SCP). Devices functioning up to this layer include hosts and gateways.

Transport Layer

The transport layer segments data from the sending host's system and reassembles the data into a data stream on the receiving host's system. The boundary between the session layer and the transport layer can be thought of as the boundary between media-layer protocols and host-layer protocols. Whereas the application, presentation, and session layers are concerned with application issues, the lower three layers are concerned with data transport issues.

The transport layer attempts to provide a data transport service that shields the upper layers from transport implementation details. Specifically, the main concern of the transport layer includes issues such as how reliable transport between two hosts is accomplished. In providing communication service, the transport layer establishes, maintains, and properly terminates virtual circuits. In providing reliable service, transport error detection and recovery, and information flow controls are used.

When the transport layer receives data from the upper layers, it breaks up the information into segments (smaller pieces) to be sent through the lower levels of the OSI model and then to the destination device.

Protocols used in this layer are listed here:

- Sequenced Package Exchange (SPX)
- Transmission Control Protocol (TCP)
- User Datagram Protocol (UDP)
- NetBIOS Extended User Interface (NetBEUI)

Services used at this layer use TCP to provide connection-oriented communication with error-free delivery and UDP to provide connectionless communications without guaranteed packet delivery (unreliable delivery). Devices functioning up to this layer include hosts and gateways.

Network Layer

The network layer is a complex layer that provides connectivity and path selection between two host systems that may be geographically separated. Layer 3 can be remembered as addressing, path selection, routing, and switching.

Protocols functioning on this layer include these routed protocols:

- IPX
- IP

The following Layer 3 protocols also are involved:

- Internet Control Message Protocol (ICMP)
- Address Resolution Protocol (ARP)

- Reverse Address Resolution Protocol (RARP) Routing Protocols
- Routing Information Protocol (RIP)
- Internet Gateway Routing Protocol (IGRP)
- Enhanced IGRP (EIGRP)
- Open Shortest Path First (OSPF)
- Exterior Gateway Protocol (EGP)
- Internet Management Group Protocol (IGMP)

The following are grouped with routed protocols but are labeled as non-routable protocols:

- NetBEUI
- DecNET

Services include software and hardware addressing, packet routing between hosts and networks, resolution of hardware and software addresses, and reports of packet delivery. Devices functioning up to this layer include routers and bridging routers (brouters).

Data Link Layer

The data link layer provides reliable transit of data across a physical link. In so doing, the data link layer is concerned with physical (as opposed to logical) addressing, network topology, network access, error notification, ordered delivery of frames, and flow control. Layer 2 can be remembered by frames and media access control.

Ethernet CSMA/CD also operates at this layer to determine which devices should transmit at a given time to avoid collisions. The NIC is also responsible for CSMA/CD on Ethernet. If two or more devices attempt to transmit signals at the same time, a collision will occur. CSMA/CD instructs the device to wait a given amount of time before transmitting another signal to avoid another collision.

The data link layer is broken down into two sublayers by the IEEE 802 standards: the Logical Link Control (LLC) sublayer and the Media Access Control (MAC) sublayer. The LLC sublayer (IEEE 802.2) establishes and maintains communication with other devices and provides connectivity with servers when data is being transferred. LLC manages link control and defines service access points (SAPs).

The MAC sublayer maintains a table of physical addresses of devices. Each device is assigned and must have a unique MAC address if the device is to participate on the network. For example, the MAC address is similar to the individual's physical residence address, which the post office uses to deliver snail mail.

Protocols used at this layer include High-Level Data Link Control (HDLC) for WAN connections, including synchronous and asynchronous transmissions. The LLC protocol (IEEE 802.2) provides flow control at this layer.

Technologies that operate at this layer include more than 18 varieties of Ethernet (specified in the IEEE 802.3 and other standards), Token Ring (IEEE 802.5), and other LAN technologies that rely on frames. Communications with the NIC are also provided.

Devices functioning up to this layer include NICs, bridges, and switches. Although routers and brouters are classified as Layer 3 devices, to perform their functions, they must operate at Layer 1 and Layer 2 as well.

Physical Layer

The physical layer (Layer 1) defines the electrical, mechanical, procedural, and functional specifications for activating, maintaining, and deactivating the physical link between end systems. Such characteristics as voltage levels, timing of voltage changes, physical data rates, maximum transmission distances, physical connectors, and other similar attributes are defined by physical layer specifications.

The physical layer is responsible for moving bits of data through physical media. Data, in the form of ones and zeros, is turned into electrical signals, pulses of light, or wireless signals. These signals are placed on the copper cables or optical fibers, or are emitted as wireless signals, using a NIC. When receiving data from the network, the NIC turns the electrical signals, pulses of light, or wireless signals back into ones and zeros to be sent up the hierarchy of the OSI model.

Protocols are the cabling, signaling, and connection standards. Services include Ethernet, Token Ring, FDDI, and other LAN technologies. Devices that function at this layer are repeaters, multiport repeaters (also called hubs), media access units (MAUs), and transceivers (transmitter/receivers for converting one signal type into another).

Networking Media

In this section, you review Category 3, Category 5, fiber optic, UTP, and STP cable.

Coaxial Cable

Coaxial cable is braided, grounded strands of wire that can provide some shielding and noise immunity (see Figure 15-6). However, the installation and the termination of the cable itself can be costly. Coaxial cabling, which uses connectors called BNC (British Naval Connector or Bayonet Nut Connector) is used, in forms of Ethernet, thicknet and thinnet, and in the older LAN technology, ARCnet, and cable TV.

FIGURE 15-6
Coaxial cable.

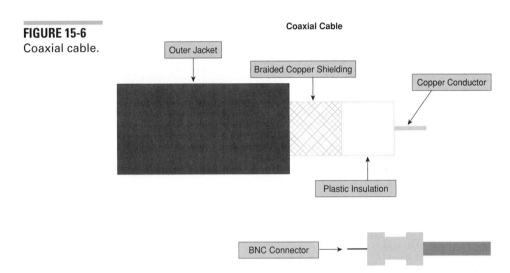

Cat 3 UTP and STP Cable

Category 3 (Cat 3) UTP and STP includes applications as voice (telephony) or data (up to 10 Mbps). More commonly, Cat 3 is used on a network for cable segments to workstations or printers. Cat 3 is not recommended for data installations because its maximum bandwidth of 10 Mbps is rapidly being exceeded by many LAN technologies.

Category 5 UTP and STP Cable

Applications for Category 5 (Cat 5) UTP and STP include voice (telephony) or data (up to 100 Mbps or, with certain technologies, 1000 Mbps). Cat 5 is sometimes used as a backbone, but it is restricted to 100 meters in length. It is currently the most popular cabling for connecting workstations and horizontal cable runs because of its low cost, high bandwidth, relative ease of installation, and ease of termination with RJ-45 connectors.

Fiber-Optic Cable

Fiber-optic cabling carries signals that have been converted from electrical to optical (pulses of light) form (see Figure 15-7). It consists of the core, which is either an extremely thin cylinder of glass or optical-quality plastic that is surrounded by a second glass or plastic layer called the *cladding*. The interface between the core and the cladding can trap light signals by a process called *total internal reflection* (TIR), in which the optical fiber acts as a light pipe.

Protective buffer and jacket materials are used to cover the cladding layer. This type of cabling is less frequently used because it is somewhat more expensive; however, it is rapidly decreasing in both raw cost and installed cost.

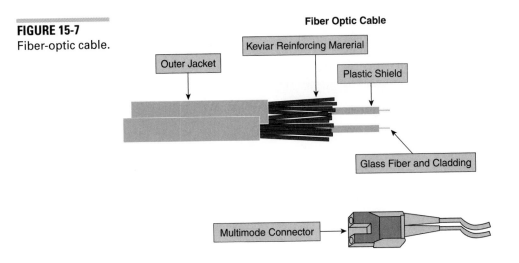

FIGURE 15-7
Fiber-optic cable.

Fiber-optic cables are not susceptible to interference, such as radio waves, fluorescent lighting, or any other source of electrical noise. This is the common cable used for network backbones and can support up to 1000 stations, carrying signals beyond 25 km. Fiber terminations include SC, ST, and a variety of proprietary connectors. Maximum data transfer rate is virtually limitless: tens and hundreds of gigabits per second, limited only by the electronics on each end of the fiber.

Unshielded Twisted-Pair Cable

Unshielded twisted-pair (UTP) cable is a set of three or four pairs of wires, with each wire in each pair twisted around the other to prevent electromagnetic interference (see Figure 15-8). UTP cabling uses RJ-45, RJ-11, RS-232, and RS-449 connectors. Because it is less expensive and easier to install, UTP is more popular than shielded twisted-pair (STP) or coaxial cabling. An example of UTP application is telephone networks, which use RJ-11 connectors, and 10BaseT networks, which use RJ-45 connectors. UTP comes in the form of Cat 2, 3, 4, and 5 grades; however, only Cat 5 is now recommended for any data applications. The maximum length is 100 meters without using any kind of signal regeneration device and a maximum data transfer rate of 1000 Mbps for Gigabit Ethernet.

FIGURE 15-8
Unshielded
twisted-pair
(UTP) cable.

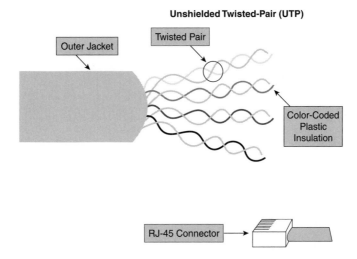

Unshielded Twisted-Pair (UTP)

Shielded Twisted-Pair Cable

Shielded twisted-pair (STP) cable, like UTP, also has four pairs of wires, with each wire in each pair twisted together (see Figure 15-9). However, the difference is that STP is surrounded with a foil shield and copper braided around the wires that allows more protection from any external electromagnetic interference. Because of the shielding, the cable is physically larger, more difficult to install and terminate, and more expensive than UTP. For applications in electrically noisy environments, STP uses RJ-45, RJ-11, RS-232, and RS-449 connectors. Like UTP, STP also comes in Cat 2, 3, 4, or 5 grades; however, only Cat 5 is recommended for any data applications. The maximum cable length without using a signal regenerating device is 100 meters, with a maximum data transfer rate of 500 Mbps.

FIGURE 15-9
Shielded
twisted-pair
(STP) cable.

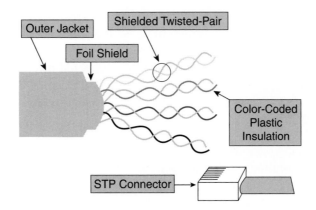

Baseband Signal

In this section, you review 10Base2, 10Base5, 10BaseT, 100BaseT, 100BaseTX, and 100BaseVG-AnyLAN.

10Base2

10Base2 cabling systems, which are also referred to as thinnet, thin wire, or coaxial, use coaxial cables. They connect no more than 30 nodes per segment, spaced at least half a meter apart. 10Base2 cabling is commonly used for small networks because it is inexpensive and easy to install.

The "10" in 10Base2, represents the rate of data transfer—in this case, 10 Mbps. "Base" is the type of signaling, either baseband or broadband; this type of cabling system uses a baseband signal. The "2" stands for the maximum distance of the cable; here, the "2" should stand for 200, but the maximum unrepeated distance is actually 185 meters. Therefore, this type of cabling system can transmit 10 Mbps, using baseband signaling, with a maximum distance of 185 meters.

10Base5

10Base5 cabling systems also use coaxial cables and are often referred to as thicknet, "Yellow Cable" (because of the outer yellow coating), or "Frozen Yellow Garden Hose." 10Base5 cabling can connect up to 100 nodes, spaced at 2.5 meters apart.

10Base5 cabling systems can transmit at 10 Mbps, using a baseband signal, and have a maximum unrepeated distance of 500 meters per cable. This type of cabling is also expensive and is usually used in circumstances that require longer distances and is used as a backbone. 10Base2 and 10Base5 cabling systems are normally used in bus topologies. However, this type of cabling is beginning to be used less often in structured cabling installations.

10BaseT

10BaseT cabling systems, which have become an extremely popular LAN technology, are normally found on Ethernet star or extended star topologies connected by UTP cables. They are usually connected into a central hub or a switch. This type of cabling system can carry 10 Mbps, using a baseband signal, with a maximum unrepeated distance of 100 meters.

100BaseT

100BaseT is the generic name for Fast Ethernet and can carry 100 Mbps, using baseband signaling, with a maximum unrepeated distance of 100 meters.

100BaseTX and 100BaseT4

100BaseTX and 100BaseT4 are two variations of 100BaseT, which are specified by the IEEE. Both cabling types carry 100 Mbps and use baseband signaling, with a maximum unrepeated distance of 100 meters per cable. 100BaseTX uses Cat 5 UTP—specifically, two pairs of twisted wires—with the capability to transmit 100 Mbps. 100BaseT4 uses Cat 3 and all four pairs of twisted wires to transmit 100 Mbps. 100BaseTX is by far the most popular copper version of Fast Ethernet.

100BaseVG-AnyLAN

100BaseVG-AnyLAN was developed by Hewlett-Packard and is similar to 100BaseVG, which can transmit 100 Mbps using baseband signaling, using a Cat 3, Cat 4, or Cat 5 UTP cable for either Ethernet or Token Ring LANs. The maximum unrepeated length is 250 meters. The primary benefit of this technology is its versatility, including the cabling it uses and the type of LAN technology with which it can be used.

Full- and Half-Duplex Operation

Three different terms are used to describe how transmitters and receivers interact during communications: simplex, half-duplex, and full-duplex. In simplex communications, the data travels only one way, and no response is needed or possible. An example of simplex communications is a school's public address (PA) system.

In half-duplex communications, data travels from a transmitter to a receiver and then from the receiver to the transmitter repeatedly, but never simultaneously. Simultaneous transmission and reception of data is not possible. Examples of half-duplex communications are walkie-talkies and 10BaseT Ethernet.

In full-duplex communications, both the transmitter and the receiver may send and receive simultaneously. Clearly, this is the fastest way to communicate, but it requires more sophisticated electronics. Examples of full-duplex communications are the telephone and 100BaseTX (Fast Ethernet).

WANs and LANs

A wide-area network (WAN) is geographically unlimited; a local-area network (LAN) is limited to a smaller region. WANs can span over cities, countries, and multiple locations; LANs are limited to a single building or school campuses.

LANs operate within a limited geographic area, connecting workstations, peripherals, and other devices on a single network. LANs provide a business with complete computer technology to share devices on a network.

WANs are geographically unlimited and vary in size. They provide an efficient way to move information from one network (a LAN) to another network.

Servers, Workstations, and Hosts

Servers are typically powerful computers that provide resources and services to other computers on a network. Workstations (clients) are devices that are capable of locally processing data; they use resources and services provided by the server. *Host* is the special name given to *any* addressable computer system on a network running TCP/IP. Examples of hosts include workstations, servers, minicomputers, mainframes, and even routers.

Server-Based Networking and Peer-to-Peer Networking

Two types of networks exist: server-based and peer-to-peer. A server-based network, also known as client/server network, connects numerous hosts to a centralized computer. This computer acts as a server, providing security functions and access to the network and resources, allowing for a central security system. As the network grows and the number of nodes increases, this type of network can add specific servers to address specific needs and resources. Examples include file and print servers, application servers, domain controllers, and directory servers.

Client/server networks typically require a powerful server computer running a network operating system, and administration by highly trained personnel. Advantages are the variety of services that can be provided and the central administration of those services; however, the disadvantages include cost and complexity.

In a peer-to-peer network, there is no centralized server or security system. Each node on the network works as its own server, granting permission to the other nodes on the network to access its resources. This type of network is limited to approximately 10 nodes connected to each other. Advantages include simplicity, low cost, and ease of administration; disadvantages include slow speed and a severely limited range of services that can be provided.

Cables, NICs, and Routers

To create a properly functioning network, the main necessities include cables, NICs, and routers. A cable is the physical media used to wire networks. The cables that can be used to wire a network include unshielded and shielded twisted-pair (UTP and STP), coaxial, fiber optic, or wireless (if no cables are required). These physical media are used in combination with the network interface card (NIC), which allows the computer to communicate with the network. Another way to look at the NIC is that it allows the workstation operating system (OS) to communicate with the local-area network operating system (NOS). A router is a Layer 3 device that performs best-path selection and packet switching and that is used to connect one or more LANs to create a WAN.

Broadband and Baseband

Two types of signaling are broadband and baseband. Broadband is an analog signaling technique normally used in cable television. This type of signaling can carry video, voice, and data across a wire. It shares the medium's bandwidth over different channels, often using different carrier frequencies. One sharing technique is called *frequency division multiplexing (FDM)*.

Baseband is a digital signaling technique that uses the entire medium's bandwidth for a single channel at a time; it allows very high throughputs (the actual measured bandwidths are possible due to this single-channel-at-a-time technique). Signals are in the form of voltage pulses on copper, light pulses on optical fiber, or electromagnetic waves in the atmosphere. A form of multiplexor (MUX) device is usually required so that multiple devices can take their turns using the medium.

Gateways

A gateway, which works as a translator, provides communication between different operating systems and frequently services the Internet. A gateway must exist if two different types of operating systems, such as Windows and UNIX, are to communicate. To communicate with a node on a different network over the Internet, the device must be connected to a LAN or a dialup connection.

Gateway also refers to default gateway, where an IP address is used to forward packets from one subnet to another subnet, if no other routing information is available.

Understanding the Physical Layer

After installing or replacing a NIC and experiencing problems accessing the network, it is important to troubleshoot the NIC and follow a logical troubleshooting methodology:

1. Determine which areas are affected. Identify what caused the problem: a protocol or a device.

2. Identify the differences of the affected areas and the unaffected areas.

3. Restart the affected hardware. Often, the problem can be resolved if the hardware of the affected area is restarted.

4. Divide the network in half and segment the area.

5. Lastly, if the problem cannot be identified by any of these methods, physical tools, from technical databases to diagnostics may be necessary.

One form of technical diagnostics is called *loopback testing*. Either an external loopback adapter or an internal device is attached to the NIC. Data is sent from the NIC and is looped back in to verify whether the data received is the same as the data that was sent. Vendor-supplied diagnostics programs are usually available through a vendor's Web page or technical support service.

The following questions provide information that a network installer must understand to properly diagnose NIC card problems.

Question 1: What does the EPROM on a NIC do?

In the Erasable Programmable Read Only Memory (EPROM) is a set of instructions built into a network adapter that allows the NIC to perform its basic functions. In a diskless workstation, commonly in larger networks, the EPROM is often replaced by a PROM. The code in the PROM is unalterable and boots a workstation that has no hard disk or diskette; this feature can be added to the NIC so that the system can be enabled to boot using files stored on the network.

Question 2: What do jumpers on a NIC do?

Jumpers are pieces of plastic and metal that connect two metal posts on a NIC. They are most commonly used to change a NIC's configuration, mainly the IRQ and the I/O addresses. Because NICs have multiple connection options, jumpers determine which transceiver needs to be used on the NIC, which transceiver to hook the cable to, and the data rate transfer setting.

Question 3: What does plug-and-play software (usually packaged with NICs) do?

Plug-and-play software works with the plug-and-play BIOS to configure expansion components on a system, such as a NIC and other devices. This involves minimal, if any, configuration issues when installing a device.

Question 4: What are network card diagnostics, such as the loopback test and vendor-supplied diagnostics?

When troubleshooting a network, two diagnostics can be used. First is the loopback test, which tests the inbound and outbound communications of a NIC. In an external loopback test, a signal is sent from the NIC, out through an adapter, and then back into the NIC. The information is then verified to determine whether the information received is the same as what was sent out. Internal loopback tests use the same idea, but no external adapter is used.

The second method in troubleshooting a NIC is using vendor-supplied diagnostic programs. Normally, the manufacturers of a NIC provide specific tests that can troubleshoot a NIC. Generic diagnostics are available, but the vendor-supplied diagnostics tests are usually more reliable. These programs can be retrieved from either the vendor's technical support lines or Web pages.

Question 5: What does it mean to resolve hardware resource conflicts, including IRQ, DMA, and I/O base address?

Because there are many devices within a personal computer, hardware conflicts may arise when one device tries to communicate with another. To avoid such conflicts, there are three main ways for devices to communicate to another within a computer.

Interrupt Request (IRQ) is a method by which a device can interrupt the processor and request a service. In a PC, 16 IRQ lines are available and are dedicated to devices such as disk controllers and serial and parallel ports. Some of the more common IRQs are IRQ 3 (for serial port COM port 2) and IRQ 5 or 10 (dedicated to NICs). In general, IRQs cannot be assigned to more than one device at a time, or a conflict will occur.

Direct memory access (DMA) is a method by which devices can access the computer's memory without involving the CPU. The DMA is managed by the DMA controller chip, which is generally faster than the CPU and works as if the CPU had managed the transfer of memory itself.

I/O (input/output) base addresses allow the CPU to access each device in the computer. Each device is assigned a unique I/O address that cannot be shared. If more than one device contains the same I/O address, neither device will be capable of functioning properly. The CPU will attempt to send information to the specified I/O address; however, because two devices are assigned the same address, both will respond and the data will be corrupted.

Hubs

Hubs, which operate at the physical layer of the OSI model, are the central location to which cabling from most topologies connect. Three types of hubs include passive, active, and intelligent hubs.

A passive hub receives information through one of its ports and then transmits the data through another port to a destination location. It has no electrical power and does not possess any signaling processing capability. Passive hubs allow communication only from one location to another to flow across the network, and they absorb some signal energy, causing a signal to weaken.

An active hub receives data through one of its ports and then works like a repeater, regenerating and retiming the signal before sending it out through another port to a destination. Active hubs are also known as multiport repeaters. Most hubs "share" bandwidth among users—more users means less bandwidth per user.

Intelligent hubs have even more electronics than active hubs, and they allow network management (a "managed" hub) or even switching (a "switching hub," or, more commonly, a "switch").

MAUs

A multistation access unit (MAU) allows multiple workstations, which are connected on a Token Ring network, to communicate with each other. Although MAUs are not a UTP hub, they are commonly referred to as a Token Ring hub. This device often has eight ports and uses Universal Data Connectors (UDC) or RJ-45 connections. MAUs are not powered devices; however, occasional lights will flash when they are connected to the network. MAUs also add fault tolerance to ring networks.

Switching Hubs

A switching hub, also called a *multiport bridge*, is a device that automatically verifies the MAC addresses of each device connected to its ports. When a packet is sent to its network, the switching hub checks the MAC address before sending the data to the specified location. Unlike a standard passive or active hub, switching hubs do not broadcast signals to each segment on the network; instead, they transmit data only to a specific destination. Switching hubs (and switches) result in dedicated bandwidth per port, whereas other hubs share the total bandwidth with the number of users.

Repeaters

When a repeater receives data from an Ethernet segment, it decodes/codes the binary information and then retransmits the signal to the destination. Advantages of a repeater include the capability to extend the network a greater distance, the capability to increase the number of devices connected to the network, added fault tolerance by isolating breaks on a network to only that cable segment, and the capability to link different cable types. A disadvantage is that repeaters enlarge collision domains: If two computers send packets at the same time, a collision occurs and CSMA/CD is applied to the entire network, thereby slowing down the network.

A repeater does not manage the flow of traffic; it only repeats signals. A maximum of four repeaters can be installed on a single-segment Ethernet network.

Transceivers

A transceiver (transmitter/receiver) is a device that transmits and receives data to and from the network This device attaches to the network interface card (NIC) in two different ways: as an onboard or external transceiver.

An onboard transceiver is usually "on board," or attached to the adapter card, such as RJ-45 receptacles and BNC connectors.

An external transceiver makes a physical connection to the NIC using a small device, called an *adapter unit interface (AUI)* or a *Digital-Intel-Xerox (DIX)* connector, that is attached by an extension cable. A common external transceiver can also connect one side to an AUI interface and the other to an RJ-45 interface.

The Data Link Layer

Bridges are devices that connect two different networks or network segments and that filter traffic from each network. The bridge builds a table of physical (hardware) addresses, learning the hosts that exist on each of its ports. The bridge examines the destination MAC address of each frame; if the destination address is local (on the same bridge port, based on the bridging table), the frame is not sent. However, if the destination MAC address is of a different bridge port than the source address, the frame is forwarded to the nonlocal destinations. Bridges provide connectivity with Layer 2 filtering. Some bridges will connect networks of differing LAN technologies (such as Ethernet to Token Ring). Because the bridge operates at Layer 2, it forwards all upper-level protocols.

802.2 Logical Link Control

802.2 is the IEEE standard that defines the LAN technology-independent logical link control (LLC). LLC manages link control and provides service access points (SAPs), all in software. LLC adds headers to encapsulated upper-layer data to identify which protocols a given frame will carry. It also provides communication between the hardware MAC sublayer and the software implementations of Layer 3.

802.3 Ethernet

802.3 defines Ethernet based on a modification of the original DIX Ethernet standard. Specifically, this standard defines the frame format to be used by a variety of specific media and topological implementations of Ethernet. The 802.3 standard also defines CSMA/CD, an algorithm for dealing with a situation in which two signals collide on a network. CSMA/CD sets the amount of time that each device must wait to send a new frame.

802.5 Token Ring

802.5 defines the "passing" of the token around a network to allow each device to transmit data across physical star or logical ring networks. A token is created by the first node and then passed along the network until another device wants to transmit data and grabs the token. The data flows along the network, past each node, until the destination node sees it and grabs the information. After the data has been received, the destination device transmits a reply to the source device to indicate that the information was received.

The Function and Characteristics of MAC Addresses

A MAC address is a unique address burned onto the memory of a NIC. Ethernet requires each computer to have a MAC address, and any computer with a MAC address is called a node. MAC addresses use a 48-bit address, which is a unique identifier for each device and is used for delivering data to a specific location. MAC addresses (Layer 2 addresses, hardware addresses, and physical addresses) are crucial to the functioning of LANs, allowing local delivery of frames and packets. A MAC address is similar to a Social Security number or a personal identification number.

The Network Layer

If the MAC address matches the address burned into the NIC card, the data link layer passes the data to the network layer. If the MAC address is all one's, the data is also passed to the network layer. When the network layer receives the packet, it uses the packet's network address to route beyond the local network. Routing allows the network layer to transfer data packets across the internetwork from a source to a destination, and to choose the most efficient path to deliver the packet.

Router

A router is a Layer 3 device that provides best-path selection and switching of data packets. To connect two different networks, a router must be used. Routers can be used to segment LANs, creating smaller collision and broadcast domains. But the most important use of routers is as the backbone devices of WANs. Networks consisting of routers, all of which can communicate using routing protocols, can be built to allow very reliable and flexible delivery of data. They make the Internet possible.

Brouter

A bridging router (brouter) is a combination of both a router and a bridge. It acts as a router for routable protocols and a bridge for nonroutable protocols. It allows the network to resolve almost all of its connection problems by using one device; therefore, it is very cost-effective. However, brouters are decreasing in prevalence because their functions are being incorporated into separate categories of devices: Layer 3 routers and Layer 2 switches.

The Difference Between Routable and Nonroutable Protocols

A routable (routed) protocol can be delivered beyond a single LAN or WAN segment; its packets can be routed. For routed protocols, a best path can be selected, and the packet can be switched to the appropriate interface for that best path. Nonroutable protocols cannot leave the LAN on which they originate. Routable (routed) protocols include IP, IPX, and AppleTalk. NetBEUI is an example of a nonroutable protocol.

The Concept of Default Gateways and Subnetworks

The connection of a LAN to a WAN is achieved through a router; therefore, LANs can be segmented by routers. The interface of a router, which resides on a LAN, is called the *default gateway* (see Figure 15-10). The default gateway is the location where all nonlocal network traffic that has no specific route to a destination is sent. The default gateway acts as an entry and exit point of a subnetwork.

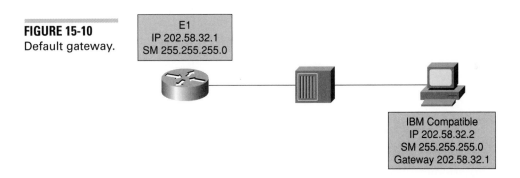

FIGURE 15-10
Default gateway.

When sending data to a remote subnetwork, the host sends the packet to the initial router specified as its default gateway. The router receives the packet and then must determine whether the destination location is on one of its local networks or whether to send the data to another router for delivery.

The Reason for Employing Unique Network IDs

Each device that participates on a network must have a unique ID: a MAC address (also known as a Layer 2 address, a hardware address, or a physical address). MAC addresses can be easily identified and maintained for LANs up to a certain size; however, the addresses become unmanageable for large unsegmented LANs or WANs. The Layer 3 or network addressing scheme, which is hierarchical, was created because a new addressing scheme was needed. By requiring that all networks connected to the router have their own network ID number, the router can refer to a group of hosts with one network layer (often IP) address. The router builds tables of device hardware and network addresses (typically MAC and IP addresses) and determines by which interface these networks can be reached. Thus, the routers use the network ID address to efficiently make best-path selection and switching decisions.

The Difference Between Static and Dynamic Routing

Two major types of routing processes exist: static and dynamic routing. Static routing is programmed by the network administrator to determine which path a packet must take to reach its destination. The administrator must maintain (including any kind of changes, additions, or deletions) the routes of each network routing device. Static paths are not flexible with changing network environments. When the static routes are programmed, the determined paths for packets do not change, regardless of changing network conditions. Static routes are most often used for security reasons.

Dynamic routing allows the router to select which path a packet must take to reach its destination. In doing so, a router uses routing protocols such as RIP, IGRP, EIGRP, or OSPF to communicate with other routers to determine which path is the fastest way to transport data across an internetwork (a network of networks). Using the routing protocols, routers "talk" to each other to update what paths are best to send data through, especially while network conditions are constantly changing. Without routing or its protocols, large networks such as the Internet would be impossible to maintain.

The Transport Layer

Connectionless communication is a fast way to send information to a destination; however, it is not reliable because there is no notification of receipt to the source location. Connectionless protocols include IP and IPX (Layer 3) and UDP (Layer 4).

Connection-oriented protocols include TCP (Layer 4) and SPX. Connection-oriented protocols, such as TCP, typically use an acknowledgment (ACK) process between source and destination. If a source does not receive an ACK from the destination, TCP retransmits the segment until an ACK is received. The processes of segmentation, handshaking/acknowledgment, flow control, and error checking are used to provide reliable transport.

The Purpose of Name Resolution

Name resolution is important for both local and remote delivery of data packets. Typically, layer hardware and Layer 3 network addresses must be resolved. IP uses ARP and IPX uses SAP to resolve hostnames ("abbreviations" of network addresses) to MAC addresses.

TCP/IP Fundamentals

TCP/IP is the most used protocol suite to date because millions of hosts worldwide and every operating system utilize this protocol. TCP/IP is popular because it is flexible, compatible, and capable of performing well in both small and large network implementations. Because of historical reasons and the quality and versatility of its protocols, TCP/IP is the de facto standard set of protocols for the Internet.

Default Gateways

IP datagrams (packets) use default gateways as entry and exit points between subnets. The subnet mask for the default gateway and the network on which it resides must be the same. A default gateway is usually the computer or router that is connected to the local subnet or other networks, which can determine the best path for delivery to the destination network ID. Packets that are too large for the gateway are fragmented with three additional pieces of information: a flag to indicate that fragmentation has occurred, a fragment ID number, and a fragment offset number for reassembling the fragments into the original packet.

DHCP, DNS, WINS, and Host Files

The Dynamic Host Configuration Protocol (DHCP) automatically distributes IP addresses to devices that are connected to the network. When a client tries to connect to the network, a request is sent to the DHCP server for configuration settings. When the server receives the message, the DHCP server sends a reply to the client that includes the configuration information, and then keeps a record of the addresses that have been assigned. DHCP uses the BOOTP protocol to communicate with clients. Clients must renew their IP addresses after 50 percent of the address lease life and again at 87.5 percent of the lease life, by sending a DHCPREQUEST message. Client hosts keep their IP address until their lease expires or until they send a DHCPRELEASE command. IPCONFIG and WINIPCFG are utilities run from the command line that allow verification of the IP address information that has been assigned to the client host.

DNS

Domain Name System (DNS) is a name-resolution service that resolves (associates) host names to IP addresses. DNS keeps a record of IP addresses and host names in a process called a domain. DNS provides services along a hierarchical chain, with a database design similar to a file tree structure (root level/top level/second level/host name). DNS also services requests for host names that cannot be resolved locally. Large internetworks have several levels of DNS servers to provide efficient name resolution.

WINS

Windows Internet Naming Service (WINS) works as DNS does to resolve IP addresses with host names. However, a difference exists between DNS and WINS. WINS uses a flat namespace by using NetBIOS instead of using a hierarchical one such as DNS. To resolve an IP address, a WINS client host registers its NetBIOS and IP addresses with the WINS server. Then the WINS client host sends a name query request to the WINS server, indicating that it desires to transmit to another host. If the desired IP address and host name are found in the server's WINS registry, they will be sent to original WINS client host. Requests made by WINS are routable. The WINS proxy agent is used for non-WINS clients such as UNIX hosts; however, WINS does not provide support for Macintosh operating systems.

HOSTS Files

The HOSTS file is a statically configured host name to IP address translation file. This file is usable in all hosts' IP protocol stacks. If present, it will be referenced for name resolution before an external DNS search. LMHOSTS provides the same services in a WINS environment and is statically configured on Windows networking clients.

TCP

The Transmission Control Protocol (TCP) is a connection-oriented protocol that operates at the transport layer of the TCP/IP and OSI models. TCP is the de facto standard of the Internet and provides full-duplex data transmission. When TCP receives data from the upper layers of the OSI model, it guarantees reliable delivery to remote networks. TCP is useful for transmitting large amounts of data reliably, but with the penalty of large ACK overhead consuming bandwidth.

UDP

The User Datagram Protocol (UDP) is a connectionless protocol that operates at the transport layer of the TCP/IP and OSI models. Because UDP is an unreliable delivery service, it does not require receiving protocols to acknowledge the receipt of a packet. An advantage that UDP has over TCP is that, because it does not concentrate on establishing a connection, it can transmit more information in a smaller amount of time than TCP. Useful for transmitting small amounts of data when reliability is less crucial, UDP lacks the overhead caused by ACKs.

POP3

Post Office Protocol version 3 (POP3), which uses TCP port 110, is a mail protocol that is responsible for holding e-mail until delivery. When an SMTP server sends an e-mail message to a POP3 server, POP3 holds on to the message until a user makes a request to have the data delivered. Thus, POP3 transfers mail files from a mail server to a mail client.

SMTP

The Simple Mail Transfer Protocol (SMTP), which uses TCP port 25, allows users to send and receive e-mail over the Internet. It is the SMTP's responsibility to make sure that the e-mail is sent to the POP3 server.

SNMP

Simple Network Management Protocol (SNMP), which uses TCP port 161, allows simple maintenance and remote monitoring of any device on a network. With SNMP, administrators can address issues such as problems with a network card in a server, a program, or service on the server, or a device such as a hub or a router.

When managing a network device using SNMP, an administrator can use the central management system and the management information base (MIB). The management system allows the administrator to view performance and operation statistics of the network devices, enabling him or her to diagnose a network remotely.

FTP

The File Transfer Protocol (FTP) is a fast, connection-oriented, error-free protocol that uses TCP ports 20 and 21. FTP allows data to be transferred between servers and clients. For FTP to connect to a remote server, the IP address or host name must be provided. FTP must be capable of resolving IP addresses to host names to establish a connection.

HTTP

Hypertext Transfer Protocol (HTTP), which uses TCP port 80, allows clients to transfer documents written in Hypertext Markup Language (HTML) over the World Wide Web for display by a browser. It is the universal display language of the Internet.

IP

The Internet Protocol (IP) is a routable (routed), connectionless protocol that operates at the network layer of the OSI and TCP/IP models. IP is the de facto standard for the Internet and provides packet delivery and addressing for source and destination.

Because IP is a connectionless delivery service, it is unreliable and does not guarantee that the packets received will be in the order sent, if they're received at all.

Internet Domain Name System

The Internet Domain Name System consists of a root and a subdomain. The root represents the upper-indexed pointers to other DNS servers. For example, when a user—for example, user@cisco.com—tries to send an e-mail to an international location—for example, a student at the University of Cambridge in England, student@cam.au.uk—the DNS server first contacts the subdomain server, which is cisco.com. The DNS server sends the e-mail to the subdomain. After the subdomain, cisco.com, has been contacted, the e-mail is then sent to the root, .com. The root passes it along the other roots to .uk, which stands for "United Kingdom." The .uk root passes the e-mail message down its hierarchy to its subdomain, .au, and then to .cam. After .cam receives the data, the e-mail message sits on the POP3 server until the mail is requested.

Class A, B, and C Addresses and Their Default Subnet Mask Numbers

IP addresses are divided into classes to accommodate different sizes of networks (see Figure 15-11). Depending on the type of IP address, the first octets (through the first, second, or third octets) are issued by ARIN or other national agencies. The IP address has three parts: the network field (assigned externally), the subnetwork field (created by the network administrator locally), and the host field (assigned locally). To create more hierarchical networks with subnets, the extended network prefix, also known as the subnet mask, which allows the decoding of the IP address into its three parts (network, subnetwork, host) is required.

The classes of IP addresses are as follows: Class A addresses begin with binary 0xxx xxxx in the first octet—that is, decimal 1 to 126 (0 and 127 are reserved for special test purposes). Class B addresses begin with binary 10xx xxxx in the first octet—that is, decimal 128 to 191. Class C addresses begin with binary 110x xxxx in the first octet—that is, decimal 192 to 223.

Class A IP addresses are reserved for the larger networks. This range allows Class A IP addresses to have a possibility of 126 networks. Each network has a capacity of more than 16 million unique hosts using a default subnet mask. The default subnet mask for this class network is 255.0.0.0.

FIGURE 15-11
IP address
classes.

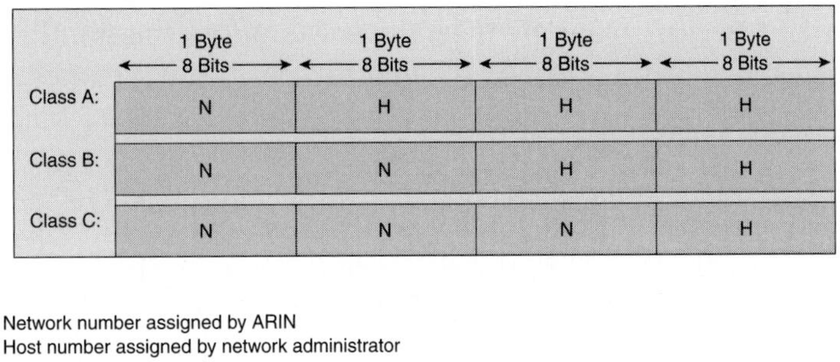

	1 Byte / 8 Bits	1 Byte / 8 Bits	1 Byte / 8 Bits	1 Byte / 8 Bits
Class A:	N	H	H	H
Class B:	N	N	H	H
Class C:	N	N	N	H

N = Network number assigned by ARIN
H = Host number assigned by network administrator

Class B IP addresses are reserved for medium-sized networks. The range dedicated for Class B networks includes IP addresses from 128.0.0.0 to 191.255.0.0. The possibility of networks available for this subnet is a little more than 16,000 networks, with each having the capacity of a few more than 65,000 unique hosts using the default subnet mask. The default subnet mask for a Class B address is 255.255.0.0.

Class C IP addresses are dedicated for small local networks. Class C networks range from 192.0.1.0 to 223.255.255.0, with a capacity of more than 2 million networks, each with a capacity of 254 unique hosts using the default subnet mask. The default subnet mask for a Class C address is 255.255.255.0.

Other classes, which are not as popular, are Class D and Class E. Class D addresses range from 224.0.0.0 to 239.255.255.255 and are used mainly for multicasting to various amounts of hosts. Class D has the potential of having more than 268 million unique multicast groups. Class E addresses, which are experimental addresses block for future use, have a range of 240.0.0.0 to 247.255.255.255.

Various solutions to the problem of IP address depletion are being implemented, including network address translation (NAT) and private addressing, variable-length subnet masking (VLSM), classless interdomain routing (CIDR), and IP version 6 (IPv6—a version of IP with longer IP addresses, and hence far more addresses to assign).

Port Numbers

Each TCP/IP protocol has at least one specifically designated port number for the flow of network traffic between client and server. Note that the use of the word *ports* here refers to structures in software, not hardware interfaces. Port numbers correspond to services to be provided for the upper layers. Well-known port numbers are normally assigned by TCP/IP on the server prior to connections; however, these numbers can be changed. Because clients have the capability to dynamically log on to the server from any location, clients do not have assigned port numbers. For instance, if an individual (client) were to call a friend (server) from anywhere in the country, the friend would be able to pick up his or her telephone. Common port numbers include HTTP (port 80), FTP (port 21), Telnet (port 23), and SMTP (port 25).

Proxies and Why They Are Used

A proxy server is a type of a "go-between" between the Internet and the users of a network. If a client needs information from the Internet, the proxy server searches for the destination and retrieves the information. This provides for higher security and faster service because the client itself does not directly connect to the destination.

A proxy server is used for a number of different reasons. Proxy servers enhance security by hiding the individual host addresses. When a server receives the request, the server sees only one address—the address of the proxy server—and not the individual host. Because all requests are being made on one server, network traffic is less busy if more than one user requests the same location, enhancing performance. The proxy server copies each of the addresses requested. When another host requests the same destination, the server sends out the cached version of that location.

Workstation Configuration

Normal configuration parameters for a workstation include the IP address and subnet mask, the DNS setting, the default gateway and subnet mask, the IP proxy, WINS, DHCP, the host name, and the Internet domain name.

IP Addresses and Subnet Masks

When assigning IP addresses, two important factors must be considered: The IP address needs to be unique, and it must be assigned a subnet mask. When a DHCP server assigns an IP address, it specifically assigns unique addresses to each device, not duplicating any address. If you are manually assigning IP addresses, it is important that no two devices have the same IP address.

Each address must also have a subnet mask to properly communicate with the network. The network and host IDs of an IP address are determined by the subnet mask; therefore, it is important that each IP address has a subnet mask.

Default Gateways and Subnet Masks

The interface of a router, which resides on a LAN, is called the default gateway. The default gateway is the location where all nonlocal network traffic that has no specific route to a destination is sent. The default gateway also acts as an entry and exit point of a subnetwork.

Host Name

A host name is assigned by the network administrator to identify each device on the network. By default, on Windows-based machines, host names are the names of the computers.

Internet Domain Name

The Internet domain name is assigned by ARIN, a company that assigns all the domain names on the Internet. The domain name consists of two parts, the host name and the domain. In the address www.cisco.com, *www* is the host name and *cisco.com* is the domain. Together, www.cisco.com becomes a fully qualified domain name (FQDN).

TCP/IP Suite: Utilities

In TCP/IP, the ARP is used to bind (associate) the physical (MAC) addresses with a specific logical (IP) addresses. When a data packet is sent to a particular destination, ARP matches the addressing information against the ARP cache for the appropriate MAC address. If no matches are made, ARP sends out a broadcast message on the network looking for the particular destination. A host will respond with the correct address and send a reply to ARP. The following table shows some variations on the **arp** command.

Commands	Action
arp -a	Displays a list of all IP and MAC addresses
arp -a -n *interface* Example: arp -a -n **146.188.144.223**	Filters the display to show only the *interface* specified
arp -s *interface MAC_address*	Is used to manually add entries
arp -d *IP_address*	Is used to manually delete a dynamically entered ARP cache

If duplicate IP addresses appear in the ARP cache, a Windows NT 4.0 TCP/IP stack is written, and a new ARP broadcast is sent to each computer affected by the ARP cache error.

Using Telnet to Test, Validate, and Troubleshoot IP Connectivity

Telnet, which uses port 23, allows users to log into and execute text-based commands when working on a remote server.

To use Telnet, the user needs to run Telnet.exe at the command prompt or from the Start Menu (choose Start, Programs, Accessories, Telnet; then select Connect, Remote System until a dialog box appears).

To connect to a host, the client must be capable of resolving the name to an IP address. The user must also specify the port to connect to (Telnet port 23) on the remote server. VT100 is the default terminal emulation used.

If a user is having problems logging onto a server, Telnet may still be functional. In this case, the user can log on using Telnet and administer the problems associated with the server. For example, if a Windows NT server crashes and displays a blue screen, and the server allows for a remote administration card to be plugged in, the user can Telnet to this card and can determine the problem of the server and reboot it.

Using NBTSTAT to Test, Validate, and Troubleshoot IP Connectivity

NBTSTAT displays information regarding NetBIOS names and corresponding IP addresses that have been resolved by a host. It is used to troubleshoot two computers trying to connect via NetBIOS over TCP/IP (NetBT) by displaying the protocol statistics and current connection with each remote host.

Using tracert to Test, Validate, and Troubleshoot IP Connectivity

The **tracert** command-line utility is used to trace the exact route that the data packet used to reach its destination. Using the Internet Control Message Protocol (ICMP), **tracert** sends out echo packets to the destination, which was the packet's original destination, to determine the exact route. Variations of the **tracert** command are shown in the table.

Command	Action
tracert *hostname* or **tracert** *ipaddress*	Displays the exact route taken by the packet to its destination
tracert -d	Specifies that an IP address should not be resolved to a host name
tracert -d -h *number_of_hops host_name* Example: **tracert -d -h 15 www.cisco.com**	Lists the maximum number of hops in a search
tracert -j *router_name local_computer*	Specifies the loose source routing to make the outbound datagram pass through the router and back
tracert -w *number*	Instructs the amount of time to wait in milliseconds before timing out

An example of displaying hops from one location to another is to use the **tracert -d -h 15 www.asu.edu** command.

Using NETSTAT to Test, Validate, and Troubleshoot IP Connectivity

NETSTAT is used to display the methods used by virtual circuits and network interfaces. NETSTAT is available for troubleshooting specific TCP/IP issues by displaying protocol statistics and current TCP/IP connections. This utility is used to show the three-step handshake method when establishing and disconnecting network sessions.

NETSTAT displays a list of protocol types, local addresses and port information, remote access and port information, and current state. The information displayed also explains what connections are open and in progress. Variations of the **netstat** command are shown in the following table.

Command	Action
netstat -a *number*	Displays connections and listening ports.
netstat -e	Includes the number of bytes received and sent, discards and errors, and unknown protocols.
netstat -s -p *ipaddress*	Displays contents of routing table. Allows users to view the current routes and active sessions and addresses.

Using netstat enables you to troubleshoot TCP/IP-based connections by monitoring TCP protocol activity (by using **netstat -a**). Error counts and Ethernet interfaces can also be monitored using netstat.

Using IPCONFIG/WINIPCONFIG to Test, Validate, and Troubleshoot IP Connectivity

IPCONFIG and WINIPCFG display the current TCP/IP configurations on the local workstation and enable the user to modify the DHCP address assigned for each interface. IPCONFIG is used in Windows NT, and WINIPCFG is used for Windows 9*x* platforms. This utility enables the user to view the IP-related settings, such as DNS and WINS servers, and the network interface's physical address. Variations on the **ipconfig** command are shown in the following table.

Command	Action
ipconfig /all or **winipcfg /all** (for Win 9*x*)	Displays all IP configuration information
ipconfig /renew or **winipcfg /renew**	Renews the DHCP lease information, if none is named
ipconfig /release or **winipcfg /release**	Releases the DHCP lease information and disables the TCP/IP on the adapter

Using FTP to Test, Validate, and Troubleshoot IP Connectivity

FTP, which uses ports 20 and 21, is designed to transfer data across a network. Variations of the **ftp** command are shown in the following table.

Command	Action
ftp -v	Suppresses any display server response
ftp -n	Prevents automatic login
ftp -l	Turns off interactive prompting during file transfer
tp -d	Displays all FTP commands between the client and server for debugging
ftp -g	Disables the gobbling capacity
ftp -s: *filename* Example: ftp -s:network.doc	Runs the text file containing specific FTP commands
ftp *hostname* Example: ftp www.cisco.com	Connects to the host

To use FTP to connect to an address or target machine, such as Telnet, FTP must be capable of resolving the host name to the IP address of the destination machine. When the connection and login has been made, users can transfer files and manage directories.

When connected with the remote computer, commands to navigate around the server include the ones in this table.

Commands	Action
CD	Changes working directory
DELETE	Deletes files
LS	Lists current directory contents
BYE	Ends connection and logs out
GET	Downloads a file
PUT	Uploads a file
VERBOSE	Turns verbose mode on and off

A common use of troubleshooting with FTP is researching and downloading patches or fixes. For example, Microsoft provides an online FTP server, where patches, upgrades, and the like can be downloaded. Most vendors provide some type of FTP server for users to retrieve these utilities.

Using ping to Test, Validate, and Troubleshoot IP Connectivity

Packet Interface Groper (ping) is a basic TCP/IP troubleshooting tool. ping is usually the first step when troubleshooting the network to verify whether a specific machine is active. Using ICMP, ping verifies connections between two servers by sending echo packets to remote servers and listening for replies.

PPP and SLIP

The Serial Line Internet Protocol (SLIP) and the Point-to-Point Protocol (PPP) allow users to log on remotely to a network using a device such as a modem (a dialup connection through an analog telephone line). Although it is available for Windows 95 and NT desktops, SLIP was originally designed to connect UNIX platforms to a remote network. SLIP was one of the first remote connectivity protocols. However, with new technology and better security, SLIP is being replaced by PPP.

PPP was designed to replace all the older technology of SLIP. It provides asynchronous and bit-oriented synchronous encapsulation, network protocol multiplexing, session negotiating, and data-compression negotiation while supporting protocols such as IPX/SPX, DECnet, and TCP/IP. PPP uses the High-Level Data Link Control (HDLC) protocol for data encapsulation during transmission and establishes and maintains connections using the Link Control Protocol (LCP). Using the Network Control Protocol (NCP) with PPP, an administrator is enabled to run different protocols simultaneously on the same line.

Advantages of PPP over SLIP include the fact that SLIP can be used only with TCP/IP, while PPP can use multinetwork protocols simultaneously during one session. PPP also uses DHCP to resolve IP addresses with the server and can handle a faster connection than SLIP. PPP supports data compression and IP address negotiation, neither of which SLIP does.

The Purpose and Function of PPTP

The Point-to-Point Tunneling Protocol (PPTP) has functions similar to that of PPP. However, it provides a secure transmission of data from the remote server. To use PPTP, the PPTP-enabled client must dial into a PPP server and gain access to the remote server. When the connection is established between the PPP and PPTP servers, the PPTP server creates a connection with the client through a process called tunneling. When a remote client sends a transmission, the transmission goes through the PPP server, is encrypted, and then is sent through the tunnel to the PPTP server. The PPTP server receives the transmission, de-encrypts it, and directs it to the appropriate host. These features of PPTP make secure connections possible across the Internet. PPTP facilitates the transfer of sensitive data: A user can log onto an ISP, use the ISP as a gateway, and then log securely into an office network.

ISDN and PSTN (POTS)

The Public Switched Telephone Network (PSTN) was originally designed to carry analog voice signals across telephone lines. A technology called Integrated Services Digital Network (ISDN) was created to convert analog signals into digital signals to allow data transfer rates faster than PSTN.

An advantage of ISDN over PSTN is speed. The fastest connection that a modem can establish using a PSTN analog line is 56 kbps. Data is converted by the modem from the PC's digital signals to analog signals and then is sent across the wires to a remote network, where the data is again converted from analog signals to digital signals. ISDN enables digital signals to travel over regular telephone lines in its digital form, transmitting data in half the time of analog modems. An ISDN BRI line can carry data at 128 kbps, and ISDN BRI lines can be aggregated to create an ISDN PRI line to carry 1.472 Mbps (T1) or 1.920 Mbps (E1). Another advantage of ISDN over PSTN is the capability to be connected to the network "all the time" without tying up the analog telephone line, which is especially useful for telecommuters.

Modem Configuration for Dialup Networking to Function

For dialup modems to work properly with the dialup network, the parameters, such as serial ports, IRQs, and I/O addresses, must be configured properly. Modems (modulators/demodulators) use a serial port for connection and attempt to use COM1 as its default. The EIA/TIA 232 serial standards determine how to connect a modem to a computer.

Serial ports, which are based on DB-9 (9 pins) or DB-25 (25 pins) connectors, are commonly known as COM1, COM2, COM3, and COM4 ports. Data terminal equipment (DTE) represents the computer side of the connection, while the data circuit-terminating equipment (DCE) represents the modem connection. Modems should be set properly; depending on the serial port, modem setup can be done through the Start menu/Control Panel/Modems.

IRQs provide a device a way to send interrupt signals to a computer. In many cases, for more than one (if not all) attempts to transfer data into a CPU, each device is issued an IRQ. An I/O address, a four-digit hexadecimal number, enables the flow of data within the computer. Addresses are used to select the information to be accessed in memory or peripherals.

The maximum port speed is the speed that a modem can support in kilobits per second. An analog line, also known as a regular telephone line, can support speeds up to 56 kbps using an analog modem.

The Requirements for a Remote Connection

The requirements for remote connection include the following:

- The user must have a valid ID and password in order to access the network remotely. This includes accounts with PPP, SLIP, or RAS.

- A remote server must be available to be accessed.

- The appropriate hardware device, such as a modem or an ISDN line, must be enabled to communicate with the server.

- Network protocols must be configured to access the remote server or network.

Security

Two types of network security exists for protecting the network: share-level security and user-level security. Said to be weak and difficult to manage, share-level security allows users to access certain information if assigned a password by the network administrator. For an individual to access information on the network, that user must provide a password, which is specifically assigned by a network administrator.

User-level security specifies the rights and privileges of each user. The network administrator assigns the user an account to access a specific computer or network. When an individual attempts to log onto the network, the computer matches the user account ID and password(s) against the security database before providing the user access.

Standard Password Practices and Procedures

In both share-level and user-level security models, passwords are given to the user for access to the network or specific data. Passwords should always be kept secure and should never be written down where unauthorized users may stumble upon them.

Passwords should not be one of the following:

- The logon, first, or last name of the user, or these names reversed
- A familiar name, such as the name of a spouse, child, pet, or relative
- Easily attainable information, such as personal information
- A word found in any language dictionary
- A combination of letters and numbers only
- A group of single digits or letters (for instance: AAAAA or 11111)

Passwords should have these characteristics:

- Be between six and eight characters in length
- Include nonalphanumeric characters
- Be set to expire periodically, ideally once every 30 days

Data Encryption

Data encryption provides the secure delivery of information being sent over the internetwork. It takes the information, which is written in plain text, and codes it into a text called ciphertext, which resembles nothing, making it unreadable. When the data is received, it is decrypted from ciphertext and converted back into its original text.

The Use of a Firewall

A firewall is used to protect the internal network from the public and insecure Internet. Firewalls may be implemented using hardware or software. A software firewall is a set of programs on the gateway that monitors all traffic flowing in and out of a network; these are often implemented using specifically configured routers. All information must go through the firewall and must be verified against a specific set of rules. If the information does not meet the specified rules, the data is bounced back and cannot continue until it meets the set standards. An example of hardware firewall is using specially configured routers to control inbound and outbound traffic.

Administrative Considerations

Before installing a network, a network administrator must consider the configurations of the network, physical location, topologies, physical structure of the network, administrative duties (including administrative and test accounts), passwords, IP addressing, IP configuration, connectivity requirements, and software.

Administrative accounts allow the administrator unrestricted access to all the information and security on the network. These accounts should be created only for individuals whose job requires the need for unrestricted access, and they should be restricted to exercise these privileges only for administrative duties. Because the role of the administrator is to protect all the data on the network, this account should be sensitive and should have a strong password that must be difficult to break.

When an administrator uses his or her administrative account to make changes on the network, a test account should be used to test and verify the changes. Test accounts are similar to that of a normal user account, resembling other user accounts and privileges.

Both administrative and test accounts need to have passwords. Passwords are a form of computer security that enables privileged users to access network information. A strong password, which should be used for administrative accounts, is a password that is difficult to "crack" by hackers. Some hackers use what is called the "brute force" attack, which uses dictionary files against a user's account. It is important to use a password that is an uncommon word not found in any dictionary, that consists of six to eight characters in length, and that is a combination of numbers, letters, and nonalphanumeric characters, as previously discussed.

Administrators must also consider IP configurations and standard operating procedures (SOPs) when building their networks. IPCONFIG is a Windows utility used to determine TCP/IP settings. This utility verifies IP addresses, default gateways, subnet masks, DNS, and other IP-related settings. IP configurations are normally determined by the desktop used.

Although most networks have different names, they use similar standard operating procedures, which is a baseline of the resources in day-to-day operation. SOPs may include backing up data on the network at the end of each day or each evening, having backup information in case a network goes down, or monitoring performance. To monitor performance, a tool called the "sniffer" may be used to monitor the amount of network traffic on the network. A sniffer is also used to analyze network traffic and provide solutions to problems affecting the infrastructure of the network.

The Impact of Environmental Factors on Computer Networks

Environmental factors should be considered when maintaining or creating a network. Computers and networking devices can easily be affected by extreme situations, such as temperature, moisture, vibrations, and electrical interference. If exposed to these situations, computers and networking devices may act irregularly and may sometimes fail.

Room conditions should be at normal humidity and temperature to prevent electrostatic discharge (ESD) and overheating. Fluorescent lighting, space heaters, televisions, radios, and other electrical devices may contribute to electromagnetic interference (EMI), especially when copper cabling is the primary networking medium. Often cooler and darker places, such as a basement, are ideal areas to store computer equipment.

Common Peripheral Ports

Common peripheral ports include the serial and parallel ports. Serial ports are often used for a workstation's mouse or keyboard, and are referred to as a slow port because data can flow only in one direction.

Parallel ports are used for devices that are quicker and that connect outside of the workstation. Data can be transmitted in both directions, making the connection faster. A printer, for example, connects to a parallel cable and port to speed up printing processes.

Data bus connectors (DB connectors) are D-shaped connectors used to connect serial and parallel cables to the computer. DB connectors are usually referred to as DB-*x*, with *x* representing the number of wires—DB-9, DB-15, and DB-25 are most commonly used.

External SCSI Connections

The Small Computer Standard Interface (SCSI) enables workstations to connect to and communicate with peripheral hardware, such as CD-ROMs, disk drives, and scanners. SCSI provides faster data transmission than the parallel port, is used for high-performance systems, and has the capability to chain together up to 7 or 15 devices.

Print Servers

Two types of print servers exist: dedicated and nondedicated print servers. Both types receive requests from end users and direct the requests to a printer pool. A print server is secure because it has no client access into the network. The difference between dedicated and nondedicated print servers is that a dedicated print server is used only as a print server; a nondedicated print server will also have some other network server functions.

Hubs

Using either twisted-pair or coaxial cabling, hubs connect a number of computers and devices together. Depending on the cabling, hubs can be used to strengthen signals if cables are not long enough and signals begin to fade. Hubs are normally used for star topologies, in which each cable segment is connected to the hub.

Routers

Routers, which operate on the third layer of the OSI model, route data packets to a destination based on the routing address provided by the data packets. Routers are responsible for addressing and translating logical addresses into the physical address of a packet.

Routers are either static or dynamic devices and are normally connected in a mesh topology with other routers. Statically configured routers cannot communicate with other routers; they have a determined fixed route, which is manually entered by the administrator. Dynamically configured routers have the capability to communicate with other routers to determine the best path to route a packet by a variety of protocols, including RIP, IGRP, EIGRP, and OSPF.

Brouters

A brouter is a device that functions as a bridge and a router. If a brouter receives a packet, it must determine the IP address. If the IP address is not connected to any of its ports, it must route the packet to another location. However, if it receives a packet with an IP address connected to one of its ports, the brouter acts as a bridge and delivers the packet to its destination.

Bridges

Bridges are devices that connect two different networks, or network segments, and that filter traffic from each network. The bridge builds a table of physical (hardware) addresses, learning the hosts that exist on each of its ports. The bridge examines the destination MAC address of each frame; if the destination address is local (on the same bridge port, based on the bridging table), the frame is not sent. However, if the destination MAC address is the address of a different bridge port from the source address, the frame is forwarded to the nonlocal destinations. Bridges provide connectivity with Layer 2 filtering. Some bridges connect networks of differing LAN technologies (such as Ethernet to Token Ring). Because the bridge operates at Layer 2, it forwards all upper-level protocols.

Patch Panels

Patch panels, which are an integral part of structured cabling installations, consist of a row of female connectors (or ports), in which every cable from different work areas connects directly to the back of the patch panel. They provide support for UTP, STP, fiber ports, and various Cat ratings of UTP cabling.

UPS

An uninterruptible power supply (UPS) provides protection from spikes and sags that may come over the electrical wires. While the server is plugged in, the battery charger constantly charges the battery. In case of a power outage, the fully charged battery will provide operations to continue or provide enough time for the server to shut down properly.

NICs

Network interface cards (NICs) allow the communication between a computer and the network, providing a physical connection. For the computer to interact with the NIC, the computer must have the proper drivers installed. Each NIC is assigned a unique address called the MAC address. This address is also the physical address and is burned onto the NIC by its manufacturer. No two MAC addresses are or can be alike.

Token Ring Media Filters

A Token Ring media filter is a passive device that is used to convert output signals from a Token Ring NIC so that it may be compatible with different media types, such as STP cable or different terminations, such as a DB-9 connector. Media filters are also designed to eliminate unwanted high-frequency emissions and to adjust inputs when using UTP cable.

Analog Modem Installation into a Digital Jack

The technologies of an analog and a digital jack are very different and are not compliant. Analog modems use a standard phone line to gain remote access; a digital jack is reserved to be used with an ISDN line or a PBX switch. A NIC or a transceiver can burn out if it is exposed to the voltages of an analog phone line. Likewise, an analog modem can be damaged if it is plugged into a digital jack.

Uses of RJ-45 Connectors, Depending on Cabling

Registered jack (RJ) connectors were previously the standard for telephone connectors. More recently, RJs have been used to connect not only the telephones, but also 10BaseT, 100BaseTX, and Token Rings.

Telephone lines use the RJ-11 connector, which connects four-wire cables, with the two inner connectors for one phone line and the two outer for another line. Modems are restricted to using RJ-11 because it is an analog connector. RJ-12, which is rarely used, is a six-wire version of the RJ-11 used for more complex telephone systems.

RJ-45 connectors have eight wires and are used for network technologies that require four pairs of wires, such as Ethernet and Token Ring networks. RJ-45 connectors are specifically designed for digital signals. If an analog modem uses an RJ-45 connector, either the connection will not function or the analog modem will stop functioning and will burn out. RJ-45 connectors are mainly used to connect 10BaseT cabling (or the like) to a hub or a bridge to connect to another media type, such as using a BNC connector for 10Base2.

Patch Cables: Contributors to the Overall Length of the Cabling Segment

Patch cables are typically 3 meters in length and often are used for either connecting two MAUs (in a Token Ring topology) or connecting two Ethernet hubs. Patch cables are also used to "patch" a system with a NIC to the digital jack on either a cube wall or a floor mount. The EIA/TIA-568-A standards govern horizontal cable installations. For Cat 5 UTP, the distance limitation is 100 meters, of which 3 meters are designated for workstation patch cables, 90 meters are designed for horizontal cable runs (from the outlet to the horizontal cross connect [HCC]), and 6 meters are reserved for patch cables/jumper cables within the HCC.

Maintaining and Supporting the Network

Test documentation normally is included with the software during packaging. Vendor patches, fixes, and upgrades usually occur after the product has been purchased. Vendors provide patches and updates of their products when bugs are found in the software or to make their software run more efficiently. If a bug is found in an earlier release, patches are provided to fix the bugs. The most current patch or fix is likely to be found on a vendor's Web page. Normally, a search feature or online support guide on the vendor's Web page is available to easily navigate the site to locate the specific patch needed.

Software upgrades are designed to improve current software and to make it more powerful. Normally, upgrades are free (or can be purchased for a fee) and can be downloaded from a vendor's Web page in the same way that a patch would be downloaded. However, a backup should be made before installation to prevent loss of data.

Without antivirus software installed on the servers and workstations, no modern network will continue working efficiently. Depending on the user's needs, a wide variety of antiviral packages are available. An ongoing network maintenance strategy should be to update virus signatures frequently. Because new viruses are spawned frequently, within a few months, what was previously protective antivirus software can become useless.

Standard Backup Procedures and Backup Media Storage Practices

Each administrator maintaining a network should have a standard backup procedure that should be implemented nightly. Backup procedures should include tape drives, tape automation, and full, incremental, and differential backups.

DAT and DLT are the two standard types of tape drives. DAT provides a complete digital recording method, which was originally used to record audio and video. DAT has a capacity of 24 GB, uses a SCSI connection, and is mostly used for medium-sized networks.

DLT have a capacity of up to 80 GB, and this is becoming the more popular method of the three backup standards. Although this method is expensive, it is very fast and reliable. Like DAT, DLT uses a SCSI connection.

Tape automation is a scheduled routine backup in which a tape backup is scheduled with an average of 20 to 25 tape rotations. The most common tape backup procedure is the 21-day tape rotation, where rotation is consistent for four days out of the week, Monday through Thursday.

Some rotations are scheduled for five days a week as well, Monday through Friday. Storing backup tape off-site is also a good idea in case of a major catastrophe that could ruin the backed-up information.

Three different types of backups exist: full, incremental, and differential. Full backup is the process in which all the information is backed up. Most companies perform full backups every day. However, this process requires the most tape out of the three backup processes.

Incremental backups back up files that have been changed since the last incremental or full backup was performed. This process is less time-consuming and uses the least amount of tape. If the database needs to be restored, the last full backup and every incremental tape afterward would be needed.

Differential backup is a process in which files that were changed since that last full backup was performed are backed up. This type of backup process takes less tape than a full backup. When restoring the information, only two tapes are required: the last full and differential backup tapes.

The Need for Periodic Application of Software Patches and Other Fixes to the Network

It is important to patch the software running on the client workstation and the server itself. There is always existing software on the client that will not be on the server, and vice versa; if software is upgraded or patched on a server and not on a workstation, problems may occur when users try to access the software with a different version.

The Need to Install Antivirus Software on the Server and Workstation

Because traffic flows from network to network via the Internet, there is a chance of a virus coming over the Internet and onto the network. To prevent a virus from destroying a system or a network, it is important to install antivirus software on the servers and workstations. Antivirus software scans all the files that come into the network off the Internet and scans all the files opened on the server that are considered to be outgoing. Without antivirus software installed on the servers and workstations, no modern network will continue working efficiently—all can be vulnerable to virus attacks and damages.

The Need to Frequently Update Virus Signatures

It is important to frequently update virus signatures that are used by the virus-scanning software when eliminating viruses. These signature files are updated by the vendor and either are mailed to the user or are available on the vendor's Web page. An ongoing network maintenance strategy should be to update virus signatures frequently. Because new viruses are developed daily, what was effective antivirus software a few months ago can become useless.

Troubleshooting the Network

An example of a troubleshooting approach involves the following four steps:

1. Determine whether the problem exists across the network. Is the problem across the network or in a portion of the network? Identifying the scale of the problem will determine how many users are affected and may provide clues as to what caused (or is causing) the problem.

2. Attempt to isolate the problem. Is one workstation not functioning? Is that client capable of connecting to the network? Or is the entire work-group not functioning? Are any of the devices capable of printing? Or, is the problem affecting the entire LAN? Is it the entire Ethernet segment that is not functioning? Or is it a WAN problem, or a problem with the LAN-WAN connection (for example, do the clients have Internet access)?

3. Determine whether the problem is consistent. Is the problem continuous and not intermittent? In other words, is the problem constantly present instead of occurring periodically or randomly? And can the problem be replicated (given the same conditions on the same machine or another, the same errors are present)? This information will help determine what may be causing the problems on the network.

4. Finally, determine whether the problems can be resolved by using tools. A set of standard tools for maintaining networks should be available. These tools include hardware tools (such as cable testers), software tools (such as protocol analyzers), workstation and server commands, software and utilities, Web-based and text-based hardware and software manuals, and diagnostics that come with various network components, such as servers, NICs, hubs, switches, and routers.

Distinguish Whether a Problem Is Attributable to the Operator or the System

To troubleshoot the network for operator or system problems, first the issue needs to be identified. Is the problem protocol-based, or is it a network issue? Second, identify what parts of the network are affected, and determine whether the problem exists on the cabling or the workstations.

When identifying the exact issue, begin with a broad view—say, the entire network. As the research is conducted, the problem should become more isolated. When dealing with network problems, re-creating the problem can provide assistance in learning the events that have occurred during the error. If the problem is complex and possibly will occur in the future, re-creating the problem may be beneficial to the troubleshooter for future reference. However, if the problem is simply to replace a NIC or a piece of hardware, re-creating the problem may not be necessary.

Isolating the cause of the problem has two benefits. First, if the problem is isolated to a specific area or number of users, the rest of the network can continue to be functional. Second, by isolating the issue, it is easier to diagnose the problem among 3 to 5 workstations than it is on 500 workstations.

After identifying the problem, correcting the problem may be even more complicated. There may also be more than one way to fix the problem. First, determine the various methods to correct the problem; sometimes a problem can be temporarily patched, or a software patch can also provide a temporary fix. There is also a possibility that when the problem is fixed, another problem will arise because of the fix.

Proper documentation (journals and equipment logs) and feedback, such as methods used to contain the problem and additional comments, can be helpful in case the problem arises in the future.

After correcting or temporarily patching the problem, another method that should be considered is to have another operator re-create the problem and test it on another workstation. This will allow verification that the problem can be re-created on other machines.

Next, have the operator re-create and test the problem against the original machine to verify that the problem can be created and fixed, and to see if any other issues arise with the affected workstation. Having the operator follow the documentation that was originally created for the problem will verify whether other operators are following the standard operating procedures as well.

Check Physical and Logical Indicators of Trouble

When isolating a problem, physical and logical indicators of trouble may exist. These indicators include the link light, power light, error display, error log and display, and performance monitors.

Link lights should be a steady green or amber, indicating that a device is connected to a network. The power light should also be a steady light. If this light is out on a machine, it could mean one of two things: first, that there is no power in the device, or, second, that the power light could have burned out. All aspects of the problem should be scoped before determining that the device has no power.

Error displays often indicate a malfunction or a failure in a device. Errors can be viewed either as a dialog box that pops up or in the LED error display of the device. Logs and error displays maintain a listing of errors that have occurred. Although error logs and displays do not provide a solution to the problem, some documentation is provided to help lead to a solution.

Performance monitoring is a tool provided by Windows NT called the Network Monitor. This monitor provides information regarding data coming in and going out of a workstation. It tracks the resources used by the components and applications. Performance monitoring is useful when trying to identify bottlenecks in the CPU, memory, disk I/O, network I/O, and error trends. This feature monitors real-time system performance and performance history. By using this monitor, an administrator can determine the capacity of the system and system configurations.

Given a Network Problem Scenario, Determine the Problem

Use the following techniques to determine the problem: recognize abnormal physical conditions; isolate and correct problems where the fault is in the physical media (patch cable or cable run); check the status of servers; check for configuration problems with DNS, WINS, and HOST files; check for viruses; check the validity of the account name and password; recheck operator logon procedures; and select and run appropriate diagnostics.

Question: What are some common issues to look for if a network is having problems?

First, abnormal physical conditions should be considered, such as power interruptions, presence of high heat or humidity where a networking device is located, or large amounts of electrical noise.

An extremely common problem, often referred to as a Layer 1 problem, is somewhere in the conducting path from a PC's NIC to the nearest networking device (typically a hub or a switch). The patch cable from the PC to the outlet could be faulty: bad terminations, bent or crushed cable, or improper wiring sequences. The horizontal cable run from the outlet to the patch panel could be bent, crushed, cut, improperly mounted, or otherwise damaged. Or, the patch and jumper cables from the patch panel to the networking device could be the incorrect type of cable or also could be damaged.

Servers should be checked to verify that all servers and resources are functioning properly. Servers and resources such as DNS, WINS, and HOST files should be checked for proper configuration. A virus scan can be done to be sure that a virus has not tapped into the network, causing problems. Workstations must have all of the proper settings.

Next, verify the validity of the user's account and password. Is the user typing in the correct user ID and password? Does the individual have access? Verify the login procedures. Finally, if the problem cannot be resolved, vendor-provided diagnostics should be run.

Summary

Now that you have completed this review chapter, you should have a firm understanding of the following topics:

- Basic networking knowledge (18 percent)
- Physical layer (6 percent)
- Data link layer (5 percent)
- Network layer (5 percent)
- Transport layer (5 percent)
- TCP/IP fundamentals (16 percent)
- TCP/IP suite utilities (11 percent)
- Remote connectivity (5 percent)
- Security (6 percent)
- Installation of the network (6 percent)
- Maintenance and support of the network (6 percent)
- Network troubleshooting (11 percent)

NOTE

The percentages indicate the weight of each topic within the Network+ Certification Exam.

CCNA Certification Exam Review

Introduction

This chapter serves as a review as you prepare for the CCNA certification exam. The first step in preparing for the exam is to review the exam objectives in conjunction with the curriculum topics. This chapter presents a review of the topics covered in the CCNA Certification Exam, which will assist in your preparation for the exam.

OSI Model

The overall goal of communication protocols is to allow a computer application on one computer to communicate with a computer application on another computer, regardless of the hardware platform or operating system of the two computers.

Application Layer

The application layer identifies the communication partner and provides functions for particular application services, such as file transfer and virtual terminals.

Typical TCP/IP applications include the following:

- Telnet
- File Transfer Protocol (FTP)
- Trivial File Transfer Protocol (TFTP)
- Simple Mail Transfer Protocol (SMTP)
- Simple Network Management Protocol (SNMP)
- Hypertext Transfer Protocol (HTTP)
- Bootstrap Protocol (BootP)
- Dynamic Host Configuration Protocol (DHCP)

The Presentation Layer

The presentation layer provides communication services by transparently converting the different data, video, sound, and graphic formats to and from a format suitable for transmission. This layer is also responsible for data compression, decompression, encryption, and decryption.

Although these can be specific protocols, they are usually built into existing application layer protocols.

Some of the presentation layer standards involved include the following:

- **Text**—ASCII, EBCDIC
- **Graphics**—TIFF, JPEG, GIF, PICT
- **Sound**—MIDI, MPEG, QuickTime

Session Layer

The session layer controls the dialogue between devices or hosts. It establishes, manages, and terminates sessions between the applications.

Examples of session layer protocols include the following:

- Network File System (NFS)
- Structured Query Language (SQL)
- Remote Procedure Call (RPC)
- X Window System
- AppleTalk Session Protocol (ASP)
- DNA Session Control Protocol (SCP)

Transport Layer

The transport layer is responsible for end-to-end delivery of information, including error recovery and flow control.

Transport layer protocols can be reliable or unreliable. Unreliable protocols may have little or no responsibility for establishing connections, acknowledgments, sequencing, and flow control. It is possible that unreliable transport layer protocols will leave this responsibility to another layer's protocol. The reliable transport layer protocols may include responsibility for the following:

- Establishing connections and closing connections, such as the three-way handshake
- Transferring data
- Acknowledging what has been received or not received
- Making sure that packets arriving out of sequence can be sequenced in their proper order
- Maintaining flow control, such as in window sizes

The TCP/IP reliable transport layer protocol is the *Transmission Control Protocol (TCP)*. Protocols that use TCP can include FTP, Telnet, and HTTP.

The TCP/IP unreliable transport layer protocol is the *User Datagram Protocol (UDP)*. Protocols that use UDP can include TFTP, SNMP, NFS, Domain Name System (DNS), and the routing protocol RIP.

Transport layer protocols include the following:

- **TCP/IP**—TCP and UDP
- **Novell**—Sequenced Packet Exchange (SPX)

Network Layer

The network layer provides connectivity and path selection between two end systems (original source and final destination) that may be located on geographically diverse networks. Network layer addressing provides addressing for the original source address and the final destination address—in TCP/IP, these are the IP addresses. These addresses do not change along the path.

Examples of network layer protocols include the following:

- Internet Protocol (IP)
- Novell's Internetwork Packet Exchange (IPX)

Data Link Layer

The data link layer provides reliable transit of data across a physical link. In doing so, the data link layer is concerned with physical (as opposed to network, or logical) addressing, network topology, line discipline (how end systems use the network link), error notification, ordered delivery of frames, and flow control.

The data link layer delivers the frame from one node to the next, such as from host to host, host to router, router to router, or router to host. The data link addresses usually change, representing the current data link address and the next-hop data link address. In terms of Ethernet, this would be the source MAC address and the destination MAC address.

Data link layer protocols include the following:

- Ethernet
- IEEE 802.3
- Token Ring
- IEEE 802.5
- High-level Data Link Control (HDLC)
- Point-to-Point Protocol (PPP)

Physical Layer

The physical layer defines the electrical, mechanical, procedural, and functional specifications for activating, maintaining, and deactivating the physical link between end systems. Such characteristics as voltage levels, timing of voltage changes, physical data rates, maximum transmission distances, physical connections, and other similar attributes are defined by physical layer specifications.

Physical layer standards include the following:

- 10BaseT
- 100BaseTX
- V.35
- RS-232

Data Encapsulation

Be sure to understand how data is encapsulated and decapsulated at different layers, as shown in Figure 16-1.

FIGURE 16-1
A data encapsulation example.

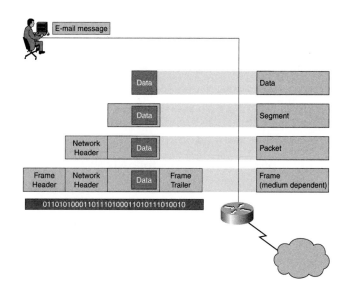

Creating Subnets

When given an IP address and a subnet mask, how can you determine other information, such as the following:

- The subnet address of this subnet
- The broadcast address of this subnet
- The range of host addresses for this subnet
- The maximum number of subnets for this subnet mask
- The number of hosts for this subnet
- The number of subnet bits and the slash number
- The number of this subnet

Subnet Planning

Knowing what subnet mask to use depends on how many subnets and host per subnets you need.

Sample Problems

Problem 1.

Network address: 172.25.0.0

Requirement: 600 hosts per subnet

Solution

Subnet mask needed: 255.255.252.0

Reason: The "252" in the third octet leaves 10 bits for the hosts or 1022 hosts per subnet. 255.255.248.0 would have been more hosts than needed, and 255.255.254.0 would not have been enough hosts.

Problem 2.

Network address: 172.25.0.0

Requirement: Eight subnets, with the greatest number of hosts possible per subnet

Solution

Subnet mask needed: 255.255.240.0

Reason: 255.255.240.0 gives you 14 subnets. 255.255.224.0 are not enough subnets, and 255.255.248.0 does not provide the maximum number of hosts per subnet.

LAN Switching

In this review of LAN switching, you will see that one way to help reduce network congestion is to use switches instead of hubs whenever possible. In addition, to increase the efficiency of the switch, you might want to utilize some or all of these switching features:

- Fast Ethernet (100 Mbps) switch ports and host NIC cards
- Full-duplex communications
- Cut-through switching

Full-Duplex and Half-Duplex Ethernet Operations

Two types of Ethernet communications exist:

- Half-duplex
- Full-duplex

Half-duplex communications allows for two or more devices to communicate with each other, but with only one device at a time (see Figure 16-2). If multiple devices attempt to communicate at the same time, a collision will occur. Those devices then back off, and a random algorithm within each NIC determines which device will send first.

FIGURE 16-2
Half-duplex
Ethernet
design
(standard
Ethernet).

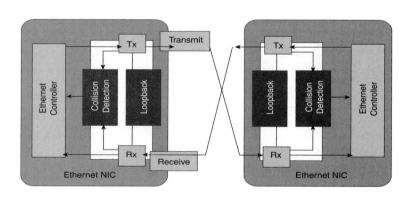

◆ Ethernet physical connection provides several circuits
◆ Most important are receive (RX), transmit (TX), and collision detection

Hosts that are connected to a hub must operate in half-duplex mode because they must be capable of detecting when a collision occurs (to stop transmitting).

Full-duplex communication allows two devices to communicate with each other simultaneously (see Figure 16-3). One of the limitations of full-duplex Ethernet is that there must be only one device connected to the switch port. That device can be a computer, a printer, a router, or another switch. If you have single devices attached to switch ports (no hubs), it is a good idea to have them operate in full-duplex mode.

FIGURE 16-3
Full-duplex
Ethernet
design.

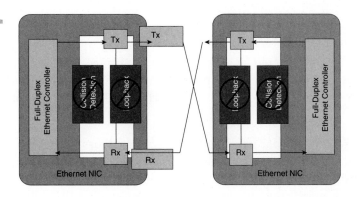

♦ Transmit circuit connects directly to receive circuit
♦ No collisions
♦ Significant performance improvement
♦ Eliminates contention on Ethernet point-to-point link
♦ Uses a single port for each full-duplex connection

Full-duplex operation doubles the amount of throughput on that link. For example, on a standard Ethernet 10-Mbps link, the throughput would be 20 Mbps—10 Mbps transmitted, plus 10 Mbps received. Virtually no collisions occur on a full-duplex connection because only two devices are in the collision domain.

Configure Both Ends

It is important that both the switch port and the device connected to the switch use the same mode of communications—either half-duplex or full-duplex. Both the NIC card in the host (or, in the case of a router, the Ethernet interface) and the switch port must use the same mode.

> **Question:** How does the computer's NIC card get configured for full-duplex or half-duplex operation?
>
> **Answer:** In older NIC cards, it was done manually, either by software that came with the NIC card or with hardware on the NIC card itself. Today, most NIC cards are autosensing and will adapt to the mode in which the switch operates.

Switches can be autosensing or software configurable, depending on the vendor and model of the switch. If both the host and the switch are autosensing and only a single device is on that switch port, the link is most likely configured to be a full-duplex link.

Configuring a Router

If a router is connected to a switch, you might need to configure the router's Ethernet interface to be either half- or full-duplex. This is a good item to check if you must troubleshoot a problem with an Ethernet interface on a router.

Mismatch Between Two Switches

NOTE

This same problem might also occur if a host and a switch are operating in different duplex modes, one in half-duplex mode and the other in full-duplex.

Another problem that you might run across occurs when two switches are interconnected, but the link seems to be slower than it should be. There might be a mismatch between the modes on the ports that link the two switches. When one switch operates in half-duplex mode and the other switch is in full-duplex mode, you might notice the collision light flashing frequently on the device running in half-duplex mode. The full-duplex device is sending at will; it does not attempt to sense whether the other device is sending frames. This causes a large number of collisions to occur as the switch operating in half-duplex mode senses no traffic on the link and forwards the frame at the same time that the switch operating in full-duplex mode sends a frame.

Ethernet Frame

In this section, you learn about the parts of the Ethernet frame (shown in Figure 16-4) and learn how internetworking devices, such as routers and switches, filter and forward these frames.

FIGURE 16-4
Ethernet frame.

Ethernet Header					Ethernet Trailer
Ethernet Header preamble	**MAC Destination Address**	**MAC Source Address**	Data Layers 3-7		FCS

Several different types of Ethernet or IEEE 802.3 frames exist. The terms "Ethernet" and "IEEE 802.3" are similar but not identical. Ethernet is a product name and a competing standard with IEEE 802.3. There are some differences and similarities between the two types, but for the purposes of this section, they are not important. To keep things simple, you will see the term "Ethernet" throughout this section, but the information applies to both Ethernet and IEEE 802.3 protocols.

The MAC Address

The *Media Access Control (MAC) address* is a Layer 2 address that is burned into the ROM chip on an Ethernet network interface card (NIC). This is a unique 48-bit number that is written as eight hexadecimal numbers.

The first 24 bits represent the vendor or maker of the of the NIC card (some vendors might have more than one 24-bit vendor code assigned to them). Each vendor code is a serial number unique to that vendor. The 24-bit vendor code, together with the 24-bit vendor-controlled and assigned serial number, makes up a unique 48-bit MAC address.

Hub Operation

In Figure 16-5, four PCs are connected to a hub. When a hub receives an Ethernet frame on one port, it forwards (repeats) it out all other ports.

FIGURE 16-5
Functions of a
MAC address—
the hub.

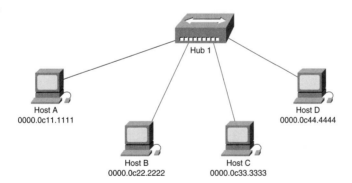

For example, if Host A is sending an Ethernet frame to Host D, Host A encapsulates the data and upper-layer headers into the Layer 2 frame field known as the "data." Normally, when data is sent from one computer to another, several frames might be needed to transmit it all. In the Ethernet frame header, as shown in Figure 16-5, Host A is the source MAC address and Host D is the destination MAC address.

> **Question:** After Host A sends out the frame, which hosts will see this frame? More specifically, where does the frame go?
>
> **Answer:** All the hosts on this network—every host connected to the hub—will see at least part of this frame.
>
> **Explanation:** When the frame is sent out from Host A to the hub, the hub forwards (repeats) the frame out all ports (except the port that the frame came in on). Therefore, each host connected to the hub begins to receive the frame. Each host copies the beginning of the frame, the MAC destination address, into the NIC card. If this destination MAC address matches the MAC address of the NIC card, then the host copies in the rest of the frame. If the destination MAC address does not match the NIC card address, then the host ignores the rest of the frame.

If any other host on the hub sends an Ethernet frame at the same time that Host A is sending its frame, as shown in Figure 16-5, a collision will occur because all four hosts are on the same collision domain.

The Switch Operation

In Figure 16-6, four hosts are all connected to a switch. Switches forward frames based on Layer 2 addresses (Ethernet MAC addresses). The switch learns these addresses by examining the Layer 2 source address of the Ethernet frame as the switch receives it.

NOTE

For more information on how switches learn addresses, review Semester 1 information.

FIGURE 16-6
Functions of a MAC address— the switch.

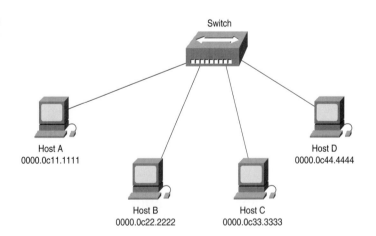

Assume that the switch has just been powered on, which means that the switch's source address table (SAT), also known as the switch table, is empty. The switch associates what devices are connected to which switch port by using the switch table. A switch associates which hosts are on which port by "learning," which is why these are sometimes called "learning switches."

When a switch is first turned on, it does not have any entries in its switching table. Each time that it sees a frame, it examines the MAC source address. If the MAC source address is not in its table, the switch enters the address into its switch table associated with the port that it was heard on.

Assume that Host A sends a Ethernet frame to Host D. When the switch receives the Ethernet frame from Host A destined for Host D, it stores the frame in its memory buffer. The switch examines the MAC source address to see if that particular MAC address is in its SAT table. In this case, it is not, so the switch adds it to the table for switch port 1. It has now "learned" that Host A, (MAC address 0000.0c11.1111) can be reached via switch port 1.

Next, the switch examines the Ethernet frame destination MAC address and searches for this address in its SAT table. Because this address does not exist in the SAT table, the switch floods it out all ports. A switch will either *filter* or *flood* frames based on its SAT table. As you just learned, a frame gets flooded (sent out all ports except for the incoming port) when the switch does not have an entry for the destination MAC address in its SAT table.

A switch filters a frame when it does have the Ethernet frame's destination MAC address in its SAT table. This means that the switch knows which port the destination MAC address can be reached and forwards the frame only out that port.

Now you will see what happens when Host D sends information back to Host A. Host D sends a frame with the destination MAC address of Host A, 0000.0c11.1111.

The switch examines the MAC source address to see if the MAC address of Host D is in its SAT table. In this case, it is not, so the switch adds it to the table for switch port 4. It has now "learned" that Host D (MAC address 0000.0c44.444) can be reached via switch port 4. Next, the switch examines the destination MAC address of the Ethernet frame, which is 0000.0c11.1111. The switch looks up this address in its SAT table and acknowledges that it is in its table. The switch forwards this frame out switch port 1 to reach Host A. This is an example of a switch filtering a frame.

> **Question:** What would happen if Host A needed to send an Ethernet frame to Host D?
>
> **Answer:** Because Host D's MAC address (0000.0c44.4444) is in the switch's SAT table, the switch would know to forward this frame only out switch port 4. As shown previously in Figure 16-6, this is another example of the switch *filtering* the frame.

NOTE

If the SAT table shows that the destination MAC address is on the same port as the incoming frame, the switch does not send the frame out any port, including the incoming port. If a switch were to ever send an Ethernet frame out an incoming port, this would cause duplicate frames on the network.

Microsegmentation of a Network

NOTE

On a switch, each switch port creates a separate collision domain.

An advantage of a switch over a hub is that a switch allows for a dedicated path between two devices on the switch, as shown in Figure 16-7. This means that pairs of devices on the same switch can communicate in parallel with a minimum number of collisions. When two or more devices attempt to send to the same device on a switch port, a collision does not occur. Instead, one frame is sent out the switch port to the destination, while the other one is held in the switch's memory or buffer. This is common when multiple clients are sending information to the same server.

FIGURE 16-7
Microsegmentation of the network.

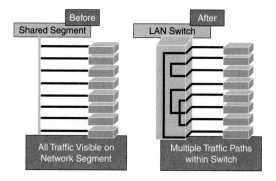

♦ Dedicated paths between sender and receiver hosts.

In Figure 16-8, assume that Host A sends a frame to Host D; at the same time, Host B sends a frame to Host C. Within the switch, Hosts A and D are communicating in parallel with Hosts B and C, giving two different dedicated paths between senders and receivers. No collisions occur in this example.

However, a collision might occur if the switch is forwarding a frame at the same time that the host on that port is sending a frame toward the switch. This is assuming that the switch and host are operating in half-duplex mode.

Switches and Buffers

Another advantage to a switch is that it has a *buffer*, or memory. If two hosts send a frame (or frames) to the same destination, instead of a collision occurring, those frames get buffered by the switch. The switch sends frames out the port to the destination one frame at a time. The advantage of the switch buffering these frames is that the source hosts do not need to resend the frame.

They are completely unaware that there is contention with another host for that destination. For example, if Host A and Host B were both sending frames to Host D, as shown in Figure 16-8, the switch would send one of the frames to Host D and then would send the next one.

FIGURE 16-8
Microsegmen-
tation of the
network using
switches.

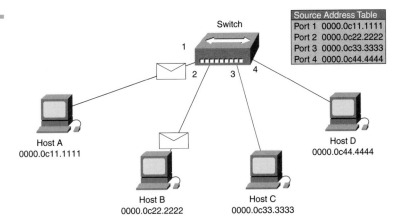

A Flat Network

In many LANs, hubs and switches are interconnected as a series. This means that the switches must not only maintain MAC address for hosts that are directly connected to one of its switch ports, but also MAC addresses of hosts connected to other switches and hubs.

In Figure 16-9, Switch 1 and Switch 2 are interconnected. If Hosts A, B, C, and D send information to Server H, Switch 2 will "learn" that these hosts (their MAC addresses) can all be reached via Switch 2's port 1. Figure 16-9 shows what the Switch 2 SAT table would like. Remember that, if the switch does not have the destination MAC address in its SAT table, it must flood the frame out all ports.

A completely switched network with all switches (and hubs) is known as a *flat network*. A flat network is a LAN made up entirely of hubs and switches, with no routers. All hosts on this LAN are on the same network or subnetwork. These networks are easy to maintain because there are no routers, so adding a new host or another device is relatively simple.

However, a flat network has several disadvantages, including a single Layer 3 broadcast domain. As we will see later, a Layer 2 broadcast, such as an ARP request, will travel to every host and device on the LAN. These and other Layer 2 broadcasts can use up a great deal of a LAN's available bandwidth.

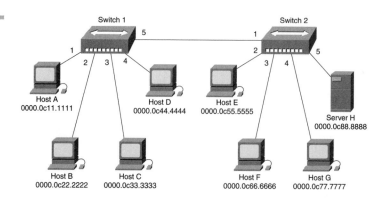

FIGURE 16-9
A flat network.

A flat network has other disadvantages as well, including less manageability of network traffic and security. In a flat network, after the switches learn about what MAC addresses are on which ports, the network traffic flows accordingly. Except for the placement of the switches, the network administrator has little or no control over the path of the frames.

LAN Segmentation Using Routers

NOTE

The information explained in this section is a simplification of the actual ARP process. Although conceptually accurate, the actual process is slightly different and more complex. However, for the purposes of this curriculum, the explanation contained in this section provides a good basis of understanding.

Remember that the LAN interfaces on routers, such as an Ethernet interface, perform both the Layer 2 function of a switch and the Layer 3 function of a router. Like switches, routers segment each LAN interface into a separate collision domain, as shown in Figure 16-10. However, routers separate LAN and WAN segments into different networks or subnetworks (Layer 3). This means that routers not only separate interfaces into their own segments, but they also do not propagate (forward) Layer 2 broadcast requests, such as ARP requests, out other interfaces.

Routers interconnect different networks or subnetworks. In Figure 16-11, the router is connecting two different subnetworks, 172.30.1.0/24 and 172.30.2.0/24. The router has an Ethernet interface on each subnetwork, Ethernet 0 with the IP address 172.30.1.1/24, and Ethernet 1 with the IP address 172.30.2.1/24. The router will forward packets from one subnetwork to the other only if the destination IP address is on the other subnetwork. Because the destination IP address is a Layer 3 address, as opposed to the Layer 2 addresses, the router will *not* forward Layer 2 broadcast addresses such as ARP requests. Therefore, the router separates, or segments, the network into separate broadcast domains.

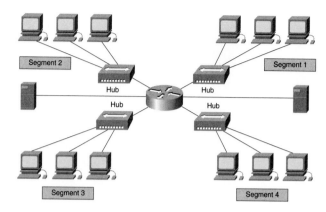

FIGURE 16-10
LAN segmentation using routers.

♦ More manageable, greater functionality, multiple active paths
♦ Smaller Broadcast
♦ Operates at Layers 3 and 4

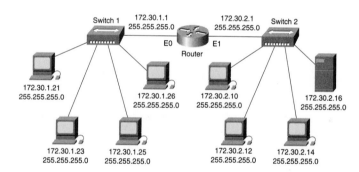

FIGURE 16-11
Router connecting two different subnetworks.

♦ Two subnets
♦ Several collision domains
  ♦ One per switch port
♦ Communication between subnets

ARP Request/Reply

ARP is a Layer 3 protocol, one of many protocols within the TCP/IP suite of protocols. An ARP request is used when a sending device knows the IP address for the destination host, but does not know its MAC address. Before the IP packet can be encapsulated into the Ethernet frame, the sending device needs to know the destination MAC address. This relationship of IP to the MAC address is normally kept in an ARP table or cache, as shown in Figure 16-12. This table is dynamically updated based on local network activity. If the IP and MAC address of the destination is not in the ARP table, the device must send out an ARP request to get the MAC address.

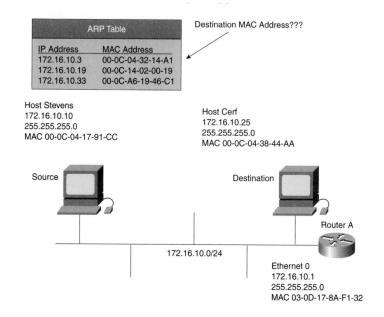

FIGURE 16-12
ARP request/
reply.

Question: Why do devices need to map a MAC address to an IP address?

Address: The simple answer is to deliver the IP packet inside an Ethernet frame to the next device along the way to reach its final destination. The next device may very well be the final destination, or it may be a router. An example is shown in Figure 16-13.

For example, Host Stevens has an IP packet it wants to send to Host Cerf. Host Stevens needs to send this packet to either the final destination, Host Cerf, or the default gateway, the router, so that it can forward the packet onward to its final destination.

FIGURE 16-13
Two devices (hosts) on the same subnetwork.

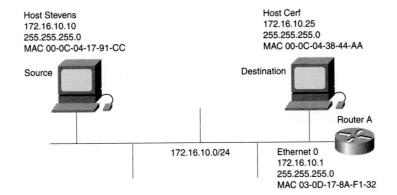

> **Question:** How does Host Stevens know where it needs to send this packet?
>
> The answer depends on your client software.
>
> **Answer 1:** Host Stevens will look for host Cerf's IP address of 172.16.10.25 in its ARP table. If it is not found, Host Stevens will send an ARP for the MAC address that is paired to Cerf's IP address. In this example, Host Cerf would respond with an ARP reply containing its MAC address, and the packet could be sent. But what if Host Cerf wasn't on the same local network? If the router has proxy ARP enabled, it would send a response of its own MAC address back to Host Stevens after it calculated that the destination IP address wasn't on the same subnetwork as the source device. Host Stevens would then create a relationship between the destination IP address, Host Cerf, and the router's MAC address in its ARP table. From then on, Host Stevens, based on the destination IP address, would send packets to the router for the first hop of the trip to the destination, Host Cerf. The router would forward the packet, based on its IP address, to the destination host or the next-hop router.
>
> *continues*

Answer 2: In this answer, Host Stevens has a default gateway and subnet mask entry stored in its TCP/IP configuration. This is the case with Microsoft Windows clients. In this situation, Host Stevens will do an AND operation on both the source and the destination IP addresses using the stored subnet mask. If the results of the AND operation results in the same subnetwork address, the two hosts are on the same network segment. Host Stevens then looks in its ARP table for the destination IP and MAC address pair. If it can't find the pair, it issues an ARP request. The destination host responds, and the packet is sent. If the resulting subnetwork addresses are different after ANDing, Host Stevens will use the default gateway's MAC address, along with the destination IP address, to get the packet to the router for the first hop of the trip to the destination host. The router would forward the packet, based on its IP address, to the destination host or the next-hop router.

Example 1: The ARP Request and Reply

In the example given in Figure 16-14, Host Cerf's IP address does not appear in Host Stevens' ARP table. Host Stevens must send out an ARP request for the IP address 172.16.10.25, Host Cerf's IP address. Once again, Host Stevens knows that it can do an ARP request directly for Host Cerf because it had determined that they are both on the same subnetwork.

As also shown Figure 16-14, the ARP request is encapsulated within an Ethernet frame.

ARP Request from Host Stevens at 172.16.10.10

The ARP request is a Layer 2 broadcast, which means that there are all binary 1s in the destination MAC address. This is normally written in hexadecimal as all Fs (FF-FF-FF-FF-FF-FF).

The IP address that Host Stevens is looking for is in the field Target IP Address. All hosts on the LAN receive and process this ARP request because it is a Layer 2 broadcast. The hosts examine the target IP Address to see if their IP address matches.

ARP Reply from Host Cerf at 172.16.10.25

The host with the IP address that matched 172.16.10.25 will reply. This reply is unicast, meaning that only the host that matches the MAC address will process it. Notice that in the ARP reply, the information in the Sender and Target fields is reversed from the ARP request. This is because the source is now Host Cerf instead of Host Stevens.

FIGURE 16-14
The ARP request and reply.

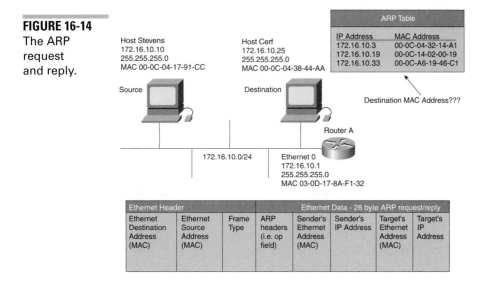

Data Transmission from Host Stevens

Host Stevens receives the ARP reply and enters Host Cerf's IP address and MAC address into its ARP table. Host Stevens now encapsulates the IP packet into the Ethernet frame and sends the packet directly to Host Cerf.

Symmetric and Asymmetric Switching

Symmetric switching is a switch with ports of the same bandwidth, as shown in Figure 16-15. Switching can be optimized through even distribution of network traffic.

Asymmetric switching is a switch with ports of different bandwidth, as shown in Figure 16-16. Asymmetric switching is appropriate when certain switch ports have devices that need more bandwidth, such as servers. Another use for switch ports that need higher bandwidth is when that port is connected to another switch.

Whether that switch port needs higher bandwidth depends on the amount of network traffic that is received and transmitted through that port. Proper LAN design, network analysis, and network traffic monitoring will help network administrators determine which switch ports need the additional bandwidth.

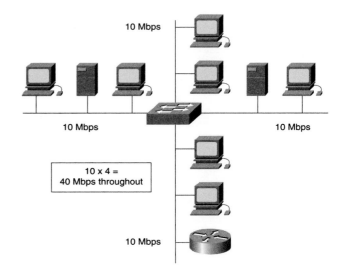

FIGURE 16-15
Symmetric
switching.

10 Mbps

10 Mbps

10 Mbps

10 x 4 =
40 Mbps throughout

10 Mbps

♦ Provides switching between like bandwidths (10/10 or 100/100 Mbps)
♦ Multiple simultaneous conversations increase throughput

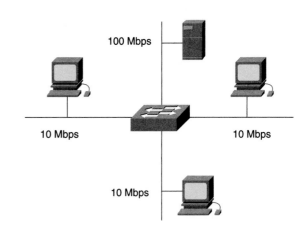

FIGURE 16-16
Asymmetric
switching.

100 Mbps

10 Mbps

10 Mbps

10 Mbps

♦ Provides switching between unlike bandwidths (10/100 Mbps)
♦ Requires the switch to use memory buffering

Cut-Through and Store-and-Forward LAN Switching

The two main types of switching methods are *store-and-forward* and *cut-through switching*. Depending on the switch, this can be a configurable parameter on each individual port.

Store-and-Forward Switching

Store-and-forward switching is typically the default method on most switches. Before a switch forwards an Ethernet frame out another interface (by looking up the destination MAC address in the switch's source address table), it copies the entire frame into its buffers and checks the frame check sequence (FCS) against its own calculations. If the FCS and its own calculations match, the frame is forwarded out the proper port. If the FCS does not match its own calculations, the frame is dropped. Checking the FCS takes time—that is, causes additional latency in the switch—but all errors are filtered.

Cut-Through Switching

Two types of cut-through switching are available on most Cisco switches:

- Fast-forward
- Fragment-free

Fast-forward switching begins to forward a frame out the proper switch port immediately after reading the Layer 2 destination address and looking that address up that address in the switch's source address table. The frame begins to be forwarded out that interface before the rest of the frame is copied into the switch. The FCS is not checked with fast-forward switching, so there is no error checking.

Fragment-free switching performs like cut-through switching, but it waits until the first 64 bytes of the frame are received before forwarding the first bytes of the frame out the outgoing switch port. According to Ethernet and 802.3 specifications, collisions should be detected during the first 64 bytes of a frame. Just as with fast-forward switching, in fragment-free switching, the FCS is not checked, so there is no error checking. Fragment-free switching is faster (less latency) than store-and-forward switching, but slower (more latency) than fast-forward switching.

The Benefits of Virtual LANs

Virtual LANs (VLANs) are used for several reasons, including the creation of separate broadcast domains within a switched network. We will see that routers are necessary to pass information between different VLANs.

NOTE

VLANs are *not* necessary to have separate subnetworks on a switched network, but as you will see, they provide more advantages when it comes to things such as data link layer (Layer 2) broadcasts.

A VLAN can be thought of as a subnetwork. There are several ways to implement VLANs, but one of the most common methods is to separate subnetworks into separate VLANs.

Without VLANs, a Layer 2 broadcast, such as an ARP request, would be seen by all hosts on the switched network. On a large switched network, these ARP requests can consume unnecessary network bandwidth and host processing cycles. Normally, only routers would stop the propagation of Layer 2 broadcast, such as these ARP requests.

Notice in Figure 16-17 that the hosts are on different subnetworks, yet the ARP request is being received by all the computers. This can be an issue especially in a network with Windows 95/98 computers. Windows 95/98 computers keep entries in their ARP tables for only 120 seconds. This means that if the ARP table hasn't communicated with a device for 120 seconds, it will erase its IP address-to-MAC address mapping from the ARP table. The next time that the host needs to communicate with this same device, it will need to do another ARP request. UNIX computers, on the other hand, normally keep entries in their ARP tables for about 20 minutes.

FIGURE 16-17
All switched networks—two networks.

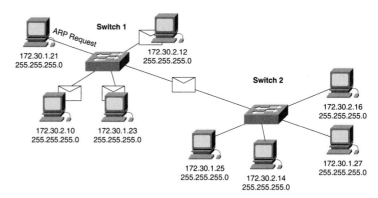

- Two Subnets
- Several Collision Domains
- One switch per port
- One Broadcast Domain

Why Use Port-Centric VLANs?

The network in Figure 16-18 has a network address of 172.30.0.0. The network has been divided into subnetworks using the subnet mask 255.255.255.0. Therefore, two subnetworks exist on the network: 172.30.1.0/24 and 172.30.2.0/24.

FIGURE 16-18
Two VLANS.

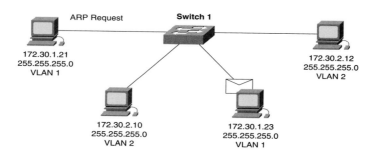

♦ Two Subnets

> **Question:** If you didn't use VLANs, what would happen with a Layer 2 broadcast, such as an ARP request?
>
> **Answer:** All hosts, regardless of what subnetwork they belong to, receive the ARP request, as long as they are on the same switched network and no router is between them and the ARP request.

Now you will see what happens if you use port-centric VLANs. In port-centric VLANs, the network administrator assigns each switch port to a specific VLAN. It is important that the VLAN assignment on the switch matches the subnetwork assignment on the host that is connected to that switch port.

For example, what would happen with ARP requests on the network, but with the use of VLANs? Remember: The VLAN assignment is actually done at the switch. No VLAN assignment is done on the individual hosts.

For a host on the 172.30.1.0 subnetwork, the switch port will be configured as VLAN 1.

For a host on the 172.30.2.0 subnetwork, the switch port will be configured as VLAN 2.

This time, only hosts on the same VLAN (VLAN 2) that are also on the same subnetwork receive the Layer 2 broadcast, the ARP request. Because Layer 2 broadcasts are meant only for hosts within the same subnetwork, the VLAN mapping on the switch keeps the unwanted, unnecessary Layer 2 broadcast from being forwarded on links that do not need to receive those frames.

Notice that the switch is doing this filtering. This happened because the network administrator assigned the proper VLAN assignment to the proper switch port. The switch is configured as described in Table 16-1.

TABLE 16-1   Switch Port VLAN

1	1
2	2
3	1
4	2

Routing and VLANs

Just like subnetworks (remember subnetworks = VLANs), a router is needed to route information between different VLANs. There are several different ways to do this with the router.

One way is to have a router with a separate Ethernet interface for every VLAN (subnetwork). Figure 16-19 shows the router with two Ethernet interfaces. The Ethernet 0 interface is configured with an IP address of 172.30.1.1/24 and will be a member of VLAN 1 on the switch; the Ethernet 1 interface is configured with an IP address of 172.30.2.1/24 and will be a member of VLAN 2 on the switch.

FIGURE 16-19
Routing and
VLANs.

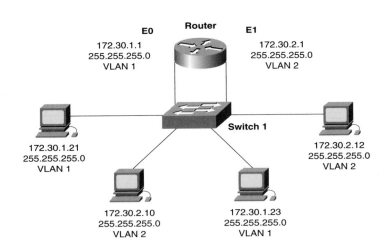

Router
E0   E1
172.30.1.1   172.30.2.1
255.255.255.0   255.255.255.0
VLAN 1   VLAN 2

Switch 1

172.30.1.21   172.30.2.12
255.255.255.0   255.255.255.0
VLAN 1   VLAN 2

172.30.2.10   172.30.1.23
255.255.255.0   255.255.255.0
VLAN 2   VLAN 1

♦ Two Subnets
♦ Communication between VLANs
♦ NOTE: VLANs assigned only to the ports

Figure 16-20 shows how the switch and router interconnect.

FIGURE 16-20
Switch and router.

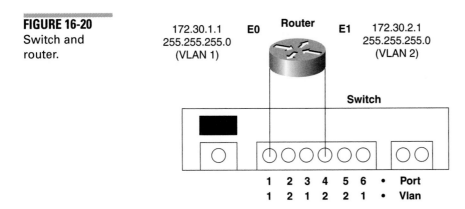

If information is needed to be sent from a host on one VLAN (subnetwork) to a host on another VLAN (subnetwork), these packets will need to be sent to and routed through the router (see Figure 16-21).

NOTE

The router must be running a routing protocol to route between the two subnetworks.

FIGURE 16-21
Communication between VLANs.

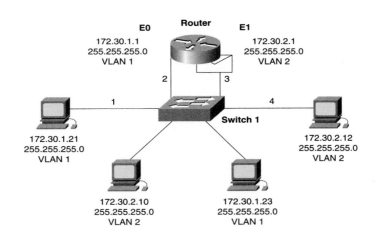

♦ Two Subnetworks
♦ Communication between VLANs
♦ NOTE: VLANs assigned only to the ports

Consider this example:

```
Router(config)# router rip
Router(config-router)# network 172.30.0.0
```

NOTE

You can use secondary addresses instead of subinterfaces to accomplish this, but secondary addresses will eventually be no longer supported in future versions of the Cisco IOS.

One of the disadvantages to this type of router configuration is that the router must have a separate Ethernet interface for every VLAN (subnetwork). This might not scale well for networks with many different VLANs. One solution to this problem is to use the "router-on-a-stick" or "one-armed-router" (OAR) method.

With the router-on-a-stick method, only one physical Ethernet interface is used. The physical interface is divided into subinterfaces, one for each VLANs (subnetworks) (see Figure 16-22).

FIGURE 16-22
VLANs only assigned to the ports.

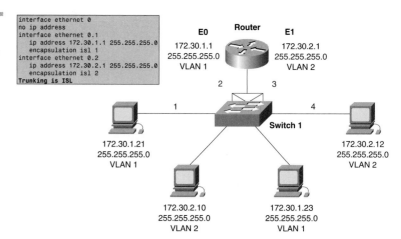

♦ Two Subnetworks
♦ Communication between VLANs using trunking
♦ NOTE: VLANs assigned only to the ports

With the use of router-on-a-stick, only one physical interface is needed. The disadvantage to this is that this single link between the router and the switch will be used for all VLAN traffic to and from the switch. The port on the switch that is connected to the router's Ethernet interface will also need to be capable of doing "trunking," either with Cisco's proprietary Inter-Switch Link (ISL) or IEEE 802.1Q.

Here is the router configuration (also shown in Figure 16-22):

```
Router# config t
Router(config)# interface ethernet 0.1
Router(config-subif)# ip address 172.30.1.1 255.255.255.0
Router(config-subif)# encapsulation isl 1 {1 = VLAN 1}
Router(config-subif)# no ip redirects {recommended}
Router(config)# interface ethernet 0.2
Router(config-subif)# ip address 172.30.2.1 255.255.255.0
Router(config-subif)# encapsulation isl 2 {2 = VLAN 2}
Router(config-subif)# no ip redirects {recommended}
```

VLAN Tagging

A normal, single link can be used to pass traffic among multiple subnetworks. However, when a single link is used to transmit multiple VLAN traffic, the switch ports or router ports that connect the two devices must be capable of "tagging." In Figure 16-23, in the link between the two switches, those switch ports must be capable of tagging.

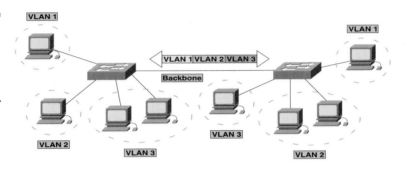

FIGURE 16-23
Specifically developed for multi-VLAN, interswitched communicators.

Again, tagging is needed between switches, or between a switch and a router, to pass VLAN traffic if a single link is used. Your switches must have ports that can do this trunking or tagging.

Some of the different tagging protocols include the following:

- IEEE 802.1q
- Inter-Switch Link (ISL) (Cisco-proprietary)
- 802.10—FDDI
- ATM LANE

Take a look at this VLAN terminology:

- **Tagging**—Used to identify which VLAN a frame belongs to
- **Trunk**—A single link that carries multiple VLANs

In Figure 16-24, you will notice that tagging is taking place on two links:

- Between Switch 1 (Port A) and Switch 2 (Port A)
- Between Switch 2 (Port B) and Router (Ethernet 0)

The links between the switches, and the switch and the router where tagging is occurring, is known as a trunk. A trunk is a link that carries multiple VLANs. (The term *trunk* also has other meanings in networking and telecommunications.)

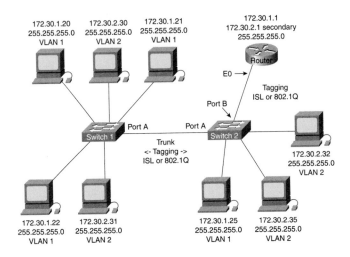

FIGURE 16-24
VLAN tagging.

This is because these links are required to carry frames belonging to multiple VLANs: VLAN 1 and VLAN 2. Not all switches and routers (or Cisco IOSs) are capable of doing the tagging, so it is important to make sure that your networking equipment can perform the tagging. On some switches, only a few ports may be configured for tagging. These are usually the higher-bandwidth ports (100 Mbps) on the switch.

In Figure 16-24, these switch ports must be capable of tagging:

- **Switch 1**—Port A
- **Switch 2**—Port A and Port B
- **Router**—Ethernet 0 (usually dependent on the Cisco IOS)

> **Question:** What would you do if your equipment did not do tagging, but you still wanted to do VLANs?
>
> **Answer:** You would need to have a separate link for every VLAN between switches, and between a switch and a router. Be sure to configure the switch ports for the proper VLANs.

Spanning-Tree Protocol

The main function of the Spanning-Tree Protocol (STP) is to allow redundant switched/bridged paths without suffering the effects of loops in the network. Spanning Tree allows for multiple links between switches, but only one link is active (forwarding mode), while all other redundant links are in standby (blocking mode) in case the primary link fails (see Figure 16-25).

FIGURE 16-25
Spanning-Tree
Protocol (STP).

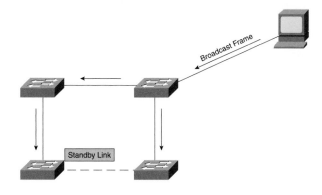

♦ Switches forward broadcast frames
♦ Prevents loops
    Loops can cause broadcast storms, and exponentially proliferate frames
♦ Allows redundant links
♦ Prunes topology to a minimal spanning tree
♦ Resilient to topology changes and device failures

Question: What would happen without Spanning Tree and if there were multiple links between two switches?

Answer: This could cause frames to be forwarded out the wrong switch ports—or, even worse, cause Layer 2 broadcast storms. Remember that a broadcast storm occurs when frames keep getting duplicated on a switched network, until it finally overwhelms the network and brings down the network.

Spanning Tree is important even in networks where there are no redundant links between switches. It is not uncommon for someone to accidentally connect a link between two switches when a connection already exists. Spanning Tree is an excellent safeguard to keep a mistake like this from bringing down a network.

Summary

Now that you have completed this review chapter, you should have a firm understanding of the following:

- OSI model
- Subnet creation
- Router commands
- Skills-based sample scenario

Chapter 17

Remote Access Technologies

Introduction

This chapter provides you with an overview of remote access technologies. More specifically, this chapter deals with one of the most rapidly evolving areas in networking: the edge referred to as access or "last mile" technologies, which are being driven by the consumer's desire for faster Internet access. This chapter covers wired to wireless remote access technologies, focusing on those that are the most widely used and those that are up-and-coming. Additionally, it discusses the pros and cons of accessing the Internet via cable modems, wireless connections, and digital subscriber lines (xDSL).

Cable Modems

Cable modems enable two-way, high-speed data transmissions using the same coaxial lines that transmit cable television. Some cable service providers promise data speeds up to 6.5 times that of T1 leased lines. This speed makes cable an attractive medium for transferring large amounts of digital information quickly, including video clips, audio files, and large chunks of data. Information that would take two minutes to download using ISDN can be downloaded in two seconds through a cable-modem connection.

Cable-modem access provides speeds superior to those of leased lines, with lower costs and simpler installation. When the cable infrastructure is in place, a firm can connect through installation of a modem, or router. Because cable modems do not use the telephone system infrastructure, no local-loop charges apply. Products, such as the Cisco uBR904 universal broadband router cable modem, make cable access an even more attractive investment by integrating a fully functional Cisco IOS router, four-port hub, and cable modem into one unit. This combination allows businesses to replace combinations of routers, bridges, hubs, and single-port cable modems with one product. (See Figure 17-1.)

FIGURE 17-1
Cisco uBR904
cable modem.

Cable modems provide a full-time connection. As soon as users turn on their computers, they are connected to the Internet. This setup removes the time and effort of dialing in to establish a connection. The "always-on" cable connection also means that a company's "information pipe" is open at all times. This setup increases the vulnerability of data to hackers and is a good reason why you should install firewalls and configure cable routers to maximize security. Fortunately, the industry is moving toward the standardization of cable modems, and this move is likely to address encryption needs. For instance, new models of the Cisco uBR904 cable modem will provide IP Security (IPSec) and firewall capabilities. These features protect company LANs and provide virtual private network (VPN) tunneling, with options for authentication and encryption.

Because the connection is permanently established, cable modems cannot dial into different networks or locations. Any network connection must take place through the Internet. For example, employees using a cable modem at home to surf the Web can connect to a company LAN only if the business connects its LAN to the Internet. Moving through the Internet in this way can restrict the speedy connection of cable modems. To address this problem, many cable access service providers are developing services that combine cable and T1 connections to provide fast and reliable remote office-to-corporate network connections.

Availability might be the biggest barrier to cable-modem adoption by businesses because only a few office buildings have been outfitted for cable reception, compared to almost 85 percent of households in North America that are wired for cable. Some cable operators are in the process of replacing traditional one-way cable systems with the two-way architecture known as *hybrid fiber coaxial (HFC)*.

How Cable Modems Work

Like telephone modems, cable modems modulate and demodulate data signals. However, cable modems incorporate more functionality designed for today's high-speed Internet services. Data flowing from the network to the user is referred to as *downstream*, and data flowing from the user to the network is referred to as *upstream*. From a user perspective, a cable modem is a 64/256 quadrature amplitude modulation (QAM) radio frequency (RF) receiver capable of delivering up to 30 to 40 Mbps of data in one 6-MHz cable channel. This is almost 500 times faster than a 56-Kbps modem. The head end manages traffic flow from both directions (see Figure 17-2). Head ends have facilities that do the following:

- Receive programming (for example, from NBC, CBS, and cable networks such as MTV and ESPN)

- Convert each channel to the channel frequency desired; scramble channels as needed (for example, the premium channels)

- Combine all the frequencies onto a single medium using frequency-division multiplexing (FDM)

- Broadcast the combined analog stream downstream to subscribers

FIGURE 17-2
The head end manages traffic flow.

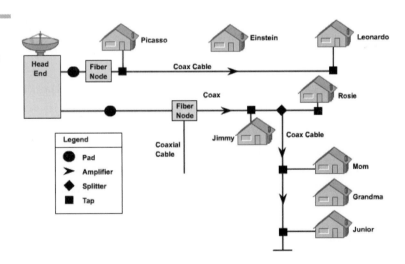

The upstream and downstream data rates can be configured to meet the needs of the subscribers. For example, a business service can be programmed to both transmit and receive at relatively high rates. A residential user, on the other hand, can have service configured to receive higher bandwidth access to the Internet while limited to low-bandwidth transmission to the network.

A subscriber can continue to receive cable television service while simultaneously receiving data on a cable modem to be delivered to a personal computer with the help of a simple one-to-two splitter (see Figure 17-3). The data service offered by a cable modem can be shared by up to 16 users in a local-area network (LAN) configuration.

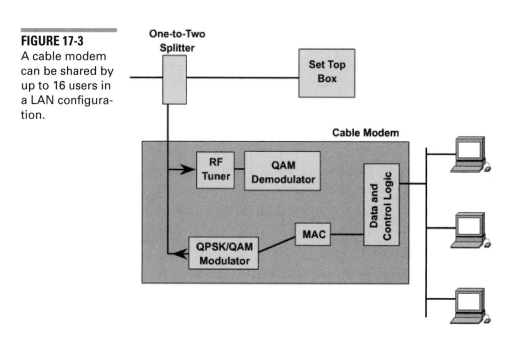

FIGURE 17-3
A cable modem can be shared by up to 16 users in a LAN configuration.

Because some cable networks are suited for only broadcast television services, cable modems can use either a standard telephone line or a QPSK/16 QAM modem over a two-way cable system to transmit data upstream from a user location to the network. When a telephone line is used in conjunction with a one-way broadcast network, the cable data system is referred to as a *telephony return interface (TRI)* system. Telephone return means that the consumer (or the subscriber modem) makes a telephone call to a terminal server when the consumer requires return-path service. At the cable head end, data from individual users is filtered by telephone-return systems for further processing by a *cable modem termination system (CMTS)*. The CMTS communicates with the cable modem to enforce the Media Access Control (MAC) protocol and RF control functions, such as frequency changes and automatic gain control.

A CMTS provides the data switching necessary to route data between the Internet and cable-modem users. The result is user data modulated into one 6-MHz channel, which is the same spectrum allocated for a cable television channel, such as ABC, NBC, or TBS, for broadcast to all users (see Figure 17-4).

FIGURE 17-4
How cable
modems work.

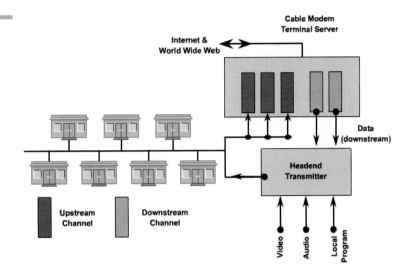

A cable head end combines the downstream data channels with the existing video, pay-per-view, audio, and local advertiser programs that are received by television subscribers. The combined signal is now ready to be transmitted throughout the cable distribution network. When the signal arrives at the user's site, the television signal is received by a converter box generally located on the top of a television, while user data is separately received by a cable modem or router and sent to a PC.

The CMTS, an important new element for the support of data services, integrates upstream and downstream communication over a cable data network. The number of upstream and downstream channels in any particular CMTS can be designed and adjusted based on the size of the serving area, the number of users, and data rates offered to each user.

Another important element in the operations and day-to-day management of a cable data system is an *element management system (EMS)*. An EMS is an operations system designed specifically to configure and manage a CMTS and associated cable-modem subscribers. These operations include provisioning, day-to-day administration, monitoring, alarms, and testing of various components of a CMTS. From a central Network Operations Center (NOC), a single EMS can support many CMTS systems in a particular geographic region.

Beyond modulation and demodulation, a cable modem or router incorporates many features necessary to extend broadband communications to wide-area networks (WANs). The Internet Protocol (IP) is used at the network layer to support Internet services such as e-mail, Hypertext Transfer Protocol (HTTP), and File Transfer Protocol (FTP). The data link layer comprises three sublayers, including the Logical Link Control (LLC) sublayer, a link security sublayer conforming to the security requirements, and a MAC sublayer suitable for cable-system operations. Cable systems use the Ethernet frame format for transmission on data channels. The downstream data channels and the associated upstream data channels on a cable network basically form an Ethernet WAN. As the number of subscribers increases, the cable operator can add more upstream and downstream data channels to meet the additional bandwidth requirements.

The link security sublayer is defined in three (sub)sets of requirements: baseline privacy interface (BPI), security system interface (SSI), and removable security module interface (RSMI). BPI provides cable-modem users with data privacy across the cable network by encrypting data traffic between the user's cable modem and CMTS. The operational support provided by the EMS allows a CMTS to map cable-modem identities to paying subscribers and thereby authorize subscriber access to data network services. These privacy and security requirements protect user data and prevent unauthorized use of cable data services.

Cable Data Network Architecture

A CMTS provides an extended Ethernet network over a WAN with a geographic reach up to 100 miles. The cable data network can be fully managed by the local cable operations unit, or operations can be aggregated at a regional NOC for better scaling. A given geographic or metropolitan region might have a few cable television head end locations that are connected by fiber links. The day-to-day operations and management of a cable data network can be consolidated at a single location, such as a regional center, while other head end locations can be economically managed as local centers.

A basic distribution center is a minimal data network configuration that exists within a cable television head end. A typical head end is equipped with satellite receivers, fiber connections to other regional head end locations, and upstream RF receivers for pay-per-view and data services (see Figure 17-5). The minimal data network configuration includes a CMTS system capable of upstream and downstream data transport, and an IP router to connect to the regional location.

A regional center is a cable head end location with additional temperature-controlled facilities to house a variety of computer servers, which are necessary to run cable data networks. The servers include file transfer, user authorization and accounting, log control (syslog), IP address assignment and administration (Dynamic Host Configuration Protocol [DHCP] servers), Domain Name System (DNS) servers, and Data-over-Cable Service Interface Specifications (DOCSIS) control servers. In addition, a regional center might contain support and network management systems necessary for television and data network operations.

FIGURE 17-5
A minimal
data network
configuration
exists within a
cable television
head end.

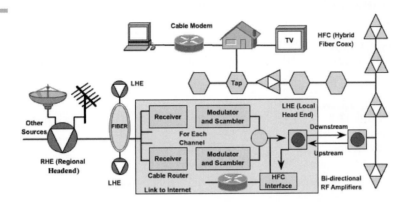

User data from local and regional locations is received at a regional data center
for further aggregation and is distribution throughout the network (see Figure
17-6). A regional data center supports DHCP, DNS, and log control servers
necessary for the cable data network administration. A regional data center
provides connectivity to the Internet and the World Wide Web, and contains
the server farms necessary to support Internet services. These servers include
e-mail, Web hosting, news, chat, proxy, caching, and streaming-media servers.

FIGURE 17-6
Cable data
network
architecture.

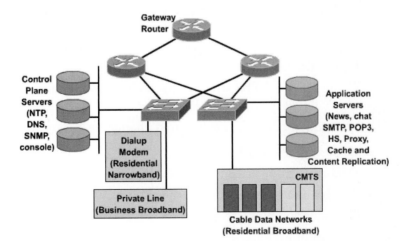

Cable and the OSI Model

The cable data system comprises many different technologies and standards (see Figure 17-7). For cable modems to be mainstreamed, modems from different vendors must be interoperable.

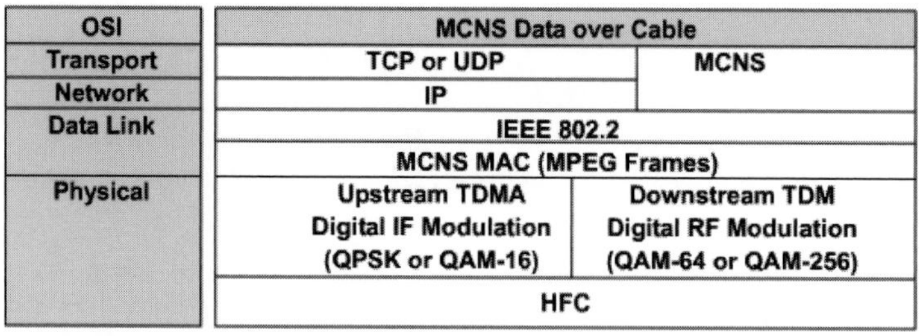

FIGURE 17-7
Cable and the
OSI model.

OSI	MCNS Data over Cable		
Transport	TCP or UDP		MCNS
Network	IP		
Data Link	IEEE 802.2		
	MCNS MAC (MPEG Frames)		
Physical	Upstream TDMA Digital IF Modulation (QPSK or QAM-16)		Downstream TDM Digital RF Modulation (QAM-64 or QAM-256)
	HFC		

Physical Layer

At the physical layer, the downstream data channel is based on North American digital video specifications (specifically, International Telecommunications Union–Telecommunication Standardization Sector [ITU-T] Recommendation J.83 Annex B) and includes the following features:

- 64 and 256 QAM
- 6-MHz occupied spectrum that coexists with other signals in the cable plant
- Variable-length interleaving support, both latency-sensitive and latency-insensitive data services
- Contiguous serial bit stream with no implied framing, providing complete physical (PHY) and MAC-layer decoupling

The upstream data channel is a shared channel featuring the following:

- QPSK and 16 QAM formats
- Data rates from 320 Kbps to 10 Mbps
- Flexible and programmable cable modem under control of CMTS
- Time-division multiple access
- Support of both fixed-frame and variable-length protocol data units (PDUs)

Data Link Layer

The data link layer provides the general requirements for many cable-modem subscribers to share a single upstream data channel for transmission to the network. Among these requirements are collision detection and a retransmission capability. The large geographic reach of a cable data network poses special problems as a result of the transmission delay between users close to the head end versus users at a distance from the cable head end. To compensate for cable losses and delay as a result of distance, the MAC layer performs ranging, by which each cable modem can assess time delay in transmitting to the head end.

The MAC layer supports timing and synchronization, bandwidth allocation to cable modems at the control of CMTS, error detection, handling and error recovery, and procedures for registering new cable modems.

Network Layer

Cable data networks use IP for communication from the cable modem to the network. The Internet Engineering Task Force (IETF) DHCP forms the basis for all IP address assignment and administration in the cable network.

Transport Layer

Cable data networks support both the Transmission Control Protocol (TCP) and the User Datagram Protocol (UDP) at the transport layer.

Application Layer

All the Internet-related application layer protocols are supported at the application layer. These applications include HTTP, FTP, e-mail, Trivial File Transfer Protocol (TFTP), news applications, chat applications, and Simple Network Management Protocol (SNMP). The use of SNMP provides for management of the CMTS and cable data networks.

Cable Conclusion

Many people are tuning into the Internet channel on their TVs. Of all the high-speed Internet access solutions, cable TV systems are probably the most talked about. That's partly because they take advantage of existing broadband cable TV networks and partly because they promise to deliver high-speed access at an affordable price.

Internet access via cable is spreading rapidly. However, to reach the main-stream, cable operators face an uphill battle. Like phone companies offering ISDN service, cable operators must gain expertise in data communications if they're going to earn and keep customers.

Technical hurdles abound: Cable modems can work in both directions if cable operators convert their one-way networks to two-way HFC networks. After this is accomplished, the technology could offer the best price/performance combination of any Internet access method to date, delivering close to 10-Mbps speeds at less than $50 per month, which is significantly better than the price/performance factor of ISDN access.

As discussed, making the cable-to-PC connection requires a cable modem to modulate and demodulate the cable signal into a stream of data. The similarity with analog modems ends there. Cable modems also incorporate a tuner (to separate the data signal from the rest of the broadcast stream); parts from network adapters, bridges, and routers (to connect to multiple computers); network-management software agents (so that the cable company can control and monitor its operations); and encryption devices (so that your data isn't intercepted or sent someplace else by mistake).

Each cable modem has an Ethernet port that connects to the computer (or network) on one side and a port for the coaxial cable connection on the other (see Figure 17-8). You install an Ethernet adapter in the PC and then connect it to the cable modem Ethernet port with a standard Ethernet cable. As far as your PC is concerned, it's hooked directly to the Internet via an Ethernet cable. There are no phone numbers to dial and no limitations on serial port throughput (as is the case with ISDN modems). What you do get is high-speed throughput: Downlinks vary from 500 Kbps to 30 Mbps, while uplinks can range from 96 Kbps to 10 Mbps.

FIGURE 17-8
A cable modem.

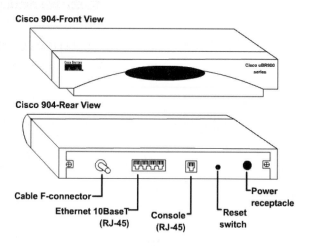

Wireless Network Access

Tremendous strides have been made on wired networks. Twisted-pair and fiber networks dominate the Layer 1 space. The transmission capacity of wired networks is almost limitless because carriers can arbitrarily add bandwidth as demand increases.

Despite the capacity of wired networks, wireless networks have had the greatest success among consumers. Broadcast television, cellular telephone, paging, and direct broadcast satellite are all wireless services that have met with commercial success, despite the fact that wireless networks typically carry lower bit rates and higher costs than wired networking.

When you install cables underground, you might be forced to obtain permission from residents. Product managers who roll out wired services struggle with marketing and demographic studies to determine the best neighborhoods in which to introduce services.

Even after the right neighborhoods are identified, it is expensive and time-consuming to dig or install overhead cables. Furthermore, permits and easements must be obtained. To some observers, the fixed networks of wired systems look like vulnerable high-capital assets in a world of fast-changing technologies.

Numerous wireless access network technologies are intended by their proponents to serve the business or consumer market. These are direct broadcast satellite (DBS), Multichannel Multipoint Distribution Services (MMDS), and Local Multipoint Distribution Services (LMDS). Figure 17-9 illustrates the network architecture of a typical wireless network. The return-path (upstream) flows, if any, travel through wired networks.

FIGURE 17-9
Wireless
network access.

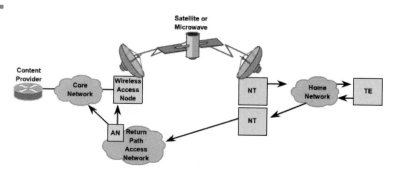

The content provider forwards content through the core network and to the wireless access node. This access node reformats data and modulates it for satellite or land-based microwave transmission. A receiving antenna at the home end forwards traffic through the home network to the terminal equipment, which is either a TV set-top box or a PC.

In the return path, the consumer uses either the same network used for the forward transmission or another access network. Another access network is needed when using most current DBS services, which are one-way networks. The return-path network could be telephone return, xDSL, or another wireless service, such as digital personal communications services (PCS). PCS service includes wireless voice, a digital form of cellular telephony, and wireless data.

Because forward- and return-path traffic can use different physical media, traffic sources must be matched so that a single bidirectional session exists between the content provider and the terminal equipment. This matching can be performed by the wireless access node or another switching/routing device inside the core network.

Direct Broadcast Satellite

While cable operators only talked about digital TV, DBS companies actually achieved it, which took the entire cable industry by surprise. Early entrants were Primestar, DirecTV, and United States Satellite Broadcasting (USSB), all of which launched in 1994.

In the United States, DBS is viewed as a commercial success. DBS signed a surprising five million customers in its first three years of operation. This response is particularly strong considering the fact that customers initially paid up to $800 for a home satellite dish and installation. Such a strong start has cable TV operators concerned. Even more troubling for U.S. cable operators is that the average DBS subscriber spends about 50 percent more per month than the average cable subscriber (about $52 versus $35 per month). This difference is partly due to sales of premium sports and movie packages.

DBS Architecture

Architecturally, DBS is a simple concept. As shown in Figure 17-10, DBS operators receive analog TV reception from the various networks at a single giant head end. The DirecTV head end, for example, is in Castle Rock, Colorado. The analog programming is encoded into Motion Picture Experts Group (MPEG) format for digital retransmission. A control function regulates the amount of bandwidth accorded to each MPEG stream and determines how the MPEG knobs (control parameters), such as the length of a group of pictures, are specified.

The settings of the knobs are closely guarded secrets of the DBS operators. ESPN, for example, tends to require more bandwidth than the Food Network. ESPN has more motion; more importantly, it has a larger audience and greater advertising revenue. How much more would ESPN pay for access than the

NOTE

Much of the success of DBS is due to imaginative programming packages. In particular, aggressive marketing of sports packages (including college basketball and professional football) has created varied content for which DBS has found an eager market.

Food Network? How much extra bandwidth is ESPN getting, and for how much? What MPEG knobs should the carrier use, and what knobs does its competition use? This is not public information.

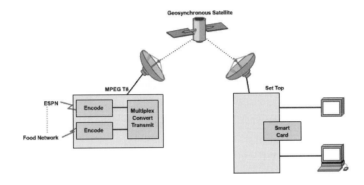

FIGURE 17-10
DBS architecture.

ESPN, the Food Network, and all other channels are encoded into MPEG transport streams, are multiplexed together, and are converted to the uplink frequency.

The major North American geosynchronous satellites for DBS so far are placed at longitudes 85° west (Primestar), 101° west (DirecTV), and 119° west (Echostar). The Primestar slot rests on the longitude that passes through the East Coast of the United States, the DirecTV longitude bisects the center of North America, and the Echostar longitude passes through the West Coast. From these orbits, each satellite can broadcast over the contiguous United States, southern Canada, and Mexico.

The satellite receives a signal and remodulates it to the designated spectrum for DBS. DBS occupies 500 MHz in the 12.2 KU band. The Ku band occupies the frequency range from 10.7 GHz to 12.75 GHz. DBS satellites are allowed by regulation to broadcast at a higher power (120W) than that used to broadcasting to the larger C-band satellite dishes currently used by many households. This enables reception on small satellite dishes. This higher-powered transmission and smaller dish distinguishes DBS from other forms of satellite reception.

The DBS uses QPSK modulation to encode digital data on the RF carriers. DirecTV encodes using MPEG-2 format to enable a density of up to 720×480 pixels on the user's monitor. Primestar uses a proprietary video compression system developed by General Instruments called DigiCipher-1. Echostar also uses a transmission system based on the European Digital Video Broadcast (DVB) standard. DVB uses the MPEG-2 and standardizes control elements of the total system, such as conditional access.

Although 720×480 is the maximum resolution offered today, DBS is capable of higher pixel resolution. In fact, DBS could be an early delivery vehicle for high-definition TV (HDTV) programming.

Data Service

DirecTV partnered with Microsoft to produce a push-mode data service over DBS. The service broadcasts approximately 200 popular Web sites, which are cached in the consumer's PC. Some content will be cached at the service provider's site. Instead of having a point-to-point connection with the Internet, consumers access content on the hard drive or service-provider cache. In addition to Web sites, other data services, such as AgCast or stock quotes, can be offered, either by continuous feeds or by caching on the consumer's PC. The problem with this model is that you cannot access a Web site that is not part of the service because no point-to-point return-path connection exists.

One form of point-to-point data service, called DirecPC, can reach the Internet. DirecPC is jointly owned by DirecTV and Hughes Network Systems. DirecPC reserves 12 Mbps of downstream service and uses a standard telephone line as a return path.

Because the footprint (the portion of the Earth's surface covered by the signal from a communications satellite) is so large for geosynchronous satellites, it is possible that thousands of users will want to use the common 12 Mbps of service concurrently. The more concurrent users there are, the less bandwidth each user gets. To provide a balance between bit rate and the number of concurrent users, DirecPC offers approximately 400 Kbps of service to concurrent users.

Low Earth Orbit Satellites

Unlike their geosynchronous brethren, which are located at 35,800 km above the equator, Low Earth Orbit (LEO) satellites orbit the planet at low altitudes. Depending on the system, the altitude of these orbits ranges from 780 to 1400 km, which is above the Earth's atmosphere but below the Van Allen radiation belt. At these altitudes, a LEO satellite is in view of 2 to 4 percent of the Earth's surface, which means that the footprint of any given LEO satellite is 4000 to 6000 km in diameter.

The low altitude provides two advantages for the consumer. First, latency is short. Phone calls through GEOs incur a 239 ms one-way delay; a round-trip delay is therefore nearly half a second. This causes annoying pauses during voice conversations. One-way latency for LEOs is about 6 ms. The second advantage is lower power consumption. LEOs travel so low that a handset requires little power to reach it, as compared with a GEO.

LEO Architecture

Because LEOs fly at low orbit, they move with respect to the Earth. This means that as a user on the ground communicates with the LEO, the LEO passes over the horizon and communication stops. To maintain the session, the original LEO must hand off the session to the following satellite. By succeeding hand-offs, the session can be maintained. The frequency of hand-offs is determined largely by the distance of the LEO from Earth, which determines the footprint size of the LEO. The lower the satellite, the faster it moves with respect to Earth, creating more frequent hand-offs. There are possibly hundreds of satellites communicating with each other, handing off user sessions. The original Teledesic system had nearly 900 satellites until a recent redesign reduced that number to 288. Lower orbits increase the number of satellites, which is an important component of system cost.

Launch Capacity

Finding satellite launch space will be a challenge. More than 1700 satellite launches are planned for the next 10 years for uses other than LEOs. LEOs will require the launch of more than 400 satellites over the next five to seven years. Considering that there were 22 rocket launches worldwide in 1996—which placed 29 satellites in orbit—the launch business needs to add capacity quickly to meet launch demand. To make things worse, about 10 percent of launches fail. Insurance premiums in some cases are nearly 25 percent of payload value. Incidentally, only about 30 percent of satellite launches are handled by the United States. About 60 percent of the world's launches are made by the European space consortium, Ariane. Others in the launch business are China and Russia.

Cost Issues

In general, there is widespread skepticism about lifecycle costs for LEOs. The following list details some of the cost concerns of particular relevance for LEOs:

- Capital costs for satellite development, construction, and launch. For example, data communications equipment must be modified for operation in space to accommodate environmental factors such as temperature and radiation. These costs are unknown at present.
- Technical innovations required, such as satellite-to-satellite communications at multimegabit rates.
- Continuing requirement for ground stations and associated settlement costs.
- Damage due to solar activity and small projectiles.
- Development of new handsets and customer terminals.

■ The concept of LEOs exhibits a boldness not found except in science fiction, with many carriers buying into the concept. LEOs offer global roaming, a simple worldwide dialing plan, and instant voice infrastructure for developing countries. More broadly, if successful, LEOs can substantially alter how we think about global communications.

Wireless Local-Area Networking

In the simplest of terms, a *wireless local-area network (WLAN)* does exactly what the name implies: It provides all the features and benefits of traditional LAN technologies, such as Ethernet and Token Ring, without the limitations of wires or cables (see Figure 17-11). But if you view a WLAN just in terms of the cables it does not have, you might miss the point: WLANs redefine the way we view LANs. Connectivity no longer implies attachment. Local areas are measured not in feet or meters, but in miles or kilometers. An infrastructure does not need to be buried in the ground or hidden behind the walls—an "infrastructure" can move and change at the speed of the organization. This technology has several immediate applications, especially for the following people and organizations:

■ IT professionals or business executives who want mobility within the enterprise, probably to access a traditional wired network from anywhere

■ Business owners or IT directors who need flexibility for frequent LAN wiring changes, either throughout the site or in selected areas

■ Any company whose site is not conducive to LAN wiring because of building or budget limitations, such as older buildings, leased space, or temporary sites

■ Any company that needs the flexibility and cost savings offered by a line-of-sight, building-to-building bridge to avoid expensive trenches, leased lines, or right-of-way issues

WLANs use a transmission medium, just like wired LANs. Instead of using twisted-pair or fiber-optic cable, WLANs use the air, transmitting frequencies in either light or RF ranges. Of the two, RF is far more popular for its longer range, higher bandwidth, and wider coverage. Most wireless LANs today use the 2.4-GHz frequency band, the only portion of the RF spectrum reserved around the world for unlicensed devices. The freedom and flexibility of wireless networking can be applied both within buildings and between buildings.

FIGURE 17-11
Wireless
local-area
networking.

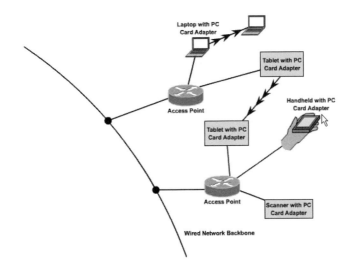

In-Building WLANs

WLAN technology can take the place of a traditional wired network or can extend its reach and capabilities. Much like their wired counterparts, in-building WLAN equipment consists of a PC card, a Personal Computer Interface (PCI), Industry-Standard Architecture (ISA) client adapters, and access points, which perform functions similar to wired networking hubs (see Figure 17-12). Similar to wired LANs for small or temporary installations, a WLAN can be arranged in a peer-to-peer or improvised topology using only client adapters. For added functionality and range, access points can be incorporated to act as the center of a star topology while simultaneously bridging with an Ethernet network.

Building-to-Building WLANs

In much the same way that a commercial radio signal can be picked up in all sorts of weather, miles from its transmitter, WLAN technology applies the power of radio waves to truly redefine the "local" in LAN. With a wireless bridge, networks located in buildings miles from each other can be integrated into a single LAN. When bridging between buildings with traditional copper or fiber-optic cable, freeways, lakes, and even local governments can be impassible obstacles. A wireless bridge makes them irrelevant, transmitting data through the air and requiring no license or right-of-way.

Without a wireless alternative, organizations frequently resort to wide-area networking (WAN) technologies to link separate LANs. Contracting with a local telephone provider for a leased line presents a variety of drawbacks. Installation is typically expensive and rarely immediate. Monthly fees are often high for bandwidth that, by LAN standards, is very low. A wireless bridge can be purchased and installed in an afternoon for a cost that is often comparable to a T1 installation charge alone. After the investment is made, no recurring charges exist. And today's wireless bridges provide the bandwidth that one would expect from a technology rooted in data, rather than voice, communications.

FIGURE 17-12
In-building
WLANs.

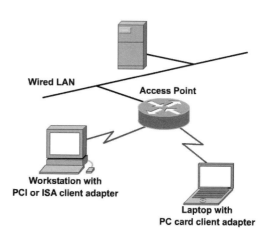

Wired LAN

Access Point

Workstation with
PCI or ISA client adapter

Laptop with
PC card client adapter

The Wireless LAN Standard

In the wired world, Ethernet has grown to become the predominant LAN technology. Its evolution parallels, and indeed foreshadows, the development of the wireless LAN standard. Defined by the Institute of Electrical and Electronics Engineers (IEEE) with the 802.3 standard, Ethernet provides an evolving, high-speed, widely available, and interoperable networking standard. It has continued to evolve to keep pace with the data rate and throughput requirements of contemporary LANs. Originally providing for 10-Mbps transfer rates, the Ethernet standard evolved to include the 100-Mbps transfer rates required for network backbones and bandwidth-intensive applications. The IEEE 802.3 standard is open, decreasing barriers to market entry and resulting in a wide range of suppliers, products, and price points from which Ethernet users can choose. Perhaps most importantly, conformance to the Ethernet standard allows for interoperability, enabling users to select individual products from multiple vendors while secure in the knowledge that they will all work together.

The first wireless LAN technologies were low-speed (1 to 2 Mbps) proprietary offerings. Despite these shortcomings, the freedom and flexibility of wireless technology allowed these early products to find a place in vertical markets, such as retail and warehousing, where mobile workers use hand-held devices for inventory management and data collection. Later, hospitals applied wireless technology to deliver patient information right to the bedside. As computers made their way into the classrooms, schools and universities began installing wireless networks to avoid cabling costs and to share Internet access. The pioneering wireless vendors soon realized that, for the technology to gain broad market acceptance, an Ethernet-like standard was needed. The vendors joined together in 1991, first proposing and then building a standard based on contributed technologies. In June 1997, the IEEE released the 802.11 standard for wireless local-area networking.

Similar to the 802.3 Ethernet standard that allows for data transmission over twisted-pair and coaxial cable, the 802.11 WLAN standard allows for different transmission methods. Compliant methods include infrared light, which is unlicensed, and two types of radio transmission within the unlicensed 2.4-GHz frequency band: frequency-hopping spread spectrum (FHSS) and direct sequence spread spectrum (DSSS). Spread spectrum is a modulation technique developed in the 1940s that spreads a transmission signal over a broad set of radio frequencies. This technique is ideal for data communications because it is less susceptible to radio noise and creates little interference.

FHSS is limited to a 2-Mbps data transfer rate and is recommended for only very specific applications. For all other wireless LAN applications, DSSS is the better choice. The recently released evolution of the IEEE standard, 802.11b, provides for a full Ethernet-like data rate of 11 Mbps over DSSS.

The Future of WLANs

The history of technology improvement in the wired LANs can be summed up with the mantra, "Faster, better, and cheaper." WLAN technology has already started down that road: Data rates have increased from 1 to 11 Mbps, interoperability became reality with the introduction of the IEEE 802.11 standard, and prices have dramatically decreased. The recent improvements are just the beginning.

Performance

IEEE 802.11b standard 11-Mbps WLANs operate in the 2.4-GHz frequency band where there is room for increased speed. Using an optional modulation technique within the 802.11b specification, it is possible to double the current data rate. Cisco already has 22 Mbps on the road map for the future. Wireless LAN manufacturers migrated from the 900-MHz band to the 2.4-GHz band to improve data rate. This pattern promises to continue, with a broader frequency band capable of supporting higher bandwidth available at 5.7 GHz. The IEEE already issued a specification (802.11a) for equipment operating at 5.7 GHz that supports up to a 54-Mbps data rate. This generation of technology might likely carry a significant price premium when it is introduced later in 2001. This premium will decrease over time while data rates increase: The 5.7-GHz band promises to allow for the next breakthrough wireless data rate of 100 Mbps.

Security

The wired equivalent privacy (WEP) option to the 802.11 standard is only the first step in addressing customer security concerns. Security is currently available today for wireless networking, offering up to 128-bit encryption and supporting both the encryption and authentication options of the 802.11 standard. The algorithm with a 40- or 128-bit key is specified in the standard. When WEP is enabled, each station (clients and access points) has up to four keys. The keys are used to encrypt the data before it is transmitted through the air. If a station receives a packet that is not encrypted with the appropriate key, the packet will be discarded and never delivered to the host. Figure 17-13 shows an outside user being rejected because of an incorrect ID.

FIGURE 17-13

The outside user is rejected because of an incorrect ID.

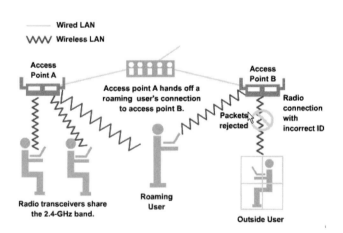

Although the 802.11 standard provides strong encryption services to secure the WLAN, the means by which the secure keys are granted, revoked, and refreshed is still undefined. Fortunately, several key administration architectures are available for use in the enterprise. The best approach for large networks is centralized key management, which uses centralized encryption key servers. A popular strategy includes the addition of encryption key servers to ensure that valuable data is protected. Encryption key servers provide for centralized creation of keys, distribution of keys, and ongoing key rotation. Key servers enable the network administrator to command the creation of RSA public/private key pairs at the client level that are required for client authentication. The key server will also provide for the generation and distribution to clients and access points of the keys needed for packet encryption. This implementation eases administration and helps avoid compromising confidential keys.

Mobility Services

A primary advantage of WLANs is mobility, but no industry standard currently addresses the tracking or management of mobile devices in its *Management Information Base (MIB)*. This omission would prohibit users from roaming between wireless access points that cover a common area, such as a complete floor of a building. Individual companies, such as Cisco Systems, have addressed this issue, providing their own versions of mobility algorithms that facilitate roaming within an IP domain (such as a floor) with an eye toward optimizing roaming across IP domains (such as an enterprise campus).

Management

Wireless access points share the functions of both hubs and switches. Wireless clients that associate with access points share the wireless LAN, similar to the way a hub functions, but the access point can additionally track movement of clients across its domain and permit or deny specific traffic or clients from communicating through it. For network managers to use these services to their advantage, it is necessary to instrument the access point like a hub and a switch.

The Cisco WLAN devices are manageable through common Telnet or SNMP (I or II) services and a Web browser interface to facilitate its monitoring and control. In addition to bridge statistics and counters, the access point offers additional features that make it powerful and manageable, including mapping of wireless access points and their associated clients, as well as monitoring and reporting of client statistics. Access points can also control access and the flow of traffic through the wireless LAN via MAC and protocol-level access lists. Configuration parameters, as well as code images for access points, can be centrally configured and managed to facilitate consistency of WLAN network policy.

WLANs Conclusion

Today, the WLAN has redefined what it means to be connected. It has stretched the boundaries of the LAN. It makes an infrastructure as dynamic as it needs to be. And it has only just begun: The standard is less than three years old, with the high-speed 802.11b yet to reach its first birthday. With standard and interoperable wireless products, LANs can reach scales unimaginable with a wired infrastructure. They can make high-speed interconnections for a fraction of the cost of traditional wide-area technologies. In a wireless world, users can roam not just within a campus, but within a city, while maintaining a high-speed link to extranets, intranets, and the Internet itself.

Digital Subscriber Line

Digital subscriber line (DSL) technology is a modem technology that uses existing twisted-pair telephone lines to transport high-bandwidth data, such as multimedia and video, to service subscribers Figure 17-14 shows you how DSL works.

The term *xDSL* covers numerous similar yet competing forms of DSL, including asymmetric DSL (ADSL), single-line DSL (SDSL), high-data-rate DSL (HDSL), rate-adaptive DSL (RADSL), and very-high-data-rate DSL (VDSL). xDSL is drawing significant attention from implementers and service providers because it promises to deliver high-bandwidth data rates to dispersed locations with relatively small changes to the existing telco infrastructure. xDSL services constitute dedicated, point-to-point, public network access over twisted-pair copper wire on the local loop ("last mile") between a network service provider's (NSP's) central office and the customer site, or on local loops created either intrabuilding or intracampus. Currently, the primary focus in xDSL is the development and deployment of ADSL and VDSL technologies and architectures. This section covers the characteristics and operations of ADSL and VDSL.

FIGURE 17-14
How DSL works.

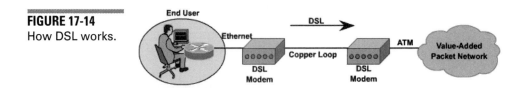

Asymmetric Digital Subscriber Line

As its name suggests, *asymmetric digital subscriber line (ADSL)* technology is asymmetric. It allows more bandwidth downstream—from an NSP's central office to the customer site—than upstream from the subscriber to the central office (see Figure 17-15). This asymmetry, combined with always-on access (which eliminates call setup), makes ADSL ideal for Internet/intranet surfing, video on demand, and remote LAN access. Users of these applications typically download more information than they send.

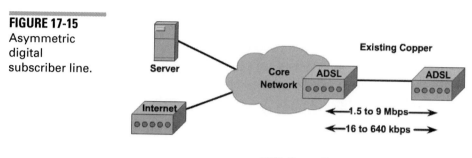

FIGURE 17-15
Asymmetric digital subscriber line.

ADSL transmits more than 6 Mbps to a subscriber, and as much as 640 Kbps more in both directions, as shown in Figure 17-15. Such rates expand existing access capacity by a factor of 50 or more without new cabling. ADSL can literally transform the existing public information network from one limited to voice, text, and low-resolution graphics to a powerful, universal system capable of bringing multimedia, including full-motion video, to every home this decade.

Over the next decade, ADSL will become crucial as telephone companies enter new markets to deliver information in video and multimedia formats. New broadband cabling might take decades to reach all prospective subscribers. Success of these new services depends on reaching as many subscribers as possible during the first few years of availability. By bringing movies, television, video catalogs, remote CD-ROMs, corporate LANs, and the Internet into homes and small businesses, ADSL will make these markets viable and profitable for telephone companies and application vendors.

ADSL Services Architecture

Figure 17-16 illustrates a typical end-to-end ADSL services architecture. It consists of customer premises equipment (CPE) and supporting equipment at the ADSL point of presence (POP). Network access providers (NAPs) manage Layer 2 network cores, while NSPs manage Layer 3 network cores. These roles are divided or shared among incumbent local exchange carrier (ILEC), competitive local exchange carrier (CLEC), and tier 1 and tier 2 Internet service provider (ISP) businesses. Over time, it's expected that market forces might redefine current relationships between ADSL providers: Some NAPs might add Layer 3 capabilities or extend service across the core.

FIGURE 17-16
Basic DSL network topology.

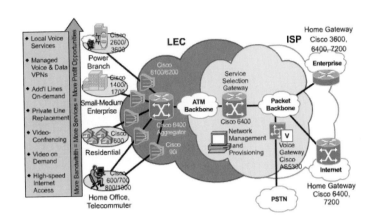

CPE represents any combination of end-user PCs or workstations, remote ADSL terminating units (ATU-Rs), and routers (see Figure 17-17). For instance, a residential user might have a single PC with an integrated ADSL modem on a peripheral component interface card, or perhaps a PC with an Ethernet or universal serial bus (USB) interface to a stand-alone ADSL modem (the ATU-R). In contrast, business users will more often connect many end-user PCs to a router with an integrated ADSL modem or a router plus ATU-R pair.

FIGURE 17-17
Basic DSL network components.

 DSL CPE
    Customer premise equipment
    PC NICs, bridges/routers, enterprise routers

 DSLAM
    DSL Access Multiplexer
    Concentrates individual subscriber lines from CPE

 Aggregator/Service Selection Gateway
    Concentrates ATM feeds (T-1,DS3,OC-3) from DSLAMs
    PPP termination, Layer 2 & 3 service selection
    On-demand, personalized sevices
    Accounting and billing

At the ADSL point of presence (POP), the NAP deploys one or more DSL access multiplexers (DSLAMs) servicing the copper loops between the POP and CPE. In a process called *subtending*, DSLAMs can be chained together to enhance ATM pipe utilization. DSLAMs connect locally or via an inter-central office (CO) link to a local-access concentrator (LAC) that provides ATM "grooming," PPP tunneling, and Layer 3 termination to local or cached content. A service selection gateway (SSG) can be colocated with the LAC, so customers can dynamically select destinations. From the LAC/SSG, services extend over the ATM core to the NSP or IP network core.

Three different architectures are applicable to wholesale ADSL services:

- **ATM point-to-point**—Cross-connects subscribers to their ISP or enterprise destination with permanent virtual circuits (PVCs) from the CPE to the endpoint.

- **Aggregation**—Aggregates multiple subscriber virtual circuits (VCs) into trunk PVCs to reduce the number of VC connections across the network core; instead of one VC per subscriber, this uses one VC for many subscribers to the same destination.

- **SVC and MPLS**—Uses switched virtual circuits (SVCs) to autoprovision connections from the CPE through the DSLAM to an edge label switch router (edge LSR), where it enters the Multiprotocol Label Switching (MPLS)–enabled network core.

Figure 17-18 outlines the end-to-end protocol stack used with xDSL.

FIGURE 17-18
The end-to-end DSL protocol stack.

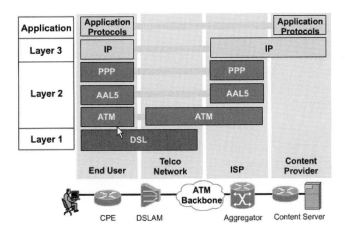

ADSL Capabilities

An ADSL circuit connects an ADSL modem on each end of a twisted-pair telephone line, creating three information channels: a high-speed downstream channel, a medium-speed duplex channel, and a basic telephone-service channel (see Figure 17-19). The basic telephone service channel is split off from the digital modem by filters, thus guaranteeing uninterrupted basic telephone service (even if ADSL fails). The high-speed channel ranges from 1.5

to 6.1 Mbps, and duplex rates range from 16 to 640 Kbps. Each channel can be submultiplexed to form multiple lower-rate channels.

FIGURE 17-19
ADSL and POTS.

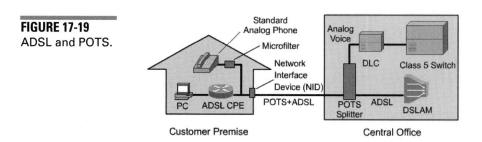

ADSL modems provide data rates consistent with North American T1 1.544-Mbps and European E1 2.048-Mbps digital hierarchies, and can be purchased with various speed ranges and capabilities. The minimum configuration provides 1.5 or 2.0 Mbps downstream and a 16-Kbps duplex channel; others provide rates of 6.1 Mbps and 64-Kbps duplex. Products with downstream rates up to 8 Mbps and duplex rates up to 640 Kbps are available today as well. ADSL modems interoperates with Asynchronous Transfer Mode (ATM) transport with variable rates and compensation for ATM overhead, as well as IP protocols.

Downstream data rates depend on many factors, including the length of the copper line, its wire gauge, the presence of bridged taps, and cross-coupled interference. Line attenuation increases with distance from the transmitter and frequency and decreases as wire diameter increases.

Although the measure varies from telco to telco, these capabilities can cover up to 95 percent of a loop plant, depending on the desired data rate. Customers beyond these distances can be reached with fiber-based digital loop carrier (DLC) systems. As these DLC systems become commercially available, telephone companies can offer virtually ubiquitous access in a relatively short time.

Many applications envisioned for ADSL involve digital compressed video. As a real-time signal, digital video cannot use link- or network-level error-control procedures commonly found in data communications systems. ADSL modems, therefore, incorporate forward error correction (FEC) that dramatically reduces errors caused by impulse noise. Error correction on a symbol-by-symbol basis also reduces errors caused by continuous noise coupled into a line.

ADSL Technology

ADSL depends on advanced digital signal processing and creative algorithms to squeeze so much information through twisted-pair telephone lines. In addition, many advances have been required in transformers, analog filters, and analog/digital (A/D) converters. Long telephone lines might attenuate signals at 1 MHz (the outer edge of the band used by ADSL) by as much as 90 decibels (dB), which forces analog sections of ADSL modems to work hard to realize large dynamic frequency ranges, separate channels, and maintain low noise figures. On the outside, ADSL looks simple—transparent synchronous data pipes at various data rates over ordinary telephone lines. The inside, where all the transistors work, is a technological miracle. Figure 17-20 displays the ADSL transceiver network end.

To create multiple channels, ADSL modems divide the available bandwidth of a telephone line in one of two ways—FDM or echo cancellation—as shown in Figure 17-21. Frequency-division multiplexing (FDM) assigns one band for upstream data and another band for downstream data. The downstream path is then divided by time-division multiplexing (TDM) into one or more high-speed channels and one or more low-speed channels. The upstream path is also multiplexed into corresponding low-speed channels. Echo cancellation assigns the upstream band to overlap the downstream, and separates the two by means of local echo cancellation, a technique well known in V.32 and V.34 modems. With either technique, ADSL splits off a 4-kHz region for basic telephone service at the DC end of the band.

FIGURE 17-20
The ADSL transceiver network end.

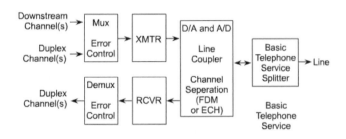

An ADSL modem organizes the aggregate data stream created by multiplexing downstream channels, duplex channels, and maintenance channels together into blocks, and attaches an error-correction code to each block. The receiver then corrects errors that occur during transmission up to the limits implied by the code and the block length. At the user's option, the unit also can create superblocks by interleaving data within subblocks; this allows the receiver to correct any combination of errors within a specific span of bits. This, in turn, allows for effective transmission of both data and video signals.

FIGURE 17-21
ADSL technology.

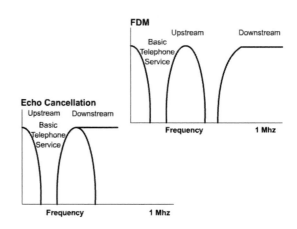

ADSL Standards and Associations

The American National Standards Institute (ANSI) Working Group T1E1.4 recently approved an ADSL standard at rates up to 6.1 Mbps (ANSI Standard T1.414). The European Technical Standards Institute (ETSI) contributed an annex to T1.414 to reflect European requirements. T1.414 currently embodies a single terminal interface at the premises end. Issue II, now under study by T1E1.4, will expand the standard to include a multiplexed interface at the premises end, protocols for configuration and network management, and other improvements.

The ATM Forum and the Digital Audio-Visual Council (DAVIC) have both recognized ADSL as a physical layer transmission protocol for unshielded twisted-pair (UTP) media.

The ADSL Forum formed in December 1994 to promote the ADSL concept and facilitate development of ADSL system architectures, protocols, and interfaces for major ADSL applications. The ADSL Forum has more than 200 members, representing service providers, equipment manufacturers, and semiconductor companies throughout the world. At present, the ADSL Forum's formal technical work is divided into the following six areas, each of which is dealt with in a separate working group within the technical committee:

- ATM over ADSL (includes transport and end-to-end architecture aspects)
- Packet over ADSL (a working group that recently completed its work)
- CPE/CO configurations and interfaces
- Operations
- Network management
- Testing and interoperability

Very-High-Data-Rate Digital Subscriber Line

It is becoming increasingly clear that telephone companies around the world are making decisions to include existing twisted-pair loops in their next-generation broadband access networks. DLC, a shared-access medium well suited to analog and digital broadcast, comes up somewhat short when used to carry voice, interactive video, and high-speed data communications at the same time. Fiber to the home (FTTH) is still prohibitively expensive in the marketplace. An attractive alternative, soon to be commercially viable, is a combination of fiber cables feeding neighborhood optical network units (ONUs) and last-leg-premises copper connections. This topology, which is often called fiber to the neighborhood (FTTN), encompasses fiber to the curb (FTTC) with short drops and fiber to the basement (FTTB), serving tall buildings with vertical drops.

One of the enabling technologies for FTTN is VDSL. In simple terms, VDSL transmits high-speed data over short reaches of twisted-pair copper telephone lines, with a range of speeds depending on actual line length (see Figure 17-22). The maximum downstream rate under consideration is between 51 and 55 Mbps over lines up to 1000 feet (300 m) long. Downstream speeds as low as 14 Mbps over lengths beyond 4000 feet (1500 m) are also common. Upstream rates in early models will be asymmetric, just like ADSL, at speeds from 1.6 to 2.3 Mbps. Both data channels will be separated in frequency from bands used for basic telephone service and Integrated Services Digital Network (ISDN), enabling service providers to overlay VDSL on existing services. At present, the two channels are separated from each other in frequency. As needs arise for higher-speed upstream channels or symmetric rates, VDSL systems might need to use echo cancellation.

FIGURE 17-22
VDSL.

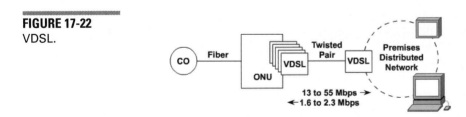

VDSL Projected Capabilities

Although VDSL has not achieved the same degree of definition as ADSL, it has advanced far enough that we can discuss realizable goals, beginning with data rate and range. Downstream rates derive from fractional multiples of the

Synchronous Optical Network (SONET) and Synchronous Digital Hierarchy (SDH) canonical speed of 155.52 Mbps—namely, 51.84 Mbps, 25.92 Mbps, and 12.96 Mbps. Each rate has a corresponding target range.

Upstream rates under discussion fall into three general ranges:

- 1.6 to 2.3 Mbps
- 19.2 Mbps
- Equal to downstream

Early versions of VDSL almost certainly incorporate the slower asymmetric rate. Higher upstream and symmetric configurations might be possible only for very short lines. Like ADSL, VDSL must transmit compressed video, a real-time signal unsuited to error retransmission schemes used in data communications. To achieve error rates compatible with those of compressed video, VDSL must incorporate FEC with sufficient interleaving to correct all errors created by impulsive noise events of some specified duration. Interleaving introduces delay, on the order of 40 times the maximum length correctable impulse.

Data in the downstream direction is broadcast to every CPE on the premises or is transmitted to a logically separated hub that distributes data to addressed CPE based on cell or TDM within the data stream itself.

Upstream multiplexing is more difficult. Systems using a passive network termination (NT) must insert data onto a shared medium, by either a form of time-division multiple access (TDMA) or a form of FDM. TDMA may use a type of token control called cell grants passed in the downstream direction from the ONU modem, or contention, or both (contention for unrecognized devices, cell grants for recognized devices). FDM gives each CPE its own channel, obviating the need for a MAC protocol, but either limiting data rates available to any one CPE or requiring dynamic allocation of bandwidth and inverse multiplexing at each CPE. Systems using active NTs transfer the upstream collection problem to a logically separated hub that (typically) uses Ethernet or ATM upstream multiplexing.

Migration and inventory considerations dictate VDSL units that can operate at various (preferably all) speeds, with automatic recognition of a newly connected device to a line or to a change in speed. Passive network interfaces need to have hot insertion, whereas a new VDSL premises unit can be put on the line without interfering with the operation of other modems.

VDSL Technology

VDSL technology resembles ADSL to a large degree, although ADSL must face much larger dynamic ranges and is considerably more complex as a result.

Line-Code Candidates

Four line codes have been proposed for VDSL:

- **Carrierless amplitude modulation/phase modulation (CAP)**—A version of suppressed carrier quadrature amplitude modulation (QAM). For passive NT configurations, CAP would use quadrature phase shift keying (QPSK) upstream and a type of TDMA for multiplexing (although CAP does not preclude an FDM approach to upstream multiplexing).

- **Discrete multitone (DMT)**—A multicarrier system using discrete Fourier transforms to create and demodulate individual carriers. For passive NT configurations, DMT would use FDM for upstream multiplexing (although DMT does not preclude a TDMA multiplexing strategy).

- **Discrete wavelet multitone (DWMT)**—A multicarrier system using wavelet transforms to create and demodulate individual carriers. DWMT also uses FDM for upstream multiplexing, but it also allows TDMA.

- **Simple line code (SLC)**—A version of four-level baseband signaling that filters the based band and restores it at the receiver. For passive NT configurations, SLC would most likely use TDMA for upstream multiplexing, although FDM is possible.

Channel Separation

Early versions of VDSL use FDM to separate downstream from upstream channels and both of them from basic telephone service and ISDN, as shown in Figure 17-23. Echo cancellation might be required for later-generation systems featuring symmetric data rates. A rather substantial distance, in frequency, will be maintained between the lowest data channel and basic telephone service to enable very simple and cost-effective basic telephone service splitters. Normal practice would locate the downstream channel above the upstream channel. However, the DAVIC specification reverses this order to enable premises distribution of VDSL signals over coaxial cable systems.

Forward Error Control

Forward Error Control (FEC) will no doubt use a form of Reed Soloman coding and optional interleaving to correct bursts of errors caused by impulse noise. The structure will be very similar to ADSL, as defined in T1.414. An outstanding question is whether FEC overhead (in the range of 8 percent) will be taken from the payload capacity or will be added as an out-of-band signal. The former reduces payload capacity but maintains nominal reach, whereas the latter retains the nominal payload but suffers a small reduction in reach. ADSL puts FEC overhead out of band.

FIGURE 17-23
VDSL
technology.

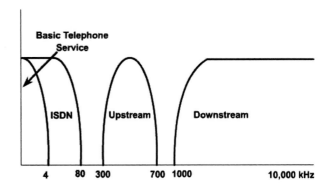

Upstream Multiplexing

If the premises VDSL unit comprises the network termination (an active NT), then the means of multiplexing upstream cells or data channels from more than one CPE into a single upstream becomes the responsibility of the premises network. The VDSL unit simply presents raw data streams in both directions. As illustrated in Figure 17-24, one type of premises network involves a star connecting each CPE to a switching or multiplexing hub; such a hub could be integral to the premises VDSL unit.

FIGURE 17-24
Active Network
Termination.

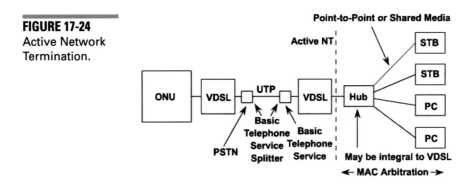

In a passive NT configuration, each CPE has an associated VDSL unit. (A passive NT does not conceptually preclude multiple CPE per VDSL, but then the question of active versus passive NT becomes a matter of ownership, not a matter of wiring topology and multiplexing strategies; see Figure 17-25.) Now the upstream channels for each CPE must share a common wire. Although a collision-detection system could be used, the desire for guaranteed bandwidth indicates one of two solutions. The first invokes a cell-grant protocol in which downstream frames generated at the ONU or farther up the network contain a few bits that grant access to specific CPE during a specified period subsequent to receiving a frame. A granted CPE can send one upstream cell during this period. The transmitter in the CPE must turn on, send a preamble to condition the ONU receiver, send the cell, and then turn itself off. The protocol must insert enough silence to let line ringing clear. One construction of this protocol uses 77 octet intervals to transmit a single 53-octet cell.

FIGURE 17-25
Passive Network
Termination.

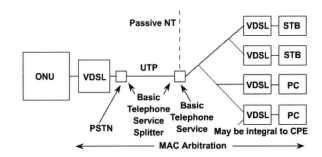

The second method divides the upstream channel into frequency bands and assigns one band to each CPE. This method has the advantage of avoiding any MAC with its associated overhead (although a multiplexer must be built into the ONU), but it either restricts the data rate available to any one CPE or imposes a dynamic inverse multiplexing scheme that lets one CPE send more than its share for a period.

VDSL Issues

VDSL is still in the definition stage; some preliminary products exist, but not enough is known yet about telephone line characteristics, radio frequency interface emissions and susceptibility, upstream multiplexing protocols, and information requirements to frame a set of definitive, standardizable properties. One large unknown is the maximum distance that VDSL can reliably realize for a given data rate. This is unknown because real line characteristics at the frequencies required for VDSL are speculative, and items such as short bridged taps or unterminated extension lines in homes (which have no effect on telephony) or ISDN may have very detrimental affects on VDSL in certain configurations.

Furthermore, VDSL invades the frequency ranges of amateur radio, and every above-ground telephone wire is an antenna that both radiates and attracts energy in amateur radio bands. Balancing low signal levels to prevent emissions that interfere with amateur radio with higher signals needed to combat interference by amateur radio could be the dominant factor in determining line reach.

A second dimension of VDSL that is far from clear is the services environment. It can be assumed that VDSL will carry information in ATM cell format for video and asymmetric data communications, although optimum downstream and upstream data rates have not been ascertained. What is more difficult to assess is the need for VDSL to carry information in non-ATM formats (such as conventional Plesiochronous Digital Hierarchy [PDH] structures) and the need for symmetric channels at broadband rates (above T1/E1). VDSL will not be completely independent of higher-layer protocols, particularly in the upstream direction, where multiplexing data from more than one CPE may require knowledge of link layer formats (that is, ATM or not).

A third difficult subject is premises distribution and the interface between the telephone network and CPE. Cost considerations favor a passive network interface with premises VDSL installed in CPE and upstream multiplexing handled similarly to LAN buses. System management, reliability, regulatory constraints, and migration favor an active network termination, just like ADSL and ISDN, that can operate like a hub, with point-to-point or shared-media distribution to multiple CPE on-premises wiring that is independent and physically isolated from network wiring.

However, costs cannot be ignored. Small ONUs must spread common equipment costs, such as fiber links, interfaces, and equipment cabinets, over a small number of subscribers compared to DLC. Furthermore, VDSL for passive NTs may (only *may*) be more expensive than VDSL for active NTs, but the elimination of any other premises network electronics may make it the most cost-effective solution and highly desired, despite the obvious benefits of an active NT.

Standards Status

At present, five standards organizations/forums have begun work on VDSL:

- **T1E1.4**—The U.S. ANSI standards group T1E1.4 has just begun a project for VDSL, making a first attack on system requirements that will evolve into a system and protocol definition.

- **European Telecommunication Standards Institute (ETSI)**—The ETSI has a VDSL standards project, under the title High-Speed Metallic Access Systems, and has compiled a list of objectives, problems, and requirements. Among its preliminary findings are the need for an active NT and payloads in multiples of SDH virtual container VC-12, or 2.3 Mbps. ETSI works very closely with T1E1.4 and the ADSL Forum, with significant overlapping attendees.

- **DAVIC**—DAVIC has taken the earliest position on VDSL. Its first specification due to be finalized will define a line code for downstream data, another for upstream data, and a MAC for upstream multiplexing based on TDMA over shared wiring. DAVIC is specifying VDSL only for a single downstream rate of 51.84 Mbps and a single upstream rate of 1.6 Mbps over 300 m or less of copper. The proposal assumes (and is driven to a large extent by) a passive NT and further assumes premises distribution from the NT over new coaxial cable or new copper wiring.

- **The ATM Forum**—The ATM Forum has defined a 51.84-Mbps interface for private-network User-Network Interfaces (UNIs) and a corresponding transmission technology. It has also addressed the question of CPE distribution and delivery of ATM all the way to premises over the various access technologies described previously.

- **The ADSL Forum**—The ADSL Forum has just begun consideration of VDSL. In keeping with its charter, the Forum will address network, protocol, and architectural aspects of VDSL for all prospective applications, leaving line code and transceiver protocols to T1E1.4 and ETSI and higher-layer protocols to organizations such as the ATM Forum and DAVIC.

Relationship of VDSL to ADSL

VDSL has an odd technical resemblance to ADSL. VDSL achieves data rates nearly ten times greater than those of ADSL, as shown in Figure 17-26, but ADSL is the more complex transmission technology, in large part because ADSL must contend with much larger dynamic distances than VDSL. However, the two are essentially cut from the same cloth. ADSL employs advanced transmission techniques and FEC to realize data rates from 1.5 to 8 Mbps over twisted-pair wiring, ranging in distance to 18,000 feet; VDSL employs the same advanced transmission techniques and FEC to realize data rates from 14 to 55 Mbps over twisted-pair wiring, ranging to 4500 feet. Indeed, the two can be considered a continuum, a set of transmission tools that delivers about as much data as theoretically possible over varying distances of existing telephone wiring.

VDSL is clearly a technology suitable for a full-service network (assuming that "full service" does not imply more than two HDTV channels over the highest-rate VDSL). It is equally clear that telephone companies cannot deploy ONUs overnight, even if all the technology were available. ADSL may not be a full-service network technology, but it has the singular advantage of offering service over lines that exist today, and ADSL products are more widely available than VDSL. Many new services being contemplated today—such as videoconferencing, Internet access, video on demand, and remote LAN access—can be delivered at speeds at or below T1/E1 rates. For such services, ADSL/VDSL provides an ideal combination for network evolution. On the longest lines, ADSL delivers a single channel. As line length shrinks, either from natural proximity to a central office or from deployment of fiber-based access nodes, ADSL and VDSL simply offer more channels and capacity for services that require rates above T1/E1 (such as digital live television and virtual CD-ROM access).

FIGURE 17-26
VDSL's relationship to ADSL.

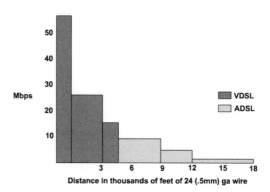

Summary

Remote access technologies are evolving to address the time-sensitive and bandwidth-intensive nature of voice, video, data, and multimedia applications. In this chapter, technologies from cable modems to wireless were compared in terms of popularity, cost, complexity, and future prospects. Additionally, this chapter covered the available options for residential and business customers, and compared them in terms of speed, cost, availability, and future potential. Some of the technologies discussed included cable, fixed wireless, DSL, and satellite technologies. Finally, this chapter discussed the application and situations in which one might be the better choice than another.

Objectives

After reading this chapter, you will be able to

- Describe VPN operation
- Describe VPN implementation
- Describe Cisco Systems VPNs
- Describe tunneling
- Describe Cisco's L2F implementation
- Describe the end-to-end virtual dialup process
- Describe highlights of the virtual dial-up service

Virtual Private Networks

Introduction

Networking is driven by the need to enable communications between applications and individuals in a faster, cheaper, and more robust way. In the majority of cases, networking is not driven by the need to handle these communications securely. Virtual private networking establishes a clear case for security as an enabler and a basic mechanism to do something new and different: to use public networks for private communications.

Virtual Private Network Operation

A *virtual private network (VPN)* is a communications environment in which access is controlled to permit peer connections only within a defined community of interest. It's constructed through some form of partitioning of a common underlying communications medium. This communications medium provides services to the network on a nonexclusive basis. A simpler, more approximate, and less formal definition of a VPN follows:

> A VPN is private network that is constructed within a public network infrastructure, such as the global Internet.

Although VPNs might be constructed to address a number of specific business needs or technical requirements, a comprehensive VPN solution provides support for dial-in and other remote access, support for multiple remote sites connected by leased lines (or other dedicated means), the capability of the VPN service provider (SP) to host various services for the VPN customers (for example, Web hosting), and the capability to support not just intra-VPN connectivity, but also inter-VPN connectivity, including connectivity, to the global Internet.

VPN Advantages

Virtual private networking has significant advantages over previous forms of channel encryption and alternatives. Some of these advantages include the following:

- A single virtual private networking technology can provide privacy for multiple TCP/IP applications. Application-level encryption requires different methods for different services. Support for multiple protocols is also possible through tunneling IP using the Point-to-Point Tunneling Protocol (PPTP), the Layer 2

Tunneling Protocol (L2TP), or the Layer 2 Forwarding (L2F) protocol. Providing privacy for multiple TCP/IP applications is especially important in environments where you want to provide secure access for partners or telecommuters.

■ Encryption services can be provided for all TCP/IP communications between the trusted client and the virtual private networking server. This has the advantage of being transparent to the end user. Because encryption is turned on, the server can enforce it.

Types of VPNs

A VPN is defined as customer connectivity deployed on a shared infrastructure with the same policies as a private network (see Figure 18-1). The shared infrastructure can leverage a service provider IP, Frame Relay, ATM backbone, or the Internet. Three types of VPNs exist that align how businesses and organizations use VPNs:

■ **Access VPN**—Provides remote access to a corporate intranet or extranet over a shared infrastructure with the same policies as a private network. Access VPNs enable users to access corporate resources whenever, wherever, and however they require. Access VPNs encompass analog, dial, Integrated Services Digital Network (ISDN), digital subscriber line (DSL), mobile IP, and cable technologies to securely connect mobile users, telecommuters, or branch offices.

■ **Intranet VPN**—Links corporate headquarters, remote offices, and branch offices over a shared infrastructure using dedicated connections. Businesses enjoy the same policies as a private network, including security, quality of service (QoS), manageability, and reliability.

■ **Extranet VPN**—Links customers, suppliers, partners, or communities of interest to a corporate intranet over a shared infrastructure using dedicated connections. Businesses enjoy the same policies as a private network, including security, QoS, manageability, and reliability.

Service-Level Agreements

At this point, it's worthwhile to briefly examine the importance of *service-level agreements (SLAs)* regarding the deployment of VPNs. SLAs are negotiated contracts between VPN providers and their subscribers; they contain the service criteria to which the subscriber expects specific services to be delivered. The SLA is arguably the only binding tool at the subscriber's disposal to ensure that the VPN provider delivers the service(s) to the level and quality agreed to; it is in the subscriber's best interest to monitor the criteria outlined in the SLA for compliance. However, SLAs present some challenging technical issues for both the provider and the subscriber.

FIGURE 18-1
A logical
topology view
of a VPN.

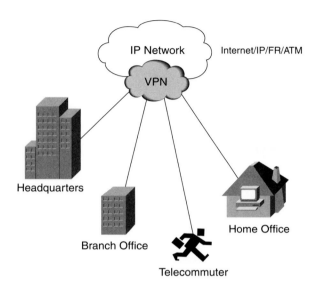

For the subscriber, the challenge of SLAs is to devise and operate service-measurement tools that can provide a reasonable indication of the extent to which the provider honors the SLA. Note that a subscriber might use an SLA to bind one or more providers to a contractual service level, but if the subscriber's VPN spans multiple providers' domains, the SLA must also encompass the issue of provider interconnection and end-to-end service performance.

For the provider, the challenge of SLAs lies in honoring multiple SLAs from a number of service providers. In the case of an Internet public data network (PDN) provider, the common mode of best-effort service levels is not conducive to meeting SLAs, given the unpredictable nature of the host's resource-allocation mechanisms. In such environments, either the provider must ensure that the network is generously engineered in terms of the ratio of subscriber access capacity to internal switching capacity, or the provider can deploy service differentiation structures to ensure that minimum resource levels are allocated to each SLA subscriber. Note that the first course of action tends to reduce the benefit of aggregation of traffic, which has an ultimate cost implication; the second course of action has implications in terms of operational management complexity and scalability of the network.

An Example VPN

In the example illustrated in Figure 18-2, Network A sites have established a VPN (depicted by the dashed lines) across the service provider's backbone network, whereas Network B is completely unaware of its existence. Networks A and B harmoniously coexist on the same backbone infrastructure.

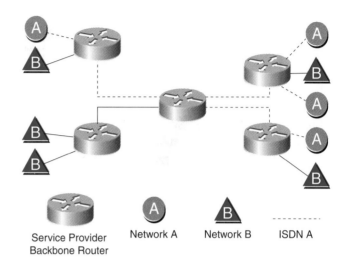

FIGURE 18-2
A virtual private
network of A
sites.

Service Provider
Backbone Router

Network A   Network B   ISDN A

VPNs of Network A Sites

The most common type of VPN has geographically diverse subnetworks that belong to a common administrative domain, interconnected by a shared infrastructure outside their administrative control (such as the global Internet or a single service provider backbone). The principal motivation in establishing a VPN of this type is that most of the communications between devices within the VPN community may be sensitive. (Again, a decision on the required level of privacy rests solely on a risk analysis performed by the administrators of the VPN.) Yet, the total value of the communications system does not justify the investment in a fully private communications system that uses discrete transmission elements.

On a related note, the level of privacy that a VPN might enjoy depends greatly on the technology used to construct the VPN. For example, if the communications between each VPN subnetwork (or between each VPN host) are securely encrypted as they transit the common communications infrastructure, the privacy aspect of the VPN is relatively high.

In fact, the granularity of a VPN implementation can be broken down to a single end-to-end, one-to-one connectivity scenario. Examples of these types of one-to-one VPNs are single dial-up users who establish a VPN connection to a secure application (such as an online banking service), or a single user establishing a secure, encrypted session between a desktop and a server application (such as a purchasing transaction conducted on the Internet). This type of one-to-one VPN becomes more prevalent as secure electronic commerce applications become more mature and are further deployed in the Internet.

NOTE

The concept of virtualization in networking has also been considered in regard to deploying both research and production services on a common infrastructure. The challenge in the research and education community is how to satisfy both network research and production requirements.

VPNs also have been considered as a method to segregate traffic in a network so that research and production traffic behave as ships in the night, oblivious to one another's existence. They are so oblivious that major events, such as major failures or instability, within one community of interest are completely transparent to the other.

VPNs can be constructed to span more than one host communications network so that the state of the VPN can be supported on one or more VPN provider networks. This scenario is perhaps at its most robust when all the providers explicitly support the resultant distributed VPN environment. However, other solutions that do not necessarily involve knowledge of the overlay VPN are occasionally deployed with mixed results.

VPN Implementation

After the decision is made to implement a VPN, steps must be taken to ensure that the infrastructure is adequately secured and that the application and its goals are well defined before implementation begins.

Security Audit

Running a security audit ensures that vulnerability in a firewall, remote-access application, or an authentication method is not exposed to a wider audience after the VPN's implementation. These security issues justify a full audit of at least the network's perimeter, which might be attacked from inside and outside. This evaluation should audit all inbound connections to the intranet, including remote-access servers, router-based connections to subsidiaries, and extranet connections. In the case of an extranet VPN, this evaluation should also include the perimeter of an enterprise's partner organizations.

The Scope and Application Needs

After a security audit is performed, you must define the scope of the VPN by identifying the end-user constituencies (such as partners, contractors, or telecommuters) that might access the VPN and the applications. This step includes evaluating the applications that the constituents will use and the sensitivity of the data they will transmit. Evaluating these applications allows for the selection of appropriate security services and adequate encryption.

Next, you must define and test the latency and QoS needs of all the applications that the VPN will support. Even applications that might be considered store-and-forward applications can have latency sensitivities in some configurations. These sensitivities affect whether the application is feasible for the VPN and help determine the nature of the underlying network.

Documentation

In the case of the extranet VPN, the enterprise should draft a statement of understanding for the extranet VPN users. In the remote-access case, the enterprise should update its remote-access policy to ensure that it incorporates this new form of access.

Security Policy

In the extranet case, for example, a virtual private networking policy regulates authentication and authorization.

Authorization should be based on generic roles that are defined by participating enterprises. (These roles should be mapped to individuals in the participating enterprises.) The generic role should have basic privileges, including network access and Web server access to the stock levels of the suppliers' products. These roles should then be mapped to a defined set of data and should be enforced through the VPN. Extranet policy should always be incorporated in a statement of understanding among the involved users.

The virtual private networking remote-access policy should not differ radically from the already established remote-access policy. Key differences from traditional remote-access policy can include an "acceptable use" for access to the Internet, where applicable. Just as any Internet-based access should also have two-factor, token-based authentication in place, the policy should include a statement about how these tokens can be used most securely.

The Cisco Systems VPN Design

NOTE

Currently, no standards exist that outline the software and hardware components of a VPN. Every vendor that provides a VPN service performs it in a method that is best supported by its own hardware platforms and software applications.

Cisco's end-to-end hardware and Cisco IOS software networking products provide sophisticated security for sensitive private transmissions over the public infrastructure, QoS through traffic differentiation, reliability for mission-critical applications, scalability for supporting large bandwidths of data, and comprehensive network management to enable a complete access VPN solution.

The following sections discuss how Cisco network access servers (NASs) and routers with Cisco IOS software provide new functionality with virtual dial-up services. This functionality is based on the L2F protocol Internet Engineering Task Force (IETF) draft Request For Comments (RFC). The L2F protocol provides a standards-based tunneling mechanism for transporting link layer frames of higher-layer protocols—such as High-Level Data Link Control (HDLC), async Point-to-Point Protocol (PPP), Serial Line Internet Protocol (SLIP), or PPP Integrated Services Digital Network (ISDN). By using such tunnels, it is possible to divorce the location of the initial dial-up server from the location at which the dial-up protocol connection is terminated and the location at which access to the network is provided (usually a corporate gateway).

Tunneling

A key component of the virtual dial-up service is *tunneling*, a vehicle that encapsulates packets inside a protocol that is understood at the entry and exit points of a given network. These entry and exit points are defined as *tunnel interfaces*. The tunnel interface is similar to a hardware interface but is configured in software. Figure 18-3 shows the format in which a packet would traverse the network within a tunnel.

FIGURE 18-3
An overview of a tunneling packet format.

IP/UDP	L2F	PPP (Data)
Carrier Protocol	Encapsulating Protocol	Passenger Protocol

Tunneling involves the following three types of protocols (see Figure 18-3):

- **Passenger protocol**—The protocol being encapsulated. In a dial-up scenario, this protocol might be PPP, SLIP, or text dialog.

- **Encapsulating protocol**—Creates, maintains, and tears down the tunnel. Cisco supports several encapsulating protocols, including the L2F protocol, which is used for virtual dial-up services.

- **Carrier protocol**—Carries the encapsulated protocol. IP is the first carrier protocol used by the L2F protocol because of its robust routing capabilities, ubiquitous support across different media, and deployment within the Internet.

No dependency exists between the L2F protocol and IP. In subsequent releases of the L2F functionality, Frame Relay, X.25 virtual circuits (VCs), and Asynchronous Transfer Mode (ATM) switched virtual circuits (SVCs) could be used as a direct Layer 2 carrier protocol for the tunnel.

Tunneling has evolved to become one of the key components in defining and using VPNs. Cisco IOS provides virtual dial-up service through a telecommuting form of a VPN.

Cisco's Virtual Dial-Up Services

The following definitions fully describe the virtual dialup service that Cisco Systems provides in its Cisco IOS software:

- **Remote user**—The client who dials ISDN/Public Switched Telephone Network (PSTN) from either a home or another remote location.
- **NAS**—The telecommuting device that terminates the dial-up calls over either analog (basic telephone service) or digital (ISDN) circuits.
- **Internet service provider (ISP)**—The supplier that provides the dial-up services, can provide for services itself through the Network Access Server (NAS), or can deliver the dial-up remote user to a designated corporate gateway.
- **Corporate gateway**—The destination router that provides access to the services the remote user requests. The services could be a corporation or even another ISP.

Remote users (using either asynchronous PPP or ISDN) access the corporate LAN as if they were dialed in directly to the corporate gateway (although their physical dialup is through the ISP NAS). See Figure 18-4 to get a topological view of how these conventions would be deployed within a virtual dial-up service.

Cisco's L2F Implementation

The key management requirements of service provided by Cisco's L2F implementation are the following:

- Neither the remote end system nor its corporate hosts should require any special software to use this service in a secure manner.
- Authentication is provided by dial-up PPP, the Challenge Handshake Authentication Protocol (CHAP), or the Password Authentication Protocol (PAP)—including Terminal Access Controller Access Control System Plus (TACACS+) and Remote Authentication Dial-In User Service (RADIUS) solutions, as well as support for smart cards and one-time passwords. The authentication will be manageable by the user independently of the ISP.
- Addressing will be as manageable as dedicated dialup solutions; the address will be assigned by the remote user's respective corporation—not by the ISP.
- Authorization will be managed by the corporation's remote users, as it would be in a direct dialup solution.
- Accounting will be performed by both the ISP (for billing purposes) and by the user (for chargeback and auditing purposes).

These requirements are primarily achieved because of the functionality provided by tunneling the remote user directly to the corporate location using the L2F protocol. In the case of PPP, all Link Control Protocol (LCP) and Network Control Protocol (NCP) negotiations take place at the remote user's corporate location. PPP is allowed to flow from the remote user and terminate at the corporate gateway. Figure 18-4 illustrates this process.

FIGURE 18-4
The remote user establishes a PPP connection with the corporate network to complete the virtual dial-up topology.

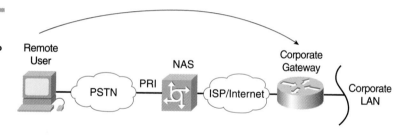

End-to-End Virtual Dial-Up Process

To illustrate how the virtual dial-up service works, the following example describes what might happen when a remote user initiates access. Figure 18-5 gives you step-by-step details of this end-to-end process.

The remote user initiates a PPP connection to an ISP over the PSTN or over ISDN. The NAS accepts the connection, and the PPP link is established. (See Figure 18-5, Step 1.)

The ISP uses CHAP or PAP to authenticate the end system/user. Only the username field is interpreted to determine whether the user requires a virtual dial-up service. It is expected that usernames will be structured (for example, smith@cisco.com) or that the ISP will maintain a database mapping users to services. In the case of virtual dial-up, mapping will name a specific endpoint—the corporate gateway. This endpoint is the IP address of the corporate gateway known to the public as the ISP network. (See Figure 18-5, Step 2.)

If a virtual dial-up service is not required, traditional access to the Internet can be provided by the NAS. All address assignment and authentication would be locally performed by the ISP in this situation.

If no tunnel connection currently exists to the desired corporate gateway, one is initiated. The details of such tunnel creation are outside the scope of this specification; L2F requires only that the tunnel media provide point-to-point connectivity. Examples of such media are User Datagram Protocol (UDP), Frame Relay, ATM, and X.25 VCs. Based on UDP using a carrier protocol of IP, any media supporting IP supports the virtual dial-up functionality. (See Figure 18-5, Step 3.)

After the tunnel connection is established, the NAS allocates an unused multiplex ID (MID) and sends a connect indication to notify the corporate gateway of this new dialup session. The MID identifies a particular connection within the tunnel. Each new connection is assigned a MID that's currently unused within the tunnel. The corporate gateway either accepts or rejects the connection. Rejection might include a reason indication, which might be displayed to the dialup user. After the indication displays, the call should be disconnected.

NOTE

If permitted by the organization's security policy, the authorization of the dial-in user at the NAS can be performed only on a domain name within the username field, not on every individual username. This setup can substantially reduce the size of the authorization database.

FIGURE 18-5
Eight steps are required for a remote VPN client and a corporate LAN to communicate.

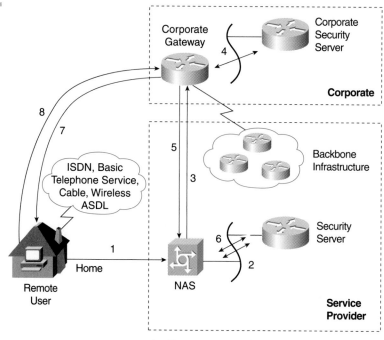

1. Remote user initiates PPP connection, NAS accepts call.
2. NAS identifies remote user.
3. NAS initiates L2F tunnel to desired corporate gateway.
4. Corporate gateway authenticates remote user and accepts or declines tunnel.
5. Corporate gateway confirms acceptance of call and L2F tunnel.
6. NAS logs acceptance/traffic optional.
7. Corporate gateway exchanges PPP negotiations with remote user. IP address can be assigned by corporate gateway at this point.
8. End-to-end data tunneled from remote user and corporate gateway.

The initial setup notification might include the authentication information required to allow the corporate gateway to authenticate the user and decide to accept or reject the connection. In the case of CHAP, the setup packet includes the challenge, the username, and a raw password. For PAP, it includes the username and a clear-text password. The corporate gateway can be configured to use this information to complete its authentication and avoid an additional cycle of authentication. The authentication takes place at the corporate customer, which allows the corporation to impose its own security and corporate policy on the remote users accessing its network. This way, the organization doesn't have to fully trust the authentication that the ISP performed. (See Figure 18-5, Step 4.)

If the corporate gateway accepts the connection, it creates a virtual interface for PPP in a manner analogous to what it would use for a direct-dialed connection. With this virtual interface in place, link layer frames can pass over this tunnel in both directions. (See Figure 18-5, Step 5.) Frames from the remote user are received at the NAS, stripped of any link-framing or transparency bytes, encapsulated in L2F, and forwarded over the appropriate tunnel. In the first release, the carrier protocol used by the L2F protocol within the tunnel is IP, requiring the frames to also be encapsulated within IP.

The corporate gateway accepts these frames, strips L2F, and processes the frames as normal incoming frames for the appropriate interface and protocol. The virtual interface behaves much like a hardware interface, except that the hardware, in this case, is physically located at the ISP NAS. The reverse traffic direction behaves analogously, with the corporate gateway encapsulating the packet in L2F, and the NAS stripping L2F encapsulation before transmitting it out the physical interface to the remote user.

In addition, NAS can optionally log the acceptance of the call and any relevant information with respect to the type of services provided to the remote user, such as duration of the call, the number of packets/bytes transferred, and the protocol ports accessed. (See Figure 18-5, Step 6.)

At this point, the connectivity is a point-to-point PPP connection whose endpoints are the remote user's networking application on one end and the termination of this connectivity into the corporate gateway's PPP support on the other. Because the remote user has become simply another dialup client of the corporate gateway access server, client connectivity can now be managed using traditional mechanisms with respect to further authorization, address negotiation, protocol access, accounting, and filtering. (See Figure 18-5, Steps 7 and 8.)

Because L2F connection notifications for PPP clients contain sufficient information for a corporate gateway to authenticate and initialize its LCP state machine, the remote user is not required to be queried for CHAP authentication a second time, nor is the client required to undergo multiple rounds of LCP negotiation and convergence. These techniques are intended to optimize connection setup and are not intended to circumvent any functions required by PPP specification.

NOTE

The functionality provided by Cisco's network access servers is intended to provide for both the virtual dial-up and traditional dial-up services.

Highlights of Virtual Dial-Up Service

The following sections discuss some of the significant differences between the standard Internet access service and the virtual dial-up service with respect to authentication, address allocation, authorization, and accounting.

Authentication and Security

In a traditional dial-up scenario, the ISP using a NAS in conjunction with a security server follows an authentication process by challenging the remote user for both the username and the password. If the remote user passes this phase, the authorization phase begins.

For the virtual dial-up service, the ISP pursues authentication to discover the user's apparent identity (and, by implication, the user's desired corporate gateway). At this point, no password interaction is performed. As soon as the corporate gateway is determined, a connection initiates with the authentication information that the ISP gathered. The corporate gateway completes the authentication by either accepting or rejecting the connection. (For example, the connection is rejected in a PAP request when the username or password is incorrect.) When the connection is accepted, the corporate gateway can pursue another phase of authentication at the PPP layer. These additional authentication activities are outside the scope of the specification but might include proprietary PPP extensions or textual challenges carried within a TCP/IP Telnet session.

For each L2F tunnel established, L2F tunnel security generates a unique random key to resist spoofing attacks. Within the L2F tunnel, each multiplexed session maintains a sequence number to prevent the duplication of packets. Cisco provides the flexibility of allowing users to implement compression at the client end. In addition, encryption on the tunnel can be done using IP security (IPSec).

Authorization

When providing a traditional dial-up service, the ISP maintains per-user profiles that define the authorization. Thus, a security server can interact with NAS to provide policy-based usage to connect users based on their authentication. These policy statements range from simple source/destination filters for a handful of sites to complex algorithms that determine specific applications, time-of-day access, and a long list of permitted or denied destinations. This process can become burdensome to the ISP, especially if the ISP must provide access to remote users on behalf of corporations that require constant change to this policy.

In a virtual dial-up service, the burden of providing detailed authorization based on policy statements is given directly to the remote user's corporation. By allowing end-to-end connectivity between remote users and their corporate gateway, all authorization can be performed as if the remote users are directly dialed into the corporate location. This setup frees the ISP from maintaining a large database of individual user profiles based on many different corporations. More importantly, the virtual dial-up service becomes more secure to corporations using it. The virtual dial-up service allows corporations to quickly react to changes in their remote user communities.

Address Allocation

For a traditional Internet service, the user accepts that the IP address might be allocated dynamically from a pool of service-provider addresses. This model often means that remote users have little or no access to their corporate network's resources because firewalls and security policies deny external IP addresses access to the corporate network.

For the virtual dial-up service, the corporate gateway can exist behind the corporate firewall and allocate addresses that are internal (and, in fact, can be RFC 1597 addresses or non-IP addresses). Because L2F tunnels operate exclusively at the frame layer, the actual policies of such address management are irrelevant to correct virtual dial-up service; for all purposes of PPP protocol handling, the dial-in user appears to have connected at the corporate gateway.

Accounting

The requirement for both NAS and the corporate gateway to provide accounting data can mean that they may count packets, octets, and connection start and stop times. Because virtual dial-up is an access service, accounting for connection attempts (in particular, failed attempts) is of significant interest. The corporate gateway can reject new connections based on the authentication information gathered by the ISP, with corresponding logging. In cases where the corporate gateway accepts the connection and continues with further authentication, the corporate gateway might subsequently disconnect the client. In such scenarios, the disconnection indication back to the ISP can also include a reason.

Because the corporate gateway can decline a connection based on the authentication information collected by the ISP, accounting can easily draw a distinction between a series of failed connection attempts and a series of brief successful connections. Without this facility, the corporate gateway must always accept connection requests and would need to exchange numerous PPP packets with the remote system.

Summary

What is a virtual private network? As you learned, a VPN can take several forms: It can exist between two end systems, or it can exist between two or more networks. A VPN can be built by using tunnels, encryption, or one of the virtual router methods. A VPN can consist of networks connected to a service provider's network by leased lines, Frame Relay, or ATM, or a VPN can consist of dial-up subscribers that connect to centralized services or other dial-up subscribers.

The pertinent conclusion? Although a VPN can take many forms, it's built to solve some basic common problems that can be listed as virtualization of services and segregation of communications to a closed community of interest, while simultaneously exploiting the financial opportunity of economies of scale in the underlying common host communications system.

Every organization has problems that it must solve, and each of the tools mentioned in this chapter can be used to construct a certain type of VPN to address a particular set of functional objectives. More than one tool is available to address these problems, and network engineers should be cognizant that VPNs are an area in which many people use the term generically—there is a broad problem with many possible solutions. Each solution has numerous strengths, weaknesses, and vulnerabilities. No single mechanism exists for VPNs that will supplant all others in the months and years to come. Instead, a diversity of technological choices in this area of VPN support will continue to emerge.

Objectives

After reading this chapter, you will be able to

- Describe network security design
- Describe security mechanisms
- Select security solutions

Chapter 19

Developing Network Security and Network Management Strategies

Introduction

Security is one of the most important aspects of logical network design. It's often overlooked during the design of a network because security is considered an operational issue rather than a design issue. However, if you consider security before you design your network, you can avoid scalability and performance problems that occur when security is added to the completed design. In addition, you can consider trade-offs while your network is still in the logical design phase, and you can plan a solution that can meet security goals.

Security designs should be completed before the start of the physical design phase, just in case the security designs affect the physical design. This chapter helps you work with your network design customer to develop effective security strategies, and it helps you select the right tools and products to implement the strategies.

Network Security Design

To enterprise network designers, security is an especially hot topic these days because of increased Internet and extranet connections, increased e-commerce on the Internet, and more telecommuters and mobile users accessing enterprise networks from remote sites.

To help you address the issues associated with increasing security requirements, this chapter discusses the steps to develop a security strategy. This chapter also covers some common security techniques and solutions for typical security challenges, such as securing the Internet connection, securing dialup network access, securing network services, and securing user services.

The following steps help you design a network with security issues in mind:

Step 1   Identify network assets.

Step 2   Analyze security risks.

Step 3   Analyze security requirements and trade-offs.

Step 4   Develop a security plan.

Step 5   Define a security policy.

Step 6   Develop procedures for applying security policies.

Step 7   Develop a technical implementation strategy.

Step 8   Achieve buy-in from users, managers, and technical staff.

Step 9   Train users, managers, and technical staff.

Step 10 Implement the technical strategy and security procedures.

Step 11 Test the security and update it if any problems are found.

Step 12 Maintain security by scheduling periodic independent audits, reading audit logs, responding to incidents, reading current literature and agency alerts, continuing to test and train, and updating the security plan and policy.

Identifying Network Assets and Analyzing Risks

Network assets can include network hosts (including the hosts' operating systems, applications, and data), internetworking devices (such as routers and switches), and network data that traverses the network. Less obvious but still important, assets can include intellectual property, trade secrets, and a company's reputation.

Risks can range from hostile intruders to untrained users who download Internet applications that contain viruses. Hostile intruders can steal data, change data, and cause service to be denied to legitimate users. (These denial-of-service attacks have become increasingly common in the last few years.)

Analyzing Security Requirements and Trade-offs

As is the case with most technical design requirements, achieving security goals means making *trade-offs*. Trade-offs must be made between security goals and goals for affordability, usability, performance, and availability. Also, security adds to the amount of management work because user login IDs, passwords, and audit logs must be maintained.

Security also affects network performance. Security features such as packet filters and data encryption consume CPU power and memory on hosts, routers, and servers. Encryption can use upward of 15 percent of available CPU power on a router or server. Encryption can be implemented on dedicated devices instead of on shared routers or servers, but there is still an effect on network performance because of the delay that packets experience while they are being encrypted or decrypted.

Encryption can reduce network redundancy. If all traffic must go through an encryption device, the device becomes a single point of failure. This makes it difficult to meet availability goals. It also makes it harder to offer load balancing. To maximize performance and minimize security complexity, a router running encryption probably should not also offer load balancing. Load balancing can still be used, but only if it is done transparently to the routers providing encryption. Devices in between routers offering encryption services can provide the load balancing.

Developing a Security Plan

One of the first steps in security design is to develop a *security plan*. A security plan is a high-level document that proposes what an organization must do to meet security requirements. The plan specifies the time, people, and other resources that are required to develop a security policy and achieve technical implementation of the policy. As the network designer, you can help your customer develop a plan that is practical and pertinent. The plan should be based on the customer's goals and the analysis of network assets and risks.

A security plan should reference the network topology and include a list of network services that will be provided (for example, FTP, Web, e-mail, and so on). This list must specify who provides the services, who has access to the services, how access is provided, and who administers the services.

As the network designer, you help the customer evaluate which services are definitely needed based on the customer's business and technical goals. Sometimes new services are added unnecessarily simply because they are the latest trend. Adding services might require new packet filters on routers and firewalls to protect the services or might necessitate additional user-authentication processes to limit access to the services, adding complexity to the security strategy. You should avoid overly complex security strategies because they can be self-defeating. Complicated security strategies are difficult to implement correctly without introducing unexpected security holes.

One of the most important aspects of the security plan is a specification of the people who must be involved in implementing network security. Because of this, it's important to ask the following questions:

- Will specialized security administrators be hired?
- How will end users and their managers get involved?
- How will end users, managers, and technical staff be trained on security policies and procedures?

For a security plan to be useful, it must have the support of all levels of employees within the organization. It is especially important for corporate management to fully support the security plan. Technical staff and end users at headquarters and at remote sites should buy into the plan.

Defining a Security Policy

A *security policy* is a formal statement of the rules by which people who are given access to an organization's technology and information assets must abide. A security policy informs users, managers, and technical staff of their obligations for protecting technology and information assets. The policy must specify the mechanisms by which these obligations can be met. Just like the security plan, employees, managers, executives, and technical personnel must buy into the security policy.

Developing a security policy is the job of security and network administrators. Administrators get input from managers, users, network designers and engineers, and possibly legal counsel. As a network designer, you must work closely with the security administrators to understand how policies might affect the network design.

After a security policy is developed with the engagement of users, staff, and management, it should be explained to everyone by top management. (Many enterprises require personnel to sign a statement indicating that they have read, understood, and agreed to abide by a policy.)

Components of a Security Policy

In general, a policy needs to include at least the following:

- **An access policy**—Defines access rights and privileges. Should provide guidelines for connecting external networks, connecting devices to a network, and adding new software to systems.
- **An accountability policy**—Defines the responsibilities of users, operations staff, and management. Should specify an audit capability and provide guidelines on reporting security problems.
- **An authentication policy**—Establishes trust through an effective password policy and sets up guidelines for remote location authentication.
- **Computer-technology purchasing guidelines**—Specify the requirements for acquiring, configuring, and auditing computer systems and networks for compliance with the policy.

Developing Security Procedures

Security procedures implement security policies. Procedures define configuration, login, audit, and maintenance processes. Security procedures should be written for end users, network administrators, and security administrators. Security procedures should specify how to handle incidents (such as what to

---

NOTE

A security policy is a living document. Because organizations constantly change, security policies must be regularly updated to reflect new business directions and technological changes.

do and who to contact if an intrusion is detected). Security procedures can be communicated to users and administrators in instructor-led and self-paced training classes.

Security Mechanisms

This section describes some typical ingredients of secure network designs. You can select from these ingredients when you design solutions for common security challenges.

Authentication

Authentication identifies who requests network services. The term *authentication* usually refers to authenticating users, but it might also refer to verifying a software process. For example, some routing protocols support *route authentication*, when a router must pass some criteria before another router accepts its routing updates.

Most security policies state that, to access a network and its services, a user must enter a login ID and a password that a security server authenticates. To maximize security, one-time (dynamic) passwords can be used. With one-time password systems, a user's password always changes. This is often accomplished with a security card. A *security card* is a physical device about the size of a credit card. The user types a *personal identification number (PIN)* into the card. (The PIN is an initial level of security that simply gives the user permission to use the card.) The card provides a one-time password that accesses the corporate network for a limited time. The password is synchronized with a central security card server that resides on the network. Security cards are commonly used by telecommuters and mobile users. (They are not usually used for LAN access.)

Authorization

Authentication controls who can access network resources, but *authorization* says what they can do after they access the resources. Authorization grants privileges to processes and users. Authorization lets a security administrator control parts of a network, such as directories and files on servers.

Authorization varies from user to user, partly depending on a user's department or job function. For example, a policy might state that only Human Resources employees should see salary records for people they don't manage. Explicitly listing the authorized activities of each user with respect to every resource is difficult, so techniques are used to simplify the process. For example, a network manager can create user groups for users with the same privileges.

CAUTION

The audit process should not collect passwords. Collecting passwords creates a potential security breach if the audit records are improperly accessed. (Neither correct nor incorrect passwords should be collected. An incorrect password often differs from the valid password by only a single character or transposition of characters.)

NOTE

Data that is encrypted is called *ciphered data* (or simply *encrypted data*). Data that is not encrypted is called *plain text* or *clear text*.

Accounting (Auditing)

To effectively analyze the security of a network and to respond to security incidents, procedures should be established for collecting network activity data. Collecting data is called *accounting* or *auditing*.

For networks with strict security policies, audit data should include all attempts to achieve authentication and authorization by any person. It is especially important to log "anonymous" or "guest" access to public servers. The data should also log all attempts by users to change their access rights.

The collected data should include usernames and host names for login and logout attempts, and previous and new access rights for a change of access rights. Each entry in the audit log should be timestamped.

A further extension of auditing is the concept of *security assessment*. With security assessment, the network is internally examined by professionals who are trained in the vulnerabilities exploited by network invaders. Part of any security policy and audit procedure should be periodic assessments of the vulnerabilities in a network. The result should be a specific plan for correcting deficiencies, which might be as simple as retraining staff.

Data Encryption

Encryption is a process that scrambles data to protect it from being read by anyone besides the intended receiver. An *encryption device* encrypts data before placing it on a network. A *decryption device* decrypts the data before passing it to an application. A router, server, end system, or dedicated device can act as an encryption or decryption device.

Encryption is a useful security feature because it provides data confidentiality. It also can be used to identify the sender of data. Although authentication and authorization should also protect the confidentiality of data and identify senders, encryption is a good security feature to implement, just in case the other types fail.

Encryption should be used when a customer has analyzed security risks and identified severe consequences if data is not confidential and if the identity of senders of data is not guaranteed. On internal networks and networks that use the Internet simply for Web browsing, e-mail, and file transfer, encryption is usually not necessary. For organizations that connect private sites via the Internet by using virtual private networking (VPN), encryption is recommended to protect the confidentiality of the organization's data.

Encryption has two parts:

- **Encryption algorithm**—A set of instructions to scramble and unscramble data

- **Encryption key**—A code used by an algorithm to scramble and unscramble data

Children sometimes play with encryption by using a simple algorithm, such as "find the letter on the top row and use the letter on the bottom row instead." A key might look something like this:

```
A B C D E F G H I J K L M N O P Q R S T U V W X Y Z
I N B Y G L S P T A R W Q H X M D K F U O C Z V E J
```

In this example, LISA is encrypted as WTFI. The key shows only uppercase letters, but many other possibilities are likely, including lowercase letters, digits, and so on.

The goal of encryption is that, even if the algorithm is known, an intruder cannot interpret the message without the appropriate key. This type of key is called a *secret key*. When both the sender and the receiver use the same secret key, it is called a *symmetric key*. The Data Encryption Standard (DES) is the best-known example of a symmetric key system. DES encryption is available for most routers and many server implementations.

Although secret keys are reasonably simple to implement between two devices, as the number of devices increases, the number of secret keys also increases, which can be difficult to manage. For example, a session between Station A and Station B uses a different key than a session between Station A and Station C, and so on. Asymmetric keys can solve this problem.

Public/Private Key Encryption

Public/private key encryption is the best-known example of an asymmetric key system. With public/private key systems, each secure station on a network has a public key that is openly published or easily determined. All devices can use a station's public key to encrypt data to send to the station.

The receiving station decrypts the data using its own private key. Because no other device has the station's private key, no other device can decrypt the data; therefore, data confidentiality is maintained. (Mathematicians and computer scientists have written computer programs that identify special numbers to use for the keys so that the same algorithm can be used by both the sender and the receiver, even though different keys are used.) Figure 19-1 shows a public/private key system for data confidentiality.

Public/private key systems provide both confidentiality and authentication features. Using asymmetric keys, a recipient can verify that a document really came from the user or host that it appears to come from. For example, let's say that you are sending your tax returns to the Internal Revenue Service (IRS). The IRS needs to know that the returns came from you and not from a hostile third party that wants to make it look like you owe more than you do.

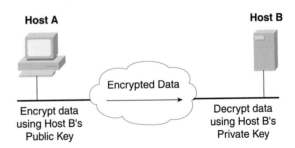

FIGURE 19-1
A public/private key system ensures data confidentiality.

You can encrypt your document or a part of your document with your private key, resulting in what is known as a *digital signature*. The IRS can decrypt the document using your public key, as shown in Figure 19-2. If the decryption is successful, the document definitely came from you because no one else should have your private key.

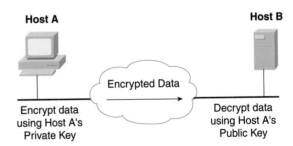

FIGURE 19-2
A public/private key system for sending a digital signature.

The digital signature feature of asymmetric keys can be used with the feature for data confidentiality. After you encrypt your document with your private key, you also can encrypt the document with the IRS's public key. The IRS decrypts the document twice. If the result is plain-text data, the IRS knows that the document came from you and that you meant for the document to go to no one but the IRS.

Some examples of asymmetric key systems include the Rivest, Shamir, and Adleman (RSA) standard; the Diffie-Hellman public key algorithm; and the Digital Signature Standard (DSS). Cisco Systems uses the DSS standard to authenticate peer routers during the setup of an encrypted session. The peer routers use the Diffie-Hellman algorithm to send information on a secret key to use that encrypts data. The actual data is encrypted by using the DES algorithm and the secret key.

Packet Filters

Packet filters can be set up on routers and servers to accept or deny packets from particular addresses or services. Packet filters augment authentication and authorization mechanisms. They help protect network resources from unauthorized use, theft, destruction, and denial-of-service (DoS) attacks.

A security policy should state whether packet filters implement one or the other of the following policies:

- Deny specific types of packets and accept all else
- Accept specific types of packets and deny all else

The first policy requires a thorough understanding of specific security threats and can be hard to implement. The second policy is easier to implement and more secure because the security administrator does not have to predict future attacks for which packets should be denied. The second policy is also easier to test because there is a finite set of accepted uses of the network. To do a good job implementing the second policy, you must have a thorough understanding of network requirements. The network designer should work with the security administrator to determine what types of packets should be accepted.

Cisco implements the second policy in its packet filters, which Cisco calls *access control lists (ACLs)*. An ACL on a router or switch running the Cisco Internetwork Operating System (IOS) software always has an implicit **deny-all** statement at the end. Specific **accept** and **deny** statements are processed before the implicit **deny-all** statement. (The statement is implicit because the administrator does not have to actually enter it, although it is a good idea to enter it to make the behavior of the list more obvious.)

ACLs let you control whether network traffic is forwarded or blocked at interfaces on a router or switch. ACL definitions provide criteria to be applied to packets that enter or exit an interface. Typical criteria can include the packet source address, the packet destination address, or the upper-layer protocol in the packet.

Because Cisco IOS software tests a packet against each criteria statement in the list until a match is found, ACLs should be designed with care to provide good performance. By studying traffic flow, you can design the list so that most packets match the earliest conditions. Fewer conditions to check per packet means better throughput. Good advice for ACLs: Order the list with the most general statements at the top and the most specific statements at the bottom, with the last statement being the general, implicit **deny-all** statement.

Firewalls

A *firewall* is a system or combination of systems that enforces security policies at the boundary between two or more networks. A firewall can be a router with ACLs, a dedicated hardware box, or software running on a PC or UNIX system. Firewalls are especially important at the boundary between the enterprise network and the Internet.

Intrusion Detection

Intrusion detection refers to the real-time monitoring of network activity and analysis of data for potential vulnerabilities and attacks in progress. Internal, authorized users who conduct unauthorized activity on the network—such as trying to transmit confidential documents over the Internet or illegally modifying network access privileges—can be detected in real time and stopped immediately. An external intruder who tries to break into the network can be handled in the same manner.

Real-time capability (as opposed to a periodic review of log files) can significantly reduce potential damage and recovery costs of an attack by eliminating the intruder from the network. A good intrusion system has the following characteristics:

- It runs continually without human supervision. The system must be reliable enough to allow it to run in the background of the system being observed.
- It must be fault-tolerant; that is, it must survive a system crash and not require its knowledge base to be rebuilt at restart.
- It must resist subversion. The system can monitor itself to ensure that it has not been subverted.
- It must impose minimal overhead on the system. A system that slows a computer to a crawl will simply not be used.
- It must observe deviations from normal behavior and immediately alert someone if abnormal behavior occurs.
- It must cope with changing system behavior over time as new applications are added.

The capability to write customized detection rules for proprietary purposes should also be of interest to you. You might want to write customized detection rules to prevent a document labeled "confidential" from being e-mailed outside the network or to address vulnerabilities for custom or legacy systems. Such customization allows the system to be modified for use in almost any environment, even if those uses are not common enough to be included as standard features of a commercial product.

Physical Security

Physical security refers to limiting access to key network resources by keeping the resources behind a locked door. Physical security also refers to protecting resources from natural disasters such as floods, fires, storms, and earthquakes. Because physical security is such an obvious requirement, it is easy to forget to plan for it, but it should never be overlooked or considered less important than other goals.

Depending on your particular network design customer, physical security should be installed to protect core routers, demarcation points, cabling, modems, servers, hosts, backup storage, and so on. Work with your customer during the early stages of the network design project to make sure equipment will be placed in computer rooms that have card key access or security guards. Computer rooms should also be equipped with uninterruptible power supplies, fire alarms, fire abatement mechanisms, and water removal systems. To protect equipment from earthquakes and high winds during storms, equipment should be installed in racks that attach to the floor or wall.

Selecting Security Solutions

The previous section described some typical ingredients of network security designs. This section provides a few recipes for putting together the ingredients to meet the following security challenges:

- Securing the Internet connection
- Securing dialup access
- Securing network services
- Securing user services

Securing the Internet Connection

The Internet connection should be secured with a set of overlapping security mechanisms, including firewalls, packet filters, physical security, audit logs, authentication, and authorization. Public servers, such as the World Wide Web and possibly File Transfer Protocol (FTP) servers, can allow unauthenticated access, but all other servers should require authentication and authorization. Public servers should be placed on a free-trade–zone network that is protected from other networks via firewalls.

If a customer can afford two separate servers, security experts recommend that FTP services should not run on the same server as Web services. FTP users have more opportunities for reading and possibly changing files than Web users. A hacker could use FTP to damage a company's Web site, thus damaging the company's image and possibly compromising Web-based e-commerce and other applications. Security experts recommend that you never allow Internet access to Trivial File Transfer Protocol (TFTP) servers because TFTP offers no authentication features.

Adding Common Gateway Interface (CGI) scripts or other types of scripts to Web servers should be done with great care. Scripts should be thoroughly tested for security leaks. E-commerce applications should be installed on Web servers only if the applications are compatible with the Secure Sockets Layer (SSL) standard.

E-mail servers have long been a source for intruder break-ins, probably because e-mail protocols and implementations have been around for a while and hackers can easily understand them. In addition, by its very nature, an e-mail server must allow outsider access. To secure e-mail servers, network administrators should keep up-to-date on well-known bugs and security leaks by subscribing to mailing lists dedicated to security information.

Securing Internet Domain Name System Services

Domain Name System (DNS) servers should be carefully controlled and monitored. Name-to-address resolution is critical to the operation of any network. An attacker who can successfully control or impersonate a DNS server can wreak havoc on a network. DNS servers should be protected from security attacks using packet filters on routers, as well as versions of DNS software that incorporate security features.

Traditionally, DNS had no security capabilities. In particular, there was no way to verify information returned in a DNS response to a query. A hacker could hijack the query and return a counterfeit name-to-address mapping. Digital signatures and other security features are being added to the protocol to address this issue and other security concerns.

Logical Network Design and the Internet Connection

A good rule for enterprise networks is that the network should have well-defined exit and entry points. An organization with only one Internet connection can manage Internet-security problems more easily than an organization with many Internet connections. Some very large organizations require more than one Internet connection for performance and redundancy reasons, however. This is fine as long as the connections are managed and monitored. Departments or users that add Internet connections without coordination from corporate network engineers should not be tolerated.

When selecting routing protocols for the Internet connection, to maximize security, you should select a protocol that offers route authentication (such as RIP Version 2, OSPF, or BGP4). Static and default routing is also a good option because, with static and default routing, no routing updates could be compromised. Internet routers should be equipped with packet filters to prevent DoS attacks.

When securing the Internet connection, Network Address Translation (NAT) can be used to protect internal network addressing schemes. NAT hides internal network numbers from outside networks. NAT translates internal network numbers when outside access is required.

Organizations that use VPN services to connect private sites via the Internet should use NAT, firewalls, and data encryption. In VPN topologies, private data travels across the public Internet, so encryption is a must. The Layer 2 Tunneling Protocol (L2TP) is an emerging Internet Engineering Task Force (IETF) standard for tunneling private data over public networks.

The IP Security Protocol

The *IP Security Protocol (IPSec)* is a set of open standards that provides data confidentiality, data integrity, and authentication between participating peers at the IP layer. As IPSec gains industry acceptance, customers require support for it in internetworking products that they purchase. Although IPSec is relatively new, many router and server manufactures support it. (IPSec is documented in RFCs 1825 through 1829.)

IPSec enables a system to select security protocols and algorithms, and establish cryptographic keys. The Internet Key Exchange (IKE) protocol provides authentication of IPSec peers. It also negotiates IPSec keys and security associations. IKE uses the following technologies:

- **DES**—Encrypts packet data
- **Diffie-Hellman**—Establishes a shared, secret session key
- **Message Digest 5 (MD5)**—Is a hash algorithm that authenticates packet data
- **Secure Hash Algorithm (SHA)**—Is a hash algorithm that authenticates packet data
- **RSA encrypted nonces**—Provides repudiation
- **RSA signatures**—Provides nonrepudiation

Securing Dial-Up Access

Security is critical for dial-up access. It should consist of firewall technologies, physical security, authentication and authorization mechanisms, auditing

> **NOTE**
>
> *Repudiation* is a security feature that prevents a third party from proving that a communication between two other parties took place. This is a desirable feature if you do not want your communication to be traceable. *Nonrepudiation* is just the opposite: A third party can prove that a communication between two other parties took place. Nonrepudiation is desirable if you want to be able to trace your communications and prove that they occurred.

capabilities, and possibly encryption. Authentication and authorization are the most important features for dialup access security. One-time passwords with security cards make sense in this arena.

Remote users and remote routers that use the Point-to-Point Protocol (PPP) should be authenticated with the Challenge Handshake Authentication Protocol (CHAP). The Password Authentication Protocol (PAP) offers less security than CHAP and is not recommended.

Another option for authentication, authorization, and accounting is the *Remote Authentication Dial-In User Server (RADIUS) protocol*. Livingston, Inc., developed RADIUS a few years ago; it has become an industry standard and is documented in RFC 2138. RADIUS gives an administrator the option of having a centralized database of user information. The database includes authentication and configuration information and specifies the type of service permitted by a user (for example, PPP, Telnet, rlogin, and so on). RADIUS is a client/server protocol. An access server acts as a client of a RADIUS server.

Dialup services should be strictly controlled. Users should not be allowed to attach modems and analog lines to their own workstations or servers. (Some companies actually fire employees who do this.) It is helpful to have a single dial-in point (for example, a single large modem pool or access server) so that all users are authenticated in the same way. A different set of modems should be used for any dial-out services. Both dial-in and dial-out services should be authenticated.

If the modems and access servers support *callback* (which most do), callback should be used. With callback, when a user dials in and is authenticated, the system disconnects the call and calls back on a specified number. Callback is useful because the system calls back the actual user, not a hacker who might be masquerading as the user. Callback can easily be compromised, however, and should not be the only security mechanism used.

Many operational security considerations with dialup networks are outside the scope of a design book. Suffice it to say that modems and access servers should be carefully configured and protected from hackers reconfiguring them. Modems should be programmed to reset to the standard configuration at the start and end of each call, and modems and access servers should terminate calls cleanly. Servers should force a logout if the user hangs up unexpectedly.

Securing Network Services

Many of the recommendations for securing the Internet connection apply to securing internal enterprise networks also. Internal network services can make use of authentication and authorization, packet filters, audit logs, physical security, encryption, and so on.

To protect internal network services, it is important to protect internetworking devices, such as routers and switches. Login IDs and passwords should be required to access these devices whether the user accesses the device through a console port or through the network. A first-level password can be used by administrators who simply need to check the status of the devices. A second-level password should be used by administrators who have permission to view or change configurations.

If modem access to the console ports of internetworking devices is allowed, the modems must be secured just as standard dial-in user modems are, and the phone numbers should be unlisted and unrelated to the organization's main number(s). The phone numbers should also be changed when staff changes occur.

For customers with numerous routers and switches, a protocol such as the *Terminal Access Controller Access Control System (TACACS)* can be used to manage large numbers of router and switch user IDs and passwords in a centralized database. TACACS also offers auditing features.

Limiting the use of the Simple Network Management Protocol (SNMP) should be considered on enterprise networks where security goals outweigh manageability goals. One of the main issues with SNMP is the **set** operation that allows a remote station to change management and configuration data. A new version of SNMP (SNMPv3) is under development; it will support authentication for use with the **set** operation and other SNMP operations.

As was the case with Internet connections, internal networks should run the most secure versions of DNS, FTP, and Web software. Implementations of Network Information Services (NIS) and other types of naming and addressing servers should also be carefully selected based on the level of security offered.

Although it is obvious that services within a network (such as file servers) should require authentication and authorization, it might be less obvious that the network itself should also require these security mechanisms. Before a user can get to the point of logging into servers, the user should first be required to log into the network.

Securing User Services

User services include end systems, applications, hosts, file servers, database servers, and other services. File servers and other servers should obviously offer authentication and authorization features. End systems can also offer these features if users are concerned about other people using their systems. Users should be encouraged to log out of sessions when leaving their desks for long periods of time and to turn off their machines when leaving work to protect against unauthorized people walking up to a system and accessing services and applications. Automatic logouts can also be deployed to automatically log out a session that has had no activity for a period of time.

Security policies and procedures should specify accepted practices regarding passwords: when they should be used, how they should be formatted, and how they can be changed. In general, passwords should include both letters and numbers, should be at least six characters, should not be a "common" word, and should be changed often.

On servers, root password knowledge (or the non-UNIX equivalent) should be limited to a few people. If possible, guest accounts should be avoided. Protocols that support the concept of trust in other hosts should be used with caution. (Examples include rlogin and rsh on UNIX systems.) Hosts that permit guest accounts and support trusted hosts should be isolated from other hosts, if possible.

Kerberos is an authentication system that provides user-to-host security for application-level protocols such as FTP and Telnet. If requested by the application, Kerberos can also provide encryption. Kerberos relies on a symmetric key database that uses a key distribution center (KDC) on a Kerberos server. See the Kerberos Frequently Asked Questions (FAQ) document for the latest information on Kerberos (available at www.ov.com/misc/krb-faq.html).

A security policy should specify which applications are allowed to run on networked PCs and should give guidelines restricting the downloading of unknown applications from the Internet or other sites. Security procedures also should specify how users can install and update virus-protection software; virus protection is one of the most important aspects of user-services security.

Depending on the network topology, user-services security might incorporate encryption. Encryption is sometimes done at servers and end systems instead of within the network. Vendors such as Microsoft, Netscape, and Sun Microsystems offer encryption software for end systems, workstations, and servers.

To guarantee security at the user-services level, known security bugs in applications and network operating systems should be identified and fixed. Administrators should be required to stay current on the latest hacker tricks and viruses.

Summary

As a network designer, your goal is to help your customers develop strategies and processes for implementing security. You should also help your customers select tools and products to implement these strategies and processes. Security is a major concern for most customers because of the increase in Internet connectivity and Internet applications, and because more users access the enterprise network from remote sites.

This chapter provided information to help you select the right processes and tools to meet a customer's goals for network security. The tasks involved with security design parallel the tasks involved with overall network design: analyzing requirements and goals, making trade-offs, characterizing network traffic flow, and developing an appropriate topology.

Security is often overlooked during the design of a network because it is considered an operational issue rather than a design issue. However, by considering security issues up front instead of waiting until the end of the design process or after the network is operational, your design will be more scalable and robust.

e-Lab Activity Index

CD Number	e-Lab Title	Description	Filename
1.1	**ping**	In this activity, you demonstrate the use of the **ping** command to verify workstation connectivity.	command_ping.swf
1.2	**ip address**	In this activity, you demonstrate how to use the **ip address** command to connect to another router via the serial port.	command_ip_address.swf
1.3	**router rip**	In this activity, you demonstrate how to use the **router rip** command to select RIP as the routing protocol.	command_router_rip.swf
5.1	Routed and Routing Protocols	In this activity, you work through several tasks to discover which routed and routing protocols are currently running or active on a router.	routed_routing_protocols.swf
5.2	Migrating RIP to IGRP	In this activity, you work through several tasks for migrating from RIP to IGRP.	migrating_rip_to_igrp.swf
5.3	**router igrp**	In this activity, you demonstrate how to use the **router igrp** command to select RIP as the routing protocol.	router_igrp.swf

continues

CD Number	e-Lab Title	Description	Filename
5.4	timers basic	In this activity, you demonstrate how to use the **timers basic** command to control how often IGRP sends updates.	timers_basic.swf
5.5	Configuring IGRP	In this activity, you work through several tasks for configuring IGRP.	configuring_igrp.swf
6.1	access-list	In this activity, you demonstrate how to use the **access-list** command to define a standard IP ACL.	access_list_standard.swf
6.2	show access-lists	In this activity, you demonstrate how to use the **show access-lists** command to display the contents of all current ACLs.	show_access_lists.swf
6.3	Standard ACLs	In this activity, you work through several tasks for configuring standard ACLs.	standard_acls.swf
6.4	access-list	In this activity, you demonstrate how to use the **access-list** command to define an extended IP ACL.	access_list_extended.swf
6.5	ACL	Use access list parameters to block traffic.	acl.swf
6.6	ip access-list	In this activity, you demonstrate how to use the **ip access-list** command to name a ACL.	ip_access_list_named.swf

CD Number	e-Lab Title	Description	Filename
6.7	deny	In this activity, you demonstrate how to use the **deny** command to set conditions for a named ACL.	deny.swf
6.8	show ip interface	In this activity, you demonstrate how to use the **show ip interface** command to display IP interface information.	show_ip_interface.swf
6.9	Extended ACLs	In this activity, you work through several tasks for configuring extended ACLs.	extended_acls.swf
7.1	show protocols	In this activity, you demonstrate how to use the **show protocols** command to display the configured protocols.	show_protocols.swf
7.2	ipx routing	In this activity, you demonstrate how to use the **ipx routing** command to enable IPX routing.	ipx_routing2.swf
7.3	ipx routing	In this activity, you work through several tasks for configuring IPX.	ipx_routing.swf
7.4	show ipx interface ethernet 0	Use **show ipx interface** to display the status of the IPX interfaces configured in the Cisco IOS software and the parameters configured on each interface.	show_ipx_intfc_eth_0.swf

continues

CD Number	e-Lab Title	Description	Filename
7.5	show ipx route	In this activity, you demonstrate how to use the **show ipx route** command to display the content of the IPX routing table.	show_ipx_route.swf
7.6	show ipx servers	In this activity, you demonstrate how to use the **show ipx servers** command to display the IPX server list.	show_ipx_servers.swf
7.7	show ipx traffic	In this activity, you demonstrate how to use the **show ipx traffic** command to display the number and type of packets.	show_ipx_traffic.swf
7.8	debug ipx routing activity	In this activity, you demonstrate how to use the **debug ipx routing activity** command to display information about IPX routing update packets that are transmitted or received.	debug_ipx_rout_activity.swf
7.9	debug ipx sap	Use the **debug ipx sap** command to display information about IPX SAP packets that are transmitted or received.	debug_ipx_sap.swf
7.10	privileged IPX ping	In this activity, you demonstrate how to use the **privileged IPX ping** command to check host reachability and network connectivity.	ping_privileged_ipx.swf

CD Number	e-Lab Title	Description	Filename
7.11	user IPX ping	In this activity, you demonstrate how to use the **user IPX ping** command to check host reachability and network connectivity.	ping_ipx_user.swf
11.1	show interfaces	In this activity, you demonstrate how to use the **show interfaces** command to displays statistics for all interfaces configured on the router or access server.	command_show_interface.swf
11.2	encapsulation ppp	In this activity, you demonstrate how to use the **encapsulation ppp** command to set PPP as the encapsulation method used by a serial or ISDN interface.	command_encapsulation_ppp.swf
11.3	**username** *name* **password** *password*	In this activity, you demonstrate how to use the **username** *name* **password** *password* command to specify the password to be used in CHAP caller identification and PAP.	command_username_name_passw.swf
11.4	PPP Configuration	In this activity, you work through several tasks for configuring PPP.	routing_and_switching.swf

continues

CD Number	e-Lab Title	Description	Filename
11.5	**ppp chap hostname** *hostname*	In this activity, you demonstrate how to use the **ppp chap hostname** *hostname* to create a pool of dialup routers that all appear to be the same host when authenticating with CHAP.	command_ppp_chap_hostname_h.swf
12.1	**interface** *interface-type inter-face-number*	In this activity, you demonstrate how to use the **interface** *interface-type interface-number* command to configure an interface type and enter interface configuration mode.	interface_interface_type.swf
12.2	**isdn switch-type**	In this activity, you demonstrate how to use the **isdn switch-type** command to specify the central office switch type on the ISDN interface.	isdn_switch_type_switch.swf
12.3	**isdn spid**	In this activity, you demonstrate how to use the **isdn spid** command to define, at the router, the *service profile identifier (SPID)* number that has been assigned by the ISDN service provider for the B1 channel.	isdn_spid1_spid1.swf

CD Number	e-Lab Title	Description	Filename
12.4	show isdn status	In this activity, you demonstrate how to use the **show isdn status** command to display the status of all ISDN interfaces or, optionally, a specific *digital signal link (DSL)* or a specific ISDN interface.	show_isdn_status.swf
12.5	ping	Use the **ping** command to confirm connectivity.	ping.swf
13.1	show interfaces	In this activity, you demonstrate how to use **show interfaces serial** command to check the DLCI information on serial 0.	show_serial_0.swf
13.2	show interfaces	In this activity, you demonstrate how to use **show interfaces serial** command to check the DLCI information on serial 1.	show_interface_serial_1.swf
13.3	show frame-relay map	In this activity, you demonstrate how to use the **show frame-relay map** command to display the current map entries and information about the connections.	show_frame_relay_map.swf
13.4	ping	In this activity, you demonstrate how to use the **ping** command to confirm connectivity.	ping_user_mode.swf

continues

CD Number	e-Lab Title	Description	Filename
13.5	interface serial 0	In this activity, you demonstrate how to use the **interface serial 0** commnand to configure the serial interface for Frame Relay packet encapsulation.	interface_serial_0.swf
13.6	show frame-relay pvc	In this activity, you demonstrate how to use the **show frame-relay pvc** command to display statistics about PVCs for Frame Relay interfaces.	show_frame_relay_pvc.swf
13.7	interface serial	In this activity, you demonstrate how to use the **interface serial** command to select the interface and enter interface configuration mode.	intfc_serial_1_1_pt_to_pt.swf
13.8	keepalive	In this activity, you demonstrate how to use the **keepalive** command to enable the LMI mechanism for serial lines using Frame Relay encapsulation.	keepalive.swf
13.9	Frame Relay Config	In this activity, you work through several tasks for configuring basic Frame Relay.	frame_relay_config.swf

Check Your Understanding Answer Key

This appendix contains the answers to the "Check Your Understanding" questions at the end of most chapters.

Chapter 1

1. C. The physical layer

2. A. It sends data by using flow control.

3. B. Path determination and switching

4. C. Distance-vector and link-state

5. A. Converged

6. Each layer depends on the service function of the OSI reference model layer below it. To provide this service, the lower layer uses encapsulation to put the PDU from the upper layer into its data field; then, it can add whatever headers and trailers the layer will use to perform its function.

7. Transport-layer services allow reliable data transport between hosts and destinations. To obtain such reliable transport of data, a connection-oriented relationship is used between the communicating end systems.

8. ICMP is implemented by all TCP/IP hosts. ICMP messages are carried in IP datagrams and are used to send error and control messages. Examples of ICMP messages are **ping** and destination unreachable.

9. Windowing is a method to control the amount of information transferred end-to-end. Windowing is an end-to-end agreement between sender and receiver on how much data will be sent between acknowledgments.

10. The network layer provides best-effort end-to-end packet delivery. The network layer sends packets from the source network to the destination network based on the IP routing table.

11. B. **router rip**
    network *network-number*

12. B. Supports all standard physical and data-link protocols.

13. C. Frame header, network header, data, frame trailer

14. A. Acknowledgement and retransmission

15. C. Adjusts automatically to topology or traffic changes.

16. A. Uses the TCP protocol to segment and reassemble data into a data stream.

17. A. Every 30 seconds

18. C. The address that is at the data link layer and hard-coded into the network interface card is the MAC address.

19. D. All of the above.

20. B. Consults its routing tables to determine which of its ports it will need to send the data out on in order for it to reach its destination network.

Chapter 2

1. B. A data frame

2. B. 800 ns

3. D. A (Dedicated paths between sender and receiver hosts) and B (Multiple traffic paths within the switch)

4. D. Multiport bridges operating at Layer 2

5. A. Client/server network traffic where the "fast" switch port is connected to the server

6. B. Cut-through; store-and-forward

7. D. Redundant network paths, without suffering the effects of loops in the network

8. In store-and-forward switching, the entire frame is received before any forwarding takes place, whereas, in cut-through switching, the switch reads the destination address before receiving the entire frame. The frame then starts to be forwarded before the entire frame arrives.

9. In half-duplex Ethernet, the transmit (TX) and the receive (RX) circuits contend for the right to use the same single shared medium. In full-duplex Ethernet, TX and RX are separate circuits and, therefore, there is no contending for the right to transmit data across the media.

10. The main function of the Spanning-Tree Protocol is to allow redundant switched/bridged paths without suffering the effects of loops in the network.

11. C. Collision domain

12. D. All of the above

13. D. Lower response times, longer file transfers, and network delays

14. B. Half-duplex

15. D. Buffering is required in cut-through packet switching if the network connection or link is slow.

16. B. They are very high-speed multiport bridges.

17. D. Sixteen

18. D. Increased available bandwidth

19. B. Switches read the source address of packet entering through a port.

20. A. To provide switch connections on ports with the same bandwidths.

Chapter 3

1. VLAN benefits include tighter network security with establishment of secure user groups, better management and control of broadcast activity, microsegmentation of the network, and the relocation of workgroup servers into secured, centralized locations.

2. Broadcast traffic within one VLAN is not transmitted outside the VLAN. Conversely, adjacent ports do not receive any of the broadcast traffic generated from other VLANs.

3. Port-centric VLANs, static VLANs, and dynamic VLANs

4. VLAN frame tagging is an approach that places a unique VLAN identifier in the header of each frame as it is forwarded throughout the network backbone.

5. A. The ability to increase networks without creating collisions domains

6. D. All of the above

7. C. Hub; switch

8. D. They automatically configure ports when new stations are added.

9. D. All of the above are criteria by which VLANs can be created.

10. A. Switches do not need to be configured.

11. C. Bridges form one of the core components of VLAN communications.

12. D. VLANs

13. B. Router

14. B. Layer 2

15. C. Frame filtering; frame tagging

16. A. Switches do need configuring.

17. A. True

18. A. Multicast control

19. D. Both A and B.

Chapter 4

1. The four main goals of any network design are functionality, scalability, adaptability, and manageability.

2. The purpose of Layer 2 devices in the network is to provide flow control, error detection, and error correction, and to reduce congestion in the network.

3. Implementation of Layer 3 devices, such as routers, allows for segmentation of the LAN into unique physical and logical networks. Routers also allow for connectivity to WANs, such as the Internet.

4. The two major categories of servers in a network design are enterprise servers and workgroup servers. Enterprise servers support all the users on the network, such as those using e-mail or DNS. Workgroup servers support a specific set of users.

5. Any network documentation should include a physical network map, a logical network map, and an addressing map. Having these dramatically decreases problem resolution time.

6. D. All of the above

7. D. Too many network segments

8. C. Layer 2; Layer 1

9. B. Max length = 400 meters

10. D. All of the above

11. A. 1 and 8; 2 and 6; 3 and 7; 4 and 5

12. C and D. Asymmetric and full-duplex

13. D. Both B and C

14. A. Router

15. D. Both A and B

16. D. Increases the size of the LAN

17. B. DNS server for a school district

18. D. Both A and C

19. D. Both B and C

20. D. All of the above

Chapter 5

1. Path determination occurs at Layer 3, the network layer. The path determination function enables a router to evaluate the available paths to a destination and to establish the preferred path of a packet across the network.

2. The router examines the packet header to determine the destination network and then references the routing table that associates networks with outgoing interfaces.

3. In multiprotocol routing, routers are capable of supporting multiple independent routing protocols and maintaining routing tables for several routed protocols concurrently. This capability allows a router to deliver packets from several routed protocols, such as IP and IPX, over the same data links.

4. The success of dynamic routing depends on two basic router functions:

   ■ Maintenance of a routing table

   ■ Timely distribution of knowledge—in the form of routing updates—to other routers (that is, convergence)

5. When all routers in a network are operating with the same knowledge, the network is said to have converged.

6. D. Switching the packet

7. D. B (Maintaining a routing table) and C (Periodic routing updates)

8. A. Distance-vector; link-state

9. D. IGRP uses all of these.

10. D. **router igrp**

11. C. Distance-vector

12. C. Adjusts automatically to topology or traffic changes

13. D. Hop count

14. D. RouterA(config-router)#network 10.0.0.0

15. B. False

16. D. Both A and C

17. A. Autonomous System

18. C. Measures the "reliability" of an IP routing protocol

19. C. At the router, it is a rute manually defined as the path to take when no route to the destination in known.

20. D. Both B and C.

Chapter 6

1. ACLs offer another powerful tool for network data packet control. ACLs filter the packet flow that flows in or out of a router's interfaces.

2. Standard ACLs check the source address of packets that could be routed. The result permits or denies output of the packet, based on the network, subnet, or host address.

3. Extended ACLs permit or deny with more precision than do standard ACLs. Extended ACLs check for both source and destination packet addresses. They also can check for specific protocols, port numbers, and other parameters.

4. ACL statements operate in sequential, logical order. They evaluate packets from the top of the list, down to the last statement in the list. Only if the packet does not match conditions of the first test does it drop to the next ACL statement.

5. Standard ACLs are identified with a number in the range 1 to 99. Extended ACLs are identified with a number in the range 100 to 199.

6. C. **show ip interface**

7. A. Wildcard bits

8. C. "Permit my network only"

9. A. True

10. B. Monitor ACL statements

11. B. Router (config)#access-list access-list number {permit | deny} {test conditions}

12. A. Decrease the amount of content in routing updates

13. B. Standard; extended

14. B. False

15. C. Access lists; packets; WAN; impeding

16. C. **show ip interface**

17. C. **show access-lists**: Displays interface information.

18. C. The source subnet/host/network of the packets.

19. B. Router

20. B. "Permit a specific host."

Chapter 7

1. A MAC address

2. **ipx maximum-paths**

3. Global configuration mode

4. **show ipx interface**

5. **debug ipx sap**

6. C. Network number; node number

7. D. Always A (Novell servers) and B (Cisco routers)

8. B. RIP; SAP

9. A. **ipx routing** [*node*]

10. B. **show ipx interface; show ipx route; show ipx servers**

11. C. Router subinterface; attached network

12. C. **show ipx interface**

13. D. 12 hexadecimal

14. A. 8 hexadecimal

15. A. The use of the IPX node number in the protocol eliminates the need for address resolution.

16. B. **ipx maximum-paths**

17. D. **sap**

18. C. Ethernet: novell-ether

19. C. Network number assigned to a specific subinterface

20. A. Displays number and types of packets

Chapter 8

1. B. Daily backup

2. C. Disk duplexing

3. D. Performance

4. A. Client to client

5. C. NTFS

6. A. Cut sheet

7. C. 3

8. B. Rights

9. C. 127.0.0.1

10. D. Use a grounding strap.

Chapter 9

1. B. One
2. C. The physical layer
3. D. DCE
4. D. None of the above
5. A. Frame Relay
6. C. Customer premises equipment
7. D. All of the above
8. D. All of the above
9. B. Frame Relay
10. B. LCP
11. A. Serial
12. B. HDLC
13. B. ISDN
14. C. Terminal adapter
15. C. Windowing is not supported.
16. A. PPP
17. B. Frame Relay
18. C. The ISDN BRI offers 23 B channels (of 64 kbps) and one D channel (of 64 kbps).
19. D. All of the above

Chapter 10

1. D. All of the above
2. A. The busiest time
3. B. Close to the users
4. C. A flat topology
5. A. Efficient use of bandwidth
6. B. Routers

7. C. Access

8. D. Access

9. A. Server

10. B. Routers

11. D. Fast Ethernet

12. D. Data path decision point

13. B. At the distribution layer

14. C. To switch packets

15. C. The distribution layer

Chapter 11

1. SLIP

2. Asynchronous serial, ISDN, and synchronous serial

3. D. All of the above

4. B. Encapsulate multiple protocols

5. C. Protocol

6. A. Establishment, maintenance, and termination of the point-to-point connection

7. C. Four

8. B. Two-way

9. C. router# **show interfaces**

10. C. When the workstation needs dialup access to the Internet

11. A. PPP

12. D. Multilink

13. D. The originating node sending Link Control Protocol (LCP) frames to configure the data link

14. A. Negotiate configureation parameters, and send and receive a configuration acknowledgment frame

15. D. LCP informs the network layer protocols.

Chapter 12

1. 128 kpbs
2. 2 B channels
3. 1 D channel
4. An SPID
5. The D channel
6. B. Router
7. A. A large concentration of users at the site
8. A. Telephone network standards
9. C. PPP
10. D. router(config)# **isdn switch-type**
11. A. ISDN
12. C. The same as if they were logging in locally
13. B. It's faster.
14. C. ISDN is faster.
15. D. ISDN

Chapter 13

1. B. It multiplexes the circuits.
2. B. Upper-layer protocols
3. C. It sends out multicasts.
4. A. Committed information rate
5. D. The service provider
6. B. The address field
7. C. Keepalives
8. D. It uses the IP address-to-DLCI mapping table.
9. C. A Frame Relay map

10. B. To prevent routing loops

11. B. Layer 2

12. B. The older versions of Frame Relay are referred to collectively as the Local Management Interface (LMI).

13. D. # interface serial0

14. C. The Frame Relay connection is active.

15. A. Displays information about the multicast DLCI, the DLCIs used on the Frame Relay configured serial interface, and the LMI DLCI used for the Local Management Interface.

16. B. Congestion-notification mechanisms

17. D. Provide a logical, bidirectional communication path between network devices.

18. B. Perform error-checking functions

19. A. Algorithmically generated MAC addresses

Chapter 14

1. C. SNMP

2. B. IPCONFIG

3. B. Divide and conquer

4. C. IP

5. E. Logging on

6. A. SNMP

7. C. Count *x* number of pings

8. D. Probes

9. A. Redundant

Command Summary

This appendix contains a summary of the commands used in this book and is intended to provide a quick reference. Each command is listed with a short description. In addition, this table contains cross-references to the chapter in which the command is introduced and explained. This appendix should add to your understanding of the commands used to configure Cisco routers.

Command	Description	Chapter
access-group	Applies access control lists (ACLs) to an interface.	6
access-list	Defines a standard IP ACL.	6
clear interface	Resets the hardware logic on an interface.	12
debug dialer	Shows such information as what number the interface is dialing.	12
debug ipx routing activity	Displays information about Routing Information Protocol (RIP) update packets.	7
debug ipx sap	Displays information about Service Advertising Protocol (SAP) update packets.	7
debug isdn q921	Displays data link layer (Layer 2) access procedures that are taking place at the router on the D channel (LAPD) of its Integrated Services Digital Network (ISDN) interface.	12
debug ppp	Displays information on traffic and exchanges in an internetwork implementing Point-to-Point Protocol (PPP).	9
deny	Sets the conditions for a named IP ACL.	6
dialer-group	Controls access by configuring an interface to belong to a specific dialing group.	12
dialer idle-timeout	Specifies the idle time before the line is disconnected.	12
dialer-list protocol	Defines a DDR dialer list to control dialing by protocol or by a combination of protocol and ACL.	12

continues

Command	Description	Chapter
dialer map	Configures a serial interface to call one or multiple sites.	12
dialer wait-for-carrier-time	Specifies how long to wait for a carrier.	12
enable password	Specifies a password to prevent unauthorized access to the router.	13
encapsulation frame-relay	Enables Frame Relay encapsulation.	13
encapsulation novell-ether	Specifies that Novell's unique frame format is used on a network segment.	7
encapsulation ppp	Sets PPP as the encapsulation method used by a serial or ISDN interface.	9, 11, 12
encapsulation sap	Specifies that Ethernet 802.2 frame format is used on a network segment. Cisco's keyword is **sap**.	7
end	Exits configuration mode.	13
exec-timeout	Sets the interval that the EXEC command interpreter waits until user input is detected.	13
exit	Exits any configuration mode or closes an active terminal session and terminates the EXEC.	13
frame-relay local-dlci	Enables the Local Management Interface (LMI) mechanism for serial lines using Frame Relay encapsulation.	13
hostname	Configures the router with a hostname, which is used in prompts and default configuration filenames.	13
interface	Configures an interface type and enters interface configuration mode.	6, 7, 9, 12
interface serial	Selects the interface and enters interface configuration mode.	13
ip access-group	Controls access to an interface.	6
ip address	Sets the logical network address of the interface.	1, 6, 13

Command	Description	Chapter
ip unnumbered	Enables Internet Protocol (IP) processing on a serial interface without assigning an explicit IP address to the interface.	13
ipx delay	Sets the tick count.	7
ipx ipxwan	Enables the IPXWAN protocol on a serial interface.	7
ipx maximum-paths	Sets the number of equal-cost paths the Cisco IOS software uses when forwarding packets.	7
ipx network	Enables Internetwork Packet Exchange (IPX) routing on a particular interface and optionally selects the type of encapsulation (framing).	7, 13
ipx router	Specifies the routing protocol to use.	7
ipx routing	Enables IPX routing.	7
ipx sap-interval	Configures less frequent SAP updates over slow links.	7
ipx type-20-input-checks	Restricts the acceptance of IPX type 20 propagation packet broadcasts.	7
isdn spid1	Defines at the router the service profile identifier (SPID) number that has been assigned by the ISDN service provider for the B1 channel.	12
isdn spid2	Defines at the router the SPID number that has been assigned by the ISDN service provider for the B2 channel.	12
isdn switch-type	Specifies the central office switch type on the ISDN interface.	12
keepalive	Enables the LMI mechanism for serial lines using Frame Relay encapsulation.	13
line console	Configures a console port line.	13
line vty	Specifies a virtual terminal for remote console access.	13
login	Enables password checking at terminal session login.	13

continues

Command	Description	Chapter
metric holddown	Keeps new IGRP routing information from being used for a certain period of time.	5
network	Assigns a NIC-based address to which the router is directly connected. Associates networks with an IGRP routing process. Enables Enhanced IGRP on a network in IPX router configuration mode.	1, 5, 7
network-number	Specifies a directly connected network.	1
permit	Sets conditions for a named IP ACL.	6
ping	Sends ICMP echo request packets to another node on the network. Checks host reachability and network connectivity. Diagnoses basic network connectivity.	1, 7, 12, 13
ppp authentication	Enables Challenge Handshake Authentication Protocol (CHAP) or Password Authentication Protocol (PAP) or both, and specifies the order in which CHAP and PAP authentication are selected on the interface.	11, 12
ppp chap hostname	Creates a pool of dialup routers that all appear to be the same host when authenticating with CHAP.	11
ppp chap password	Configures a password that will be sent to hosts that want to authenticate the router. This command limits the number of username/password entries in the router.	11
ppp pap sent-username	Enables remote PAP support for an interface and uses **sent-username** and **password** in the PAP authentication request packet to the peer.	11
protocol	Defines an IP routing protocol, which can be either RIP, Interior Gateway Routing Protocol (IGRP), Open Shortest Path First (OSPF), or Enhanced IGRP.	1
router igrp	Enables an IGRP routing process.	5
router rip	Selects RIP as the routing protocol.	1
show access-lists	Displays the contents of all current ACLs.	6

Command	Description	Chapter
show dialer	Displays general diagnostics for serial interfaces configured for DDR.	12
show frame-relay lmi	Displays statistics about the LMI.	13
show frame-relay map	Displays the current map entries and information about the connections.	13
show frame-relay pvc	Displays statistics about PVCs for Frame Relay interfaces.	13
show interfaces	Displays statistics for all interfaces configured on the router or access server.	9, 11, 12
show interfaces serial	Displays information about a serial interface.	13
show ip interface	Lists a summary of an interface's IP information and status.	6
show ip route	Displays the current state of the routing table.	12
show ipx interface	Displays the status of the IPX interfaces configured in the Cisco IOS software and the parameters configured on each interface.	7
show ipx route	Displays the content of the IPX routing table.	7
show ipx servers	Displays the IPX server list.	7
show ipx traffic	Displays the number and type of packets.	7
show isdn active	Displays current call information, including called number, the time until the call is disconnected, AOC charging units used during the call, and whether the AOC information is provided during calls or at the end of calls.	12
show isdn status	Displays the status of all ISDN interfaces or, optionally, a specific digital signal link (DSL) or a specific ISDN interface.	12
show protocols	Displays the configured protocols.	7
show spantree	Displays spanning-tree information for a virtual local-area network (VLAN).	2

continues

Command	Description	Chapter
show status	Displays the current status of the ISDN line and both B channels.	12
term ip netmask-format	Specifies the format in which network masks are displayed in **show** command output.	1
timers basic	Controls how often IGRP sends updates.	5
username password	Specifies the password to be used in CHAP caller identification and PAP.	11

Movie Index

Movie Name	Description	Chapter
Movie 1.1	**The OSI Model Conceptual Framework** Protocols enabling communication.	1
Movie 1.2	**Determining Network Address** The IP destination retrieves an internal subnet mask.	1
Movie 1.3	**Router Function** Path determination.	1
Movie 1.5	**Router Can't Deliver** ICMP destination unreachable message.	1
Movie 1.6	**Reachability** TCP/IP host sends ICMP echo request.	1
Movie 1.7	**Address Resolution** Finding the MAC address.	1
Movie 1.8	**Link-State Protocols** A complex database of topology information.	1
Movie 1.9	**OSPF Routers** Link-state advertisements.	1
Movie 1.10	**Distance-Vector Protocols** Routing updates.	1
Movie 1.11	**Connection-Oriented Services** Three phases: connection establishment, data transfer, and connection termination.	1
Movie 1.12	**Three-Way Handshake** Sequence of messages exchanged to ensure transmission synchronization.	1
Movie 1.13	**TCP Host Sends Packet** Window size.	1
Movie 1.14	**Windowing** Window size, acknowledgment.	1

continues

Movie Name	Description	Chapter
Movie 1.15	**PAR** Positive acknowledgment and retransmission.	1
Movie 2.1	**Ethernet and 802.3 LANs** Broadcast networks.	2
Movie 2.2	**CSMA/CD LANs** Ethernet and 802.3.	2
Movie 2.3	**Collisions** Backoff protocols that determine when to retransmit.	2
Movie 2.4	**Repeater Advantages** Repeater cleans, amplifies, and resends.	2
Movie 2.5	**Repeater Disadvantages** Can't filter traffic.	2
Movie 2.6	**Bridge Examines MAC Addresses** Store-and-forward devices.	2
Movie 2.7	**LAN Switching** Dedicated collision-free communication between devices.	2
Movie 2.8	**Symmetric Switching** Switch connections between ports of equal bandwidth.	2
Movie 2.9	**Asymmetric Switching** Switch connections between ports with different bandwidth.	2
Movie 2.10	**Store-and-Forward Switching** Copies frame on board, checks frame's length and CRC.	2
Movie 2.11	**Cut-Through Switching** Switch reads the destination address before receiving the entire frame.	2
Movie 3.1	**Broadcast Transmission** Source node to network.	3
Movie 5.1	**Router Function** Sending data packets.	5
Movie 5.2	**Path Switching** The network layer finds a path to the destination.	5

Movie Name	Description	Chapter
Movie 5.3	**IP Routing Table** Destination network address and next-hop pairs.	5
Movie 5.4	**Route Processor** Using routing protocols to determine optimum paths.	5
Movie 5.5	**IGRP** Multipath routing.	5
Movie 5.6	**IGRP Update** Timer controls frequency of router update messages.	5
Movie 7.1	**Large Novell Installations** Hundreds of file, print, and gateway services available.	7
Movie 7.2	**Novell NetWare** Based on client/server architecture.	7
Movie 7.3	**Simple Split Horizon** Prevents routing loops.	7
Movie 7.4	**SAP** Network resources advertise services.	7
Movie 9.1	**WAN Technology** Identify WAN components.	9
Movie 9.2	**Data** Goes through layers, is given a header at each layer, and is passed on to next layer.	9
Movie 9.3	**Sending Packets Through Network** Paths selected dynamically.	9
Movie 9.4	**DLCIs Become Unique Network Addresses for DTE Devices** Frame Relay network changes to reflect origin of source.	9
Movie 9.5	**Dial Backup** Activates backup serial line to be used when traffic is too heavy or when primary line fails.	9
Movie 9.6	**ISDN BRI Service** B channel and D channel.	9

continues

Movie Name	Description	Chapter
Movie 11.1	**PPP Components** Three components: HDLC Encapsulation, Link Control Protocol, Network Control Programs (NCPs).	11
Movie 11.2	**PPP Link Establishment** Establish communications.	11
Movie 11.3	**PPP Configuration Acknowledgment** Negotiate parameters.	11
Movie 11.4	**LCP: Link Quality Determination** Test links.	11
Movie 11.5	**Network-Layer Protocols** Configuration by appropriate NCP.	11
Movie 11.6	**LCP Link Termination** LCP can terminate the link at any time.	11
Movie 12.1	**ISDN Applications** Integration of telecommuting services.	12
Movie 13.1	**Congestion Handled by FECN** Frame Relay switch recognizes congestion in the network.	13
Movie 13.2	**Multicast Transmission** Data packets sent through network.	13

This glossary defines many of the terms and abbreviations related to networking. It includes all the key terms used throughout the book, as well as many other terms related to networking. As with any growing technical field, some terms evolve and take on several meanings. Where necessary, multiple definitions and abbreviation expansions are presented. Multiword terms are alphabetized as if there were no spaces; hyphenated terms, as if there were no hyphens.

Terms in this glossary typically are defined under their abbreviations. Each abbreviation expansion is listed separately, with a cross-reference to the abbreviation entry. In addition, many definitions contain cross-references to related terms.

We hope that this glossary adds to your understanding of internetworking technologies.

Numerics

2B+D In reference to the ISDN BRI service, two B channels and one D channel.

4B/5B local fiber 4-byte/5-byte local fiber. Fibre Channel physical medium used for FDDI and ATM. Supports speeds of up to 100 Mbps over multimode fiber.

4-byte/5-byte local fiber See 4B/5B local fiber.

8B/10B local fiber 8-byte/10-byte local fiber. Fiber Channel physical medium that supports speeds up to 149.76 Mbps over multimode fiber.

8-byte/10-byte local fiber See 8B/10B local fiber.

10Base2 A 10-Mbps baseband Ethernet specification using 50-ohm thin coaxial cable. 10Base2, which is part of the IEEE 802.3 specification, has a distance limit of 185 meters per segment. *See also* Ethernet and IEEE 802.3.

10Base5 A 10-Mbps baseband Ethernet specification using standard (thick) 50-ohm baseband coaxial cable. 10Base5, which is part of the IEEE 802.3 baseband physical-layer specification, has a distance limit of 500 meters per segment. *See also* Ethernet and IEEE 802.3.

10BaseF A 10-Mbps baseband Ethernet specification that refers to the 10BaseFB, 10BaseFL, and 10BaseFP standards for Ethernet over fiber-optic cabling. *See also* 10BaseFB, 10BaseFL, 10BaseFP, and Ethernet.

10BaseFB A 10-Mbps baseband Ethernet specification using fiber-optic cabling. 10BaseFB is part of the IEEE 10BaseF specification. It is not used to connect user stations, but provides a synchronous signaling backbone that allows additional segments and repeaters to be connected to the network. 10BaseFB segments can be up to 2000 meters long. *See also* 10BaseF and Ethernet.

10BaseFL A 10-Mbps baseband Ethernet specification using fiber-optic cabling. 10BaseFL is part of the IEEE 10BaseF specification. 10BaseFL segments can be up to 1000 meters long if used with FOIRL, and up to 2000 meters if 10BaseFL is used exclusively. *See also* 10BaseF and Ethernet.

10BaseFP A 10-Mbps fiber-passive baseband Ethernet specification using fiber-optic cabling. 10BaseFP is part of the IEEE 10BaseF specification. It organizes a number of computers into a star topology without the use of repeaters. 10BaseFP segments can be up to 500 meters long. *See also* 10BaseF and Ethernet.

10BaseT A 10-Mbps baseband Ethernet specification using two pairs of twisted-pair cabling (Category 3, 4, or 5): one pair for transmitting data and the other for receiving data. 10BaseT, which is part of the IEEE 802.3 specification, has a distance limit of approximately 100 meters per segment. *See also* Ethernet and IEEE 802.3.

10Broad36 A 10-Mbps broadband Ethernet specification using broadband coaxial cable. 10Broad36, which is part of the IEEE 802.3 specification, has a distance limit of 3600 meters per segment. *See also* Ethernet and IEEE 802.3.

100BaseFX A 100-Mbps baseband Fast Ethernet specification using two strands of multimode fiber-optic cable per link. To guarantee proper signal timing, a 100BaseFX link cannot exceed 400 meters in length. Based on the IEEE 802.3 standard. *See also* 100BaseX, Fast Ethernet, and IEEE 802.3.

100BaseT A 100-Mbps baseband Fast Ethernet specification using UTP wiring. Like the 10BaseT technology on which it is based, 100BaseT sends link pulses over the network segment when no traffic is present. However, these link pulses contain more information than do those used in 10BaseT. Based on the IEEE 802.3 standard. *See also* 10BaseT, Fast Ethernet, and IEEE 802.3.

100BaseT4 A 100-Mbps baseband Fast Ethernet specification using four pairs of Category 3, 4, or 5 UTP wiring. To guarantee proper signal timing, a 100BaseT4 segment cannot exceed 100 meters in length. Based on the IEEE 802.3 standard. *See also* Fast Ethernet and IEEE 802.3.

100BaseTX A 100-Mbps baseband Fast Ethernet specification using two pairs of either UTP or STP wiring. The first pair of wires is used to receive data; the second is used to transmit. To guarantee proper signal timing, a 100BaseTX segment cannot exceed 100 meters in length. Based on the IEEE 802.3 standard. *See also* 100BaseX, Fast Ethernet, and IEEE 802.3.

100BaseX A 100-Mbps baseband Fast Ethernet specification that refers to the 100BaseFX and 100BaseTX standards for Fast Ethernet over fiber-optic cabling. Based on the IEEE 802.3 standard. *See also* 100BaseFX, 100BaseTX, Fast Ethernet, and IEEE 802.3.

100VG-AnyLAN A 100-Mbps Fast Ethernet and Token Ring media technology using four pairs of Category 3, 4, or 5 UTP cabling. This high-speed transport technology, developed by Hewlett-Packard, can be made to operate on existing 10BaseT Ethernet networks. Based on the IEEE 802.12 standard. *See also* IEEE 802.2.

A

A&B bit signaling A procedure used in T1 transmission facilities in which each of the 24 T1 subchannels devotes 1 bit of every sixth frame to the carrying of supervisory signaling information.

ABM Asynchronous Balanced Mode. An HDLC (and derivative protocol) communication mode supporting peer-oriented, point-to-point communications between two stations, where either station can initiate transmission.

access layer The layer at which a LAN or a group of LANs, typically Ethernet or Token Ring, provide users with frontline access to network services.

access method 1. Generally, the way in which network devices access the network medium. 2. Software within an SNA processor that controls the flow of information through a network.

ACK See acknowledgment.

acknowledgment A notification sent from one network device to another to acknowledge that some event (for example, receipt of a message) has occurred. Sometimes abbreviated ACK.

ACL (access control list) A list kept by a Cisco router to control access to or from the router for a number of services (for example, to prevent packets with a certain IP address from leaving a particular interface on the router). *See also* extended ACL and standard ACL.

active monitor A device responsible for performing maintenance functions on a Token Ring network. A network node is selected to be the active monitor if it has the highest MAC address on the ring. The active monitor is responsible for ring maintenance tasks such as ensuring that tokens are not lost and that frames do not circulate indefinitely.

adapter See NIC (network interface card).

address A data structure or logical convention used to identify a unique entity, such as a particular process or network device.

address mapping A technique that allows different protocols to interoperate by translating addresses from one format to another. For example, when routing IP over X.25, the IP addresses must be mapped to the X.25 addresses so that the IP packets can be transmitted by the X.25 network.

address mask A bit combination used to describe which portion of an address refers to the network or subnet and which part refers to the host. Sometimes referred to simply as mask.

address resolution Generally, a method for resolving differences between computer addressing schemes. Address resolution usually specifies a method for mapping network layer (Layer 3) addresses to data link layer (Layer 2) addresses.

Address Resolution Protocol See ARP.

adjacency A relationship formed between selected neighboring routers and end nodes for the purpose of exchanging routing information. Adjacency is based on the use of a common media segment.

Advanced Research Projects Agency See ARPA.

advertising A router process in which routing or service updates are sent so that other routers on the network can maintain lists of usable routes.

AEP (AppleTalk Echo Protocol) A protocol used to test connectivity between two AppleTalk nodes. One node sends a packet to another node and receives a duplicate, or echo, of that packet.

AFP (AppleTalk Filing Protocol) A presentation-layer protocol that allows users to share data files and application programs that reside on a file server. AFP supports AppleShare and Mac OS file sharing.

agent 1. Generally, software that processes queries and returns replies on behalf of an application. 2. In NMSs, a process that resides in all managed devices and reports the values of specified variables to management stations.

algorithm See protocol.

ANSI (American National Standards Institute) A voluntary organization composed of corporate, government, and other members that coordinates standards-related activities, approves U.S. national standards, and develops positions for the U.S. in international standards organizations. ANSI helps develop international and U.S. standards relating to, among other things, communications and networking. ANSI is a member of the IEC and the International Organization for Standardization.

API (application programming interface) A specification of function-call conventions that defines an interface to a service.

AppleTalk A series of communications protocols designed by Apple Computer consisting of two phases. Phase 1, the earlier version, supports a single physical network that can have only one network number and be in one zone. Phase 2 supports multiple logical networks on a single physical network and allows networks to be in more than one zone. *See also* zone.

application A program that performs a function directly for a user. FTP and Telnet clients are examples of network applications.

application layer Layer 7 of the OSI reference model. This layer provides network services to user applications. For example, a word processing application is serviced by file transfer services at this layer. *See also* OSI reference model.

APPN (Advanced Peer-to-Peer Networking) An enhancement to the original IBM SNA architecture. APPN handles session establishment between peer nodes, dynamic transparent route calculation, and traffic prioritization for APPC traffic.

ARA (AppleTalk Remote Access) A protocol that provides Macintosh users direct access to information and resources at a remote AppleTalk site.

area A logical set of network segments (CLNS, DECnet, or OSPF based) and their attached devices. Areas are usually connected to other areas via routers, making up a single autonomous system.

ARP (Address Resolution Protocol) An Internet protocol used to map an IP address to a MAC address. Defined in RFC 826. Compare with RARP.

ARPA (Advanced Research Projects Agency) A research and development organization that is part of the U.S. Department of Defense. ARPA is responsible for numerous technological advances in communications and networking. ARPA evolved into DARPA, and then back into ARPA again in 1994.

ARPANET Advanced Research Projects Agency Network. A landmark packet-switching network established in 1969. ARPANET was developed in the 1970s by BBN and funded by ARPA (and later DARPA). It eventually evolved into the Internet. The term ARPANET was officially retired in 1990.

AS (autonomous system) A collection of networks under common administration sharing a common routing strategy. Also referred to as a routing domain. The AS is assigned a 16-bit number by the Internet Assigned Numbers Authority.

ASBR (autonomous system boundary router) An ABR located between an OSPF autonomous system and a non-OSPF network. ASBRs run both OSPF and another routing protocol, such as RIP. ASBRs must reside in a nonstub OSPF area.

ASCII (American Standard Code for Information Interchange) An 8-bit code (7 bits plus parity) for character representation.

asymmetric switching A type of switching that provides switched connections between ports of unlike bandwidth, such as a combination of 10-Mbps and 100-Mbps ports.

Asynchronous Balanced Mode See ABM.

asynchronous circuit A signal that is transmitted without precise clocking. Such signals generally have different frequencies and phase relationships. Asynchronous transmissions usually encapsulate individual characters in control bits (called start and stop bits) that designate the beginning and end of each character. *See also* synchronous circuit.

Asynchronous Transfer Mode See ATM.

ATM (Asynchronous Transfer Mode) An international standard for cell relay in which multiple service types (such as voice, video, or data) are conveyed in fixed-length (53-byte) cells. Fixed-length cells allow cell processing to occur in hardware, thereby reducing transit delays. ATM is designed to take advantage of high-speed transmission media, such as E3, SONET, and T3.

ATM Forum An international organization jointly founded in 1991 by Cisco Systems, NET/ADAPTIVE, Northern Telecom, and Sprint that develops and promotes standards-based implementation agreements for ATM technology. The ATM Forum expands on official standards developed by ANSI and ITU-T, and develops implementation agreements in advance of official standards.

ATP (AppleTalk Transaction Protocol) A transport-level protocol that provides a loss-free transaction service between sockets. The service allows exchanges between two socket clients in which one client requests the other to perform a particular task and to report the results. ATP binds the request and response together to ensure the reliable exchange of request/response pairs.

attenuation Loss of communication signal energy.

AUI (attachment unit interface) An IEEE 802.3 interface between a MAU and a network interface card. The term AUI can also refer to the rear panel port to which an AUI cable might attach, such as those found on a Cisco LightStream Ethernet access card. Also called a *transceiver cable*.

AURP (AppleTalk Update-Based Routing Protocol) A method of encapsulating AppleTalk traffic in the header of a foreign protocol, allowing the connection of two or more discontiguous AppleTalk internetworks through a foreign network (such as TCP/IP) to form an AppleTalk WAN. This connection is called an *AURP tunnel*. In addition to its encapsulation function, AURP maintains routing tables for the entire AppleTalk WAN by exchanging routing information between exterior routers.

authentication In security, the verification of the identity of a person or process.

B

backbone The structural core of the network, which connects all the components of the network so that communication can occur.

backbone cabling Cabling that provides interconnections between wiring closets, between wiring closets and the POP, and between buildings that are part of the same LAN.

backoff The retransmission delay enforced when a collision occurs.

balanced-hybrid routing protocol A protocol that combines aspects of the link-state and distance-vector protocols. *See also* link-state routing protocol and distance-vector routing protocol.

bandwidth The difference between the highest and lowest frequencies available for network signals. Also, the rated throughput capacity of a given network medium or protocol.

bandwidth reservation The process of assigning bandwidth to users and applications served by a network. It involves assigning priority to different flows of traffic based on how critical and delay sensitive they are. This makes the best use of available bandwidth, and if the network becomes congested, lower-priority traffic can be dropped. Sometimes called *bandwidth allocation*.

Banyan VINES *See* VINES.

Basic Rate Interface *See* BRI.

B channel (bearer channel) In ISDN, a full-duplex, 64-kbps channel used to send user data. *See also* 2B+D, D channel, E channel, and H channel.

BECN (backward explicit congestion notification) A bit set by a Frame Relay network in frames traveling in the opposite direction of frames encountering a congested path. DTE devices receiving frames with the BECN bit set can request that higher-level protocols take flow control action as appropriate. *See also* FECN.

best-effort delivery Delivery that occurs when a network system does not use a sophisticated acknowledgment system to guarantee reliable delivery of information.

BGP (Border Gateway Protocol) An interdomain routing protocol that replaces EGP. BGP exchanges reachability information with other BGP systems and is defined by RFC 1163.

binary A numbering system characterized by ones and zeros (1 = on; 0 = off).

bit A binary digit used in the binary numbering system. Can be zero or one. *See also* byte.

bit bucket The destination of discarded bits as determined by the router.

BOOTP (Bootstrap Protocol) A protocol used by a network node to determine the IP address of its Ethernet interfaces to affect network booting.

bootstrap A simple, preset operation to load instructions that in turn cause other instructions to be loaded into memory, or cause entry into other configuration modes.

Bootstrap Protocol *See* BOOTP.

border router A router situated at the edges, or end, of the network boundary, which provides a basic security from the outside network or from a less controlled area of the network into a more private area of the network.

BPDU (bridge protocol data unit) A Spanning-Tree Protocol hello packet that is sent out at configurable intervals to exchange information among bridges in the network.

BRI (Basic Rate Interface) An ISDN interface composed of two B channels and one D channel for circuit-switched communication of voice, video, and data. Compare with PRI.

bridge A device that connects and passes packets between two network segments that use the same communications protocol. Bridges operate at the data link layer (Layer 2) of the OSI reference model. In general, a bridge filters, forwards, or floods an incoming frame based on the MAC address of that frame.

bridging A technology in which a bridge connects two or more LAN segments.

broadcast A data packet that is sent to all nodes on a network. Broadcasts are identified by a broadcast address. Compare with multicast and unicast. *See also* broadcast address, broadcast domain, and broadcast storm.

broadcast address A special address reserved for sending a message to all stations. Generally, a broadcast address is a MAC destination address of all ones. Compare with multicast address and unicast address. *See also* broadcast.

broadcast domain The set of all devices that will receive broadcast frames originating from any device within the set. Broadcast domains are typically bounded by routers because routers do not forward broadcast frames. *See also* broadcast.

broadcast storm An undesirable network event in which many broadcasts are sent simultaneously across all network segments. A broadcast storm uses substantial network bandwidth and, typically, causes network timeouts. *See also* broadcast.

bus topology A linear LAN architecture in which transmissions from network stations propagate the length of the medium and are received by all other stations. Compare with ring topology, star topology, and tree topology.

byte A series of consecutive binary digits that are operated on as a unit (for example, an 8-bit byte). *See also* bit.

C

cable range A range of network numbers that is valid for use by nodes on an extended AppleTalk network. The cable range value can be a single network number or a contiguous sequence of several network numbers. Node addresses are assigned based on the cable range value.

caching A form of replication in which information learned during a previous transaction is used to process later transactions.

call setup time The time required to establish a switched call between DTE devices.

CAM (content-addressable memory) Memory that maintains an accurate and functional forwarding database.

carrier An electromagnetic wave or alternating current of a single frequency, suitable for modulation by another, data-bearing signal.

carrier network A service provider's network.

catchment area A zone that falls within an area that can be served by an internetworking device, such as a hub.

Category 1 cabling One of five grades of UTP cabling described in the EIA/TIA 568B standard. Category 1 cabling is used for telephone communications and is not suitable for transmitting data. *See also* UTP.

Category 2 cabling One of five grades of UTP cabling described in the EIA/TIA 568B standard. Category 2 cabling is capable of transmitting data at speeds up to 4 Mbps. *See also* UTP.

Category 3 cabling One of five grades of UTP cabling described in the EIA/TIA 568B standard. Category 3 cabling is used in 10BaseT networks and can transmit data at speeds up to 10 Mbps. *See also* UTP.

Category 4 cabling One of five grades of UTP cabling described in the EIA/TIA 568B standard. Category 4 cabling is used in Token Ring networks and can transmit data at speeds up to 16 Mbps. *See also* UTP.

Category 5 cabling One of five grades of UTP cabling described in the EIA/TIA 568B standard. Category 5 cabling can transmit data at speeds up to 100 Mbps. *See also* UTP.

CCITT (Consultative Committee for International Telegraph and Telephone) An international organization responsible for the development of communications standards. Now called the *ITU-T*. *See* ITU-T.

CDDI (Copper Distributed Data Interface) An implementation of FDDI protocols over STP and UTP cabling. CDDI transmits over relatively short distances (about 100 meters), providing data rates of 100 Mbps using a dual-ring architecture to provide redundancy. Based on the ANSI Twisted-Pair Physical Medium Dependent (TPPMD) standard. Compare with FDDI.

Challenge Handshake Authentication Protocol *See* CHAP.

CHAP (Challenge Handshake Authentication Protocol) A security feature supported on lines using PPP encapsulation that prevents unauthorized access. CHAP does not itself prevent unauthorized access, but it identifies the remote end; the router or access server then determines whether that user is allowed access.

CIDR (classless interdomain routing) A technique supported by BGP and based on route aggregation. CIDR allows routers to group routes together in order to cut down on the quantity of routing information carried by the core routers. With CIDR, several IP networks appear to networks outside the group as a single, larger entity.

CIR (committed information rate) The rate, in bits per second, at which the Frame Relay switch agrees to transfer data.

circuit A communications path between two or more points.

circuit group A grouping of associated serial lines that link two bridges. If one of the serial links in a circuit group is in the spanning tree for a network, any of the serial links in the circuit group can be used for load balancing. This load-balancing strategy avoids data ordering problems by assigning each destination address to a particular serial link.

circuit switching A switching system in which a dedicated physical circuit path must exist between the sender and the receiver for the duration of the "call." Used heavily in the telephone company network. Circuit switching can be contrasted with contention and token passing as a channel-access method, and with message switching and packet switching as a switching technique.

Cisco IOS (Internetwork Operating System) software Cisco system software that provides common functionality, scalability, and security for all products under the CiscoFusion architecture. The Cisco IOS software allows centralized, integrated, and automated installation and management of internetworks, while ensuring support for a wide variety of protocols, media, services, and platforms.

client A node or software program (front-end device) that requests services from a server. *See also* server.

client/server The architecture of the relationship between a workstation and a server in a network.

client/server application An application that is stored centrally on a server and accessed by workstations, thus making it easy to maintain and protect.

client/server computing Distributed computing (processing) network systems in which transaction responsibilities are divided into two parts: client (front end) and server (back end). Both terms (client and server) can be applied to software programs or actual computing devices. Also called *distributed computing* (processing). Compare with peer-to-peer computing.

client/server model A common way to describe network services and the model user processes (programs) of those services. Examples include the nameserver/nameresolver paradigm of the DNS and fileserver/file-client relationships such as NFS and diskless hosts.

CMIP (Common Management Information Protocol) An OSI network management protocol created and standardized by ISO for the monitoring and control of heterogeneous networks. *See also* CMIS.

CMIS (*Common Management Information Services*)   An OSI network management service interface created and standardized by ISO for the monitoring and control of heterogeneous networks. *See also* CMIP.

CO (*central office*)   The local telephone company office to which all local loops in a given area connect and in which circuit switching of subscriber lines occurs.

coaxial cable   Cable consisting of a hollow outer cylindrical conductor that surrounds a single inner wire conductor. Two types of coaxial cable are currently used in LANs: 50-ohm cable, which is used for digital signaling, and 75-ohm cable, which is used for analog signal and high-speed digital signaling.

coding   Electrical techniques used to convey binary signals.

collision   In Ethernet, the result of two nodes transmitting simultaneously. The frames from each device collide and are damaged when they meet on the physical medium.

collision domain   In Ethernet, the network area within which frames that have collided are propagated. Repeaters and hubs propagate collisions; LAN switches, bridges, and routers do not.

common carrier   A licensed, private utility company that supplies communication services to the public at regulated prices.

concentrator   *See* hub.

congestion   Traffic in excess of network capacity.

congestion avoidance   A mechanism by which an ATM network controls traffic entering the network to minimize delays. To use resources most efficiently, lower-priority traffic is discarded at the edge of the network if conditions indicate that it cannot be delivered.

connectionless   Data transfer without the existence of a virtual circuit. Compare with connection-oriented. *See also* virtual circuit.

connection-oriented   Data transfer that requires the establishment of a virtual circuit. *See also* connectionless and virtual circuit.

console   A DTE through which commands are entered into a host.

contention   An access method in which network devices compete for permission to access the physical medium.

convergence   The speed and ability of a group of internetworking devices running a specific routing protocol to agree on the topology of an internetwork after a change in that topology.

core layer The layer that provides fast wide-area connections between geographically remote sites, tying a number of campus networks together in a corporate or enterprise WAN.

cost An arbitrary value, typically based on hop count, media bandwidth, or other measures, that is assigned by a network administrator and used to compare various paths through an internetwork environment. Cost values are used by routing protocols to determine the most favorable path to a particular destination: the lower the cost, the better the path.

count to infinity A problem that can occur in routing algorithms that are slow to converge, in which routers continuously increment the hop count to particular networks. Typically, some arbitrary hop-count limit is imposed to prevent this problem.

CPE (customer premises equipment) Terminating equipment, such as terminals, telephones, and modems, supplied by the telephone company, installed at customer sites, and connected to the telephone company network.

CSMA/CD (carrier sense multiple access collision detect) A media-access mechanism wherein devices ready to transmit data first check the channel for a carrier. If no carrier is sensed for a specific period of time, a device can transmit. If two devices transmit at once, a collision occurs and is detected by all colliding devices. This collision subsequently delays retransmissions from those devices for some random length of time. CSMA/CD access is used by Ethernet and IEEE 802.3.

CSU/DSU (channel service unit/digital service unit) A digital interface device that connects end-user equipment to the local digital telephone loop.

cut sheet A rough diagram indicating where cable runs are located and the numbers of rooms they lead to.

cut-through A packet-switching approach that streams data through a switch so that the leading edge of a packet exits the switch at the output port before the packet finishes entering the input port. A device using cut-through packet switching reads, processes, and forwards packets as soon as the destination address is looked up and the outgoing port is determined. Also known as *on-the-fly packet switching*.

D

DARPA (Defense Advanced Research Projects Agency) The U.S. government agency that funded research for and experimentation with the Internet. Evolved from ARPA, and then, in 1994, back to ARPA. *See also* ARPA.

DAS (dual attachment station) A device attached to both the primary and the secondary FDDI rings. Dual attachment provides redundancy for the FDDI ring: If the primary ring fails, the station can wrap the primary ring to the secondary ring, isolating the failure and retaining ring integrity. Also called a *Class A station*. Compare with SAS.

data Upper-layer protocol data.

data flow control layer Layer 5 of the SNA architectural model. This layer determines and manages interactions between session partners, particularly data flow. Corresponds to the session layer of the OSI reference model. *See also* data link control layer, path control layer, physical control layer, presentation services layer, transaction services layer, and transmission control layer.

datagram A logical grouping of information sent as a network-layer unit over a transmission medium without prior establishment of a virtual circuit. IP datagrams are the primary information units in the Internet. The terms *cell*, *frame*, *message*, *packet*, and *segment* are also used to describe logical information groupings at various layers of the OSI reference model and in various technology circles.

data link control layer Layer 2 in the SNA architectural model. Responsible for the transmission of data over a particular physical link. Corresponds roughly to the data link layer of the OSI reference model. *See also* data flow control layer, path control layer, physical control layer, presentation services layer, transaction services layer, and transmission control layer.

data link layer Layer 2 of the OSI reference model. This layer provides reliable transit of data across a physical link. The data link layer is concerned with physical addressing, network topology, line discipline, error notification, ordered delivery of frames, and flow control. The IEEE has divided this layer into two sublayers: the MAC sublayer and the LLC sublayer. Sometimes simply called *link layer*. Roughly corresponds to the data link control layer of the SNA model. *See also* OSI reference model.

DCE (data circuit-terminating equipment) The device used to convert the user data from the DTE into a form acceptable to the WAN service's facility. Compare with DTE.

D channel (delta channel) A full-duplex, 16-kbps (BRI) or 64-kbps (PRI) ISDN channel. *See also* B channel, E channel, and H channel.

DDN (Defense Data Network) A U.S. military network composed of an unclassified network (MILNET) and various secret and top-secret networks. DDN is operated and maintained by DISA.

DDP (Datagram Delivery Protocol) An AppleTalk network-layer protocol responsible for the socket-to-socket delivery of datagrams over an AppleTalk internetwork.

DDR (dial-on-demand routing) A technique with which a router can dynamically initiate and close circuit-switched sessions as transmitting end stations need them.

DECnet A group of communications products (including a protocol suite) developed and supported by Digital Equipment Corporation. DECnet/OSI (also called DECnet Phase V) is the most recent iteration and supports both OSI protocols and proprietary Digital protocols. Phase IV Prime supports inherent MAC addresses that allow DECnet nodes to coexist with systems running other protocols that have MAC address restrictions.

DECnet Routing Protocol *See* DRP.

dedicated link A communications link that is indefinitely reserved for transmissions, rather than switched as transmission is required. *See also* leased line.

default route A routing table entry that is used to direct frames for which a next hop is not explicitly listed in the routing table.

delay The time between the initiation of a transaction by a sender and the first response received by the sender. Also, the time required to move a packet from source to destination over a given path.

demarcation The point at which the CPE ends and the local loop portion of the service begins. Often occurs at the POP of a building.

demultiplexing The separating of multiple input streams that have been multiplexed into a common physical signal back into multiple output streams. *See also* multiplexing.

designated router An OSPF router that generates LSAs for a multiaccess network and has other special responsibilities in running OSPF. Each multiaccess OSPF network that has at least two attached routers has a designated router that is elected by the OSPF Hello protocol. The designated router enables a reduction in the number of adjacencies required on a multiaccess network, which in turn reduces the amount of routing protocol traffic and the size of the topological database.

destination address An address of a network device that is receiving data. *See also* source address.

destination service access point *See* DSAP.

DHCP Dynamic Host Configuration Protocol. A protocol that provides a mechanism for allocating IP addresses dynamically so that addresses automatically can be reused when hosts no longer need them.

dial-on-demand routing *See* DDR.

dialup line A communications circuit that is established by a switched-circuit connection using the telephone company network.

distance-vector routing protocol A routing protocol that iterates on the number of hops in a route to find a shortest-path spanning tree. Distance-vector routing protocols call for each router to send its entire routing table in each update, but only to its neighbors. Distance-vector routing protocols can be prone to routing loops, but are computationally simpler than link-state routing protocols. Also called *Bellman-Ford routing algorithm*. Compare with balanced-hybrid routing protocol and link-state routing protocol.

distribution layer The layer in which the distribution of network services occurs to multiple LANs within a WAN environment. This layer is where the WAN backbone network is found, typically based on Fast Ethernet.

DLCI (data-link connection identifier) A value that specifies a PVC or an SVC in a Frame Relay network. In the basic Frame Relay specification, DLCIs are locally significant (that is, connected devices can use different values to specify the same connection). In the LMI extended specification, DLCIs are globally significant (that is, DLCIs specify individual end devices).

DNS (Domain Name System) A system used in the Internet for translating names of network nodes into addresses.

DoD (Department of Defense) The U.S. government organization that is responsible for national defense. The DoD has frequently funded communication protocol development.

dotted-decimal notation The common notation for IP addresses in the form a.b.c.d, where each number represents, in decimal, 1 byte of the 4-byte IP address. Also called *dotted notation* or *four-part dotted notation*.

DRP (DECnet Routing Protocol) A proprietary routing scheme introduced by Digital Equipment Corporation in DECnet Phase III. In DECnet Phase V, DECnet completed its transition to OSI routing protocols (ES-IS and IS-IS).

DSAP (destination service access point) The SAP of the network node designated in the Destination field of a packet. Compare with SSAP. *See also* SAP (service access point).

DTE (data terminal equipment) A device at the user end of a user-to-network interface that serves as a data source, destination, or both. A DTE connects to a data network through a DCE device (for example, a modem) and typically uses clocking signals generated by the DCE. DTEs includes such devices as computers, protocol translators, and multiplexers. Compare with DCE.

dual attachment station See DAS.

dual counter-rotating rings A network topology in which two signal paths, whose directions are opposite each other, exist in a token-passing network. FDDI and CDDI are based on this concept.

dual-homed station A device attached to multiple FDDI concentrators to provide redundancy.

dual homing A network topology in which a device is connected to the network by way of two independent access points (points of attachment). One access point is the primary connection, and the other is a standby connection that is activated in the event of a failure of the primary connection.

dynamic routing Routing that adjusts automatically to network topology or traffic changes. Also called *adaptive routing*. Compare with static routing.

dynamic VLAN A VLAN that is based on the MAC addresses, the logical addresses, or the protocol type of the data packets. Compare with static VLAN. *See also* LAN and VLAN.

E

E1 A wide-area digital transmission scheme used predominantly in Europe that carries data at a rate of 2.048 Mbps. E1 lines can be leased for private use from common carriers. Compare with T1.

E3 A wide-area digital transmission scheme used predominantly in Europe that carries data at a rate of 34.368 Mbps. E3 lines can be leased for private use from common carriers. Compare with T3.

E channel (echo channel) A 64-kbps ISDN circuit-switching control channel. The E channel was defined in the 1984 ITU-T ISDN specification, but was dropped in the 1988 specification. Compare with B channel, D channel, and H channel.

echo channel See E channel.

EEPROM (electrically erasable programmable read-only memory) EPROM that can be erased using electrical signals applied to specific pins.

EIA (Electronic Industries Association) A group that specifies electrical transmission standards. EIA and TIA have developed numerous well-known communications standards together, including EIA/TIA-232 and EIA/TIA-449.

EIA/TIA 568 A standard that describes the characteristics and applications for various grades of UTP cabling.

Enhanced IGRP (Enhanced Interior Gateway Routing Protocol) An advanced version of IGRP developed by Cisco. Provides superior convergence properties and operating efficiency, and combines the advantages of link-state protocols with those of distance-vector protocols. Compare with IGRP. *See also* OSPF and RIP.

encapsulate To wrap data in a particular protocol header. For example, Ethernet data is wrapped in a specific Ethernet header before network transit. Also, when bridging dissimilar networks, the entire frame from one network is simply placed in the header used by the data link layer protocol of the other network.

encapsulation Wrapping of data in a particular protocol header. For example, upper-layer data is wrapped in a specific Ethernet header before network transit. Also, when bridging dissimilar networks, the entire frame from one network can simply be placed in the header used by the data link layer protocol of the other network. *See also* tunneling.

encoding The process by which bits are represented by voltages.

enterprise network A corporation, agency, school, or other organization's network that ties together its data, communication, computing, and file servers.

enterprise server A server that supports all the users on a network by offering services such as e-mail or Domain Name System (DNS). Compare with workgroup server.

EPROM (erasable programmable read-only memory) Nonvolatile memory chips that are programmed after they are manufactured and, if necessary, can be erased by some means and reprogrammed. Compare with EEPROM and PROM.

ES-IS (End System-to-Intermediate System) An OSI protocol that defines how end systems (hosts) announce themselves to intermediate systems (routers). *See also* IS-IS.

Ethernet A baseband LAN specification invented by Xerox Corporation and developed jointly by Xerox, Intel, and Digital Equipment Corporation. Ethernet networks use CSMA/CD and run over a variety of cable types at 10 Mbps. Ethernet is similar to the IEEE 802.3 series of standards. *See also* Fast Ethernet.

excess rate Traffic in excess of the insured rate for a given connection. Specifically, the excess rate equals the maximum rate minus the insured rate. Excess traffic is delivered only if network resources are available and can be discarded during periods of congestion. Compare with insured rate and maximum rate.

extended ACL (extended access control list) An ACL that checks for source address and destination address. Compare with standard ACL. *See also* ACL.

exterior protocol A protocol that is used to exchange routing information between networks that do not share a common administration. Compare with interior protocol.

F

Fast Ethernet Any of a number of 100-Mbps Ethernet specifications. Fast Ethernet offers a speed increase ten times that of the 10BaseT Ethernet specification, while preserving such qualities as frame format, MAC mechanisms, and MTU. Such similarities allow the use of existing 10BaseT applications and network management tools on Fast Ethernet networks. Based on an extension to the IEEE 802.3 specification. *See also* Ethernet.

fast-forward switching Switching that offers the lowest level of latency by immediately forwarding a packet after receiving the destination address.

fault management Five categories of network management—accounting management, configuration management, performance management, and security management—defined by ISO for management of OSI networks. Fault management attempts to ensure that network faults are detected and controlled.

FDDI (Fiber Distributed Data Interface) A LAN standard, defined by ANSI X3T9.5, specifying a 100-Mbps token-passing network using fiber-optic cable, with transmission distances of up to 2 km. FDDI uses a dual-ring architecture to provide redundancy. Compare with CDDI and FDDI II.

FDDI II An ANSI standard that enhances FDDI. FDDI II provides isochronous transmission for connectionless data circuits and connection-oriented voice and video circuits. Compare with FDDI.

FECN (forward explicit congestion notification) A bit set by a Frame Relay network to inform DTE devices receiving the frame that congestion was experienced in the path from source to destination. DTE devices receiving frames with the FECN bit set can request that higher-level protocols take flow-control action as appropriate. *See also* BECN.

Fiber Distributed Data Interface *See* FDDI.

fiber-optic cable A physical medium capable of conducting modulated light transmission. Compared with other transmission media, fiber-optic cable is more expensive, but is not susceptible to electromagnetic interference, and is capable of higher data rates. Sometimes called *optical fiber.*

File Transfer Protocol *See* FTP.

filter Generally, a process or device that screens network traffic for certain characteristics, such as source address, destination address, or protocol, and determines whether to forward or discard that traffic based on the established criteria.

firewall A router or an access server, or several routers or access servers, designated as a buffer between any connected public networks and a private network. A firewall router uses access control lists and other methods to ensure the security of the private network.

firmware Software instructions set permanently or semipermanently in ROM.

Flash memory Nonvolatile storage that can be electrically erased and reprogrammed so that software images can be stored, booted, and rewritten as necessary. Flash memory was developed by Intel and is licensed to other semiconductor companies.

flash update The process of the sending of an update sooner than the standard periodic update interval for notifying other routers of a metric change.

flat addressing A scheme of addressing that does not use a logical hierarchy to determine location.

flat network A network in which there are no routers placed between the switches, broadcasts and Layer 2 transmissions are sent to every switched port, and there is one broadcast domain across the entire network.

flooding A traffic-passing technique used by switches and bridges in which traffic received on an interface is sent out all the interfaces of that device except the interface on which the information was originally received.

flow A stream of data traveling between two endpoints across a network (for example, from one LAN station to another). Multiple flows can be transmitted on a single circuit.

flow control A technique for ensuring that a transmitting entity does not overwhelm a receiving entity with data. When the buffers on the receiving device are full, a message is sent to the sending device to suspend the transmission until the data in the buffers has been processed. In IBM networks, this technique is called *pacing.*

forwarding A process of sending a frame toward its ultimate destination by way of an internetworking device.

fragment A piece of a larger packet that has been broken down into smaller units. In Ethernet networks, also sometimes referred to as a frame less than the legal limit of 64 bytes.

fragment-free switching A switching technique that filters out collision fragments, which are the majority of packet errors, before forwarding begins.

fragmentation The process of breaking a packet into smaller units when transmitting over a network medium that cannot support the original size of the packet.

frame A logical grouping of information sent as a data link–layer unit over a transmission medium. Often refers to the header and trailer, used for synchronization and error control, that surround the user data contained in the unit. The terms *datagram*, *message*, *packet*, and *segment* are also used to describe logical information groupings at various layers of the OSI reference model and in various technology circles.

frame forwarding A mechanism by which frame-based traffic, such as HDLC and SDLC, traverses an ATM network.

Frame Relay An industry-standard, switched data link–layer protocol that handles multiple virtual circuits using HDLC encapsulation between connected devices. Frame Relay is more efficient than X.25, the protocol for which it is generally considered a replacement.

FTP (File Transfer Protocol) An application protocol, part of the TCP/IP protocol stack, used for transferring files between network nodes. FTP is defined in RFC 959.

full duplex The capability for simultaneous data transmission between a sending station and a receiving station. Compare with half duplex and simplex.

full-duplex Ethernet A capability for simultaneous data transmission between a sending station and a receiving station. Compare with half-duplex Ethernet.

fully meshed topology A topology in which every Frame Relay network device has a PVC to every other device on the multipoint WAN.

G

gateway In the IP community, an older term referring to a routing device. Today, the term router is used to describe nodes that perform this function, and gateway refers to a special-purpose device that performs an application-layer conversion of information from one protocol stack to another. Compare with router.

gateway of last resort A router to which all unroutable packets are sent.

Gb (gigabit) Approximately 1,000,000,000 bits.

Gbps (gigabytes per second) A rate of transfer speed.

Get Nearest Server See GNS.

gigabit See Gb.

GNS (Get Nearest Server) A request packet sent by a client on an IPX network to locate the nearest active server of a particular type. An IPX network client issues a GNS request to solicit either a direct response from a connected server or a response from a router that tells it where on the internetwork the service can be located. GNS is part of IPX SAP.

GUI (graphical user interface) A user environment that uses pictorial as well as textual representations of the input and output of applications and the hierarchical or other data structure in which information is stored. Conventions such as buttons, icons, and windows are typical, and many actions are performed using a pointing device (such as a mouse). Microsoft Windows and the Apple Macintosh are prominent examples of platforms utilizing GUIs.

H

half duplex A capability for data transmission in only one direction at a time between a sending station and a receiving station. Compare with full duplex and simplex.

half-duplex Ethernet A capability for data transmission in only one direction at a time between a sending station and a receiving station. Compare with full-duplex Ethernet.

handshake A sequence of messages exchanged between two or more network devices to ensure transmission synchronization before sending user data.

hardware address See MAC address.

H channel (high-speed channel) A full-duplex ISDN primary rate channel operating at 384 kbps. Compare with B channel, D channel, and E channel.

HCC (horizontal cross-connect) A wiring closet where the horizontal cabling connects to a patch panel that is connected by backbone cabling to the MDF.

HDLC (High-Level Data Link Control) A bit-oriented synchronous data link–layer protocol developed by ISO. HDLC specifies a data encapsulation method on synchronous serial links by using frame characters and checksums.

header Control information placed before data when encapsulating that data for network transmission.

hello packet A multicast packet that is used by routers using certain routing protocols for neighbor discovery and recovery. Hello packets also indicate that a client is still operating and network ready.

hexadecimal (base 16) A number representation using the digits 0 through 9, with their usual meaning, plus the letters A through F, to represent hexadecimal digits with values 10 to 15. The rightmost digit counts ones, the next counts multiples of 16, the next is $16^2=256$, and so on.

holddown An IGRP feature that rejects new routes for the same destination for some period of time.

hop The passage of a data packet between two network nodes (for example, between two routers).

hop count A routing metric used to measure the distance between a source and a destination. RIP uses hop count as its sole metric.

horizontal cross-connect *See* HCC.

host A computer system on a network. Similar to node, except that host usually implies a computer system, whereas node generally applies to any networked system, including access servers and routers. *See also* node.

host address *See* host number.

host number The part of an IP address that designates which node on the subnetwork is being addressed. Also called a *host address*.

HTML (Hypertext Markup Language) A simple hypertext document formatting language that uses tags to indicate how a given part of a document should be interpreted by a viewing application, such as a Web browser.

HTTP (Hypertext Transfer Protocol) The protocol used by Web browsers and Web servers to transfer files, such as text and graphics files.

hub 1. Generally, a device that serves as the center of a star-topology network. Also called a *multiport repeater.* 2. A hardware or software device that contains multiple independent but connected modules of network and internetwork equipment. Hubs can be active (where they repeat signals sent through them) or passive (where they do not repeat, but merely split, signals sent through them).

hybrid network An internetwork made up of more than one type of network technology, including LANs and WANs.

Hypertext Markup Language *See* HTML.

Hypertext Transfer Protocol *See* HTTP.

I

IAB (Internet Architecture Board) A board of internetwork researchers who discuss issues pertinent to Internet architecture. Responsible for appointing a variety of Internet-related groups such as the IANA, IESG, and IRSG. The IAB is appointed by the trustees of the ISOC. *See also* IANA and ISOC.

IANA (Internet Assigned Numbers Authority) An organization operated under the auspices of the ISOC as a part of the IAB. IANA delegates authority for IP address-space allocation and domain-name assignment to the InterNIC and other organizations. IANA also maintains a database of assigned protocol identifiers used in the TCP/IP stack, including autonomous system numbers.

ICMP (Internet Control Message Protocol) A network-layer Internet protocol that reports errors and provides other information relevant to IP packet processing. Documented in RFC 792.

IDF (intermediate distribution facility) A secondary communications room for a building using a star networking topology. The IDF is dependent on the MDF.

IEC (International Electrotechnical Commission) An industry group that writes and distributes standards for electrical products and components.

IEEE (Institute of Electrical and Electronic Engineers) A professional organization whose activities include the development of communications and network standards. IEEE LAN standards are the predominant LAN standards today.

IEEE 802.2 An IEEE LAN protocol that specifies an implementation of the LLC sublayer of the data link layer. IEEE 802.2 handles errors, framing, flow control, and the network layer (Layer 3) service interface. Used in IEEE 802.3 and IEEE 802.5 LANs. *See also* IEEE 802.3 and IEEE 802.5.

IEEE 802.3 An IEEE LAN protocol that specifies an implementation of the physical layer and the MAC sublayer of the data link layer. IEEE 802.3 uses CSMA/CD access at a variety of speeds over a variety of physical media. Extensions to the IEEE 802.3 standard specify implementations for Fast Ethernet. Physical variations of the original IEEE 802.3 specification include 10Base2, 10Base5, 10BaseF, 10BaseT, and 10Broad36. Physical variations for Fast Ethernet include 100BaseTX and 100BaseFX.

IEEE 802.5 An IEEE LAN protocol that specifies an implementation of the physical layer and MAC sublayer of the data link layer. IEEE 802.5 uses token passing access at 4 or 16 Mbps over STP or UTP cabling and is functionally and operationally equivalent to IBM Token Ring. *See also* Token Ring.

IETF (Internet Engineering Task Force) A task force consisting of more than 80 working groups responsible for developing Internet standards. The IETF operates under the auspices of ISOC.

IGRP (Interior Gateway Routing Protocol) A protocol developed by Cisco to address the problems associated with routing in large, heterogeneous networks.

Institute of Electrical and Electronic Engineers *See* IEEE.

insured rate The long-term data throughput, in bits or cells per second, that an ATM network commits to support under normal network conditions. The insured rate is 100 percent allocated; the entire amount is deducted from the total trunk bandwidth along the path of the circuit. Compare with excess rate and maximum rate.

Integrated Services Digital Network *See* ISDN.

interior protocol A protocol that is used for routing networks that are under a common network administration.

intermediate distribution facility *See* IDF.

International Organization for Standardization *See* ISO.

interface 1. A connection between two systems or devices. 2. In routing terminology, a network connection. 3. In telephony, a shared boundary defined by common physical interconnection characteristics, signal characteristics, and meanings of interchanged signals. 4. A boundary between adjacent layers of the OSI reference model.

Internet The largest global internetwork, connecting tens of thousands of networks worldwide and having a culture that focuses on research and standardization based on real-life use. Many leading-edge network technologies come from the Internet community. The Internet evolved in part from ARPANET. At one time called the DARPA Internet, not to be confused with the general term internet.

internet Short for internetwork. Not to be confused with the Internet. *See* internetwork.

Internet Control Message Protocol *See* ICMP.

Internet protocol Any protocol that is part of the TCP/IP protocol stack. *See* IP. *See also* TCP/IP.

Internet Protocol *See* IP.

internetwork A collection of networks interconnected by routers and other devices that functions (generally) as a single network

internetworking The industry devoted to connecting networks together. The term can refer to products, procedures, and technologies.

Internetwork Packet Exchange *See* IPX.

InterNIC An organization that serves the Internet community by supplying user assistance, documentation, training, registration service for Internet domain names, network addresses, and other services. Formerly called NIC (Network Information Center).

interoperability The capability of computing equipment manufactured by different vendors to communicate with one another successfully over a network.

intranet An internal network that is to be accessed by users who have access to an organization's internal LAN.

IOS (Internetwork Operating System) *See* Cisco IOS software.

IP (Internet Protocol) A network-layer protocol in the TCP/IP stack offering a connectionless internetwork service. IP provides features for addressing, type-of-service specification, fragmentation and reassembly, and security. Defined in RFC 791. IPv4 (Internet Protocol version 4) is a connectionless, best-effort packet switching protocol. *See also* IPv6.

IP address A 32-bit address assigned to hosts by using TCP/IP. An IP address belongs to one of five classes (A, B, C, D, or E) and is written as 4 octets separated by periods (that is, dotted-decimal format). Each address consists of a network number, an optional subnetwork number, and a host number. The network and subnetwork numbers together are used for routing, and the host number is used to address an individual host within the network or subnetwork. A subnet mask is used to extract network and subnetwork information from the IP address. Also called an *Internet address*.

IP datagram A fundamental unit of information passed across the Internet. Contains source and destination addresses along with data and a number of fields that define such things as the length of the datagram, the header checksum, and flags to indicate whether the datagram can be (or was) fragmented.

IPv6 (IP version 6) A replacement for the current version of IP (version 4). IPv6 includes support for flow ID in the packet header, which can be used to identify flows. Formerly called IPng (IP next generation).

IPX (Internetwork Packet Exchange) A NetWare network-layer (Layer 3) protocol used for transferring data from servers to workstations. IPX is similar to IP and XNS.

IPXWAN (IPX wide-area network) A protocol that negotiates end-to-end options for new links. When a link comes up, the first IPX packets sent across are IPXWAN packets negotiating the options for the link. When the IPXWAN options are successfully determined, normal IPX transmission begins. Defined by RFC 1362.

IS-IS (Intermediate System-to-Intermediate System) An OSI link-state hierarchical routing protocol based on DECnet Phase V routing whereby ISs (routers) exchange routing information based on a single metric to determine network topology. *See also* ES-IS and OSPF.

ISO (International Organization for Standardization) An international organization that is responsible for a wide range of standards, including those relevant to networking. ISO developed the OSI reference model, a popular networking reference model.

ISDN (Integrated Services Digital Network) A communication protocol, offered by telephone companies, that permits telephone networks to carry data, voice, and other source traffic.

ISOC (Internet Society) An international nonprofit organization, founded in 1992, that coordinates the evolution and use of the Internet. In addition, ISOC delegates authority to other groups related to the Internet, such as the IAB. ISOC is headquartered in Reston, Virginia, U.S.A. *See also* IAB.

ITU-T (International Telecommunication Union Telecommunication Standardization Sector) Formerly the Committee for International Telegraph and Telephone (CCITT), an international organization that develops communication standards. *See also* CCITT.

K

kb (kilobit) Approximately 1000 bits.

kB (kilobyte) Approximately 1000 bytes.

kbps (kilobits per second) A rate of transfer speed.

kBps (kilobytes per second) A rate of transfer speed.

keepalive A message sent by one network device to inform another network device that the virtual circuit between the two is still active.

keepalive interval The period of time between each keepalive message sent by a network device.

kilobit *See* kb.

kilobits per second *See* kbps.

kilobyte *See* kB.

kilobytes per second *See* kBps.

L

LAN (local-area network) A high-speed, low-error data network covering a relatively small geographic area (up to a few thousand meters). LANs connect workstations, peripherals, terminals, and other devices in a single building or other geographically limited area. LAN standards specify cabling and signaling at the physical and data link layers of the OSI model. Ethernet, FDDI, and Token Ring are widely used LAN technologies. Compare with MAN and WAN. *See also* VLAN.

LAN switch A high-speed switch that forwards packets between data-link segments. Most LAN switches forward traffic based on MAC addresses. LAN switches are often categorized according to the method they use to forward traffic: cut-through packet switching or store-and-forward packet switching. An example of a LAN switch is the Cisco Catalyst 5000.

LAPB (Link Access Procedure, Balanced) A data link-layer protocol in the X.25 protocol stack. LAPB is a bit-oriented protocol derived from HDLC. *See also* HDLC and X.25.

LAPD (Link Access Procedure on the D channel) An ISDN data link-layer protocol for the D channel. LAPD was derived from LAPB and is designed primarily to satisfy the signaling requirements of ISDN basic access. Defined by ITU-T Recommendations Q.920 and Q.921.

LAT (local-area transport) A network virtual terminal protocol developed by Digital Equipment Corporation.

latency The delay between the time a device requests access to a network and the time it is granted permission to transmit.

layering The separation of networking functions used by the OSI reference model, which simplifies the tasks required for two computers to communicate with each other.

LCP (Link Control Protocol) A protocol that provides a method of establishing, configuring, maintaining, and terminating the point-to-point connection.

leased line A transmission line reserved by a communications carrier for the private use of a customer. A leased line is a type of dedicated line. *See also* dedicated link.

link A network communications channel consisting of a circuit or transmission path and all related equipment between a sender and a receiver. Most often used to refer to a WAN connection. Sometimes referred to as a *line* or a *transmission link*.

Link Access Procedure, Balanced *See* LAPB.

Link Access Procedure on the D channel *See* LAPD.

Link Control Protocol *See* LCP.

link layer *See* data link layer.

link-layer address *See* MAC address.

link-state routing protocol A routing protocol in which each router broadcasts or multicasts information regarding the cost of reaching each of its neighbors to all nodes in the internetwork. Link-state protocols create a consistent view of the network and are therefore not prone to routing loops, but they achieve this at the cost of relatively greater computational difficulty and more widespread traffic (compared with distance-vector routing protocols). Compare with balanced-hybrid routing protocol and distance-vector routing protocol.

LLC (logical link control) The higher of the two data link–layer sublayers defined by the IEEE. The LLC sublayer handles error control, flow control, framing, and MAC-sublayer addressing. The most prevalent LLC protocol is IEEE 802.2, which includes both connectionless and connection-oriented variants.

LMI (Local Management Interface) A set of enhancements to the basic Frame Relay specification. LMI includes support for a keepalive mechanism, which verifies that data is flowing; a multicast mechanism, which provides the network server with its local DLCI and the multicast DLCI; global addressing, which gives DLCIs global rather than local significance in Frame Relay networks; and a status mechanism, which provides an ongoing status report on the DLCIs known to the switch.

load. The amount of activity on a network resource, such as a router or link.

load balancing. In routing, the capability of a router to distribute traffic over all its network ports that are the same distance from the destination address. Good load-balancing algorithms use both line speed and reliability information. Load balancing increases the use of network segments, thus increasing effective network bandwidth.

load sharing. The use of two or more paths to route packets to the same destination evenly among multiple routers to balance the work and improve network performance.

local access rate. The clock speed (port speed) of the connection (local loop) to the Frame Relay cloud. It is the rate at which data travels into or out of the network.

local-area network. See LAN.

local loop. Cabling (usually copper wiring) that extends from the demarc into the WAN service provider's central office.

Local Management Interface. See LMI.

local traffic filtering. A process by which a bridge filters out (drops) frames whose source and destination MAC addresses are located on the same interface on the bridge, thus preventing unnecessary traffic from being forwarded across the bridge. Defined in the IEEE 802.1 standard.

logical link control. See LLC.

loop. A route where packets never reach their destination but simply cycle repeatedly through a constant series of network nodes.

loopback test. A test in which signals are sent and then directed back toward their source from some point along the communications path. Loopback tests are often used to test network interface usability.

LSA (link-state advertisement). A broadcast packet used by link-state protocols that contains information about neighbors and path costs. LSAs are used by the receiving routers to maintain their routing tables. Sometimes called *link-state packet* (LSP).

M

MAC (Media Access Control) The part of the data link layer that includes the 6-byte(48-bit) address of the source and destination, and the method of getting permission to transmit. *See also* data link layer and LLC.

MAC (Media Access Control) address A standardized data link-layer address that is required for every port or device that connects to a LAN. Other devices in the network use these addresses to locate specific ports in the network and to create and update routing tables and data structures. MAC addresses are each 6 bytes long, and they are controlled by the IEEE. Also known as a *hardware address*, a *MAC-layer address*, or a *physical address*. Compare with network address.

MAC address learning A service that characterizes a learning switch in which the source MAC address of each received packet is stored so that future packets destined for that address can be forwarded only to the switch interface on which that address is located. Packets destined for unrecognized broadcast or multicast addresses are forwarded out every switch interface except the originating one. This scheme helps minimize traffic on the attached LANs. MAC address learning is defined in the IEEE 802.1 standard.

MAC-layer address *See* MAC address.

MAN (metropolitan-area network) A network that spans a metropolitan area. Generally, a MAN spans a larger geographic area than a LAN, but a smaller geographic area than a WAN. Compare with LAN and WAN.

Management Information Base *See* MIB.

mask *See* address mask and subnet mask.

MAU (media attachment unit) A device used in Ethernet and IEEE 802.3 networks that provides the interface between the AUI port of a station and the common medium of the Ethernet. The MAU, which can be built into a station or can be a separate device, performs physical-layer functions including the conversion of digital data from the Ethernet interface, collision detection, and injection of bits onto the network. Sometimes referred to as a *media access unit*, also abbreviated MAU, or as a *transceiver*.

maximum rate The maximum total data throughput allowed on a given virtual circuit, equal to the sum of the insured and uninsured traffic from the traffic source. The uninsured data might be dropped if the network becomes congested. The maximum rate, which cannot exceed the media rate, represents the highest data throughput the virtual circuit will ever deliver, measured in bits or cells per second. Compare with excess rate and insured rate.

Mb (megabit) Approximately 1,000,000 bits.

MB (megabyte) Approximately 1,000,000 bytes.

Mbps (megabits per second) A rate of transfer speed.

MDF (main distribution facility) The primary communications room for a building. The central point of a star networking topology where patch panels, hub, and router are located.

media Plural of medium. The various physical environments through which transmission signals pass. Common network media include twisted-pair, coaxial, and fiber-optic cable, and the atmosphere (through which microwave, laser, and infrared transmission occurs). Sometimes called *physical media*.

Media Access Control *See* MAC.

media access unit *See* MAU.

media attachment unit *See* MAU.

megabit *See* Mb.

megabits per second *See* Mbps.

megabyte *See* MB.

memory buffer The area of memory where the switch stores the destination and transmission data.

mesh A network topology in which devices are organized in a manageable, segmented manner with many, often redundant, interconnections strategically placed between network nodes. *See also* fully meshed topology and partially meshed topology.

message An application-layer logical grouping of information, often composed of a number of lower-layer logical groupings such as packets. The terms *datagram*, *frame*, *packet*, and *segment* are also used to describe logical information groupings at various layers of the OSI reference model and in various technology circles.

metric A standard of measurement (for example, path length) that is used by routing protocols to determine the optimal path to a destination.

MIB (Management Information Base) A database of network management information that is used and maintained by a network management protocol such as SNMP. The value of a MIB object can be changed or retrieved by using SNMP commands, usually through a GUI network management system. MIB objects are organized in a tree structure that includes public (standard) and private (proprietary) branches.

microsegmentation The division of a network into smaller segments, usually with the intention of increasing aggregate bandwidth to network devices.

modem (modulator-demodulator) A device that converts digital and analog signals. At the source, a modem converts digital signals to a form suitable for transmission over analog communication facilities. At the destination, the analog signals are returned to their digital form. Modems allow data to be transmitted over voice-grade telephone lines.

MSAU (multistation access unit) A wiring concentrator to which all end stations in a Token Ring network connect. The MSAU provides an interface between these devices and the Token Ring interface of a router. Sometimes abbreviated MAU.

MTU (maximum transmission unit) Maximum packet size, in bytes, that a particular interface can handle.

multicast Single packets copied by a network and sent out to a set of network addresses. These addresses are specified in the destination address field. Compare with broadcast and unicast.

multicast address A single address that refers to multiple network devices. Synonymous with group address. Compare with broadcast address and unicast address. *See also* multicast.

multimode fiber Optical fiber supporting propagation of multiple frequencies of light.

multiplexing A scheme that allows multiple logical signals to be transmitted simultaneously across a single physical channel. Compare with demultiplexing.

multiprotocol routing Routing in which a router delivers packets from several routed protocols, such as TCP/IP and IPX, over the same data links.

multistation access unit *See* MSAU.

multivendor network A network using equipment from more than one vendor. Multivendor networks pose many more compatibility problems than single-vendor networks. Compare with single-vendor network.

N

NAK (negative acknowledgment) A response sent from a receiving device to a sending device indicating that the information received contained errors. Compare with acknowledgment.

name resolution Generally, the process of associating a name with a network address.

name server A server connected to a network that resolves network names into network addresses.

NAT (network address translation) A mechanism for reducing the need for globally unique IP addresses. NAT allows an organization with addresses that are not globally unique to connect to the Internet by translating those addresses into globally routable address space. Also known as *network address translator*.

NAUN (nearest active upstream neighbor) In Token Ring or IEEE 802.5 networks, the closest upstream network device from any given device that is still active.

NCP (Network Control Program) A program that routes and controls the flow of data between a communications controller and other network resources.

neighboring routers In OSPF, two routers that have interfaces to a common network. On multiaccess networks, neighbors are dynamically discovered by the OSPF Hello protocol.

NetBEUI (NetBIOS Extended User Interface) An enhanced version of the NetBIOS protocol used by network operating systems such as LAN Manager, LAN Server, Windows for Workgroups, and Windows NT. NetBEUI formalizes the transport frame and adds additional functions. NetBEUI implements the OSI LLC2 protocol.

NetBIOS (Network Basic Input/Output System) An application programming interface used by applications on an IBM LAN to request services from lower-level network processes. These services might include session establishment and termination, and information transfer.

NetWare A popular distributed NOS developed by Novell. Provides transparent remote file access and numerous other distributed network services.

NetWare Link Services Protocol *See* NLSP.

NetWare Loadable Module *See* NLM.

network A collection of computers, printers, routers, switches, and other devices that are able to communicate with each other over some transmission medium.

network address A network-layer address referring to a logical, rather than a physical, network device. Also called a *protocol address*.

network address translation *See* NAT.

network administrator A person responsible for the operation, maintenance, and management of a network.

network analyzer A hardware or software device offering various network troubleshooting features, including protocol-specific packet decodes, specific preprogrammed troubleshooting tests, packet filtering, and packet transmission.

Network Basic Input/Output System *See* NetBIOS.

network byte order An Internet-standard ordering of the bytes corresponding to numeric values.

Network Control Program *See* NCP.

Network File System *See* NFS.

network interface The boundary between a carrier network and a privately owned installation.

network interface card *See* NIC.

network layer Layer 3 of the OSI reference model. This layer provides connectivity and path selection between two end systems. The network layer is the layer at which routing occurs. Corresponds roughly with the path control layer of the SNA model. *See also* OSI reference model.

network management Using systems or actions to maintain, characterize, or troubleshoot a network.

network management system *See* NMS.

network number The part of an IP address that specifies the network to which the host belongs.

network operating system *See* NOS.

networking The interconnection of workstations; peripherals such as printers, hard drives, scanners, CD-ROMs; and other devices.

next-hop address The IP address that is computed by the IP routing protocol and software.

NFS (Network File System) As commonly used, a distributed file system protocol suite developed by Sun Microsystems that allows remote file access across a network. In actuality, NFS is simply one protocol in the suite. NFS protocols include RPC and XDR. These protocols are part of a larger architecture that Sun refers to as ONC.

NIC (Network Information Center) An organization whose functions have been assumed by InterNIC. *See* InterNIC.

NIC (network interface card) A board that provides network communication capabilities to and from a computer system. Also called an *adapter.*

NLM (NetWare Loadable Module) An individual program that can be loaded into memory and function as part of the NetWare NOS.

NLSP (NetWare Link Services Protocol) A link-state routing protocol based on IS-IS. The Cisco implementation of NLSP also includes MIB variables and tools to redistribute routing and SAP information between NLSP and other IPX routing protocols.

NMS (network management system) A system responsible for managing at least part of a network. An NMS is generally a reasonably powerful and well-equipped computer such as an engineering workstation. NMSs communicate with agents to help keep track of network statistics and resources.

node An endpoint of a network connection or a junction common to two or more lines in a network. Nodes can be processors, controllers, or workstations. Nodes, which vary in routing and other functional capabilities, can be interconnected by links and serve as control points in the network. Node is sometimes used generically to refer to any entity that can access a network, and is frequently used interchangeably with device.

nonextended network An AppleTalk Phase 2 network that supports addressing of up to 253 nodes and only 1 zone.

nonseed router In AppleTalk, a router that must first obtain and then verify its configuration with a seed router before it can begin operation. *See also* seed router.

nonstub area A resource-intensive OSPF area that carries a default route, static routes, intra-area routes, interarea routes, and external routes. Non-stub areas are the only OSPF areas that can have virtual links configured across them, and are the only areas that can contain an ASBR. Compare with stub area.

NOS (network operating system) The operating system used to run a network such Novell NetWare and Windows NT.

Novell IPX See IPX.

NT1 (Network Termination Type 1) A device that connects four-wire ISDN subscriber wiring to the conventional two-wire local loop facility.

NT2 (Network Termination Type 2) A device that directs traffic to and from different subscriber devices and the NT1. The NT2 is an intelligent device that performs switching and concentrating.

NTP (Network Time Protocol) A protocol built on top of TCP that assures accurate local time-keeping with reference to radio and atomic clocks located on the Internet. This protocol is capable of synchronizing distributed clocks within milliseconds over long time periods.

NVRAM (nonvolatile RAM) RAM that retains its contents when a unit is powered off.

O

octet 8 bits. In networking, the term *octet* is often used (rather than byte) because some machine architectures employ bytes that are not 8 bits long.

ODI (Open Data-Link Interface) A Novell specification providing a standardized interface for network interface cards (NICs) that allows multiple protocols to use a single NIC.

Open Shortest Path First See OSPF.

Open System Interconnection See OSI.

Open System Interconnection reference model See OSI reference model.

OSI (Open System Interconnection) An international standardization program created by ISO and ITU-T to develop standards for data networking that facilitate multivendor equipment interoperability.

OSI presentation address An address used to locate an OSI application entity. It consists of an OSI network address and up to three selectors, one each for use by the transport, session, and presentation entities.

OSI reference model (Open System Interconnection reference model) A network architectural model developed by ISO and ITU-T. The model consists of seven layers, each of which specifies particular network functions such as addressing, flow control, error control, encapsulation, and reliable message transfer. The lowest layer (the physical layer) is closest to the media technology. The lower two layers are implemented in hardware and software, and the upper five layers are implemented only in software. The highest layer (the application layer) is closest to the user. The OSI reference model is used universally as a method for teaching and understanding network functionality. Similar in some respects to SNA. *See* application layer, data link layer, network layer, physical layer, presentation layer, session layer, and transport layer.

OSPF (Open Shortest Path First) A link-state, hierarchical routing protocol proposed as a successor to RIP in the Internet community. OSPF features include least-cost routing, multipath routing, and load balancing.

OUI (organizational unique identifier) Three octets assigned by the IEEE in a block of 48-bit LAN addresses.

P

packet A logical grouping of information that includes a header containing control information and (usually) user data. Packets are most often used to refer to network-layer units of data. The terms *datagram*, *frame*, *message*, and *segment* are also used to describe logical information groupings at various layers of the OSI reference model and in various technology circles.

packet internet groper *See* ping.

packet switching A networking method in which nodes share bandwidth with each other by sending packets.

PAP (Password Authentication Protocol) An authentication protocol that allows PPP peers to authenticate one another. The remote router attempting to connect to the local router is required to send an authentication request. Unlike CHAP, PAP passes the password and host name or username in cleartext (that is, unencrypted). PAP does not itself prevent unauthorized access, but it identifies the remote end; the router or access server then determines whether that user is allowed access. PAP is supported only on PPP lines. Compare with CHAP.

parallel transmission A method of data transmission in which the bits of a data character are transmitted simultaneously over a number of channels. Compare with serial transmission.

partially meshed topology A topology in which not every device on the Frame Relay cloud has a PVC to every other device.

Password Authentication Protocol *See* PAP.

patch panel An assembly of pin locations and ports that can be mounted on a rack or wall bracket in the wiring closet. Patch panels act like switchboards that connect workstations' cables to each other and to the outside.

path control layer Layer 3 in the SNA architectural model. This layer performs sequencing services related to proper data reassembly. The path control layer is also responsible for routing. Corresponds roughly with the network layer of the OSI reference model. *See also* data flow control layer, data link control layer, physical control layer, presentation services layer, transaction services layer, and transmission control layer.

path determination The decision of which path traffic should take through the network cloud. Path determination occurs at the network layer of the OSI reference model.

payload A portion of a cell, frame, or packet that contains upper-layer information (data).

PBX (private branch exchange) A digital or an analog telephone switchboard located on the subscriber premises and used to connect private and public telephone networks.

PDN (public data network) A network operated either by a government (as in Europe) or by a private concern to provide computer communications to the public, usually for a fee. PDNs enable small organizations to create a WAN without all the equipment costs of long-distance circuits.

PDU (protocol data unit) The OSI term for a packet.

peer-to-peer computing Peer-to-peer computing calls for each network device to run both client and server portions of an application. Also describes communication between implementations of the same OSI reference model layer in two different network devices. Compare with client/server computing.

permanent virtual circuit *See* PVC.

PHY 1. Physical sublayer. One of two sublayers of the FDDI physical layer. 2. Physical layer. In ATM, the physical layer provides for the transmission of cells over a physical medium that connects two ATM devices. The PHY is composed of two sublayers: PMD and TC.

physical address *See* MAC address.

physical control layer Layer 1 in the SNA architectural model. This layer is responsible for the physical specifications for the physical links between end systems. Corresponds to the physical layer of the OSI reference model. *See also* data flow control layer, data link control layer, path control layer, presentation services layer, transaction services layer, and transmission control layer.

physical layer Layer 1 of the OSI reference model. This layer defines the electrical, mechanical, procedural, and functional specifications for activating, maintaining, and deactivating the physical link between end systems. Corresponds with the physical control layer in the SNA model. *See also* OSI reference model.

ping (packet internet groper)   An ICMP echo message and its reply. Often used in IP networks to test the reachability of a network device.

PLP (packet level protocol)   A network-layer protocol in the X.25 protocol stack. Sometimes called *X.25 Level 3* and *X.25 Protocol. See also* X.25.

point-to-multipoint connection   One of two fundamental connection types. In ATM, a point-to-multipoint connection is a unidirectional connection in which a single source end system (known as a root node) connects to multiple destination end systems (known as leaves). Compare with point-to-point connection.

point-to-point connection   One of two fundamental connection types. In ATM, a point-to-point connection can be a unidirectional or bidirectional connection between two ATM end systems. Compare with point-to-multipoint connection.

point-to-point link   A link that provides a single, preestablished WAN communications path from the customer premises through a carrier network, such as a telephone company, to a remote network. Also called a *dedicated link* or a *leased line.*

Point-to-Point Protocol   See PPP.

poison reverse update   An IGRP feature intended to defeat larger routing loops. Poison reverse updates explicitly indicate that a network or subnet is unreachable, rather than imply that a network is unreachable by not including it in updates.

POP (point of presence)   The point of interconnection between the communication facilities provided by the telephone company and the building's main distribution facility.

port   1. An interface on an internetworking device (such as a router). 2. A female plug on a patch panel that accepts the same size plug as an RJ-45 jack. Patch cords are used in these ports to cross connect computers wired to the patch panel. It is this cross-connection that allows the LAN to function. 3. In IP terminology, an upper-layer process that receives information from lower layers. Ports are numbered, and many are associated with a specific process. For example, SMTP is associated with port 25. A port number of this type is called a *well-known address.* 4. To rewrite software or microcode so that it will run on a different hardware platform or in a different software environment than that for which it was originally designed.

port-centric VLAN A VLAN in which all the nodes in the same VLAN are attached to the same switch port.

POST (power-on self-test) A set of hardware diagnostics that runs on a hardware device when that device is powered up.

PPP (Point-to-Point Protocol) A successor to SLIP, a protocol that provides router-to-router and host-to-network connections over synchronous and asynchronous circuits.

presentation layer Layer 6 of the OSI reference model. This layer provides data representation and code formatting, along with the negotiation of data transfer syntax. It ensures that the data that arrives from the network can be used by the application, and it ensures that information sent by the application can be transmitted on the network. *See also* OSI reference model.

presentation services layer Layer 6 of the SNA architectural model. This layer provides network resource management, session presentation services, and some application management. Corresponds roughly with the presentation layer of the OSI reference model.

PRI (Primary Rate Interface) An ISDN interface to primary rate access. Primary rate access consists of a single 64-kbps D channel plus 23 (T1) or 30 (E1) B channels for voice or data. Compare with BRI.

priority queuing A routing feature in which frames in an interface output queue are prioritized based on various characteristics such as protocol, packet size, and interface type.

PROM (programmable read-only memory) ROM that can be programmed using special equipment. PROMs can be programmed only once. Compare with EPROM.

propagation delay The time required for data to travel over a network, from its source to its ultimate destination. Also called *latency.*

protocol A formal description of a set of rules and conventions that govern how devices on a network exchange information.

protocol address *See* network address.

protocol analyzer *See* network analyzer.

protocol stack A set of related communications protocols that operate together and, as a group, address communication at some or all of the seven layers of the OSI reference model. Not every protocol stack covers each layer of the model, and often a single protocol in the stack will address a number of layers at once. TCP/IP is a typical protocol stack.

proxy An entity that, in the interest of efficiency, essentially stands in for another entity.

proxy Address Resolution Protocol *See* proxy ARP.

proxy ARP (proxy Address Resolution Protocol) A variation of the ARP protocol in which an intermediate device (for example, a router) sends an ARP response on behalf of an end node to the requesting host. Proxy ARP can lessen bandwidth use on slow-speed WAN links.

PTT (post, telephone, and telegraph) A government agency that provides telephone services. PTTs exist in most areas outside North America and provide both local and long-distance telephone services.

punch tool A spring-loaded tool used for cutting and connecting wire in a jack or on a patch panel.

PVC (permanent virtual circuit) A virtual circuit that is permanently established. PVCs save bandwidth associated with circuit establishment and teardown in situations where certain virtual circuits must exist all the time. Compare with SVC.

Q

Q.931 A protocol that recommends a network layer between the terminal endpoint and the local ISDN switch. Q.931 does not impose an end-to-end recommendation. The various ISDN providers and switch types can and do use various implementations of Q.931.

QoS (quality of service) A measure of performance for a transmission system that reflects its transmission quality and service availability.

queue 1. Generally, an ordered list of elements waiting to be processed. 2. In routing, a backlog of packets waiting to be forwarded over a router interface.

queuing A process in which ACLs can designate certain packets to be processed by a router before other traffic, on the basis of a protocol.

queuing delay The amount of time that data must wait before it can be transmitted onto a statistically multiplexed physical circuit.

R

RAM (random-access memory) Volatile memory that can be read and written by a microprocessor.

random-access memory *See* RAM.

RARP (Reverse Address Resolution Protocol) A protocol in the TCP/IP stack that provides a method for finding IP addresses based on MAC addresses. Compare with ARP.

RBOC (regional Bell operating company) A local or regional telephone company that owns and operates telephone lines and switches in one of seven U.S. regions. The RBOCs were created by the divestiture of AT&T.

reassembly The putting back together of an IP datagram at the destination after it has been fragmented either at the source or at an intermediate node.

redirect Part of the ICMP and ES-IS protocols that allows a router to tell a host that using another router would be more effective.

redundancy 1. In internetworking, the duplication of devices, services, or connections so that, in the event of a failure, the redundant devices, services, or connections can perform the work of those that failed. 2. In telephony, the portion of the total information contained in a message that can be eliminated without loss of essential information or meaning.

reference point A specification that defines the connection between specific devices, depending on their function in the end-to-end connection.

regional Bell operating company *See* RBOC.

reliability The ratio of expected to received keepalives from a link. If the ratio is high, the line is reliable. Used as a routing metric.

repeater A device that regenerates and propagates electrical signals between two network segments.

Request for Comment *See* RFC.

Reverse Address Resolution Protocol *See* RARP.

RFC (Request for Comment) A document series used as the primary means for communicating information about the Internet. Some RFCs are designated by the IAB as Internet standards. Most RFCs document protocol specifications such as Telnet and FTP, but some are humorous or historical. RFCs are available online from numerous sources.

ring A connection of two or more stations in a logically circular topology. Information is passed sequentially between active stations. Token Ring, FDDI, and CDDI are based on this topology.

ring topology A network topology that consists of a series of repeaters connected to one another by unidirectional transmission links to form a single closed loop. Each station on the network connects to the network at a repeater. Although logically rings, ring topologies are most often organized in a closed-loop star. Compare with bus topology, star topology, and tree topology.

RIP (Routing Information Protocol) A protocol supplied with UNIX BSD systems. The most common Interior Gateway Protocol (IGP) in the Internet. RIP uses hop count as a routing metric.

RMON (remote monitoring) A MIB agent specification described in RFC 1271 that defines functions for the remote monitoring of networked devices. The RMON specification provides numerous monitoring, problem detection, and reporting capabilities.

ROM (read-only memory) Nonvolatile memory that can be read, but not written, by the microprocessor.

routed protocol A protocol that can be routed by a router. A router must be able to interpret the logical internetwork as specified by that routed protocol. Examples of routed protocols include AppleTalk, DECnet, and IP. Compare with routing protocol.

route map A method of controlling the redistribution of routes between routing domains.

route summarization The consolidation of advertised network numbers in OSPF and IS-IS. In OSPF, this causes a single summary route to be advertised to other areas by an area border router.

router A network-layer device that uses one or more metrics to determine the optimal path along which network traffic should be forwarded. Routers forward packets from one network to another based on network layer information. Occasionally called a *gateway* (although this definition of gateway is becoming increasingly outdated).

routing The process of finding a path to a destination host. Routing is very complex in large networks because of the many potential intermediate destinations a packet might traverse before reaching its destination host.

routing metric A method by which a routing protocol determines that one route is better than another. This information is stored in routing tables. Metrics include bandwidth, communication cost, delay, hop count, load, MTU, path cost, and reliability. Sometimes referred to simply as a *metric*.

routing protocol A protocol that accomplishes routing through the implementation of a specific routing protocol. Examples of routing protocols include IGRP, OSPF, and RIP. Compare with routed protocol.

routing table A table stored in a router or some other internetworking device that keeps track of routes to particular network destinations and, in some cases, metrics associated with those routes.

Routing Table Maintenance Protocol *See* RTMP.

routing update A message sent from a router to indicate network reachability and associated cost information. Routing updates are typically sent at regular intervals and after a change in network topology. Compare with flash update.

RPC (remote-procedure call) The technological foundation of client/server computing. RPCs are procedure calls that are built or specified by clients and executed on servers, with the results returned over the network to the clients.

RPF (Reverse Path Forwarding) A multicasting technique in which a multicast datagram is forwarded out of all but the receiving interface if the receiving interface is the one used to forward unicast datagrams to the source of the multicast datagram.

RSVP (Resource Reservation Protocol) A protocol that supports the reservation of resources across an IP network. Applications running on IP end systems can use RSVP to indicate to other nodes the nature (bandwidth, jitter, maximum burst, and so forth) of the packet streams they want to receive. RSVP depends on IPv6. Also known as *Resource Reservation Setup Protocol*.

RTMP (Routing Table Maintenance Protocol) Apple Computer's proprietary routing protocol. RTMP establishes and maintains the routing information that is required to route datagrams from any source socket to any destination socket in an AppleTalk network. Using RTMP, routers dynamically maintain routing tables to reflect changes in topology. RTMP was derived from RIP.

RTP (Routing Table Protocol) A VINES routing protocol based on RIP. Distributes network topology information and aids VINES servers in finding neighboring clients, servers, and routers. Uses delay as a routing metric.

RTP (Rapid Transport Protocol) A protocol that provides pacing and error recovery for APPN data as it crosses the APPN network. With RTP, error recovery and flow control are done end-to-end rather than at every node. RTP prevents congestion rather than reacts to it.

RTP (Real-Time Transport Protocol) One of the IPv6 protocols. RTP is designed to provide end-to-end network transport functions for applications transmitting real-time data, such as audio, video, or simulation data, over multicast or unicast network services. RTP provides services such as payload type identification, sequence numbering, timestamping, and delivery monitoring to real-time applications.

S

SAP (Service Advertising Protocol) An IPX protocol that provides a means of informing network clients, via routers and servers, of available network resources and services.

SAS (single attachment station). A device attached only to the primary ring of an FDDI ring. Also known as a *Class B station*. Compare with DAS. *See also* FDDI.

scalability. The ability of a network to grow, without any major changes to the overall design.

SDLC (Synchronous Data Link Control). An SNA data link–layer communications protocol. SDLC is a bit-oriented, full-duplex serial protocol that has spawned numerous similar protocols, including HDLC and LAPB.

secondary station. In bit-synchronous data link–layer protocols such as HDLC, a station that responds to commands from a primary station. Sometimes referred to simply as a *secondary*.

seed router. A router in an AppleTalk network that has the network number or cable range built in to its port descriptor. The seed router defines the network number or cable range for other routers in that network segment and responds to configuration queries from nonseed routers on its connected AppleTalk network, allowing those routers to confirm or modify their configurations accordingly. Each AppleTalk network must have at least one seed router.

segment. 1. A section of a network that is bounded by bridges, routers, or switches. 2. In a LAN using a bus topology, a continuous electrical circuit that is often connected to other such segments with repeaters. 3. In the TCP specification, a single transport-layer unit of information. The terms *datagram*, *frame*, *message*, and *packet* are also used to describe logical information groupings at various layers of the OSI reference model and in various technology circles.

segmentation. The process of splitting a single collision domain into two or more collision domains in order to reduce collisions and network congestion.

Sequenced Packet Exchange. See SPX.

serial transmission. A method of data transmission in which the bits of a data character are transmitted sequentially over a single channel. Compare with parallel transmission.

server A node or software program that provides services to clients. *See also* client.

service access point A field defined by the IEEE 802.2 specification that is part of an address specification.

Service Advertising Protocol *See* SAP.

session 1. A related set of connection-oriented communications transactions between two or more network devices. 2. In SNA, a logical connection enabling two network addressable units to communicate.

session layer Layer 5 of the OSI reference model. This layer establishes, maintains, and manages sessions between applications. *See also* OSI reference model.

shortest-path routing Routing that minimizes distance or path cost through application of an algorithm.

signal reference ground The reference point used by computing devices to measure and compare incoming digital signals.

signaling In the ISDN context, the process of call setup used, such as call establishment, call termination, information, and miscellaneous messages, including setup, connect, release, user information, cancel, status, and disconnect.

simplex The capability for transmission in only one direction between a sending station and a receiving station. Broadcast television is an example of a simplex technology. Compare with full duplex and half duplex.

single-vendor network A network using equipment from only one vendor. Single-vendor networks rarely suffer compatibility problems. *See also* multivendor network.

sliding window A window whose size is negotiated dynamically during the TCP session.

sliding window flow control A method of flow control in which a receiver gives a transmitter permission to transmit data until a window is full. When the window is full, the transmitter must stop transmitting until the receiver advertises a larger window. TCP, other transport protocols, and several data link-layer protocols use this method of flow control.

SLIP (Serial Line Internet Protocol) A standard protocol for point-to-point serial connections using a variation of TCP/IP. The predecessor of PPP.

small office/home office *See* SOHO.

SMI (Structure of Management Information) A document (RFC 1155) specifying rules used to define managed objects in the MIB.

SNA (Systems Network Architecture) A large, complex, feature-rich network architecture developed in the 1970s by IBM. Similar in some respects to the OSI reference model, but with a number of differences. SNA is essentially composed of seven layers. *See* data flow control layer, data link control layer, path control layer, physical control layer, presentation services layer, transaction services layer, and transmission control layer.

SNMP (Simple Network Management Protocol) A network management protocol used almost exclusively in TCP/IP networks. SNMP provides a means to monitor and control network devices and to manage configurations, statistics collection, performance, and security.

socket 1. A software structure operating as a communications endpoint within a network device (similar to a port). 2. An addressable entity within a node connected to an AppleTalk network; sockets are owned by software processes known as *socket clients*. AppleTalk sockets are divided into two groups: SASs, which are reserved for clients such as AppleTalk core protocols, and DASs, which are assigned dynamically by DDP upon request from clients in the node. An AppleTalk socket is similar in concept to a TCP/IP port.

socket number An 8-bit number that identifies a socket. A maximum of 254 socket numbers can be assigned in an AppleTalk node.

SOHO (small office/home office) A small office or home office consisting of a few users requiring a connection that provides faster, more reliable connectivity than an analog dialup connection.

source address An address of a network device that is sending data.

spanning tree A loop-free subset of a Layer 2 (switched) network topology.

spanning-tree algorithm An algorithm used by the Spanning-Tree Protocol to create a spanning tree. Sometimes abbreviated as STA.

Spanning-Tree Protocol A bridge protocol that utilizes the spanning-tree algorithm, enabling a learning bridge to dynamically work around loops in a network topology by creating a spanning tree. Bridges exchange BPDU messages with other bridges to detect loops, and then remove the loops by shutting down selected bridge interfaces. Refers to both the IEEE 802.1 Spanning-Tree Protocol standard and the earlier Digital Equipment Corporation Spanning-Tree Protocol on which it is based. The IEEE version supports bridge domains and allows the bridge to construct a loop-free topology across an extended LAN. The IEEE version is generally preferred over the Digital version.

SPF (shortest path first) protocol A routing protocol that iterates on length of path to determine a shortest-path spanning tree. Commonly used in link-state routing protocols. Sometimes called *Dijkstra's algorithm*.

SPID (service profile identifier) A number that some service providers use to define the services to which an ISDN device subscribes. The ISDN device uses the SPID when accessing the switch that initializes the connection to a service provider.

split horizon An IGRP feature designed to prevent routers from picking up erroneous routes. Split horizon prevents loops between adjacent routers and keeps down the size of update messages.

split-horizon updates A routing technique in which information about routes is prevented from exiting the router interface through which that information was received. Split-horizon updates are useful in preventing routing loops.

spoofing 1. A scheme used by routers to cause a host to treat an interface as if it were up and supporting a session. The router spoofs replies to keepalive messages from the host in order to convince that host that the session still exists. Spoofing is useful in routing environments such as DDR, in which a circuit-switched link is taken down when there is no traffic to be sent across it in order to save toll charges. 2. The act of a packet illegally claiming to be from an address from which it was not actually sent. Spoofing is designed to foil network security mechanisms such as filters and ACLs.

SPP (Sequenced Packet Protocol) A protocol that provides reliable, connection-based, flow-controlled packet transmission on behalf of client processes. Part of the XNS protocol suite.

SPX (Sequenced Packet Exchange) A reliable, connection-oriented protocol that supplements the datagram service provided by network-layer protocols. Novell derived this commonly used NetWare transport protocol from the SPP of the XNS protocol suite.

SQE (signal quality error) In Ethernet, a transmission sent by a transceiver back to the controller to let the controller know whether the collision circuitry is functional. Also called *heartbeat*.

SS7 (Signaling System 7) A standard common channel signaling system developed by Bellcore, used in ISDN, that uses telephone control messages and signals between the transfer points along the way to the called destination.

SSAP (source service access point) The SAP of the network node designated in the Source field of a packet. Compare with DSAP. *See also* SAP.

standard A set of rules or procedures that are either widely used or officially specified.

standard ACL (standard access control list) An ACL that filters based on a source address and mask. Standard ACLs permit or deny the entire TCP/IP protocol suite. *See also* ACL and extended ACL.

star topology A LAN topology in which endpoints on a network are connected to a common central switch by point-to-point links. A ring topology that is organized as a star implements a unidirectional closed-loop star, instead of point-to-point links. Compare with bus topology, ring topology, and tree topology.

static routing Routing that is explicitly configured and entered into the routing table. Static routes take precedence over routes chosen by dynamic routing protocols. Compare with dynamic routing.

static VLAN A VLAN in which the ports on a switch are statically assigned. Compare with dynamic VLAN. *See also* LAN and VLAN.

store-and-forward A packet-switching technique in which frames are completely processed before being forwarded out the appropriate port. This processing includes calculating the CRC and checking the destination address. In addition, frames must be temporarily stored until network resources (such as an unused link) are available to forward the message.

STP (shielded twisted-pair) A two-pair wiring medium used in a variety of network implementations. STP cabling has a layer of shielded insulation to reduce EMI. Compare with UTP.

stub area An OSPF area that carries a default route, intra-area routes, and interarea routes, but does not carry external routes. Virtual links cannot be configured across a stub area, and they cannot contain an ASBR. Compare with nonstub area.

stub network A network that has only a single connection to a router.

subinterface One of a number of virtual interfaces on a single physical interface.

subnet *See* subnetwork.

subnet address A portion of an IP address that is specified as the subnetwork by the subnet mask.

subnet mask A mask used to extract network and subnetwork information from the IP address.

subnetwork 1. A network that is segmented into a series of smaller networks. 2. In IP networks, a network sharing a particular subnet address. Subnetworks are networks arbitrarily segmented by a network administrator in order to provide a multilevel, hierarchical routing structure while shielding the subnetwork from the addressing complexity of attached networks. Sometimes called a *subnet*. 3. In OSI networks, a collection of ESs and ISs under the control of a single administrative domain and using a single network access protocol.

surge Any voltage increase above 110% of the normal voltage carried by a power line.

SVC (switched virtual circuit) A virtual circuit that is dynamically established on demand and is torn down when transmission is complete. SVCs are used in situations in which data transmission is sporadic. Compare with PVC.

switch A network device that filters, forwards, and floods frames based on the destination address of each frame. The switch operates at the data link layer of the OSI reference model.

switching The process of taking an incoming frame from one interface and delivering it out through another interface.

synchronous circuit A signal that is transmitted with precise clocking. Such signals have the same frequency, with individual characters encapsulated in control bits (called *start bits* and *stop bits*) that designate the beginning and end of each character.

Synchronous Data Link Control *See* SDLC.

T

T1 A digital WAN carrier facility that transmits DS-1-formatted data at 1.544 Mbps through the telephone-switching network, using AMI or B8ZS coding. Compare with E1.

T3 A digital WAN carrier facility that transmits DS-3-formatted data at 44.736 Mbps through the telephone switching network. Compare with E3.

TA (terminal adapter) A device used to connect ISDN BRI connections to existing interfaces such as EIA/TIA-232. Essentially, an ISDN modem.

TACACS (Terminal Access Controller Access Control System) An authentication protocol, developed by the DDN community, that provides remote access authentication and related services, such as event logging. User passwords are administered in a central database rather than in individual routers, providing an easily scalable network security solution.

TCP (Transmission Control Protocol) A connection-oriented transport-layer protocol that provides reliable full-duplex data transmission. TCP is part of the TCP/IP protocol stack.

TCP/IP (Transmission Control Protocol/Internet Protocol). A common name for the suite of protocols developed by the U.S. DoD in the 1970s to support the construction of worldwide internetworks. TCP and IP are the two best-known protocols in the suite.

TDM (time-division multiplexing). A circuit-switching signal used to determine the call route, which is a dedicated path between the sender and the receiver.

TE1 (Terminal Equipment Type 1). A device that is compatible with the ISDN network. A TE1 connects to a network termination of either Type 1 or Type 2.

TE2 (Terminal Equipment Type 2). A device that is not compatible with ISDN and requires a terminal adapter.

Telnet. A standard terminal emulation protocol in the TCP/IP protocol stack. Telnet is used for remote terminal connection, enabling users to log in to remote systems and use resources as if they were connected to a local system. Telnet is defined in RFC 854.

TFTP (Trivial File Transfer Protocol). A simplified version of FTP that allows files to be transferred from one computer to another over a network.

throughput. The rate of information arriving at, and possibly passing through, a particular point in a network system.

TIA (Telecommunications Industries Association). An organization that develops standards relating to telecommunications technologies. Together, TIA and EIA have formalized standards, such as EIA/TIA-232, for the electrical characteristics of data transmission.

tick. The delay on a data link using IBM PC clock ticks (approximately 55 milliseconds). One tick is a second.

timeout. An event that occurs when one network device expects to hear from another network device within a specified period of time but does not. The resulting timeout usually results in a retransmission of information or the dissolving of the session between the two devices.

Time To Live. See TTL.

token. A frame that contains control information. Possession of the token allows a network device to transmit data onto the network.

token bus A LAN architecture using token passing access over a bus topology. This LAN architecture is the basis for the IEEE 802.4 LAN specification.

token passing An access method by which network devices access the physical medium in an orderly fashion based on possession of a small frame called a *token*. Compare with circuit switching and contention.

Token Ring A token-passing LAN developed and supported by IBM. Token Ring runs at 4 or 16 Mbps over a ring topology. Similar to IEEE 802.5.

TokenTalk Apple Computer's data-link product that allows an AppleTalk network to be connected by Token Ring cables.

toll network The collective switches and facilities (called *trunks*) inside the WAN provider's cloud.

topology A physical arrangement of network nodes and media within an enterprise networking structure.

traceroute A program available on many systems that traces the path a packet takes to a destination. It is mostly used to debug routing problems between hosts. There is also a traceroute protocol defined in RFC 1393.

traffic management Techniques for avoiding congestion and shaping and policing traffic. Allows links to operate at high levels of utilization by scaling back lower-priority, delay-tolerant traffic at the edge of the network when congestion begins to occur.

trailer Control information appended to data when encapsulating the data for network transmission. Compare with header.

transaction services layer Layer 7 in the SNA architectural model. Represents user application functions, such as spreadsheets, word processing, or electronic mail, by which users interact with the network. Corresponds roughly with the application layer of the OSI reference model. *See also* data flow control layer, data link control layer, path control layer, physical control layer, presentation services layer, and transmission control layer.

transmission control layer Layer 4 in the SNA architectural model. This layer is responsible for establishing, maintaining, and terminating SNA sessions, sequencing data messages, and controlling session level flow. Corresponds to the transport layer of the OSI reference model. *See also* data flow control layer, data link control layer, path control layer, physical control layer, presentation services layer, and transaction services layer.

Transmission Control Protocol See TCP.

transport layer Layer 4 of the OSI reference model. This layer segments and reassembles data into a data stream. The transport layer has the potential to guarantee a connection and offer reliable transport. *See also* OSI reference model.

trap A message sent by an SNMP agent to an NMS, a console, or a terminal to indicate the occurrence of a significant event, such as a specifically defined condition or a threshold that was reached.

tree topology A LAN topology similar to a bus topology, except that tree networks can contain branches with multiple nodes. Transmissions from a station propagate the length of the medium and are received by all other stations. Compare with bus topology, ring topology, and star topology.

TTL (Time To Live) A field in an IP header that indicates how long a packet is considered valid.

tunneling An architecture that is designed to provide the services necessary to implement any standard point-to-point encapsulation scheme.

U

UDP (User Datagram Protocol) A connectionless transport-layer protocol in the TCP/IP protocol stack. UDP is a simple protocol that exchanges datagrams without acknowledgments or guaranteed delivery, requiring that error processing and retransmission be handled by other protocols. UDP is defined in RFC 768.

UNI (User-Network Interface) A specification that defines an interoperability standard for the interface between products (a router or a switch) located in a private network and the switches located within the public carrier networks. Also used to describe similar connections in Frame Relay networks.

unicast A message sent to a single network destination.

unicast address An address specifying a single network device. Compare with broadcast address and multicast address.

uniform resource locator See URL.

UPS (uninterruptible power supply) A backup device designed to provide an uninterrupted power source in the event of a power failure. UPSs are commonly installed on file servers and wiring hubs.

URL (uniform resource locator) A standardized addressing scheme for accessing hypertext documents and other services using a browser.

UTP (unshielded twisted-pair) A four-pair wire medium used in a variety of networks. UTP does not require the fixed spacing between connections that is necessary with coaxial-type connections. Five types of UTP cabling are commonly used: Category 1 cabling, Category 2 cabling, Category 3 cabling, Category 4 cabling, and Category 5 cabling. Compare with STP.

User Datagram Protocol *See* UDP.

User-Network Interface *See* UNI.

V

VCC (vertical cross-connect) A connection that is used to interconnect the various IDFs to the central MDF.

vertical cabling Backbone cabling.

vertical cross-connect *See* VCC.

VINES (Virtual Integrated Network Service) An NOS developed and marketed by Banyan Systems.

virtual circuit A logical circuit created to ensure reliable communication between two network devices. A virtual circuit is defined by a VPI/VCI pair and can be either permanent (a PVC) or switched (an SVC). Virtual circuits are used in Frame Relay and X.25. In ATM, a virtual circuit is called a *virtual channel*. Sometimes abbreviated VC.

VLAN (virtual LAN) A group of devices on a LAN that are configured (using management software) so that they can communicate as if they were attached to the same wire, when in fact they are located on a number of different LAN segments. Because VLANs are based on logical instead of physical connections, they are extremely flexible.

W

WAN (wide-area network) A data communications network that serves users across a broad geographic area and often uses transmission devices provided by common carriers. Frame Relay, SMDS, and X.25 are examples of WAN technologies. Compare with LAN and MAN.

WAN link A WAN communications channel consisting of a circuit or transmission path and all related equipment between a sender and a receiver.

watchdog packet A method used to ensure that a client is still connected to a NetWare server. If the server has not received a packet from a client for a certain period of time, it sends that client a series of watchdog packets. If the station fails to respond to a predefined number of watchdog packets, the server concludes that the station is no longer connected and clears the connection for that station.

watchdog spoofing A subset of spoofing that refers specifically to a router acting especially for a NetWare client by sending watchdog packets to a NetWare server to keep the session between client and server active. Useful when the client and server are separated by a DDR WAN link.

watchdog timer 1. A hardware or software mechanism that is used to trigger an event or an escape from a process unless the timer is periodically reset. 2. In NetWare, a timer that indicates the maximum period of time that a server will wait for a client to respond to a watchdog packet. If the timer expires, the server sends another watchdog packet (up to a set maximum).

wildcard mask A 32-bit quantity used in conjunction with an IP address to determine which bits in an IP address should be ignored when comparing that address with another IP address. A wildcard mask is specified when setting up an ACL.

window The number of octets that the sender is willing to accept.

window size The number of messages that can be transmitted while awaiting an acknowledgment.

workgroup server A server that supports a specific set of users and offers services such as word processing and file sharing, which are services that only a few groups of people would need. Compare with enterprise server.

X–Z

X.25 An ITU-T standard that defines how connections between DTEs and DCEs are maintained for remote terminal access and computer communications in public data networks. Frame Relay has to some degree superseded X.25.

XNS (Xerox Network Systems) A protocol suite originally designed by PARC. Many PC networking companies, such as 3Com, Banyan, Novell, and UB Networks used or currently use a variation of XNS as their primary transport protocol.

ZIP (Zone Information Protocol) An AppleTalk session-layer protocol that maps network numbers to zone names. ZIP is used by NBP to determine which networks contain nodes that belong to a zone.

zone In AppleTalk, a logical group of network devices.

zone multicast address A data-link-dependent multicast address at which a node receives the NBP broadcasts directed to its zone.

Hey, you've got enough worries.

Don't let IT training be one of them.

Get on the fast track to IT training at InformIT,
your total Information Technology training network.

 | **www.informit.com** |

■ Hundreds of timely articles on dozens of topics ■ Discounts on IT books
from all our publishing partners, including Cisco Press ■ Free, unabridged books
from the InformIT Free Library ■ "Expert Q&A"—our live, online chat
with IT experts ■ Faster, easier certification and training from our Web- or
classroom-based training programs ■ Current IT news ■ Software downloads
■ Career-enhancing resources

InformIT is a registered trademark of Pearson. Copyright ©2001 by Pearson.